Course   Business Law 1
                Intro. to Contracts, Liability
                Issues & Intellectual Property

Course Number

                B-LAW 341
                Smeal College of Business

http://create.mcgraw-hill.com

ISBN-10: 1121657605   ISBN-13: 9781121657601

Contents

Online Supplements 477

Credits

Chapter 1. Law as a Foundation for Business

Law as a Foundation for Business

📖 Learning Objectives

In this chapter you will learn:

1-1. To recognize why the legal systems of nations contribute to making the economies of some nations much stronger than the economies of other nations.

1-2. To explain that "property" in the law refers not to something that is owned but to the right of ownership itself, which gives maximum incentive for wealth creation.

1-3. To analyze why *stare decisis* is different in common law nations than in civil law nations.

1-4. To classify what legal sources lawyers turn to in answering legal questions from their clients, and the hierarchy of those sources.

>> Introduction

To understand the legal and regulatory environment of business, you must appreciate the role of law as the foundation for business practice in the private market system. The purpose of this book is to explain the legal system and its rules and regulations that provide the foundation for the private market. Note that Chapter 1 maintains, however, that not just any kind of law creates a basis for modern business practice. Only a property-based legal system does this.

In 2008 the worst recession in over 70 years hit the United States. Millions of people lost their jobs, millions more lost their homes. Tens of thousands of businesses closed. The stock market collapsed. Giant financial institutions considered "too big to fail" had to be rescued by the federal government, which had to borrow a trillion dollars it did not have to bail out these businesses. What do these unfortunate events have to do with the legal and regulatory environment of business? What does the legal system have to do with this terrible recession?

Your authors suggest that law and the legal system have a great deal to do with what happens economically in our country. As you read this book, note that we refer again and again to the influence of law on the environment of business. To understand the legal and regulatory environment of business, you must appreciate the role of law as the foundation for business practice in the private market system. Chapter 1 introduces you to the legal foundation of the private market. Not just any kind of law creates the basis for modern business practice. Only a property-based legal system does.

Before examining this system, we first should give you some hints about how to read and study *The Legal and Regulatory Environment of Business.*

>> How to Study this Textbook

To read this textbook we highly recommend a certain method called Survey, Question, Read, Recite, Review (SQ3R). SQ3R is much more effective than simply starting at the beginning of a chapter and reading straight through to the end. But it should not take much longer than reading straight through.

If you are allowing two hours for the reading of a chapter, first take no more than five or six minutes and "survey" the chapter. Flip through the chapter and look at all of the main headings and subheadings of the sections, perhaps also looking at the first sentences of several paragraphs in each section. In surveying you are not trying to learn or even understand the material but rather to get an idea of what the chapter is about.

After surveying the material, develop a "question" for each section as you read. If the section heading says "Why Nations Are Economically Weak or Strong," turn the heading into a question, like "Why are some nations economically weak and others economically strong?" Then "read" the section with the purpose of answering your question. When you finish reading, "recite" aloud or silently to yourself the answer to the question.

The last "R" refers to "review." Spend the last 10 minutes of your study time reviewing the chapter. A good way to do this is to go back to your questions and answer them again. If you will study by this method, we guarantee more effective results than if you simply read the chapter straight through. We have included a longer explanation of SQ3R as Appendix 1 in the back of the book, along with an explanation of the case briefing system, which you may need beginning with Chapter 3.

LO 1-1

1. WHY NATIONS ARE ECONOMICALLY WEAK OR STRONG

Why some nations are economically weak and others economically strong is of great importance in the world today. According to the United Nations, 30,000 children worldwide die every day from malnourishment and largely preventable diseases. Most of these children are located in economically weak countries. In economic poverty lies the roots of much hunger, disease, discontent, despair, revolution, and terrorism.

According to Nobel economist Douglass North, 500 years ago all nations of the world were poor. Today, however, some are much wealthier than others. A 2010 International Monetary Fund study shows that 43 nations have average national incomes per person, adjusted for purchasing power, above $20,000 a year, with the figure in the United States being $47,123. In contrast, 44 countries have adjusted per person incomes of less than $2,000 per year. The economically stronger nations tend to be in Europe, North America, and along the Pacific Rim, with the economically weaker nations being found in the rest of the world. But sometimes they are side by side. For instance, although the United States and Mexico share a common border, the former has three times the national adjusted income per person of the latter. Also sharing a common border are Singapore and Malaysia, with the former nation enjoying per person almost 14 times the adjusted income of the latter.

Several explanations attempt to show why national economies are weak or strong.

- Dependency theory. This theory argues that economically strong nations exploit the resources and labor of weaker nations through trade. It asserts that some nations grow and flourish at the expense of keeping others economically poor. Yet nations with stronger economies invest and trade much more with each other than they do with nations having weaker economies, and international trade usually accounts for only a small fraction of national income in even the poorest countries. Lack of conditions encouraging internal economic activity rather than overdependence on international trade causes weak national economies.

- Natural resources. Whether or not a nation has abundant natural resources has been offered to explain economic prosperity. Yet economically wealthy Japan has relatively few natural resources and little fertile land while economically weak Russia has an abundance of both. Many economically poor regions of South America and Africa possess much fertile land, various minerals, and considerable other natural resources. Even those small nations that are comparatively well-off because they have a large amount of a single natural resource like oil are wealthy only because they are able to sell to other nations with strong, diverse economies.

  Wealthy Singapore has almost no natural resources or fertile land. Its wealth comes from shipping and financial services.

- Education and technology. Economically strong nations usually have more schools and implement technology more quickly than economically weak nations. Technology and education are certainly important to the continuing economic strength of wealthy nations, but in some parts of the world, well-educated people have few job opportunities, and powerful technologies are easily transferred between countries. Widespread education and rapid technology implementation in nations seem to be more a result rather than the primary cause of strong economies.

  In economically weaker countries like Egypt, many college graduates can get jobs only with the government because there are few jobs available in private business that require education.

- Climate. Some geographers have thought that climate helps explain whether nations are economically strong or weak. They believe that when temperatures average too hot, people are less able to work, especially outdoors. However, strong economies can exist in hot climates. Singapore

6   **PART 1**   Introduction

lies near the equator and has one of the world's most prosperous economies and highest national per person incomes.

- Private market. According to many economists, the presence or absence of a modern private market is the single most significant reason why some economies are strong and others are weak. Yet the mere existence of a private market may not be enough to create an economically prosperous economy. After the former Soviet Union collapsed, Russia ended much state planning, leaving individuals free to carry on business privately. Many economists expected the Russian economy to take off. Instead, it declined 41% over the next seven years.

- Law and the legal system. An adequately enforced system of equally applied law is increasingly recognized as a necessary foundation for strong, productive economies. A certain framework of law is necessary for maximum incentive to entrepreneurs, investors, and inventors. The law of property, contract, tort, and various government regulations provides a foundation for institutions such as corporations, banks, and securities exchanges. Law secures the elements of trust and certainty that are vital to economic transactions among strangers. No nations with weak economies have adequate legal systems, and all nations that have these systems are economically strong in comparison.

Abundant natural resources, education and technology, a temperate climate, and the institutions of the private market all contribute to strong national economies. However, a certain type of legal system is most fundamental to national wealth creation.

>> Law, the Rule of Law, and Property

Three concepts establish a necessary framework for the most effectively functioning market in the modern nation: law, the rule of law, and property. Note how they connect to each other.

2. LAW

In the last 10,000 years, human society has moved from roving bands of hunter-gatherers to large modern nations with populations in the hundreds of millions. The social forces that hold together societies range from custom and religion to law and economic ties. In the modern nation, however, the most significant of the social forces is **law** because law can glue together diverse peoples of different backgrounds into very large, organized groups. Law is known by everyone as being intended to tell members of society what they can or cannot do. Strangers to a society may not understand or appreciate complex and subtle customs of behavior, but they can observe the formal laws governing what kinds of activities are permitted and prohibited in society. Lawyers, judges, and other trained interpreters of the rules can help them in this process.

A simple definition of law follows:

- Law is made up of rules.
- These rules are laid down by the state and backed up by enforcement.

Law is a formal social force, meaning that laws come from the state and are usually written down and accessible so those who need to understand and obey them can. To maintain order in society, adequate enforcement institutions such as courts and the police are a necessary part of the legal system. As the countries of the former Soviet Union are finding out, written laws mean little unless they can be promptly and fairly enforced. Without adequate enforcement, resources can be taken from those who have them, and agreements can be disregarded. The certainty and trust necessary to make complex, long-term business arrangements are absent. People must spend much of their time guarding their resources rather than developing them.

The first known written set of laws was the Code of Hammurabi, named after the Babylonian king of the 18th century BC.

3. THE RULE OF LAW

In a modern nation, law is important to implement either the commands of a dictator or the will of the people in a democracy. However, only in democracies is there true concern for the rule of law, which goes beyond merely thinking of law as governmental commands backed up by force. Under the **rule of law,** laws that are made are *generally* and *equally* applicable. They apply to all or most members of society and they apply to various groups in the same way.

Under the rule of law, law applies to lawmakers as well as to the rest of society. Thus, lawmakers have an incentive to make laws that benefit everyone. Rule-of-law nations adopt laws supporting the private market because it is in everyone's interest, including the lawmakers'.

In today's international business environment, more and more voices are calling for the rule of law. The secretary-general of the United Nations says that "without confidence based on the rule of law; without trust and transparency—there could be no well-functioning markets." The managing director of the International Monetary Fund asserts that "high quality" economic growth depends "in particular on the rule of law" which is a "lodestar for all countries." Observes the managing director of J. P. Morgan and Co.: "An environment in which courts cannot be relied upon to adhere to the rule of law is an environment in which businesses will be reluctant to invest and in which development will be stunted." He calls the rule of law "a cornerstone of free trade."

Unfortunately, the rule of law is an ideal rather than a complete fact in even the most democratic nation. Special interest groups attempt to persuade lawmakers to benefit these groups at the expense of others. And it is not always clear what it means to apply laws generally and equally. Still, in a democracy well-educated voters who understand the importance of the rule of law can hold to account lawmakers who excessively favor special interests. Judges also play a vital role in maintaining the rule of law. (See Sidebar 1.1.)

Almost all wealthy countries embrace the rule of law; for example, most European countries. Article 6 of the Treaty on European Union, called the Maastricht Treaty, says the EU is "founded" on "the rule of law." There are no countries with strong, diverse economies that do not have the rule of law. As former President Eisenhower warned, "The clearest way to show what the rule of law means to us in everyday life is to recall what has happened when there is no rule of law."

"Without the rule of law, major economic institutions such as corporations, banks, and labor unions would not function, and the government's many involvements in the economy—regulatory mechanisms, tax systems, customs structure, monetary policy, and the like—would be unfair, inefficient, and opaque."

–ThomasCarothers, Director, Democracy and Rule of Law Project, Carnegie Endowment for International Peace

"While economic growth can occur in the short run with autocratic regimes, long-run economic growth entails the development of the rule of law."

–Douglas C.North, acceptance speech for the Nobel Prize in Economics, 1993

>> *sidebar* 1.1

The Chief Justice and the Rule of Law

Before someone can become a justice of the U.S. Supreme Court, the president must nominate and the U.S. Senate must confirm that person. The Senate must also confirm the president's choice to be chief justice. During the confirmation, the senators always ask questions about the rule of law. Here is how Chief Justice John Roberts responded to a confirmation question about the rule of law.

> Somebody asked me . . ., "Are you going to be on the side of the little guy," he said. And you obviously want to give an

immediate answer, but, as you reflect on it, if the Constitution says that the little guy should win, the little guy's going to win in court before me. But if the Constitution says that the big guy should win, well, then the big guy's going to win, because my obligation is to the Constitution.

Compare Chief Justice Roberts' statement to a similar observation made by former Chief Justice Warren E. Burger: "Judges rule on the basis of law, and not public opinion, and they should be totally indifferent to the pressures of the times."

LO 1-2

4. PROPERTY

Property is a legal right that allows you to exclude others from your resources. It makes what is yours "yours."

The third concept necessary for a successful private market in the modern nation is **property.** In a dictionary, property has two common meanings: (1) something that is owned, and (2) ownership. We will be using the word in its second definition as **"ownership."** In law the word "property" (or "ownership") means the right to turn to public authorities like the police or the courts to help you keep others from interfering with what you own. Property is a legal fence that keeps others out without your permission. It allows you to exclude others from something without your permission.

Three types of ownership fences are

- Public property, which applies to public resources owned by the government (or "state") like roads, public buildings, public lands, and monuments.
- Private property, which applies to resources that you own as an individual.
- Common property, which applies to resources like land that more than one individual owns jointly.

Do remember that the property right gives a major incentive to develop resources.

Property right helps the poor as much as the wealthy. Why?

So important is the right of private property that in this book we often just refer to private property as "property." We will specifically say "public property" or "common property" if we mean those applications of exclusionary right.

It is through the law of property that individuals and business organizations can possess, use, and transfer their private resources. The enforcement of the property right under the rule of law gives people incentive to develop the resources they own. Something deeply natural to human beings encourages them to exert the greatest productive effort only when they can prevent others from taking the resources they produce. Only when people control what they produce will they give production their maximum effort. It is a property-based legal system that enables such control by allowing people to exclude others from interfering with what their efforts produce. Importantly, such a system protects and assists the poor as well as the wealthy. (See Sidebar 1.2.)

>> *sidebar* 1.2

How Property Protects the Poor

Many people have difficulty grasping how property protects the poor. After all, do the poor even have "property"? Legally, the answer is "yes," because property is an exclusive right to keep others from interfering with one's resources, not the resources themselves, and under the rule of law, this right protects the resources of the poor as well as those of the wealthy.

In many parts of the world that have no adequate property systems, poor "squatters" lack formally recognized ownership of the land they live on. They spend much of their time defending their possession and cannot use their houses and land to secure loans that would allow them to start small businesses. Peru, however, has begun recognizing and registering the legal ownership of these squatters in their homes.

Princeton graduate student Erica Field compared areas of Peru where legal property has been formally secured with areas where it is yet to be recognized.

She found the granting of the right of property to the "average squatter family" was associated with a 17% total household work increase, a 47% increase in the probability of working outside the home, and a 28% decline in the likelihood of child labor in the family. Her 2002 study concluded that formal ownership means the families no longer have to spend as much time protecting their homes and can engage in more productive work, which makes them less poor.

The ownership program in Peru was initiated following the ideas of economist Hernando de Soto. De Soto's ideas and work have spread to other countries, and he has gained support from many world leaders, including Presidents George W. Bush and Bill Clinton. De Soto believes that Western and Pacific Rim nations are the world's most wealthy because they have had the rule of law and the law of property the longest. He maintains that law is the "hidden architecture" of the modern private market.

The exclusionary right of property provides a basis for the private market and modern business. Scholars have traced the economic flourishing of Western civilization during the last several hundred years to the increasing recognition of the right of property in the nations of the West.

Consider the following. If a nation with a property-based legal system averages only 2% a year greater productivity than a nation without such a system, in 34.5 years the first nation has twice the annual total income (called Gross National Income or GNI) of the second nation. In 206 years, the first nation has 64 times the annual GNI of the second nation. Note that abundant goods and services, educational excellence, rapidly developing technology, food availability, and sufficient medical service are usually related to the economic wealth of GNI.

5. PROPERTY IN ITS BROADEST SENSE

Property can be thought of as the central concept underlying Western legal systems. (See Figure 1.1.) Most of the topics discussed in this book relate to the exclusionary right of property. Contract law enables an owner to exchange resources (Chapters 8 and 9), especially at a future date. Tort law compensates owners whose resources are wrongfully harmed by the actions of others (Chapter 10). Criminal law punishes those who harm an owner's resources in particular ways, for example, by theft (Chapter 13). The law of business organizations identifies how individuals can own and use private resources in groups (Chapter 14).

*Property is the central concept of Western legal systems.

Figure 1.1 *The wheel of property*

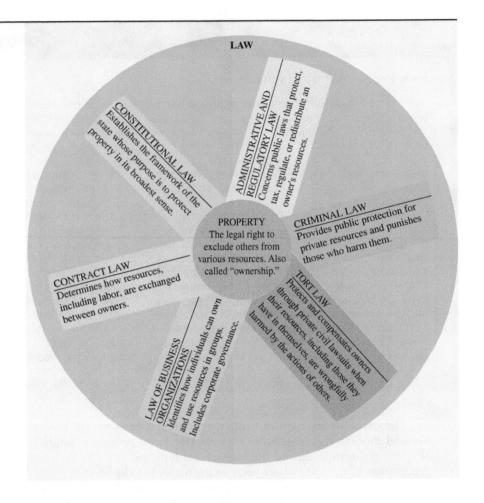

To say that you have a "right" means that legally you can keep others from interfering with that right. To be able to exclude others is the essence of property.

Regulatory law both protects ownership and sets limits on private resource use (Chapter 15). Antitrust law forbids owners from monopolizing classes of resources and sets rules for how businesses can compete to acquire ownership in new resources (Chapter 16). Securities laws regulate the transfer of ownership in certain profit-making opportunities (Chapter 17). Environmental law controls how owners can use their resources when creating pollution (Chapter 19). Even labor laws and antidiscrimination laws involve property in the sense they protect the employees' right to exclude employers from interfering with certain self-ownership interests of the employees (Chapters 20, 21, and 22). Finally, a theme of the entire book, corporate governance, specifically concerns the law protecting the owners of a business organization from the managers who run it for them. Generally speaking, corporate governance also refers to any law regulating and limiting private owners' productive resources and their use.

In its broadest sense, property includes an ownership of individual constitutional and human rights in ourselves that excludes the state from interfering with these rights. Today, we usually call our relationship to these rights "liberty," but liberty and property in this sense have almost identical meanings. John Locke, the seventeenth-century English philosopher who greatly influenced the framers of the Constitution, asserted that private property begins with the right we have in ourselves and in our efforts and actions. He said that an individual is the "proprietor [owner] of his own person, and the actions or labour of it" and that this is "the great foundation of property." Later, James Madison wrote that property "in its larger and juster meaning. . . embraces everything to which a man may attach value and have a right . . . . [A] man has property in his opinions and free communication of them. . . . In a word, as a man is said to have a right to his property, he may be equally said to have a property in his rights." For Madison and other constitutional framers, property protected not only physical resources like land but also human rights like freedom of speech, freedom of religion, and freedom from unreasonable intrusion by the government. The individual's very relationship to society was defined by the word *property*. Scholars have pointed out that the modern understanding of human rights began with the concept of property.

Nearly two million students study business in the United States; one hundred thousand of them are from other countries. As necessary as it is for them to grasp business subjects involving computers, debits and credits, balance sheets, financial statements, employee and consumer behavior, and stakeholder theory, it is equally vital for them to appreciate how law and the legal concept of property establish conditions for the private market in society. The secret to economic prosperity and the wealth of nations lies in the foundation of property law and the legal system to implement it under the rule of law. Modern private markets within nations simply do not work well without generally and equally applied property law.

>> sidebar 1.3

Russia's Property Problems

When the former Soviet Union collapsed, many observers thought that the new private market would promptly improve Russia's economy. However, that economy went into a serious decline from which it has been slow to recover. Why? Most now consider that Russia's lack of the rule of law and the law of property accounts for its poor economy.

The government still controls over half of the resources in Russia. Much of what private control of resources exists in Russia has been gotten through force, fraud, and corruption. One study in Moscow found that small business owners must pay over $30,000 a year in bribes to corrupt officials and extortionists. Developing property law in Russia often does not allow a single individual to control all the ways that land can be used. When disputes over agreements arise, businesses cannot depend on the courts to resolve issues justly and impartially. Recently, the Russian economy has been strengthened by the sale of oil to wealthy countries, but per person income in Russia remains low. In comparison, per person income in the United States is still approximately 3 times that in Russia.

Generally and equally applied property rights, their transfer by contract, and the support of adequate enforcement institutions like courts will provide a necessary basis to move the Russian economy toward prosperity. But the Russian people will have to be educated about the legal foundation of the wealth of nations.

6. JURISPRUDENCE

Jurisprudence is the philosophy of law.

Over the centuries, several ideas have developed that help explain the origin of law and its justification. We call these ideas (or philosophies) of law **jurisprudence.** Briefly, the main types or "schools" of jurisprudence include the following:

- Natural law. Going back to Aristotle and other ancient philosophers, natural law theory asserts that law contains universal moral principles. These principles are observable in nature, and we can determine them through human reason. John Locke, the British philosopher whose writing influenced the framers of the U.S. Constitution, thought that "property" was part of natural law. Merely human laws that contradict the principles of natural law are improper. Compare natural law to "formalism," discussed in Chapter 2.

> "True law is right reason in agreement with nature; it is of universal application, unchanging and everlasting. . . ."
>
> **–Cicero, Roman historian**

- Positive law. Positive law jurisprudence believes that law is simply the commands of the state backed up by force and punishments. It is contrary to the philosophy of natural law. Eighteenth-century philosopher Jeremy Bentham ridiculed the idea of natural law as "nonsense upon stilts." Compare positive law to "consequentialism," discussed in Chapter 2.

The definition of law at the beginning of this chapter is taken from positive law jurisprudence.

- Historical school. The historical school of jurisprudence emphasizes that contemporary law should focus on legal principles that have withstood the test of time in a nation. The historical school believes that law reflects the cultural traditions of a people and recognizes that different nations may have different traditions and, consequently, different laws. Friedrich Savigny, a prominent German legal philosopher, helped develop this jurisprudence.

- Sociological jurisprudence. Sociological jurisprudence supports the idea that law can and should change to meet new developments in society. From this point of view, the Second Amendment to the U.S. Constitution, which asserts the right to "bear arms," or weapons, should not be interpreted today to allow citizens to own and carry lightweight fully automatic rifles that can fire hundreds of rounds a minute. When the Second Amendment was written, a highly trained person carrying a 25-pound rifle could fire only about two rounds a minute.

- Legal realism. Legal realism tries to go beyond just the words of law to examine what police, administrators, prosecutors, and judges are actually doing as they enforce, interpret, and apply laws. When Supreme Court Justice Oliver Wendell Holmes, Jr., said that "law is what officials do about it," he reflected the jurisprudence of legal realism. For instance, the posted speed limit around the Atlanta perimeter highway, Interstate 285, is 55 mph. However, almost no one drives within the posted speed limit and traffic police rarely ticket drivers until they go faster than 75 mph. In terms of legal realism, what is the actual speed limit on Atlanta's perimeter highway?

Several of these types of jurisprudence overlap. For instance, sociological jurisprudence and legal realism are types of legal positivism. Jurisprudence may also certainly influence the actual rules of law, but jurisprudence is a philosophy about law rather than the law itself. However, complicating matters is that the word *jurisprudence* also refers to the general body of law interpretations by judges as different from legislation passed by legislators.

>> Classifications of Law

Even when you understand jurisprudence and grasp the significance of our property-based legal system to the private marketplace, you still have much left to know about the legal and regulatory environment of business. In large part, learning about law demands an extensive vocabulary of legal terms and concepts. It will be useful in organizing this vocabulary to examine several major classifications of law.

7. COMMON LAW AND CIVIL LAW

The world has two major legal systems: common law and civil law. The United Kingdom, the United States, Canada, Jamaica, India, Nigeria, New Zealand, and a few other countries—all colonized by England—follow the common law. The **common law** legal system emphasizes the role of judges in determining the meaning of laws and how they apply. It arose beginning in the eleventh and twelfth centuries as the English monarch appointed royal judges to ride circuits around the English countryside and to resolve disputes in the name of the king (or queen). As there was little formal law to apply to many disputes, the decisions handed down by the judges literally made the law.

By the time the English legislature (Parliament) emerged, a huge body of written judicial decisions was "common" to all of England. The role of judges in making and interpreting law was in place. English colonists then brought the common law to what became the United States and various other countries. The common law continues its development even today, and so significant is the role of judges in the United States that they determine the meaning of the Constitution and can declare void the legislation of Congress and the acts of the president.

The world's nations not colonized by England generally observe civil law legal systems. The **civil law** relies more on legislation than judicial decisions to determine what the law is. Like common law courts, courts in civil law nations decide the facts in a disputed case (for example, who did what, who committed a crime or breached a contract), but civil law courts do not make law nor do their judges think themselves obligated to follow prior judicial decisions, called *precedents,* as they do in common law nations, although they do refer to "settled" cases. Essentially, judges play a much more important role in determining law and its meaning in common law nations than in civil law nations. Only Louisiana among the U.S. states, follows a partial civil law system. This is due to Louisiana's historical ties with France, a civil law nation.

8. PUBLIC AND PRIVATE LAW

Another way of classifying the law is to divide it into matters of public law and matters of private law. **Public law** includes those matters that involve the regulation of society as opposed to individuals interacting. In each of these matters, a government official represents society, or "the people," and the official is responsible for seeking justice to achieve the ends of society. The main types of public law include:

- **Constitutional law,** which involves the interpretation and application of either the federal or state constitutions.
- **Administrative law,** which covers the legal principles that apply to government agencies, bureaus, boards, or commissions.

LO 1-3

Common law emphasizes the role of judges in determining the meaning of laws.

Civil law relies more on legislation than judicial decisions for law.

Public law includes constitutional law, administrative law, and criminal law.

*Special areas of property concern land, goods, copyrights, patents, and trademarks.

- **Criminal law,** which specifies various offenses against the proper order of the state.

    Private law covers those legal problems and issues that concern your private resource relationships with other people. Private law traditionally includes:

- **Property law,** which involves the recognition of exclusive right in both tangible (physically touchable) and intangible resources. Special areas of property law concern land, goods, copyrights, trademarks, patents, and trade secrets.
- **Contract law,** which covers the rules of how owners transfer resources by exchanging them. Contracts often involve enforceable promises to exchange resources in the future.
- **Tort law,** which establishes rules for compensation when an owner's legal boundaries are wrongfully crossed by another. Tort law often but not always requires actual injury to the owner's resources.

    Note that although we mention property law as only one kind of private law, actually, in its broad sense, property in our legal system is at the heart of both public and private law. See Sidebar 1.4.

Don't confure our reference to *civil* (or noncriminal) lawsuits with a *civil* law legal system, which is one emphasizing the importance of the legislature in determining the meaning of laws.

9. CIVIL LAW AND CRIMINAL LAW

Another means of classifying the law is to divide it into civil law and criminal law. For administrative purposes, courts usually separate criminal actions from all other lawsuits. *Civil* cases may include suits for breach of contract or

---

>> *sidebar* 1.4

Public and Private Law as Subsets of Property

The Lord Mayor of London, John Wilkes, said before the American Revolution, "If the colonists can be taxed without their consent [meaning representation in Parliament], they have no property, nothing they can call their own." The first rallying cry of the Revolution was "Liberty, Property, and No Stamps." Without any opposition at the Constitutional convention, several members attending asserted that the only reason for having a *constitution* was the protection of property.

Important to remember here is that the framers had a view of property that included, in the words of James Madison, not only "land and merchandise" but also "a larger and juster view." The Father of the Constitution was also thinking about property as central to our Constitution when he said in 1792 that we "have a property" in our "rights." An exclusive legal fence surrounds our free speech and practice of religion even as it protects our land and other resources from being taken by the state (except with democratic consent by taxation or just compensation). In this sense property and liberty become quite similar concepts. It is fair to say then that property is the central concept of the Constitution and its amendments.

Other types of public law also have property at their heart. Most **administrative law** protects us from having others harm what is privately proper to people. Likewise, **criminal law** punishes people for theft, fraud, and other violations of private property, such as crimes of violence against one's body, which in an important sense one owns. For instance, famous philosopher John Locke said that the ownership of oneself is the basis for all property.

Private law begins with **property law** about land ownership and most movable things. It also includes **contract law,** which covers how owners legally transfer ownership in a property-based legal system such as ours. Finally, private law includes **tort law,** which sets up rules for compensation when someone legally injures what is privately proper to owners, including the owners' bodies and sometimes their mental well-being.

It is fair to say that in our legal system, public and private law are subsets of property, of the exclusive legal fence that make things privately proper to people. Your book covers all of these areas of public and private law.

tort cases, such as suits for personal injuries. Typically, they involve a request for damages or other appropriate relief that does not involve punishment of the wrongdoer. *Criminal* cases involve a representative of government attempting to prove the wrong committed against society and seeking to have the wrongdoer punished by the court system.

10. SUBSTANTIVE LAW AND PROCEDURAL LAW

Another important classification or distinction in law is between substance and procedure. **Substantive law** defines the legal relationship of people with other people or between them and the state. Thus, the rules of law governing the creation or enforcement of a contractual promise are substantive in nature. **Procedural law** deals with the method and means by which substantive law is made and administered. The time allowed for one party to sue another and the rules of law governing the process of the lawsuit are examples of procedural laws. Thus, substantive rules of law define rights and duties, while procedural rules of law provide the machinery for enforcing those rights and duties.

> That a plaintiff must prove the defendant failed to use reasonable care in order to establish the tort of negligence is an example of substantive law.

Judicial procedures involve the conduct of lawsuits and appeals and the enforcement of judgments. The rules for conducting civil trials are different from those for criminal trials. For example, each party may call the other party to the witness stand for cross-examination in a civil trial, but the defendant may not be required to testify in a criminal case. Procedural problems sometimes arise concerning papers filed in lawsuits, the admission of evidence, and various other techniques involved in trying the case. They are the rules of the game. In Chapter 4 , you will study these procedural aspects of law in greater depth.

>> Sources of Law

LO 1-4

For Sections 11–14 consider that you have a dry cleaning business and have gone to a lawyer to ask what the law says about your emitting certain chemical cleaning pollutants into the air. What sources of law will the lawyer have to be familiar with in order to answer your questions? The following sources form a hierarchy of law, which means that if a lower source of law conflicts with a higher source of law, it is legally void; that is, the higher source trumps, or prevails over, the lower.

11. FEDERAL LAW

Federal law is a very important source of law. It includes the U.S. Constitution, which is the supreme law of the nation. Any law, federal or state, that conflicts with the **Constitution** is said to be void and has no legal effect. In consulting sources of law, your attorney will look closely indeed to determine how the Constitution affects any other rules of law that adversely affect you. Chapter 6 examines more closely how the U.S. Constitution in particular applies to business practice.

> "The American Constitution is the most wonderful work ever struck off at a given time by the brain and purpose of man."
>
> **–William Gladstone, four-time prime minister of Great Britain in the 1800s**

Next in the hierarchy of federal law comes the **legislation** passed by Congress, also called "**acts**" or "**statutes**" (collections of legislation, often on the same subject, are **codes**). The Clean Air Act discussed in Chapter 19 is an example of such legislation that will be very important in answering the legal questions you have. Federal legislation that is constitutional prevails over all other sources of law. Finally, in federal law your attorney will also have to look at administrative law, specifically, administrative law that regulates business. Administrative law or regulation is made by agencies of the federal government like the Environmental Protection Agency. To answer your legal questions, the Environmental Protection Agency's regulation will be the most important regulatory law of the 15 independent regulatory agencies of the federal government. Chapter 15 will tell you more about administrative regulation in general.

12. STATE LAW

All federal law prevails over all state law in the hierarchy of our sources of law. But state law will still be very important in answering your legal questions about dry cleaning and putting certain pollutants into the air. At the state level, the hierarchy of law sources begins with the state constitution, followed by the statutes or acts adopted by the state legislature, like its commercial code (you will study the **Uniform Commercial Code** or **UCC** in Chapters 8 and 9). Then there is also the regulatory law of the state administrative agencies. Even lower in the hierarchy of law at the state level is the law in the counties and cities called **ordinances.** Counties and cities also sometimes have administrative agencies that help plan local development, such as zoning boards that specify where businesses and housing can be located.

13. JUDICIAL DECISIONS OR CASE LAW

Don't forget that there are court systems in all 50 states plus a federal system. According to the U.S. Department of State, more than 31,000 judges nationwide make numerous decisions every year, adding to the volume of case law.

Finally, your attorney must consult the decisions of judges as a source of law. Even after considering constitutional language, reading legislation, and referring to administrative regulation, your attorney must still know the judicial decisions, called *case law,* that apply to your legal problem. These decisions interpret the relevant constitutional, legislative, and regulatory laws. As previously discussed, judges also make and interpret the common law.

When judges, especially judges who decide appeals from trial courts, make decisions on legal issues, they write their decisions, or **opinions,** setting out reasons. These case opinions are collected and published in book volumes known as "reporters," and these opinions now become **precedents** for future cases involving similar facts and legal issues. To locate prior precedents, it is helpful to know the **citation** for the case where a precedent is found. For example, a case opinion cited as 313 N.W.2d 601 (1982) can be located on page 601 of volume 313 of the *Northwestern Reporter,* second edition, a case decided in 1982. Knowing a case citation, you can easily locate the case in a library or through computer databases.

The extensive reliance of our legal system on judicial case law has both advantages and disadvantages. It is useful to summarize these.

"Stare decisis is the viaduct over which the law travels in transporting the precious cargo of justice."

—Bosely v. Andrews, **393 Pa. 161 (1958)**

Advantages **Stare decisis** is the doctrine of prior precedents. The Latin meaning of these words is "let the prior decision stand." Under *stare decisis,* judges in current cases follow whenever possible the interpretation of law determined by judges in prior cases. This doctrine arose from the desire for certainty and predictability in the law. One important advantage of *stare decisis* was people became secure in their right of property. They then became willing to invest resources in fixed locations for factories and other immovable valuables because they were certain the state would not seize these resources for its own use. Case law helps specify in great detail the boundaries of our property-based legal system, and it protects what is "proper" to people from the interference of others.

Disadvantages Several disadvantages of case law are also important to know. Keep in mind, however, that we do not believe these disadvantages destroy the benefits of certainty, predictability, and stability provided by case law and *stare decisis*. Disadvantages of case law include:

- Volume of cases. Even with computers, searching through hundreds of thousands of cases and then identifying and reading the significant ones is often a very great task. At the very least, it is both time consuming for the attorney and expensive for the client.

- Conflicting precedents. Sometimes in searching prior cases, attorneys find cases in which judicial decisions conflict with each other. Conflicting precedents do not create confidence in the certainty of law.

- Dicta. Increasing the difficulty of determining how to follow prior precedent is the distinction between the **holding** in a prior case and mere **dicta**. The holdings in prior cases are precisely what was necessary to the decision reached. Dicta are whatever else the court said. Judges in future cases are not so likely to follow the dicta in prior cases as they are the holdings.

- Rejection of precedent. Because of *stare decisis,* courts usually hesitate to reject the precedents of prior cases, but sometimes they do. They may think that prior cases were wrongly decided, or they may think that times have changed. In constitutional law the idea that courts should understand the meaning of the Constitution relative to the times in which they interpret it is known as **constitutional relativity. Originalism** is the opposite of constitutional relativity. It stands for the idea that courts should interpret the Constitution only according to the intentions of those who wrote it.

- Conflicts of law. A buyer in Georgia orders equipment by telephone from a seller's representative in Illinois. The buyer directs the seller to ship the equipment to New York. When the equipment breaks down while being used in Pennsylvania, the buyer sues the seller in Ohio where the seller is incorporated. What state's law applies? Courts resolve such problems by applying **conflicts of law** rules, but even these rules may vary from state to state. A better solution is for the buyer and seller to specify in the contract which state's law will apply in case of a dispute. In a tort case, the usual conflicts of law rule applies the law of the state where the injury occurred, no matter where the injury occurred. If a contract specifies no particular state's law for the parties to a dispute to follow, a court interpreting the contract will usually apply the law of the state where the contract was made.

A baseball fan is hurt by a foul ball and sues the baseball team's owner. The court writes, "Whether a fan is injured by a foul ball or an accidentally thrown bat, the result is the same. The fan cannot recover damages against the team because the fan assumes the risk." The comment about "thrown bat" is dicta because the case involved only a foul ball. Bats are heavier and more dangerous than balls, and a judge in a future case may not feel obligated to follow the dicta in this case concerning bats.

Regarding case law, you should note that courts are the institution in our legal system that interpret the meaning of the law, whether that law is the U.S. Constitution, legislation, administrative law, or the common law. Because there are an infinite number of possible cases, each a little bit different on its facts, the power of courts to interpret meaning is very important. Consider the Second Amendment to the Constitution: It says that "the right to bear arms shall not be infringed." What do these words mean? Do they apply constitutionally only to protect seven-foot muskets weighing 20 pounds that a well-trained person could only fire twice a minute? Do they apply constitutionally to protect possession of semiautomatic pistols that an eight-year-old child can fire 20 times a minute? Do they apply to protect ownership of machine guns that can be fired hundreds of times a minute? Now are you beginning to understand the powerful role that courts play in interpreting the meaning not only of the Constitution but of all laws in our legal system?

Do make sure to include a provision for the payment of attorney's fees in any contract loaning money or extending credit to someone.

14. SOURCES OF LAW HIERARCHY IN REVIEW

So your lawyer has to know many sources of law and how they interact in order to answer your question about the pollutants from your cleaning business. It is mistaken to think that lawyers know all of the law that applies to every legal question that you may ask them. However, they should know how to go about answering your questions, including the fact that some questions may not have answers that can be known in advance and that require formal dispute resolution, that is, they require that a judge, or perhaps an arbitrator, decide them.

The hierarchy of the sources of law, however, is well understood. That hierarchy is as follows. Remember that each higher source of law voids, or prevails, over every lower source of law in the hierarchy, except that in many instances there will be no conflict between higher and lower sources of law and in other instances it may not be clear whether or not a higher source of law (such as a constitutional right of speech) conflicts with a lower source of law (such as a law regulating advertising expression).

Hierarchy of sources of law from highest to lowest:

- U.S. Constitution and Amendments.
- Statutes (also called "acts" or "legislation") of Congress.
- Federal administration regulation.
- State constitutions (apply only in individual states).
- State statutes (apply only in individual states).
- State administrative regulation (applies only in individual states).
- Local ordinances (apply only in cities, towns, and other such areas).
- Case law (court cases, as they interpret all of the other sources, may or may not void sources lower than the source being interpreted).

15. LEGAL SANCTIONS

The enforcement of the law is vital to the rule of law and a "proper" legal system. Law enforcement officials and the courts use several methods to encourage or to force compliance with the obedience to the law. These methods, often called **sanctions,** may be used against a person who has failed to comply with the law. The sanctions are in effect a form of punishment for violating the law. Sanctions also have a preventive function. The threat of sanctions usually results in compliance with the requirements of law.

Because punishment is used to secure obedience to the law, the Fourteenth Amendment to the Constitution of the United States provides in part: "No State shall . . . deprive any person of life, liberty or property without due process of law." This provision recognizes that the law is enforced by taking a person's life, freedom, or the resources that he or she owns. The taking of an owner's resources may be (1) for the benefit of society generally, as when land is taken through eminent domain; (2) to punish someone, as with a traffic fine; or (3) for the benefit of another person, as an award of damages. The right of an individual to take another person's resources (especially money) because that person has failed to meet the requirements of the law (e.g., the breach of a contract) is known as a **remedy.** As you study the following sections, identify the remedies available to those seeking through the courts what belongs to another, and keep in mind how important that adequately and fairly enforced sanctions are to a property-based legal system and how nations lacking adequate enforcement sanctions tend to be poor even when they claim to believe in private property.

16. SANCTIONS FOR CRIMINAL CONDUCT

A *crime* is a public wrong against society. Criminal cases are brought by the government on behalf of the people. The people are represented by a state's attorney or U.S. attorney or other public official. When a person is convicted of a crime, one of the following punishments may be imposed:

Do remember that the law divides crimes into misdemeanors and felonies.

- Death.
- Imprisonment.
- Fine.
- Removal from office.
- Disqualification from holding any office and from voting.

Among the purposes of such punishments are to protect the public and to deter persons from wrongful conduct.

17. SANCTIONS FOR BREACH OF CONTRACT

Legally enforceable agreements, called *contracts* (see Chapter 8), are vitally important to business because they allow buyers and sellers to exchange resources and shape their agreements any legal way they wish. When one party to a contract fails to do what he or she agreed to do, a **breach of contract** occurs. The usual remedy for a breach is a suit for dollar damages. These damages, called **compensatory damages,** are awarded to make the victim of the breach "whole" in the economic sense. Such damages compensate the party for all losses that are the direct and foreseeable result of the breach of contract. The objective is that the party be in as good a position as he or she would have been in had the contract been performed. Damages do not make most parties totally "whole," however, because they do not as a general rule include attorney's fees. Unless the contract or some special law provides to the contrary, parties to the contract litigation pay their own attorneys.

Compensatory damages awarded for breach of contract attempt to make a plaintiff "whole," as though in an economic sense the defendant had not breached the contract.

In addition to compensatory damages, breach-of-contract cases may award consequential damages when the breaching party knew or had reason to know that special circumstances existed that would cause the other party to suffer additional losses if the contract were breached.

There are other remedies available for a breach of contract. If a breach by one party is serious enough, the other party may be permitted to rescind or cancel the contract. In some circumstances, the remedy of an injured party may be a decree of **specific performance**—an order by the court commanding the other party actually to perform a bargain as agreed. The single largest number of lawsuits today, especially in the federal courts, involves one business suing another business for breach of contract.

18. SANCTIONS FOR TORTIOUS CONDUCT

A **tort** is a civil wrong other than a breach of contract. Torts involve improper crossing of property boundaries, usually causing injury to our person or other things we own. The boundaries may be physical as when someone trespasses across the boundaries of another's land. Boundaries may also be behavioral as when someone acts unreasonably and injures another.

Tort law helps protect property boundaries by providing *compensation* when someone wrongfully crosses such boundaries.

The law divides torts into the following three categories:

- **Intentional torts.** These torts all require the plaintiff (the person who initiates a lawsuit) to prove the defendant intended to cross the boundaries protecting the plaintiff. Intentional torts include assault (intentionally placing someone in apprehension of his physical safety), battery (intentionally making offensive, unconsented to physical contact with someone), conversion (intentionally depriving someone of goods owned), and trespass (intentionally crossing someone else's land boundaries without permission).
- **Negligence.** This tort requires the plaintiff to show that the defendant injured what was proper to the plaintiff through unreasonable behavior.
- **Strict liability.** Strict liability torts usually require the plaintiff to prove only that the defendant has injured something proper to the plaintiff. Injury caused by an ultrahazardous activity like blasting is an example.

In law, the sanction (or remedy) for tortious conduct is money damages. The damages compensate injured plaintiffs for medical expenses, lost wages or earning power, pain and suffering, and damages to other owned goods and land. **Punitive damages**—also called **exemplary damages**—are also appropriate when the tort is intentional or the unreasonable conduct is extremely severe.

> **Punitive damages** are a civil punishment for intentional or extremely negligent wrongdoing. Their purpose is to deter others from such conduct in the future.

19. SANCTIONS FOR VIOLATING STATUTES AND REGULATIONS

Statutes at both the federal and state levels of government impose a variety of sanctions for violating the statutes or regulations of administrative agencies adopted to accomplish statutory purposes. These sanctions are often similar to those imposed for criminal conduct, breach of contract, or tortious conduct. Many statutes, for example, impose a fine for a violation and authorized damages to injured parties as well. Although common law did not make a defendant pay a plaintiff's attorney fees, many statutes do require so in various circumstances.

You should keep in mind that the sanctions imposed for violating statutes or administrative agency regulations are an important part of enforcing the property-based legal system. These laws help define boundaries and protect us from the boundary infringements of others. Regulations often set boundaries of what it is proper for businesses to do in producing and selling goods and competing with other producers in the market. Many of the chapters in this book examine the boundaries set by various business regulations.

concept >> *summary*

1. Persons and businesses convicted of criminal conduct may be fined, imprisoned, or both.
2. A party who breaches a contract may be required to pay as compensatory damages to the other party the sum of money required to make the victim whole. In addition, special circumstances may justify consequential damages.
3. A tort victim is entitled to collect as damages the amount of money necessary to compensate the injured party for the total harm caused by the intentional or negligent conduct of the wrongdoer.
4. Punitive damages may be awarded in the case of intentional torts.
5. Statutes and regulations issued by government agencies often authorize sanctions similar to those used in the criminal law, contracts, and torts. They usually go further by using a multiplier for damages and award attorney's fees as well.

>> A Property-Based Legal System and Corporate Governance

Under the rule of law in a property-based legal system, all persons have an equal right to their resources. Property problems arise when one person harms another's resources or takes them without permission or authorization. When a stranger takes your car without permission, we call this "theft," and it is easy to appreciate how it violates your right of property under the rule of law. However, more complex property problems can arise.

Much, if not most, business in the United States is transacted through large corporate business organizations. A **corporation** is a business chartered by the state to do business as a legal person in a certain form of organization. Chapter 11 will explain to you the details of corporate legal ownership but, briefly, a corporation is owned by *shareholders* who have *stock* in the business. They vote to elect the *board of directors* who legally run the business but who often hire *managers* to be in charge of day-to-day business operations. In large corporations, few shareholders sit on the board of directors or are managers of these businesses, and thus ownership is usually separate from resource control.

> **Corporations** are businesses chartered by the state to do business as legal persons.

20. THE SPECIFIC SENSE OF CORPORATE GOVERNANCE

Because of the separation of ownership and control, corporate governance is very important. **Corporate governance** refers to the legal rules that structure, empower, and regulate the *agents* (primarily the board of directors and managers) of corporations and define their relationship to the owners (shareholders). Specifically, *corporate governance rules protect the property interest that the owners have in corporations.*

> **Corporate governance** defines the legal relationship between corporate agents like managers or boards of directors and the shareholder owners of the corporation.

Because of the complexity of modern corporations, there are sometimes breakdowns in corporate governance. Managers like the president, vice presidents, or chief financial officer of a corporation can abuse their control of its resources to benefit themselves in ways that impair or even destroy the corporation's value to the shareholders. For example, often these top managers have salaries, bonuses, or stock options that are tied to the corporation's profitability or stock price. If they manipulate the corporation's profit by puffing up assets or concealing debts, they may be able to raise their incomes by millions of dollars even as they mislead the owners about the true value of the corporation and risk corporate collapse when the true situation is disclosed. Other examples of corporate misgovernance include managers' engaging in insider trading of stock, running up stock prices in order to exercise stock options, and taking advantage of business opportunities that rightfully belong to the corporation and its shareholders.

Corporate governance can fail even when corporate managers do nothing illegal. An economically painful recession began in 2008 in part because lenders at large banks allowed and encouraged risky loans that loan applicants could not repay unless the market value of their homes went up substantially. Millions of homeowners borrowed under these conditions. When the market value of housing did not increase and borrowers could not repay their loans, the entire banking system came close to collapse.

Businesses depend on credit, and when they could not borrow money from banks because of the near collapse, many businesses either failed or

PART 1   Introduction

had to lay off employees. Much harm was done to investors and others because those in control of the banks took risks they should not have. Why did they take these risks? That the risky loans they generated led to large salary increases, personal bonuses, stock options, and resale commissions and profits on packaged loans was a significant reason. Bank executives and managers chose to ignore the risk that the housing market might stop its rapid increase in value. After all, the risk was being taken not with their personal money, but with the money of the bank's shareholders and investors. As Nobel laureate Paul Krugman wrote, "[I]t was mainly about gambling with other people's money. The financial industry took big, risky bets with borrowed funds—bets that paid high returns until they went bad—but was able to borrow cheaply because investors didn't understand how fragile the industry was."

21. THE GENERAL SENSE OF CORPORATE GOVERNANCE

In a broad general sense, corporate governance includes the legal property relations that large businesses have with each other, with their customers, and with society.

In a general sense, corporate governance also applies to the legal relationships that businesses have with each other, with their customers, and with society. The economic collapse of 2008 illustrates the need for corporate governance in this general sense. As previously explained, a major factor in the collapse was the risky homeowner lending practice of banks, added to by the risky practices of other financial institutions that repackaged, sold, and resold hundreds of billions of dollars of poor-quality housing loans that were inadequately secured. As long as housing prices were rising, many people made a great deal of money, but when the housing bubble burst and prices began to decline, economic collapse occurred, affecting not only the financial institutions but also the entire economy because credit was too expensive or unavailable. It has been suggested that lack of adequate corporate governance has allowed the risky lending practices that ultimately have led to the biggest recession since the Great Depression of the 1930s. A number of the chapters that follow discuss the general corporate governance that has followed this recession.

>> Key Terms

Act 15	Constitution 15	Holding 17
Administrative law 13	Constitutional law 13	Intentional torts 20
Breach of contract 19	Constitutional relativity 17	Jurisprudence 12
Citation 16	Contract law 14	Law 6
Civil law 13	Corporate governance 21	Legislation 15
Codes 15	Corporation 21	Negligence 20
Common law 13	Criminal law 14	Opinion 16
Compensatory damages 19	Dicta 17	Ordinances 16
Conflicts of law 17	Exemplary damages 20	Originalism 17

Ownership 8
Precedent 16
Private law 14
Procedural law 15
Property 8
Property law 14
Public law 13

Punitive damages 20
Remedy 18
Rule of law 7
Sanctions 18
Specific performance 19
Stare decisis 16
Statute 15

Strict liability 20
Substantive law 15
Tort 19
Tort law 14
Uniform Commercial Code
   (UCC) 16

>> Review Questions and Problems

Introduction
1. *Why Nations Are Economically Weak or Strong*
   (a) Identify several reasons put forth to explain why nations are prosperous or poor.
   (b) What does this section say is the foundation of the private market and prosperity?

Law, the Rule of Law, and Property
2. *Law*
   (a) Define law. Compare and contrast law and custom.
   (b) What role do the courts and police play in the legal system?
3. *The Rule of Law*
   (a) Define the rule of law. How does the rule of law differ from law as the commands of the state?
   (b) Explain why the rule of law is "an ideal rather than a complete fact."
4. *Property*
   (a) What is property? How does property differ from "resources"?
   (b) Why is property important to society? To private enterprise?
5. *Property in Its Broadest Sense*
   (a) Explain why property can be thought of as the central concept underlying Western legal systems.
   (b) What does James Madison mean when he says we have property in our opinions "and free communication of them"?
6. *Jurisprudence*
   (a) Define jurisprudence and name four schools of jurisprudence.
   (b) Describe the main difference between the jurisprudences of natural law and sociological jurisprudence.

Classifications of Law
7. *Common Law and Civil Law*
   (a) What is "common law"? Why is the United States a "common law country"?
   (b) What is the primary distinction between common law and civil law legal systems?
8. *Public and Private Law*
   (a) What is public law? Give three examples of public law.
   (b) Explain private law. Give three examples.
9. *Civil Law and Criminal Law*
   (a) What is the difference between civil law and criminal law?
   (b) Explain the two ways that the words *civil law* are used in this chapter.

10. *Substantive Law and Procedural Law*

   (a) Define substantive law and procedural law.

   (b) Is contract law substantive law or procedural law? How about a rule specifying that a defendant has 30 days to respond to a complaint?

Sources of Law

11. *Federal Law*

   (a) Explain what it means to say that constitutions are the "highest laws of the nation."

   (b) Explain the important distinctions between state and federal constitutions.

12. *State Law*

   (a) Give two additional terms for legislation.

   (b) Why is uniformity of law important to business? How can legislators achieve uniformity of the laws affecting business? What is the most significant uniform law affecting business?

   (c) For what purposes do administrative agencies exist?

13. *Judicial Decisions or Case Law*

   (a) Define *stare decisis*. What are its advantages? Disadvantages?

   (b) What is the distinction between a precedent and dicta in judicial decisions, and how does this distinction relate to stare decisis?

   (c) Alex was on a coast-to-coast trip by automobile. While passing through Ohio, Alex had a flat tire. It was fixed by Sam's Turnpike Service Station, and later, while Alex was driving in Indiana, the tire came off and Alex was injured. Alex was hospitalized in Indiana, so he sued Sam in Indiana for the injuries. What rules of substantive law will the Indiana court use to determine if Sam is at fault? Explain.

14. *Sources of Law Hierarchy in Review*

   (a) Explain the relationship of case law to the other sources of law.

15. *Legal Sanctions*

   (a) Why are legal sanctions important in a property-based legal system?

   (b) What is the difference between a sanction and a remedy?

16. *Sanctions for Criminal Conduct*

   (a) What are the sanctions for criminal conduct.

   (b) Name three purposes of criminal sanctions.

17. *Sanctions for Breach of Contract*

   (a) What is the purpose of compensatory damages?

   (b) What is specific performance of a contract?

18. *Sanctions for Tortious Conduct*

   (a) What are the two premises of tort liability?

   (b) When are punitive damages appropriate in a tort case?

19. *Sanctions for Violating Statutes and Regulations*

   (a) What types of sanctions are used for the violation of statutes and regulations?

   (b) What is an injunction?

A Property-Based Legal System and Corporate Governance

20. *The Specific Sense of Corporate Governance*

   (a) What is the "specific" sense of corporate governance?

   (b) Why might some managers try to artificially raise or "puff up" the market price of their stocks? Describe several ways they could do this.

21. *The General Sense of Corporate Governance*
    (a) What is the "general" sense of corporate governance?
    (b) Discuss how effective corporate governance contributes to the creation of economic wealth.

business >> *discussions*

1. As the vice president of finance for a company producing and selling electronic switchboards, you are considering foreign investment to build a plant to assemble electronic components. A source in Russia advises you that a town near Moscow may be an excellent location for a new plant. Russians are well educated and willing to work for reasonable wages. Projected construction costs are acceptable. Both rail lines and airports are nearby, and the current Russian government seems politically stable. The town even has a technical college that will be an excellent source for skilled employees. The plant will ship most of the finished electronic components back to the United States.

> Do you know everything you need to make an investment decision?
> If not, what else do you need to know about investment in foreign countries?
> What does it mean to say that law is the foundation of the private enterprise system?

2. Three years ago the Darden Corporation bought a thousand acres of land that borders the Potowac River in Washam County. While waiting on development opportunities, Darden cut timber to help repay the mortgage loan it took out to buy the land. On March 2, the Washam County Commission proposed an ordinance to establish a 250-foot-wide greenway along the south side of the Potowac that will effectively ban both development and timbering on nearly 80 acres of Darden's land. The same day in an unrelated accident a Darden truck ran over a hunter who was hunting without permission on the company's land. Darden immediately contacted an attorney in Washam City.

- What is law?
- What does it mean to say that Darden has "property" in the land? That the hunter has "property" in himself?
- What sources of law will the attorney have to understand in order to advise Darden about the proposed greenway? The company's potential responsibility to the hunter?

Chapter 3. The Court System

3 The Court System

Learning Objectives

In this chapter you will learn:

3-1. To recognize the role of key personnel associated with the courts.

3-2. To know the organization of the state and federal court systems.

3-3. To understand the power of judicial review and the philosophies of judicial restraint and judicial activism.

3-4. To appreciate and contrast the background and judicial alignment of the justices of the U.S. Supreme Court.

3-5. To analyze a sample case from the U.S. Supreme Court, including the majority, concurring, and dissenting opinions.

A viable court system is crucial to maintaining the rule of law. This chapter deals with the court system and the court's authority to decide disputes between parties. First, it examines the personnel who operate our courts, including the role of judges, jurors, and lawyers in a case. It next explores the organizational structure of both the state and federal courts and the differences between trial courts and appellate courts. Finally, the chapter examines the U.S. Supreme Court and the concept of judicial review and the role of courts in interpreting the Constitution, state and federal legislation, and the making of common law in the process of deciding cases (*stare decisis*).

By the time you have completed this chapter, you should have an understanding of the court system and a greater sensitivity for how the courts apply the law. You will understand the importance of every citizen willingly serving on a

Managers often are involved in the litigation process as either parties or witnesses in a case.

jury and receiving the cooperation of employers and the protection of the government for doing so. You will appreciate the difficult questions jurors must answer and the complex cases juries must decide. Finally, you will appreciate the difficulty that arises in resolving legal disputes.

>> *sidebar* 3.1

The Soaring Cost of Legal Representation

When a lawsuit is filed, how much does it cost to defend a company and its executives? How much can it cost to defend against a criminal prosecution? In some cases, the mere investigation may run into tens of millions of dollars. Massive legal expenses are a major concern for both executives and shareholders. Defense costs can bankrupt a small business. In an accounting fraud investigation, Qwest

Communications spent $75 million on legal fees in one year. Tyco International spent about $50 million to defend and investigate its practices. In 2011, it is estimated that Galleon Group LLC co-founder Raj Rajaratnam spent as much as $40 million unsuccessfully defending an insider trading criminal action. His legal bills were about two-thirds of the amount he allegedly made from the trades.

LO 3-1   >> Personnel

Before we look at the court system, you should have some background and understanding of the individuals who operate our court system. Judges apply the law to the facts, jurors find or determine the facts from conflicting evidence, and the facts as found by the jury are given great deference. In the process of representing clients, lawyers present evidence to the jury and argue the law to the court. Collectively, these persons conduct the search for truth. The court system is the way we enforce our laws in a property-based legal system. Without the courts, our legal system could not operate.

1. JUDGES AND JUSTICES

"Facts are stubborn things; and whatever may be our wishes, our inclinations, or the dictates of our passion, they cannot alter the state of facts and evidence."

–John Adams

The individuals who operate our courts are called judges or magistrates. In some appellate courts, such as the U.S. Supreme Court, members of the court are called justices. In this discussion, we will refer to trial court persons as judges and reviewing court persons as justices.

In all cases, the function of the trial judge is to determine the applicable rules of law to be used to decide the case. Such rules may be procedural or substantive. In cases tried without a jury, the judge is also responsible for finding the facts. In cases tried before a jury, the function of the jury is to decide questions of fact. The judge still is responsible for deciding questions of law.

Most cases are resolved before trial and even fewer cases lead to an appeal.

Trial judges are the main link between the law and the citizens it serves. The trial judge renders decisions that deal directly with people in conflict. These judges have the primary duty to observe and to apply constitutional limitations and guarantees. They bear the burden of upholding the dignity of the courts and maintaining respect for the law.

Justices do more than simply decide an appeal—they often give reasons for their decisions. These reasoned decisions become precedent and a part of our body of law that may affect society as a whole, as well as the litigants. So in deciding cases, justices must consider not only the result between the parties but also the total effect of the decision on the law. In this sense, their role is similar to that of legislators. When reviewing appeals, justices are essentially concerned with issues of *law;* issues of *fact* normally are resolved at the trial court level.

For these reasons, the personal characteristics required for a justice or appellate judge are somewhat different from those for a trial judge. The manner of performing duties and the methods used also vary between trial and reviewing courts. A trial judge who has observed the witnesses is able to use knowledge gained from participation as an essential ingredient in his or her decisions. A justice must spend most of the time studying the briefs, the record of proceedings, and the law in reaching decisions.

The judiciary, because of the power of judicial review, has perhaps the most extensive power of any branch of government. This issue will be extensively examined later in the chapter. Lower court judges' decisions may be reviewed by a reviewing court, but they have personal immunity from legal actions against them based on their judicial acts.

*Judges and justices often sacrifice considerable financial opportunities by giving up the practice of law in the prime of their careers.

2. JURORS

It is important to understand the role of the jury as a fact-finding body. Since litigation may involve both questions of law and questions of fact, the deference given to the decisions of a jury is very important. Trial by jury is a cherished right guaranteed by the Bill of Rights. The Sixth and Seventh Amendments to the Constitution guarantee the right of trial by jury in both criminal and civil cases. The **petit jury** is the trial jury that returns a verdict in both situations.

Although juries are used in only a very small percentage of all cases, they remain critical to the administration of justice. In civil cases the right to trial by a jury is preserved in suits at common law when the amount in controversy exceeds $20. State constitutions have similar provisions guaranteeing the right of trial by jury in state courts.

Historically, a jury consisted of 12 persons. Today many states and some federal courts have rules of procedure that provide for smaller juries in both criminal and civil cases. Such provisions are acceptable since the federal law does not specify the *number* of jurors—only the *types* of cases that may be brought to trial before a jury at common law. Several studies have found no discernible difference between results reached by a six-person jury and those reached by a 12-person jury. As a result, many cases are tried before six-person juries today.

In most states, a jury's decision must be unanimous because many believe that the truth is more nearly to be found and justice rendered if the jury acts only on one common conscience. However, there is growing evidence that the requirement of unanimity is taking its toll on the administration of justice in the United States. Holdout jurors contribute to mistrials and many cases are routinely deadlocked by margins of 11–1 or 10–2. Many states have eliminated the requirement of unanimity in their courts in civil cases and two states have done so in criminal cases. Several legal commentators have argued

Rule 48 of the Federal Rules of Civil Procedure states that the "court shall seat a jury of not fewer than six and not more than twelve members." Local rules allow district courts to set the number of jurors consistent with this rule.

*The quality of a jury depends upon the ability to get competent and dedicated citizens to serve.

that unanimous jury verdicts are not constitutionally mandated and should be eliminated to help restore public confidence in our jury system.

Thanks to a series of sensationalized trials, the jury system has been subject to much criticism. Many argue that jurors are not qualified to distinguish fact from fiction, that they vote their prejudices, and that their emotions are too easily swayed by skilled trial lawyers. However, most members of the bench and bar feel the right to be tried by a jury of one's peers in criminal cases is the most effective method of discovering the truth and giving the accused his or her "day in court."

>> *sidebar* 3.2

Jury Consultants and Technical Support: Other Key Parties in Litigation

Jury consultants and technical support services are often a key aspect of litigation. The following list provides a sense of the ways in which they offer trial support:

- Coaching attorneys
- Conducting community attitude surveys
- Providing focus groups

- Developing *voir dire* to elicit attitudes and experiences
- Creating a theme for the case
- Preparing sophisticated demonstrative exhibits, including timelines
- Helping with media management for high-profile cases

> "I do not assert that the jury trial is an infallible mode of ascertaining truth. Like everything human, it has its imperfection. I only say, that it is the best protection for innocence and the surest mode of punishing guilt that has yet been discovered. It has borne the test of longer experience, and borne it better than any other legal institution that ever existed among men."
>
> —Jeremiah Black, defense attorney in the case of *Ex Parte Milligan*, 71 U.S. 2 (1886).

Jurors normally do not give reasons for their decisions, although some special verdicts may require juries to answer a series of questions. Actually, it would be almost impossible for the jury to agree on the reasons for its verdict. A jury may agree as to the result but disagree on some of the facts, and different jurors may have different ideas or understandings of the testimony.

Many individuals attempt to avoid jury duty. Some lose money because of time away from a job or profession. Others feel great stress in having to help make important decisions affecting the lives of many people. Because so many potential jurors seek relief from jury duty, many trials often end up with more jurors who are unemployed or retired than should be the case. Today, there is a strong trend toward requiring jury duty of all citizens, irrespective of any hardship that such service may entail. Courts often refuse to accept excuses because jury duty is a responsibility of all citizens in a free society.

One of the most difficult issues facing the judicial system is the right to a trial by jury in very complex and complicated cases that frequently take a long time to try. For example, many antitrust cases involve economic issues that baffle economists, and such cases may last for several months or even years. The average juror may not comprehend the meaning of much of the evidence, let alone remember it when it is time to make a decision. As a practical matter, many persons cannot serve on a jury for several weeks or months. How does a free and democratic society deliver a trial by jury of one's peers, if busy people are excused from jury service? For these and other reasons, some experts recommend that the right to a trial by jury be abolished in very complex and time-consuming cases.

Many of the largest jury verdicts involve medical malpractice, products liability, fraud, or breach of contract. Juries have been increasingly generous to plaintiffs who suffer death or serious physical injury. Many plaintiffs' lawyers now contend that million dollar awards—once the standard for measuring a successful case—are no longer indicative of a major victory.

3. LAWYERS

Our court system is an adversarial one. Although private parties may represent themselves without a lawyer, as a practical matter, lawyers are required in most cases. Since knowledge of court procedures and substantive law is required as a bare minimum in most cases, lawyers serve as the representative advocates in our court system. They present the evidence, the points of law, and the arguments that are weighed by juries and judges in making their decisions.

A lawyer's first duty is to the administration of justice. As an officer of the court, he or she should see that proceedings are conducted in a dignified and orderly manner and that issues are tried on their merits only. The practice of law should not be a game or a battle of wits, but a means to promote justice. The lawyer's duties to each client require the highest degree of fidelity, loyalty, and integrity.

A lawyer serves in three capacities: counselor, advocate, and public servant. As a counselor, a lawyer by the very nature of the profession knows his or her client's most important secrets and affairs. A lawyer is often actively involved in the personal decisions of clients, ranging from their business affairs and family matters such as divorce to their alleged violations of the criminal law. These relationships dictate that a lawyer meet the highest standards of professional and ethical conduct.

The tension between the business community and the legal profession has been growing in recent years. This conflict has been fueled by the increasing number of lawsuits filed by lawyers on behalf of their clients, by resistance from organized lawyer advocacy groups like the American Bar Association to reforms, and by the high costs of attorney fees that businesses must absorb. As the size and revenue generated by law firms grows every year, many of the nation's largest law firms take on the look of a large business enterprise. Table 3.1 provides you with a sense of the size and scope of larger law firms today. The big law firm surge has been fueled by the demand for high-end legal services needed by corporations and other large businesses.

Lawyers can be sanctioned for unethical conduct and some have gone to jail for illegal conduct.

*Lawyers may have many clients and often handle complex and complicated cases. The American Bar Association reported over 1 million licensed lawyers in the United States in 2005.

table 3.1 >> 2010 Law Firm Gross Revenues

Firm	Gross Revenue	Change from 2009	Lawyers/Equity Partners
Baker & McKenzie	$2.104 billion	–.04%	3,738/717
Skadden	$2.1 billion	0%	1,859/430
DLA Piper	$1.961 billion	n/a	3,348/416
Latham & Watkins	$1.929 billion	5.9%	1,931/451
Hogan Lovells	$1.664.5 billion	n/a	2,363/512

Source: www.americanlawyer.com/amlaw100

Obviously, if a lawyer is to give competent advice, he or she must know to the fullest extent possible all the facts involved in any legal problem presented by the client. To encourage full disclosure by a client, the rules of evidence provide that confidential communications to a lawyer are privileged. The law does not permit a lawyer to reveal such facts and testify against a client, even if called to do so at a trial. This is the attorney-client privilege, and it may extend to communications made to the lawyer's employees in certain cases. This is especially important today because law firms frequently use paralegals (legal assistants) to gather facts and assist attorneys.

concept >> *summary*

Personnel

1. Trial judges determine the applicable law and, in cases without a jury, they also are responsible for finding the facts.
2. Appellate courts act as reviewing courts and generally are concerned with issues of law.
3. The petit jury is the trial jury that returns a verdict.
4. The nation's top 10 jury verdicts include 3 over $500 million.
5. Lawyers serve three roles: counselor, advocate, and public servant.

LO 3-2 >> Organization of the Court System

There are two major court systems in the United States: the federal courts and the 50 state courts. The federal court system and those in most states contain three levels—trial courts, courts of appeals, and supreme courts. Lawsuits begin at the **trial court** level, and the results may be reviewed at one or more of the other two **appellate court** levels. Critical to every lawsuit is the question of subject matter jurisdiction.

4. SUBJECT MATTER JURISDICTION

Jurisdiction refers to the power of a court, at the state or federal level, to hear a case. For any court to hear and decide a case at any level, it must have **subject matter jurisdiction,** which is the power over the issues involved in the case. Some state trial courts have what is called general jurisdiction, or the power to hear any type of case. Other state courts have only limited jurisdiction, or the power to hear only certain types of cases. Jurisdiction may be limited as to subject matter, amount in controversy, or area in which the parties live.

Courts, especially those of limited jurisdiction, may be named according to the subject matter with which they deal. Probate courts deal with wills and the estates of deceased persons, juvenile courts with juvenile crime and dependent children, criminal and police courts with violators of state laws and municipal ordinances, and traffic courts with traffic violations.

Courts of different scope and subject matter jurisdiction help create order and efficiency.

Even trial courts (courts of general jurisdiction) cannot attempt to resolve every dispute or controversy that may arise. Some issues are simply nonjusticiable. For example, courts would not attempt to referee a football or basketball game. They would not hear a case to decide how English or math should be taught in the public schools. Moreover, courts do not accept cases involving trivial matters.

5. STATE COURTS

State court systems are created, and their operations are governed, from three sources. First, state constitutions provide the general framework for the court system. Second, the state legislature, pursuant to constitutional authority, enacts statutes that add body to the framework. This legislation provides for various courts, establishes their jurisdiction, and regulates the tenure, selection, and duties of judges. Other legislation may establish the general rules of procedure to be used by these courts. Each court sets forth its own rules of procedure within the statutory bounds. These rules are detailed and may specify, for example, the times when various documents must be filed with the court clerk.

> Currently, 39 states elect judges at some level.

Trial Courts Depending upon the particular state, a general trial court can take on any number of names: the *superior court,* the *circuit court,* or the *district court.* In the trial courts, parties file their lawsuits or complaints seeking to protect their property rights or redress a wrongdoing. The complaint describes the parties (John Doe versus Sally Smith), the facts and law giving rise to a cause of action, the authority of the court to decide the case, and the relief requested from the court. (See Chapter 4 for a more complete explanation of the litigation process including a sample complaint.) The trial court is responsible for determining both the facts and the law in the case.

Appellate Courts The parties to litigation are entitled as a matter of right to a review of their case by a higher court, or an **appeal,** if the requirements of procedural law are followed in seeking the review. In some states there is only one appellate court, which is usually called the supreme court of the state. In more populous states, there often are

> 95% to 98% of all complaints are settled or fully resolved at the trial court level. Very few cases, by comparison, are appealed.

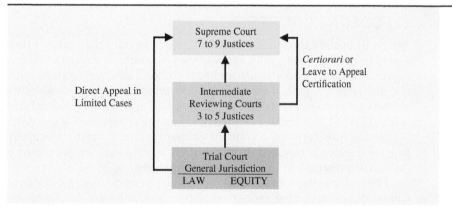

Figure 3.1 *Typical state court system*

two levels of reviewing courts—an intermediate level and a court of final resort. In states with two levels of review, the intermediate courts are usually called the **courts of appeal,** and the highest court is again called the **supreme court.** In states with two levels of reviewing courts, most appeals are taken to the lower of the two courts, and the highest court of the state will review only very important cases. Intermediate courts of review typically consist of three to five judges. A state supreme court typically has seven to nine judges.

Reviewing courts review are essentially concerned with questions of law. Although a party is entitled to one trial and one appeal, he or she may obtain a second review if the higher reviewing court, in the exercise of its discretion, agrees to such a review. The procedure for requesting a second review is called in some states a *petition for leave to appeal* and in others a petition for a ***writ of certiorari.*** The process for requesting a review is explained more fully in Section 7 in this chapter. Deciding such requests is a major function of the highest court in each state. As a practical matter, less than 5% of all such requests are granted.

>> *sidebar* 3.3

Small-Claims Courts

One court of limited jurisdiction, falling below the trial court, is especially important to the business community. This court, usually known as **small-claims court,** handles much of the litigation between businesses and its customers. Small-claims courts are used by businesses to collect accounts and by customers to settle disputes with the business community that are relatively minor from a financial perspective. Such suits are often quite important from the standpoint of principle. Landlord-tenant disputes are an example of controversies decided in these courts. Small-claims courts have low court costs and simplified procedures. The informality of the proceedings speeds up the flow of cases. The services of a lawyer are not usually required, and some states do not allow lawyers to participate in these proceedings. Lawsuits filed in small-claims courts usually are subject to a dollar limitation, such as a maximum of $25,000, often ranging from $500 to $5,000.

---

6. FEDERAL COURTS

Article III of the Constitution (see Appendix) provides that judicial power be vested in the Supreme Court and such lower courts as Congress may create. Figure 3.2 shows you the hierarchy of the federal court system. The judicial power of the federal courts has been limited by Congress. Essentially, it extends to matters involving (1) questions of federal law (federal question cases), (2) the United States as a party, (3) controversies among the states, and (4) certain suits between citizens of different states (diversity of citizenship). Federal question cases and diversity of citizenship cases require further discussion as presented in the following paragraphs.

*Federal courts have subject matter jurisdiction over federal question cases and diversity of citizenship cases.

Federal question cases may be based on issues arising out of the U.S. Constitution or out of federal statutes. Any amount of money may be

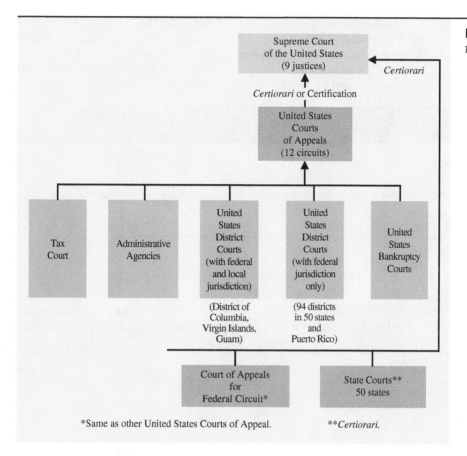

Figure 3.2 *The federal court system*

involved in such a case, and it need not be a suit for damages. For example, a suit to enjoin a violation of a constitutional right can be filed in a federal court as a federal question case. These civil actions may involve matters based on federal laws such as those dealing with patents, copyrights, trademarks, taxes, or employment discrimination. The rights guaranteed by the Bill of Rights of the Constitution also may be the basis for a federal question case.

Diversity of citizenship requires that all plaintiffs be citizens of different states from all defendants. If a case involves a party on one side that is a citizen of the same state as a party on the other, there will then be no diversity of citizenship and thus no federal jurisdiction. Courts have held that it is the citizenship of the party in the case that determines whether diversity of citizenship exists. For example, diversity jurisdiction is based on the citizenship of all members of a partnership.

The fact that business corporations, which are considered persons before the law, are frequently incorporated in one state and have their principal place of business in another state also causes problems in determining when diversity of citizenship exists. For purposes of diversity jurisdiction, a corporation is a citizen of the state of incorporation and also a citizen of the state in which it has its principal place of business. Thus, a Delaware corporation with its principal place of business in Illinois is a citizen of both Delaware and Illinois for purposes of diversity. If any party on the other side of a lawsuit with such a corporation is a citizen of either Illinois or Delaware, there is then no diversity and no federal jurisdiction.

>> *sidebar* 3.4

Circuit Scoreboard

The following chart illustrates the number of cases granted certiorari by the U.S. Supreme Court:

CIRCUIT	NUMBER OF CASES	%	DECIDED	% AFF'D	% REV'D
CA1	2	2%	1	100%	0%
CA2	4	5%	0		
CA3	5	6%	3	67%	33%
CA4	4	5%	2	50%	50%
CA5	5	6%	3	33%	67%
CA6	6	7%	3	0%	100%
CA7	5	6%	3	0%	100%
CA8	4	5%	2	50%	50%
CA9	25	31%	16	13%	87%
CA10	—				
CA11	3	4%	1	0%	100%
CA DC	—				
CA Fed	7	9%	2	0%	100%
State	9	11%	2	0%	100%
Dist. Ct	1	1%			
Original	1	1%			

Source: Scotus Blog http://sblog.s3.amazonaws.com/wp-content/uploads/2011/05/SB_stat_pack_050311.pdf for the October Term 2010 through May 3, 2011.

In diversity of citizenship cases, the federal courts have a jurisdictional amount of more than $75,000. If a case involves multiple plaintiffs with separate and distinct claims, *each* claim must satisfy the jurisdictional amount. Thus, in a class-action suit, the claim of each plaintiff must be greater than the $75,000 jurisdictional amount.

One of the reasons Congress provides for diversity of citizenship jurisdiction is to guard against state court bias against the nonresident party in a lawsuit. Since the biggest increase in federal lawsuits in recent years has been over businesses suing one another in contract disputes, diversity jurisdiction preserves the sense of fairness in such situations when one of the parties is out of state.

District Courts The federal district courts are the trial courts of the federal judicial system. There is at least one such court in every state and the District of Columbia. These courts have subject matter jurisdiction over all the cases mentioned above. These courts have the authority to review lawsuits, receive evidence, evaluate testimony, impanel juries, and resolve disputes. Most significant federal litigation begins in this court. The **Federal Rules of Civil Procedure** provide the details concerning procedures to be followed in federal court litigation. These rules are strictly enforced by the courts and must be followed by the parties in every lawsuit.

An adverse decision from a federal district court in Atlanta may be appealed to the Eleventh Circuit Court of Appeals.

Appellate Courts Under its constitutional authorization, Congress has created 12 U.S. Courts of Appeal plus a special Court of Appeals for the Federal Circuit as intermediate appellate courts in the federal system. This special reviewing court, located in Washington, D.C., hears appeals from special courts such as the U.S. Claims Court and Contract Appeals as well as from administrative decisions such as those made by the Patent and Trademark Office. Other courts, such as the Court of Appeals for Armed Forces, have been created to handle special subject matter. Figure 3.3 illustrates the location of the Courts of Appeals.

7. DECISIONS BY THE U.S. SUPREME COURT

In addition to the court of appeals, the federal court system provides for a Supreme Court. Because the litigants are entitled to only one review, or appeal, a subsequent review by the U.S. Supreme Court must be obtained through a petition for a *writ of certiorari* to the Supreme Court.

A petition for a *writ of certiorari* is a request by the losing party in the court of appeals for permission to file an appeal with the U.S. Supreme Court. In such situations, the Supreme Court has discretion as to whether or not it will grant the petition and allow another review. This review is not a matter of right. *Writs of certiorari* are granted primarily in cases of substantial federal importance or where there is an obvious conflict between decisions of two or more U.S. Circuit Courts of Appeal in an important area of the law that needs clarification. Pursuant to the U.S. Constitution (Art. III. Sec. 2), the Supreme Court also has original jurisdiction over a small range of cases, including those affecting ambassadors and in which the state is a party. The Supreme Court's decision becomes the law of the land and reconciles the division of opinion between the lower courts.

*Four U.S. Supreme Court justices must vote yes to grant a petition for a *writ of certiorari.*

When the U.S. Supreme Court reviews petitions for a *writ of certiorari,* the writ is granted if four of the nine justices vote to take the case. The Supreme Court spends a great deal of time and effort in deciding which cases it will hear. It is able to pick and choose those issues with which it will be involved and to control its caseload. The Supreme Court normally resolves cases involving major constitutional issues or interpretation of federal law. In recent years, the Court has been very reluctant to review many lower court decisions. In the 2006–2007 term of the U.S. Supreme Court, only 75 cases were heard. (See Sidebar 3.5.)

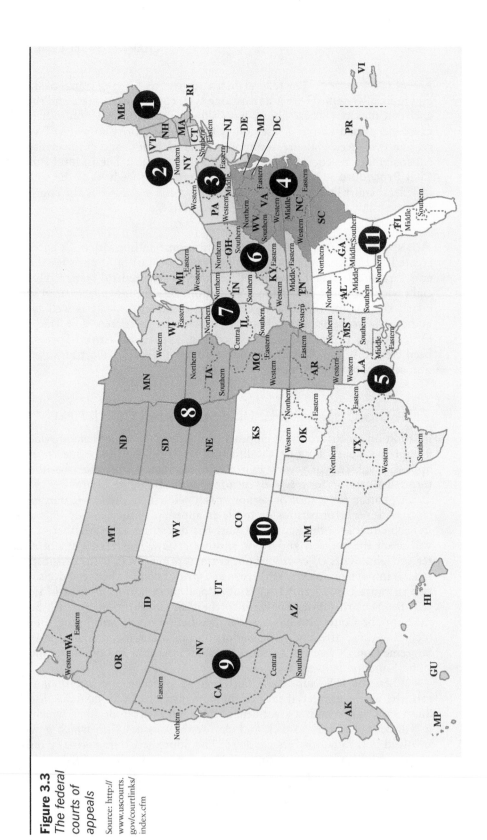

Figure 3.3
The federal courts of appeals

Source: http://
www.uscourts.
gov/courtlinks/
index.cfm

>> *sidebar* 3.5

Very Slim Odds

Every year, thousands of petitions are filed in the U.S. Supreme Court by parties seeking review of adverse decisions by federal circuit courts of appeal or state supreme courts. The Supreme Court grants only a fraction of the petitions filed. During the 2001–02 term, the Supreme Court agreed to hear 88 cases; then, during the 2004–05 term, that number fell to 80 cases. Of the 8,517 petitions filed in the Court's 2005–06 term, 78 were granted argument (0.9%). For the 2010–11 term, 81 merits opinions are expected. For ongoing updates, see The U.S. Supreme Court Blog: http://www.scotusblog.com/.

Sources: David Thompson & Melanie Wachtell, "An Analysis of Supreme Court Petition Procedures," 16:2 *George Mason Law Review*, 240 (2009) and Scotus Blog http://sblog.s3.amazonaws.com/wp-content/uploads/2011/05/SB_stat_pack_050311.pdf for the October Term 2010 through May 3, 2011.

The Supreme Court is far more likely to review and reverse a decision rendered by the Ninth Circuit Court of Appeals—treating it, as one commentator noted, like a wayward child. Many commentators attribute the difference to the judicial activism of the Ninth Circuit, which often is at odds with the philosophy of judicial restraint found in the Supreme Court in recent years. In contrast, decisions rendered by the Fourth Circuit Court of Appeals tend to be far more conservative or consistent with the philosophy of judicial restraint. A more thorough discussion of these two philosophies will follow in Sections 8 and 9 of this chapter.

*Supreme Court case reviews have been steadily declining in recent years.

The federal district courts and the courts of appeal cannot review, retry, or correct judicial errors charged against a state court. Final judgments or decrees rendered by the highest court of a state are reviewed only by the

>> *sidebar* 3.6

The Role of the Reviewing Court

Since reviewing courts create case law or precedent in the process of deciding cases, most final decisions of reviewing courts are published in order to make the precedent of each case available for inclusion into the total body of law. The opinions usually include the procedures which have been followed, the facts of the case, the law applicable to the facts, the decision of the court, and the reasons for the decision. Opinions may be written in the name of the author of the opinion or they may be written *per curiam*—by the court without identifying the author.

It is not surprising that the decisions of a reviewing court often are not unanimous. Some Supreme Court decisions are closely divided and 5–4 or 6–3 decisions in cases involving highly controversial issues are quite common. The *Roe v. Wade* decision legalizing abortions, and the cases involving abortions which followed, often have been decided 5–4 or 6–3. Presidential appointments to the Supreme Court are evaluated, in part, on their potential effect on the court alignment as perceived in the close decisions of the past.

The written opinions in the cases in this textbook reflect the majority opinion of the reviewing court and as such they reflect the current status of the law. Dissenting opinions of the court also make a contribution to our jurisprudence and to the public debate on important social and public policy issues. Dissents often provide the foundation for changes in public policy and they often provide guidance to legislative bodies on issues under consideration.

Supreme Court of the United States. State cases reviewed by the U.S. Supreme Court must concern a federal question involving the validity of state action on the grounds that the statute under review is repugnant to the Constitution, treaties, or laws of the United States. If the case does not involve a federal question, the decision of the highest state court is not subject to review by the Supreme Court of the United States.

concept >> *summary*

Organization of the Court System

1. The court system—both at the federal and state level—operates on three levels: the trial court, the court of appeals, and the supreme court.

2. Trial courts focus on the law and facts while reviewing courts focus only on the law.

3. The parties to litigation are entitled as a matter of right to one review of their case by a higher court.

4. Subject matter jurisdiction must exist for a court to hear a case.

5. Federal courts typically obtain jurisdiction upon diversity of citizenship or federal questions.

6. The highest legal authority in the United States is the U.S. Supreme Court.

7. Parties seek permission to bring their case to the Supreme Court through a petition for a *writ of certiorari*.

LO 3-3 >> The Power of Judicial Review

*Judicial review is the ultimate power to invalidate actions by the president or the Congress.

In the United States the most significant power of the courts, or "judiciary," is **judicial review,** which is the power to review laws passed by the legislative body and to declare them to be unconstitutional and void. It also allows the courts to review actions taken by the executive branch and to declare them unconstitutional. Although the Constitution does not expressly provide that the judiciary shall be the overseer of the government, the net effect of this power is to make it so. Chief Justice John Marshall in *Marbury v. Madison,* 5 U.S. 137 (1803), announced the power of judicial review using in part the following language and reasoning:

> It is a proposition too plain to be contested, that the constitution controls any legislative act repugnant to it; or, that the legislature may not alter the constitution by an ordinary act. . . .
>
> It is emphatically the province and duty of the judicial department to say what the law is. Those who apply the rule to particular cases, must of necessity expound and interpret that rule. If two laws conflict with each other, the courts must decide on the operation of each. So, if a law be in opposition to the constitution; if both the law and the constitution apply to a particular case, so that the court must either decide that case, conformably to the law, disregarding the constitution; or conformably to the constitution, disregarding the law; the court must determine which of these conflicting rules governs the case: this is of the very essence of judicial duty. If then, the courts are to regard the constitution, and the constitution is superior to any ordinary act of the legislature, the constitution, and not such ordinary act, must govern the case to which they both apply.

In practice, the U.S. Supreme Court rarely exercises its extraordinary powers and has developed carefully crafted rules as self-imposed limits on its authority as individual jurists.

As individual jurists exercise the power of judicial review, they do so with varying political attitudes and philosophies. Some judges believe that judicial power should be used very sparingly, although others are willing to use it more often. Those who believe that the power should not be used except in unusual cases are said to believe in **judicial restraint.** Those who think that the power should be used whenever the needs of society justify its use believe in **judicial activism.** All members of the judiciary believe in judicial restraint and all are activists to some extent. Often a jurist may be an activist in one area of the law and a firm believer in judicial restraint in another. Both judicial restraint and judicial activism describe attitudes or tendencies by matters of degree. Both terms are also used to describe general attitudes toward the exercise of the power of judicial review.

In recent years, judicial restraint has been associated with conservative judges often appointed by Republican presidents. Judicial activism primarily is linked to liberal judges generally appointed by Democratic presidents. The tension between these philosophies has become more pronounced in the past several years often leading to bitterly divided confirmation hearings before the U.S. Senate where less attention often is paid to a nominee's qualifications than to his or her political views. It is important to remember, however, that conservative judges may take activist positions. Court decisions should be analyzed on their merits with an open mind. Sidebar 3.7 describes the process of becoming a Supreme Court justice. Sidebar 3.8 highlights the first five years of the Roberts court.

The terms judicial restraint and judicial activism are not exclusive to particular judges. Many judges may share aspects of both in their judicial philosophy.

>> *sidebar* 3.7

Choosing a Supreme Court Justice

In the federal system, the U.S. Constitution gives the president the power to appoint federal judges, including Supreme Court justices, subject to the advice and consent of the U.S. Senate. In practical terms, this means a majority of the U.S. Senate must vote to confirm the president's nominee. Typically, after the president announces his nominee, interest groups on both sides search out information, including past decisions, about the candidate. The nominee is questioned by the Senate Judiciary Committee, which also hears testimony from others about the nominee's qualifications and judicial philosophy. If the Judiciary Committee approves the nominee, the nomination is forwarded to the entire Senate for debate before a vote is taken. The confirmation process can take months and is often subject to bitter conflict between Republican and Democratic senators and the White House.

8. JUDICIAL RESTRAINT

The philosophy of judicial restraint developed naturally from the recognition that, in exercising the power of judicial review, the courts are overseeing coequal branches of government. When the power of judicial review is used to set aside decisions by the other branches of government, the courts are wielding great power. A commitment to the constitutional system dictates that this almost unlimited power be exercised with great restraint.

Those who believe in judicial restraint think that many constitutional issues are too important to be decided by courts unless absolutely necessary and are to be avoided if there is another legal basis for a decision. They believe the proper use of judicial power demands that courts refrain from determining the constitutionality of an act of Congress unless it is absolutely necessary to a decision of a case. This modest view of the role of the judiciary is based on the belief that litigation is not the appropriate technique for bringing about social, political, and economic change.

The philosophy of judicial restraint is sometimes referred to as *strict constructionism,* or *judicial abstention.* Strict constructionists believe that the Constitution should be interpreted in light of what the Founding Fathers intended. They place great weight on the debates of the Constitutional Convention and the language of the Constitution. Those who promote judicial abstention hold that courts should decide only those matters they must to resolve actual cases and controversies before them. Courts should abstain from deciding issues whenever possible, and doubts about the constitutionality of legislation should be resolved in favor of the statute. Cases should be decided on the facts if possible and on the narrowest possible grounds.

Those who believe in judicial restraint believe that social, political, and economic change in society should result from the political process rather than from court action.

*Followers of judicial restraint favor a very limited role for the courts in our system of government.

>> *sidebar* 3.8

The First Five Years of the Roberts Court

An analysis of the first five years of the U.S. Supreme Court led by Chief Justice John G. Roberts, Jr. (2005–2010) illustrates the conservative nature of the court:

- The Court issued conservative decisions 58% of the time, with the number at 65% at the end of the 2009 term.
- Chief Justice Roberts and Justices Scalia, Alito, and Thomas are considered to be among the most conservative justices on the court since 1937.
- Although the number of laws deemed unconstitutional and precedents revered is consistent with

the rate of other courts, the "ideological direction of the court's activism has undergone a marked change toward conservative results."

Here are the results of a 2009 survey asking "Is the U.S. Supreme Court too conservative, too liberal, or about right?"

22% Too Conservative   29% Too Liberal   47% About Right

Source: Adam Liptak, "The Most Conservative Court in Decades," *The New York Times* (July 25, 2010). The article cites Nathaniel Persily (Columbia Law School) and Stephen Ansolabehere (Harvard University) for the survey.

Judges who identify with judicial restraint give great deference to the political process. They believe that the courts, especially the federal courts, ought to defer to the actions of the states and of the coordinate branches of government unless these actions are clearly unconstitutional. They allow the states and the federal legislative and executive branches wide latitude in finding solutions to the nation's problems.

Judicial restraint jurists have a deep commitment to precedent. They overrule cases only when the prior decision is clearly wrong. They try to refrain from writing their personal convictions into the law. They do not view the role of the lawyer and the practice of law as that of social reform. To them, reform is the function of the political process.

Followers of judicial restraint often take a pragmatic approach to litigation. Whenever possible, decisions are based on the facts rather than a principle of law. Reviewing courts exercising judicial restraint tend to accept the trial court decisions unless they are clearly wrong on the facts or the law. If there is any reasonable basis for the lower court decision, it will not be reversed. Such courts often engage in a balancing approach to their decisions. They weigh competing interests. For example, justices who adhere to judicial restraint often weigh the rights of the person accused of crime with the interests of the victim and of society in determining the extent of the rights of the accused in criminal cases.

Throughout most of our history, judicial restraint has been the dominant philosophy. Today, a majority of the justices of the U.S. Supreme Court usually follow this philosophy, but all courts to some degree also are activist. Sidebar 3.9 illustrates some typical judicial restraint decisions. The Court allowed these decisions by other branches of government and the political process to stand.

>> *sidebar* 3.9

Typical Judicial Restraint Decisions

1. Male-only draft is not a denial of equal protection of the law.
2. States can regulate nuclear power.
3. States can tax the foreign income of multinational corporations.
4. Prayer in the legislature does not violate the First Amendment.
5. Unanimous verdicts are not required, and juries may consist of fewer than 12 persons.
6. A federal law cannot require state law enforcement officers to conduct background checks on gun purchasers.
7. Class-action suits require actual notice to members of the class.
8. Congress cannot create religious freedoms pursuant to Section 5 of the Fourteenth Amendment.
9. Seniority has preference over affirmative action layoffs.
10. State and local employees are subject to the Federal Fair Labor Standards Act.

9. JUDICIAL ACTIVISM

Those who believe in the philosophy of judicial activism believe that courts have a major role to play in correcting wrongs in our society. To them, courts must provide leadership in bringing about social, political, and economic change

*Followers of judicial activism favor a more expansive role for the courts in our system of government.

because the political system is often too slow or unable to bring about those changes necessary to improve society. Activists tend to be innovative and less dependent on precedent for their decisions. They are value oriented and policy directed. Activist jurists believe that constitutional issues must be decided within the context of contemporary society and that the meaning of the Constitution is relative to the times in which it is being interpreted. Activists believe that the courts, and especially the Supreme Court, sit as a continuing constitutional convention to meet the needs of today.

Although dissenting opinions are not usually included in this textbook, they remain an important part of the judicial process and may become the law of the land in the future as the composition of the Supreme Court changes over time. See Justice Scalia's dissent in the sample case.

During the 1950s and 1960s, there was an activist majority on the Supreme Court. This activist majority brought about substantial changes in the law, especially in such areas as civil rights, reapportionment, and the criminal law. For example, the activist court of this period ordered desegregation of public schools and gave us the one-man, one-vote concept in the distributing of legislative bodies. Earl Warren, chief justice during that period, used to request that lawyers appearing before the Court address themselves to the effect of their clients' positions on society. "Tell me why your position is 'right' and that of your opponent is 'wrong' from the standpoint of society" was a common request to lawyers arguing cases before him.

Activist courts tend to be more result conscious and to place less reliance on precedent. Activists are often referred to as liberals, but that description is too narrow to explain their belief in the role of the judiciary as an instrument of change. Activists also believe that justices must examine for themselves the great issues facing society and then decide these issues in light of contemporary standards. Otherwise, they believe we are governed by the dead or by people who are not aware of all of the complexities of today's problems.

Sidebar 3.10 illustrates typical judicial activist decisions. These examples are of decisions in which that judiciary has imposed its will on society.

>> *sidebar* 3.10

Typical Judicial Activist Decisions

1. Welfare recipients have a right to travel among states and be treated like others in their new states.
2. The Pledge of Allegiance is an unconstitutional endorsement of religion when recited in public schools because of the reference to "under God."
3. No prayer is permitted in school.
4. The *Miranda* warning shall be given to all criminal suspects prior to interrogation.
5. Statutes outlawing abortion are unconstitutional.
6. Female pensions must be the same as male pensions, even though, on average, females live longer.
7. There shall be equal pay for comparable worth.
8. Residency requirements for public assistance violates equal protection.
9. State laws that require teaching "creation science" as well as evolution are unconstitutional.
10. Certain public employees, such as public defenders, cannot be fired because of political affiliation.

Sidebar 3.11 provides insight into the general alignment of the justices. It is important to understand, however, that this overall perspective does not translate into predicatbility. It is often fascinating to analyze each justice's position as set forth in concurring and dissenting opinions.

>> *sidebar* 3.11

Typical Alignment of Justices

LEFT	SWING	RIGHT
Ginsburg		Roberts
Bryer		Scalia
Sotomayor		Thomas
Kagan		Alito
	Kennedy	

Mirroring societal trends, the Supreme Court's divided decisions are often peppered with angry words about each other. Justices use phrases like "scanty and equivocal evidence" and "analytical confusion" and words such as "unrealistic" and "indefensible" in response. The importance of the issues and the close division of the Court contributes to the tension found in many divided opinions. Sidebar 3.12 offers another perspective on the differences found on the Supreme Court.

>> *sidebar* 3.12

Labeling Judges As Liberal or Conservative

Some legal scholars do not think it is fair to label judges as liberal or conservative. Professor Lawrence Friedman notes, "[H]owever easy it may be for commentators and the general public to label Supreme Court justices with politically loaded terms like 'conservative' and 'liberal,' in reality this tendency may be less informative and merely simplistic." Peter G. Verniero, a former justice of the New Jersey Supreme Court, made the following argument against this traditional approach: "In particular, labeling judges as 'conservative' or 'liberal' can result in false impressions of the judiciary. Those labels wrongly suggest that judges should resolve disputes on the basis of partisan ideology. . . . Jurists are not robots. When the law is unclear, judges must do their best to determine the intent of the lawmakers. That process of judicial decision-making is not activism—it's judging. In an earlier, less partisan era, terms like 'conservative' or 'liberal' might have communicated something useful about the philosophies of sitting or potential jurists. Indeed, there's nothing inherently bad about being known by either label. Still, in today's climate, use of those terms can have a polarizing effect and erode confidence in judges by casting them in a purely political way. That weakens the judiciary, to everyone's detriment."

Source: Lawrence Friedman, "The Limitations of Labeling: Justice Anthony M. Kennedy and the First Amendment," 20 Ohio N.U.L.Rev. 225 (1993) and *Atlanta Constitution*, April 22, 2008.

10. A SAMPLE U.S. SUPREME COURT CASE

We present the following case at the outset of this edition as an example of how the Supreme Court influences critically important areas of the law.

Case 3.1, *Citizens United v. Federal Election Commission,* involves political speech and the First Amendment. The petitioner Citizens United is a nonprofit corporation with an annual budget of about $12 million. In January 2008, it released the film *Hillary: The Movie* ("*Hillary*"). The movie is a 90-minute documentary about then Senator Hillary Clinton, who was a candidate in the Democratic Party's 2008 presidential primary elections. The film includes interviews with political commentators and others critical of Hillary Clinton. Citizens United wanted to release *Hillary* via video-on-demand to allow digital cable subscribers to watch the program at any time, including within 30 days of the 2008 primary elections. It also wanted to run ads to promote the film. The film had already been already released in theaters and on DVD, but Citizens United sought to increase distribution on cable.

Because Citizens United was concerned that *Hillary* and the ads would be prohibited by the Bipartisan Campaign Reform Act of 2002 (BCRA), it asked the Supreme Court to address this question:

> For the proper disposition of this case, should the Court overrule either or both *Austin v. Michigan Chamber of Commerce,* 494 U.S. 652 (1990), and the part of *McConnell v. Federal Election Comm'n,* 540 U.S. 93 (2003), which addresses the facial validity of Section 203 of the Bipartisan Campaign Reform Act of 2002, 2 U.S.C. §441b?

In essence, Citizens United argued that (1) §441b is unconstitutional as applied to *Hillary,* and (2) that the BCRA's disclaimer and disclosure requirements are also unconstitutional as applied to *Hillary* and the ads promoting the movie.

In a 5–4 decision, the Court overturned *Austin* and *McConnell,* declaring that the government may not ban political spending by corporations. As you can see in the case excerpts in Case 3.1, the opinion contains strong language about the significance of the First Amendment. The case invoked strong feelings from the justices, many of whom were moved to write their own opinions. Justices Roberts, Scalia, and Alito all joined the majority opinion. In addition to the majority opinion, several other opinions were filed: Justice Roberts filed a concurring opinion, joined by Justice Alito; Justice Scalia filed a concurring opinion joined by Justice Alito and, in part, by Justice Thomas; Justice Stevens filed an opinion concurring in part and dissenting in part, joined by Justices Ginsburg, Breyer, and Sotomayor; and Justice Thomas filed an opinion concurring in part and dissenting in part. Taken together, the decision is 176 pages long.

The decision was met with opposition from a number of individuals and groups concerned about corporate money in political elections. President Obama immediately issued a statement expressing his disagreement with the majority:

> With its ruling today, the Supreme Court has given a green light to a new stampede of special interest money in our politics. It is a major victory for big oil, Wall Street banks, health insurance companies, and the other powerful interests that marshal their power every day in Washington to drown out the voices of everyday Americans.

Again during the 2010 State of the Union address, President Obama criticized the decision. In response, Justice Alito shook his head and appeared to mouth the phrase "not true." Justice Alito's reaction created quite a stir, as Supreme Court Justices generally do not express any emotion—not even clapping—during the State of the Union.

>> *sidebar* 3.13

Supreme Court Justices

John Roberts, Chief Justice of the United States (born 1955). He received his B.A. from Harvard College and his J.D. from Harvard Law School. President George W. Bush nominated him as chief justice, and he took office in 2005.

Anthony Kennedy, Associate Justice (born 1936). He received his B.A. from Stanford University and the London School of Economics, and his LL.B. from Harvard Law School. President Reagan nominated him as an associate justice of the Supreme Court, and he took office in 1983.

Antonin Scalia, Associate Justice (born 1936). He received his A.B. from Georgetown University and the University of Fribourg, Switzerland, and his LL.B. from Harvard Law School. President Reagan nominated him as an associate justice of the Supreme Court, and he took office in 1986.

Clarence Thomas, Associate Justice (born 1948). He attended Conception Seminary and received an A.B., cum laude, from Holy Cross College, and a J.D. from Yale Law School. President George H. W. Bush nominated him as an associate justice of the Supreme Court, and he took office in 1991.

Ruth Bader Ginsburg, Associate Justice (born 1933). She received her B.A. from Cornell University, attended Harvard Law School, and received her LL.B. from Columbia Law School. President Clinton nominated her as an associate justice of the Supreme Court, and she took office in 1993.

Stephen Breyer, Associate Justice (born 1938). He received an A.B. from Stanford University, a B.A. from Magdalen College, Oxford, and an LL.B. from Harvard Law School, magna cum laude. President Clinton nominated him as an associate justice of the Supreme Court, and he took office in 1994.

Samuel Alito, Associate Justice (born 1950). He received his A.B. from Princeton University and his J.D. from Yale Law School. President George W. Bush nominated him as associate justice, and he took office in 2006.

Sonia Sotomayor, Associate Justice (born 1954). She received her B.A. from Princeton University, summa cum laude, and a J.D. from Yale Law School. President Obama nominated her as an associate justice of the Supreme Court, and she took office in 2009.

Elena Kagan, Associate Justice (born 1960). She received her A.B. from Princeton University, summa cum laude, an M. Phil from Oxford University, and her J.D. from Harvard Law School, graduating magna cum laude. President Obama nominated her as an associate justice of the Supreme Court, and she took office in 2010.

case 3.1 >>

CITIZENS UNITED v. FEDERAL ELECTION COMMISSION
558 U.S. 50 (2010)

In January 2008, appellant Citizens United, a nonprofit corporation, released a documentary, Hillary: The Movie *("Hillary"), critical of then Senator Hillary Clinton, a candidate for her party's presidential nomination. Anticipating that it would make* Hillary *available on cable television through video-on-demand within 30 days of primary elections, Citizens United produced television ads to run on broadcast and cable television.*

Concerned about possible civil and criminal penalties for violating §44 1b of the Bipartisan Campaign Reform Act of 2002 (BCRA), it sought declaratory and injunctive relief, arguing that (1) §441b is unconstitutional as applied to Hillary, *and (2) BCRA's disclaimer, disclosure, and reporting requirements (§§201 and 311) were unconstitutional as applied to* Hillary *and the ads. The District Court denied Citizens United a preliminary injunction and granted appellee Federal Election Commission (FEC) summary judgment.*

JUSTICE KENNEDY delivered the opinion of the Court. Federal law prohibits corporations and unions from using their general treasury funds to make independent expenditures for speech defined as "electioneering communication" or for speech expressly advocating the election or defeat of a candidate. 2 U. S. C. §441b. Limits on electioneering communications were upheld in *McConnell v. Federal Election Comm'n*, 540 U. S. 93, 203-209 (2003). The holding of *McConnell* rested to a large extent on an earlier case, *Austin v. Michigan Chamber of Commerce*, 494 U. S. 652 (1990). *Austin* had held that political speech may be banned based on a speaker's corporate identity.

In this case we are asked to reconsider *Austin* and, in effect, *McConnell*. It has been noted that "*Austin* was a significant departure from ancient First Amendment principles" . . . We agree with that conclusion and hold that *stare decisis* does not compel the continued acceptance of *Austin*. The government may regulate corporate political speech through disclaimer and disclosure requirements, but it may not suppress that speech altogether . . . the Court cannot resolve this case on a narrower ground without chilling political speech, speech that is central to the meaning and purpose of the First Amendment. . . .

The First Amendment provides that "Congress shall make no law . . . abridging the freedom of speech." Laws enacted to control or suppress speech may operate at different points in the speech process. . . . The law before us is an outright ban, backed by criminal sanctions. Section 441b makes it a felony for corporations—including nonprofit advocacy corporations—either to expressly advocate the election or defeat of candidates or to broadcast electioneering communications within 30 days of a primary election and 60 days of a general election. . . . Section 441b is a ban on corporate speech notwithstanding the fact that a PAC created by a corporation can still speak. . . .

Speech is an essential mechanism of democracy, for it is the means to hold officials accountable to the people. . . For these reasons, political speech must prevail against laws that would suppress it, whether by design or inadvertence. Laws that burden political speech are "subject to strict scrutiny," which requires the Government to prove that the restriction "furthers a compelling interest and is narrowly tailored to achieve that interest." . . .

We find no basis for the proposition that, in the context of political speech, the Government may impose restrictions on certain disfavored speakers. Both history and logic lead us to this conclusion. . . .

There is simply no support for the view that the First Amendment, as originally understood, would permit the suppression of political speech by media corporations. The Framers may not have anticipated modern business and media corporations. . . . Yet television networks and major newspapers owned by media corporations have become the most important means of mass communication in modern times. The First Amendment was certainly not understood to condone the suppression of political speech in society's most salient media. It was understood as a response to the repression of speech and the press that had existed in England and the heavy taxes on the press that were imposed on the colonies. . . .

Austin interferes with the "open marketplace" of ideas prohibited by the First Amendment. . . . When Government seeks to use its full power, including the criminal law, to command where a person may get his or her information or what distrusted source he or she may not hear, it uses censorship to control thought. This is unlawful. The First Amendment confirms the freedom to think for ourselves. . . .

Due consideration leads to this conclusion: *Austin* . . . should be and now is overruled. . . . the Government may not suppress political speech on the basis of the speaker's corporate identity. No sufficient

[continued]

governmental interest justifies limits on the political speech of nonprofit or for-profit corporations. . . .

Citizens next challenges BCRA's disclaimer and disclosure provisions as applied to *Hillary* and the three advertisements for the movie. Under BCRA §311, televised electioneering communications funded by anyone other than the candidate must include a disclaimer that "'_____ is responsible for the content of this advertising.'" . . . there has been no showing that, as applied in this case, these requirements would impose a chill on speech or expression. . . .

Some members of the public might consider *Hillary* to be insightful and instructive; some might find it to be neither high art nor a fair discussion on how to set the Nation's course; still others simply might suspend judgment on these points but decide to think more about issues and candidates. Those choices and assessments, however, are not for the Government to make. "The First Amendment underwrites the freedom to experiment and to create in the realm of thought and speech. Citizens must be free to use new forms, and new forums, for the expression of ideas. The civic discourse belongs to the people, and the Government may not prescribe the means used to conduct it." . . .

The judgment of the District Court is reversed with respect to the constitutionality of 2 U. S. C. §441b's restrictions on corporate independent expenditures. The judgment is affirmed with respect to BCRA's disclaimer and disclosure requirements. The case is remanded for further proceedings consistent with this opinion.

It is so ordered.

ROBERTS, C.J., CONCURRING: The Government urges us in this case to uphold a direct prohibition on political speech. It asks us to embrace a theory of the First Amendment that would allow censorship not only of television and radio broadcasts, but of pamphlets, posters, the Internet, and virtually any other medium that corporations and unions might fund useful in expressing their views on matters of public concern. . . . The First Amendment protects more than just the individual on the soapbox and the lonely pamphleteer.

STEVENS, J., DISSENTING IN PART: At the bottom, the Court's opinion is thus a rejection of the common sense of the American people, who have recognized a need to prevent corporations from undermining self-government since the founding, and who have fought against the distinctive corrupting potential of corporate electioneering since the days of Theodore Roosevelt. It is a strange time to repudiate that common sense. While American democracy is imperfect, few outside the majority of this Court would have thought its flaws included a dearth of money in politics. I would affirm the judgment of the District Court.

>> CASE QUESTIONS

1. What is the procedural background of this lawsuit resulting in this Supreme Court decision?
2. What legal questions did the Supreme Court address?
3. What major differences are there between the majority decision, concurring decision and dissenting decision?
4. From what you have learned about judicial restraint and judicial activism, which do you think the majority was exercising in this opinion?
5. How do you believe that the majority decision will affect elections?

11. THE NATURE OF THE JUDICIAL PROCESS

In deciding cases and in examining the powers discussed in the prior sections, courts are often faced with several alternatives. They may decide the case by use of existing statutes and precedents and demonstrate a deep commitment to the common law system. They may also refuse to apply existing case law or declare a statute to be void as unconstitutional. If there is no statute or case law, the court may decide the case and create law in the process. However, case law as a basis for deciding controversies often provides only the point of departure from which the difficult labor of the court begins. The court must examine and compare cases cited as authority to it so it can determine not only which is correct, but also whether the principles should continue to be followed. In reaching its decision, the court must consider whether the ruling will provide justice in the particular case and whether it will establish sound precedent for future cases.

The foregoing alternatives raise several questions: Why do courts reach one conclusion rather than another in any given case? What formula, if any, is used in deciding cases and in determining the direction of the law? What forces tend to influence judicial decisions when the public interest is involved?

There is no simple answer to these questions. Many people assume that logic is the basic tool of the judicial decision. But Justice Oliver Wendell Holmes stated, "the life of the law has not been logic; it has been experience."[1] Others argue that courts merely reflect the attitudes of the times and simply follow the more popular course in decisions where the public is involved.

Justice Benjamin Cardozo, in a series of lectures on the judicial process,[2] discussed the sources of information judges utilize in deciding cases. He stated that if the answer were not clearly established by statute or by unquestioned precedent, the problem was twofold: "He [the judge] must first extract from the precedents the underlying principle, the *ratio decidendi;* he must then determine the path or direction along which the principle is to work and develop, if it is not to wither or die." The first part of the problem is separating legal principles from dicta so that the actual precedent is clear.

In Cardozo's judgment, the rule of analogy also was entitled to certain presumptions and should be followed if possible. He believed that the judge who molds the law by the method of philosophy is satisfying humanity's deep-seated desire for certainty. History, in indicating the direction of precedent, often illuminates the path of logic and plays an important part in decisions in areas such as real property. Custom or trade practice has supplied much of the direction of the law in the area of business. All judicial decisions are at least in part directed by the judge's viewpoint on the welfare of society. The end served by law must dictate the administration of justice, and ethical considerations, if ignored, will ultimately overturn a principle of law.

Noting the psychological aspects of judges' decisions, Cardozo observed that it is the subconscious forces that keep judges consistent with one another. He recognized that all persons, including judges, have a philosophy that gives coherence and direction to their thought and actions whether they admit it or not.

> All their lives, forces which they do not recognize and cannot name, have been tugging at them—inherited instincts, traditional beliefs, acquired conviction; and the resultant is an outlook on life, a conception of social needs, . . . which when reasons are nicely balanced, must determine where choice shall fall. In this mental background every problem finds its setting. We may try to see things as objectively as we please. None the less, we can never see them with any eyes except our own. To that test they are all brought—a form of pleading or an act of parliament, the wrongs of paupers or the rights of princes, a village ordinance or a nation's charter.

In the following comments, Cardozo summarized his view of the judicial process.

[1]*Holmes, The Common Law 1 (1938).*
[2]*Cardozo, The Nature of the Judicial Process (1921). Excerpts are used by permission from the Yale University Press.*

case 3.2 >>

THE NATURE OF THE JUDICIAL PROCESS
Benjamin N. Cardozo

. . . My analysis of the judicial process comes then to this, and little more: logic, and history, and custom, and utility, and the accepted standards of right conduct are the forces which singly or in combination shape the progress of the law. Which of these forces shall dominate in any case must depend largely upon the comparative importance or value of the social interests that will be thereby promoted or impaired. One of the most fundamental social interests is that law shall be uniform and impartial. There must be nothing in its action that savors of prejudice or favor or even arbitrary whim for fitfulness. Therefore in the main there shall be adherence to precedent. There shall be symmetrical development, consistently with history or custom when history or custom has been the motive force, or the chief one, in giving shape to existing rules, and with logic or philosophy when the motive power has been theirs. But symmetrical development may be bought at too high a price. Uniformity ceases to be a good when it becomes uniformity of oppression. The social interest served by symmetry or certainty must then be balanced against the social interest served by equity and fairness or other elements of social welfare. These may enjoin upon the judge the duty of drawing the line at another angle, of staking the path along new courses, of marking a new point of departure from which others who come after him will set out upon their journey.

If you ask how he is to know when one interest outweighs another, I can only answer that he must get his knowledge just as the legislator gets it, from experience and study and reflection; in brief, from life itself. Here, indeed, is the point of contact between the legislator's work and his. The choice of methods, the appraisement of values, must in the end be guided by like considerations for the one as for the other. Each indeed is legislating within the limits of his competence. No doubt the limits for the judge are narrower. He legislates only between gaps. He fills the open spaces in the law. How far he can go without traveling beyond the walls of the interstices cannot be staked out for him upon a chart. He must learn it for himself as he gains the sense of fitness and proportion that comes with years of habitude in the practice of an art. Even within the gaps, restrictions not easy to define, but felt, however impalpable they may be, by every judge and lawyer, hedge and circumscribe his action. They are established by the traditions of the centuries, by the example of other judges, his predecessors and his colleagues, by the collective judgment of the profession, and by the duty of adherence to the pervading spirit of the law. . . . Nonetheless, within the confines of these open spaces and those of precedent and tradition, choice moves with a freedom which stamps its action as creative. The law which is the resulting product is not found, but made. The process, being legislative, demands the legislator's wisdom. . . .

concept >> *summary*

Judicial Review

1. Judicial review allows the courts to review actions taken by legislative and executive branches of government.

2. The philosophy of judicial restraint is sometimes referred to as strict constructionism or a conservative approach.

3. Supporters of judicial activism believe the courts are the appropriate body to bring about social, political, and economic change.

4. The Supreme Court is deeply divided between these two competing views of judicial decision making.

>> Key Terms

Appeal 71	Judicial activism 79	Trial court 70
Appellate court 70	Judicial restraint 79	*Writ of certiorari* 72
Courts of appeal 72	Judicial review 78	
Diversity of citizenship 73	Petit jury 67	
Federal question cases 72	Small-claims court 72	
Federal Rules of Civil	Subject matter jurisdiction 70	
Procedure 75	Supreme court 72	

>> Review Questions and Problems

Personnel

  1. *Judges and Justices*

     What are the essential responsibilities of a trial judge?

  2. *Jurors*

     Why have several states eliminated the requirement of unanimity in jury trials?

  3. *Lawyers*

     Name the three critical roles a lawyer serves in society. Why have many lawyers and their business clients had such conflict in recent years?

Organization of the Court System

  4. *Subject Matter Jurisdiction*

     Mark, a citizen of Georgia, was crossing a street in Atlanta when he was struck by a car driven by David, a citizen of New York visiting Atlanta. The car was owned by David's employer, a Delaware corporation that has its principal place of business in Atlanta, Georgia. Mark sues both David and the corporation in federal district court in Atlanta alleging damages in the amount of $500,000. Does the court have subject matter jurisdiction? Why or why not?

  5. *State Courts*

     What role do reviewing or appellate courts play in the judicial process? How do they differ from trial courts?

  6. *Federal Courts*

     XYZ makes and markets a product that it believes will help control weight by blocking the human body's digestion of starch. The Food and Drug Administration (FDA) has classified the product as a drug and orders it removed from the market until it can evaluate its use through testing. XYZ disputes the FDA's action and seeks to bring suit in the federal courts. Will the federal courts have jurisdiction to hear the case? Why or why not?

  7. *Decisions by the U.S. Supreme Court*

     Susan files a petition for certiorari in the U.S. Supreme Court following an adverse decision in the Illinois Supreme Court on a claim arising under a breach of contract. What chance does Susan have of the Supreme Court granting the petition? What special circumstances would she need to show?

The Power of Judicial Review

  8. *Judicial Restraint*

     Define the power of judicial review. How do advocates of judicial restraint exercise that power?

  9. *Judicial Activism*

     Define judicial activism. Compare and contrast judicial restraint and judicial activism.

10. *A Sample U.S. Supreme Court Case*

Why are concurring and dissenting opinions important?

11. *The Nature of the Judicial Process*

What are the forces that Justice Cardozo says shape the judicial process? How is the law made? In light of the liberal versus conservative divisions in the courts, are Cardozo's observations still relevant?

business >> *discussion*

1. You have spent the past four weeks away from work serving as a juror in a case deciding whether a pharmaceutical company should be held liable for the heart attack of a woman who took its painkiller, Oxxy-1. The lengthy case has taken a toll on your professional career, and you have many unanswered questions as jury deliberations begin.

- Where does your duty lie in serving on a jury?
- Are you protected against adverse employment action by your firm for missing work to serve on a jury?
- How do you reconcile the woman's prior heart palpitations from years ago with her recent attack? Was her heart already compromised before she began taking the painkiller Oxxy-1?
- Why didn't the pharmaceutical company withdraw the painkiller from the market at the first sign of a problem?

2. You are the president of a large corporation which is in the business of manufacturing, among other things, chemical products used to eradicate termites. You have just reviewed a confidential report, prepared by one of your top scientists, questioning the effectiveness of the product and the claims your business has been making to homeowners, pesticide treatment firms, and the general public. You have heard rumors that a lawsuit will be filed shortly against your corporation claiming that this product is ineffective.

Who should you turn to for advice?
Should you destroy the report?
In which court can a lawsuit be filed?
If you lose the lawsuit at trial, can you appeal?

Chapter 5. Alternative Dispute Resolution

5

Alternative Dispute Resolution

Learning Objectives

In this chapter you will learn:

5-1. To understand why disputing parties seek alternatives to the litigation process as methods to revolve their differences.

5-2. To appreciate the importance of effective negotiation and to recognize the basic methods of negotiation.

5-3. To evaluate the various forms of ADR systems so that efficient choices can be made as to the means of resolving disputes.

5-4. To explain the differences between arbitration and mediation and to know when each is the most appropriate method of ADR.

5-5. To comprehend why courts have a very limited role in reviewing the actions of arbitrators and mediators.

From the preceding chapter, you should appreciate that the litigation process within the court system imposes tremendous costs in terms of time, money, emotional stress, and harmony in relationships. This fact is a major reason why you probably have very little personal experience with litigation. It also is the reason most businesses try to avoid litigation and use it as a means of last resort to resolve disputes.

One way to confirm how seldom we litigate is to examine some data. Ask yourself, have I ever had a conflict with someone? Maybe a better question is, does a day go by without me experiencing one or more conflicts? We constantly and consistently deal with conflicts, and even disputes, without filing a lawsuit to resolve our problems.

However, sometimes lawsuits are necessary. Even after beginning the litigation process, most parties reach some type of resolution before the case is presented to a jury for a verdict and judgment. The general rule, usually cited, is 95 percent or more of the lawsuits filed settle prior to the completion of the litigation process.

The litigation process provides individuals and businesses with a formal method to enforce agreements. It can be said that business cannot be conducted without the existence of the court system to protect property interests. A more accurate statement probably is we transact business, personally and professionally, in a way that hopefully avoids the need to use litigation as our dispute resolution system.

In this chapter, you will study a variety of alternatives to litigation. Prior to reviewing more formal alternative dispute resolution (ADR) systems, we take a look at the distinction between conflicts and disputes and how negotiation is a skill we each use all the time.

>> Conflicts and Negotiation

In answer to one of the earlier questions, a day doesn't go by without encountering conflicts at home, on the road, and at work. Only a day of total isolation might be the exception. Even then the lonely person likely experiences internal conflicts over how best to utilize this time alone.

In the following sections, the distinction between a conflict and a dispute helps emphasize the importance of how people negotiate.

1. CONFLICTS AND DISPUTES

Conflict is ubiquitous and can be productive.

Conflict exists whenever there are two or more points of view. Even in productive relationships, involving amicable co-workers or happily married couples, conflict is always present. Conflicts are not negative; indeed, conflict can stimulate significant thoughts and produce great discoveries. So, why do we shy away from conflict? Why do most of us perceive conflict as bad and try to avoid it?

Conflict + Claim that is rejected = Dispute

The answer likely lies in the fact that conflict leads to disputes. A **dispute** arises when one party makes a claim that another party denies. For example, two co-workers may have a conflict because they both think they need to use a copy machine right now. This conflict escalates when one person asks the other to move aside and the request is refused. These parties now are in dispute as to who gets to use the copier first. In essence, the process of both workers claiming a right to the machine likely causes the dispute to become more emotional and thus uncomfortable for both involved.

Does this example prove disputes are bad and conflicts should be left alone? Not necessarily. Suppose one worker simply stood in line and waited for the other to finish. The worker doing the copying may not know about the frustration and angst that exists inside the co-worker. On the other hand, the worker waiting may be expressing impatience through comments or sighs without ever asking or claiming to go ahead. The worker making the copies may feel this pressure and become upset by what is perceived as rudeness or a lack of respect. Leaving the conflict unresolved may cause larger problems among those co-workers later. Thus, it may be more beneficial to everyone involved to have the conflict become a dispute so the parties can more easily express their emotions. Such expressions may lead to an earlier resolution between these co-workers.

2. STYLES AND METHODS OF NEGOTIATION

All of us instinctively engage in some form of negotiation. Even as evidence of a conflict is exhibited (through comments or sighs or groans), the parties are negotiating. **Negotiation** is the process used to persuade or coerce someone to do what you want them to do. All of us negotiate all the time with ourselves, our family members, our co-workers, and even with strangers.

The issue to focus on is not *when* do I negotiate but *how* do I negotiate. Think again about the co-workers and the copy machine. The actual request (or claim) to make copies first is the beginning of a negotiation. How the other worker responds to this request likely will set a tone for the negotiation process. An examination of how this tone is set can be viewed through the illustration in Sidebar 5.1.

"When do we negotiate? Always!"

–Dialogue from the movie *The Devil's Advocate*

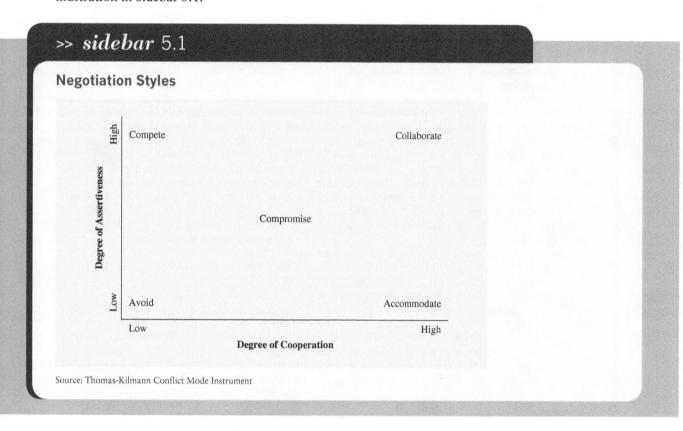

>> *sidebar* 5.1

Negotiation Styles

Source: Thomas-Kilmann Conflict Mode Instrument

Can you imagine the conversation between these two co-workers that illustrates each style listed? Avoiding could be seen through the person at the copier ignoring the request by pretending not to hear. Accommodating occurs if the request to go first is granted. Competing comes into play if the worker at the copier turns around and tells the co-worker who requested priority to stand in line and be patient. Collaborating might exist if the worker making the copies agrees to use another copier or explains to the co-worker how another machine is available to use. Compromising is the hardest to demonstrate even though it is a common response in a negotiation. Perhaps a compromise occurs in this example if these two co-workers get into a discussion/

argument and a third worker takes over the use of the copier such that neither of the disputing parties gets the work done.

Understanding the styles used in negotiations is not enough. Analyses of negotiation processes also need to focus on the methods used by the negotiators. The next two sections examine two of the most studied methods of negotiations. To help illustrate these methods, consider the factual situation in Sidebar 5.2.

>> *sidebar* 5.2

A Business Dispute

Mickey Shears and Naomi Hamilton operate a business that manufactures large (40+ inches) flat-screen 3-D televisions. The business name is M&N TVs, Inc. The principal market for M&N televisions has been buyers for home use. M&N's reputation is based on assembling a high-quality TV for a relatively low price. M&N's biggest problem has been maintaining a large enough, qualified sales force while keeping the price for its TVs below the market average.

William Dalton operates a nationwide chain of discount department stores. This chain is known as Bill's Discount Centers. One year ago, Bill's Discount Centers agreed to buy from M&N a minimum of 250 TVs (with specifications stated in the contract) per month for six months. The agreed-upon price of each TV was $1,250.

The relationship between M&N and Bill's worked very well. In the fifth month of this initial contract, Bill's agreed to increase its minimum purchase per month to 750 TVs, and Bill's committed to this monthly purchase for a twelve-month period to begin after the sixth month of the original contract. The price per TV was to remain at $1,250.

M&N was delighted with the arrangement since it allowed M&N to concentrate on increasing its production capacity while reducing the costs of maintaining a large active sales force.

Unlike the success of its initial relationship with M&N, Bill's began receiving complaints from its customers about the lack of quality of M&N's TVs. These complaints were traced by Bill's customer service representatives to the newer TVs that M&N was assembling under its expanded production program. Despite its knowledge of these quality-related problems, Bill's never informed M&N of its findings.

The complaints continued to become more numerous. During the fifth month of the twelve-month period, Bill's purchased only 350 TVs from M&N. When M&N sent an invoice for the 750 TVs specified as the monthly minimum, Bill's refused to pay for any TVs over the 350 actually purchased. In the second week of the sixth month, Bill's sent M&N written notice that it was canceling the remainder of the sales contract due to declining quality of M&N's TVs. M&N offered to reduce the price per TV to $1,050, but Bill's refused to withdraw its termination letter.

M&N wants to sue Bill's for $7,062,500. This figure is based on the shortfalls of 400 TVs in the fifth month times $1,250/TV plus 750 TVs times 7 months times $1,250/TV. Prior to filing suit, M&N wants to explore the chances for a negotiated settlement in the hope of salvaging a constructive relationship with Bill's.

---

3. POSITIONAL NEGOTIATION

Most people instinctively use a negotiation method called **positional bargaining**. Typically, these parties begin in a competitive style by stating their respective expectations. For example, in a sales transaction, the seller starts with as high an asking price as is considered reasonable. Likewise, the buyer begins with the lowest reasonable price. The gap between these two opening prices provides room for give and take. If the negotiation remains focused on the sales price, all the parties do is change their respective positions on the acceptable price. This process of exchange moves the parties toward the middle of the gap.

In the factual situation in Sidebar 5.2 , Bill's is saying that it owes nothing to M&N. On the other side, M&N is demanding payment of more than $7 million. The difference between these two positions is so wide that it may be difficult to bring these parties into agreement.

Even if Bill's was willing to buy some TVs at a revised price and even if M&N agreed to a reduced quantity or selling price, the issue of quality is not being addressed. Does Bill's gain any market advantage in selling an inferior product, albeit at a lower price, to its customers? Clearly not.

If the positions on quantity and price are the only items open for negotiation, Bill's and M&N are unlikely to reach a satisfactory compromise. Hence, the chances of a negotiated settlement through positional bargaining are minimal. This result occurs because positional bargaining does not focus on the underlying conflicts.

There is another method of negotiation that might help these parties. This alternative is discussed in the next section.

4. PRINCIPLED NEGOTIATION

A better approach to negotiating among disputing parties has been described as **principled, interest-based negotiations** in the book *Getting to Yes* by Roger Fisher, William Ury, and Bruce Patton.[1] These authors present seven elements that should become the focus of negotiators. The elements will vary in importance depending on the factual situation in dispute and on the parties' individual perspectives. However, concentrating on these elements can help remove some of the barriers created by positional negotiation. A quick focus on these elements illustrates how M&N and Bill's can be more productive in their negotiation efforts.

Communication First, as expressed in the factual situation above, Bill's has not openly explained to M&N the nature of its dissatisfaction. Sharing customer complaints, either in general or with specificity, might help M&N locate a production operations problem. Likewise, M&N does not appear to be informing Bill's of any difficulties it faced as it expanded production capacities. Clear communication between these parties may assist them in becoming joint problem solvers. Without this exchange of information, these parties are likely to continue blaming each another. To change from a "game" of blaming, effective negotiators put significant energy into listening to the other party. Communication involves a balance of talking and listening.

Relationship Second, these parties would likely benefit by discussing how each could benefit by continuing their relationship of customer and supplier. Can they solve the current problem and maintain, if not enhance,

Positional Bargaining

The Seven Elements of Interest-Based Negotiation:
  Communication
  Relationship
  Interests
  Options
  Legitimacy
  Alternatives
  Commitment

"If negotiation is half talking and half listening, the more important half is listening."

–Roger Fisher

[1] *Penguin Books, 3d ed., 2011.*

their future business opportunities together? Maintaining, or even enhancing, the relationship may be possible if these parties focus on effective communications.

Interests   Third, have M&N and Bill's communicated their real interests to each other? Perhaps these interests are not mutually exclusive. For example, Bill's might want to expand its offerings in TV technology to customers. M&N might want to dissolve its sales force and concentrate on production of a variety of TVs. These interests, once communicated, may help the parties realize that a continuing relationship is in their mutual best interests.

Options   Fourth, M&N and Bill's should brainstorm possible options or solutions to their dispute. This exploration process is best done with the parties agreeing that an option mentioned is not necessarily a proposal for compromise. One attractive option might be for Bill's to agree to buy all the TVs M&N can produce and for Bill's to market these TVs under its own name. Rather than severing their business relationship, M&N could become the exclusive supplier of store-brand TVs. The renaming of these products also can help overcome the "quality problems" customers associate with M&N's TVs.

Legitimacy   Fifth, legitimacy involves the application of accepted standards to the topic negotiated—rather than having the parties state unsupported propositions. Bill's probably will not be impressed by M&N stating it will improve the quality of its TVs. Instead the parties should focus on how quality can be improved and how customers will accept the improvements. Production engineers may help address the former issue while specific test marketing plans may assist in legitimizing the latter.

Alternatives   Sixth, alternatives are outcomes that are possible without the agreement of the other party. In essence, alternatives are the thing that parties to a negotiation can do away from the bargaining table. If the parties understand their alternatives to negotiating a settlement and understand the unattractive nature of these alternatives, the desire to negotiate, instead of litigating, is enhanced. M&N, for example, may perceive that bankruptcy is a very likely result if this dispute is not resolved. Bill's, on the other hand, may believe that another supplier is readily available. The desirable result of any negotiation is to agree on an outcome that is better than both parties' alternatives.

Commitment   Seventh, any successful negotiation must conclude with the parties making realistic commitments that can be put into practice. Perhaps an initial commitment that assists the overall process of negotiation is to have the parties agree that they will continue to meet and focus on these seven elements. Hopefully, the conclusion of the negotiation will be an agreement between the parties that avoids the expense (dollars, time, and emotions) of litigation. If that commitment is not a settlement, then it might be an agreement to utilize one of the following ADR systems.

concept >> *summary*

Conflicts, Disputes, and Negotiation

1. Conflicts are everywhere; each personal interaction can cause conflicts or be impacted by them.
2. Conflicts may be insignificant and easily avoided, or they may produce significant anxiety if ignored.
3. A dispute arises from a conflict when one party makes a claim that another denies or refuses to honor.

4. Conflicts and disputes can be managed and perhaps resolved through negotiations.
5. Styles of negotiation include avoiding, accommodating, competing, compromising, and collaborating.
6. Two methods of negotiation include positional bargaining and principled (interest-based) bargaining.

>> Alternative Dispute Resolution (ADR) Systems

Negotiations occur in everything we do. Thus, even as we present the following material on formal and informal alternative dispute resolution (ADR) systems, remember the negotiation processes still govern the success or failure of such ADR systems.

It is important to remember several things at the outset of this discussion. First, litigation does not preclude the use of ADR techniques. Indeed, it is very common for disputes to be arbitrated, mediated, or settled through negotiations during the pretrial process discussed in the preceding chapter.

Second, disputing parties do not have to begin a lawsuit to use any form of ADR. In the rest of this chapter, you will study how ADR systems relate to formal litigation and how they are utilized independently from the litigation process.

Third, ADR systems used by disputing parties may be part of a contractual relationship between these parties. For example, even before any problem arises, it is an effective dispute resolution tool to have the parties' contract specify a preferred ADR system. Disputing parties also may agree to use an ADR technique after the dispute arises even if they did not foresee the possibility of needing to use a dispute resolution system at the time of their original agreement.

Fourth, effective use of ADR systems can save disputing parties many of the costs associated with litigation. Especially important is the preservation of an ongoing business relationship. The ability to keep doing business often is destroyed through litigation. ADR systems, when used appropriately, help ensure the productive relationships needed for successful business transactions.

5. RANGE OF OPTIONS

Figure 5.1 illustrates an array of ADR systems. These are arranged along a spectrum of high cost (in dollars, time, emotions, and relationships) to lowest cost. Although any given factual situation may cause the items on this

134   **PART 2**   Courts and Dispute Resolution

Figure 5.1
Scale of dispute resolution systems

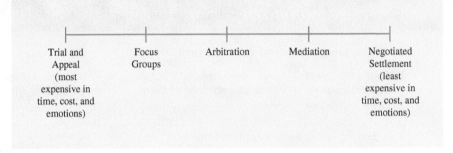

spectrum to shift places, this figure presents a generally accepted view of dispute resolution systems.

The next two sections briefly address why settlement is attractive and how lawyers utilize focus groups. Arbitration and mediation are discussed in more detail since they are the most popular ADR systems used by businesses and people attempting to resolve disputes.

6. SETTLEMENTS

The Department of Justice reports 98 percent of tort cases filed in the U.S. District Courts settled prior to either a bench or jury trial. http://bjs. ojp.usdoj.gov/content/ glance/tables/ torttrialtab.cfm

It is universally acknowledged that both parties to litigation are losers. The winning party in a lawsuit is a loser to the extent of the attorney's fees—which are often substantial. The fact that the loser usually also has to pay court costs is an added incentive to settlement without litigation.

There are also personal reasons to settle controversies. The desire to resolve differences is instinctive for many Americans. Most of us dislike trouble, and many fear going to court. The opinions of others are often a motivating force in encouraging amicable settlements.

Businesses tend to settle disputes with customers for two additional reasons. First, it is simply not good business from a goodwill and public relations standpoint to sue a customer. Second, juries are frequently sympathetic to individuals who have suits against large corporations or defendants who are covered by insurance. Juries often decide close questions of liability, as well as size of the verdict, against business organizations because of their presumed ability to pay. As a result, businesses settle many disputes even though they might possibly prevail in litigation.

Table 5.1 provides a summary of cases recently settled. The size of these settlements represents evidence that companies want to avoid the litigation process even when the settlement costs are high.

7. FOCUS GROUPS

Recognizing that a jury's function is to determine the facts, attorneys frequently use **focus groups** in significant cases. The attorneys assemble a group of citizens and present their evidence. This group then deliberates and makes findings. This dress rehearsal gives attorneys insight into possible jury reaction to the evidence and points up weaknesses in the case. Sometimes issues are tested without introducing evidence. Lawyers argue the case on the basis of assumed facts to the mock jury for a few hours, and this jury returns a verdict.

The verdicts often cause plaintiffs to take a more realistic view of the damages to which they think they are entitled. This "reality test" helps disputing

table 5.1 >> Samples of Recent Major Settlements		
Company	**Product or Action**	**Settlement**
British Petroleum (BP)	Gulf Oil Spill (Deepwater Horizon explosion)	$20 billion distributed among thousands of claimants
Merck	Vioxx linked to heart attacks and strokes	$4.85 billion to 47,000 possible claimants
Citicorp	Conspiring with Enron executives to misstate Enron's financial condition	$1.66 billion to Enron Creditors Recovery Corporation
Eli Lilly	Failure to disclose information about side effects of Zyprexa	$1.2 billion to 31,000 possible claimants
Pfizer Claims	Failure to disclose accurate information about Bextra	$669 million under False Act; $331 million for state Medicaid programs
AstraZeneca Claims	Failure to disclose accurate information about Seroquel	$520 million under False Act; $198 million in Britain
Novartis	Failure to disclose accurate information about Trileptal	$192.7 million under False Claims Act
	Gender bias in pay	$175 million to 5,600 current and former female sales representatives

parties to engage in more meaningful negotiations. Through such negotiations, these parties often settle their dispute without having to go through the formal process of either a trial or an arbitration.

>> Arbitration

To avoid the various expenses of litigation, disputing parties sometimes agree to have a third party decide the merits of the dispute. This formal ADR system is called **arbitration.** The decision maker, who should be disinterested in any financial impact of the decision and neutral regarding the issues presented in the dispute, is known as an **arbitrator.** The distinctive characteristic of this form of ADR is the arbitrator's decision on the merits. In essence, the arbitrator takes the place of the jury and judge in the litigation process.

Over the past 80 years, arbitration has played an increasingly important role in resolving business disputes. Historically, arbitration has been the most commonly used ADR system. The primary reason for the use of arbitration is the laudable goal of providing a relatively quick and inexpensive resolution of disputes. Arbitration not only helps the parties avoid the expense of litigation but also provides a means of avoiding the formalities of the courtroom. Formal pleadings, for example, and other procedural steps such as discovery and the rules of evidence are usually not used in an arbitration hearing.

Arbitration also serves to help ease congested court dockets. A primary function of arbitration is to serve as a substitute for and not a prelude to litigation. It is a private proceeding with no public record available to the press

Arbitrators are authorized to make decisions that are binding on the parties, thereby resolving the dispute.

"Studies show that employment arbitrations are resolved twice as quickly on average as lawsuits."

–Nathan Koppel, *The Wall Street Journal.*

and others. Thus, by keeping their dispute private, adversaries may be more likely to preserve their business relationship.

Arbitration also has the advantage of submitting many disputes to experts for solutions. For example, if the issue involves whether a building has been properly constructed, the matter could be submitted to an architect for resolution. If it involves a technical accounting problem, it could be submitted to a certified public accountant. The Securities and Exchange Commission (SEC) has approved an arrangement whereby investors with complaints against securities dealers must submit them for arbitration to arbitrators assigned by the various stock exchanges and the Financial Industry Regulatory Authority. These arbitrators are selected because they possess the special knowledge required to determine if a customer of a brokerage house has a legitimate complaint.

Arbitration is of special importance in labor relations, where it provides the grievance procedures under collective bargaining contracts. Arbitration is a means for industrial self-government, a system of private law for all problems that may arise in the workplace.

Sidebar 5.3 illustrates the growing importance and widespread use of arbitration as an alternative dispute resolution system.

>> *sidebar* 5.3

Examples of Contracts with Arbitration Clauses

Stockbroker and client

Commodities broker and customer

Brokerage firm and employee

Attorney* and client

Union-management collective bargaining agreements

Owner-contractor and contractor-subcontractor

Insurance company and insured

Public carrier and shipper of goods

*Most bar associations require lawyers to arbitrate disputes with clients.

Submission is the process of beginning an arbitration proceeding.

The parties authorize an arbitrator to make a decision that binds these parties and resolves their dispute. The act of referring a matter to arbitration is called **submission.** Submission to arbitration often occurs when the disputing parties agree to use this form of ADR. Such an agreement by the parties is a submission to **voluntary arbitration.** Generally, an agreement to submit an issue to arbitration is irrevocable, and a party that thinks the process is not going well cannot withdraw from the arbitration and resort to litigation. Another form of a submission occurs when a statute or court requires parties to arbitrate. This type of submission results in a **mandatory arbitration.**

After the submission, a hearing is conducted by the arbitrator or arbitrators. Both parties are allowed to present evidence and to argue their own points of view. Then a decision, known as an **award,** is handed down. In most states the arbitrator's award must be in writing. The award is valid as long as it settles the entire controversy and states which party is to pay the other a sum of money.

Sidebar 5.4 discusses trends in the use and popularity of arbitration. It will be interesting, throughout your business careers, to see how arbitration is utilized when compared to other ADR systems.

>> *sidebar* 5.4

Trends in Arbitration

Throughout the second half of the twentieth century, businesses increasingly included arbitration clauses in various types of contracts. Most common among these examples have been business-to-business contracts (e.g., customer-supplier), employment contracts, and securities broker-investor contracts. Beginning in 2007, pressures mounted to provide employees and investors with options to either pursue arbitration or to litigate. To achieve this system of choice, the Arbitration Fairness Act has been proposed each year from 2007 to 2010 in both the U.S. House and Senate; however, no final legislative enactment has occurred. Advocates for litigation cite studies showing that arbitration in securities brokerage cases tends to favor the broker-age firm. To counter this perceived bias, the Financial Industry Regulatory Authority, FINRA, administers arbitrations involving investors. FINRA recently completed a pilot project allowing investors to use non-industry experts as arbitrators. This process, known as an all-public panel of arbitrators, has been submitted to the SEC for final approval. "'Giving each individual investor the option of an all-public panel will enhance confidence in and increase the perception of fairness in the FINRA arbitration process,' said Richard Ketchum, FINRA's chief executive officer. FINRA spokeswoman Nancy Condon said 23 of the pilot cases went through to a ruling, with the rest reaching settlements. Among 17 cases heard by all-public panels, investors were awarded damages 71% of the time."[1] This argument in favor of litigation is contradicted by statistics and polls about efficiency. "A poll . . . finds that most Americans do not want their day in court. Rather they prefer cheaper and faster methods of settling arguments. When asked how they'd like to settle a dispute with a company, 82% chose arbitration, which avoids the time and expense of going to court. Only 15% opted for litigation. Americans are not confident that a lawsuit will produce a fair result, but a solid majority looks favorably on mediation and arbitration."[2] The 2010 law providing reforms of financial institutions and services empowers the Bureau of Consumer Financial Protection to protect consumers by restricting and even prohibiting arbitration clauses. In the years ahead, the trend may be toward mediation clauses, rather than arbitration clauses, in contracts. In mediation, parties maintain control over the outcome of dispute and decide whether to settle or continue litigation. This choice may be preferable over the arbitration process.

[1]Joseph A. Giannone, "FINRA Arbitration Change Seen Aiding Investors," *Reuters* September 28, 2010.

[2]Editorial, *The Wall Street Journal*, April 5, 2008.

8. SUBMISSIONS

Submission by contract occurs if the parties enter into an agreement to arbitrate an existing dispute. The arbitration agreement is the submission in this case. In addition, the parties may contractually agree to submit to arbitration all issues that may arise in the future. Submission in these circumstances occurs when a demand to arbitrate is served on the other party.

Most state statutes authorizing voluntary arbitration require the agreement to arbitrate to be in writing. Since the goal of arbitration is to obtain a quick resolution of disputes, most statutes require submission within a stated time period, usually six months, after the dispute arises.

In the absence of a statute, the rights and duties of the parties to a submission are described and limited by their agreement. Parties that have contracted to arbitrate are not required to arbitrate any matters other than those they contractually agree to arbitrate. Sidebar 5.5 contains an example of an agreement to arbitrate.

>> *sidebar* 5.5

Sample Arbitration Clause

All disputes, claims, or controversies arising from or relating to this contract shall be resolved by binding arbitration by one arbitrator selected by the parties from an American Arbitration Association list of qualified arbitrators. This arbitration contract is made pursuant to a transaction in interstate commerce, and it shall be governed by the Federal Arbitration Act.

The parties voluntarily and knowingly waive any right they have to a jury trial. The parties agree and understand the arbitrator shall have all powers provided by the law and this contract. These powers shall include all legal and equitable remedies, including, but not limited to, money damages, declaratory relief, and injunctive relief.

The issues submitted to arbitration, as framed in the submission, may be questions of fact, questions of law, or mixed questions of fact and law. They may include the interpretation of the arbitration agreement. Sometimes a dispute arises as to whether the parties have agreed to submit an issue to arbitration. In such a case, one party refuses to arbitrate and the other files suit to compel arbitration. The court hearing the case decides the issue of arbitrability but does not decide the basic issue between the parties. The U.S. Supreme Court explained these distinct roles of the court and the arbitrator in a case summarized in Sidebar 5.6.

>> *sidebar* 5.6

To Arbitrate or Litigate

The communication workers union, as the bargaining agent of employees working for AT&T Tech., Inc., negotiated a contract that contained an arbitration clause covering disputes that might arise. Another provision of the contract allowed management to make decisions regarding hiring, placement, and termination of employees. Exercising its authority, management laid off 79 employees due to a lack of work. The union challenged this action by claiming there was no lack of work justifying the layoffs. The union sought to have this dispute arbitrated; however, management refused to arbitrate claiming its authority to terminate employees was clear. The union filed suit and asked the court to compel arbitration.

Does a judge or an arbitrator decide what issues should be submitted to arbitration?

The question of whether the parties agreed to arbitrate is decided by a judge, not an arbitrator. However, in deciding what issues can be arbitrated, a judge is not to rule on the merits of the underlying claim. Judges should presume arbitration is appropriate; thus, any doubt should be resolved in favor of arbitration over litigation.[1] Later, the Supreme Court discussed "gateway issues" and whether an arbitrator or judge decides such matters. The Court ruled the application of a statute of limitations should be decided by the arbitrator.[2] However, the Court has held that a judge must determine the ratification date of a collective bargaining agreement.[3]

[1]*AT&T Tech., Inc. v. Communications Workers*, 106 S. Ct. 1414 (1986).
[2]*Howsam v. Dean Witter Reynolds, Inc.*, 123 S. Ct. 588 (2002).
[3]*Granite Rock Company v. International Brotherhood of Teamsters*, 130 S. Ct. 2847 (2010).

9. ARBITRATORS

Arbitrators generally are chosen by the disputing parties. A provision in the agreement to arbitrate or in the statute that requires the arbitration describes how the arbitrator is selected. Of concern in the selection process are the expertise of the arbitrator and the number of arbitrators to be chosen.

Expertise One reason arbitration is frequently preferable to litigation is the use of an expert to resolve the dispute. Appraisers can be used to decide disputes about the value of real estate, medical doctors can be used to decide health care disputes, and academicians can be used to decide issues within their area of expertise.

This use of experts is especially important in labor-management relations. Arbitration is the technique used in collective-bargaining contracts to settle grievances of employees against their employers. Arbitration is able to resolve disputes arising out of labor contracts without resorting to judicial intervention. It is quick and efficient and minimizes disruption in the workplace. Labor arbitration has attracted a large number of experts—both lawyers and academicians.

Arbitration provides for decision making by experts with experience in the particular industry and with knowledge of the customs and practices of the particular work site. Parties expect the arbitrator to look beyond strictly legal criteria to other factors that bear on the proper resolution of a dispute. These factors may include the impact of a particular result on productivity, its consequences to morale, and whether tensions will be heightened or diminished. The ablest judge usually does not bring the same experience and competence to bear upon the determination of a grievance, because the judge cannot be as informed as the expert arbitrator.

Number Chosen Another issue relates to the number of arbitrators to hear a dispute. It is common to use one arbitrator who is considered objective and impartial. Any person the disputing parties agree upon can be an arbitrator. There are no licensing requirements an arbitrator must satisfy. However, an arbitrator often is chosen from a list of qualified arbitrators provided by the arbitration service. The disputing parties are not limited to the list unless they have agreed to make their selection from this list.

It is also common to have a panel of three arbitrators. In such cases, each party selects an arbitrator and the two so selected choose a third. It is not surprising that when this procedure is used, allegations of bias are often made by the losing party. Courts generally do not allow such allegations to form a basis for overturning a panel's award unless there is evidence of overt corruption or misconduct in the arbitration proceedings. Since such evidence usually is difficult to obtain, allegations of bias normally do not impact the results of arbitration.

Authority over Certain Matters What arbitrators have authority to decide has been a topic of controversy and litigation. The following case attempts to clarify whose responsibility it is to decide preliminary matters prior to the actual arbitration. You should read this case as clarification of the cases discussed in Sidebar 5.6.

For information about available arbitrators and their expertise, examine the following websites:

- *American Arbitration Association* www.adr.org
- *JAMS* www.jamsadr.com/professionals
- *National Arbitration Forum* www.arb-forum.com
- *Arbitrator.com* (listing by states) www.arbitrator.com

"Although arbitration does not guarantee well-reasoned decisions or moderate damage awards, the conventional wisdom is that arbitrators tend to be both more predictable in decision-making and reasonable in awarding damages than juries."

Robert M. Shea at www.mbbp.com/ resources/employment/ pdfs/arbitration.pdf

The number of arbitrators is based on the agreement of the parties.

case **5.1** >>

RENT-A-CENTER, WEST, INC., v. ANTONIO JACKSON
130 S. Ct. 2772 (2010)

Antonio Jackson works for Rent-A-Center. As a condition of this employment, Jackson signed a Mutual Agreement to Arbitrate Claims (Agreement). This Agreement provides that all disputes arising out of Jackson's employment will be submitted to arbitration. The Agreement specifically states that claims for discrimination and claims for violations of any federal law would be arbitrated, not litigated. Furthermore, the Agreement provided that the "Arbitrator, and not any federal, state, or local court or agency, shall have exclusive authority to resolve any dispute relating to the interpretation, applicability, enforceability or formation of this Agreement including, but not limited to any claim that all or any part of this Agreement is void or voidable." On February 1, 2007, Jackson filed a federal lawsuit claiming that Rent-A-Center had discriminated against Jackson based on his race.

Rent-A-Center filed a motion to dismiss or stay the lawsuit and to compel arbitration. Jackson responded, claiming that the Agreement to arbitrate is unconscionable under Nevada law and is unenforceable. Rent-A-Center argued that the issue of unconscionability and unenforceability are matters for the arbitrator, not the courts, to decide. The District Judge agreed with Rent-A-Center and compelled arbitration. The Ninth Circuit Court of Appeals reversed, deciding that the threshold question of unconscionability is for the court to decide. Upon Rent-A-Center's petition, the Supreme Court granted certiorari.

SCALIA, J.: . . . The [Federal Arbitration Act] FAA reflects the fundamental principle that arbitration is a matter of contract. Section 2, the primary substantive provision of the Act, provides:

> "A written provision in . . . a contract evidencing a transaction involving commerce to settle by arbitration a controversy thereafter arising out of such contract . . . shall be valid, irrevocable, and enforceable, save upon such grounds as exist at law or in equity for the revocation of any contract."

The FAA thereby places arbitration agreements on an equal footing with other contracts and requires courts to enforce them according to their terms. Like other contracts, however, they may be invalidated by generally applicable contract defenses, such as fraud, duress, or unconscionability.

The Act also establishes procedures by which federal courts implement §2's substantive rule. Under §3, a party may apply to a federal court for a stay of the trial of an action "upon any issue referable to arbitration under an agreement in writing for such arbitration." Under §4, a party "aggrieved" by the failure of another party "to arbitrate under a written agreement for arbitration" may petition a federal court "for an order directing that such arbitration proceed in the manner provided for in such agreement." The court "shall" order arbitration "upon being satisfied that the making of the agreement for arbitration or the failure to comply therewith is not in issue."

The Agreement here contains multiple written provisions to settle by arbitration a controversy. Two are relevant to our discussion. First, the section titled "Claims Covered By The Agreement" provides for arbitration of all "past, present or future" disputes arising out of Jackson's employment with Rent-A-Center. Second, the section titled "Arbitration Procedures" provides that "[t]he Arbitrator . . . shall have exclusive authority to resolve any dispute relating to the . . . enforceability . . . of this Agreement including, but not limited to any claim that all or any part of this Agreement is void or voidable." The current controversy between the parties is whether the Agreement is unconscionable. It is the second provision, which delegates resolution of that controversy to the arbitrator, that Rent-A-Center seeks to enforce. Adopting the terminology used by the parties, we will refer to it as the delegation provision.

The delegation provision is an agreement to arbitrate threshold issues concerning the arbitration agreement. We have recognized that parties can agree to arbitrate "gateway" questions of "arbitrability," such as whether the parties have agreed to arbitrate or whether their agreement covers a particular controversy. . . . An agreement to arbitrate a gateway issue is simply an additional, antecedent agreement the party seeking arbitration asks the federal court to enforce, and the FAA operates on this additional arbitration agreement just as it does on any other. The additional agreement is valid under §2 "save upon such

[continued]

grounds as exist at law or in equity for the revocation of any contract," and federal courts can enforce the agreement by staying federal litigation under §3 and compelling arbitration under §4. The question before us, then, is whether the delegation provision is valid under §2.

There are two types of validity challenges under §2: One type challenges specifically the validity of the agreement to arbitrate, and the other challenges the contract as a whole, either on a ground that directly affects the entire agreement (*e.g.*, the agreement was fraudulently induced), or on the ground that the illegality of one of the contract's provisions renders the whole contract invalid. In a line of cases neither party has asked us to overrule, we held that only the first type of challenge is relevant to a court's determination whether the arbitration agreement at issue is enforceable. . . .

If a party challenges the validity under §2 of the precise agreement to arbitrate at issue, the federal court must consider the challenge before ordering compliance with that agreement under §4. . . . [I]f the claim had been fraud in the inducement of the arbitration clause itself, then the court would have considered it. . . . In some cases the claimed basis of invalidity for the contract as a whole will be much easier to establish than the same basis as applied only to the severable agreement to arbitrate. Thus, in an employment contract many elements of alleged unconscionability applicable to the entire contract (outrageously low wages, for example) would not affect the agreement to arbitrate alone. But even where that is not the case, . . . we nonetheless require the basis of challenge to be directed specifically to the agreement to arbitrate before the court will intervene.

Here, the written provision to settle by arbitration a controversy, that Rent-A-Center asks us to enforce is the delegation provision—the provision that gave the arbitrator "exclusive authority to resolve any dispute relating to the . . . enforceability . . . of this Agreement." . . . [U]nless Jackson challenged the delegation provision specifically, we must treat it as valid under §2, and must enforce it under §3 and 4, leaving any challenge to the validity of the Agreement as a whole for the arbitrator.

The District Court correctly concluded that Jackson challenged only the validity of the contract as a whole. Nowhere in his opposition to Rent-A-Center's motion to compel arbitration did he even mention the delegation provision. . . .

Jackson's appeal to the Ninth Circuit confirms that he did not contest the validity of the delegation provision in particular. His brief noted the existence of the delegation provision, but his unconscionability arguments made no mention of it. He also repeated the arguments he had made before the District Court, that the entire agreement favors Rent-A-Center and that the limitations on discovery further his contention that the arbitration agreement as a whole is substantively unconscionable. Finally, he repeated the argument made in his District Court filings, that under state law the unconscionable clauses could not be severed from the arbitration agreement. The point of this argument, of course, is that the Agreement *as a whole* is unconscionable under state law.

Jackson repeated that argument before this Court. At oral argument, counsel stated: "There are certain elements of the arbitration agreement that are unconscionable and, under Nevada law, which would render the *entire arbitration agreement* unconscionable." . . .

We reverse the judgment of the Court of Appeals for the Ninth Circuit.

Reversed.

>> CASE QUESTIONS

1. What is Jackson's basis for filing a lawsuit instead of arbitrating his claim of racial discrimination?

2. Why does Rent-A-Center seek to have the lawsuit dismissed?

3. What rule does the Supreme Court use to decide the proper roles of a judge and an arbitrator?

4. What conclusion is reached by the Supreme Court in this case?

10. AWARDS

An **award** is the decision by an arbitrator.

Generally an arbitrator's award does not need to set forth findings of fact, conclusions of law, or the reasons for the award. However, a disclosure of findings and the reasons must be given if the applicable statute, arbitration agreement, or submission so requires. When the arbitrator does provide the basis for decision in the form of an opinion or letter, that document becomes a part of the award.

Because the parties themselves, by virtue of the submission, frame the issues to be resolved and define the scope of the arbitrator's powers, the parties are generally bound by the resulting award. A court will make every reasonable presumption in favor of the arbitration award and the arbitrator's acts and proceedings. The U.S. Supreme Court favors a broad scope of the arbitrators' authority. Restrictions on this authority will be allowed only when the disputing parties clearly state such limits.

An arbitrator's award is final on all issues submitted, and it will be enforced by the courts as if it were a judgment of the court. As is discussed in Section 14, awards are not subject to judicial review on the merits of the decision. Only when fraud or other clearly inappropriate action by the arbitrator can be shown is a court willing to reverse the award granted in a voluntary arbitration proceeding.

After the award is made by the arbitrator, it is usually filed with the clerk of an appropriate court. If no objections are filed within a statutory period, it becomes final and enforceable, like a judgment.

11. THE FEDERAL ARBITRATION ACT

The Federal Arbitration Act encourages disputing businesses to utilize arbitration.

The important role and positive perception of arbitration among businesses today probably would not exist without the Federal Arbitration Act (FAA). Prior to the enactment of the FAA, our common law system preferred litigation over arbitration as a means of resolving disputes. In 1925, congressional enactment of the FAA began to change this presumed way of dispute resolution. However, it was not until after the revision and reenactment of the FAA in 1947 that courts began to encourage disputing parties to use arbitration instead of litigation. Clearly, the FAA changed public policy perceptions of arbitration and how states can regulate its use. These two impacts of the FAA are discussed now.

Impact on Policy The FAA covers any arbitration clause in a contract that involves interstate commerce. Under it, courts are "rigorously" to enforce arbitration agreements. A court assumes arbitration was intended unless it can say with positive assurance that the arbitration clause was not intended to include the particular dispute. The federal policy clearly favors arbitration of commercial disputes. The FAA provides that arbitration agreements "shall be valid, irrevocable, and enforceable, save upon such grounds as exist at law or in equity for the revocation of any contract."

The U.S. Supreme Court, through its decisions, gives strong support to the use of arbitration. However, this deference is not absolute. For example, the Supreme Court does not allow a collective-bargaining agreement's arbitration clause to prevent an individual worker from using the court to pursue a Title VII claim of discrimination.

The Supreme Court continues to search for the proper balance between encouraging arbitration and allowing access to the court system. When legislation clearly grants the disputing parties the right to litigate claims, arbitration clauses signed by these parties do not prevent access to the courts. However, the Supreme Court, in the following case, clarifies its support of arbitration when the statute does not prohibit ADR. Case 5.2 discusses several opinions that must now be read as providing narrow restrictions on the use of arbitration.

 case 5.2 >>

14 PENN PLAZA LLC. v. PYETT
129 S. Ct. 1456 (2009)

The Service Employees International Union is the exclusive bargaining representative of its members. These members are building cleaners, porters, and doorpersons working in New York City. The union has a collective bargaining agreement (CBA) with the Realty Advisory Board on Labor Relations, Inc. (RAB), a multiemployer bargaining association for the New York City real estate industry.

The CBA contains a commitment to non-discrimination based on race, creed, color, age, disability, national origin, sex, union membership, or any other characteristic protected by law. The CBA further states that all claims of discrimination shall be subject to arbitration procedures specified in the CBA as the sole and exclusive remedy for such violations.

14 Penn Plaza LLC is a member of the RAB. As an owner of an office building, 14 Penn Plaza hired unionized workers as night lobby watchmen. Later, 14 Penn Plaza, with the union's consent, employed licensed security guards to staff the lobby and entrances of its building. This hiring resulted in the night lobby watchmen being reassigned as night porters and cleaners. These latter jobs paid less than the watchmen positions. These union members, including Mr. Pyett, filed a complaint with the Equal Employment Opportunity Commission (EEOC) on the grounds of age discrimination by 14 Penn Plaza, their employer. The EEOC did not find a violation but granted the employees/union members the right to sue their employer.

A lawsuit alleging age discrimination was filed, and 14 Penn Plaza sought to have the case dismissed. A motion to compel arbitration, as required under the CBA, was denied by the District Court for the Southern District of New York. On appeal, the Second

Circuit affirmed this decision stating that a CBA cannot deny an employee's opportunity to litigate federal statutory protected right. The Supreme Court granted certiorari to review that decision.

THOMAS, J.: The question presented by this case is whether a provision in a collective-bargaining agreement that clearly and unmistakably requires union members to arbitrate claims arising under the Age Discrimination in Employment Act of 1967 (ADEA) is enforceable. The United States Court of Appeals for the Second Circuit held that this Court's decision in *Alexander* v. *Gardner-Denver Co.*, 415 U. S. 36 (1974), forbids enforcement of such arbitration provisions. We disagree and reverse the judgment of the Court of Appeals. . . .

In this instance, the Union and the RAB, negotiating on behalf of 14 Penn Plaza, collectively bargained in good faith and agreed that employment-related discrimination claims, including claims brought under the ADEA, would be resolved in arbitration. This freely negotiated term between the Union and the RAB easily qualifies as a condition of employment that is subject to mandatory bargaining . . . . The decision to fashion a CBA to require arbitration of employment-discrimination claims is no different from the many other decisions made by parties in designing grievance machinery.

Respondents, however, contend that the arbitration clause here is outside the permissible scope of the collective-bargaining process because it affects the employees' individual, non-economic statutory rights. We disagree. Parties generally favor arbitration precisely because of the economics of dispute resolution. As in any contractual negotiation, a union may

[continued]

agree to the inclusion of an arbitration provision in a collective-bargaining agreement in return for other concessions from the employer. Courts generally may not interfere in this bargained-for exchange. Judicial nullification of contractual concessions . . . is contrary to what the Court has recognized as one of the fundamental policies of the National Labor Relations Act—freedom of contract.

As a result, the CBA's arbitration provision must be honored unless the ADEA itself removes this particular class of grievances from the NLRA's broad sweep. It does not. This Court has squarely held that the ADEA does not preclude arbitration of claims brought under the statute.

In *Gilmer,* the Court explained that "[a]lthough all statutory claims may not be appropriate for arbitration, 'having made the bargain to arbitrate, the party should be held to it unless Congress itself has evinced an intention to preclude a waiver of judicial remedies for the statutory rights at issue.'" And "if Congress intended the substantive protection afforded by the ADEA to include protection against waiver of the right to a judicial forum, that intention will be deducible from text or legislative history." The Court determined that "nothing in the text of the ADEA or its legislative history explicitly precludes arbitration." The Court also concluded that arbitrating ADEA disputes would not undermine the statute's remedial and deterrent function. In the end, the employee's generalized attacks on the adequacy of arbitration procedures were insufficient to preclude arbitration of statutory claims, because there was no evidence that Congress, in enacting the ADEA, intended to preclude arbitration of claims under that Act.

The *Gilmer* Court's interpretation of the ADEA fully applies in the collective-bargaining context. Nothing in the law suggests a distinction between the status of arbitration agreements signed by an individual employee and those agreed to by a union representative. This Court has required only that an agreement to arbitrate statutory antidiscrimination claims be explicitly stated in the collective-bargaining agreement. . . .

Examination of the two federal statutes at issue in this case, therefore, yields a straightforward answer to the question presented: The NLRA provided the Union and the RAB with statutory authority to collectively bargain for arbitration of workplace discrimination claims, and Congress did not terminate that authority with respect to federal age-discrimination claims in the ADEA. Accordingly, there is no legal basis for the Court to strike down the arbitration clause in this CBA, which was freely negotiated by the Union and the RAB, and which clearly and unmistakably requires respondents

to arbitrate the age discrimination claims at issue in this appeal. Congress has chosen to allow arbitration of ADEA claims. The Judiciary must respect that choice.

The CBA's arbitration provision is also fully enforceable under the *Gardner-Denver* line of cases. Respondents interpret *Gardner-Denver* and its progeny to hold that a union cannot waive an employee's right to a judicial forum under the federal antidiscrimination statutes because allowing the union to waive this right would substitute the union's interests for the employee's antidiscrimination rights. The combination of union control over the process and inherent conflict of interest with respect to discrimination claims, they argue, provided the foundation for the Court's holding in *Gardner-Denver* that arbitration under a collective-bargaining agreement could not preclude an individual employee's right to bring a lawsuit in court to vindicate a statutory discrimination claim. We disagree. . . .

[The Supreme Court summarized the holding of Gardner-Denver concluding that arbitration in that collective bargaining agreement was designed to resolve "differences between the Company and the Union as to the meaning and application of the provisions of this Agreement" and "any trouble in the plant." The Court notes that in Gardner-Denver there was no language that the arbitration clause was to cover discrimination claims. Thus, the Gardner-Denver decision is not as broad as the respondents claim.]

The Court's decisions following *Gardner-Denver* have not broadened its holding to make it applicable to the facts of this case. In *Barrentine* v. *Arkansas-Best Freight System, Inc.,* 450 U. S. 728 (1981), the Court considered "whether an employee may bring an action in federal district court, alleging a violation of the minimum wage provisions of the Fair Labor Standards Act, . . . after having unsuccessfully submitted a wage claim based on the same underlying facts to a joint grievance committee pursuant to the provisions of his union's collective bargaining agreement." The Court held that the unsuccessful arbitration did not preclude the federal lawsuit. Like the collective-bargaining agreement in *Gardner-Denver,* the arbitration provision under review in *Barrentine* did not expressly reference the statutory claim at issue. The Court thus reiterated that an "arbitrator's power is both derived from, and limited by, the collective-bargaining agreement" and "[h]is task is limited to construing the meaning of the collective-bargaining agreement so as to effectuate the collective intent of the parties."

McDonald v. *West Branch,* 466 U. S. 284 (1984), was decided along similar lines. The question presented in that case was "whether a federal court may accord preclusive effect to an unappealed arbitration award in a case brought under [42 U. S. C. §1983]." The Court

[continued]

declined to fashion such a rule, again explaining that "because an arbitrator's authority derives solely from the contract, an arbitrator may not have authority to enforce §1983" when that provision is left unaddressed by the arbitration agreement. Accordingly, as in both *Gardner-Denver* and *Barrentine,* the Court's decision in *McDonald* hinged on the scope of the collective-bargaining agreement and the arbitrator's parallel mandate.

The facts underlying *Gardner-Denver, Barrentine,* and *McDonald* reveal the narrow scope of the legal rule arising from that trilogy of decisions. Summarizing those opinions in *Gilmer,* this Court made clear that the *Gardner-Denver* line of cases did not involve the issue of the enforceability of an agreement to arbitrate statutory claims. Those decisions instead involved the quite different issue whether arbitration of contract-based claims precluded subsequent judicial resolution of statutory claims. Since the employees there had not agreed to arbitrate their statutory claims, and the labor arbitrators were not authorized to resolve such claims, the arbitration in those cases understandably was held not to preclude subsequent statutory actions. *Gardner-Denver* and its progeny thus do not control the outcome where, as is the case here, the collective-bargaining agreement's arbitration provision expressly covers both statutory and contractual discrimination claims.

We recognize that apart from their narrow holdings, the *Gardner-Denver* line of cases included broad dicta that was highly critical of the use of arbitration for the vindication of statutory antidiscrimination rights. That skepticism, however, rested on a misconceived view of arbitration that this Court has since abandoned. . . . The Court was correct in concluding that federal antidiscrimination rights may not be prospectively waived, but it confused an agreement to arbitrate those statutory claims with a prospective waiver of the substantive right. The decision to resolve ADEA claims by way of arbitration instead of litigation does not waive the statutory right to be free from workplace age discrimination; it waives only the right to seek relief from a court in the first instance. This Court has been quite specific in holding that arbitration agreements

can be enforced under the FAA without contravening the policies of congressional enactments giving employees specific protection against discrimination prohibited by federal law. The suggestion in *Gardner-Denver* that the decision to arbitrate statutory discrimination claims was tantamount to a substantive waiver of those rights, therefore, reveals a distorted understanding of the compromise made when an employee agrees to compulsory arbitration. . . .

Gardner-Denver mistakenly suggested that certain features of arbitration made it a forum well suited to the resolution of contractual disputes, but a comparatively inappropriate forum for the final resolution of rights created by Title VII. . . .

These misconceptions have been corrected. For example, the Court has recognized that arbitral tribunals are readily capable of handling the factual and legal complexities of antitrust claims, notwithstanding the absence of judicial instruction and supervision and that there is no reason to assume at the outset that arbitrators will not follow the law. An arbitrator's capacity to resolve complex questions of fact and law extends with equal force to discrimination claims brought under the ADEA. Moreover, the recognition that arbitration procedures are more streamlined than federal litigation is not a basis for finding the forum somehow inadequate; the relative informality of arbitration is one of the chief reasons that parties select arbitration. Parties trade the procedures and opportunity for review of the courtroom for the simplicity, informality, and expedition of arbitration. In any event, it is unlikely that age discrimination claims require more extensive discovery than other claims that we have found to be arbitrable, such as RICO and antitrust claims. . . .

We hold that a collective-bargaining agreement that clearly and unmistakably requires union members to arbitrate ADEA claims is enforceable as a matter of federal law. The judgment of the Court of Appeals is reversed, and the case is remanded for further proceedings consistent with this opinion.

Reversed and remanded.

>> CASE QUESTIONS

1. What means of dispute resolution is exclusively provided for in the collective bargaining agreement?
2. How does the Supreme Court distinguish this exclusive remedy from the arbitration clauses in *Gardner-Denver, Barrentine,* and *McDonald* cases?
3. Why does the Court find that arbitration is viewed more favorably now than in the past?

146   **PART 2**   Courts and Dispute Resolution

An interesting question remains following the decision in Case 5.2. What if the EEOC had decided to pursue the claim of age discrimination on behalf of Pyett? Sidebar 5.7 describes a case in which the Supreme Court concludes other federal laws provide the EEOC the right to litigate even though an employee signed an arbitration clause.

>> *sidebar* 5.7

Do Agreements to Arbitrate Limit the EEOC's Remedies?

The Equal Employment Opportunity Commission (EEOC) has authority to bring enforcement actions against employers whenever the EEOC believes illegal discrimination has occurred. An employee of Waffle House was discharged from employment because he had a seizure at work. This employee did not pursue the contractual remedy of arbitration; however, he did file a complaint with the EEOC. His complaint alleged Waffle House fired him because of his disability. After investigating the factual situation, the EEOC filed a lawsuit against Waffle House in federal district court. Waffle House sought to have the suit dismissed since the remedy provided by the employment contract was arbitration, and the employee did not seek arbitration. Waffle House argues that the EEOC takes the place of the employee and therefore cannot avoid the requirement of arbitration.

The Supreme Court reviews the legislative history of the EEOC by examining the Civil Rights Act of 1964, the Equal Employment Opportunity Act of 1972, and the Civil Rights Act of 1991. The Court finds that the EEOC can be a plaintiff in its own right and not simply a representative of an aggrieved employee. Due to the authority given to the EEOC, it can pursue court-ordered victim-specific relief, such as backpay, reinstatement, and damages for violations involving discrimination without first resorting to arbitration. The power of the EEOC to avoid agreed-upon arbitration does not extend to nongovernmental third parties. Investors in tax-sheltered organizations may not sue tax advisors to these organizations when the tax shelter fails. Instead, these investors are subject to the arbitration agreement that exists in the contract between the organizations and the tax advisors. When third parties, like these investors, benefit from the contracts of other parties, the third parties are bound by the original parties' agreement to arbitrate.

Source: *Arthur Andersen LLP v. Carlisle*, 129 S. Ct. 1896 (2009).
Source: *Equal Employment Opportunity Commission v. Waffle House, Inc.*, 122 S. Ct. 754 (2002).

State laws cannot prevent arbitration of disputes if the parties are engaged in or impact interstate commerce.

Impact on State Laws The federal policy favoring arbitration frequently conflicts with state laws favoring litigation as the means to resolve a dispute. Sometimes a state law specifically provides that designated matters are not to be submitted to arbitration. Are these state laws constitutional when applied to businesses engaged in interstate commerce? The Commerce Clause and the Supremacy Clause of the U.S. Constitution are often used to set aside such state laws that deny arbitration of certain disputes.

Sidebar 5.8 summarizes two additional cases in which the Supreme Court reiterates the deference to arbitration and the authority of the arbitrator.

>> *sidebar* 5.8

Who Decides? Judge, Agency, or Arbitrator?

As a customer of Buckeye Check Cashing, Inc., John Cardegna signed a contract that included a standard arbitration clause covering "any claim, dispute, or controversy arising from or related to this Agreement." This customer filed a lawsuit alleging Buckeye Check Cashing's charge of an excessive interest rate rendered the contract illegal, void, and unenforceable. Buckeye Check Cashing asked the trial judge to order the parties to arbitrate the issue of an illegal interest rate.

The U.S. Supreme Court agreed to hear this case and ruled "regardless of whether the challenge is brought in federal or state court, a challenge to the validity of the contract as a whole, and not specifically to the arbitration clause, must go to the arbitrator." This case provides further support for the general proposition that judges must defer to arbitrators when an arbitration clause has been signed by the parties.

More recently, the Supreme Court decided who has authority—the arbitrator or an administrative agency. This issue arose between Alex Ferrer, known as Judge Alex on FOX television, and Arnold Preston. Preston seeks money for services rendered to Judge Alex under a contract that includes an arbitration clause. Preston seeks arbitration and Judge Alex asks the California Labor Commissioner to declare that Preston is not properly licensed as a talent agent and thus is not eligible to collect his fees.

The Supreme Court, after reviewing a number of decisions, decides that the Federal Arbitration Act overrides a state law that attempts to vest authority in an administrative agency to make an initial decision. Thus, Judge Alex is subject to the arbitration process pursuant to the clause he signed. Arbitrators, not administrators, have the authority to make initial determinations in cases covered by the Federal Arbitration Act.

Sources: Buckeye Check Cashing, Inc. v. Cardegna, 126 S. Ct. 1204 (2006) and Preston v. Ferrer, 128 S. Ct. 978 (2008).

12. STATUTORILY MANDATED ARBITRATION

Another reason why arbitration has become more widespread during the last few decades is that legislation may require disputing parties to submit to arbitration. A growing number of states have adopted statutes that require mandatory arbitration for certain types of disputes. Those whose disputes fall within the boundaries of the mandatory arbitration statute must submit the dispute to arbitration prior to being allowed to litigate. On the basis of studies showing that a dispute requiring three days for resolution before a 12-person jury takes only two to four hours for resolution by an arbitrator, the mandatory arbitration statute is clearly a viable alternative for controlling court congestion.

The arbitrators in the mandatory arbitration process are retired judges and practicing lawyers, usually experienced trial attorneys. A list of eligible arbitrators is maintained by court officials in charge of the mandatory process. Although the parties may agree on using only one arbitrator, mandatory arbitration cases are usually presented to a panel of three. Arbitrators are paid a per-diem fee. The parties involved in the arbitration are responsible for paying these costs.

Types of Cases Mandatory arbitration statutes cover only a few types of cases. A typical statute might apply the procedure to claims exclusively for money of a small amount, such as those for less than $15,000, not including

Do check with your state and local courts to determine which cases are subject to mandatory arbitration.

interest and costs. Some statutes require arbitration of specific subject matter, like issues arising out of divorces. In addition, arbitration is required only in those cases in which a party has demanded a jury trial, as it can be assumed that a judge hearing a case is basically as efficient as an arbitrator.

Procedures Mandatory arbitration, while requiring substantially less time than litigation, does not necessarily provide speedy justice. The usual procedure for a claim filed in court that is covered by the mandatory arbitration law is to place the claim in the arbitration track at time of filing. At this time the date and time of hearing are assigned, typically eight months from the date of filing.

Discovery procedures may be used prior to the hearing on arbitration. Since no discovery is permitted after the hearing without permission of the court, an early and thorough degree of preparation is necessary to achieve a full hearing on the merits of the controversy. This preparation also prevents the hearing from being used as an opportunity to discover the adversary's case en route to an eventual trial. Most discovery is by interrogatories rather than by deposition.

The arbitrators have the power to determine the admissibility of evidence and to decide the law and the facts of the case. Rulings on objections to evidence or on other issues that arise during the hearing are made by the arbitrators. States have different rules relating to the admissibility of evidence. In most states the established rules of evidence must be followed by the arbitrators. Several jurisdictions, however, do not require hearings to be conducted according to the established rules of evidence. New Jersey law, for example, provides: "The arbitrator shall admit all relevant evidence and shall not be bound by the rules of evidence." Other states leave to the discretion of the arbitrator the extent to which the rules of evidence apply.

13. VOLUNTARY/CONTRACT-BASED ARBITRATION

Although the statutes that mandate arbitration of certain types of disputes clearly have increased the use of this ADR method, the larger growth in the number of arbitration cases comes from disputing parties agreeing to arbitrate, not litigate.

These agreements to voluntarily arbitrate come in two basic forms. One is known as the **predispute arbitration clause.** Such clauses commonly appear in business contracts. In essence, the contracting parties show good judgment in understanding conflicts exist, conflicts give rise to disputes, and disputes are better resolved through arbitration rather than by litigating.

Don't rely on getting a party to sign a postdispute arbitration agreement; relying on a predispute arbitration clause is smarter.

People often view a contract as the beginning of a productive business relationship. They do not want to lessen the forthcoming opportunities with any expectation that problems might occur. And they view including an arbitration clause in the contract as an indication that bad things will happen. These people may need to utilize a **postdispute arbitration agreement.** Such agreements arise when parties already in dispute decide that arbitration is better than litigation.

On the basis of your study of this chapter, we trust you understand why a predispute arbitration is the wiser and ultimately more efficient approach to ADR than the postdispute agreement. An obvious disadvantage to relying on the latter approach is that disputing parties may not be able to find the common ground to agree to arbitrate.

To encourage businesspeople to use voluntary arbitration, the goal of an efficient and affordable alternative to litigation must be achieved. When arbitration is as expensive and time-consuming as litigation, the attractiveness of the ADR system declines. Sidebar 5.9 discusses how the Supreme Court interprets arbitration agreements that limit claims to single parties, thereby prohibiting class action arbitrations.

>> *sidebar* 5.9 Arbitration Agreements

Single Claims v. Class Actions

When a party with a complaint suffers a small amount of damages, it is not feasible to litigate. The same might be said of arbitration, even though this process is intended to be simpler and less expensive than a lawsuit. To increase the chance of a satisfactory result, a party claiming a wrong with little damages would like to create a class action involving similarly situated parties.

This was the situation after the Concepcions enrolled for cellular phone service with AT&T. As a part of the subscription for this service through AT&T, the Concepcions signed a voluntary arbitration agreement indicating they would arbitrate any dispute with AT&T. This arbitration clause clearly stated the process would be limited to only the Concepcions' dispute.

As a party of the contract with AT&T, the Concepcions were told they would receive two "free" phones. Instead of getting the phones free of all charges, the Concepcions were billed for the sales tax on the retail value of these phones. The total amount of this tax was $30.22. When the Concepcions discovered this charge, they filed a class action suit in federal district court claiming they and other customers had been defrauded. AT&T sought to have this action dismissed, claiming the Concepcions' dispute had to be arbitrated.

The impact of AT&T's argument would be to prohibit class-action litigation and even class-action arbitration. The Concepcions sought to have the arbitration agreement declared invalid, arguing it was unconscionable under California law to deny them the right to bring this class action. Even though the District Court and 9th Circuit Court of Appeals ruled for the Concepcions, holding the prohibition of class actions was unconscionable, the U.S. Supreme Court reverses and upholds the arbitration agreement.[1] The Court's majority finds that the Federal Arbitration Act preempts the California law on unconscionability as it applies to this situation. The Court's decision upholds the belief that arbitration is preferred over litigation.

The impact of this decision and a previous one[2] by the Court appears to be that consumers will have to negotiate to preserve the right to arbitrate class action claims. If the arbitration agreement clearly states that the parties limit the arbitration to their personal claims, such class actions will be prohibited.

[1]*AT&T Mobility LLC v. Concepcion*, 131 S. Ct. 1740 (2011).
[2]*Stolt-Nielsen SA v. AnimalFeeds Int'l Corp.*,130 S.Ct. 1758 (2010).

---

14. JUDICIAL REVIEW

LO 5-5

The arbitration process is less time consuming and less costly than litigation only if the parties are limited in seeking judicial review of the arbitrators' awards. From this perspective, voluntary arbitration is a more effective alternative to litigation than mandatory arbitration. The following subsections discuss the extent of judicial review of awards depending on the type of arbitration.

Review of Voluntary/Contract-Based Arbitration Awards

Generally, the award resulting from the voluntary arbitration procedure is final. The arbitrator's findings on questions of both fact and law are conclusive. The judicial review of an arbitrator's award is quite restricted and is more limited than the appellate review of a trial court's decision.

Arbitration clauses are liberally interpreted when the issue contested is the scope of the clause. If the scope of an arbitration clause is debatable or reasonably in doubt, the clause is construed in favor of arbitration.

The fact that the arbitrator made erroneous rulings during the hearing, or reached erroneous findings of fact from the evidence, is no ground for setting aside the award because the parties have agreed that he or she should be the judge of the facts. An erroneous view of the law no matter how egregious is binding because the parties have agreed to accept the arbitrator's view of the law. Error of law renders the award void only when it requires the parties to commit a crime or otherwise to violate a positive mandate of the law. Courts do not interfere with an award by examining the merits of the controversy, the sufficiency of the evidence supporting the award, or the reasoning supporting the decision. Were it otherwise, arbitration would fail in its chief purpose: to preclude the need for litigation. Instead of being a substitute for litigation, arbitration would merely be the beginning of litigation. Broad judicial review on the merits would render arbitration wasteful and superfluous.

Judicial review can correct fraudulent or arbitrary actions by an arbitrator. Further, courts of review are sometimes called upon to set aside an award when the decision is allegedly against public policy. In such cases, the reviewing court must establish that an arbitration award is contrary to the public policy which arises from laws and legal precedents. A reviewing court cannot reject an award simply because that court bases public policy on general considerations of presumed public interests. In essence, the scope of review by courts of an arbitrator's award in a voluntary/contract-based arbitration is extremely limited, as discussed in Sidebar 5.10.

>> *sidebar* 5.10

Judicial Review of Arbitrator's Award

Can a judge reject an arbitrator's factual findings and award and substitute a decision by that judge? This is the issue that the Supreme Court resolved in a case involving major league baseball. Steve Garvey sought damages of $3,000,000 after his contract with the San Diego Padres was not extended because of the team's alleged collusion with other teams. This collusion was supposedly in violation of the Major League Baseball Players Association collective bargaining agreement with the various Major League baseball clubs.

Garvey's claim was submitted to arbitration, and the arbitrator denied the claim stating that Garvey had failed to establish proof of the fact that his contract was not extended because of collusion.

Garvey sought review at the district court level, and that judge denied Garvey's motion to set aside the arbitrator's award. Garvey appealed to the Ninth Circuit Court of Appeals. This court of appeals reversed the district court's decision, vacated the arbitrator's award, and decided the case on the basis of record established by the arbitrator.

The Supreme Court reversed the decision of the court of appeals. It held when a court finds that the arbitrator made a mistake, that court should vacate the award and remand the matter to the arbitrator for further arbitration proceedings. The court should not resolve the merits of the parties' dispute.

Source: *Major League Baseball Players Association v. Garvey,* 121 S. Ct. 1724 (2001).

Review of Statutorily Mandated Arbitration   Although a party may voluntarily consent to almost any restriction upon or deprivation of a right, a similar restriction or deprivation, when compelled by government, must be in accord with procedural and substantive due process of law. Therefore, statutorily mandated arbitration requires a higher level of judicial review of the award.

Laws providing for mandatory arbitration are subject to numerous constitutional challenges. Many courts have generally held that mandatory arbitration statutes that effectively close the courts to the litigants by compelling them to resort to arbitrators for a final and binding determination are void as against public policy and are unconstitutional in that they:

1. Deprive one of property and liberty of contract without due process of law.
2. Violate the litigant's Seventh Amendment right to a jury trial and/or the state's constitutional access to courts' provisions.
3. Result in the unconstitutional delegation of legislative or judicial power in violation of state constitutional separation-of-powers provisions.

Mandatory arbitration may be constitutional, however, if fair procedures are provided by the legislature and ultimate judicial review is available. Courts throughout the United States have uniformly upheld mandatory arbitration statutory schemes as against the constitutional challenges previously mentioned where a dissatisfied party can reject the arbitrator's award and seek a **de novo judicial review** of that award. *De novo* review means that the court tries the issues anew as if no arbitration occurred.

> *De novo* hearings may be possible following a mandatory arbitration.

In mandatory arbitrations, a record of proceedings is required. Also, findings of fact and conclusions of law are essential if there is to be enough judicial review to satisfy due process. Judicial review of mandatory arbitration requires a *de novo* review of the interpretation and application of the law by the arbitrators.

The right to reject the award and to proceed to trial is the sole remedy of a party dissatisfied with the award. In a sense, the award is an intermediate step in resolving the dispute if the trial itself is desired. The right to reject the award exists without regard to the basis for the rejection. Many jurisdictions authorize fee and cost sanctions to be imposed on parties who fail to improve their positions at the trial as compared to the arbitration. Hopefully the quality of the arbitrators, the integrity of the proceedings, and the fairness of the awards will keep the number of rejections to a minimum.

The failure of a party to be present, either in person or by counsel, at an arbitration constitutes a waiver of the right to reject the award and seek *de novo* judicial review. In essence, a party's lack of participation operates as a consent to the entry by the court of a judgment on the award. Since the procedure of mandatory-court-annexed arbitration is an integral part of the judicial process of dispute resolution, its process must be utilized either to resolve the dispute or as the obligatory step prior to resolution by trial. To allow any party to ignore the arbitration would permit a mockery of this deliberate attempt to achieve an expeditious and less costly resolution of private controversies.

Review under the Federal Arbitration Act When the arbitration is pursuant to state statute, that statute determines what, if any, grounds are available to challenge an award in court. In cases that involve interstate commerce issues, the provisions of the Federal Arbitration Act control.

Section 10 of the Federal Arbitration Act provides that an arbitration award may be vacated or set aside on any one of four grounds:

(a) Where the award was procured by corruption, fraud, or other undue means.
(b) Where the arbitrators were obviously partial or corrupt.

   (c) Where the arbitrators were guilty of misconduct in refusing to postpone the hearing, upon sufficient cause shown, or in refusing to hear evidence pertinent and material to the controversy or by engaging in any other misbehavior by which the rights of any party have been prejudiced.

   (d) Where the arbitrators exceeded their powers or so imperfectly executed them that a mutual, final, and definite award upon the subject matter submitted was not made.

As set in subsection (a), the Federal Arbitration Act provides that an award can be vacated if it can be proved that it was procured by "corruption, fraud, or other undue means." "Undue means" goes beyond the merely inappropriate or inadequate nature of the evidence and refers to some aspect of the arbitrator's decision or decision-making process that was unfair and beyond the normal process contemplated by the arbitration act. The courts tend to interpret "undue means" in conjunction with the terms "corruption" and "fraud" which precede it, and thus, "undue means" requires some type of bad faith in the procurement of the award.

> The grounds for over-turning an arbitrator's award are very limited; being disappointed with an award is not a basis for changing the award.

When the disputing parties each choose an arbitrator and these arbitrators choose a third to make up a three-person panel, the disputing parties may be inclined to charge that the arbitrator chosen by the parties is partial or corrupt. Under subsection (b), the use of "partial or corrupt" in the FAA means that an arbitrator lacks the ability to consider evidence and to reach a fair conclusion.

Subsection (c) covers arbitral misconduct. The concept of arbitral "misconduct" does not lend itself to a precise definition. Among the actions found to constitute such misconduct on the part of an arbitrator that justify vacating an arbitration award are the following:

1. Participation in communications with a party or a witness without the knowledge or consent of the other party.
2. Receipt of evidence as to a material fact without notice to a party.
3. Holding hearings or conducting deliberations in the absence of a member of an arbitration panel or rendering an award without consulting a panel member.
4. Undertaking an independent investigation into a material matter after the close of hearings and without notice to the parties.
5. Accepting gifts or other hospitality from a party during the proceedings.

An award may likewise be set aside on the basis of procedural error if an arbitrator denies a reasonable request for postponement of a hearing or commits an egregious evidentiary error, such as refusing to hear material evidence or precluding a party's efforts to develop a full record.

Finally, subsection (d), involving the question of whether the arbitrators exceeded their power, relates to the arbitrability of the underlying dispute. An arbitrator exceeds powers and authority when attempting to solve an issue that is not arbitrable because it is outside the scope of the arbitration agreement. Conversely, if the issues presented to the arbitrators are within the scope of the arbitration agreement, subsection (d) does not require the court to review the merits of every construction of the contract.

Sidebar 5.11 describes how parties to an arbitration cannot grant courts greater authority to review an arbitrator's award than described in the Federal Arbitration Act.

>> *sidebar* 5.11

Standard of Review of Arbitrator's Decision—Can Parties Expand the Statute?

A complicated factual situation involving whether Mattel, Inc., as a tenant is liable to its landlord, Hall Street Associates, for the cost of an environmental cleanup forms the issue of whether parties can expand the scope of the Federal Arbitration Act. To resolve the lawsuit filed in federal district court over whether Mattel has to pay for the cost of cleaning up a manufacturing site, these parties agreed to arbitrate this dispute. These parties' agreement to arbitrate gave the U.S. District Court for the District of Oregon the authority to "vacate, modify or correct any award; (i) where the arbitrator's findings of fact are not supported by substantial evidence, or (ii) where the arbitrator's conclusions of law are erroneous."

Following arbitration resulting in a finding favoring Mattel (finding it was not liable to pay for the environmental cleanup), Hall Street Associates asked the district court judge to vacate or modify the arbitrator's findings and conclusions. The judge did vacate the arbitrator's award. The Ninth Circuit reversed the judge's order, and the Supreme Court granted certiorari. The Supreme Court states, "Under the terms of section 9, a court must confirm an arbitration award unless it is vacated, modified, or corrected as prescribed in sections 10 and 11. Section 10 lists grounds for vacating an award, while section 11 names those for modifying or correcting one."

The Justices decide that parties, even under the jurisdiction of a district court, cannot expand this quoted language. The parties cannot set a standard of review of an arbitrator's award that is different from the Federal Arbitration Act. The arbitrator's decision favoring Mattel must be reviewed in such a way as to confirm to the limits of the statute.

Source: *Hall Street Associates, LLC v. Mattel, Inc.*, 128 S. Ct. 1396 (2008).

concept >> *summary*

Voluntary versus Mandatory Arbitration

	VOLUNTARY	MANDATORY ARBITRATION
Submission	Based on parties' agreement after dispute arises or on contract clause before dispute arises.	Required by statute.
Procedures	Since process is not tied to a court, it is quick, informal, often with no discovery, and not bound by rules of evidence.	The procedure is associated with a court's supervision; discovery usually is done, and many states require arbitrators to follow the formal rules of evidence.
Review of award	The award is final with no judicial review, unless a party can prove that the arbitrator engaged in fraudulent, arbitrary, or other inappropriate actions.	The court will conduct a *de novo* hearing as if the arbitration process had not occurred.

>> Mediation

As the preceding sections document, arbitration has played a significant role in ADR, particularly throughout the last half of the twentieth century. More recently, individuals and businesses have been utilizing the process of mediation as a preferred means of ADR. **Mediation** is the process by which a third person, called a **mediator,** attempts to assist disputing parties in resolving their differences. A mediator cannot impose a binding solution on the parties. However, as an unbiased and disinterested third party, a mediator is often able to help the parties bring about an understanding of a dispute and thus avoid litigation of it. Typically, mediators utilize the principles of interest-based negotiations, discussed in Section 4.

The process of mediation may be utilized by the disputing parties as a result of their agreement to mediate. This agreement may have been made as a part of a contract before a dispute arose. On the other hand, parties to a dispute may agree that mediation should be attempted as an alternative to litigating their controversy.

A trial judge can require the disputing parties to submit to the mediation process before a complaint can be litigated formally. There is a growing movement in this court-annexed mediation as one means of controlling the heavy caseload faced by courts. Rules related to court-annexed mediation are local in nature; thus, there are wide variations as to the type of cases that courts require to be mediated. Generally, cases involving domestic-relations issues (such as divorce and child custody) and cases involving a dollar amount in dispute below a stated threshold level are examples of those that are subject to court-annexed mediation.

The number of mediations have increased for three primary reasons. First, and perhaps most important, the disputing parties retain control over when to settle and when to continue disputing. This fact allows an effective mediation procedure to help parties address the conflicts that cause the dispute to erupt. An arbitrator's award may benefit one party while punishing another; however, the award likely does not assist the parties in developing a constructive, ongoing business relationship. Since mediation typically focuses on getting the parties to negotiate through an interest-based method, existing and potential conflicts can be handled productively. Sidebar 5.12 attempts to capture this point.

> Parties in a mediation are the decision makers; mediators provide a procedure of facilitated negotiation; and the parties are responsible for finding a solution to the dispute.

> "Mediation has emerged as the primary ADR process in federal courts."
>
> **ADR and Settlement in Federal District Courts**

> Mediation often allows disputing parties to preserve or reestablish relationships.

>> *sidebar* 5.12

Bill's and M&N Revisited

At the end of Section 2 of this chapter, you were introduced to the business transactions and resulting disputes between Bill's Discount Centers and M&N TV, Inc. Let's suppose these parties litigated or arbitrated the dispute involving the quality of M&N's TVs and the reduced purchases, over time, by Bill's. What would be the likely result? The court's judgment or arbitrator's award probably would take the form of a dollar amount in favor of one party or the other. Would such a judgment or award address the underlying concerns of the parties, thereby helping them continue to do business? Probably not!

To achieve some creative result, like the one suggested in Section 4, above, the parties will have to negotiate. The mediation form of ADR is the process that focuses on the parties negotiating.

The second reason mediation is growing in popularity relates to the cost savings compared to litigation and even arbitration. Since there is no presentation of evidence in a mediation, the active role of lawyers is reduced. The resulting savings in time and money can be quite substantial. In mediations, parties are actively engaged in negotiation, which allows these parties to be more efficient with their time.

A third reason businesses are relying more and more on mediation is found in the reduction of the legal system governing the process. As Section 17 of this chapter concludes, the role of courts in mediation is minimal.

15. PROCEDURES

Despite the fact that mediations are informal and controlled by the disputing parties, the odds for a successful mediation occurring increase greatly when the mediator follows some basic procedures. Sidebar 5.13 summarizes the typical steps of the mediation process, and a more complete description follows.

> "The good news today is that there are many different ways to resolve disputes. Within a generation, the default method has moved from litigation to mediation."
>
> **http://www. adrtoolbox.com/ decision-resources/ adr-decision-tree/**

>> *sidebar* 5.13

Steps in the Mediation Process

1. Mediator's introduction and explanation of mediation.
2. Parties' opening statements.
3. Parties' exchange (or dialogue or negotiation).
4. Brainstorming possible options (or solutions).
5. The agreement (written and signed).
6. Private sessions or caucuses. (These are optional at the mediator's discretion.)

First, the mediator usually makes an opening statement. During this statement, mediators should explain the procedures to which they are asking the parties to agree. In essence, the mediator explains much of what you are reading in this section. Also, any "rules"—such as the common courtesy of not interrupting the party speaking—are specified.

Second, all parties are allowed to make a statement about their views of this dispute. These statements are made in the presence of each other and the mediator. A party's attorney may be the spokesperson; however, it often is more enlightening when the parties speak for themselves.

Third, the mediator attempts to get the parties talking to one another in what some refer to as the dialogue or exchange phase of mediation. Through an exchange based on open communication, the parties "clear the air" and hopefully begin to shift their focus from "the wrongs done in the past" to "how can business be conducted in the future."

Fourth, once the parties concentrate on how to work together or how best to end a relationship, the mutual generation of possible solutions should occur. Brainstorming options that resolve the dispute becomes the purpose of this stage of the mediation process. Skillful mediators assist parties in evaluating the possible solutions. Through productive questioning (some call

A **caucus** in mediation occurs when the mediator meets privately with one party without the other party.

"Mediators must have the facility to listen to what the negotiators are saying and to hear priorities and demands that may not be articulated explicitly. When they start making progress, more tradeoffs follow pretty quickly, once you can break the ice."

–Jerome Lefkowitz, a labor lawyer, on the end of the New York City Transit strike in December 2005 (Source: Sewell Chan and Steven Greenhouse, "From Back-Channel Contacts, Blueprint for a Deal," *The New York Times,* December 23, 2005)

Do weigh the benefits and detriments of the mediation process. Remember, some disputes can involve issues that need to be litigated for society's gain.

this reality testing) by the mediator, parties should be able to make informed choices as to the best solution. At this point, the parties hopefully are ready to make a realistic commitment to resolve their dispute and conflict.

Sometimes, the mediator may decide that the process will be more productive if the parties and their attorneys meet with the mediator outside the presence of the other disputant. This private meeting is called a **caucus.** After each side caucuses with the mediator, the mediator may call the parties back together for continued discussions, or the mediator may begin to act as a shuttle diplomat, moving back and forth between the parties who are in separate rooms. Especially during these caucuses, the mediator must win the trust and confidence of each party to the dispute.

Through the good judgment and experience of the mediator, the differences between the parties hopefully will be resolved and a common agreement can be produced. The final step to a successful mediation is the writing of the agreement and the signing of the agreement by the parties.

16. ADVANTAGES/DISADVANTAGES

The basic advantage of mediation over litigation and arbitration is that the disputing parties retain full control over the resolution (or lack thereof) of their controversy. Through retaining this control, the parties can decide how much time and effort to put into the mediation process. The fact that mediation is party driven and does not involve even an informal presentation of evidence makes the process much more efficient than other ADR systems. If parties are making progress toward a settlement, the mediation can be continued and perhaps expanded to involve a possible agreement on other potential disputes. When the mediation is not aiding the parties, any of them can stop the process by simply stating that they will not participate further.

This same aspect of the parties controlling the mediation process may be viewed as a disadvantage rather than as an advantage when compared to other ADR systems. Even in the court-annexed mediations, a party usually satisfies the court's order to mediate by simply showing up. Generally, there is no enforcement mechanism that ensures the parties will mediate in good faith.

An additional disadvantage relates to the selection of the neutral mediator. The parties must be able to agree at least on who will be their mediator. The parties can avoid the need to agree on a mediator by allowing the person or organization that administers the mediation program to select the mediator. If the disputing parties cannot "get together" to select a mediator, the mediation process cannot begin.

Finally, the requirements for training as a mediator are not universally defined. Furthermore, licensing requirements are nonexistent at present. Therefore, anyone can serve as a mediator. The disputing party should be aware of the experience (or lack thereof) of the party chosen as their mediator. The Federal Mediation and Conciliation Service, the American Arbitration Association, and other similar organizations are valuable sources of credible mediators.

17. LACK OF JUDICIAL INVOLVEMENT

LO 5-5

There is no need for judicial review of the mediation process. If mediation is successful, it is the parties' agreement that resolves the dispute. If the parties are not pleased with the mediation, they are free to end their voluntary involvement. A court-mandated mediation either will result in the parties settling their differences and dismissing the lawsuit or will result in no agreement being reached, which likely means the litigation process continues.

In essence, mediations do not involve the legal issues found in the arbitration process. Typically, the conduct of the mediator is not subject to judicial review. Furthermore, mediators usually have the disputing parties sign a consent to mediate that states the mediator cannot be subpoenaed or otherwise be made to testify in any judicial hearing.

18. COMBINATION OF ADR SYSTEMS

LO 5-4

The benefit of flexibility related to mediation allows parties to utilize this process in conjunction with other dispute resolution systems. For example, in the middle of heated litigation, parties can agree to mediate just one issue. The resolution of one issue may help the litigation of the remaining issues proceed in a more efficient manner.

One of the more popular variations has given rise to what some people are calling an additional ADR technique. This variation involves the mediation of a dispute. The parties resolve all the matters of contention that they can and they agree to arbitrate the unresolved matters. This variation has become known as **Med-Arb.** The opportunities to use mediation in beneficial ways are limited only by the creativity of the parties involved.

Some laws encourage the parties to be creative in utilizing ADR systems. For example, the Magnuson-Moss Warranty Act provides that if a business adopts an informal dispute resolution system to handle complaints about its product warranties, then a customer cannot sue the manufacturer or seller for breach of warranty without first going through the informal procedures. This law does not deny consumers the right to sue, nor does it compel a compromise solution. It simply allows a manufacturer to require mediation, for instance, before the complaining consumer can litigate.

>> Key Terms

Arbitration 135
Arbitrator 135
Award 136
Caucus 156
Conflict 128
De novo judicial review 151
Dispute 128
Focus groups 134

Mandatory arbitration 136
Med-Arb 157
Mediation 154
Mediator 154
Negotiation 129
Positional bargaining 130
Postdispute arbitration
   agreement 148

Predispute arbitration
   clause 148
Principled, interest-based
   negotiations 131
Submission 136
Voluntary arbitration 136

>> Review Questions and Problems

Conflicts and Negotiation

1. *Conflicts and Disputes*

   What are the distinguishing characteristics of a conflict versus a dispute? Think about recent conflicts that did and did not become a dispute. Think about a recent dispute and describe how you handled it.

2. *Styles and Methods of Negotiation*

   List the five instinctive responses used in negotiation and describe how each of these applies to you.

3. *Positional Negotiation*

   In business disputes, what two items are most likely to dominate a position-based negotiation?

4. *Principled Negotiation*

   (a) Summarize the seven elements of principled, interest-based negotiations.

   (b) How does focusing on these elements assist the negotiation process?

Alternative Dispute Resolution (ADR) Systems

5. *Range of Options*

   What are the various items along the spectrum of ADR systems between litigation and negotiated settlements?

6. *Settlements*

   Why do businesses have incentives to settle disputes rather than relying on jury verdicts in the litigation process?

7. *Focus Groups*

   What is the benefit to lawyers and parties of conducting a focus group?

Arbitration

8. *Submissions*

   (a) What is th e purpose of a submission in an arbitration?

   (b) What is the proper role of the courts in determining whether a submission to arbitrate is valid?

9. *Arbitrators*

   As a client of a brokerage firm, Howsam invested in four limited partnerships. These investments were made between 1986 and 1994. The client agreement signed by Howsam required all disputes with the brokerage firm to be arbitrated. When she lost money on her investments, Howsam filed for arbitration, claiming the firm misrepresented the investments in the limited partnerships. The arbitration agreement has a six-year statute of limitations. The brokerage firm filed a lawsuit seeking to have the arbitration submission enjoined, since the statute of limitations had run out. Who—a judge or an arbitrator—makes the decision concerning the application of a statute of limitations to an arbitration proceeding? Why?

10. *Awards*

    Generally, what does an arbitrator have to include in the award to make it valid?

11. *The Federal Arbitration Act*

    (a) A dispute arose between partners. The partnership agreement provided that if the parties were unable to agree on any matter, it would be submitted to arbitration. One partner filed suit asking a court to appoint a receiver for the business. The other insisted on arbitration. How will the dispute be resolved? Why?

    (b) What impact does the FAA have on state laws that prefer the litigation process to arbitration?

12. *Statutorily Mandated Arbitration*

    (a) What is meant by the phrase *statutorily mandated arbitration?*

    (b) Is arbitration required in all cases? Why or why not?

13. *Voluntary/Contract-Based Arbitration*

    The contract arising from Randolph's purchase and financing of a mobile home contained an arbitration clause covering all disputes that might arise. When a dispute arose, Randolph filed a lawsuit in federal court alleging violations of the Truth-in-Lending Act and the Equal Credit Opportunity Act. Randolph claimed the arbitration agreement was unenforceable, since it did not specify what Randolph might have to pay associated with an arbitration proceeding. Is an arbitration agreement that doesn't specify anything about costs enforceable? Why?

14. *Judicial Review*

    (a) Explain why there are different standards of review of arbitration awards depending on whether the arbitration is voluntary or statutorily mandated.

    (b) Barbara and Cole, Inc., disputed the amount of money due as "minimum royalties" under a mineral lease. They submitted the dispute to arbitration, and the arbitrators awarded Barbara $37,214.67. The court held that there was no substantial evidence in the record to support an award of less than the minimum royalty of $75,000 and directed entry of a judgment for that amount. Was it proper for the court to increase the award? Why or why not?

Mediation

15. *Procedures*

    What steps usually are followed to provide an effective and efficient mediation? Explain.

16. *Advantages/Disadvantages*

    (a) How is mediation fundamentally different from an arbitration?

    (b) What are some of the advantages and disadvantages of the mediation process?

17. *Lack of Judicial Involvement*

    What is the nature of mediation that reduces the degree of judicial supervision?

18. *Combination of ADR Systems*

    Describe how mediation can be used in conjunction with arbitration.

business >> *discussion*

1. Your employer, Let's-Get-It-Done, has a history of multiple employee disputes. These disputes range from claims of illegal discrimination to general complaints of worker dissatisfaction with supervisors. You have been assigned the task of changing the organization's culture. Since litigation is the typical method of resolving company disputes, you are considering alternatives to litigation.

> What are possible alternative dispute resolution systems (ADRs)?
> Should employees be required to sign a contract that an ADR method will be used before any lawsuit is filed against the organization?

2. As the vice president for sales of a company that manufactures and sells commercial carpet, you notice an alarming increase in the number of customers filing complaints with your company service representatives. Of particular importance is the number of complaints that involve claims in excess of $10,000. Because these large dollar amounts can lead to lawsuits being filed, you want to investigate what is causing the increase in complaints and how your company can be processing these complaints to avoid burdensome litigation.

> What steps should you take to discover, in the most accurate and efficient manner, the reasons customers are filing complaints?
> What is the distinction between mediation and arbitration?
> Should your company's sales contracts include a clause that requires the parties to attempt resolution of dispute by mediation? By arbitration? By some other mechanisms?
> If your company's sales contracts did include a dispute resolution (other than litigation) clause, when can the courts still be used?

3. After working as a consultant for the "We Can Help You" firm for seven years, you recently received a promotion to manager. In this new role, you report to a partner and are responsible for various consulting teams. You now create these teams in collaboration with the partner. These teams typically consist of four to seven consultants with a senior consultant serving as the team leader. Teams are organized or adjusted as the client demands dictate. As a new manager, you are becoming increasingly aware of conflicts among team members and disputes between the teams and clients.

> What is the difference between a conflict and a dispute?
> What steps should you take to discover, in an accurate and efficient manner, the reasons conflicts and disputes exist?
> Should your consulting firm's contracts with employees contain a dispute resolution clause? What about the firm's consulting agreement with clients? If so, what system of dispute resolution should be included?

Chapter 6. The Consitution

6 The Constitution

☐ Learning Objectives

In this chapter you will learn:

6-1. To appreciate how the structure of the U.S. Constitution provides the framework for our federal government.

6-2. To understand the importance of the supremacy clause and the contracts clause for business.

6-3. To recognize the major amendments to the U.S. Constitution.

6-4. To analyze the basic protections created by the First, Second, and Fourteenth Amendments.

The U.S. Constitution provides the legal framework of our federal government and the authority it has to regulate business activities. You should take time to read the Constitution and its amendments found in Appendix III. You may react, like many people do, by being surprised how short the Constitution is. The original document was drafted in 1787 as an alternative to the Articles of Confederation. Today, the U.S. Constitution is upheld as a cherished document of democracy. However, the Constitution was an experiment in government since the states, under the Articles of Confederation, were not acting as a nation.

In some ways, the genius of the Constitution is in its simplicity. In other ways, the Constitution is hailed for the way it balances the complexity of government. There are seven articles in the original Constitution. The first three articles establish the legislative, executive, and judicial branches, respectively.

The Constitution creates the Congress, the presidency and vice presidency, and the Supreme Court.

Do understand that an amendment must be ratified by 38 states through legislative action or by a constitutional convention. The U.S. has never held a convention for the purposes of amending the Constitution.

Article IV ensures one nation versus individual states will provide the framework for citizenship and commercial activities. This article contains the full faith and credit clause and the privileges and immunities clause.

Article V provides the process governing the amendment of the Constitution. Article VI describes how this Constitution will be the supreme law of the land. This article also clarifies that federal laws take priority when there is a conflicting state or local law.

Finally, Article VII states the Constitution will become effective upon ratification of the states. This ratification occurred in 1789. Two years later, in 1791, the first ten amendments also were ratified. These amendments, known as the Bill of Rights, provide clear statements of individuals' freedoms and protections from government action. Some of the key provisions of the Bill of Rights related directly to business are discussed in this chapter. Other provisions from these amendments are found in Chapter 13 on criminal law.

There have been a total of 27 amendments to the Constitution; thus, only 17 amendments have been approved since 1791. Twelve of these 17 amendments relate to how the federal government operates or who has the right to vote.

This leaves five amendments, beyond the Bill of Rights, that substantially impact the government and the rights of individuals. Of these five, one amendment operates to cancel out or repeal another. The Eighteenth Amendment made the manufacture and sale of alcohol illegal. This is known as the Prohibition amendment. The Twenty-first Amendment repealed Prohibition and the Eighteenth Amendment.

It can be argued that only three amendments influence social policy. The Thirteenth Amendment abolished slavery. The Fourteenth Amendment provides protection to citizens against the actions of the states. This amendment contains three important clauses—privileges and immunities, due process, and equal protection. The Sixteenth Amendment authorizes the federal income tax.

Amending the Constitution is not the typical way social policy is adopted and implemented.

table 6.1 >> First Fourteen Amendments to the U.S. Constitution

I.	Freedom of Speech, Press, Religion and Petition (1791)
II.	Right to Keep and Bear Arms (1791)
III.	Conditions for the Quarters of Soldiers (1791)
IV.	Right of Search and Seizure (1791)
V.	Provisions Regarding Prosecution (1791)
VI.	Right to a Speedy Trial, Witnesses, etc. (1791)
VII.	Right to a Trial By Jury (1791)
VIII.	Excessive Bail and Cruel Punishment (1791)
IX.	Rule of Construction of the Constitution (1791)
X.	Rights of States (1791)
XI.	State Sovereign Immunity (1798)
XII.	Electoral College (1804)
XIII.	Abolishment of Slavery and Involuntary Servitude (1865)
XIV.	Due Process and Equal Protection (1868)

>> Basic Concepts

The Constitution contains many concepts that frame how the federal government operates and interacts with state and local governments. Three of these are of great significance to the creation of a strong centralized, federal government. They are the separation of powers concept, the supremacy clause, and the contract clause. Each is discussed in the following sections.

1. SEPARATION OF POWERS

Historians describe the success of "the constitutional experiment" as founded in the division of powers. The concept of checks and balances among the three branches of the federal government is well known. A lesser emphasized separation of powers is that between the federal government and governments at the state and local levels.

This **separation of powers** between levels of government is known as **federalism.** This concept recognizes that each level of government has a separate and distinct role to play. The federal government recognizes that it was created by the states and that states have some sovereignty. The Tenth Amendment reserves some powers to the states and to the people. Congress may not impair the ability of state government to function in the federal system. Likewise, state government may not limit the federal government's exercise of powers. Federalism, the separation of powers between the federal and state/local governments, is an important topic facing the Supreme Court every year.

2. SUPREMACY CLAUSE

In allocating power between federal and state levels of government, the Constitution, in Article VI, makes it clear that the Constitution is supreme under all laws and that federal law is supreme over a state law or local ordinance. Under the **supremacy clause,** courts may be called upon to decide if a state law is invalid because it conflicts with a federal law. They must construe or interpret the two laws to see if they are in conflict. A conflict exists if the state statute would prevent or interfere with the accomplishment and execution of the full purposes and objectives of Congress.

When various laws are not consistent, the order of priority is (1) U.S. Constitution, (2) U.S. laws, (3) state and local laws.

It is immaterial that a state did not intend to frustrate the federal law if the state law in fact does so. For example, an Arizona statute provided for the suspension of licenses of drivers who could not satisfy judgments arising out of auto accidents, even if the driver was bankrupt. The statute was declared unconstitutional since it was in conflict with the federal law on bankruptcy. The purpose of the Bankruptcy Act is to give debtors new opportunity unhampered by the pressure and discouragement of preexisting debt. The challenged state statute hampers the accomplishment and execution of the full purposes and objectives of the Bankruptcy Act enacted by Congress.

Preemption Sometimes a federal law is said to preempt an area of law. If a federal law preempts a subject, then any state law that attempts to regulate the same activity is unconstitutional under the supremacy clause. The concept of **preemption** applies not only to federal statutes but also to the rules and regulations of federal administrative agencies. Sidebar 6.1 lists several examples of business-related cases in which the courts have found federal preemption of areas involving business regulations. The federal laws in this list are covered throughout this book. When you study these laws, remember the constitutional issues related to preemption. This concept helps explain the vast authority of the federal government.

In an important decision for business, the U.S. Supreme Court ruled that the state of Michigan cannot regulate the mortgage lending subsidiary of a major national bank.[1] This ruling reaffirms that the federal Office of the Comptroller of the Currency (OCC) has greater authority than a state to regulate banks and associated activities. In 2011, the U.S. Supreme Court upheld an Arizona law that penalizes employers who knowingly hire unauthorized foreign workers. In *Chamber of Commerce v. Whiting*, the Court ruled that federal immigration law does not preempt the Arizona statute. For more about this Arizona law, see Chapter 21 employment laws.

>> *sidebar* 6.1

Examples of State Laws Preempted by Federal Law

STATE OR LOCAL LAW PREEMPTED BY	FEDERAL LAW
A city conditions renewal of taxicab franchise on settlement of a labor dispute.	National Labor Relations Act
Municipal zoning ordinance governs size, location, and appearance of satellite dish antennas.	Federal Communications Commission Regulation
A state statute permits indirect purchasers to collect damages for overcharges resulting from price-fixing conspiracies.	Sherman Antitrust Act
A state law authorizes a tort claim by workers that a union has breached its duty to ensure a safe workplace.	Labor-Management Relations Act (Landrum-Griffin)
A state law prohibits repeat violators of labor laws from doing business with the state.	National Labor Relations Act
A state nuisance law purports to cover out-of-state sources of water pollution.	Clean Water Act
State criminal prosecution for aggravated battery is filed against corporate officials because of unsafe workplace conditions.	Occupational Safety and Health Act
State statute prohibits use of the direct molding process to duplicate unpatented boat hulls or knowing sale of hulls so duplicated.	Patent Law

---

3. CONTRACT CLAUSE

Article I, Section 10, of the Constitution says, "No State shall . . . pass any . . . Law impairing the Obligation of contracts." This is the **contract clause.** It does not apply to the federal government, which does in fact frequently enact laws and adopt regulations that affect existing contracts. For example, the Department of Agriculture from time to time embargoes grain sales to foreign countries, usually as a result of problems in foreign affairs. Prohibitions of

[1] *Watters v. Wachovia Bank NA, 127 S.Ct. 1559 (2007).*

sales of electronic equipment to certain nations are upheld if the federal government prohibits such sales.

Under the contract clause, states cannot enact laws that impact rights and duties under existing contracts. Suppose your company has a contract to provide natural gas to customers for stated minimum costs. A state or local government cannot impose new lower minimum prices on these existing contracts. The new minimum prices would be applicable only to newly created contracts.

The limitation on state action impairing contracts has not been given a literal application. As a result of judicial interpretation, some state laws that affect existing contracts have been approved, especially when the law is passed to deal with a specific emergency situation. On the other hand, this constitutional provision does generally limit alternatives available to state government and prevents the enactment of legislation that changes existing contract rights.

> The contract clause regulates state and local government; it does not restrict the federal govenrnment's power to impact contractual relationships.

>> Amendments and Basic Protections

LO 6-3

The original seven constitutional articles created basic, fundamental concepts or principles of a centralized government. However, the language of the original Constitution was criticized for not restricting the newly formed federal government in some important ways. The first ten amendments, known as the Bill of Rights, establish a variety of important protections. Oftentimes we do not think of the protections in a business context. Instead, we think of them as the personal rights of individuals living in a free society. Indeed, many of the basic protections are referred to as freedoms. As you read this chapter keep in mind how constitutional protections relate to economic opportunity and business activities.

As you study the impact of these basic protections keep four important aspects in mind. First, basic constitutional rights are not absolute. Second, the extent of any limitation on a basic constitutional guarantee depends upon the nature of the competing public policy. Cases involving the Bill of Rights almost always require courts to strike a balance either between some goal or policy of society and the constitutional protection involved or between competing constitutional guarantees. For example, such cases may involve conflict between the goal of protecting an individual's or business's reputation and the right of another to speak freely about the reputation. The courts are continually weighing the extent of constitutional protections.

> **Do** remember constitutional rights are not absolute.

Third, constitutional guarantees exist in order to remove certain issues from the political process and the ballot box. They exist to protect the minority from the majority. Freedom of expression (press and speech) protects the unpopular idea or viewpoint. Freedom of assembly allows groups with ideologies foreign to most of us to meet and express their philosophy.

Finally, constitutional rights vary from time to time and may be narrowly interpreted during emergencies such as war or civil strife. Even during peacetime, constitutional principles are constantly reapplied and reexamined.

The next four sections cover topics arising from the Bill of Rights. Then Section 6 examines provisions of the Fourteenth Amendment that extend constitutional protections by restricting the authority of state and local governments.

4. FIRST AMENDMENT PROTECTIONS

>> *sidebar* 6.2

How Does the IRS Define "Churches"?

The term *church* is found, but not specifically defined, in the Internal Revenue Code. Certain characteristics are generally attributed to churches. These attributes of a church have been developed by the IRS and by court decisions. They include:

- Distinct legal existence
- Recognized creed and form of worship
- Definite and distinct ecclesiastical government
- Formal code of doctrine and discipline
- Distinct religious history
- Membership not associated with any other church or denomination
- Organization of ordained ministers
- Ordained ministers selected after completing prescribed courses of study
- Literature of its own
- Established places of worship
- Regular congregations
- Regular religious services
- Sunday schools for the religious instruction of the young
- Schools for the preparation of its members

The IRS generally uses a combination of these characteristics, together with other facts and circumstances, to determine whether an organization is considered a church for federal tax purposes.

Source: http://www.irs.gov/charities/churches/article/0,,id=155746,00.html.

Freedom of Religion The First Amendment states that Congress shall make no law "respecting an establishment of religion" (the **establishment clause**) "or prohibiting the free exercise thereof" (the **free exercise clause**). These clauses guarantee freedom of religion through the separation of church and state.

Most business-related freedom of religion cases involve the free exercise clause. The Supreme Court has held that the denial of unemployment benefits to a worker who refused a position because the job would have required him to work on Sunday violated the free exercise clause of the First Amendment. The constitution requires that the owner of the business either allow the person to have Sunday off or allow the state to pay unemployment compensation and increase the business's taxes. Most businesses are likely to face this issue in employment discrimination claims brought under Title VII. These issues appear in detail in Chapter 20.

Freedom of religion has been used to challenge legislation requiring the closing of business establishments on Sunday. Although the motive for such legislation may be, in part, religious, there are also economic reasons for such legislation. As a result, if a law is based on economic considerations, it may be upheld if its classifications are reasonable and in the public interest. However, many such laws have been held invalid as a violation of the First Amendment.

Other examples of freedom of religion cases that concern business appear in Sidebar 6.3.

>> *sidebar* 6.3

Examples of Freedom of Religion Issues Affecting Business

	CASE DECISIONS	
	YES	NO
Is it constitutional to apply the Fair Labor Standards Act (minimum-wage law) to a nonprofit religious organization?	X	
Is it constitutional to apply the labor laws relating to union elections to parochial school teachers?		X
Is a state law constitutional when it provides Sabbath observers with an absolute and unqualified right not to work on their Sabbath?		X
Is religious belief justification for refusing to participate in the Social Security system?		X
Does the 1964 Civil Rights Act, which obligates employers to make reasonable accommodations of employees' religious beliefs, violate the First Amendment's establishment clause?		X
May a state impose a 6 percent sales tax on religious merchandise sold in the state by religious organizations?	X	
May a state exempt religious periodicals from a sales tax that applies to all other periodicals?		X

Freedom of Speech Freedom of speech, sometimes referred to as freedom of expression, covers both verbal and written communications. This protection relates to governmental action that restricts our ability to express ourselves. The Amendment protection does not apply to private action. Whether a restriction is imposed by the government or a private company is critical to understand. The First Amendment does not apply to action by private companies.

Free speech also covers conduct or actions considered **symbolic speech.** Although freedom of speech is not absolute, it is as close to being absolute as any constitutional guarantee. It exists to protect the minority from the majority. It means freedom to express ideas antagonistic to those of the majority. Freedom of speech exists for thoughts many of us hate and for ideas that may be foreign to us. It means freedom to express the unorthodox, and it recognizes that there is no such thing as a false idea.

As was seen in *Citizens United v. Federal Election Commission* (Chapter 3, Case 3.1), corporations have First Amendment rights in the political speech arena.

Not all speech, however, is protected. "Fighting words," or speech inciting a hostile reaction, is unprotected. In *Chaplinsky v. State of New Hampshire* (1942), the Court held words that "inflict injury or tend to incite an immediate breach of the peace" are not subject to First Amendment protection. The Court held "that such utterances are no essential part of any exposition of ideas, and are of such slight social value as a step to truth that any benefit may be derived from them is clearly outweighed by the social interest in order and morality." Similarly, in *Brandenburg v. Ohio,* the Court held that to be unprotected, such speech must be an "incitement to imminent lawless action."

Obscenity is also unprotected speech. To determine if speech is legally obscene, the following test should be applied from the perspective of the "average person, applying contemporary community standards":*

- Whether the work, taken as a whole, appeals to the prurient interest in sex
- Whether the work depicts or describes, in a patently offensive way, sexual conduct specifically defined by applicable state law
- Whether the work, taken as a whole, lacks serious literary, artistic, political, or scientific value (*Miller v. California*, 413 U.S. 15 (1973))

This test for obscenity evolved in the twentieth century as the result of a number of challenges to laws and ordinances prohibiting a range of speech in books, records, films, and pamphlets. Well-known literary works by writers such as James Joyce, D.H. Lawrence, Allen Ginsberg, and Henry Miller formed the basis of obscenity prosecutions. With the exception of child pornography, very little material is prohibited in the U.S. as legally obscene. See Sidebar 6.4 for examples of art exhibits challenged as obscene.

>> *sidebar* 6.4

Art and Obscenity

Art exhibits can also be subject to obscenity challenges. One notorious trial involved the photography exhibit *Robert Mapplethorpe: The Perfect Moment* in Cincinnati. Of the approximately 175 photographs in the exhibit, seven portraits were at issue, primarily depicting sadomasochistic acts. The Contemporary Arts Center and its director, Dennis Barrie, were indicted for displaying obscene material. The openly homosexual nature of Mapplethorpe's work generated negative public attention. Ultimately, Barrie and the museum were acquitted at trial.

Another high-profile action involved an exhibit at the Brooklyn Museum, *Sensation: Young British Artists from the Saatchi Collection.* Then-mayor Rudolph Giuliani threatened to cut off city funding for the museum if it did not remove a number of works from the exhibit. One work at issue, Chris Ofili's painting "The Holy Virgin Mary," uses elephant dung and cutouts from pornographic magazines. Viewed as "Catholic-bashing" and an attack on religion, the mayor wanted it removed from the exhibit. The Brooklyn Museum refused to remove the piece. After New York City stopped funding the museum, the director filed a First Amendment lawsuit. Many actors, artists, and writers spoke out in support of the museum. A federal judge subsequently ordered New York City to restore the denied funding and to refrain from continuing its ejection action.

Both cases are viewed as reaffirming First Amendment protection of art.

The Federal Communications Commission (FCC) has the power to restrict certain speech. It prohibits legally obscene broadcasts at all times, and it is a violation of FCC rules to air "indecent programming or profane language" between 6 A.M. and 10 P.M. on broadcast radio and television. The FCC defines "indecency" as "language or material that, in context, depicts or describes, in terms patently offensive as measured by contemporary community standards for the broadcast medium, sexual or excretory organs or activities." Although this material does not rise to the level of being legally obscene, its broadcast may be restricted during the day when children may be in the audience. Sidebar 6.5 contains examples of two high-profile FCC actions.

>> *sidebar* 6.5

The FCC Is Not Amused

 During the 2004 Super Bowl, MTV, a Viacom subsidiary, produced the half-time show, featuring Janet Jackson and Justin Timberlake. According to the FCC decision, the "joint performance by Ms. Jackson and Mr. Timberlake culminated in Mr. Timberlake pulling off part of Ms. Jackson's bustier and exposing her bare breast." The FCC was not persuaded by CBS's argument that "the exposure . . . was unexpected and the duration of the exposure was for only 19/32 of a second." The FCC found that "the nudity here was designed to pander to, titillate and shock the viewing audience." The FCC fined CBS $550,000 for violating indecency rules.

Following the Super Bowl incident, the FCC also fined:

- Clear Channel Communications $755,000 for graphic drug and sex talk on a "Bubba the Love Sponge" radio program
- Clear Channel $175 million for indecency complaints against Howard Stern and other radio personalities

In 2009, the U.S. Supreme Court held that the FCC may penalize even the occasional use of certain expletives on the airwaves. In *FCC v. Fox Television Stations* (129 S.Ct. 1800), the Court made it clear that companies may be fined for "fleeting expletives" (primarily the "F-word"). The litigation involved nonscripted expletives uttered by a number of celebrities, including Bono, Cher, and Nicole Richie.

For more examples of FCC actions, see http://transition.fcc.gov/eb/oip/Actions.html.

The issue of freedom of speech arises in many other business situations. Sidebar 6.6 discusses several situations that arise when considering the protection of picketing and the limitation of free speech.

>> *sidebar* 6.6

Picketing as Free Speech

Cases involving picketing, for example, especially with unions, often are concerned with the issue of free speech. The right to picket peacefully for a lawful purpose is well recognized. A state or local law that prohibits all picketing would be unconstitutional since the act of picketing, itself, is a valuable form of communication. However, a state law that limits picketing or other First Amendment freedoms may be constitutional if:

- The regulation is within the constitutional power of government.
- It furthers an important or substantial governmental interest.
- It is unrelated to suppression of free expression.
- The incidental restriction on First Amendment freedoms is no greater than is essential to further the government's interest.

Under these principles, laws that prevent pickets from obstructing traffic and those designed to prevent violence would be constitutional. For example, a Texas statute that prohibits "mass picketing," defined as picketing by more than two persons within 50 feet of any entrance or of one another, does not violate the First Amendment. The Supreme Court has held that a city ordinance prohibiting picketing in front of an individual residence was constitutional. The law was enacted to prevent picketing of the homes of doctors who perform abortions.

Courts may limit the number of pickets to preserve order and promote safety, but they will not deny pickets the right to express opinions in a picket line. For example, a court order preventing a client from picketing her lawyer was held to be a violation of the First Amendment. Freedom of speech even extends to boycotts of a business for a valid public purpose such as the elimination of discrimination.

case **6.1** >>

SNYDER v. PHELPS
131 S.CT. 1207 (2011)

Father of deceased military service member brought action against fundamentalist church and its members, stemming from defendants' anti-homosexual demonstration near service member's funeral, and asserting claims for intentional infliction of emotional distress (IIED), invasion of privacy by intrusion upon seclusion, and civil conspiracy. A jury awarded Snyder $2.9 million in compensatory damages and $8 million in punitive damages. Following jury's verdict for father, the United States District Court for the District of Maryland remitted aggregate punitive damages award to $2.1 million, but otherwise denied posttrial motions. Defendants appealed. The United States Court of Appeals for the Fourth Circuit reversed, concluding that Westboro's statements were entitled to First Amendment protection. The U.S. Supreme Court granted certiori.

ROBERTS, C.J., A jury held members of the Westboro Baptist Church liable for millions of dollars in damages for picketing near a soldier's funeral service. The picket signs reflected the church's view that the United States is overly tolerant of sin and that God kills American soldiers as punishment. The question presented is whether the First Amendment shields the church members from tort liability for their speech in this case. . . .

Fred Phelps founded the Westboro Baptist Church in Topeka, Kansas, in 1955. The church's congregation believes that God hates and punishes the United States for its tolerance of homosexuality, particularly in America's military. The church frequently communicates its views by picketing, often at military funerals. In the more than 20 years that the members of Westboro Baptist have publicized their message, they have picketed nearly 600 funerals. Brief for Rutherford Institute as *Amicus Curiae* 7, n. 14. Marine Lance Corporal Matthew Snyder was killed in Iraq in the line of duty. Lance Corporal Snyder's father selected the Catholic church in the Snyders' hometown of Westminster, Maryland, as the site for his son's funeral. Local newspapers provided notice of the time and location of the service. Phelps became aware of Matthew Snyder's funeral and decided to travel to Maryland with six other Westboro Baptist parishioners (two of his daughters and four of his grandchildren) to picket.

On the day of the memorial service, the Westboro congregation members picketed on public land adjacent to public streets near the Maryland State House, the United States Naval Academy, and Matthew Snyder's funeral. The Westboro picketers carried signs that were largely the same at all three locations . . . The church had notified the authorities in advance of its intent to picket at the time of the funeral, and the picketers complied with police instructions in staging their demonstration. The picketing took place within a 10-by 25-foot plot of public land adjacent to a public street, behind a temporary fence. App. to Brief for Appellants in No. 08-1026(CA4), pp. 2282–2285 (hereinafter App.). That plot was approximately 1,000 feet from the church where the funeral was held. Several buildings separated the picket site from the church. *Id.,* at 3758. The Westboro picketers displayed their signs for about 30 minutes before the funeral began and sang hymns and recited Bible verses. None of the picketers entered church property or went to the cemetery. They did not yell or use profanity, and there was no violence associated with the picketing. . . . The funeral procession passed within 200 to 300 feet of the picket site. Although Snyder testified that he could see the tops of the picket signs as he drove to the funeral, he did not see what was written on the signs until later that night, while watching a news broadcast covering the event . . . .

Whether the First Amendment prohibits holding Westboro liable for its speech in this case turns largely on whether that speech is of public or private concern, as determined by all the circumstances of the case. "[S]peech on 'matters of public concern' . . . is 'at the heart of the First Amendment's protection.'" . . .

Speech deals with matters of public concern when it can "be fairly considered as relating to any matter of political, social, or other concern to the community," . . .

Deciding whether speech is of public or private concern requires us to examine the "'content, form, and context'" of that speech, "'as revealed by the whole record.'" . . .

The "content" of Westboro's signs plainly relates to broad issues of interest to society at large, rather than matters of "purely private concern." . . .

The placards read "God Hates the USA/Thank God for 9/11," "America is Doomed," "Don't Pray

[continued]

for the USA," "Thank God for IEDs," "Fag Troops," "Semper Fi Fags," "God Hates Fags," "Maryland Taliban," "Fags Doom Nations," "Not Blessed Just Cursed," "Thank God for Dead Soldiers," "Pope in Hell," "Priests Rape Boys," "You're Going to Hell," and "God Hates You." App. 3781–3787. While these messages may fall short of refined social or political commentary, the issues they highlight—the political and moral conduct of the United States and its citizens, the fate of our Nation, homosexuality in the military, and scandals involving the Catholic clergy—are matters of public import. The signs certainly convey Westboro's position on those issues, in a manner designed, unlike the private speech in *Dun & Bradstreet,* to reach as broad a public audience as possible. And even if a few of the signs—such as "You're Going to Hell" and "God Hates You"—were viewed as containing messages related to Matthew Snyder or the Snyders specifically, that would not change the fact that the overall thrust and dominant theme of Westboro's demonstration spoke to broader public issues.

. . . Given that Westboro's speech was at a public place on a matter of public concern, that speech is entitled to "special protection" under the First Amendment. Such speech cannot be restricted simply because it is upsetting or arouses contempt. "If there is a bedrock principle underlying the First Amendment, it is that the government may not prohibit the expression of an idea simply because society finds the idea itself offensive or disagreeable." . . .

Snyder argues that even assuming Westboro's speech is entitled to First Amendment protection generally, the church is not immunized from liability for intrusion upon seclusion because Snyder was a member of a captive audience at his son's funeral. . . . As a general matter, we have applied the captive audience doctrine only sparingly to protect unwilling listeners from protected speech . . . .

Here, Westboro stayed well away from the memorial service. Snyder could see no more than the tops of the signs when driving to the funeral. And there is no indication that the picketing in any way interfered with the funeral service itself. We decline to expand the captive audience doctrine to the circumstances presented here. Because we find that the First Amendment bars Snyder from recovery for intentional infliction of emotional distress or intrusion upon seclusion—the alleged unlawful activity Westboro conspired to accomplish-we must likewise hold that Snyder cannot recover for civil conspiracy based on those torts . . . Our holding today is narrow. . . .

Speech is powerful. It can stir people to action, move them to tears of both joy and sorrow, and—as it did here—inflict great pain. On the facts before us, we cannot react to that pain by punishing the speaker. As a Nation we have chosen a different course to protect even hurtful speech on public issues to ensure that we do not stifle public debate. That choice requires that we shield Westboro from tort liability for its picketing in this case. The judgment of the United States Court of Appeals for the Fourth Circuit is affirmed.

It is so ordered.

Justice ALITO, dissenting.

Our profound national commitment to free and open debate is not a license for the vicious verbal assault that occurred in this case. Petitioner Albert Snyder is not a public figure. He is simply a parent whose son, Marine Lance Corporal Matthew Snyder, was killed in Iraq. Mr. Snyder wanted what is surely the right of any parent who experiences such an incalculable loss: to bury his son in peace. But respondents, members of the Westboro Baptist Church, deprived him of that elementary right. They first issued a press release and thus turned Matthew's funeral into a tumultuous media event. They then appeared at the church, approached as closely as they could without trespassing, and launched a malevolent verbal attack on Matthew and his family at a time of acute emotional vulnerability. As a result, Albert Snyder suffered severe and lasting emotional injury . . . The Court now holds that the First Amendment protected respondents' right to brutalize Mr. Snyder. I cannot agree.

>> CASE QUESTIONS

1. Why did the Court hold that the picketing pertained to a matter of "public concern"?

2. What does it mean to be a "captive audience"?

3. Why does Justice Alito dissent?

In some free-speech cases, an individual whose own speech or conduct may not be prohibited is nevertheless permitted to challenge a statute limiting speech because it also threatens other people not before the court. The person is allowed to challenge the statute because others who may desire to engage in legally protected expression may refrain from doing so. They may fear the risk of prosecution, or they may not want to risk having a law declared to be only partially invalid. This is known as the **overbreadth doctrine.** It means that the legislators have gone too far in seeking to achieve a goal.

> The overbreadth doctrine was used by the courts to declare certain versions of child pornography laws unconstitutional. Governmental restrictions on expression must be narrowly drafted.

For example, an airport authority resolution declared the central terminal area "not open for First Amendment activities." The resolution was unconstitutional under the First Amendment overbreadth doctrine. The resolution reached the "universe of expressive activity" and in effect created a "First-Amendment-Free Zone" at the airport. Nearly every person who entered the airport would violate the resolution, since it bars all First Amendment activities, including talking and reading.

As you can see, the freedom of speech is cherished as a fundamental right of citizenship. While this right's importance provides significant protection, it sometimes can contradict other critical interests, such as the right of privacy. Sidebar 6.7 highlights the balance that courts often seek to find.

>> *sidebar* 6.7

Free Speech versus an Individual's Right of Privacy

Through wiretapping and electronic surveillance statutes, the federal government and most states make it illegal to intercept and record oral, wire, and electronic conversations. A more complicated issue arises when an illegally obtained conversation involving public issues is broadcast or published by someone who is not involved in the illegal activity. For example, does the free speech clause protect a radio commentator who broadcasts a cell phone conversation when that conversation is illegally recorded but when the commentator is not the party who illegally taped the conversation?

The U.S. Supreme Court holds it would be most unusual to hold "speech by a law-abiding possessor of information can be suppressed in order to deter conduct by a non-law-abiding third party." When the recorded conversation involves public issues (such as the pay of public school teachers), the publication of this public information is protected compared to the interest of individuals to have their conversation remain private.

Source: *Bartnicki v. Vopper,* 121 S. Ct. 1753 (2001).

Commercial Speech Historically, **commercial speech** was not protected by the First Amendment. However, in the 1970s the Supreme Court began to recognize that free commercial speech was essential to the public's right to know. Therefore, today, freedom of speech protects corporations as well as individuals. The public interests served by freedom of expression protect the listener as well as the speaker. Freedom of expression includes freedom of information or the rights of the public to be informed. Since corporations may add to the public's knowledge and information, they also have the right to free speech. As was seen in *Citizens United v. Federal Election Commission*

(Chapter 3, Case 3.1), corporations have First Amendment rights in the political speech arena.

Freedom of speech for corporations may not be as extensive as the right of an individual. However, a government cannot limit commercial speech without a compelling state interest expressed to justify the restriction. State regulatory commissions often seek to limit the activities of public utilities. Such attempts usually run afoul of the First Amendment. Sidebar 6.8 explains why and to what extent commercial speech is protected.

>> sidebar 6.8

Balancing the Protection of Commercial Speech

The Food and Drug Administration Modernization Act (FDAMA) of 1997 allows drug compounding and the advertisement of such services. However, this law prohibits the advertising or any other promotional announcement that a specific compounded drug is available. Pharmacists, fearing their promotional materials related to drug compounds might be found to violate the FDAMA, sought a declaratory judgment that this law's prohibition on advertising specific compounded drugs was unconstitutional.

The Supreme Court reviews the four tests used to protect commercial speech. The compounding of drugs, as practiced by the pharmacists involved in this case, is a lawful activity. The government's interests in limiting the availability of compound drugs, which are not thoroughly tested by the FDA, are significant and substantial. The ban on advertisement of specific compound drugs does directly relate to the government's interest stated above. However, the Court discusses numerous examples of how the FDA could restrict the compounding drugs without resorting to a restriction on commercial advertisement. Since the FDA did not show why these less-restrictive examples were not feasible, the Court affirms the lower courts' decisions that the FDAMA violates the First Amendment's free speech clause.

Source: *Secretary of Health and Human Services v. Western Medical Center*, 122 S. Ct. 1497 (2002).

>> sidebar 6.9

Cigarette Warning Labels

The regulation of advertising of tobacco products is an example of a limitation on commercial speech. Tobacco advertising is one of the most regulated forms of marketing in the U.S., as well as in many other counties. The Family Smoking Prevention and Tobacco Control Act requires that cigarette packages and advertisements have larger and more visible graphic health warnings. The warnings are quite explicit, such as:

- Smoking can kill you.
- Cigarettes cause cancer.
- Tobacco smoke can harm your children.
- Cigarettes cause fatal lung disease.
- Cigarettes are addictive.

Source: Food and Drug Administration, www.fda.gov/TobaccoProducts/Labeling/CigaretteProductWarningLabels/default.htm.

case **6.2** >>

BROWN v. ENTERTAINMENT MERCHANTS ASSOCIATION
564 U.S. _____ (2011)

*Respondents, representing the video-game and soft-
ware industries, filed a pre-enforcement challenge to
a California law that restricts the sale or rental of violent video games to minors. The Federal District Court
concluded that the Act violated the First Amendment
and permanently enjoined its enforcement. The Ninth
Circuit affirmed. In a 7-2 decision, the Supreme Court
affirmed the Ninth Circuit decision. Justice Scalia
delivered the opinion of the Court in which Justices
Kennedy, Ginsburg, Sotomayor and Kagan joined. Justice Alito filed a concurring opinion in which Chief
Justice Roberts joined. Justices Thomas and Breyer
filed dissenting opinions.*

SCALIA, J.: We consider whether a California law
imposing restrictions on violent video games comports
with the First Amendment.

I California Assembly Bill 1179 (2005), Cal. Civ.
Code Ann. §§1746–1746.5 (West 2009) (Act), prohibits the sale or rental of "violent video games" to minors,
and requires their packaging to be labeled "18." The
Act covers games "in which the range of options available to a player includes killing, maiming, dismember-
ing, or sexually assaulting an image of a human being,
if those acts are depicted" in a manner that "[a] reasonable person, considering the game as a whole, would
find appeals to a deviant or morbid interest of minors,"
that is "patently offensive to prevailing standards in
the community as to what is suitable for minors," and
that "causes the game, as a whole, to lack serious literary, artistic, political, or scientific value for minors."
§1746(d)(1)(A). Violation of the Act is punishable by a
civil fine of up to $1,000. §1746.3.

Respondents, representing the video-game and
software industries, brought a preenforcement challenge to the Act in the United States District Court for
the Northern District of California. That court concluded that the Act violated the First Amendment and
permanently enjoined its enforcement. The Court of
Appeals affirmed, and we granted certiorari.

California correctly acknowledges that video
games qualify for First Amendment protection. The
Free Speech Clause exists principally to protect discourse on public matters, but we have long recognized
that it is difficult to distinguish politics from entertainment, and dangerous to try. "Everyone is familiar with
instances of propaganda through fiction. What is one

man's amusement, teaches another's doctrine." *Winters
v. New York,* 333 U. S. 507, 510 (1948). Like the protected books, plays, and movies that preceded them,
video games communicate ideas—and even social messages—through many familiar literary devices (such
as characters, dialogue, plot, and music) and through
features distinctive to the medium (such as the player's
interaction with the virtual world). That suffices to
confer First Amendment protection. Under our Constitution, "esthetic and moral judgments about art
and literature . . . are for the individual to make, not
for the Government to decree, even with the mandate
or approval of a majority." *United States* v. *Playboy
Entertainment Group, Inc.,* 529 U. S. 803, 818 (2000).
And whatever the challenges of applying the Constitution to ever-advancing technology, "the basic principles of freedom of speech and the press, like the First
Amendment's command, do not vary" when a new and
different medium for communication appears.

> The most basic of those principles is this: "[A]s a
> general matter, . . . government has no power to
> restrict expression because of its message, its ideas,
> its subject matter, or its content.". . . There are of
> course exceptions. "'From 1791 to the present,' . . .
> the First Amendment has 'permitted restrictions
> upon the content of speech in a few limited areas,'
> and has never 'include[d] a freedom to disregard
> these traditional limitations.'" *United States* v.
> *Stevens,* 559 U. S. _____, _____ (2010) (slip op.,
> at 5) (quoting *R. A. V.* v. *St. Paul,* 505 U. S. 377,
> 382–383 (1992)). These limited areas—such as
> obscenity, *Roth* v. *United States,* 354 U. S. 476,
> 483 (1957), incitement, *Brandenburg* v. *Ohio,* 395
> U. S. 444, 447–449 (1969) *(per curiam),* and fight-
> ing words, *Chaplinsky* v. *New Hampshire,* 315 U.
> S. 568, 572 (1942)—represent "well-defined and
> narrowly limited classes of speech, the preven-
> tion and punishment of which have never been
> thought to raise any Constitutional problem," *id.,*
> at 571–572.

Last Term, in *Stevens,* we held that new categories of unprotected speech may not be added to the
list by a legislature that concludes certain speech is too
harmful to be tolerated. *Stevens* concerned a federal
statute purporting to criminalize the creation, sale, or
possession of certain depictions of animal cruelty. See
18 U. S. C. §48 (amended 2010). The statute covered

[continued]

depictions "in which a living animal is intentionally maimed, mutilated, tortured, wounded, or killed" if that harm to the animal was illegal where the "the creation, sale, or possession t[ook] place," §48(c)(1). A saving clause largely borrowed from our obscenity jurisprudence, see *Miller* v. *California,* 413 U. S. 15, 24 (1973), exempted depictions with "serious religious, political, scientific, educational, journalistic, historical, or artistic value," §48(b). We held that statute to be an impermissible content-based restriction on speech. There was no American tradition of forbidding the *depiction of* animal cruelty—though States have long had laws against *committing* it.

> The Government argued in *Stevens* that lack of a historical warrant did not matter; that it could create new categories of unprotected speech by applying a "simple balancing test" that weighs the value of a particular category of speech against its social costs and then punishes that category of speech if it fails the test. *Stevens,* 559 U. S., at _____ (slip op., at 7). We emphatically rejected that "startling and dangerous" proposition. *Ibid.* "Maybe there are some categories of speech that have been historically unprotected, but have not yet been specifically identified or discussed as such in our case law." *Id.,* at _____ (slip op., at 9). But without persuasive evidence that a novel restriction on content is part of a long (if heretofore unrecognized) tradition of proscription, a legislature may not revise the "judgment [of] the American people," embodied in the First Amendment, "that the benefits of its restrictions on the Government outweigh the costs." *Id.,* at _____ (slip op., at 7).

That holding controls this case. As in Stevens, California has tried to make violent-speech regulation look like obscenity regulation by appending a saving clause required for the latter. That does not suffice. Our cases have been clear that the obscenity exception to the First Amendment does not cover whatever a legislature finds shocking, but only depictions of "sexual conduct" . . . Because speech about violence is not obscene, it is of no consequence that California's statute mimics the New York statute regulating obscenity-for-minors that we upheld in *Ginsberg* v. *New York,* 390 U. S. 629 (1968). That case approved a prohibition on the sale to minors of *sexual* material that would be obscene from the perspective of a child . . .

The California Act is something else entirely. It does not adjust the boundaries of an existing category of unprotected speech to ensure that a definition designed for adults is not uncritically applied to children. California does not argue that it is empowered to prohibit selling offensively violent works *to adults*—and it is wise not to, since that is but a hair's breadth from the

argument rejected in *Stevens.* Instead, it wishes to create a wholly new category of content-based regulation that is permissible only for speech directed at children. That is unprecedented and mistaken . . .

California's argument would fare better if there were a longstanding tradition in this country of specially restricting children's access to depictions of violence, but there is none. Certainly the *books* we give children to read—or read to them when they are younger—contain no shortage of gore. Grimm's Fairy Tales, for example, are grim indeed. As her just deserts for trying to poison Snow White, the wicked queen is made to dance in red hot slippers "till she fell dead on the floor, a sad example of envy and jealousy." The Complete Brothers Grimm Fairy Tales 198 (2006 ed.). Cinderella's evil stepsisters have their eyes pecked out by doves. *Id.,* at 95. And Hansel and Gretel (children!) kill their captor by baking her in an oven. *Id.,* at 54.

High-school reading lists are full of similar fare [citing *The Odyssey of Homer,* the *Inferno* and *Lord of the Flies*] . . . California claims that video games present special problems because they are "interactive," in that the player participates in the violent action on screen and determines its outcome. The latter feature is nothing new: Since at least the publication of The Adventures of You: Sugarcane Island in 1969, young readers of choose-your-own adventure stories have been able to make decisions that determine the plot by following instructions about which page to turn to . . .

Because the Act imposes a restriction on the content of protected speech, it is invalid unless California can demonstrate that it passes strict scrutiny—that is, unless it is justified by a compelling government interest and is narrowly drawn to serve that interest . . . California cannot meet that standard . . . The State's evidence is not compelling . . . [The studies relied on by California] do not prove that violent video games *cause* minors to *act* aggressively (which would at least be a beginning) . . . California cannot show that the Act's restrictions meet a substantial need of parents who wish to restrict their children's access to violent video games but cannot do so. The video-game industry has in place a voluntary rating system designed to inform consumers about the content of games. . . . California's legislation straddles the fence between (1) addressing a serious social problem and (2) helping concerned parents control their children. Both ends are legitimate, but when they affect First Amendment rights they must be pursued by means that are neither seriously under inclusive nor seriously over inclusive . . . Legislation such as this, which is neither fish nor fowl, cannot survive strict scrutiny.

Affirmed.

179

[continued]

>> CASE QUESTIONS

1. What is the issue before the Court?
2. What is the basis for the Court's holding?
3. Should violent speech be protected by the First Amendment?

Do realize that the concept of prohibiting prior restraints means a community must allow a performance to occur; the community can charge the actors with violating a local ordinance if the performance is inappropriate.

Freedom of the Press The publishing business is the only organized private business given explicit constitutional protection. The First Amendment states that "Congress shall make no law . . . abridging the freedom of . . . the press." This guarantee essentially authorizes a private business to provide organized scrutiny of government.

Freedom of the press is not absolute. The press is not free to print anything it wants without liability. Rather, freedom of the press is usually construed to prohibit **prior restraints** on publications. If the press publishes that which is illegal or libelous, it has liability for doing so. This liability may be either criminal or civil for damages. See Sidebar 6.10 about how WikiLeaks is presenting challenges to this doctrine.

>> *sidebar* 6.10

WikiLeaks and Freedom of the Press

According to its website,

> Wikileaks is a non-profit media organization dedicated to bringing important news and information to the public. We provide an innovative, secure and anonymous way for independent sources around the world to leak information to our journalists. We publish material of ethical, political and historical significance while keeping the identity of our sources anonymous, thus providing a universal way for the revealing of suppressed and censored injustices.

WikiLeaks is challenging the bounds of freedom of the press. Its release of thousands of confidential messages about controversial subjects, such as the wars in Iraq and Afghanistan, as well as thousands of U.S. Embassy diplomatic cables, sparked international debate. What are the implications for traditional media outlets? Under U.S. law, even if government documents are illegally obtained, news organizations may publish the material. The most famous case on this point is *New York Times v. United States,* 403 U.S. 713 (1971), upholding the right to publish the Pentagon Papers (about U.S. involvement in Vietnam), which were classified at the time.

Sources: WikiLeaks, http://www.wikileaks.ch/ and Alan Greenblatt, "Wiki-Leaks Fallout: Unease Over Web Press Freedoms," *NPR* (Dec. 8, 2010).

Don't forget to determine whether a person is a public or private figure when deciding if defamation exists.

A major area of litigation involving freedom of the press involves **defamation.** The tort theory known as **libel** is used to recover damages as a result of printed defamation of character. Libel cases compensate individuals for harm inflicted by defamatory printed falsehoods. Since the threat of a libel suit could have a chilling effect on freedom of the press and on the public's rights to information, the law has a different standard for imposing liability when the printed matter concerns an issue of public interest and concern. If the person involved is a public official or figure, a plaintiff seeking damages for emotional distress caused by offensive publications must prove actual **malice** in order to recover. *Actual malice* includes knowledge that the printed statements are false or circumstances showing a reckless disregard for whether they are true or not. If the plaintiff is not a public figure or public official, there is liability for libelous statements without proof of malice. Defamation is also discussed in more detail in Chapter 10 in the context of torts.

Second Amendment: The Right to Possess Guns Unlike the extensive litigation that defines the meaning of the First Amendment, there have been very few Supreme Court opinions involving the Second Amendment. The language of this amendment is as follows: "A well regulated Militia, being necessary to the security for a free State, the right of the people to keep and bear Arms, shall not be infringed."

In 2008, the U.S. Supreme Court addressed the meaning of the Second Amendment as it applies to the maintenance of a militia versus an individual's right to possess and use guns in their homes.[2] By a 5–4 margin, the Court ruled that the Second Amendment is not limited by its introductory phrase. The Court struck down, as unconstitutional, the District of Columbia's ban on handguns and its requirement that other guns, such as rifles, be kept unloaded or disassembled, or subject to a trigger-locking mechanism. The Court's majority concluded individuals in the District of Columbia can possess handguns in their homes and can have their guns loaded and ready for use in self-defense.

Even as this opinion was announced, commentators speculate that this decision will lead to increases in litigation under the Second Amendment. Regulation of guns by states and cities will be challenged since this Supreme Court opinion is very narrow even as it strikes down, as unconstitutional, a very broad restriction. The Supreme Court's majority opinion simply affirms the right to possess guns, including handguns, in one's home and to have them ready for use in self-defense. Left unanswered are many questions. For example, can individuals carry guns, especially concealed handguns, in public places like restaurants, parks, transit systems, and even airports? These and other issues related to the language of the Second Amendment should become a significant part of future constitutional cases. Two years after the Heller case, the Court considered a challenge to Chicago's gun laws. See Sidebar 6.11 for details about this case.

Guns are big business. According to industry reports, the U.S. firearms industry consists of 200 companies with annual revenue of $2 billion.

[2]*District of Columbia v. Heller, 554 U.S. 570 (2008).*

>> *sidebar* 6.11

The Second Amendment After the *Heller* Case

In *District of Columbia v. Heller* (554. U.S. 570 (2008), the U.S. Supreme Court held that the Second Amendment protects the right to keep and bear arms for the purpose of self-defense, and it struck down a Washington, D.C., law that banned the possession of handguns in the home. This decision led to a challenge of Chicago and Oak Park, IL, laws effectively banning handgun possession by almost all private citizens. In a 5–4 decision, the Court held that the Second

Amendment is fully applicable to the States. In other words, the right to keep and bear arms recognized in the Heller case applies to the States. Justices Stevens, Ginsburg, Breyer, and Sotomayor dissented, contending that the Heller decision remains incorrect, that "the Framers did not write the Second Amendment in order to protect a private right of armed self-defense."

Source: *McDonald v. City of Chicago*, 561 U.S. _____ , 130 S. Ct. 3020(2010).

The Fourteenth Amendment: Equal Protection and Due Process of Law The Fourteenth Amendment to the Constitution states, "No state shall make or enforce any law which shall abridge the privileges or immunities of citizens of the United States; nor shall any state deprive any person of life, liberty or property, without due process of law, nor deny to any person within its jurisdiction the equal protection of the laws." Two of this amendment's provisions are of very special importance to businesspeople—the **due process clause** and the **equal protection clause.**

> The Fourteenth Amendment restricts actions by state and local governments.

Prior to reading about these clauses, look again at the language quoted in the preceding paragraph. It is critical to understand that the first ten amendments describe individual protections against action by the federal government. The Fourteenth Amendment explicitly clarifies that certain restrictions also apply to state (and local) governments.

5. DUE PROCESS OF LAW

The term *due process of law* as used in the Fourteenth Amendment probably arises in more litigation than any other constitutional phrase. It cannot be narrowly defined. The term describes fundamental principles of liberty and justice. Simply stated, due process means "fundamental fairness and decency." It means that *government* may not act in a manner that is arbitrary, capricious, or unreasonable. The clause does not prevent private individuals or corporations, including public utilities, from acting in an arbitrary or unreasonable manner. The due process clause applies only to governmental bodies; it does not apply to the actions of individuals or businesses.

Procedural due process cases involve whether proper notice has been given and a proper hearing has been conducted. Such cases frequently involve procedures established by statute. However, many cases involve procedures that are not created by statute. For example, the due process clause has been used to challenge the procedure used in the dismissal of a student from a public university.

In essence, the due process clause can be invoked anytime procedures of government are questioned in litigation. For example, in recent years, the Supreme Court has used the due process clause as its justification for defining the limits for a jury awarding punitive damages to a plaintiff in a civil lawsuit. Sidebar 6.12 illustrates this use of the due process clause.

Incorporation Doctrine The due process clause has played a unique role in constitutional development—one that was probably not anticipated at the time of its ratification. This significant role has been to make most of the provisions of the Bill of Rights applicable to the states. The first phrase of the First Amendment begins: "Congress shall make no law." How then are state and local governments prohibited from making such a law? Jurists have used the due process clause of the Fourteenth Amendment to "incorporate" or "carry over" the Bill of Rights and make these constitutional provisions applicable to the states. Starting in 1925, the Supreme Court began applying various portions of the first eight amendments to the states using the due process clause of the Fourteenth Amendment as the reason for this incorporation and application.

> The concept of incorporation through the due process clause has made the protections of the Bill of Rights applicable to individuals subject to state and local regulations.

The role of the due process doctrine goes well beyond incorporation. For example, the Fifth Amendment contains a due process clause applicable to the federal government. The Fourteenth Amendment contains a due process clause applicable to state and local governments. Due process essentially means the same thing under both amendments. Through the due process clause, all of the constitutionally guaranteed freedoms we discuss in this chapter and in Chapter 13 have been incorporated into the Fourteenth Amendment and are applicable to the state government's regulation of our personal and professional lives.

>> *sidebar* 6.12

Punitive Damages and the Supreme Court

In a series of decisions over the past several years, the U.S. Supreme Court describes how the due process clause limits the authority of trial juries and judges to award punitive damages, the type of awards intended to punish a wrongdoer.

The Campbells had their car insured with State Farm. The Campbells were involved in a car accident and were sued. A State Farm representative told the Campbells that their insurance would protect them and that they did not need their own lawyer. The Campbells were found liable for an amount greater than their insurance coverage. The Campbells then sued State Farm claiming the company's bad faith misrepresentations resulted in the Campbells' damages. Using evidence that State Farm had been involved in similar claims throughout the United States, the Campbells won a jury verdict of $2.6 million in compensatory damages and $145 million in punitive damages. The trial judge reduced the compensatory damages to $1 million and the punitive damages to $25 million. Following appeals, the Utah Supreme Court reinstated the $145 million in punitive damages. State Farm asked the U.S. Supreme Court to declare that these punitive damages violated the due process clause of the Fourteenth Amendment.

The Court expresses concern that the degree of reprehensibility of State Farm's bad faith is unreasonably increased by the evidence from cases outside of Utah. In addressing a proper ratio of punitive damages to compensatory damages, the Court seems to want to limit such ratio to a single digit. In light of Utah's civil sanction for State Farm's bad faith being limited to $10,000, the Court finds the $145 million in punitive damages is unreasonable, arbitrary, and unconstitutional under the Fourteenth Amendment's due process clause.

In 2007, a jury awarded the estate of a deceased smoker $21,000 in economic damages, $800,000 in noneconomic damages, and $79.5 million in punitive damages. These awards arose out of a lawsuit against Philip Morris, the manufacturer of Marlboros, the preferred cigarette of the deceased. This lawsuit was not a class-action; it involved only one plaintiff.

The U.S. Supreme Court vacated the punitive damages award on the basis that the jury cannot punish a defendant for its action involving people (other smokers) who are not parties to the litigation. The Court does not issue a ruling that the nearly 100:1 ratio of punitive to nonpunitive damages is grossly excessive. Before deciding that issue, the Supreme Court wants the lower court to decide whether the jury considered other smokers, who are not involved in the lawsuit, when deciding on the amount of the punitive damages. If so, the punitive damages award would be unconstitutional since it would be a taking of Philip Morris's property without due process.

In 2008, the U.S. Supreme Court addressed the punitive damages awarded to commercial fishermen and native Alaskans against the Exxon Shipping Company for the harm created by the oil spill from the *Exxon Valdez* running aground. A jury awarded $5 billion in punitive damages, and this amount was reduced to $2.5 billion by the Ninth Circuit Court of Appeals. These awards were in addition to $507 million in compensatory damages.

In applying federal maritime law, instead of constitutional principles, the Supreme Court concluded that no more than a 1:1 ratio of punitive damages to compensatory damages was reasonable. Thus, the justices reduced the $2.5 billion punitive damages award to approximately $500 million, a five-fold reduction.

Sources: *State Farm Mutual Automobile Insurance Company v. Campbell*, 123 S. Ct. 1513 (2003); *Philip Morris USA v. Williams*, 127 S. Ct. 1057 (2007); *Exxon Shipping Company v. Baker*, 128 S. Ct. 2605 (2008).

6. EQUAL PROTECTION

The Fourteenth Amendment's equal protection language is also involved in a great deal of constitutional litigation. No law treats all persons equally; laws draw lines and treat people differently. Therefore, almost any state or local law imaginable can be challenged under the equal protection clause. It is obvious that the equal protection clause does not always deny states the power to treat different persons in different ways. Yet the equal protection clause embodies the ethical idea that law should not treat people differently without a satisfactory reason. In deciding cases using that clause to challenge state and local laws, courts use three distinct approaches. One is the traditional, or **minimum rationality,** approach, and a second is called the **strict scrutiny** approach. Some cases are analyzed as falling in between these approaches. Courts in these cases use the **quasi-strict scrutiny** approach.

As a practical matter, if the traditional (minimum rationality) approach is used, the challenged law and its classifications are usually found *not* to be a violation of equal protection. On the other hand, if the strict scrutiny test is used, the classifications are usually found to be unconstitutional under the equal protection clause.

Do understand the role of each test under the equal protection clause.

Minimum Rationality   Under the minimum rationality approach, a law creating different classifications will survive an equal protection challenge if it has a *rational* connection to a *permissible* state end. A permissible state end is one not prohibited by another provision of the Constitution. It qualifies as a legitimate goal of government. The classification must have a reasonable basis (not wholly arbitrary), and the courts will assume any statement of facts that can be used to justify the classification. These laws often involve economic issues or social legislation such as welfare laws.

Such laws are presumed to be constitutional because courts recognize that the legislature must draw lines creating distinctions and that such tasks cannot be avoided. Only when no rational basis for the classification exists is it unconstitutional under the equal protection clause. For example, a state law restricting advertising to company-owned trucks was held valid when the rational-basis test was applied to it because it is reasonable to assume less advertising on trucks provides for safer roads. Therefore, under this state law, a trucking company could not use the sides of its trucks to carry other companies' ads. Sidebar 6.13 provides an additional case example of the rational-basis test.

Strict Scrutiny   Under the strict scrutiny test, a classification will be a denial of equal protection unless the classification is necessary to achieve a *compelling* state purpose. It is not enough that a classification be permissible to achieve any state interest; it must be a compelling state objective. To withstand constitutional challenge when this test is used, the law must serve important governmental objectives and the classification must be substantially related to achieving these objectives.

The strict scrutiny test is used if the classification involves either a suspect class or a fundamental constitutional right. A suspect class is one that has such disabilities, has been subjected to such a history of purposeful unequal treatment, or has been placed in such a position of political powerlessness that it commands extraordinary protection from the political process of the

>> *sidebar* 6.13

Economic Regulations and the Rational-Basis Test

The state of Iowa taxes revenues from slot machines on riverboats at a maximum rate of 20 percent. Iowa provides a maximum tax rate of 36 percent on revenues from slot machines at racetracks. A group of racetracks and an association of dog owners filed a lawsuit to have these different tax rates declared unconstitutional under the equal protection clause.

The U.S. Supreme Court wrote that these tax rates are subject to the rational-basis test under the equal protection analysis, stating:

> The Equal Protection Clause is satisfied so long as there is a plausible policy reason for the classification, the legislative facts on which the classification is apparently based rationally may have been considered to be true by the governmental decisionmaker, and the relationship of the classification to its goal is not so attenuated as to render the distinction arbitrary or irrational.

The Court finds that the Iowa legislators could rationally support riverboats by providing a lower tax on slot machines. This action does not unconstitutionally harm the racetracks since this case simply involves an economic decision of the legislature.

Source: *Fitzgerald v. Racing Association of Central Iowa*, 123 S. Ct. 2156 (2003).

majority. For example, classifications directed at race, national origin, and legitimacy of birth are clearly suspect. As a result, the judiciary strictly scrutinizes laws directed at them. Unless the state can prove that its statutory classifications have a compelling state interest as a basis, the classifications will be considered a denial of equal protection. Classifications that are subject to strict judicial scrutiny are presumed to be unconstitutional. The state must convince the court that the classification is fair, reasonable, and necessary to accomplish the objective of legislation that is compelling to a state interest.

Case 6.3 focuses on the application of racial consideration in the award of government contracts.

 case **6.3** >>

ADARAND CONSTRUCTORS, INC. v. PENA
115 S. Ct. 2097 (1995)

O'CONNOR, J.: In 1989, the Central Federal Lands Highway Division (CFLHD), which is part of the United States Department of Transportation (DOT), awarded the prime contract for a highway construction project in Colorado to Mountain Gravel & Construction Company. Mountain Gravel then solicited bids from subcontractors for the guardrail portion of the contract. Adarand, a Colorado-based highway construction company specializing in guardrail work, submitted the low bid. Gonzales Construction Company also submitted a bid.

The prime contract's terms provide that Mountain Gravel would receive additional compensation if it hired subcontractors certified as small businesses controlled by "socially and economically disadvantaged individuals." Gonzales is certified as such a business;

[continued]

Adarand is not. Mountain Gravel awarded the subcontract to Gonzales, despite Adarand's low bid. Federal law requires that a subcontracting clause similar to the one used here must appear in most federal agency contracts, and it also requires the clause to state that "the contractor shall presume that socially and economically disadvantaged individuals include Black Americans, Hispanic Americans, Native Americans, Asian Pacific Americans, and other minorities, or any other individual found to be disadvantaged by the [Small Business] Administration pursuant to section 8(a) of the Small Business Act." Adarand claims that the presumption set forth in that statute discriminates on the basis of race in violation of the Federal Government's Fifth Amendment obligation not to deny anyone equal protection of the laws. . . .

The contract giving rise to the dispute in this case came about as a result of the Surface Transportation and Uniform Relocation Assistance Act of 1987, a DOT appropriations measure. Section 106(c)(1) of STURAA provides that "not less than 10 percent" of the appropriated funds "shall be expended with small business concerns owned and controlled by socially and economically disadvantaged individuals." STURAA adopts the Small Business Act's definition of "socially and economically disadvantaged individual," including the applicable race-based presumptions, and adds that "women shall be presumed to be socially and economically disadvantaged individuals for purposes of this subsection.". . .

After losing the guardrail subcontract to Gonzales, Adarand filed suit against various federal officials in the United States District Court for the District of Colorado, claiming that the race-based presumptions involved in the use of subcontracting compensation clauses violate Adarand's right to equal protection. The District Court granted the Government's motion for summary judgment. The Court of Appeals for the Tenth Circuit affirmed. It understood our decision in *Fullilove v. Klutznick,* 100 S. Ct. 2758 (1980), to have adopted "a lenient standard, resembling intermediate scrutiny, in assessing" the constitutionality of federal race-based action. Applying that "lenient standard," as further developed in *Metro Broadcasting, Inc. v. FCC,* 110 S. Ct. 2997 (1990), the Court of Appeals upheld the use of subcontractor compensation clauses. We granted certiorari. . . .

In 1978, the Court confronted the question whether race-based governmental action designed to benefit such groups should also be subject to "the most rigid scrutiny." *Regents of Univ. of California v. Bakke,* 98 S. Ct. 2733, involved an equal protection challenge to a state-run medical schools' practice of reserving a number of spaces in its entering class for minority students. The petitioners argued that "strict scrutiny" should apply only to "classifications that disadvantage 'discrete and insular minorities.'" *Bakke* did not produce an opinion for the Court, but Justice Powell's opinion announcing the Court's judgment rejected the argument. In a passage joined by Justice White, Justice Powell wrote that "the guarantee of equal protection cannot mean one thing when applied to one individual and something else when applied to a person of another color." He concluded that "racial and ethnic distinctions of any sort are inherently suspect and thus call for the most exacting judicial examination.". . .

Two years after *Bakke,* the Court faced another challenge to remedial race-based action, this time involving action undertaken by the Federal Government. In *Fullilove v. Klutznick,* the Court upheld Congress' inclusion of a 10% set-aside for minority-owned businesses in the Public Works Employment Act of 1977. As in *Bakke,* there was no opinion for the Court. Chief Justice Burger, in an opinion joined by Justices White and Powell, observed that "any preference based on racial or ethnic criteria must necessarily receive a most searching examination to make sure that it does not conflict with constitutional guarantees." That opinion, however, "did not adopt, either expressly or implicitly, the formulas of analysis articulated in such cases as [*Bakke*]." It employed instead a two-part test which asked, first, "whether the objectives of the legislation are within the power of Congress," and second, "whether the limited use of racial and ethnic criteria, in the context presented, is a constitutionally permissible means for achieving the congressional objectives." It then upheld the program under that test. . . .

In *Wygant v. Jackson Board of Ed.,* 106 S. Ct. 1842 (1986), the Court considered a Fourteenth Amendment challenge to another form of remedial racial classification. The issue in *Wygant* was whether a school board could adopt race-based preferences in determining which teachers to lay off. Justice Powell's plurality opinion observed that "the level of scrutiny does not change merely because the challenged classification operates against a group that historically has not been subject to governmental discrimination," and stated the two-part inquiry as "whether the layoff provision is supported by a compelling state purpose and whether the means chosen to accomplish that purpose are narrowly tailored." In other words, "racial classifications of any sort must be subjected to 'strict scrutiny.'" The plurality then concluded that the school board's interest in "providing minority role models for its minority students, as an attempt to alleviate the effects of societal discrimination," was not a compelling interest that could justify the use of a racial classification.

[continued]

It added that "societal discrimination, without more, is too amorphous a basis for imposing a racially classified remedy," and insisted instead that "a public employer . . . must ensure that, before it embarks on an affirmative-action program, it has convincing evidence that remedial action is warranted. That is, it must have sufficient evidence to justify the conclusion that there has been prior discrimination.". . .

The Court's failure to produce a majority opinion in *Bakke*, *Fullilove*, and *Wygant* left unresolved the proper analysis for remedial race-based governmental action.

The Court resolved the issue, at least in part, in 1989. *Richmond v. J. A. Croson Co.*, 109 S. Ct. 706 (1989), concerned a city's determination that 30% of its contracting work should go to minority-owned businesses. A majority of the Court in *Croson* held that "the standard of review under the Equal Protection Clause is not dependent on the race of those burdened or benefited by a particular classification," and that the single standard of review for racial classifications should be "strict scrutiny." As to the classification before the Court, the plurality agreed that "a state or local subdivision . . . has the authority to eradicate the effects of private discrimination within its own legislative jurisdiction," but the Court thought that the city had not acted with "a 'strong basis in evidence for its conclusion that remedial action was necessary.'" The Court also thought it "obvious that [the] program is not narrowly tailored to remedy the effects of prior discrimination."

With *Croson*, the Court finally agreed that the Fourteenth Amendment requires strict scrutiny of all race-based action by state and local governments. But *Croson* of course had no occasion to declare what standard of review the Fifth Amendment requires for such action taken by the Federal Government. . . .

A year later, however, the Court took a surprising turn. *Metro Broadcasting, Inc. v. FCC* involved a Fifth Amendment challenge to two race-based policies of the Federal Communications Commission. In *Metro Broadcasting*, the Court repudiated the long-held notion that "it would be unthinkable that the same Constitution would impose a lesser duty on the Federal Government" than it does on a State to afford equal protection of the laws. It did so by holding that "benign" federal racial classifications need only satisfy intermediate scrutiny, even though *Croson* had recently concluded that such classifications enacted by a State must satisfy strict scrutiny. "Benign" federal racial classifications, the Court said, "—even if those measures are not *remedial* in the sense of being designed to compensate victims of past governmental or societal discrimination—are constitutionally permissible to the extent that they serve important

governmental objectives within the power of Congress and are substantially related to achievement of those objectives.". . .

By adopting intermediate scrutiny as the standard of review for congressionally mandated "benign" racial classifications, *Metro Broadcasting* departed from prior cases in two significant respects. First, it turned its back on *Croson*'s explanation of why strict scrutiny of all governmental racial classifications is essential. . . .

Second, *Metro Broadcasting* squarely rejected one of the three propositions established by the Court's earlier equal protection cases, namely, congruence between the standards applicable to federal and state racial classifications, and in so doing also undermined the other two—skepticism of all racial classifications and consistency of treatment irrespective of the race of the burdened or benefited group. Under *Metro Broadcasting*, certain racial classifications ("benign" ones enacted by the Federal Government) should be treated less skeptically than others; and the race of the benefited group is critical to the determination of which standard of review to apply. *Metro Broadcasting* was thus a significant departure from much of what had come before it.

The three propositions undermined by *Metro Broadcasting* all derive from the basic principle that the Fifth and Fourteenth Amendments to the Constitution protect persons, not groups. It follows from that principle that all governmental action based on race . . . should be subjected to detailed judicial inquiry to ensure that the personal right to equal protection of the laws has not been infringed. These ideas have long been central to this Court's understanding of equal protection, and holding "benign" state and federal racial classifications to different standards does not square with them. . . . Accordingly, we hold today that all racial classifications, imposed by whatever federal, state, or local governmental actor, must be analyzed by a reviewing court under strict scrutiny. In other words, such classifications are constitutional only if they are narrowly tailored measures that further compelling governmental interests. To the extent that *Metro Broadcasting* is inconsistent with that holding, it is overruled. . . .

Because our decision today alters the playing field in some important respects, we think it best to remand the case to the lower courts for further consideration in light of the principles we have announced. The Court of Appeals, following *Metro Broadcasting* and *Fullilove*, analyzed the case in terms of intermediate scrutiny. It upheld the challenged statutes and regulations because it found them to be "narrowly tailored to achieve [their] significant governmental purpose of providing subcontracting opportunities for small disadvantaged business

[continued]

enterprises." The Court of Appeals did not decide the question whether the interests served by the use of sub-contractor compensation clauses are properly described as "compelling." It also did not address the question of narrow tailoring in terms of our strict scrutiny cases, by asking, for example, whether there was "any consideration of the use of race-neutral means to increase minority business participation" in government contracting, or whether the program was appropriately limited such that it "will not last longer than the discriminatory effects it is designed to eliminate.". . .

The question whether any of the ways in which the Government uses subcontractor compensation clauses can survive strict scrutiny, and any relevance distinctions such as these may have to that question, should be addressed in the first instance by the lower courts.

Accordingly, the judgment of the Court of Appeals is vacated, and the case is remanded for further proceedings consistent with this opinion.

Vacated and remanded.

>> CASE QUESTIONS

1. Why was Adarand Constructors, as low bidder on the guardrail subcontract, not awarded the job?
2. What were the holdings of *Bakke, Fullilove,* and *Wygant?* Why did these decisions not resolve the standard of review question?
3. What is the conflict between the opinions in *Croson* and *Metro Broadcasting?*
4. Why is the holding in this case so important? Does this opinion stand for the proposition that affirmative action programs are unconstitutional?
5. Why did the Supreme Court decide not to resolve the issue of which party should be awarded the guardrail subcontract?

Strict judicial scrutiny is applied to a second group of cases involving classifications directed at fundamental rights. If a classification unduly burdens or penalizes the exercise of a constitutional right, it will be stricken unless it is found to be necessary to support a compelling state interest. Among such rights are the right to vote, the right to travel, and the right to appeal. Doubts about such laws result in their being stricken by the courts as a denial of equal protection.

>> *sidebar* 6.14

Same-Sex Marriage and the Constitution

In 2008, California voters approved Proposition 8, The Marriage Protection Act, adding a new provision to the California Constitution providing that "only marriage between a man and a woman is valid or recognized in California." Supporters of gay marriage brought an action for declaratory and injunctive relief against the enforcement of Proposition 8. In 2010, Judge Vaughn Walker overturned Proposition 8, holding that based on the Due Process and Equal Protection Clauses of the Fourteenth Amendment California cannot deny gay and lesbian couples a marriage license. Judge Walker states that "[a]lthough Proposition 8 fails to possess even a rational basis, the evidence presented at trial shows that gays and lesbians are the type of minority strict scrutiny was designed to protect." Over 50 pages of Judge Walker's opinion are "findings of fact," laying the groundwork to support gay marriage in subsequent legal challenges. In short, Judge Walker concluded that Proposition 8 is unconstitutional. An appeal is pending.

Source: *Perry v. Schwarzenegger,* 704 F.3d 921 (N.D. Cal. 2010).

Quasi-Strict Scrutiny Some cases actually fall between the minimum rationality and strict scrutiny approaches. These cases use what is sometimes called quasi-strict scrutiny tests because the classifications are only partially suspect or the rights involved are not quite fundamental. For example, classifications directed at gender are partially suspect. In cases involving classifications based on gender, the courts have taken this position between the two tests or at least have modified the strict scrutiny approach. Such classifications are unconstitutional unless they are *substantially* related to an *important* government objective. This modified version of strict scrutiny has resulted in holdings that find laws to be valid as well as unconstitutional.

Equal protection cases run the whole spectrum of legislative attempts to solve society's problems. For example, courts have used the equal protection clause to require the integration of public schools. In addition, the meaning and application of the equal protection clause have been central issues in cases involving:

- Apportionment of legislative bodies.
- Racial segregation in the sale and rental of real estate.
- Laws distinguishing between the rights of legitimates and illegitimates.
- The makeup of juries.
- Voting requirements.
- Welfare residency requirements.
- Rights of aliens.

Sidebar 6.15 summarizes the legal approaches courts use when analyzing equal protection cases.

> One reason gender has not been moved to the strict scrutiny analysis is cases involving gender discrimination are so infrequent; states understand that unequal protection on the basis of gender is unacceptable.

>> *sidebar* 6.15

Analysis of Equal Protection

	MINIMUM RATIONALITY	QUASI-STRICT SCRUTINY	STRICT SCRUTINY
Classifications Must Be	Rationally connected to a permissible or legitimate government objective	Substantially related to an important government interest	Necessary to a compelling state interest
	Presumed Valid	*Quasi-Suspect Classes*	*Suspect Classes*
Examples	Height	Gender	Race
	Weight		National origin
	Age		Legitimacy
	Testing		*Fundamental Rights*
	School desegregation		To vote
	Veteran's preference		To travel
	Marriage		To appeal

The equal protection clause is the means to the end, or goal, of equality of opportunity. As such, it may be utilized by anyone claiming unequal treatment in any case. At the same time the clause will not prevent states from remedying the effect of past discrimination. As you will study in Chapter 20, courts have upheld laws that provide for preferential treatment of minorities if this remedy is narrowly tailored to serve a compelling governmental interest in eradicating past discrimination against the minority group.

>> Key Terms

Commercial speech 176	Free exercise clause 170	Prior restraints 180
Contract clause 168	Libel 180	Procedural due process 182
Defamation 180	Malice 181	Quasi-strict scrutiny 184
Due process clause 182	Minimum rationality 184	Separation of powers 167
Equal protection clause 182	Obscenity 172	Strict scrutiny 184
Establishment clause 170	Overbreadth doctrine 176	Supremacy clause 167
Federalism 167	Preemption 167	Symbolic speech 171

>> Review Questions and Problems

Basic Concepts

1. *Separation of Powers*

   Describe the two concepts that (a) balance power within the federal government and (b) provide distinctions in the role of the federal, state, and local governments.

2. *Supremacy Clause*

   In 1916, the federal government passed a law that allows national banks to sell insurance in towns with a population of less than 5,000. In 1974, Florida passed a law prohibiting insurance agents from associating with financial institutions that are owned by or affiliated with a bank holding company. A bank located in a small Florida town is affiliated with a national bank. This bank wants to sell insurance through licensed insurance agents. Can the bank successfully challenge the Florida prohibition as being preempted by the federal law? Explain your reasoning.

3. *Contract Clause*

   (a) Does this provision of the Constitution apply to the federal government, state government, or both? Explain.

   (b) Does this provision of the Constitution apply to present contractual relationships, future ones, or both? Explain.

Amendments and Basic Protections

4. *Freedom of Religion*

   Explain the purposes of and distinction between the establishment clause and the free exercise clause.

5. *Freedom of Speech*

   Silvia, an attorney in Florida, also was a licensed certified public accountant (CPA) and a certified financial planner (CFP). Silvia placed an ad in the yellow pages listing her credentials, including the CPA and CFP designations. The Florida Board of Accountancy reprimanded Silvia for using both the CPA and CFP credentials in an ad essentially emphasizing her legal work. Silvia challenged the board's right to issue this reprimand. What is the legal basis for Silvia's challenge? Explain.

6. *Freedom of the Press*

   (a) A promoter of theatrical productions applied to a municipal board (charged with managing a city-leased theater) for a license to stage the play *Hair*. Relying on outside reports that because of nudity the production would not be in the best interests of the community, the board rejected the application. The promoter sought a court order permitting it to use the auditorium. Why should the court allow the production to proceed?

   (b) What are the distinctions in how the law treats public persons versus private persons with respect to defamation?

7. *Right to Possess Guns*

   The Supreme Court recently interpreted the Second Amendment for the first time in decades. Based on that decision, can individuals have guns in their homes for self-defense or is the right to possess guns limited only to members of a governmental-approved militia unit?

8. *Due Process of Law*

   Explain what is meant by the Incorporation Doctrine and how it was used to expand the impact of the due process clause.

9. *Equal Protection*

   There are three levels of judicial scrutiny under this clause. Describe what these levels are and when they are applicable.

business >> *discussions*

1. Other retail businesses in the mall in which your sports shoes shop is located have decided to open on Sundays from 12 noon to 6 P.M. You decide to follow suit, but two of your employees refuse to go along, saying it is against their religious beliefs to work on the Sabbath. You terminate their employment. They apply for unemployment compensation, and contend their unemployed status is your fault. If the state grants them benefits, you will be penalized since your unemployment compensation taxes will go up.

Should you contest their claim?
What would be the result if the employees refuse to work on Sunday because of their desire to play golf on that day?

2. The Mayor of the City of New York took issue with a number of works in a Brooklyn Museum temporary exhibit titled "Sensation: Young British Artists from the Saatchi Collection." Especially troubling to him was a painting by Nigerian artist Chris Ofili, entitled "The Holy Virgin Mary." In that work, Ofili depicted Mary with African features, and attached a clump of elephant dung as well as photographs of female genitalia to his work. The Mayor termed Ofili's painting "sick" and "disgusting." He insisted that a city-supported museum had no right to display the exhibit.

Could the mayor prohibit the work from appearing in the show?
Why or why not? Explain your answer using the appropriate legal standard.

Chapter 7. The Property System

The Property System

7

Learning Objectives

In this chapter you will learn:

7-1. To critique property as an exclusive legal fence and to identify applications of property even when they are not traditionally called "property."

7-2. To recognize the connection between a property-based legal system and prosperity.

7-3. To organize and apply the rules of security interests.

7-4. To analyze the statement that private property promotes the common good and be able to furnish examples.

At the Constitutional Convention in 1789, no fewer than 5 of the 55 delegates asserted without any opposition that the state (or government) comes into being to protect property, meaning what is privately proper to people. Likely, all or almost all of the delegates held this opinion, which was not controversial in the late 1700s. As you read this chapter and study many of the specific rules applying the legal fence that is property, keep in mind that property is something very basic and important to our nation.

>> Introduction to the Property-Based Legal System

Think of property not as a physical fence but as a legal fence that protects resources inside the fence from the acquisitiveness of others.

The dictionary gives two definitions of "property." First, it defines property as "something that is owned," but this does not help us understand property in the legal sense. Second, the dictionary defines property as "ownership." This definition, too, is not helpful unless we have a good idea of what "ownership" means. Here is our definition of property: **Property** *is the legal right to exclude others from resources that are originally possessed or are acquired without force, theft, or fraud.* What follows are some additional definitions that will help you to understand property:

- By "exclude," we mean that you can have the police or courts keep someone from interfering with what is yours. You can *exclude* those who would interfere. Property, then, is a type of legal fence that surrounds and protects resources the law recognizes as belonging to you. People who interfere with what properly belongs to you can often be punished or required to compensate you.

- "Resources" include anything that someone may need or want. It includes land, widgets, and other physical things, but it also includes the *uses* of those things. Physical things do not mean much to us unless we can use them. James Madison, who played an important role in the writing of the Constitution, said that we have property in our speech and even our practice of religion. It is important that you understand "property" protects the uses of things.

- "Originally possessed" resources refer to what comes from you, like your work or expressions. The philosopher John Locke said that people own themselves and that this self-ownership is the basis for all property.

- Acquiring resources "without force, theft, or fraud" means basically that if we illegally take away what belongs to others, we lack the protections of the legal fence regarding those resources.

"It is true that 'property' is frequently used as a shorthand method of referring to a thing which is owned, but . . . when we refer to an object [resource] as 'property', we are forgetting that the 'property' is not the object itself, but rather a legal category which gives a person certain rights over the object."

**Margaret Davies,
Property: Meanings,
Histories, Theories
(2007)**

Property is *absolute* but not *infinite*, and its boundaries can be *ambiguous*. By "absolute" we mean that legally you can either seek the police or the courts to protect some resource or you cannot. You either have the protections of the legal fence or you do not. By "is not infinite" we mean that the uses protected by the legal fence do not go on forever. You cannot use your motorcycle to chase the cows in my pasture! The resources you own must stop short of harming the resources that I own. Further, exactly where your boundaries stop and mine begin can be "ambiguous," i.e., unclear or uncertain. This is why we have courts to resolve the disputes that arise from ambiguous property boundaries, especially boundaries involving the uses of something. Legislation and regulation also help resolve issues of ambiguous or disputed property boundaries.

This definition makes property very central to the whole legal system. Refer back to Chapter 1 and Figure 1.1 to help you understand that property is the hub of our entire legal system. We defined property in this very broad way to help business students fully appreciate its importance to the study of business. Many legal scholars define property as "a bundle of stick-like rights," and say that if you have "property," you have the right to *possess* some resource, to *control* it, *to use* it in various ways, to *transfer* it, to *gain income* from it, and so forth. Rather than regarding property as a bundle of rights, we regard it as a single right—the right to exclude. If you can legally exclude others from some resource, whether it is a physical resource or various uses of something physical, you have a private property in that resource. The legal system will protect you and allow you to exclude others from interfering with that resource.

Exactly what resources can or cannot be the objects of property protection is very important in society. For instance, in every state you can own a piece of land, but in most states, you cannot own the use of that land to grow marijuana or own the marijuana that you grow on the land. Those are not private resources that are protected by the exclusive legal fence of property. Likewise, you can own bald eagle feathers, but you do not own as a resource the use of those feathers for sale. The same thing is true of prescription drugs, which you cannot sell or even give away so that another person will have property in them. Which resources society protects by the private property fence are determined in our legal system by tradition, decisions of courts, legislation, and regulation. In our legal system, many resources can be privately owned, and property is the foundation of the "free" market (see Sidebar 7.1), but be very clear that people cannot privately own every resource, especially not every resource of use.

>> *sidebar* 7.1

Property as the Foundation of the Private Market

People are often very sloppy in the way they use words. For instance, we talk about the "free" market when what we really mean is the "private" market—that is, *the private property market.* What we call the free market is really a market in the resources people privately own that others want and need. Economists know that we can have a market in things we do not own, but we would not want to live in a system where society did not legally define and protect private property in the resources that people want and need. In a market system without private property, the transfer of goods and services would be way too costly, since everyone could take what everyone else held. Each person would have to protect what he or she held all the time to keep it from being taken by others.

We often do not think about the importance of our legal system, but in parts of the world that are poor, there is inadequate enforcement of the law establishing private property. The market is "free," but it does not produce goods and services nearly so well as a system where the law enforces private property fences adequately. People in really free markets have to spend most of their time guarding what they possess and have very little time to produce more than they can consume and to transfer it to others, which is what business is all about. Business is truly based on law, the law of private property, and the modern private market arises out of which resources society legally protects by the private property fence.

Property law does not function well when it is not adequately enforced. Honest police are needed to deter robbery and theft. Impartial courts are required to settle disputes over who owns what and whether X has wrongfully injured

Y's resources. Property becomes not just an exclusionary right but also an entire system, and it is upon this property system of law that business depends.

This chapter explores the benefits of the property system and many of the rules that apply the property fence to different kinds of resources. It concludes with an examination of how various principles of property protect the common good. As you read the chapter, you should note that the various rules you study are not themselves "property," which is the principle of the legally exclusive private fence. The rules you study simply describe different ways of applying the fence. You should finish this chapter with a deeper knowledge of the central significance of property law to business. Quite simply, property is the necessary foundation for private enterprise and the market in the modern nation.

>> The Property System

Arguably, the most significant issue for any society is how it orders the relationships among people concerning limited and valued resources, resources needed to survive and flourish. As long as people need or want more resources than they have available to them, society will order how people relate to each other in acquiring and possessing these resources. Such resources include land, food, raw materials, manufactured products, and even some types of information. Importantly, limited resources also include useful applications of the physical world and the human effort necessary for these applications. In other words, limited resources include the uses of physical raw materials and of yourself.

1. THE PROBLEM OF LIMITED RESOURCES

In Western political theory, the state comes into being in response to the problem of limited resources. Through law, the state establishes a framework for handling the problem. At least two basic legal frameworks exist. In one framework the state itself, represented by a ruler or legislature, makes the major decisions about the production and distribution of resources. The state takes ownership of resources or acquires them through taxation. It also may direct people in how, when, and where to work, thus assuming rights over the resources people have in themselves, their efforts, and talents. Distribution of resources occurs through state planning.

Communism is one system providing such a framework. The state requires that its citizens produce according to their abilities and share according to the needs of everyone else. The communist state expects people to want to do this, but it legally coerces them when necessary.

A second legal framework that orders how people relate to each other concerning scarce resources is private property. Private property, which we will just call "property," is a system of law under which the state recognizes and enforces an individual's rights to acquire, possess, use, and transfer scarce resources. (As for property other than private property, see Sidebar 7.2). In the property system, the state does not plan what people should have nor does it acquire and redistribute resources to them. Rather, the people themselves determine how resources are distributed through voluntary exchange, usually for money that they use to acquire other resources they need or want. The role of the state is to recognize legally when people have exclusive property rights in scarce resources and to allow them to enforce their rights through legal institutions like courts.

>> *sidebar* 7.2

The Three Faces of Property

Legal scholars divide the word "property" into three main usages: private, public, and common. *Private property* protects private persons and allows them to exclude others, including in most instances the state, from interfering with resources that are acquired without force, theft, or fraud. *Public property* refers to the state's right under various circumstances to exclude people from state monuments, buildings, equipment, land, and other public resources.

Common property has two meanings. First, it refers to the right we all have to common resources like the air, rivers, or oceans. However, this meaning is appropriate only to the extent we can legally exclude others from interfering with our usage of these resources, for example, as when anyone who uses a river can sue to prevent or stop its illegal pollution. Second, "common property" sometimes refers to the private ownership by two or more people of a specific resource such as a piece of land.

For studying the legal and regulatory environment of business, private property is most important. It provides the foundation for the conduct of the modern market, and it is often just called "property."

All nations recognize some applications of private property. Even the most communist society may allow individuals some right as to how they use their productive efforts, and it usually allows them exclusive control over limited personal possessions and food consumption. On the other hand, societies founded on private property law always have legal limitations on how owners can use their resources, prohibiting harm to others and recognizing both some state taxation and regulation over property. The difference in the two frameworks is a matter of degree, and most societies have mixed frameworks for dealing with the reality of limited resources.

However, if the goal of society is to produce more of what people need and want (i.e., to increase the total amount of limited resources), one of the legal frameworks is superior to the other. The available evidence suggests that a property system produces more for a society than a state planning system. And if "freedom" is measured as individual autonomy and the absence of state coercion, then a property system also makes people more free.

For the property system to function most effectively in promoting prosperity, it should be applied according to the rule of law, which means it should be applied generally and equally to everyone. All members of society must have an equal guarantee of exclusive rights to their resources. The following section discusses more specifically how property promotes prosperity.

> What does it mean to say that all nations recognize private property?

2. PROPERTY AND PROSPERITY

Property is central to the legal environment of business. It is also central to society's achievement of prosperity. In fact, property creates some of the maximum conditions known for producing and sustaining prosperity. Since property refers to a particular system of laws, rather than to useful resources, it is fair to conclude that certain laws are a major contributing factor to prosperity. Let us examine how property helps generate prosperity.

Private property
establishes maximum
conditions for wealth
creation through
promoting incentive.

First, property powerfully promotes *incentive*. By allowing people to keep and benefit from what they produce, property motivates effort in a way that Chapter 1 suggested is very natural to human beings. Whether the activity is growing crops, manufacturing cars, or starting a new business, people will generally expend more effort when they have a protected property in what they produce than when they do not. Likewise, they are willing to produce more when they do not have to spend much of their time defending their homes or other acquisitions from those who may desire to take them. Under conditions where others are likely to take through force, theft, fraud, or even government mandate what people have or produce, there comes a point at which people will simply not work as hard, take as many risks, nor innovate as much. We may debate where that point is (e.g., how much people can be taxed before they slow their efforts), but the fact that property and incentive bear a direct relationship seems beyond debate.

Next, property helps generate prosperity by establishing the conditions necessary for *capital formation,* which refers to that quality of resources that produces new or different resources. For example, property enables people to borrow money at reasonable cost. In the United States most entrepreneurs start businesses by capitalizing the resource they have in their houses. They borrow money, and in a **mortgage** agreement put up their houses to secure the loans. (See Section 13.)

Private property also
promotes capital
formation.

Lenders are willing to loan money at affordable rates primarily because property law guarantees (1) that a borrower's house is on an identifiable piece of land recognized by the state, (2) that the state recognizes a borrower's claim to the house, and (3) that the state permits lenders to enforce the mortgage agreement through the courts and sell a borrower's house to satisfy the loan if the borrower fails to repay it. The law of property enables entrepreneurs to change the form of their resources from houses to money, so they can start a business. This type of capital formation may seem curiously obvious to business students in the United States. However, as Sidebar 7.3 discusses, it is virtually unavailable in the poorer nations of the world due to the absence of adequate property law.

>> *sidebar* 7.3

The Mystery of Capital

In the book *The Mystery of Capital,* Peruvian economist Hernando de Soto asserts that the reason "why capitalism triumphs in the West but fails everywhere else" is because of the secure system of property law that exists in Western nations. Not new technology, hard work, a superior culture, better management techniques, nor "exploitation" account principally for prosperity in the West, but rather the willingness of lenders in an adequate property system to risk their money to entrepreneurs with business ideas. De Soto's research team estimates that in less-developed countries there exists $9 trillion of "dead capital"—resources that

people possess which they cannot capitalize because the laws in their countries do not adequately guarantee property in these resources, and affordable collateral-secured loans are unavailable. Without the legal recognition of property, many resources may also be difficult to sell since a buyer cannot be sure that the state will recognize and protect a seller's right to transfer the resources. This problem is especially acute with the sale of land and buildings. The lack of an adequate property law system may not account totally for poverty in less-developed countries, but it is arguably the most important contributing factor.

Of course, the relationship of capital formation to property law means more than just mortgages or other collateral-secured loans. Large-scale businesses are capitalized by investors who buy ownership shares. For instance, corporations capitalize by selling stock shares, which are legally recognized property interests in a corporation. This method of capitalization is feasible only because the law recognizes stockholders' property interests in corporations (see Chapter 14). Likewise, securities markets (i.e., markets for stocks, bonds, and other ownership interests in businesses) are not possible without law enforcing the property interests in what these markets sell. Securities markets are vital to capital formation and prosperity in modern nations. Both corporate stock shares and securities markets enable businesses to change a property interest in future profit potential into the money necessary for business operation.

A final contribution property makes to prosperity is to make resources easily divisible. *Divisibility* also relates to capital formation and refers to how property permits resources to be broken into parts and used in many ways while the owner still retains a property interest in each part. Under property law, an owner of a single piece of land can sell part of it outright (change it into money), sell another part of it on credit and hold a mortgage to ensure payment, lease part of it to tenants who pay rent, incorporate part of it and sell shares to investors, and secure a loan against part of it in order to start an Internet business. In each of these transactions regarding the single piece of land, the owner retains identifiable and protected property interests. Each transaction is made practically possible because the law of property enables resources to be subdivided as an owner may find advantageous.

This feature of property facilitates the development of resources, which creates new wealth and causes prosperity. The next section further elaborates the divisibility of property.

3. TWO BASIC DIVISIONS OF PROPERTY

The preceding section asserted that the easy divisibility of property contributes to prosperity, and it gave several examples of how property can be divided. This section introduces the two basic legal divisions of property: real property and personal property. **Real property** law applies ownership to land and interests in land such as mining rights or leases. All other types of resources are protected under the law of **personal property.**

Real property law applies to land and interests in land. All other resources are protected by **personal property** law.

Because of the historical importance of land, real property rules are very formal. As Chapter 8 on contracts discusses, agreements transferring interests in land ownership should be written, and many special rules apply to the registration and taxation of land ownership. Land ownership is also known as *real estate* or *realty.*

A particular kind of interest in land is the fixture. A **fixture** is an object of personal property that has become an object of real property (1) by physical annexation (attachment) to the land or its buildings, or (2) whose use has become closely associated with the use to which the land is put. Unless sellers and buyers agree differently when they sell land, the fixtures go with the land to the buyers. Manufacturing equipment is a fixture when it is sold along with a manufacturing plant. Carpeting is a fixture if it is nailed down or glued to the floor. Not being attached to the land, rugs are usually not fixtures. To prevent misunderstandings in land sales, sellers and buyers should identify which things are fixtures and stay with the buyers and which things remain protected under personal property and go with the sellers.

Personal property applies to movable resources, those things that people do not annex to the land. The law divides personal property into rules applying to tangible and intangible resources. *Tangible property* applies to things one can touch, that is, to physical things. Computers, cars, and carrots are such touchable things. The sale of tangible things, also known as "goods," is controlled by the Uniform Commercial Code, a type of contract law explained in the next chapter. Chapter 17 discusses the sale of corporate stock, which is an intangible thing. Real property rules and personal property rules are often different as are rules applying personal property to tangible or intangible things.

>> Acquiring Resources in a Property System

How do you come to own resources in a property system? In other words, how does the right of property to something attach to a specific person? Although you can acquire resources in many ways, including by force (called "robbery"), theft (various forms of stealing), and fraud (intentionally lying and harming others to get what belongs to them), there are only five basic legal ways to become an owner of something in a property system. As you read what follows, consider that **ownership** means the same thing as "property." Both terms refer to the legal right that makes resources exclusive, that makes resources "mine," instead of "yours," or "no one's."

4. ACQUIRING RESOURCES THROUGH EXCHANGE

The most common way of coming to have a property in something is through exchanging resources. For example, when you buy a car, or buy a company, you exchange one form of resources you own (money) for another form of resources (car or company). You are now the legal owner of the car or company. Resources have been switched but property (or ownership) remains. Likewise, when you exchange your services for a paycheck, you become the owner of the paycheck and the money it represents. The employer becomes the owner of your services and what they produce.

Contract rules control the way owners make agreements to exchange resources in the property-based legal system.

The rules under which people exchange resources in a property system are called the rules of **contract.** Contract rules are the subject of Chapters 8 and 9, but you should understand now that contract rules make agreements to exchange resources between owners legally binding and enforceable. In particular, the rules of contract make it possible for owners to commit legally to future exchange of resources. These rules also make it possible for one owner to sue another if agreements to exchange resources in the future are broken by one of the owners. Further, contract rules allow lawsuits against those who have not adequately performed their agreements. If owner A agrees to sell goods to owner B in 30 days and then does not deliver them, owner B may sue owner A for damages. Likewise, owner B may sue owner A if owner A does deliver the goods, but they turn out to be defective. In addition to damages, contract rules may specify other remedies for contract breach.

It is difficult to overemphasize the importance of contract rules in the property system. Professor Philip Nichols of the Wharton School asserts that observing legally enforceable contracts is the single most significant indicator that a country's economy is ready for international trade. If the right of property is the foundation for the modern private market, the rules of contract are perhaps the keystone of that foundation.

5. ACQUIRING RESOURCES THROUGH POSSESSION

Sometimes you can become an owner of something merely through possession, that is, by physically holding and controlling it. The **rule of first possession** is that the first person to reduce previously unowned things to possession becomes their owner. In Sylacauga, Alabama, a meteorite crashed through the roof of a rented house in 1954 and struck the tenant on the leg, the only recorded instance in history when a meteorite has struck a person. Initially, both the owner of the house and the tenant (owner of the lease) claimed the meteorite, but because the tenant was the first person to reduce it to possession, she acquired the right of property to it.

Similar to the rule of first possession, is the rule that when someone has *abandoned* what they own, the first person to reduce it to possession owns it. The law determines whether or not someone has abandoned what they previously owned by measuring *intent,* whether the previous owner intended to abandon something. The law measures intent by the circumstances of the situation. If it looks like someone meant to abandon something, we say they intended to do it. When it is not clear who is the first person to reduce previously unowned or abandoned resources to possession, lawsuits may follow. See Sidebar 7.4.

> The rule of first possession is that the first person to reduce previously unowned things to possession becomes their owner.

>> *sidebar* 7.4

Barry Bonds Home-Run Ball

When Barry Bonds blasted his record-setting 73rd home run ball into the stands of PacBell Park on October 7, 2001, ownership of the ball was abandoned. Unlike in football, where a ball that goes into the stands must be returned, Major League baseball— the association of team owners—deliberately abandons the balls and allows fans to keep them. But who had the right of property in the record-setting ball, Alex Popov who initially appeared to catch it before a wild crowd of fans knocked him to the ground, or Patrick Hayashi who shortly afterward saw the ball rolling free, grabbed it, and stuck it in his pocket?

Popov sued Hayashi, arguing that he was the owner because he had caught and first possessed the ball, which had an estimated value of $1 million. After trial, Judge Kevin McCarthy recognized that the principle of first possession applied to the ball, but did Popov or Hayashi first possess it? The facts were not clear as to whether Popov caught or dropped the ball. The judge stated, "An award of the ball to Mr. Popov would be unfair to Mr. Hayashi. It would be premised on the assumption that Mr. Popov would have caught the ball. That assumption is not supported by the facts. An award of the ball to Mr. Hayashi would unfairly penalize Mr. Popov. It would be based on the assumption that Mr. Popov would have dropped the ball. That conclusion is also unsupported by the facts."

With the facts unclear, Judge McCarthy ruled that it was fairest to divide the ownership of the ball. "The court therefore declares that both plaintiff and defendant have an equal and undivided interest in the ball. . . . In order to effectuate this ruling, the ball must be sold and the proceeds divided equally between the parties." Rather than appeal, Popov and Hayashi agreed they would sell the ball and divide the proceeds.

202   **PART 3**   Legal Foundations for Business

Lost Items   Things that are *lost* also can acquire a new owner through possession. The finder of a lost item becomes its owner by reducing it to possession and following a statutory procedure, which may require the finder to turn the item over to the police and to advertise it in a local paper for a period of time to allow the original owner to claim it. But at the end of the specified statutory period the finder becomes the new owner.

Can you distinguish between things that are lost and things that are merely mislaid?

The law distinguishes things that have been lost from things that have simply been mislaid. Things that have been lost go to the first person who subsequently reduces them to possession, but things that have been *mislaid* go to the person who owns the premises where the item was mislaid. A $100 bill on the table in the library has been mislaid, but if it is on the floor it has been lost. The difference in the way the law treats these two situations is based on an assumption that the original owner will know where to come back and reclaim mislaid things. Consider the following instance: A man who had a box in a bank vault was examining the contents of his box at a table in the vault room when he found $25,000 in a pile under the table. A lawsuit arose over whether the money was lost or mislaid and whether it went to the bank or to the finder. The court held that since the money was under the table the money had been lost and belonged to the finder. Question: Why didn't the person who "lost" the money come forward and claim it? Was it because the money had been acquired illegally, or because tax had not been paid on it?

Adverse Possession   Another form of ownership through possession arises through **adverse possession.** Adverse possession gives you ownership of land (and it only applies to land) under state statute when the possession is:

- Open and notorious. The possessor must occupy the land in such a way as to put the true owner of the land on notice.
- Actual and exclusive. The possessor must physically occupy the land. However, the building of a fence around the land or construction of a building on it constitutes physical occupation.
- Continuous. Possession must not be interrupted.
- Wrongful. The possessor must not have the owner's permission to be on the land, for example, under a lease.
- For a prescribed period of time. Most states specify an adverse possession of between 10 and 20 years before the possessor becomes the new owner.

You should appreciate that there may be more than one solution to a property problem.

In one instance, the author was teaching about adverse possession when a student suddenly jumped up and ran out of class. Later the student reported that he had called his parents because about the time the student had been born, their neighbor had built a fence for half a mile about five or ten feet onto land belonging to the student's parents. To maintain good relations, the parents had simply said nothing to their neighbor about the wrongful location of the fence. The student had wanted to notify his parents about the rule of adverse possession. The author asked the class what the student's parents might do in this situation, assuming wrongful possession. Some students said to confront the neighbor and tear down the fence if the 20-year time required by the statute had not expired. But what about the good relations with the neighbor? Eventually, the students concluded that the parents could either sell the strip of land to the neighbor, or give the neighbor permission to have the fence on the land, meaning that the occupation of the land would no longer be "wrongful." Even if the 20-year period for adverse possession had expired, the neighbor might have been willing to deed back the land to the student's parents.

The Homestead Act of 1862 illustrates ownership through possession. This act allowed those who lived on certain public land to obtain legal ownership of it by possessing it for five years and making certain improvements. Upward of a half million settlers possessed and then gained title to the 160-acre homesteads under the act.

In parts of the world today, governments are granting ownership of land to "squatters" who possess it without legal right. Studies show that this is one of the best ways to distribute land in poor nations. Squatters become owners and can then capitalize land by selling it or borrowing money and putting up the land as collateral.

Some have criticized the "squatter-to-owner" process because many of the new owners sell their land. However, the process enables poor squatters to raise money for the first time. It is also less violent than a situation where squatting alone occurs, and squatters may have to defend their possession by force. Further, it is more efficient than for the government to specify that the land cannot change ownership. In U.S. history there were numerous instances in which legal title was given to settlers who at first possessed land by squatting. Many of them, too, sold their land after receiving legal title to it.

> Peruvian economist Hernando de Soto believes that nations can strengthen their economies through the "squatter-to-owner" process.

6. ACQUIRING RESOURCES THROUGH CONFUSION

Ownership through **confusion** arises when *fungible* goods (i.e., goods that are identical) are mixed together. The common example involves grain in a silo when two or more batches of separately owned grain are mixed together. If the confusion occurs by honest mistake or agreement, the owners of the originally separate goods now own a proportional share of the confused goods. Careful records of who owned what grain must be kept since lacking evidence, a court in the case of dispute will assume that everyone claiming the confused mass owns an equal share. If a court determines that the confusion was intentionally wrongful, perhaps done by someone willfully attempting to defraud another, the court will grant ownership of the entire confused mass to the innocent party.

The doctrine of confusion also illustrates the importance of *boundaries* to the concept of property, and it explains one determination of ownership when resource boundaries are not certain. Problems of where boundaries lie are common, however, to various types of resources. Boundaries to the ownership of the water in a creek that crosses your land may be measured by a certain volume of water per minute. Landowners upstream may legally not be able to divert that flow.

> Be aware that disputes arise concerning not only boundary problems involving physical location but they concern also boundaries of permissible uses of things.

7. ACQUIRING RESOURCES THROUGH ACCESSION

When the owner of an old airplane engine has it restored and has an airplane built around it, the owner of the engine now owns the entire airplane through the doctrine of **accession,** which refers to something "added." Normally, this is not a problem, but suppose a thief steals the engine, repairs it, and builds it into an airplane. A court will likely grant ownership of the entire airplane to the engine's owner.

However, if the builder *accidentally* picked up someone else's engine and builds it into an airplane, a court will probably give ownership of the airplane to the builder, requiring only that the builder adequately compensate the engine's original owner. An exception gives ownership of the entire airplane to the engine's owner if the engine is substantially more valuable than the additions to it. The court may even require the engine's owner to pay for the valuable additions.

The law of accession also explains that when you apply your efforts or ingenuity to any raw materials you own and change their nature into finished products, you own the finished products. Generally, because you own your efforts, you own what they produce, whether it is an airplane, a paycheck (through exchange), or a work of art. Much of the property foundation of the modern private market arises from the right to exclude others legally from what you own and what you add to that.

The philosopher John Locke, whose ideas were very important to the framers of the U.S. Constitution, said that the principle of property was justified when someone contributed labor to a previously unowned natural resource. In other words, if people own themselves and their work efforts and transform something previously unowned into something new by their work, they also own the new thing. This view and the rule of accession have strong similarities.

> Can you explain how Locke used the concept of **accession** to justify how people come to own previously unowned things?

8. ACQUIRING RESOURCES THROUGH GIFT

Receiving a **gift** is also a way of acquiring ownership. In the making of a gift, no mutual exchange of resources occurs. Instead, a *donor* who owns something gives it to a *donee*, who becomes the new owner. The rules of gift specify that the gift does not generally take place until the donor (1) *intends* to make the gift, and (2) *delivers* the gift by physical transfer to the donee. Note that in some instances, a *constructive delivery*, like turning over the keys to a car or the deed to land, constitutes an adequate delivery.

A particular kind of gift is a *testamentary gift*, or one that is made through a will. The rules of such a gift pass ownership not by delivery but upon the death of the donor (called a "testator") and the proving of a valid will that specifies the gift. Some people believe that the purpose of a property system is to stimulate efforts to generate further wealth which benefits society. They argue that permitting people to pass property to vast fortunes through testamentary gifts does not give incentive to those who receive such gifts. What do you think? How would the behavior of owners change during their lifetimes if they could not make testamentary gifts?

> In your opinion, what justifies people being able to pass large wealth on to their children through testamentary gifts?

9. TYPES OF OWNERSHIP

The law allows division of resource ownership into various types, or degrees. This division is another indication of how sensitive property law is in allowing owners to do exactly what they need and want with their resources: Not all states still use the common law terms that follow, but all states recognize the various aspects of ownership that the terms represent. *These terms usually apply to land ownership, but ownership of movable and intangible things can be held practically in the same way.*

1. Fee simple. The bundle of rights and powers of land ownership are called an **estate. Fee simple** represents the maximum estate allowed under law, the owner having the fullest legal rights and powers to possess, use, and transfer the land. The fee simple *absolute* estate has no limitations or conditions attached. The fee simple *defeasible* may have a condition attached to its conveyance (transfer). For example, a seller may convey land to a buyer "as long as it is used for agricultural purposes." If the new owner (buyer) develops the land for other than agricultural purposes, the ownership goes back to the original owner (seller).

2. Life estate. A **life estate** grants an ownership in land for the lifetime of a specified person. "To Brodie Davis for her life" grants such an estate. Upon Brodie Davis's death the land reverts to the original grantor who is said to keep a *reversion* interest in the land. If the land goes to someone other than the grantor upon Brodie Davis's death, that person has a *remainder* interest. Reversion and remainder property interests are also called *future* interests as opposed to the life estate, which is a *present* interest. Subject to any attached conditions, all of these estates can be capitalized or transferred. For example, it is possible to borrow upon or sell a future interest.

   > Having a **life estate** means that the property fence only protects your interest in something for your lifetime.

3. Leasehold estate. A **leasehold estate** is simply the property right granted to tenants by a landlord. Although it is not common to think of tenants as "owners," they do in a meaningful way have an estate or property. Tenants have a qualified possession, use, and transfer of the land, qualified in that they cannot *waste* the land, which means do something that substantially reduces the value of the land. For an apartment tenant to rip up carpeting and knock holes in the walls would be a waste of the interest in the land. The landlord could terminate the lease and sue the tenant.

   > When you lease an apartment for a year, what is it that you own?

   Unless prohibited by the lease, the rights owned by tenants can be capitalized by transfer to someone else. Thus, unless prohibited, a tenant who is paying $3,000 per month under a two-year lease of an office can sell the balance of time remaining on the lease at $5,000 per month. Many leases, however, do require that a tenant obtain approval from a landlord, or even of the other tenants, before transferring lease rights.

   A landlord may lease land for a *definite duration* of time like two years, or for an *indefinite duration* with rent payable at periodic intervals like monthly, or simply *at will*, which means "for as long as both shall agree." State law generally specifies that the landlord and tenant must give each other written notice of 30 days or 60 days in order to terminate a lease that does not run for a definite duration.

4. Concurrent ownership. Both personal and real property interests can have concurrent owners. That is, more than one person can own the same thing. The ownership is undivided, meaning that no concurrent owner owns a specific piece of the resources that are owned. The shareholders of a corporation are concurrent owners as are the partners of a partnership. In fact, concurrent ownership greatly facilitates almost all forms of modern private enterprise.

   Other forms of concurrent ownership include the **joint tenancy** and the **tenancy in common.** In both of these forms of ownership, the property interest is undivided, but the tenants in common can own different shares of the resource (e.g., two-thirds and one-third), whereas the joint

   > The surviving tenant in a joint tenancy with right of survivorship becomes the sole owner of the entire resource, usually interests in land.

tenants must have equal ownership shares (e.g., one-half and one-half). On the other hand, joint tenants, but not tenants in common, can have the *right of survivorship.* This right means that if one of the joint tenants dies, the remaining tenant becomes the sole owner of the entire resource. To create a joint tenancy requires special words, such as "convey to X and Y as joint tenants, and not as tenants in common, together with the right of survivorship."

The owners themselves, or the creditors, of a joint tenancy or tenancy in common can usually force the separation of these concurrent owner-ships under the doctrine of *partition.*

10. TITLE AND PROPERTY REGISTRATION

Land, automobiles, and in many states, boats, require a registration of ownership called title.

Ownership is frequently referred to by the term **title.** Thus, someone who owns something has title to it. When an owner transfers ownership, the owner is said to "pass title." For specific types of resources the law requires that the title be represented by a physical document registered with the state. The title to an automobile is one example of such an ownership document that must be registered with the state. Many states also require the registration of boat titles.

A **deed** is the document of title that transfers ownership of land. The deed contains a precise legal description of the land that specifies the exact loca-tion and boundaries according to a mapping or surveying system. Without this description, few buyers or lenders would be willing to risk their money on the land. That exact, accepted boundaries identify land ownership pro-vides the basis for much capital formation.

What does it mean to say that a quitclaim deed does not convey ownership?

Even knowing the precise location of the land does not always ensure that there are no problems with the ownership. A lender may have a mortgage claim against the land, or the grantor of a deed may have conveyed the land to more than one person. There are two protections against these problems. First, the kind of deed the buyer receives from the seller can protect the buyer. A *warranty deed* promises the grantee (usually, the buyer) that the grantor (seller) has good ownership and the full power to convey it. The buyer can sue the seller if someone else claims the land. A *special warranty deed* speci-fies that certain legal claims against the land, like mortgages, exist but guar-antees that no other claims exist. A *quitclaim deed* makes no guarantees other than that the grantor surrenders all claim against the land. Several other types of deeds may apply in certain states.

Second, buyers and lenders are protected by registration statutes. The law enables buyers to register their deeds to land and lenders to register their mortgage claims against land. Potential buyers or other lenders are thus put on notice regarding the land, and the legal owner or claimant is legally and publicly identified. By going to the county courthouse or other place of record, you can often trace the ownership history of a piece of land for 200 years or more.

>> Specialty Applications of Property

The following sections discuss specialty applications of property. Generally, the private legal fence of property allows an owner to exclude others from interfering with (1) the possession of an object or resource, (2) the transfer of the object or interest by gift or through exchange with other owners, and (3) all uses of the object that do not harm other owners in what belongs to them. However, a number of specialty applications are quite narrow and one or more of the three general property characteristics may be lacking. In fact, many scholars do not recognize some of the specialty applications discussed here to apply to property at all. However, we note that all of these specialty applications involve some object or interest that is legally exclusive in some important fashion, leading us to believe these applications deserve the name "property."

11. EASEMENTS

An **easement** places a particular use of land behind the exclusive legal fence. Usually, this use involves the right of passage across the land, for example, when a timbering company has purchased the right to bring its harvest of trees out across an owner's land. Once the easement has been acquired, the timbering company can exclude others, especially the titleholder of the land, from interfering with passage of its trucks across the land. An easement can also be reserved in a deed, for example, when Martina sells a piece of her land to George and the deed reserves an easement for George to cross over Martina's remaining land. Easements can also involve such uses as the laying of water pipes or the stringing of power wires across land.

An **easement** is often a right to cross over land.

An easement can be acquired in various ways. For instance, it can be bought directly from a titleholder, or reserved in a deed as part of the purchase and sale of land. At common law owners of land also had a *natural easement* (also called easement by necessity) to get from their land to the nearest public road. A *negative easement* means that an adjoining landowner cannot do anything that would cause your land to cave in or collapse, such as digging a ditch that would cause the land on your side to collapse. Finally, an *easement by prescription* arises when one person has used another's land, such as by crossing it openly, wrongfully, and continuously for a period of years (frequently 20), and once an easement by prescription arises, a titleholder of the land can no longer prevent a person from continuing to use the land by crossing it. The titleholder cannot now use the land in such a way to prevent the easement holder from crossing it, and the easement holder can legally exclude a titleholder from trying to prevent passage.

Statutes in many states set standards for easements and their acquisition. The easements mentioned here merely give you a general idea about these specialty applications of property.

12. BAILMENTS

In many common situations, an owner puts an object protected by personal property into the intentional possession of another person with the understanding that the other person must return the object at some point or otherwise dispose of it. This property arrangement is known as a **bailment,** with the owner known as the **bailor** and the possessor of the object known as the **bailee.** Bailments arise when you store something in a warehouse, rent furniture from the rental store, lease a piece of equipment, loan your lawnmower to a neighbor, or store your car in a friend's garage while you are on vacation.

Can you figure out in each instance who is the bailor and who is the bailee? Bailments fall into three categories:

- For the sole benefit of the bailor.
- For the sole benefit of the bailee.
- For the mutual benefit of both parties.

Can you explain the three different types of bailments?

Think about the examples mentioned above. Do you understand that storing your car in a friend's garage while you are on vacation is a bailment for the sole benefit of the bailor and that the furniture and equipment rentals are mutual benefit bailments? The loan of your mower to your neighbor to mow the grass is a bailment for the sole benefit of the bailee. Consider the following situation: you go to a business meeting at a hotel, removing your expensive leather coat, and hanging it on a hanger in a small room provided by the hotel. The coat turns up missing. Is the hotel responsible as a bailee? Would the situation have been different if the hotel had someone taking care of coats? The answers depend on whether or not the hotel has taken *intentional* possession of the coat, and it is likely that merely by providing a coat hanger, the hotel is not taking intentional possession of the coat. But if a hotel employee hangs up the coat for you, the hotel becomes a bailee.

In the business world, most bailments are of mutual benefit to both parties. Although the bailee has an absolute duty to return the object to the bailor (or to dispose out of it as the bailor directs), and becomes liable to the bailor for failing to do so correctly, an issue often arises when something happens to the object while it is in the bailee's possession and control. What if someone steals it? What if a natural disaster, called "an act of God," destroys it, or it is damaged in an accident? To understand the potential liability from these events, you have to understand the legal duty the bailee is under. In a mutual benefit bailment, such as a rental arrangement, the bailee is under a duty to use "reasonable care" in taking care of the object in possession, but if an Act of God destroys or damages the object, the bailee is not likely liable to the bailor. However, see Sidebar 7.5.

>> *sidebar* 7.5

Follow Instructions or Else

Roger, a graduate student, leases a car from Acme Car Dealership in Texas. The lease contract contains a clause that limits Roger's driving to the United States. However, Roger drives the car over the border down to Mexico City where an earthquake causes a building to collapse on the car after Roger parks it on the street. Although in mutual benefit bailments such as this one, the bailee is not often responsible to the bailor for acts of God, in this instance by using a car in a way specifically prohibited by the bailor, Roger becomes liable to the car dealership in spite of the fact his fault did not cause the damage to the car. When a bailee uses an object in a way not authorized or prohibited by the bailor, the bailee becomes absolutely liable as an "insurer" for anything that happens to it.

Another example of this liability arises when a bailee returns an object improperly. In one instance a wealthy woman bought expensive jewelry on approval from Tiffany's, promising the manager to return the jewelry to him personally if she did not wish to keep it. Several days later there was a knock on her door and a man dressed in a Tiffany's uniform asked if she wished to return the jewelry, which she did, and she returned the jewelry to the man, who turned out to be a thief in a stolen uniform. Tiffany's sued for the jewelry's price and won because the bailee became absolutely liable for loss when she returned the jewelry improperly.

In a bailment for the sole benefit of a bailor, the bailee owes only a slight duty of care while the object is in the bailee's possession, but in a bailment for the sole benefit of the bailee, such as where the bailee has borrowed the object, the bailee owes a very high duty of care, one that is greater than merely what is "reasonable." These duties of care become important when the parties are negotiating a settlement, or when a judge is instructing a jury about the bailee's responsibility to the bailor. Many times it may be difficult for a bailor who sues a bailee to prove why the object in the bailee's possession has been damaged and how the bailee has breached the duty of care. Therefore, the law presumes that the bailee has breached the duty of care when the bailee cannot return the object to the bailor in proper condition, placing the burden of proof on the bailee to prove that she has met the duty of care.

The following case illustrates the bailee's liability for failing to return some pieces of sculpture in the proper condition.

> When your roommate borrows your car and returns it with a dent in it, the law makes your roommate liable unless she can prove she has met the duty of extremely high care.

 case **7.1** >>

SEMOON v. THE WOOSTER SCHOOL CORP.
2010 Conn. Super. LEXIS 1816

OZALIS, JUDGE: . . . The plaintiff, Suk Semoon, commenced this action against the defendants, the Wooster School Corporation (the Wooster School) and the Wooster Community Art Center (WCAC). This case arises out of the alleged loan by the plaintiff of seven pieces of sculpture to the defendant WCAC which allegedly was controlled and operated by the defendant Wooster School.

The plaintiff has alleged . . . that the defendants Wooster School and WCAC in September 2001 willingly took possession of seven of the plaintiff's outdoor sculptures and displayed them in plain view on its campus. The plaintiff further alleges that when she asked for the return of the seven sculptures, she was advised that three were missing and one had been damaged. The plaintiff alleges that the defendants Wooster School and WCAC failed to redeliver all of the seven sculptures to her at her request . . . and are therefore liable for the full value of the missing/damaged sculptures. . . .

In order to prove a bailment, the plaintiff must prove that she delivered the seven sculptures to the defendants. In this action, there is no dispute as to this issue and in fact the parties stipulated that the seven sculptures were delivered to the defendant WCAC. It is also undisputed in this action that . . . the director

of the defendant WCAC accepted the delivery of the sculptures and intended to and did use them as an outdoor sculpture garden to enhance the landscape of the defendants' facilities. It is clear, based on the evidence at trial, that the director had authority to accept the sculptures on behalf of the defendants. It is also undisputed that the plaintiff in 2006 asked for the return of all seven sculptures, but only three were fully returned. The court finds that a mutual benefit bailment did in fact exist between the parties as the loan of the sculptures benefited the defendants and the plaintiff as well, as she had a place to exhibit her artwork and contribute to the community.

"Once a bailment has been established and the bailee is unable to redeliver the subject of the bailment in an undamaged condition a presumption arises that the damage to or loss of the bailed property was the result of the bailee's negligence [failure to use reasonable care]." . . . "This presumption prevails unless and until the bailee proves the actual circumstances involved in the damaging of the property. If these circumstances are proved, then the burden is upon the bailor [the plaintiff here who put her artwork in the hands of the defendants] to satisfy the court that the bailee's conduct in the matter constituted negligence. . . . The circumstances which a bailee must prove must be something

[continued]

more than those indicating the immediate cause of damage. The proof must go so far as to establish what, if any, human conduct materially contributed to that immediate cause. . . . The bailee must prove something more if he is to overcome the presumption. The bailee must prove the actual circumstances connected with the origin of the damage, and these include the precautions taken to prevent the loss.". "Whether the bailee has proved the actual circumstances of the loss and overcome the presumption of negligence in that the bailee has taken reasonable precautions under the circumstances is a question of fact for the trier [the judge]."

This court agrees with the plaintiff that the defendants . . . have put forth no evidence as to the actual circumstances surrounding the loss of sculptures one, two and three. Accordingly, the court finds that the

presumption arises that the loss of sculptures one, two and three was due to the defendants' negligence. With respect to the destruction of sculpture seven, the defendants Wooster School and WCAC have put forth no evidence that it took any efforts, let alone reasonable efforts, to secure or protect this sculpture from being destroyed or damaged during construction. The court finds that the defendants' actions were woefully inadequate in protecting this sculpture from the construction that was occurring and that the loss that occurred was due to the defendants' negligence.

For the reasons set forth above, the court finds that the plaintiff has met her burden of proof as to the breach of bailment contract and judgment shall enter in favor of the plaintiff in the amount of $26,100.

>> CASE QUESTIONS

1. Why does the court decide that this is a mutual benefit bailment?
2. What does the court mean when it says there is a "presumption" regarding the bailee's possession of the sculptures? How does this presumption affect the burden of proof in bailment cases?
3. In the broad general definition of property used in this chapter, does the bailee in this case have property in the sculptures? Explain.

The bailor also has duties to the bailee. In a mutual benefit bailment, the bailor must pay the bailee for storing or otherwise keeping possession of something, such as when the bailee is a warehouse. According to the type of bailment, the bailor also warrants or guarantees that she has no knowledge of defects in the objects bailed or no knowledge of defects that could have been discovered through reasonable inspection. In a number of states, courts have made merchants in mutual benefit bailments liable for any defect in a bailed object that causes personal injury.

You should read the terms of a bailment contract very carefully.

Many states have laws that apply to particular kinds of bailments, such as those involving common carriers, warehouses, and innkeepers (hotels). In particular, these bailees are often able to limit their potential liability to bailors for damage to the bailed objects, for example, by inserting contractual terms that limit compensation to a certain value. Common carriers, which include airlines, railroads, and public trucking companies, carry packages for the public. Common carriers are also not responsible for acts of God or of public enemies, the acts of the bailor in failing to package properly, defects in the packaged object itself, or acts of the public authority (such as the stopping of a truck carrying produce at a state border because of concern about plant disease).

In legal terms, a bailee is usually not considered to have "property" regarding the bailed object. However, the bailee has both possession and control over the object and can exclude the rest of the world, including the bailee in some instances, from interfering with this possession and control. For this reason, we are treating bailments as a specialty application of property, although they are often a very narrow one.

>> Property and Security Interests

In a property-based legal system resources can be highly divisible. Importantly, they are divisible both in specific type and by time. Sellers can transfer resources to buyers now and depend upon getting paid for these resources later. That is a subject of contract law, which begins in the next chapter. The following sections, however, deal with how sellers can increase their confidence in the risky business of transferring goods, rendering services, and making loans by securing particular types of property interests in something usually possessed by the buyer. These property interests are usually conditional and end when a buyer-debtor fulfills some condition, frequently repayment of what is owed. The two principal types of **security interests** are mortgages and secured transactions under Article 9 of the Uniform Commercial Code.

Many scholars do not appreciate that these security interests are in fact property applications because these interests are not physical objects. But they involve a legal fence that protects the holder of the security interest from the general claims of all other persons, and if the buyer-debtor (from here on, just *debtor*), fails to comply with the condition, the seller-creditor (from here on, just *creditor* or *secured party*) can usually seize (and/or sell) the object of the security interest to help satisfy the obligation of repayment. Identifying security interests as applications of property helps explain why we say that property, the concept of the private fence, is the central concept of capitalism and private markets.

> How is a security interest a property arrangement?

13. SECURITY INTERESTS IN LAND

Security interests in land and the structures on the land include mortgages, deeds of trust, and land sales contracts. As observed at the beginning of this chapter, the major way that small business owners raise money to begin their businesses is through mortgaging their homes. They borrow money from a bank or financial institution and in return give that creditor a security interest called a *mortgage* on their homes and the land associated with their homes. In recent years it has also become quite common for homeowners in their capacity as consumers to take out a mortgage on their homes in order to access the value of their homes for purchases they wish to make.

Similar to mortgages are **deeds of trust.** Under the deed of trust, a borrower signs a *note,* which shows the borrower's debt to the lender, and then signs a deed of trust, which grants the lender a security interest in the building and land put up to secure the loan. The deed is held by a third party called a *trustee* who holds full legal ownership to the land. Under this arrangement the debtor will obtain legal ownership, or *title,* only when the deed has been repaid.

> The major way that small business owners raise money to begin their businesses is through mortgaging their homes.

Unimproved land and farmland are often sold through land sales contracts. Under a **land sales contract,** the owner of land sells it by contract subject to the condition that the seller retains title to the land until the buyer pays the purchase price. Until that time, the buyer has the legal right to possess and use the land and is responsible for paying taxes and insurance.

Recording Statutes   Generally, mortgages and deeds of trust must be registered in a recording office in the county where the land is located. Recording gives notice of the security interest to potential buyers of the land and to potential lenders who will then consider that fact in determining whether or not to buy the land or to loan money. That potential buyers or lenders become aware of the mortgage is important since the land is subject to satisfy the mortgagee's debt whether or not the land is sold or a subsequent mortgage is taken out on the land.

If **mortgagees** (the creditors) fail to record mortgages, new buyers of the lands who are unaware of mortgages will take the lands free and clear of the mortgages, although the debts will still be owed by the **mortgagors** (debtors). Likewise, a creditor who registers a subsequent mortgage on land, being unfamiliar with the unrecorded first mortgage, will have priority over the first mortgage.

> If mortgagees failed to record mortgages, new buyers of the lands who are unaware of mortgages will take the lands free and clear of the mortgages.

Foreclosure, Deficiency, and Redemption   Almost all states regulate how mortgagees can exercise their property interest when the obligation owed to them is not satisfied. **Foreclosure** is the term used for the exercise of the secured property interest, and foreclosure usually means that the creditor must go through the court system to ensure that procedures are properly followed before debtors lose their homes and land. Foreclosure as it relates to land sales contracts is generally simpler and less expensive to exercise than foreclosure of mortgages and deeds of trust. Foreclosure means that the court will order the land sold to satisfy the debt owed, usually by auction to the highest bidder, with any excess after payment of what is owed to the secured creditor going to the debtor.

You should appreciate that the property represented by these types of security interests is separate from the loan obligation owed by the debtor-mortgagor. In many states, if foreclosure and auction does not produce enough money to satisfy the debt owed by the mortgagor, the creditor-mortgagee can still sue the debtor for the balance owed, called a **deficiency.** Some states, however, have passed statutes, called *antideficiency judgment statutes,* that prevent mortgagees from obtaining anything else from mortgagors once the land has been foreclosed and auctioned. These statutes generally only apply to protect homeowners.

Before the actual foreclosure, most states permit a **right of redemption,** which allows the mortgagor to get back the land upon payment of the full amount of the debt, including all interest and costs. Even after foreclosure some states have a statutory period of redemption, usually six months or one year after foreclosure, in which the mortgagor can redeem the land from a new buyer. If a first mortgagor fails to redeem, most states permit second mortgage holders to redeem the land.

> The **right of redemption** allows a mortgagor, before foreclosure, to get back land upon payment of the full amount of the debt. Statutory redemption allows a mortgagor to regain ownership of the land upon payment of all interest and costs for a period of time after foreclosure.

In 2008, following a collapse of the mortgage due to poor lending practices, the right of redemption did not prevent many homeowners from losing their homes. See Sidebar 7.6.

>> *sidebar* 7.6

Financial Collapse and Recession

In 2008, a financial collapse and recession occurred, caused in major part by lenders offering "subprime mortgages" to borrowers. These subprime mortgages had little to do with the mortgage rules discussed here, but related to the eagerness of borrowers to obtain homes that they could not afford to buy, and the willingness of lenders to take risks by loaning to these borrowers, by obtaining mortgages based on poor credit worthiness, and then by turning around and reselling the mortgages loans as investments in complex financial packages called "derivatives." Repayment of these subprime mortgage loans, however, depended on housing prices continuing to increase rapidly so the loans could be renegotiated and become affordable. When prices stopped going up and loans could not be renegotiated and repaid, millions of homeowners were unable to meet their loan payments, the housing market collapsed, the derivatives market was devastated, many financial institutions went into bankruptcy, credit became difficult to obtain, businesses had to lay off millions of workers, and a very serious recession followed.

Why did financial institutions make so many poor-quality mortgage loans? Consider Nobel economist Paul Krugman's opinion: "In a nutshell, bank executives are lavishly rewarded if they deliver big short-term profits but aren't correspondingly punished if they later suffer even bigger losses. This encourages excessive risk taking. Some of the people most responsible for the current crisis walked away immensely rich from the bonuses they earned in the good years, even though the high-risk strategies that led to those bonuses eventually destroyed their companies, taking down a large part of the financial system in the process."

14. SECURED TRANSACTIONS

Article 9 of the Uniform Commercial Code is the principal set of laws controlling security interests in objects of personal property. Article 9 contains the law of **secured transactions.** This law is highly complicated and technical, and what follows merely introduces you to some of the concepts found in Article 9. A secured transaction involves a creditor who has sold something on credit or made a loan to a debtor who agrees to give the creditor a security interest in a valuable object, called **collateral.**

Secured transaction law applies to a variety of things, including consumer goods (which are not bought for business purposes), farm products, inventory, equipment, stocks, bonds, negotiable instruments (orders or promises to pay in a certain form, such as checks), valuable documents such as those transferring goods, accounts receivable (money owed, but not in a certain form like negotiable instruments), and "general intangibles" like interests in patents, trademarks, and copyrights. A security interest in any of these things arises when it attaches. **Attachment** takes place when (1) a secured party has given value, (2) the debtor owns the collateral, and (3) a security agreement is given. This agreement must be in writing, signed by the debtor, and contain a reasonable description of the collateral. The collateral may include not only things currently owned by the debtor but collateral known as *after-acquired property* that the debtor acquires in the future. Proceeds realized from the sale of the collateral can also be covered by the security interest.

Article 9 of the Uniform Commercial Code covers the law of secured transactions.

Explain to yourself how **attachment** takes place.

Perfection As soon as the security interest attaches it is effective against the debtor, but to be effective against third parties, such as other creditors and people to whom the collateral may be sold or transferred, the secured party must *perfect* the security interest. **Perfection** arises when a security interest has attached and the creditor has taken all proper steps required by Article 9. A creditor perfects a security interest differently according to the type of collateral.

The general way of perfecting a security interest under Article 9 is to file a **financing statement.** The form of the financing statement differs from state to state, but the statement should contain the names and addresses of the creditor and debtor, a reasonable description of the collateral, and the signature of the debtor. Financing statements expire five years after the date of filing unless a maturity date is stated and are usually filed in the county where the collateral is located or with an office of the state government, depending on the state and the type of collateral. Financing statements are appropriate to perfect any type of collateral except negotiable ones, which can always be transferred free of a secured creditor's claim unless they are kept in the creditor's possession.

Some types of security interests are perfected by attachment alone, for example, a **purchase money security interest (PMSI)** in consumer goods, meaning a security interest that secures the purchase price of goods bought for personal or household use. Such security interests perfect as soon as they properly attach. Similarly, there is a temporary 21-day perfection in negotiable instruments or documents as soon as they attach, which allows the creditor time to take possession of these valuables. An automatic 10-day perfection in proceeds realized from the sale of collateral also exists even if the perfected security interest in the original collateral did not mention proceeds.

> Be able to discuss all the different ways that **perfection** can take place.

> A PMSI secures the purchase price of goods bought for personal or household use.

15. PRIORITY PROBLEMS AND EXAMPLES

Consider the following problems and examples that illustrate the complexity of determining the outcomes of several different situations involving secured creditors. Are you sure you want to be a business attorney?

> Generally, a creditor with an attached security interest has priority over a creditor without a security interest, a creditor with a perfected security interest has priority over one whose security interest has not been perfected, and when two creditors have perfected security interests the one whose interest was perfected first has priority.

1. A secured creditor with an attached security interest has priority over a creditor without a security interest. However, a secured creditor does not have priority over a purchaser who gives value for collateral and takes it before a security interest is perfected.

2. John loans Carl $5,000 and attaches a security interest in Carl's printing machinery. John's security interest takes priority against a judgment creditor who tries to seize the machinery to satisfy a damage award. An attached security interest wins over an unattached creditor's claim, but if neither a creditor's claim nor a security interest has attached, the first to attach has priority.

3. A perfected security interest has priority over one that is not perfected but merely attached. If John loans Carl $5,000 on April 5 and attaches a security interest in the printing machinery on that day, John will lose priority to the bank that has filed a financing statement perfecting a security interest in the same machinery on April 15.

4. In the same situation, if John perfects his security interest on April 18, he still loses to the bank. Generally, when two creditors each have a perfected security interest, the creditor to perfect first has priority over the other, and the times the security interests attached are not important.

5. However, an exception to the rule in (3) occurs in that a PMSI in noninventory collateral, such as a printing machine for a print shop, which is received on August 1, takes priority over a bank's perfected financing statement in "all equipment presently owned or after acquired" that is perfected in the printing shop's equipment on July 9, *but only if the August 1 creditor perfects within a statutory period defined by state law, frequently 20 days.*

6. Likewise, if a publishing company sells books to a retail bookstore on credit, and has a purchase money security interest in the books sold, which will go into the inventory of the bookstore, the publishing company will have priority over a secured creditor like a bank that has previously filed a financing statement on the bookstore's "present inventory and after-acquired inventory," but *only if the publishing company has perfected its interest in the inventory at the time the bookstore receives the books.* Also, the publisher must check financing statements covering the bookstore's inventory, which are a matter of public record, and inform previously perfected security interests of the publisher's PMSI, and must describe the new inventory to them.

7. Print shop B that buys a piece of printing machinery from print shop A in another town will find that the machinery is still subject to the security interest held by a bank that has filed a proper financing statement on the machinery prior to B's purchase. However, a **buyer in the ordinary course of business** will have priority over a perfected security interest, meaning that if the seller of the printing machinery is a manufacturer of that machinery and is selling *in the ordinary course of business*, a buyer would take the machinery free and clear of a bank's previously perfected security interest. Note that in this latter instance the bank does continue to have a security interest for a period of time in the proceeds realized from the sale of the machinery that will have priority over a judgment creditor or a trustee in bankruptcy.

> A **buyer in the ordinary course of business** has priority over a perfected security interest.

8. Susan sells her computer to Greg for his personal use and a computer store holding a PMSI in the computer attempts to repossess it from Greg. The rule is that if Greg had no knowledge of the security interest he takes the computer free and clear of the computer store's perfected interest.

9. Artisan's liens and mechanic's liens usually have priority over even perfected Article 9 security interests. See Sidebar 7.7.

After a debtor has defaulted, which usually means it has failed to repay the credit that the secured creditor extended, the secured creditor may peacefully repossess the collateral without going to court unless the debtor orally protests the repossession, in which case the secured party will have to obtain a court order to repossess. Following repossession, the secured creditor can dispose of the collateral in any "commercially reasonable" fashion, such as sale or lease, and must return to the debtor any excess money realized over the amount owed. The secured party can also propose to keep the collateral in complete satisfaction of the debt.

> A secured creditor can repossess collateral only if the repossession is peaceful.

>> *sidebar* 7.7

Artisan's Liens and Mechanic's Liens

You take your car to the garage for a new transmission but when the work is complete, the credit card company refuses to extend additional credit, asserting that your limit has been reached. You are unable to pay the garage for its materials and labor. The garage can legally refuse to release your car until you have paid it. This is because the garage has an **artisan's lien** on your car, a narrow property interest that arises when someone who contributes parts and/or services to an object of personal property is not paid. This lien has priority over even an Article 9 perfected security interest held by the bank that loaned you the money to buy the car. This result is so because the garage has added value to the car by its parts and labor, and if the garage has to sell the car, it can only realize the value of the parts and labor it added. An artisan's lien is *possessory,* meaning that generally the lien has priority only as long as the creditor keeps possession of the collateral.

A **mechanic's lien** arises when someone contributes materials and/or services to real estate, usually a building, and is not paid. Unlike the artisan's lien, this lien is not possessory and has priority only if it is perfected by the filing of a written notice, usually in the county where the real estate is found. This lien also has priority over an Article 9 perfected security interest when a fixture, an object of personal property like a carpet, is incorporated into real estate by becoming a physical part of it. The carpet can be subject to a perfected security interest that will follow the carpet's incorporation into the real estate if the owner of the real estate receives the required notice. However, a mechanic's lien that adds value to the real estate has priority over a perfected security interest in a fixture.

 >> Limitations on Property and the Common Good

Some people consider private property to be an unacceptably selfish social principle. Karl Marx said in the *Communist Manifesto* that the first thing communists should do when coming to power is to abolish "private property." Yet this chapter argues that the tremendous national wealth created by a fairly enforced private property system justifies the institution of private property. In other words, private property serves the common good or general welfare of the nation. Importantly, private property has limits, and these limits tell us that an individual private property right is always subject at some point to the right of others. Further, individual private property gives way to the common good of society both through eminent domain and taxation, which are recognized by the U.S. Constitution. Read the sections that follow and develop your own view of private property and the common good.

16. PROPERTY, THE USE OF RESOURCES, AND THE EQUAL RIGHT OF OTHERS

In law, property is not a *thing*. It is an owner's *right* to exclude others from resources. One of the most important resources is the use owners can make of another resource, for example, a piece of land. Owners can build a house, a shopping mall, or a skyscraper on their land. Or farm it. Or leave it unoccupied. They can take their money and open a computer store with it, or save it for retirement, or invest it in the stock market. All of these ways of using resources come within the legal guarantee of property. Implied in the exclusive rights to private resources is the legal protection to use them in many ways. This quality helps make the marketplace dynamic and responsive to needs and wants.

In an important and meaningful sense, owners also have a property in using their efforts. They have an exclusive right to direct their resource in themselves any way they wish. They can use it to pursue any line of employment, or they can leave the job market and do volunteer work for Meals on Wheels. Or go back to school for an MBA. Or retire on their savings and garden, travel, or watch football.

Having a property right to direct the resources of one's efforts and to be able to exclude others from the further resources one acquires with these efforts is closely related to other concepts like "freedom" and "liberty." The American colonists and the framers of the Constitution certainly thought so. John Dickinson, who helped draft the Constitution, observed that Americans "cannot be happy, without freedom; nor free, without security of property; nor so secure, unless the sole power to dispose of it be lodged within themselves." Revolutionary War diplomat Arthur Lee wrote, "The right of property is the guardian of every other right, and to deprive people of this, is in fact to deprive them of their liberty." In 1768 a colonial American observed, "Liberty and Property are not only join'd in common discourse, but are in their own natures so nearly ally'd [allied], that we cannot be said to possess the one without the other." The early Americans firmly believed they had a property not only in their material possessions but also in liberty, speech, and other rights. In summary, they had an exclusive right to use freely their resource in themselves and the resources produced by their efforts.

Generally speaking, owners are prohibited from using their resources in ways that harm or injure the resources of other owners. See also Sidebar 7.8. As James Madison explained, the concept of property "leaves to everyone else a like advantage." Under the rule of law, a property system protects the equal

> Explain what it means to say that you have a property in your efforts. How is such a property related to *liberty*?

>> *sidebar* 7.8

The Property System and Corporate Governance

Chapter 1 explained why the issues of corporate governance are property issues. The explanation bears reemphasizing.

The property system allows us to enjoy exclusive resources. It protects our resources from the harm of others, but at the same time it limits us from harming the resources of others. Corporate governance illustrates how this property system functions.

In the *specific* sense, corporate governance laws protect the investment resources of corporate owners, or shareholders. These laws define the authority and responsibility of the board of directors, who are elected by the shareholders. The laws also regulate the managers appointed by the board.

In the *broad* sense, corporate governance also includes those laws that protect the resources of others from harm by the corporation. Such laws include antitrust laws, employment discrimination and employee protection laws, environmental protection laws, and a great many antifraud laws.

Sometimes the law does not protect the boundary between what is *mine* and what is *yours*. Sometimes there is disagreement about where proper boundaries lie. Sometimes we have failures of corporate governance. But under a system that permits private resource ownership, corporate governance issues are property issues.

right of all to their resources, including the resources they have in themselves. Tort law (Chapter 10), criminal law (Chapter 13), and much of the regulatory law discussed throughout this book attempt to prevent owners from using their resources to injure the resources that belong to others.

Two limits on land use that protect the equal right of all landowners is especially relevant to this chapter. They involve the law of nuisance and zoning.

17. NUISANCE AND ZONING

The law limits certain uses of one's land through the doctrine of nuisance. What constitutes a nuisance is somewhat vague, but in most jurisdictions the common law cases have been put in statutory form. Several common elements exist in the law of nuisance in most states. To begin with, there are two types of nuisance: public and private.

A **public nuisance** is one arising from some use of land that causes inconvenience or damage to the public. For example, discharging industrial waste from one's land that kills the fish in a river constitutes a public nuisance since fishing rights are publicly held. Public nuisance claims may be brought only by a public official, not private individuals, unless the latter have suffered some special damage to their property as a result of the public nuisance. Note that many public nuisances can also violate various regulatory laws, such as environmental laws (see Chapter 19).

A **private nuisance** is an *unreasonable* use of one's property so as to cause substantial interference with the enjoyment or use of another's land.

Any unreasonable use of one's property so as to cause substantial interference with the enjoyment or use of another's land establishes a common law **private nuisance.** The unreasonableness of the interference is measured by a balancing process in which the character, extent, and duration of harm to the plaintiff is weighed against the social utility of the defendant's activity and its appropriateness to its location. Since society needs industrial activity as well as natural tranquility, people must put up with a certain amount of smoke, dust, noise, and polluted water if they live in concentrated areas of industry. But what may be an appropriate industrial use of land in a congested urban area may be a private nuisance if it occurs in a rural or residential location.

Once the plaintiff establishes a substantial and unreasonable interference with the use or enjoyment of his or her property, the court must decide what remedy the plaintiff is entitled to. The court may award damages if the plaintiff has suffered economic loss, but when damages are inadequate the court may also order the defendant to do something, like correct the problem, or else cease the nuisance-creating activity. In determining whether to issue an injunction, the court will take into consideration (1) the relative economic hardship that will be placed upon the parties if such relief is granted, and (2) the public interest in the continuation of the defendant's activity. This balancing of interests required by nuisance law can bring about some unusual remedies.

In the following case, the court requires the defendants to move their house.

case 7.2 >>

COOK v. SULLIVAN
829 A.2d 1059 (N.H. Sup. Ct. 2003)

DALIANIS, J: . . . The defendants, John and Diane Sullivan, appeal a decision of the Superior Court finding that they created a nuisance on the plaintiffs' property by filling in wetlands and constructing a home on their property.

Since 1946, the plaintiffs [the Cooks] have owned property on Lake Winnipesaukee in Moultonboro. Over the years, they have built various structures on the property, including a main house, a garage, and a guest house. In 1996, the defendants purchased adjoining property.

At the time of the purchase, the defendants [Sullivans] . . . had a three-bedroom modular house placed on their property. In the course of construction, the defendants used large quantities of fill in the area where they were building the house. In 1997, the plaintiffs began experiencing increased wetness, which they claim lasted for extended periods of time, on their property. Specifically, the plaintiffs claimed, among other things, that, since the construction, standing water accumulated in their garage and underneath the house, and that the water has interfered with their ability to use their property as they had in the past. They also claimed that this condition persisted each summer from 1997 to 2001.

In 1999, the plaintiffs complained to the defendants, who attempted to remedy the problem by removing some fill along the parties' common boundary line, digging a drainage ditch and moving a wall. The plaintiffs, however, claimed that the condition of their land did not change [and they sued].

The trial court ruled that the defendants' construction activities constituted a nuisance that damaged the plaintiffs' property, and that the remedy was to remove the fill and foundation from the jurisdictional wetlands, which would necessarily require the defendants' house to be moved. . . . [T]his appeal followed.

A private nuisance exists when an activity substantially and unreasonably interferes with the use and enjoyment of another's property. "To constitute a nuisance, the defendants' activities must cause harm that exceeds the customary interferences with land that a land user suffers in an organized society,

and be an appreciable and tangible interference with a property interest." In determining whether an act interfering with the use and enjoyment is so unreasonable and substantial as to amount to a nuisance and warrant an injunction, a court must balance the gravity of the harm to the plaintiff against the utility of the defendant's conduct, both to himself and to the community. It is the plaintiffs' burden to prove the existence of a nuisance by a preponderance of the evidence.

The evidence supports the trial court's finding of nuisance. At trial, witnesses testified that large portions of the defendants' lot were swampy and had pools of standing water prior to construction. The plaintiffs' expert, Randall Shuey, a certified soil scientist, testified that he conducted extensive testing of the defendants' property subsequent to their construction and stated that the defendants' activities had had caused subsurface waters to divert to the plaintiffs' property.

Further, the plaintiffs testified that their property was substantially wetter after the defendants built their house. The defendants assert that there was insufficient evidence to support this finding, or that the wetness problems continued to exist at the time of final hearing, because the plaintiffs' property was wet before construction. While there was evidence that portions of the plaintiffs' property were wet prior to the defendants' construction, numerous witnesses testified that the water levels increased following the defendants' construction. This testimony was corroborated by Shuey's statement that the defendants' construction altered the elevation of the defendants' land as well as the flow of subsurface waters, causing increased wetness on the plaintiffs' property. While there was evidence introduced of flooding in 1998, Shuey stated that, while having a short-term effect, the flooding did not cause the prolonged wetness the plaintiffs experienced in later years. Moreover, the plaintiffs testified that this condition on their property repeated each spring and early summer from 1997 to 2001.

The plaintiffs also illustrated various problems associated with the increased wetness. For example,

[continued]

they testified that following the construction, there was standing water on their property, both on a large portion of the lawn, including the backyard between the house and the garage, and under the garage and chalet. They explained that because of the increased wetness, they were forced to move dog pens that they traditionally kept in the lower part of their property, and that they could no longer hang a clothesline or stack firewood in the backyard, or use the backyard for recreational activities. Plaintiffs testified that they had trouble mowing the lawn because of the water. The plaintiffs also explained that they could no longer store things directly on their garage floor due to standing water in the spring and early summer months. Further, they testified that there was a strong, musty odor in the house after water began collecting under the foundation, which prevented them from using the house during those months when the windows are closed.

Given the evidence in the record, we cannot hold that the trial court erred in finding that the defendants' construction created a nuisance resulting in damages to the plaintiffs' property.

Having concluded that there was sufficient evidence to support the trial court's findings that the defendants' activities constitute a nuisance, we now must determine whether the remedy was appropriate. In evaluating the appropriateness of injunctive relief, the court utilizes the same balancing test that is used to first identify whether a nuisance exists, "although the scales must weigh more heavily in the [plaintiff's] favor because of the extraordinary nature of this form of relief." The propriety of affording relief in a particular case rests in the sound discretion of the trial court. . . . We will uphold a trial court's order unless its decision constitutes an unsustainable exercise of discretion. If the defendants' activity can be carried on without causing unreasonable interference to the plaintiffs, then they should not be required to remove their house. On the other hand, an order requiring such removal is justified if there is no other way to abate the private nuisance.

The defendants challenge the ordered remedy, arguing that the trial court neglected to balance the hardships between the parties and that there was insufficient evidence to support its decision.

With regard to remedying the nuisance, Shuey stated specifically that "the only way to guarantee that we're not going to have any additional impacts on the property, or to restore it to what it was previously, is to move that house and all that fill out of the jurisdictional area, out of the jurisdictional wetlands." He also stated that this could be accomplished by moving the defendants' house and foundation back forty or fifty feet on the property.

The defendants did propose a less stringent remedy to the trial court, which involved removing fill within twenty feet of the plaintiffs' boundary and constructing a ditch near the boundary for water discharge. Shuey testified, however, that he could not guarantee that the plaintiffs' property would be restored to its condition prior to the defendants' construction. The defendants did not offer any expert testimony at trial in support of their proposed remedy nor did they offer any other alternate remedies.

The record reflects that the trial court took the hardships of both parties into consideration when deciding the remedy. For example, the trial court explained in its final verdict that it was prepared to decide what remedy "would be equitable and fair under all the circumstances." Further, the court told the parties during trial that it was considering the equities of both parties when considering the appropriate remedy. Moreover, the court adopted the unusual procedure of viewing the property both before and after it took testimony and reviewed the exhibits. Having considered the evidence before the trial court, we agree that the gravity of harm to the plaintiffs resulting from the defendants' nuisance is significant enough to support the trial court's remedy.

Consequently, we find sufficient evidentiary support for the trial court's remedy and uphold its decision. *Affirmed.*

>> CASE QUESTIONS

1. What did the defendants do with their land that the plaintiffs considered "unreasonable and substantial"?

2. How does the court decide whether or not a use of land is unreasonable? What kind of thinking process does the court go through?

3. Do you believe that courts in nuisance cases are acting in the general welfare or common good of the public? Discuss.

Can you see now how nuisance law attempts to balance the equal right of all in the property system? It does so by preventing landowners from *unreasonably* interfering with other publicly and privately owned resources. Determining what is unreasonable is an ongoing and controversial process in a property-based legal system. You should understand now that property boundaries of use are not infinite and may be ambiguous until a court order legislature sets them.

Through their exercise of the police powers, states and local governments protect the public health, safety, morals, and general welfare. It is under the police powers that a major governmental regulation of land use takes place: zoning. **Zoning ordinances** are generally laws that divide counties or municipalities into use districts designated residential, commercial, or industrial. Zoning limits the use to which land can be put to that specified. For instance, industrial facilities cannot be built in residential districts. Zoning may also specify the height, size, number, and location of buildings that can be built on land. Restricting buildings in a commercial district to no more than eight stories in height is an example. Zoning may additionally impose aesthetic requirements concerning color and exterior design. Zoning boards (or commissions), which are generally agencies of local governments, enforce the zoning ordinances. Owners should always check to determine how zoning limits land use.

> Do you agree with the principle of **zoning ordinances** or not?

An owner can ask a zoning board for a *variance* to allow use of land in a way not permitted under a zoning ordinance. The board is likely to grant a variance only when the owner can prove that the ordinance prevents a reasonable economic return on the land as zoned. Zoning ordinances allow uses of land that existed prior to passage of the ordinances. Such uses are called "nonconforming" uses.

Like nuisance law, zoning regulations are highly controversial because they involve limits on how owners can use their land. The purpose of zoning laws may be to protect the right of all to their lands, but not everyone is going to agree with the limits that zoning laws establish.

18. PROPERTY LIMITATIONS AND THE COMMON GOOD

Even limitations on property illustrate that this exclusive right serves the common good. Several property-related concepts illustrate that when society believes that property no longer promotes the general public welfare, owners lose the resources protected by property:

- Duration limitations
- Eminent domain
- Taxation

Duration Limitations on Property   Do not believe for a minute that when you own something you own it forever. For instance the Constitution grants patents and copyrights—only for "limited Times." The reasoning behind the limitation is to ensure that inventions and creative expressions enter the public domain so to serve the common good as quickly as possible after allowing for the profit necessary to encourage people to create new things in the first place.

> *The **rule against perpetuities** serves the common good by preventing dead owners from indefinitely limiting the new productive ways that resources can be used.

Patents and copyrights, however, are not the only property concept that limits the duration of an owner's exercise of exclusive right over resources. The **rule against perpetuities** limits all exercise of property over resources to a duration of "lives in being plus twenty-one years." The rule prevents an owner from controlling resources through many future generations by setting up *trust* arrangements, under which trustees are legally required to carry out the wishes of the owner for extended duration. As it is, a trust may not extend the control of an owner beyond twenty-one years of the death of someone who is alive at the time of the owner's death.

19. EMINENT DOMAIN

Zoning and many regulatory limitations on property protect some owners from being harmed by other owners. Eminent domain, however, is quite different. This important concept specifically exists to limit the exclusive right of property in order to serve the common good by allowing the government to take away property-protected resources from owners.

Eminent Domain and the Common Good Jeremy Bentham, a philosopher who lived a century after John Locke, thought that Locke's ideas about property being a natural right from God were "nonsense upon stilts." He called the right of property the "noblest triumph" but believed that property served only the common good, which he defined as the "greatest happiness for the greatest number." This definition is similar to the one expressed earlier that the common good reflects the maximum conditions for providing what people need and want. It assumes only that satisfying what people need and want makes them happy.

The takings clause of the Fifth Amendment to the Constitution favors Bentham's view that property serves the common good. It allows the government to take specific resources (usually but not always land) away from private owners for "public use" upon the payment of "just compensation." The clause recognizes the existence and importance of private ownership, but allows the government to "condemn" and take specific private resources for money under the power called **eminent domain.**

Eminent domain means the government can take private property for public use upon paying just compensation.

Three significant questions of interpretation arise:

- What constitutes a "taking"?
- What is a "public use"?
- What is "just compensation"?

As to the first question, it is clear that when the government builds a public road through private land, it has *taken* the land and must pay compensation. But what if the government merely limits specific uses of the land, perhaps for environmental purposes? Does it have to pay compensation? The cases have been unclear, but they seem to say that as long as some economic use has been left to the landowner, no taking has occurred. One way to determine whether regulation is a taking is to see if it is necessary to protect an established property right of others that concerns safety, health, or other general welfare. The courts do not consider such regulation a taking. It is merely determining the location of boundaries, often boundaries of use.

Over the years *public use* has come to mean *public purpose.*

Public Use The easiest way to define *public use* is to say it is a use *by* the public. A public road, a public park, a public building, a public sewage treatment plant or landfill—taking a private owner's land for any of these uses is a public use. What about the government's taking a right to string power wires across your land, then selling it to a private electric company that charges you for electricity? Is that a public use?

Courts have certainly allowed the government to take private property right for use by electric and other private utility companies. These companies benefit the public greatly. Over the years public use has come to mean *public purpose,* that is, any *purpose* that benefits the public, whether the public uses the resource or not.

What about the government's taking of land in order to sell it for private development in order to stimulate employment and increase the public tax base? Is employment stimulation and increased tax revenue a public use, or at least a public purpose? Consider Case 7.3.

case 7.3 >>

KELO v. CITY OF NEW LONDON, CONNECTICUT
125 S.Ct. 2655 (2005)

In 2000, the city of New London, Connecticut, approved a development plan that was projected to create in excess of 1,000 jobs, increase tax and other revenues, and revitalize an economically distressed community. In assembling the land needed for this project, the city's development agency, the New London Development Corporation (NLDC), purchased property from willing sellers and initiated condemnation proceedings against the plaintiffs for the remainder of the land. The plaintiffs are nine landowners of property within the area where the new development was planned.

The trial court prohibited NLDC from taking part of the land but on appeal the Supreme Court of Connecticut reversed, allowing the NLDC to take all of the land. The U. S. Supreme Court granted Ms. Kelo's petition for a writ of certiorari to decide the question of whether a city's decision to take property for the purpose of economic development satisfies the "public use" requirement of the Fifth Amendment.

STEVENS, J: . . . Two polar propositions are perfectly clear. On the one hand, it has long been accepted that the sovereign may not take the property of *A* for the sole purpose of transferring it to another private property *B*, even though *A* is paid just compensation. On the other hand, it is equally clear that a State may transfer property from one private party to another if future "use by the public" is the purpose of the taking; the condemnation of land for a railroad with common-carrier duties is a familiar example. Neither of these propositions, however, determines the disposition of this case.

The disposition of this case therefore turns on the question whether the City's development plan serves a "public purpose." Without exception, our cases have defined that concept broadly, reflecting our longstanding policy of deference to legislative judgments in this field.

In *Berman v. Parker,* 348 U.S. 26 (1954), this Court upheld a redevelopment plan targeting a blighted area of Washington, D.C., in which most of the housing for the area's 5,000 inhabitants was beyond repair. Under the plan, the area would be condemned and part of it utilized for the construction of streets, schools, and other public facilities. The remainder of the land would be leased or sold to private parties for the purpose of redevelopment, including the construction of low-cost housing.

The owner of a department store located in the area challenged the condemnation, pointing out that his store was not itself blighted and arguing that the creation of a "better balanced, more attractive community" was not a valid public use. Writing for a unanimous Court, Justice Douglas refused to evaluate this claim in isolation, deferring instead to the legislative and agency judgment that the area "must be planned as a whole" for the plan to be successful. The Court explained that "community redevelopment programs need not, by force of the Constitution, be on a piecemeal basis—lot by lot, building by building." The public use underlying the taking was unequivocally affirmed:

> We do not sit to determine whether a particular housing project is or is not desirable. The concept of the public welfare is broad and inclusive. . . . The values it represents are spiritual as well as physical, aesthetic as well as monetary. It is within the power of the legislature to determine that the community should be beautiful as well as healthy, spacious as well as clean, well-balanced as well as carefully patrolled.

[continued]

Viewed as a whole, our jurisprudence has recognized that the needs of society have varied between different parts of the Nation, just as they have evolved over time in response to changed circumstances. . . . For more than a century, our public use jurisprudence has wisely eschewed rigid formulas and intrusive scrutiny in favor of affording legislatures broad latitude in determining what public needs justify the use of the takings power. . . .

The City has carefully formulated an economic development plan that it believes will provide appreciable benefits to the community, including but by no means limited to new jobs and increased tax revenue. . . . To effectuate this plan, the City has invoked a state statute that specifically authorizes the use of eminent domain to promote economic development. . . . Because that plan unquestionably serves a public purpose, the takings challenged here satisfy the public use requirement of the Fifth Amendment.

To avoid this result, petitioners urge us to adopt a new bright-line rule that economic development does not qualify as a public use. Putting aside the unpersuasive suggestion that the City's plan will provide only purely economic benefits, neither precedent nor logic supports petitioners' proposal. Promoting economic development is a traditional and long accepted function of government. There is, moreover, no principled way of distinguishing economic development from the other public purposes that we have recognized. . . . It would be incongruous to hold that the City's interest in the economic benefits to be derived from the development has less of a public character than any of those other interests. Clearly, there is no basis for exempting economic development from our traditionally broad understanding of public purpose.

Petitioners contend that using eminent domain for economic development impermissibly blurs the boundary between public and private takings. Again, our cases foreclose this objection. Quite simply, the government's pursuit of a public purpose will often benefit individual private parties. . . . The owner of the department store in *Berman* objected to "taking from one businessman for the benefit of another businessman," referring to the fact that under the redevelopment plan land would be leased or sold to private developers for redevelopment. Our rejection of that contention has particular relevance to the instant case: The public end may be as well or better served through an agency of private enterprise than through a department of government—or so the Congress might conclude. We cannot say that public ownership is the sole method of promoting the public purposes of community redevelopment projects. . . .

It is further argued that without a bright-line rule nothing would stop a city from transferring citizen *A*'s property to citizen *B* for the sole reason that citizen *B* will put the property to a more productive use and thus pay more taxes. Such a one-to-one transfer of property, executed outside the confines of an integrated development plan, is not presented in this case. While such an unusual exercise of government power would certainly raise a suspicion that a private purpose was afoot, the hypothetical cases posted by petitioners can be confronted if and when they arise. They do not warrant the crafting of an artificial restriction on the concept of public use. . . .

Just as we decline to second-guess the City's considered judgments about the efficacy of its development plan, we also decline to second-guess the City's determinations as to what lands it needs to acquire in order to effectuate the project. It is not for the courts to oversee the choice of the boundary line nor to sit in review on the size of a particular project area. Once the question of the public purpose has been decided, the amount and character of land to be taken for the project and the need for a particular tract to complete the integrated plan rests in the discretion of the legislative branch. . . .

The judgment of the Supreme Court of Connecticut is affirmed.

It is so ordered.

DISSENT: THOMAS, J.: Long ago, William Blackstone wrote that "the law of the land . . . postpone[s] even public necessity to the sacred and inviolable rights of private property." The Framers embodied that principle in the Constitution, allowing the government to take property not for "public necessity," but instead for "public use." Defying this understanding, the Court replaces the Public Use Clause with a "'[P]ublic [P]urpose'" Clause, a restriction that is satisfied, the Court instructs, so long as the purpose is "legitimate" and the means "not irrational." This deferential shift in phraseology enables the Court to hold, against all common sense, that a costly urban-renewal project whose stated purpose is a value promise of new jobs and increased tax revenue, but which is also suspiciously agreeable to the Pfizer Corporation, is for a "public use."

I cannot agree. If such "economic development" takings are for a "public use," any taking is, and the Court has erased the Public Use Clause from our Constitution. I do not believe that this Court can eliminate liberties expressly enumerated in the Constitution. Regrettably, however, the Court's error runs deeper than this. Today's decision is simply the latest in a string of our cases construing the Public Use Clause to be a virtual nullity, without the slightest nod to its original meaning. In my view, the Public Use Clause, originally understood, is a meaningful limit on the government's eminent domain power. Our cases have strayed from the Clause's original meaning, and I would reconsider them.

[continued]

The Fifth Amendment provides: "No person shall. . . . be deprived of life, liberty, or property, without due process of law; *nor shall private property be taken for public use without just compensation.*" (Emphasis added.)

In my view, it is "imperative that the Court maintain absolute fidelity to" the Clause's express limit on the power of the government over the individual, no less than with every other liberty expressly enumerated in the Fifth Amendment or the Bill of Rights more generally. . . .

The most natural reading of the Clause is that it allows the government to take property only if the government owns, or the public has a legal right to use, the property, as opposed to taking it for any public purpose or necessity whatsoever. . . .

More fundamentally, *Berman* erred by equating the eminent domain power with the police power of States. . . . The question whether the State can take property using the power of eminent domain is therefore distinct from the question whether it can regulate property pursuant to the police power. . . .

The consequences of today's decision are not difficult to predict, and promise to be harmful. So-called "urban renewal" programs provide some compensation for the properties they take, but no compensation is possible for the subjective value of these lands to the individuals displaced and the indignity inflicted by uprooting them from their homes. Allowing the government to take property solely for public purposes is bad enough, but extending the concept of public purpose to encompass any economically beneficial goal guarantees that these losses will fall disproportionately on poor communities. Those communities are not only systematically less likely to put their lands to the highest and best social use, but are also the least politically powerful. . . .

I would reverse the judgment of the Connecticut Supreme Court.

>> CASE QUESTIONS

1. What constitutional issue did the Supreme Court take the case to answer, and what was its answer?
2. How does the majority opinion address the point that if NLDC can take this land, the state can take any private land and pass it along to any private person?
3. In his dissent, Justice Thomas says, "Allowing the government to take property solely for public purposes is bad enough. . . ." What do you think he means by this statement? Do you agree?
4. Does private property exist under our legal system for the common good? Discuss in light of the *Kelo* case opinions.

A national uproar arose after *Kelo* over whether private property interest should *ever* be taken and turned over for private development. Note that state and local governments have been taking private land and turning it over in this way for many years. The *Kelo* case merely represents the first time the Supreme Court has squarely decided the issue. The Supreme Court did not require that state governments take anyone's land for private development. It merely decided that it was a constitutional public use to do so under the given circumstances. Under pressure from voters, a number of states have passed laws preventing the units of government from taking private land for private development purposes.

*A number of states have passed laws preventing the units of government (cities and counties) from taking private land for private development purposes.

Just Compensation The government can only take what belongs to private owners upon payment of "just compensation." The courts have generally defined just compensation in terms of market value. In most instances the government offers compensation to an owner, a negotiation follows, and an amount is agreed upon as a just compensation. However, courts have ruled that due process requires that an owner can go to court and have a jury determine a just compensation if the owner cannot agree with the government's offer.

PART 3   Legal Foundations for Business

*Public use means basically the same thing as common good. These terms are also similar to general welfare.

Do you understand now how eminent domain illustrates that property right is limited by the common good? *Public use* means basically the same thing as *common good*. When the state decides to take an owner's resources, it is determining that the right of property in these resources no longer serves the common good and that the greater common good requires that the resources be taken. Even so, the owner who has lost a property interest through eminent domain must receive just compensation.

20. TAXATION

The justification for property may be the common good. And the common good may consist primarily of setting conditions for the maximum private production of what people need and want. However, the government provides other resources that people need and want, including public roads, public education, law enforcement, a judicial system, defense of the nation, and public assistance for the poor. These services are also a part of the general welfare (or common good) of the nation, and they are expensive. Some people believe that in the common good the government should provide even more public services such as more public health care. The taxes to support these services limit the right of private property and suggest that property's claim to promoting the common good is not absolute.

Federal taxation is a specified power of Congress, contained in Article 1, Section 8 of the Constitution: "The Congress shall have the Power to lay and collect Taxes . . . to . . . provide for the common Defense and general Welfare of the United States. . . ." Because the Supreme Court ruled that Article 1, Section 8, did not authorize indirect taxes, like the progressive income tax, the Constitution was amended in 1913 by the Sixteenth Amendment, which permits such taxes.

The CBO also reports that the top 20% of taxpayers pay 60% of all federal income tax.

According to the Congressional Budget Office, the top 1% of federal income taxpayers pay more dollars of tax than the bottom 60% of taxpayers do. On the other hand, poorer taxpayers pay a higher percentage of their incomes in state and local sales taxes than do wealthier taxpayers. The fairness of the tax system and the adequacy of public services are frequent issues around election time. One thing is certain, however: These issues intertwine with perceptions of the common good, which in turn connects with the exclusive right called property. They illustrate that property, which promotes the common good, is also limited by it.

Can property exist both as an individual right and for the common good? Discuss.

The wealth produced by the property system must actually reach people in order to produce the greatest happiness for the greatest number. Exclusive right is not an ethical or moral end in itself. Although there can be much debate about its extent, taxation of wealth generated by the incentives of the property system is part of what contributes to the common good.

21. PROPERTY: A CONCLUSION AND COMMENT

This chapter has introduced the law of property as it orders society's limited resources. Although many chapter sections have explained the rules making up property law, the chapter has also focused on the general importance of the legal property system to private enterprise and society. The key to the most rapid increase of total wealth—the greatest expansion of limited resources—is a property system that applies generally and equally to everyone's resources.

In the modern nation, property law founds the marketplace by establishing an essential framework for the voluntary and certain exchange of identifiable private resources. There is strong reason to think that a prime determinant of wealth in the world today is the presence or absence of an adequate property system under the rule of law. Thus, it is significant that business students appreciate the fundamental role of law in business and the necessity for a strong legal system even when they oppose the wisdom of specific rules or regulations.

Although effective property law may be the foundation for society's material flourishing and the liberty of the individual, it also has another side to it. Property law permits the accumulation of unequal exclusive resources, and as James Madison wrote in *The Federalist:* "The most common and durable source of factions has been the various and unequal distribution of property." A property system functions best when there is a large middle class with adequate resources, or at least a well-educated populace that understands the benefits of property. Otherwise, in a democracy the temptation is great to redistribute resources through taxation, and at some point the motivation to produce additional limited resources diminishes.

> Why does a property system function best when there is a large middle class with adequate resources?

The major issues of poverty and prosperity in the new millennium involve the understanding of property law's effects on society. To deal knowledgeably with the legal environment of business, students must grasp how law founds the private marketplace for the common good.

The next two chapters introduce you to the rules of *contract* law. As you read these chapters, keep in mind the important connection between property and contract. The rules of contract law concern the legally binding promises by which owners exchange resources in our property-based legal system. When you sign a contract to buy a new 3-D television set, you promise to exchange the ownership of money for the ownership of the television set.

>> Key Terms

Accession 203	Eminent domain 222	Perfection 214
Adverse possession 202	Estate 205	Personal property 199
Artisans lien 216	Fee simple 205	Private nuisance 218
Attachment 213	Financing statement 214	Property 194
Bailee 207	Fixture 199	Public nuisance 218
Bailment 207	Foreclosure 212	Purchase money security
Bailor 207	Gift 204	interest (PMSI) 214
Buyer in the ordinary course	Joint tenancy 205	Real property 199
of business 215	Land sales contract 212	Right of redemption 212
Collateral 213	Leasehold estate 205	Rule against perpetuities 221
Confusion 203	Life estate 205	Rule of first possession 201
Contract 200	Mechanic's lien 216	Secured transactions 213
Deed 206	Mortgage 198	Security interest 211
Deeds of trust 211	Mortgagees 212	Tenancy in common 205
Deficiency 212	Mortgagors 212	Title 206
Easement 207	Ownership 200	Zoning ordinance 221

>> Review Questions and Problems

The Property System

1. *The Problem of Limited Resources*

   The Soviet Constitution guaranteed the citizens' private property. Why then was the former Soviet Union so poor?

2. *Property and Prosperity*

   (a) How does property help generate prosperity? Discuss.

   (b) Explain the importance of the visibility of resources to the wealth of nations.

3. *Two Basic Divisions of Property*

   (a) Explain the two basic divisions of property.

   (b) Martin sold his house to Cheryl. Later, when he tried to take the beautiful chandelier in the dining room, which had belonged to his grandparents, with him, Cheryl objected. What is the issue here? Legally, who is likely to win this dispute? Discuss.

Acquiring Resources in a Property System

4. *Acquiring Resources through Exchange*

   (a) How does the law of contracts fit into our property-based legal system?

   (b) Explain why more resources are exchanged by contracts than by any other method.

5. *Acquiring Resources through Possession*

   (a) Along a winding dirt road, Lee finds an old, rusty car with no license plates. Looking through the car, which is unlocked, he finds a valuable diamond ring. Later, the original buyer of the ring comes forward and admits that he has dumped the old car along the road, but wants his ring back. Who is legally entitled to the ring? Explain.

   (b) The owner of Downtown Condos discovers that Schuyler Skyscraper actually extends 6 inches on to land belonging to Downtown. Discuss the legal ramifications.

6. *Acquiring Resources through Confusion*

   (a) What are fungible goods? Give an example.

   (b) Discuss why boundaries of use are sometimes difficult to determine.

7. *Acquiring Resources through Accession*

   (a) Explain what it means to acquire ownership by accession.

   (b) Discuss why to John Locke a doctrine similar to accession justifies who owns what.

8. *Acquiring Resources through Gift*

   (a) In terms of a gift, explain *delivery* and constructive *delivery.*

   (b) What is a testamentary gift?

9. *Types of Ownership*

   (a) What does it mean to have a fee simple defeasible estate?

   (b) What is the difference between a remainder interest and a reversion?

   (c) Arla and Jack own a house as joint tenants with right of survivorship. What is the legal significance of this?

10. *Title and Property Registration*

    (a) Name three kinds of deeds to land and explain what they mean.

    (b) Why is it important to register a deed? Discuss.

Specialty Applications of Property

11. *Easements*

    (a) In what way is an easement protected by a property fence?

    (b) Explain an easement by prescription.

12. *Bailments*

    (a) Is a lease of a mowing tractor a bailment? Explain.

    (b) A warehouse contract requires that your equipment be stored in "warehouse 314." For its own convenience the warehouseman moves your equipment to warehouse 212, and your equipment is destroyed by a tornado that sweeps through town. Is the warehouse liable to you for the value of the equipment? What if the equipment had been destroyed in warehouse 314? Would your answer be different? Because of these types of problems, what sort of arrangements do bailors and bailees often make regarding bailed goods?

    (c) How are common carriers different from other sorts of bailees?

Property and Security Interests

13. *Security Interests in Land*

    (a) Name three types of security interests in land and explain them.

    (b) Discuss why recording mortgages and deeds of trust is so important. Why is recording less important in the case of the land sales contract?

14. *Secured Transactions*

    (a) Describe the requirements for attachment of a security interest under UCC, Article 9.

    (b) Describe four different instances that demonstrate perfection of a security interest.

15. *Priority Problems*

    Roger sells his expensive mowing tractor to his neighbor Zan. Shortly after Zan takes possession, someone representing the lawn equipment company tells Zan that the store holds a purchase money security interest in the tractor. Does the store have priority regarding the mower, meaning does the security interest continue on the mower following Zan's purchase of it?

Limitations on Property and the Common Good

16. *Property, the Use of Resources, and the Equal Right of Others*

    Discuss why it is important to have a property right in the uses of things.

17. *Nuisance and Zoning*

    (a) Distinguish a public nuisance from a private nuisance. What does nuisance have to do with the common good? Discuss.

    (b) What is the "coming to the nuisance" doctrine?

18. *Property Limitations and the Common Good*

    What is the rule against perpetuities? What does it have to do with the common good?

19. *Eminent Domain*

    Several people unhappy with the majority decision in *Kelo* tried to have the city council in Justice Souter's hometown condemn his house under eminent domain, take it, and turn it over to a private bed and breakfast business. Discuss whether or not this taking would have been constitutional.

20. *Taxation*

    Why is taxation of private property legal?

21. *Property: A Conclusion and Comment*

    (a) What does James Madison think is the problem with a private property system, a system he nevertheless supported?

    (b) Suppose you say to your roommate, "I have as much property as Bill Gates," although more accurately in terms of law you should say, "I have the *same* property as Bill Gates." What do you mean by this statement? Answer by explaining the basic confusion about the term "property."

business >> *discussions*

1. While you are attending a business conference in South America, someone approaches you and says, "A private property system might work well in your country, but it will never work in mine. There are only a few wealthy families in my country who own almost everything. Our only hope for the people is for the government to confiscate their lands and administer our resources through socialism."

What do you say to this person in light of what you have read in this chapter?
What strategy might you suggest regarding getting more private land into the hands of the poor in that country?

2. Richard Epstein, a University of Chicago law professor, said in his book Takings that the principles of nuisance illustrate more clearly than any other doctrine how our property-based legal system functions.

What did he mean by this statement? Discuss.
Explain what it means to say that property is the central concept in our legal system.

Chapter 8. Contract Formation

8 Contract Formation

Learning Objectives

8-1. To describe the rationale and legal basis for contracts.

8-2. To classify contracts and articulate the terminology used to describe contracts.

8-3. To describe the requirements needed to create an enforceable contract.

8-4. To know when a particular contract form is required.

8-5. To understand how contracts can benefit parties other than the original parties to an agreement.

The average person's day is filled with agreements. Consider these activities:

- Updating a social networking page while adhering to the use rules.

- Promising to meet a friend for lunch.

- Purchasing a cup of coffee.

- Committing to work with a colleague on a group assignment.

- Downloading music from a subscription site.

Are all of these agreements or promises *contracts?* Would we expect a court to enforce them? What are the consequences if one party refuses to follow through with his or her promise?

Contracts involve promises made as commitments.

These and many other questions about contracts are fundamental to the environment in which people conduct business. Here, at the beginning of this chapter, understanding the basic definition of contracts is essential. Simply stated, a contract is a legally enforceable **promise** or an exchange of promises. Although the details of contract classifications, terminology, formation, and performance make up the bulk of this and the next chapter, remember at the heart of this topic is a promise or commitment to do or not to do something.

The preceding chapters have addressed the importance of a dependable legal framework for our free enterprise system. The enforcement of contracts is an essential component of this framework. Every day, millions of contracts are created and performed by both businesspeople and consumers. Without contracts and the court systems to enforce contracts, buyers and sellers would not be able to predict future risks or have confidence in exchanging valuable property interests. In fact, it is fair to say that no other area of the law has been as important as the law of contracts in supporting private enterprise. As you read and study this chapter and the next, keep in mind the fundamental role that contracts have in making business possible.

There are also nonlegal business considerations in every contract. If your company tries to get out of a deal a customer believes exists, you risk losing that customer's future business. Moreover, companies that use contracts to trap customers in agreements that are unexpected or unfair risk negative publicity that can undermine a good reputation for products or services. In so many ways, your business acumen is enhanced when you know the rules of contract law.

In this chapter, you will study such topics as:

- Laws governing contracts.
- When communications become a contract.
- What parties have to do when changes to a contract occur.
- Who has the capacity to create contracts.
- The necessary format of a contract.
- How third parties benefit from contracts.

The next chapter continues our examination of contracts by examining the performance and breach of contracts, as well as the authority of agents to bind a party to a contract.

>> Basic Concepts

When was the last time you entered into a contract? Was it last month when you signed an apartment or dorm lease? If so, you must be very hungry. This is because one enters a contract when buying a meal or a snack from a vending machine. Actually, most people contract daily for a great variety of goods and services that they purchase or lease. The rules of contract law underlie the private enterprise system at every turn.

LO 8-1   ## 1. CONTRACT LAW IN PRIVATE ENTERPRISE

A contract need not be a formal, written document, and those who make a contract do not have to use the word *contract* or recognize that they have made a legally enforceable promise. Still, the rules of contract law apply. If the expectations of the parties to a contract are not met, these rules affect legal negotiations and may result in a lawsuit. For instance, contract law says that a restaurant makes an implied "promise" that its food is fit to eat. Should the restaurant serve a meal that gives the buyer food poisoning, it could be liable for the injury caused by breaking its promise.

Contract law enables private agreements to be legally enforceable. Enforceability of agreements is desirable because it gives people the certainty they need to rely on promises contained in agreements. For instance, a shirt manufacturer in Los Angeles must know that it can rely on the promise of a store in Boston to pay for a thousand specially manufactured shirts. The manufacturer is more likely to agree to sew the shirts if it can enforce payment from the buyer, if necessary, under the law of contracts. In an important sense, then, the law of contracts is vital for our private enterprise economy. It helps make buyers and sellers willing to do business together.

Contract law provides enormous flexibility and precision in business dealings. It provides flexibility in that you can agree (or require agreement) to literally anything that is not illegal or against public policy. It gives precision in that with careful thinking you can make another agree to exactly the requirements that accomplish even a very complex business purpose. Sidebar 8.1 provides an example of the precise use of contractual language to accomplish a business purpose. Failure to follow this language can result in an outcome very different from the intended one.

>> *sidebar* 8.1

The Confidentiality Agreement

Many companies require employees to sign contractual confidentiality agreements. In these agreements, employees promise not to disclose certain things they learn during their employment. Confidentiality agreements are very useful in keeping employees or ex-employees from disclosing a company's research discoveries, marketing plans, customer lists, and other sensitive information.

Confidentiality agreements are important to firms in any industry where internal secrets provide a competitive advantage. This can include producers of cutting-edge, high-technology products like smartphones, but it can also impact providers of more commonplace and traditional items, like baked goods. The knowledge held by individual employees, encompassing sales techniques, corporate strategy, and even secret formulas, can be among a firm's most valuable assets. Contracts are an important way of ensuring the information does not fall into the hands of a competitor.

For example, when an executive for a company that produces well-known brands of English muffins, pastries, and other baked goods decided to move to a competitor, the company invoked the executive's contractual promise to maintain confidentiality. It argued that it was impossible for the executive to work for the competitor and not disclose proprietary information on new product plans, customer identities, and product formulas, among other things. The court agreed and issued a preliminary injunction preventing the employee from beginning work.

Source: *Bimbo Bakeries v. Chris Botticella*, 613 F.3d 102 (3d Cir. 2010).

2. SOURCES OF CONTRACT LAW

Most of the contract law outlined in this chapter is common law. Hopefully, you remember from Chapter 1 that common law comes from judges' decisions. The courts have developed principles controlling contract formation,

Do remember there are special rules applicable to the sale of goods by virtue of the Uniform Commercial Code.

performance, breach, and remedies in countless cases. This judge-made law affects many types of contracts, including real property, service, employment, and general business contracts.

Another source of contract law is legislation. Various states have enacted the common law as a part of the state statutes. A particularly important example of state-based legislation impacting contract law is the Uniform Commercial Code (UCC). Article 2 of the UCC covers the sale of **goods.** It applies to individuals as well as firms. Goods are tangible, movable items of personal property. Every state has adopted this portion of the UCC, thereby making state contract law uniform in the area of contracts involving goods. Throughout this chapter and the next, you will study both the common law principles of contracts and the UCC. Remember this distinction between these two primary sources of contract law. The UCC relates to contracts involving goods, and the common law governs other contracts.

LO 8-2

>> Contractual Classifications and Terminology

We use a number of terms to help classify different types of contracts. Learning these terms will greatly help you understand contract law. This section introduces the following contractual terminology:

- Bilateral and unilateral contracts.
- Express and implied-in-fact contracts.
- Implied-in-law or quasi-contracts.
- Enforcement terminology.
- Performance terminology.

3. BILATERAL AND UNILATERAL CONTRACTS

Bilateral contracts involve a promise-for-promise exchange.

Contracts involve either an exchange of promises by the parties or a promise conditioned on the performance of an act. A **bilateral contract** is an agreement containing mutual promises. For example, suppose Paul promises to sell his laptop computer to Pearl in exchange for her promise to pay $1,000 to Paul for the equipment. When Pearl makes her promise in response to Paul's, a bilateral contract is formed. This relationship is depicted in Figure 8.1. Notice that a bilateral contract involves two promises, two rights, and two duties.

Unilateral contracts exist when a promise is made to motivate an action.

While a bilateral contract involves a promise for a promise, a **unilateral contract** is an agreement with only one promise, and only one party is committed to perform. The maker of such a promise seeks an action rather than a promise in return. If that action does not occur, there is no breach. Suppose Pat tells Alex, "If you sell 100 units this year, I will pay you a bonus of $1,000." Here, Alex is not committed to perform, but if he does, Pat is bound to pay the promised amount. In Figure 8.2, notice that there is only one promise, one duty, and one right.

Most business contracts take the bilateral form. Indeed, courts presume a bilateral nature of an agreement whenever there is doubt about the form. Nevertheless, the party making a promise can control the application of many concepts of contract law by understanding the distinction between bilateral and unilateral contracts.

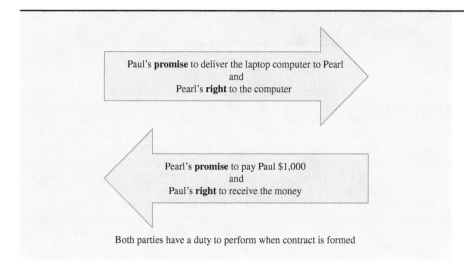

Figure 8.1 *Bilateral contract*

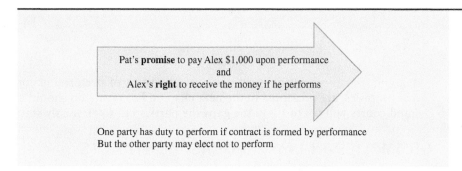

Figure 8.2 *Unilateral contract*

4. EXPRESS AND IMPLIED-IN-FACT CONTRACTS

Many contracts arise from interactions in which parties actually discuss the promised terms of their agreement. These are called **express contracts.** A negotiated purchase of land for construction of a manufacturing plant is an example of an express contract. There are also **implied-in-fact contracts,** which arise from the conduct of the parties rather than from words. For instance, asking a person such as an accountant for professional advice *implies* a promise to pay the going rate for this advice even though you do not make an *express* promise to pay for it.

In most business contracts, many conflicts and disputes can be avoided if the parties take time to express clearly the terms of the agreement. However, businesspeople can get in a hurry to complete the contract arrangements so they can begin doing business. For example in a typical customer-supplier relationship, a written contract may omit specific terms of delivery. These terms will be implied by the courts to ensure the contractual relationship is

A typical rule of thumb—parties expressing the detail of contractual commitments is better than leaving terms unstated.

>> *sidebar* 8.2

Unsolicited Ideas

A common concern for businesses is the creation of an unintended contractual obligation on receipt of an unsolicited idea. For example, imagine that an inventor develops a new idea for an improved toothbrush design and submits it to a firm that manufactures dental care products. But suppose that firm already has a similar idea in development. If the firm eventually markets the improved toothbrush design, it may appear that the idea was taken from the inventor without compensation. In such a case, it is easy to see how the inventor could perceive a breach of an implied-in-fact contract—acceptance of an idea with the understanding by both parties that compensation is owed if the idea is used—and sue on that basis.

The television and film industry faces similar issues. Writers often submit ideas for movies or TV shows in summary form to producers for consideration. There is an implication that if the idea is eventually produced, the writer is owed compensation. However, it is the nature of the entertainment industry and popular culture that similar ideas are often developed contemporaneously. Thus, there may be a question of whether the resulting TV show or movie was derived from the writer's submission or another source, and litigation may ensue.

Some businesses address this problem by refusing to accept external idea submissions. Although they may miss out on a few business opportunities, they avoid costly litigation over allegedly stolen ideas.

Source: *Montz v. Pilgrim Films & Television, Inc.*, 649 F.3d 675 (9th Cir. 2011)

ongoing. Details about delivery terms, as an aspect of performing contractual promises, are presented in the next chapter. For now, you should understand courts will try to fill in the gaps the parties fail to expressly state.

5. IMPLIED-IN-LAW OR QUASI-CONTRACTS

When one party is unjustly enriched at the expense of another, the law may imply a duty on the first party to pay the second even though there is no contract between the two parties. The doctrine that requires this result is based on an **implied-in-law contract.** Since there really is no actual contractual agreement, the phrase **quasi-contract** often is used.

Quasi-contracts are a judicial remedy to prevent one party from receiving unjust enrichment.

If a debtor overpays a creditor $5,000, the debtor can force the creditor to return that amount by suing under quasi-contract. It would be an unjust enrichment to allow the creditor to keep the $5,000. Likewise, when John has paid taxes on land, thinking that he owns it, and Mary comes along with a superior title (ownership) to the land and has John evicted, the remedy of quasi-contract requires that Mary reimburse John for the taxes paid.

It is important to understand that the remedy of quasi-contract generally applies only when no actual contract exists to cover the dispute. But note that quasi-contract is not an answer to every such situation. Over the years, courts have come to apply quasi-contract in a fairly limited number of cases based on unjust enrichment. However, as Case 8.1 illustrates, the principle of unjust enrichment under quasi-contract plays a very important role in ensuring the courts can achieve justice.

case **8.1** >>

NORTHEAST FENCE & IRON WORKS, INC. v. MURPHY QUIGLEY CO., INC.
933 A.2d 664 (Pa. Super.2007)

Murphy Quigley Co., Inc., is a general contractor for fencing and security upgrade projects at the Bucks County (Pennsylvania) Correctional Facility. The fencing contract required the installation of perimeter fencing and the creation of seven fence-enclosed recreational yards. Murphy Quigley contracted with Eagle Fence, as a subcontractor, to do the actual fencing work. Eagle Fence began this work. After completing only 10 to 15% of the required work, it quit the job due to disputes with Murphy Quigley over nonpayment.

In somewhat of an emergency situation, Murphy-Quigley granted a contract to Northeast Fence & Iron Works, Inc., to complete the unfinished fencing. Both Murphy Quigley and Northeast Fence & Iron Works agree the cost to finish the perimeter fence was $26,500. However, these parties never agreed on the specific contract price and the actual cost of the fencing of the recreational yards. Murphy Quigley thought the work would be done at the rate of $3,500 per day with a cap of $122,500. Officials at Northeast Fence & Iron Works agree with the daily rate; however, they dispute the existence of a cap. Despite the lack of a contractual agreement, Northeast Fence & Iron Works did the work. Believing it had an agreement, Murphy Quigley did not object to this work being done or try to stop it.

Having completed the fencing work, Northeast Fence & Iron Works submits invoices totaling $134,428.30. Murphy Quigley disputes this total and refused to pay. Northeast Fence & Iron Works sues Murphy Quigley. The trial judge decided these parties did not have a contract for the fencing of the recreational yards. The judge did find Northeast Fence & Iron Works was entitled to recover $114,246.06 in damages on a quasi-contract theory to avoid the unjust enrichment of Murphy Quigley. These damages were calculated by taking 15% (the work done by Eagle Fence) from the amount of the submitted invoices.

Murphy Quigley appeals the trial court's judgment.

BOWES, J.: . . . Appellant first suggests that the concept of unjust enrichment is not applicable in this case because the relationship between the parties was founded on a contract. A cause of action for unjust enrichment arises only when a transaction is not subject to a written or express contract. In this case, there was no written contract, and there also was a conflict over the contractual price during the verbal exchange. Both parties agreed on the price of the perimeter fencing and that the recreational yard work would be performed at a per diem rate of $3,500. However, Appellant claimed that there was a contractual maximum cost while Appellee denied this claim.

Thus, the evidence established the existence of a dispute over the contract price, an essential term of a contact, and supported the trial court's refusal to find the existence of an express contract. If no express contract exists between the parties due to the absence of an agreed-upon contract price, a plaintiff may recover under a quasi-contract theory of unjust enrichment. Moreover, the plaintiff can recover under this quasi-contractual theory even when the plaintiff has been partially paid if the benefit conferred on the defendant is greater than the value paid to the plaintiff. Indeed, we recently held that a subcontractor can recover based upon unjust enrichment when it performed work outside the coverage of the parties' contractual provisions.

. . . Appellant recruited Appellee to install the fencing. After the original subcontractor responsible for the work performed by Appellee left the worksite, Appellee was engaged to perform that work on an emergency basis in the face of impending contractual deadlines. . . . Appellant was the general contractor for the construction project at issue herein. Appellee submitted evidence that it performed approximately $134,000 worth of work for which it had not been paid by Appellant. This work clearly benefited Appellant because it satisfied Appellant's contractual obligations to a third party. Appellant thereafter accepted and retained Appellee's work.

. . . The benefit to Appellant was the performance of work at Appellant's request in order to satisfy Appellant's contractual obligation to the prison. Once a benefit is conferred and retained under circumstances where it would be unjust to deny payment, the evidence is sufficient to sustain a verdict based upon this cause of action. . . .

Appellant also alleges that Appellee never proved the value of the fencing because it only submitted

[continued]

invoices. . . . Our review of . . . cases establishes that they do not stand for the proposition that a subcontractor cannot establish the value of a benefit conferred on a contractor through the submission of unpaid invoices. . . .

Appellant also maintains that the trial court should have accepted its unrebutted evidence that the value of the fencing installed by Appellee was about $40,000. Specifically, Appellant contends that it presented unrebutted evidence that it paid "$75,818.82 to Northeast Fence . . . and that it incurred $26,220.14 in damages to repair Northeast Fence's defective work," and in light of this evidence, the damage award of the court cannot be upheld.

The trial court, sitting as factfinder, was free to reject Appellant's evidence of value conferred as not credible. The trial court herein specifically concluded that Appellant's evidence that it had expended money to repair Appellee's work was not worthy of belief. Furthermore, Appellant's evidence of value was indeed rebutted by Appellee, who submitted evidence that the value conferred far exceeded the amount paid. The invoices submitted by Appellee demonstrated that the amount owed, after credit for the amount paid by Appellant, was approximately $134,000. Thus, there was sufficient evidentiary support for the $114,000 damage award rendered by the trial court.

Judgment affirmed.

>> CASE QUESTIONS

1. What is the relationship between the parties in this case?
2. What caused these parties to fail to enter into a binding, express contract?
3. Why does the court conclude that a quasi-contract exists?

6. CONTRACTUAL ENFORCEMENT TERMINOLOGY

Terms used in contract law related to the enforceability of agreements include *enforceable, unenforceable, valid, void,* and *voidable.*

The ultimate purpose of a contract is the creation of an agreement that courts will order parties to perform or to pay consequences for the failure of performance. When courts uphold the validity of such promises, the resulting agreement is an **enforceable contract.** If a nonperforming party has a justifiable reason for noncompliance with a promise, the result is an **unenforceable contract.** In essence, in this latter situation, a defense exists that denies the legal enforcement of an agreement.

Valid contracts are enforceable; void contracts are unenforceable; voidable contracts are enforceable until a party with the right to do so elects to void the agreement.

When an agreement is enforceable because all the essential requirements (discussed in Sections 8–12) are present, courts refer to a **valid contract.** At the other end of the spectrum, a **void contract** is one that appears to be an agreement but lacks an essential requirement for validity and enforceability. The most typical example of a void contract is an apparent agreement that has an illegal purpose. For example, a business contract that involves the shipment of contraband is void and unenforceable. As described in Section 12 in more detail, courts usually refuse to hear arguments of parties to a void contract. Courts simply leave these parties where they are regardless of whether the illegal agreement has been partially or fully performed. Thus, in states where gambling is illegal, a bet on a football game is void. Courts will not enforce the betting agreement and do not care if the losing party has or has not paid off the bet.

A **voidable contract** is an agreement when at least one party has the right to withdraw from the promise made without incurring any legal liability. That party has the power to end the enforcement of a voidable contract. In some cases, a contract is voidable by both parties and either one can withdraw. An interesting aspect of voidable contracts involves the fact that these agreements are enforceable in court until a party with the legal right to do so decides to void the contract, thereby making the agreement unenforceable. Typically this middleground situation arises when a party to the contract lacks capacity or is disadvantaged by specific situations. This existence of voidable contracts is discussed in detail in Section 11 on page 250.

7. CONTRACTUAL PERFORMANCE TERMINOLOGY

In addition to issues related to enforcing contracts in court, the topic of parties performing their commitments is vital to contract law. The key terms related to performance are *executed* and *executory*. An **executed contract** is one in which the parties have performed their promises. When the parties have not yet performed their agreement, it is called an **executory contract.**

Since most business contracts are bilateral in nature involving an exchange of promises by the parties, most contracts are executory at some time. For example, if you promise your new employer to begin working next month and that employer promises to pay you at the end of the first month's work, this employment contract is executory from both parties' perspective.

Contracts cover a multitude of situations and these performance terms may be more or less relevant. Suppose you take a grocery item to the cashier and pay for it. The resulting contract is executed at the time of its creation. In fact, there probably was no exchange of spoken promises. The exchange of money for the item results in the performance being the proof of the contract.

In more complicated business transactions, the performance or lack thereof by one party becomes very important in determining the rights and duties under the contracts. A supplier of raw materials may ship its product and await the buyer's payment. The seller's performance is executed while the buyer's performance remains executory. How these terms impact enforceability issues is a part of the discussion in the next chapter.

>> Contract Formation

How a contract is formed is one of the most important issues to understand about contract law. Many agreements are void, and thus unenforceable, because they lack some essential element of contract formation.

The following sections (8–12) focus on the essential elements and how they come together to form contracts. Before an agreement can become a legally binding contract, someone must make a specific promise to another and also a specific demand of that person. This is the offer. The other person must accept the terms of the offer in the proper way. Both parties must give consideration to the other. Consideration is the promise to give, or the actual giving, of a requested benefit or the incurring of a legal detriment (i.e., doing something one does not have to). Both parties must be of legal age and sound mind, and the purpose of the agreement cannot be illegal or against public policy.

The five essential elements of forming a valid contract:

- Offer
- Acceptance
- Consideration
- Capacity
- Lawful purpose

8. OFFER TO CONTRACT

An **offer** contains a specific promise and a specific demand. "I will pay $15,000 for the electrical transformer" promises $15,000 and demands a specific product in return. An *offeror* (person making the offer) must intend to make the offer by making a commitment to the offeree (the person to whom the offer is made). Many issues about an offer can and do arise. For example, is the language of the offer clear enough to conclude that a valid contract can result? What if a person makes a statement ("I'll give you $100 for a ride to the mall"), intending it as a joke. Is this an offer? Courts answer this question by measuring intent from a reasonable person's perspective in the position of the offeree (person receiving the offer). This standard is known as the objective, rather than the subjective, intent of the offeror.

When does the language used in negotiation become an offer? Suppose a seller asks a potential buyer, "Would you be willing to pay $1,500 for this?" Is this an offer or an invitation to continue negotiating? The answers to these questions relate to the specificity of the language used to state a commitment or willingness to be bound. An offer is much more likely to exist when a seller says, "I am ready to sell this to you for $1,500."

Definite Terms   Under the common law of contracts, contractual terms must be definite and specific. An offer to purchase a house at a "reasonable price" cannot be the basis for a contract because of **indefiniteness.** Most advertisements, catalog, and web page price quotes are considered too indefinite to form the basis for a contract unless they are specific about the quantity of goods being offered, as well as the intended offeree. Otherwise, the retailer would be required to have sufficient stock to supply all readers of the advertisement or face multiple contract breaches.

Sidebar 8.3 presents an interesting case that emphasizes the importance of determining whether or not a definite offer exists.

>> *sidebar* 8.3

Is There a Definite Offer?

Many websites, including those for social networking services, have privacy policies that are separate from the so-called "terms of service" or "terms of use." Although it is generally acknowledged that the terms of service are an attempt to contractually set the conditions for website access, the effect of additional privacy policies is less clear. Is a website operator contractually bound to adhere to its promises to respect privacy? Or are such policies merely an aspirational expression without legal effect?

Interestingly, courts have issued inconsistent rulings in this area. In some cases, they have found that privacy policies are a part of the terms-of-service contract, and that a failure to adhere to the promises constitutes a breach. In other cases, courts have found that the policies are insufficiently definite to provide a basis for fashioning a remedy.

Even in cases where courts find a sufficiently definite offer as well as the intent to contract, damages resulting from any breach must be shown. Without any established monetary loss, the breach of contract claim may fail.

Source: Richard Raysman and Peter Brown, "Contractual Nature of Online Policies Remains Unsettled," *New York Law Journal,* August 10, 2010.

However, under the UCC, contracts for the sale of goods can leave open nonquantity terms to be decided at a future time (§2-305). For example, an agreement for the sale of 500 cameras will bind the parties even though they leave open the price to be decided on delivery in six months. Note that this rule applies only to sales of goods. It does not apply to sales of real estate or services.

Termination of Offer   Offers create a legal power in the offeree to bind the offeror in a contract. However, that legal power does not last forever. When an offer *terminates,* the offeree's legal power to bind the offeror ends. Review carefully Sidebar 8.4 describing various instances when an offer terminates.

Do be very thoughtful in the choice of spoken words; decide whether you are ready to make an offer or want to continue discussions about possible arrangements.

>> *sidebar* 8.4

When an Offer Terminates

By provision in the offer: "This offer terminates at noon Friday."

By lapse of a reasonable period of time if the offer fails to specify a time: What is "reasonable" depends on the circumstances.

By the offeree's **rejection:** "Thank you, but I do not want the flooring you are offering." A **counter-offer** is also a rejection: "Your offer of $10,000 for the land is too low. I will sell it to you for $12,500."

By the offeror's **revocation:** "I regret to inform you that I am withdrawing my offer."

By destruction of the subject matter: The carpet is destroyed by fire before the offer of their sale has been accepted.

By the offeror's death or insanity: Offeror dies before the offer has been accepted.

By the contractual performance becoming illegal: Congress declares that sales of certain computers to Iran are illegal. This terminates an offer to sell the computers to an Iranian trading company.

---

9. ACCEPTANCE OF OFFER

Acceptance of an offer is necessary to create a valid, enforceable contract. An offer to enter into a bilateral contract is accepted by the offeree's making the required promise. When Toni offers Aaron certain vinyl flooring for $2,500 to be delivered by November 30 on 90-day credit terms, and Aaron accepts, Aaron is promising to pay $2,500 on 90-day credit terms.

Unilateral contracts are accepted by performing a requested act, not by making a promise. A company's offer of a $2,500 reward for information leading to the conviction of anyone vandalizing company property is not accepted by promising to provide the information. Only the act of providing information accepts such an offer.

The language of the offer determines whether acceptance should be a promise resulting in a bilateral contract or an act resulting in a unilateral contract. The rights and duties of the contracting party can turn on the form of the acceptance.

244 **PART 3** Legal Foundations for Business

Don't change the terms of the offer unless you want to create a counteroffer.

Between merchants means both parties to a contract do business in the goods being bought and sold.

Other issues relating to the importance of acceptance in the formation of a valid contract are discussed under the following headings.

Mirror Image Rule For an acceptance to create a binding contract, standard contract law requires that the acceptance must "mirror" the offer, that is, must match it exactly. This is the **mirror image rule.** If the acceptance changes the terms of the offer or adds new terms, it is not really an acceptance. It is a *counteroffer,* and negotiations continue. Sidebar 8.5 highlights how in sales of goods contracts the UCC changes this common law principle. To fully understand these UCC provisions, you need to know that special rules apply to merchants. **Merchants** are people who deal in the business of goods.

>> *sidebar* 8.5

UCC's Battle of the Forms

Suppose your company receives a purchase order from a buyer offering to purchase an executive desk and chair for $3,500. This order states the buyer will accept delivery at its company's offices. Your company responds by sending a confirmation form agreeing to the purchase price. However, your form states delivery will be made in two weeks.

Is there a contractual agreement? If so, which terms are used to determine the rights and obligations of the parties?

The UCC changes the mirror image rule. An expression of acceptance or a written confirmation is treated as an acceptance even if such communication adds or changes terms to those stated in the offer. Under the UCC, it appears there is a contract governing the purchase and sale of the desk and chair. The issue now focuses on the different term describing the timing of delivery.

In general, contracts involving the sale of goods treat additional terms as proposals for addition to the contract. When the contract is between merchants, the additional terms become a part of the contract unless one of the following takes place:

1. The offer expressly limits acceptance to the original terms.
2. The proposed terms materially (importantly) alter the contract.
3. The offeror rejects the proposed terms.

Therefore, in the example of the desk and chair, if the buyer does not respond to the confirmation form, a contract exists and the desk and chair should arrive at the buyer's office within two weeks. Do you see how the UCC attempts to facilitate the business transactions? Of course, sometimes parties may not want these gap-filling provisions to complete or govern their contracts. In such situations, clear, specific, and definite language should be used in contract negotiations.

Source: UCC §2-207.

Don't rely on the other party's silence as evidence of acceptance. It can mislead you concerning the existence of a contract.

Silence Not Acceptance In general, an offeree's failure to reject an offer does not imply acceptance. Another way to say this is that silence alone is not acceptance. The offeree has no usual duty to reply to the offer even if the offer states that the offeror will treat silence as acceptance. Note, however, that an *action,* such as using an Internet search engine after having the opportunity to review contractual terms of use, may constitute acceptance.

There are major exceptions to this rule. For instance, parties may have a contract that specifies that future shipments of goods be made automatically unless the offeree expressly rejects them.

A related doctrine looks at the parties' prior *course of dealing*—the way they have done business in the past. Silence may well imply acceptance if the parties previously dealt with each other by having the buyer take shipments from the seller unless the buyer notified the seller in advance not to ship.

Finally, the UCC says that a contract may arise from the *conduct* of a buyer and seller of goods. Emphasis is placed on how the parties act rather than on a formal offer and acceptance of terms.

Mailbox Rule When does the acceptance become legally binding on the offeror? Unless the offeror specifies a particular time, the acceptance usually binds the parties when the offeree dispatches it. Since the offeree frequently mails the acceptance, the acceptance becomes binding when it is "deposited" with the postal service—hence the **mailbox rule,** also called the **deposited acceptance rule.**

The importance of the mailbox rule is that the offeror cannot revoke the offer once the offeree has accepted it. An added significance is that an offeror's revocation is not effective until the offeree actually receives it. Thus, a deposited acceptance creates a binding contract even though a revocation is also in the mail.

Sidebar 8.6 highlights the relevance of the mailbox rule in modern business transactions.

>> *sidebar* 8.6

Is the Mailbox Rule Still Relevant?

Many modern contracts are not accepted though the U.S. Mail or other physical delivery service, but rather through an electronic means like e-mail, fax, or a web page. Is the mailbox rule relevant in any of these situations? In general, the answer is yes. In any case where the contracting parties are not interacting simultaneously, the mailbox rule applies. While the time between an offeree's acceptance and the offeror's receipt is extremely short, the exact point at which acceptance occurs is still governed by the mailbox rule. Although this will often have little impact in electronic transactions, there may be cases where it is important.

Two states employ a modified mailbox rule when the transaction involves computer information, like software. Under the Uniform Commercial Information Transactions Act (UCITA), which only Maryland and Virginia have adopted, acceptance of such contracts is valid only when received.

Source: Valerie Watnick, *The Electronic Formation of Contracts and the Common Law "Mailbox Rule."* 56 Baylor L. Rev. 175 (2004).

As this section and the prior one illustrate, the application of finding the parties' mutual assent to a contract can become complex. Despite the variety of rules associated with offers and acceptances, the purpose of these essential contractual elements remains simple. Case 8.2, involving a very common factual situation, illustrates the basics.

case **8.2** >>

DEFONTES v. DELL, INC.
984 A.2d 1061 (R.I. 2009)

WILLIAMS, C.J.: This litigation began on May 16, 2003, when Mary E. DeFontes, individually and on behalf of a class of similarly situated persons, brought suit against Dell, alleging that its collection of taxes from them on the purchase of Dell optional service contracts violated the Deceptive Trade Practices Act . . . Dell is an international computer hardware and software corporation. Within the Dell corporate umbrella, Dell Catalog and Dell Marketing primarily are responsible for selling computers via the Internet, mail-order catalogs, and other means to individual and business consumers. Dell ships these orders throughout all fifty states from warehouses located in Texas and Tennessee. As part of these purchases, Dell offers consumers an optional service contract for on-site repair of its products, . . . Parties opting to purchase a service contract are charged a "tax," which is either paid to the State of Rhode Island directly or collected by the third-party service provider and then remitted to the state.

. . . Mr. Long purchased his computer through Dell Marketing and opted for a service contract managed by Dell. In total, he paid $3,037.73, out of which $198.73 was designated as tax paid on the service contract. . . . Several months after plaintiffs filed their amended complaint, defendants filed a motion to stay proceedings and compel arbitration, citing an arbitration provision within the parties' purported agreements. . . . The defendants argued that the arbitration provision was part of a "Terms and Conditions Agreement," which they contended plaintiffs had accepted by accepting delivery of the goods. Specifically, they averred that plaintiffs had three separate opportunities to review the terms and conditions agreement, to wit, by selecting a hyperlink on the Dell website, by reading the terms that were included in the acknowledgment/invoice that was sent to plaintiffs sometime after they placed their orders, or by reviewing the copy of the terms Dell included in the packaging of its computer products.

The hearing justice found that although plaintiffs had three opportunities to review the terms, none was sufficient to give rise to a contractual obligation. First, he noted that plaintiffs could have reviewed the terms and conditions agreement had they clicked a hyperlink that appeared on Dell's website. The hearing justice found, however, that this link was "inconspicuously located at the bottom of the web page" and insufficient

to place customers on notice of the terms and conditions. Nevertheless, the hearing justice noted that the terms and conditions agreement also appeared both in the acknowledgment that Dell sent to plaintiffs when they placed their orders and later within the packaging when the computers were delivered . . . .

We therefore evaluate whether plaintiffs are bound by the terms and conditions agreement by resorting to a careful review of the provisions of the U.C.C. Under U.C.C. §2-204, contracts for the sale of goods may be formed "in any manner sufficient to show agreement, including conduct by both parties which recognizes the existence of such a contract." . . .

If contract formation occurred at the moment Dell's sales agents processed the customer's credit card payment and agreed to ship the goods, as plaintiffs argue, then any additional terms would necessarily be treated as "[a]dditional [t]erms in [a]cceptance or [c]onfirmation" under U.C.C. §2-207 . . . or offers to modify the existing contract under U.C.C. §2-209. Yet, the modern trend seems to favor placing the power of acceptance in the hands of the buyer after he or she receives goods containing a standard form statement of additional terms and conditions, provided the buyer retains the power to "accept or return" the product.

. . . After reviewing the case law pertaining to so-called "shrinkwrap" agreements, we are satisfied that the *ProCD* [majority] line of cases is better reasoned and more consistent with contemporary consumer transactions. It is simply unreasonable to expect a seller to apprise a consumer of every term and condition at the moment he or she makes a purchase. A modern consumer neither expects nor desires to wade through such minutia, particularly when making a purchase over the phone, where full disclosure of the terms would border on the sadistic. Nor do we believe that, after placing a telephone order for a computer, a reasonable consumer would believe that he or she has entered into a fully consummated agreement. . . . Rather, he or she is aware that with delivery comes a multitude of standard terms attendant to nearly every consumer transaction.

We therefore decline to adopt the minority view, as urged by plaintiffs, that a contract is fully formed when a buyer orders a product and the seller accepts payment and either ships or promises to ship. Instead, formation occurs when the consumer accepts the full terms after receiving a reasonable opportunity to

[continued]

refuse them. Yet in adopting the so-called "layered contracting" . . . theory of formation, we reiterate that the burden falls squarely on the seller to show that the buyer has accepted the seller's terms after delivery. Thus, the crucial question in this case is whether defendants reasonably invited acceptance by making clear in the terms and conditions agreement that (1) by accepting defendants' product the consumer was accepting the terms and conditions contained within and (2) the consumer could reject the terms and conditions by returning the product.

On the first question, defendants notified plaintiffs that "[b]y accepting delivery of the computer systems, related products, and/or services and support, and/or other products described on that invoice[,] You ('Customer') agrees to be bound by and accepts those terms and conditions." This language certainly informed plaintiffs that defendants intended to bind them to heretofore undisclosed terms and conditions, but it did not advise them of the period beyond which they will have indicated their assent to those terms. The defendants argue that the meaning of the term "accepting delivery" is apparent to a reasonable consumer. We are not so sure. . . . "Acceptance of goods" has a technical meaning not easily discernable to the average consumer. A consumer may believe that simply by opening the package he or she has agreed to be bound by the terms and conditions contained therein. Indeed, many of the courts that have enforced so-called "approve-or-return" agreements cite language informing the consumer of a specific period after which he or she will have accepted the terms. . . . The more problematic issue, however, is whether plaintiffs were aware of their power to reject by returning the goods.

Significantly, the agreement sent to Ms. DeFontes, who is no longer a plaintiff in this case, contained additional language advising her of the method of rejection. . . . That this language is absent in the documents sent to current plaintiffs Mr. Long and Ms. Ricci is troubling and raises the specter that they were unaware of

both their power to reject and the method with which to do so. The introductory provision that purportedly bound plaintiffs does not mention either the "Total Satisfaction Return Policy" or the thirty-day period in which a consumer may exercise his or her right to return the product. Rather, this policy is explained, if at all, in a distinct section of the terms and conditions agreement, which confusingly informed plaintiffs that "Dell Branded Hardware systems and parts that are purchased directly from Dell by an end-user Customer may be returned by Customer in accordance with Dell's 'Total Satisfaction Return Policy' in effect on the date of the invoice." Thus, the consumer is left to construe these provisions together and infer that his or her right to reject the terms extends beyond what would commonly be understood as the moment of delivery. This separate provision not only fails to establish a clear relationship between the consumer's acceptance of the terms by retaining the goods and his or her right to reject the terms by returning the product, but it further obscures the matter by forcing the consumer to refer to a separate document if he or she wants to discover the full terms and conditions of the "Total Satisfaction Return Policy.". . .

In reviewing the language of the terms and conditions agreement it cannot be said that it was reasonably apparent to the plaintiffs that they could reject the terms simply by returning the goods. We believe that too many inferential steps were required of the plaintiffs and too many of the relevant provisions were left ambiguous. We are not persuaded that a reasonably prudent offeree would understand that by keeping the Dell computer he or she was agreeing to be bound by the terms and conditions agreement and retained, for a specified time, the power to reject the terms by returning the product. . . [W]e hold that the hearing justice properly denied the defendants' motion to compel arbitration on the ground that the plaintiffs did not agree to be bound by the terms and conditions agreement . . . .

>> CASE QUESTIONS

1. According to Dell, what were three ways the terms of its "Terms and Conditions Agreement" were delivered to DeFontes and Long? How do they differ in the likelihood that a customer will read them?
2. How did DeFontes and Long allegedly consent to Dell's Agreement?
3. What is the significance of giving customers like DeFontes and Long an opportunity to return the merchandise for a refund?
4. What should Dell have done to make a binding contract?

10. CONSIDERATION

All promises are not enforceable through legal action. There must be some incentive or inducement for a person's promise or it is not binding. The legal mechanism for evaluating the existence of this incentive is **consideration,** the receipt of a legal benefit or the suffering of a legal detriment. Courts will not enforce contractual promises unless they are supported by consideration.

> To be valid, a contract must involve the exchange of consideration between the parties.

Before Laura can enforce a promise made by David, Laura must have given consideration that induced David to make the promise. In a bilateral contract, each party promises something to the other. The binding promises are the consideration. In a unilateral contract, the consideration of one party is a promise; the consideration of the other party is performance of an act. When it is not clear whether there is consideration to support a promise, a court will often examine a transaction as a whole.

Consideration need not be money, though a promise to pay a certain amount is one type of consideration. Valid consideration can include any promise to do something one has no obligation to do, refrain from doing something one has the right to do, or in the case of a unilateral contract, a performance when there is no obligation to do so. That is the definition of a legal detriment.

Must Be Bargained For An important part of consideration is that it must be *bargained for.* Although the amount of consideration is generally not relevant, an insignificant consideration in return for a great one may raise concerns that a real exchange has not occurred. For example, a promise of $1 might be made in return for a promise to convey 40 acres of land. In such situations a court must decide whether the party promising to convey the land really bargained for the $1 or merely promised to make a gift. Promises to make gifts are not binding, because no bargained-for consideration supports the promise.

Similarly, *prior consideration* is no consideration. For instance, after many years of working at Acme Co., Bigman retires as vice president for financial planning. The company's board of directors votes him a new car every year "for services rendered." One year later the board rescinds this vote. If Bigman sues for breach of contract, he will lose. He gave no consideration to support the board's promise. The past years of service were not "bargained for" by the company's board when it took its vote. The board merely promised to give an unenforceable gift to Bigman.

> The phrase "paid in full" placed on a check offered in settlement of a disputed amount acts as an accord and satisfaction if the check is cashed or deposited.

Agreement Not to Sue When reasonable grounds for a lawsuit exist, an agreement not to sue is consideration to support a promise. If Maria is at fault in an automobile accident with Peter, and Peter accepts $100 from Maria as full compensation for his damages on the spot, Peter has been given compensation. He has promised to surrender his legal right to sue Maria.

Likewise, suppose that a consulting firm bills a client $5,000 for 50 hours of work at $100 per hour. The client disputes the bill and contends that the consulting firm worked only 25 hours and should get only $2,500. If the two parties compromise the bill at $3,500 for 35 hours, this agreement binds them both. Each has surrendered the right to have a court determine exactly what amount is owed. Such an agreement and the payment of the $3,500 to resolve a dispute over the amount owed is an **accord and satisfaction.**

Preexisting Obligation A party to an agreement does not give consideration by promising to do something that he or she is already obligated to do. For example, suppose a warehouse owner contracts to have certain repairs done for $20,000. In the middle of construction, the building contractor demands an additional $5,000 to complete the work. The owner agrees, but when the work is finished, he gives the contractor only $20,000. If the contractor sues, he will lose. The owner's promise to pay an extra $5,000 is not supported by consideration. The contractor is under a *preexisting obligation* to do the work for which the owner promises an additional $5,000. If the contractor promises to do something he was not already obligated to do, there would be consideration to support the promise of the additional $5,000. Promising to modify the repair plans illustrates such new consideration.

Sidebar 8.7 discusses how the UCC changes the legal requirement of consideration.

> Many contractual modifications are not enforceable because there is a lack of consideration. If Gerald agrees to paint your house for $2,000 and halfway through the job insists on receiving another $1,000, what consideration would you receive if you agree to pay the additional amount?

>> sidebar 8.7

Consideration Not Necessary

The preexisting obligation rule does not apply to a sale-of-goods contract. The UCC states that parties to a sale-of-goods contract may make binding modifications to it without both parties giving new consideration. If a buyer of more than $500 of supplies agrees to pay your company an additional $500 over and above the amount already promised, this buyer is bound, although your company gives only the consideration (supplies) that it is already obligated to give (§2-209(1)).

Under the UCC, the rules of consideration also do not apply to a **firm offer.** A firm offer exists when a merchant offering goods promises in writing that the offer will not be revoked for a period not to exceed three months. This promise binds the merchant, although the offeree buyer gives no consideration to support it (§2-205).

In contracts that are not between merchants selling goods, a promise to keep an offer open for a certain time period must be supported by the offeree's consideration. Such agreement to not revoke an offer is called an **option.** A typical use of options is found in real estate transactions. A seller of land may promise to let a prospective buyer have two weeks to study the deal and accept the offer at a specific price. The buyer must provide some consideration (usually a small sum of money) to the seller, or the seller's offer is not an enforceable option because it can be revoked.

An important exception to the rule requiring consideration to support a promise is the doctrine of **promissory estoppel.** This doctrine arises when a promisee justifiably relies on a promisor's promise to his or her economic injury. The promisor must know that the promisee is likely to rely on the promise. Promissory estoppel is increasingly used when the facts of a business relationship do not amount to an express or implied contract.

An example arises in situations when an employer promises its employees that they will not be terminated without finding a justifiable cause. Often

> Promissory estoppel often is used to prevent a party who has made a unilateral offer from withdrawing the offer after the requested work has begun.

these types of promises are found in employee handbooks. Courts have ruled that employers cannot withdraw the pledge in a handbook and reinstate the employee-at-will status without their employees receiving some form of consideration.[1] To achieve this change, the employer must explicitly give employees more pay, greater benefits, or some type of inducement.

The extent to which promissory estoppel can create liability for an employer that withdraws a job offer is another common issue. As courts may consider reliance on an at-will job offer to be unjustified, plaintiffs are likely to experience difficulty recovering under this theory.

11. CAPACITY OF PARTIES TO CONTRACT

Capacity refers to a person's ability to be bound by a contract. Courts have traditionally held three classes of persons to lack capacity to be bound by contractual promises:

- Minors (also called "infants").
- Intoxicated persons.
- Mentally incompetent persons.

Don't enter into contracts with minors; they have the power to affirm or void the agreement.

Minors In most states, a *minor* is anyone under age 18. Minors usually cannot be legally bound to contractual promises unless those promises involve *necessaries of life* such as food, clothing, shelter, medical care, and—in some states—education. Even for necessaries, minors often cannot be sued for the contract price, only for a "reasonable" value. In a number of states, courts will hold a minor who has misrepresented his or her age to contractual promises.

A contract into which a minor has entered is voidable at the election of the minor. The minor can *disaffirm* the contract and legally recover any consideration that has been given an adult, even if the minor cannot return the adult's consideration. On the other hand, the adult is bound by the contract unless the minor elects to disaffirm it.

The minor may disaffirm a contract anytime before reaching the age of majority (usually 18) and for a reasonable time after reaching majority. If the minor fails to disaffirm within a reasonable time after reaching majority, the minor is said to *ratify* the contract. In addition, a minor can explicitly ratify a contract and forego disaffirmance, but only after reaching the age of majority. Upon ratification, the minor loses the right to disaffirm.

Intoxicated and Mentally Incompetent Persons Except when a court has judged an adult to be mentally incompetent, that adult does not lose capacity to contract simply because of intoxication or mental impairment. In most cases involving adult capacity to contract, courts measure capacity by whether the adult was capable of understanding the nature and purpose of the contract. Obviously, the more complex a contractual transaction gets, the more likely a court is to decide that an intoxicated or mentally impaired person lacks capacity to contract and has the right to disaffirm the contract. In such factual situations, the contracts are voidable by the intoxicated or mentally impaired person.

[1]*Peters v. Gilead Sciences, Inc.*, 533 F.3d 594 (7th Cir. 2008).

Traditionally, the descriptive phrase *mentally impaired* applies to adults with a history of medically documented disabilities. With the aging of the population, the number of cases involving elderly citizens claiming contractual incapacity grows. These cases will develop additional nuances in the law of capacity to contract. Practical business advice is to be aware when contracting with an elderly person. It may be best to insist that a friend or family member assist (if not cosign with) an older contracting party. Take steps to ensure you will not be accused of taking advantage of the elderly.

Beware of signs that an elderly person may have difficulty understanding the nature of the contractual agreement.

12. LAWFUL PURPOSE

A basic requirement of a valid contract is *legality of purpose*. A "contract" to murder someone is obviously not enforceable in a court of law. Contracts that require commission of a crime or tort or violate accepted standards of behavior (*public policy*) are void. Courts will generally take no action on a void contract, and they will leave the parties to a contract where they have put themselves. Sidebar 8.8 gives a common example of a contract with legality issues.

>> *sidebar* 8.8

Unconscionable Contracts

Contracts that courts find "unconscionable" are unenforceable as illegal. In such cases, it is often said that terms or circumstances that are so unfair that they shock the conscience of the court should not be enforced against the innocent party. One common type of unconscionability involves adhesion contracts. Adhesion contracts are those that are drafted by one party and presented to the other without a substantial opportunity for revision. They include many standard form contracts. In general, adhesion contracts are often enforceable. But, in some cases, a court may find that the lack of negotiation renders such a contract unconscionable, particularly when it contains terms that are severe or detrimental to the non-drafting party.

Contracts involving a sale of goods under the UCC may be found unconscionable when a difference

in bargaining power or education leads a merchant to take unreasonable advantage of a consumer (§2-302).

The U.S. Supreme Court recently addressed the issue of unconscionability in the context of a wireless carrier contract that compelled customers to arbitrate disputes rather than sue in a class action (see Sidebar 5.9 for a more detailed discussion). California, the state in which the contract was signed, has a law that makes such clauses unenforceable. The Supreme Court held that federal law facilitating arbitration, the Federal Arbitration Act (FAA), preempted the California law. If state contract law regarding unconscionability were permitted to apply so broadly, the Court reasoned, it would frustrate the purpose of the FAA.

Source: *AT&T Mobility LLC v. Concepcion*, 131 S. Ct. 1740 (2011).

There are several exceptions to the general rule that courts will take no action on an illegal contract. A contract may have both legal and illegal provisions to it. In such a case, courts will often enforce the legal provisions and refuse to enforce the illegal ones. For instance, a contract providing services or leasing goods sometimes contains a provision excusing the service provider or lessor from liability for negligently caused injury. Courts usually will not enforce this provision but will enforce the rest of the contract.

Often, courts will allow an innocent party to recover payment made to a party who knows (or should know) that a contract is illegal. For example, courts will allow recovery of a payment for professional services made by an innocent person to a person who is unlicensed to provide such services.

In some cases courts may allow a person to recover compensation under quasi-contract for services performed on an illegal contract. Recovery may be allowed when an otherwise qualified professional lets his or her license expire and provides services to a client before renewing the license.

Contracts That Restrain Trade   Contracts that restrain trade often are illegal and void. They include contracts to monopolize, to fix prices between competitors, and to divide up markets. Chapter 16 on antitrust law discusses these contracts and their illegality.

> Any agreement not to compete that you sign must be reasonable in its restrictions on the type of business being prohibited and the time and geography covered.

Other contracts that restrain trade are important to the efficient operation of business. **Covenants not to compete** are important in protecting employers from having the employees they train leave them and compete against them. They also protect the buyer of a business from having the seller set up a competing business.

However, some covenants not to compete are illegal. Courts will declare such agreements illegal unless they have a valid business purpose, such as to protect the goodwill a business buyer purchases from the seller of the business. Covenants not to compete must also be "reasonable as to time and space." If they restrain competition for too long or in an area too large, the courts will declare them unreasonable and void them as being illegal. Four or five years is generally as long a time as the courts are willing to find reasonable, and even then the length of time must be justified. As to space, the courts will void covenants not to compete any time the area restrained exceeds the area in which the restraining business operates.

13. OTHER SITUATIONS INVOLVING VOIDABLE CONTRACTS

> A party disadvantaged by a mutual mistake can void the contract; a party who makes a unilateral mistake suffers the burden of that mistake.

Contracts based on fraud or misrepresentation are two important examples of voidable contracts. **Fraud** involves an intentional misstatement of a material (important) fact that induces one to rely justifiably to his or her injury. Intentionally calling a zircon a diamond and persuading someone to purchase it on that basis is a fraud. Sometimes failures to disclose a material fact can also be a fraud, as when a landowner sells a buyer land knowing that the buyer wishes to build a home on it and does not disclose that the land is underwater during the rainy season. The defrauded party can withdraw from the contract. **Misrepresentation** is simply a misstatement without intent to mislead. However, a contract entered into through misrepresentation is still voidable by the innocent party.

> A person finds a pretty rock while hiking through a field. This person sells the rock to a jeweler for $50. The jeweler honestly did not know what the rock was worth. If this rock turns out to be an uncut gem worth more than $10,000, does the seller have any recourse against the jeweler?

Other examples of voidable contracts are those induced by duress or undue influence. **Duress** means force or threat of force. The force may be physical or, in some instances, economic. **Undue influence** occurs when one is taken advantage of unfairly through a contract by a party who misuses a position of relationship or legal confidence. Contracts voidable because of undue influence often arise when persons weakened by age or illness are persuaded to enter into a disadvantageous contract.

What happens when each party misunderstands something very basic and material about a contract? Such a situation goes right to the heart of whether there has been a "voluntary" consent to a contract. When there is a **mutual mistake** as to a material fact inducing a contract, **rescission** is appropriate. The test of materiality is whether the parties would have contracted had they been aware of the mistake. If they would not have contracted, the mistaken fact is material.

There is a difference between a mutual, or bilateral, mistake and a unilateral mistake. A **unilateral mistake** arises when only one of the parties to a contract is wrong about a material fact. Suppose that Royal Carpet Co. bids $8.70 per yard for certain carpet material instead of $7.80 per yard as it had intended. If the seller accepts Royal Carpet's bid, a contract results even though there was a unilateral mistake.

>> Contract Form

Knowing what elements must exist to form a valid contract is only the beginning of understanding the use of contracts in business transactions. Among the other important topics is whether contracts have to be in writing and signed by the parties. The following sections examine the formality of contracts.

14. WRITTEN VERSUS ORAL CONTRACTS

Because of the importance of contracts in our personal and professional lives, people believe a contract has to be written and signed to be valid. Typically, this impression is wrong. Oral contracts generally are as enforceable as written ones. Think about the agreements you made recently.

- Have you driven through or eaten in a fast-food restaurant?
- Have you been in a store and bought anything?
- Have you purchased something from a vending machine?
- Have you agreed to help someone get some work done in return for that person helping you or giving you something (money or a ride)?

Many of our everyday transactions involve informal contracts. This does not mean we should ignore reasons for greater formality. When contracts are of significant importance or the dollars involved are larger than typical day-to-day transactions or it is important to have a record of the precise agreement, writing and signing a contract is best. In certain situations, the law requires contracts to be in a written, signed format. The next two sections discuss this requirement and explain the types of agreements that must be in writing. The impact of oral changes to written contracts is examined later, in Chapter 9.

> Oral contracts generally are valid and enforceable. Certain types of contracts must be evidenced by a writing that is signed by the party to be bound.

15. STATUTE OF FRAUDS

The law requiring that certain contracts be in writing is known as the statute of frauds. Note, however, that this rule does not address fraud in the formation of a contract. Rather, it is designed to prevent potential deception or fraud from oral contracts. The original English statute was adopted in 1677, and today, every state has its own statute of frauds. The role of these statutes requiring certain written contracts is to minimize confusion in court whenever a party claims a contract is breached. If courts have to decide the validity of an oral agreement, parties can make allegations that contradict one another. One party says to the judge, "We have a contract." The other party says, "We never finalized a contract" or "the terms are different." Judges can have difficulty knowing whom to believe. Written contracts reduce the potential for confusion, fraud, and deceit. If the required writing is not met, the parties are left with an unenforceable contract. The statute of frauds requires certain types of business-related contracts to be in writing. Sidebar 8.9 provides a list of these agreements.

>> *sidebar* 8.9

Types of Contracts Required to Be Evidenced by a Signed Writing

- Contracts involving an interest in land.
- Collateral contracts to pay the debt of another person.
- Contracts that cannot be performed within one year from the date of the agreement.
- Contracts for the sale goods of $500 or more.

Exchange of e-mail messages may satisfy the requirement of a writing.

In some states, the statute of frauds requires that the actual contract between the parties must be in writing. However, most states merely require that the contract be evidenced by writing and be signed by the party against whom enforcement is being sought. This requirement means that the party being sued must have signed a note, memorandum, or another written form short of a formal contract that describes with reasonable certainty the terms of the oral agreement. In sales of goods between merchants, the writing may not need to be signed by the party being sued. Despite these rules, the best practice is to have contracts carefully written and signed. Written documentation will save time and expense if a dispute arises. Chapter 9 provides more detail about how written contracts get interpreted.

Sale of an Interest in Land Sales of interests in land are common contracts covered by the statute of frauds. Although "sales of interests in land" covers a contract to sell land, it includes much more. Interests in land include contracts for mortgages, mining rights, and easements (rights to use another's land, such as the right to cross it with electric power wires). However, a contract to insure land or to erect a building is not an interest in land.

Collateral Promise to Pay Another's Debt A collateral promise is a secondary or conditional promise. Such a commitment arises when one person, a business shareholder for example, promises to repay the loan of the corporation if and only when that organization does not make payments. This collateral promise usually arises at a time different from the original obligation. Suppose the corporation borrows money from a bank and later finds it is having trouble making payments on time. To avoid the bank's calling the entire loan in default, the shareholder may promise to pay if the corporation does not. This promise by the shareholder is of a collateral nature and must be in writing to be enforced by the bank.

To avoid this situation of a collateral promise, banks often require a small business organization to have someone guarantee the performance of its contracts. If a shareholder makes an original promise to be responsible for the corporation's performance, this commitment is not collateral and does not have to be in writing. In essence, in such situations the corporation and the shareholder are considered equally obligated to perform the contract. There is no conditional promise by the shareholder. Although such original promises often are in writing, the law does not require a written agreement.

> Remember the difference between guaranteeing a person's performance and agreeing to become liable if a person fails to perform.

Cannot Be Performed within One Year   The statute of frauds applies to a contract the parties cannot perform within one year after its making. Courts usually interpret the one-year requirement to mean that the contract must specify a period of performance longer than one year. Thus, an oral contract for services that last 20 months or a lease of longer than one year are generally not enforceable. But an oral contract for services to be completed "by" a date 20 months away is enforceable. The difference is that the latter contract can be performed within one year, even if it actually takes longer than that to perform it.

> If it is possible, even if unlikely, to perform a contract within one year, an oral contract involving that performance is enforceable.

As interpreted by the courts, the statute of frauds applies only to executor contracts that the parties' cannot perform within a year. Once one of the parties has completed his or her performance for the other, that party can enforce an oral multiyear contract.

Sale of Goods of $500 or More   Under the UCC, the statute of frauds covers sales of goods of $500 or more. Modifications to such are also included and must be in writing. While this provision appears arbitrary with respect to the $500 amount, its purpose is clear. Contracts involving the sale and purchase of goods that are less than $500 usually are performed quickly. There is very little room for disputes about terms or performance that arise. As the dollar amount increases, the need for a written agreement also increases. This is particularly true if the contract will remain executory (not performed) for an extended period of time. As you think about this requirement in sale of goods transactions, ponder a typical transaction. Assume you go into a computer store and buy a new laptop computer for $1,500. Do you and the seller sign a written contract before completing the purchase? Probably not! The reason is there is no need for a written contract. The agreement to buy and the actual sale occur almost simultaneously—at least in very quick order. Suppose, instead of going to the store, you go online to order a laptop. The online transaction contains information telling you the laptop will be assembled and shipped within three weeks. The paperwork generated through the website likely will include a contract for you to sign electronically. This writing is needed to satisfy the statute of frauds. The written agreement governs the parties' relationship until the contract is performed—you pay and the manufacturer delivers the laptop.

Others   In addition to the basic contracts covered by the statute of frauds, other contracts must be in writing in various states. Most states require insurance policies to be written. Several states require written estimates in contracts for automobile repair.

>> *sidebar* 8.10

Are Electronic Contracts Considered Writings?

When one imagines a "written" contract, one usually has in mind terms printed on paper with handwritten signatures at the end. However, many business transactions that formerly took place face-to-face or through the mail now occur electronically. Is it possible for an electronic exchange to constitute a writing, and if so, can it be signed? The trend in the courts has been to answer in the affirmative: electronic contracts are generally as enforceable as paper contracts. A signature need not be the stylized, handwritten letters of one's name, but merely an indication that a party intends to be bound to the contract. A typed name or even a check-box will usually suffice.

Recent legislation supports the enforceability of electronic contracts. The federal Electronic Signatures in Global and National Commerce Act (ESIGN) ensures that contracts and other documents are not considered invalid solely because they are in electronic form. States have passed similar laws, such as the Uniform Electronic Transactions Act (UETA), which complements ESIGN in guaranteeing that electronic contracts satisfy the writing requirement. Therefore, consider the impact of sending that e-mail message, fax or even text message; a written contract may be the result.

Source: Jay M. Zitter, *Construction and Application of Electronic Signatures in Global and National Commerce Act (E-Sign Act)*, 29 A.L.R. Fed. 2d 519 (2008).

16. EXCEPTIONS TO THE WRITING REQUIREMENT

In addition to understanding that the statute of frauds requires certain types of contracts to be in writing, it is important to know there are exceptions to the writing requirement. If an agreement is orally stated, parties may be able to convince a judge that a contract does exist. If such proof can be established in a way that convinces the judge the contract was agreed upon, there is little chance of fraud. Under certain circumstances, oral contracts are enforceable.

Such exceptions fall into the following categories:

- Part Performance
- Rules Involving Goods
- Judicial Admissions

The part performance exception sometimes is called promissory estoppel.

Part Performance   The doctrine of part performance creates an exception to the requirement that sales of interests in land must be in writing. When a buyer of land has made valuable improvements in it, or when the buyer is in possession of it and has paid part of the purchase price, even an oral contract to sell is enforceable. The courts will enforce an oral agreement involving land title if the part performance clearly establishes the intent of the parties as buyer and seller. If a court can envision the parties in some other relationship, such as landlord and tenant, the part performance is not sufficient to substitute for a written agreement.

Rules Involving Goods   The UCC creates a number of situations that allow the enforcement of oral agreements involving the sale of goods. In essence, the law strives to facilitate transactions involving goods as long as the parties cannot deceive the judge who is asked to determine a contract's validity. Sidebar 8.11 lists exceptions to the writing requirement for transactions involving the sale of goods.

>> *sidebar* 8.11

Exceptions to Statute-of-Frauds Requirement That Sale-of-Goods Contracts Be in Writing

- Contract for goods specially manufacturer for the buyer on which the seller had begun performance.
- Contract for goods for which payment has been made and accepted or that have been received and accepted.
- Contract for goods in which the party being sued admits in court or pleadings that the contract has been made.

- Contract for goods between merchants in which the merchant sued has received a written notice from the other merchant confirming the contract and in which merchant sued does not object to the confirmation within 10 days.

Source: UCC §2–201.

The first exception is known as the specifically manufactured goods rule. If a buyer places an oral order for more than $500 worth of goods that are made especially for this buyer, the seller who has started production on this special order can enforce this agreement to avoid undue hardship. Since the seller would not be able to resell this special goods to other buyers, courts enforce the oral contact. A written confirmation between merchants is another example of how the law facilitates business transactions. A merchant can avoid the impact of this provision by simply noting its objection to any written confirmation within 10 days of receiving it.

Judicial Admissions If one party sues another party for failing to perform promises that are made orally, the defendant might argue the contract cannot be enforced since it must be in writing under the statute of frauds. This defense asks the judge to dismiss the lawsuit. Based on the historical background of the statute of frauds, a judge does not want the burden of deciding which party is telling the truth about the existence or nonexistence of an oral contract. However, if the defendant admits in court or in documents filed in court that an oral contract does exist, the judge does not have to guess about the contract's existence.

This judicial admissions exception is most important when the acknowledged oral contract is for the sale of goods. The UCC explicitly recognizes this exception [2-201(3)(b)]. Does this exception apply when the oral contract involves the sale of an interest in land, a collateral promise to pay another's debt, or performances that cannot be completed in one year? The answer is mixed among the states. Courts in a number of states permit the plaintiff to ask the defendant to admit the oral contract exists. If there is a judicial admission, the statute of fraud-based defense disappears. The judge proceeds to decide whether the oral contract is valid and enforceable.

>> Third Parties' Rights

Parties usually negotiate and enter into contracts for personal or organizational reasons. The purpose of the contractual agreement is to gain a direct benefit. Despite this common practice, sometimes third parties become involved in the performance of the contract. This occurrence could be anticipated by the original contracting parties, or it could arise due to the occurrence of unforeseen circumstances. Regardless of the factual situations, third parties and contract rights provide the focus of the concluding part of this chapter. The next two sections discuss third-party beneficiaries and assignments. The final section examines how a novation impacts the liability of the original contracting parties.

17. BENEFICIARIES

One or more of the original parties to a contract may intend for their agreement to benefit a third party. Such parties are called **third-party beneficiaries.** In general, persons who are not parties to a contract have no rights to sue to enforce the contract or to get damages for breach of contract. However, a third-party beneficiary can sue if the parties to the contract *intended* to benefit that person.

Intended third-party beneficiaries fall into two distinct categories; however, any intended beneficiary has rights to enforce the contract to gain the intended benefit. The first category involves a *creditor beneficiary.* Suppose Carl owes Terry $10,000 for work Terry already has performed. Also assume Carl does work for Chris and contracts to have Chris pay Terry. Terry is a creditor beneficiary of the Carl–Chris contract and can sue Chris for the payment owed.

When the performance under a contract is meant as a gift to a third party, that person is a *donee beneficiary.* Donee beneficiaries can sue the party who owes them a performance under a breached contract, but they cannot sue the party who contracted to make them a gift. The beneficiary of a life insurance policy is usually a donee beneficiary.

An *incidental beneficiary* is a third party who unintentionally benefits from a contract. The incidental beneficiary has no rights under a contract. If merchant A contracts to have security service patrol her property—a contract that will likely also protect the other merchants on the block—and if one evening when the service fails to show up merchant B on the block is burglarized, B cannot sue the security service for breach of contract. B is only an incidental beneficiary of the contract between A and the service.

> You are a donee beneficiary if a parent buys a car for you. If the seller does not deliver the car, you can sue.

18. ASSIGNMENT OF CONTRACTS

Contracts often are thought as involving only two parties—the offeror and the offeree. In business, such a view is overly simplistic. Contracts may involve many original parties and sometimes third parties who are not a part of the negotiation resulting in the original contract. This section discusses how these third parties become involved in the contract's performance through the process of assignment.

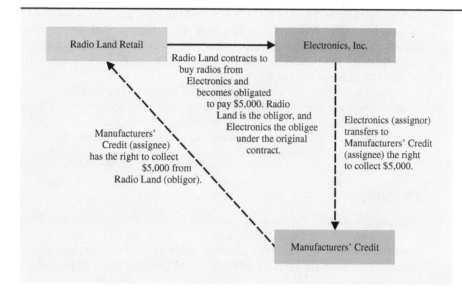

Figure 8.3
Assignment

Electronics, Inc., sells 250 radios on credit at $20 apiece to Radio Land Retail. Electronics then sells its rights under the contract to Manufacturers' Credit Co. When payment is due, can Manufacturers' Credit legally collect the $5,000 owed to Electronics by Radio Land? This transaction is controlled by the law of **assignment,** which is a transfer (generally a sale) of rights under a contract. Figure 8.3 shows the transaction and introduces important terminology.

As Figure 8.3 illustrates, in an assignment one of the original contracting parties becomes an **assignor** and assigns rights or duties or both to a third party, known as the **assignee.** If the assignment is properly structured, the assignee can enforce the original contract. When an assignor assigns rights, an implied warranty is made that the rights are valid and enforceable. If the assignee is unable to enforce the rights against the obligor because of illegality, incapacity, or breach of contract, the assignee can sue the assignor for breach of the implied warranty. However, if the obligor simply refuses to perform for the assignee, the assignee's legal claim is against the obligor, not the assignor.

Notice of Assignment   When an assignment is made, an assignee should notify the obligor immediately. Otherwise, the obligor may perform for the obligee-assignor. If Radio Land pays Electronics before being notified by Manufacturers' Credit of the assignment, Radio Land cannot be held liable to Manufacturers' Credit.

A dishonest or careless assignor may assign the same contract rights to two different assignees. Notification of the obligor is especially important in this situation. In most states, the law says that the first assignee to notify the obligor has priority no matter which assignee receives the first assignment of rights.

The order of multiple assignments is not as important as when an assignee gives notice that an assignment occurred.

Contracts That Cannot Be Assigned   Although most contracts can be assigned, certain ones cannot. An assignment that increases the burden of performance to the obligor cannot be assigned. For instance, a right to

260   **PART 3**   Legal Foundations for Business

have goods shipped to the buyer's place of business cannot be assigned by an Atlanta buyer to a Miami buyer if a New York seller has to ship the goods to Miami instead of Atlanta. Similarly, a *requirements contract* to supply a retail buyer with all the radios needed cannot be assigned because it depends upon the buyer's personal situation.

Most states regulate the assignment of wages. They limit the amount of wages a wage earner can assign to protect wage earners and their families.

A party to a contract cannot assign (delegate) performance of duties under a contract when performance depends on the character, skill, or training of that party. Otherwise, duties under a contract can be assigned as well as rights.

19. NOVATIONS

Typically, an assignor who delegates duties under a contract is not automatically relieved of future liability. In your current role as a student, suppose you find someone to take your place on your lease of an apartment or house. Assume you have six months left under the original term of the lease when you assign rights and delegate duties to the friend substituting for you. If the friend moves out and stops paying rent after only two months, you are still liable to the landlord for the last four months of rent. How can you avoid this lingering responsibility? The answer lies in understanding the impact of a novation. A **novation** is a three (or more) party contract wherein the original contracting parties agree to relieve the obligor from liability by substituting an assignee in the place of this party. For example, in your landlord-tenant-friend situation, when you have your friend take your place, you could seek an agreement with the landlord to remove you from the lease and to make your friend liable for the remainder of the lease period. This arrangement is a novation. Such agreements usually are found in business contracts when an organization is acquired through purchase or merger transactions.

>> Key Terms

>> Review Questions and Problems

Basic Concepts

1. *Contract Law in Private Enterprise*

   Discuss the importance of contract law to the private market system. How does contract law provide flexibility and precision in business dealings?

2. *Sources of Contract Law*

   (a) What is meant by the common law of contracts? *→ promise*

   (b) What is the UCC? *→ both promise → invitation to perform*

Contractual Classifications and Terminology

3. *Bilateral and Unilateral Contracts*

   (a) What is the distinction between a bilateral and a unilateral contract?

   (b) Which type is more common in business? *~ bil*

4. *Express and Implied-in-Fact Contracts*

   (a) Using an instance in which you bought or sold something in the last week describe the terms of an express contract that might arise between the supplier and the seller.

   (b) When would an implied-in-fact contract arise between the seller and a buyer? *→ Dentist*

5. *Implied-in-Law or Quasi-Contracts*

   Why are courts willing to apply contractual principles when the parties <u>fail to create</u> contractual relationships? *→ judicial remedy to prevent one party from receiving unjust enrichment.*

6. *Contractual Enforcement Terminology*

   How can someone reasonably say that a voidable contract is both enforceable and unenforceable?

7. *Contractual Performance Terminology*

   Pat hires a tailor to make a suit. The tailor completes all the sewing and now waits for Pat to pick up the suit and pay for it. Is this contractual agreement executed or executory? Explain. *not paid*

Contract Formation

8. *Offer to Contract*

   Condor Equipment Company offers to sell a dough cutting machine to Snappy Jack Biscuits, Inc. The offer states: "This offer expires Friday noon." On Thursday morning, the sales manager for Condor calls the president of Snappy Jack and explains that the machine has been sold to another purchaser. Discuss whether Condor has legally revoked its offer to Snappy Jack.

9. *Acceptance of Offer*

   Fielding Bros. offers to ship six furnaces to Central City Heating and Cooling Co. for $4,500 cash. Central City accepts on the condition that Fielding give 120 days' credit. Has a contract resulted? Explain.

10. *Consideration*

    Jefferson and Goldberg enter a contract for the sale of five acres of land at $10,000 per acre. Later, Goldberg, the buyer, asks if Jefferson will agree to modify the contract to $9,000 per acre.

    (a) Jefferson agrees. Is Jefferson's promise binding on him?

    (b) Would your answer be different if five used cars were being sold instead of five acres of land?

11. *Capacity of Parties to Contract*

    Describe the circumstances under which an adult lacks the capacity to contract.

12. *Lawful Purpose* *minority*

    Hunt signs an equipment lease contract with Edwards Rental. The contract contains a clause stating: "Lessor disclaims all liability arising from injuries caused by use of this equipment."

Because the equipment has been improperly serviced by Edwards Rental, Hunt is injured while using it. If Hunt sues, will the disclaimer clause likely be enforced? Explain.

13. *Other Situations Involving Voidable Contracts*

Laura removes the airbags from a used car, and then offers to sell the car to David without disclosing the removal. David agrees to purchase the used car without asking any questions about the airbags or investigating whether they are present. Upon discovering the missing airbags one day later, David is upset. State whether this situation involves fraud, misrepresentation, mutual mistake or unilateral mistake and explain your answer.

Contract Form

14. *Written versus Oral Contracts*

(a) In general, are oral contracts as valid and enforceable as written ones?

(b) Why should contracting parties consider reducing their agreement to writing?

15. *Statute of Frauds*

(a) Explain the purpose of requiring certain types of contracts to be in writing.

(b) List four types of contracts covered by the traditional statute of frauds.

16. *Exceptions to the Writing Requirement*

Elegante Haberdashery telephones an order to Nordic Mills for 500 men's shirts at $15 each. Each shirt will carry the Elegante label and have the Elegante trademark over the pocket. After the shirts are manufactured, Elegante refuses to accept delivery of them and raises the statute of frauds as a defense. Discuss whether this defense applies to these facts.

Third Parties' Rights

17. *Beneficiaries*

What is the distinction between an intended and an incidental beneficiary?

18. *Assignment of Contracts*

Franchetti Rifle Distributors assigns a $20,000 claim against Top Gun, Inc., to the Zenith Collection Agency. When Zenith sues Top Gun, Top Gun asserts that it rejected a shipment of rifles from Franchetti out of which the claim arose because they had defective trigger guards. Explain whether Top Gun can properly assert its defense against plaintiff Zenith.

19. *Novations*

Explain the purpose of a novation and who must be party to it.

business >> *discussion*

You are the Marketing Manager for We-Can-Furnish-It Office Supply Company. In your role, you work with your company's sales staff. This staff is divided between personnel who travel to make face-to-face calls and those who answer the phones and accept orders during these conversations. In addition to the sales staff, you also are responsible for the technicians that ensure online orders can be placed and filled.

The transactions with customers range from supplying an entire office building with furniture and everything that allows an office to function to delivering small amounts of basic office supplies. As you study the documentation, including purchase order forms and confirmation statements, of these various transactions, you wonder about the answers to the following questions:

When does the negotiation end and a binding contract exist?
If there is conflicting language in the buyer's purchase order and the seller's confirmation, which language controls?
How can you determine when a contract has been performed fully?

Chapter 9. Contractual Performance & Agency

9

Contractual Performance and Agency

Learning Objectives

In this chapter you will learn:

9-1. To understand how courts interpret contracts.

9-2. To identify when contract performance duties arise.

9-3. To understand how contractual duties are discharged.

9-4. To understand that nonperformance of contracts results in a breach unless performance is excused.

9-5. To predict the consequences of a breach of contract.

9-6. To describe the authority of agents to act on behalf of a principal in contracts and beyond.

In the preceding chapter, you studied the basics of contract terminology and classifications. You learned about the essential elements and form required to create a valid, enforceable contract. Finally, you read about how contracts impact third parties.

In this chapter, your study of contracts continues as you learn about the performance of contracts and the consequences of breach. In addition, you will learn the basic principles of agency authority related to contracts and other legal contexts. These topics are of critical importance to businesspeople. After studying this chapter, you should have answers to the following questions:

- Are there rules that businesspeople should know that determine what contract language means?

- How do parties (and courts) decide if promises in a contract have been fully performed?
- What happens if a contract is not fully performed?
- What authority do agents have to bind a party to a contract?

>> Interpretation of Contracts

If each party is satisfied with the other's performance under a contract, there is no problem with interpreting the contract's terms. But when disagreement about what a term means, or whether additional promises were made, interpretation often becomes necessary. How do we decide who is right?

One of the most important contract interpretation principles is that courts decide what a contract means. The meaning of a contract is a "question of law," which means that a judge makes the final determination. However, depending on the circumstances and issues, that determination may require factual information from the parties or other witnesses. To guide their interpretation, courts use established rules designed to reduce ambiguity in a predictable manner. Understanding these rules can ensure that a contract is not interpreted differently than you predict.

1. RULES OF INTERPRETATION

In the interpretation of contract terms, handwriting is the best evidence of intention.

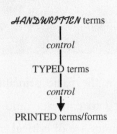

Common words are given their usual meaning. "A rose is a rose is a rose," said the poet, and a court will interpret this common word to refer to a flower. If the meaning of the word is clear on the face of the contract, courts will usually reject a party's attempt to reinterpret it later. However, if there is evidence that a word has a particular *trade usage,* courts will give it that meaning. In a contract in the wine trade, the term *rose* would not refer to a flower at all but to a type of wine.

Many businesses today use printed form contracts. Sometimes the parties to one of these printed contracts type or handwrite additional terms. What happens when the typed or handwritten terms contradict the printed terms? What if the printed terms of a contract state "no warranties," but the parties have written in a 90-day warranty? In such a case, courts interpret handwritten terms to control typed terms and typed terms to control printed ones. The written warranty will be enforced since the writing is the best evidence of the parties' true intention.

Another rule is that when only one of the parties drafts (writes) a contract, courts will interpret ambiguous or vague terms against the party that drafts them. Courts often apply this rule to the adhesion contracts discussed in Chapter 8 as well as insurance contracts and interpret the contract to give the non-drafting party the benefit of the doubt when deciding the meaning of a confusing term or phrase.

Case 9.1 illustrates how important a court's interpretation of contractual language is in determining the rights of the parties.

case **9.1** >>

CITIBANK, N.A. v. MORGAN STANLEY & CO. INTERNATIONAL, PLC
724 F. Supp. 2d 398 (S.D.N.Y. 2010).

The following case involves one of the most complex transactions in modern business, the credit default swap. This is an agreement in which one party promises to cover the losses of another in the event of a default on credit extended for a security. In exchange for this promise, the other makes payments, similar to an insurance contract. The losses covered can be quite large, and the consequence of default can be severe on the party offering coverage. As you probably know, credit default swaps played a significant role in the recent financial crises. However, at base, credit default swaps are contracts. When there is a dispute as to the meaning of the agreement, courts must use the same rules of contract interpretation that apply in more mundane situations.

The specific question before the court was whether Citibank breached the terms of a credit default swap it entered into with Morgan Stanley & Co. Internationals, PLC (MSIP) in 2006. In order to insure against losses from $366 million extended as credit to another firm called Capmark, Citibank entered into a default swap with MSPI for a payment of approximately $750,000. When Capmark defaulted in 2008, Citibank acted by liquidating Capmark's security to make up for the original debt. However, the liquidation fell short by over $246 million. According to the default swap agreement, MSIP was liable for the shortfall. MSIP argued that it was not liable for that amount because Citibank liquidated the security without first obtaining MSIP's consent as required by the contract. To determine whether consent was necessary, the court considered the terms of the credit default swap contract.

SCHEINDLIN, J.: This dispute can be resolved by reference solely to the contractual documents properly considered by the Court on this motion—the Indenture, Credit Agreement, and Swap with MSIP's admissions. Allegations and evidence extrinsic to the contractual documents, therefore, have not been considered . . .

It is undisputed that the consent rights MSIP asserts Citibank violated derive exclusively from section 6(d) of the Swap Confirmation. . . . MSIP

argues that when Citibank ordered liquidation of the Capmark VI CDO, Citibank provided a "consent of or with respect to" the Revolving Facility, thereby implicating MSIP's rights under section 6(d). Citibank counters that it did not provide a consent under section 6(d) but rather issued a "direction" pursuant to the Indenture. . . . Thus, the parties' cross motions boil down to whether Citibank's conduct implicated MSIP's consent rights under section 6(d).

MSIP admits that Citibank, in its role as Administrative Agent of the Revolving Facility, *directed* the Trustee to liquidate the Collateral. . . . Nonetheless, MSIP cites to section 6.07 of the Credit Agreement and argues that Citibank, in its role as Lender to the Revolving Facility, provided a consent pursuant to section 6(d).

MSIP argues that because this provision requires the Administrative Agent (i.e., Citibank) to obtain "authorization" before ordering the liquidation of the Capmark VI CDO, Citibank was required to *authorize* itself to take such action. Thus, according to MSIP, when Citibank caused the Trustee to liquidate the Collateral, it occurred in two separate steps: *First,* Citibank, as Lender, *authorized* itself, as Administrative Agent, to direct the Trustee. *Second,* Citibank, as Administrative Agent, *directed* the Trustee to undertake the liquidation. MSIP further argues that because the definition of "consent" in section 6(d) includes "authorisation," . . . when Citibank, as Lender, *authorized* the liquidation of the Capmark VI CDO, Citibank provided the *consent* that triggered MSIP's rights under section 6(d).

Even assuming that section 6.07 is applicable—a point Citibank does not concede . . .—MSIP's linguistic gymnastics and strained reasoning is not persuasive. First, I reject MSIP's focus on Citibank's two roles under the Credit Agreement. That Citibank was required to consent to or authorize its own action makes no sense. Because Citibank was always the sole Lender to the Revolving Facility, Citibank was always the only principal for which it was acting as Administrative Agent. Thus, under the circumstances, Citibank was simultaneously sole Lender, Controlling Class, and Administrative Agent. As such, MSIP's admission that Citibank

[continued]

directed the liquidation as Administrative Agent is tantamount to an admission that Citibank did nothing but issue a direction, which is fatal to MSIP's position.

Nor do I accept MSIP's attempt to read "direction" to fall within the definition of "consent" by way of "authorization" and "authorisation." Not only is "direction" conspicuously absent from the plain terms of section 6(d), "direction" is also not included within the definition of "consent" found in the Master Agreement. The fact that "consent" includes "authorisation" under the Master Agreement does not mean or imply that every method of "authorisation" is a "consent." Indeed, the plain language of section 6.07 makes clear that "authorization" may be effected by either a consent *or* a direction.

Furthermore—and as section 6.07 itself demonstrates—the contractual documents at issue here repeatedly distinguish between the words "direction" (or "direct") and "consent." . . . This is not surprising given that the two words have different meanings: while "consent" is a word of acquiescence, "direction" is a word of action. . . . Similarly, "authorization" and "direction" are also utilized differently in the contracts . . . —a distinction recognized in New York law.

If these highly sophisticated parties truly intended "consent" to include "direction" via "authorization" or "authorisation", they could and would have so provided. To merge these terms as if they were one would render meaningless the distinction between them.

In sum, Citibank's issuance of a direction under the Indenture did not implicate MSIP's consent rights under section 6(d) of the Swap Confirmation. Therefore, Citibank was permitted to direct the liquidation of the Capmark VI CDO without acquiring MSIP's prior written consent. MSIP's attempt to introduce ambiguity where there is none cannot prevent this result.

For the reasons stated above, Citibank's motion for judgment on the pleadings and for dismissal of MSIP's original counterclaims is granted. MSIP's motion for judgment on the pleadings is denied. . . .

>> CASE QUESTIONS

1. What obligation did MSIP argue Citibank breached, and what did MSIP believe should be the result?
2. What evidence did the court use to determine the meaning of the contract?
3. Why did the court find MSIP's suggested interpretation unpersuasive?
4. How could the parties have drafted an agreement that required MSIP's explicit consent before liquidation?

2. THE PAROL EVIDENCE RULE

The parol evidence rule prohibits testimony about the oral negotiation that results in a written contract; thus, read the contract before signing.

Like the statute of frauds, the **parol evidence rule** influences the form of contracts. This rule states that parties to a complete and final written contract cannot introduce oral evidence in court that changes the intended meaning of the written terms.

The parol evidence rule applies only to evidence of oral agreements made at the time of or prior to the written contract. It does not apply to oral modifications coming after the parties have made the written contract (although the statute of frauds may apply).

Suppose that Chris Consumer wants to testify in court that a merchant of an Ultima washing machine gave him an oral six-month warranty on the machine, even though the $450 written contract specified "no warranties." If the warranty was made after Chris signed the contract, he may testify about its existence. Otherwise, the parol evidence rule prevents him from testifying about an oral agreement that changes the terms of the written contract.

An exception to the parol evidence rule allows evidence of oral agreement that merely explains the meaning of written terms without changing the terms. Also, oral evidence that changes the meaning of written terms can be given if necessary to prevent fraud.

>> Performance

LO 9-2

The fundamental reason any of us enter into a contract is to assure the performance of the promise made or to secure the performance of the action desired. What we want is the other party's **duty of performance.** In turn, they want this same duty to be performed by us. An extremely high percentage of contracts are performed in such a way that makes the contracting parties happy. Thus, the most simple (and realistic) statement concerning performance of contracts is that it typically happens. When the parties perform, the obligations of the contract are discharged. A party to a contract is **discharged** when that party is relieved from all further responsibility of performance.

However, not all contractual obligations are fully performed. When less than full performance occurs, a number of legal issues arise. For example, a complete lack of performance results in a breach of the contract. As summarized in Figure 9.1, less than full performance results in issues about the level of performance and excuses for nonperformance. As you study this figure and read the next sections, keep in mind that contracting parties ultimately arrive at one of two conclusions: (1) they are discharged from the obligation to perform further or (2) they are liable for breaching the contract.

3. CONDITIONS OF PERFORMANCE

Parties typically put conditions in their contracts to clarify when performance is due. While conditions reflect the creativity of the contracting parties, classifications of conditions usually take three forms.

If something must take place in the future, before a party has a duty to perform, it is a **condition precedent.** For example, a building developer may contract to buy certain land "when the city annexes it." The annexation is a condition precedent to the developer's duty to purchase the land. Parties should think through their business environment and state clearly the conditions governing their performance. For example, in a supplier-customer contract, the parties should state whether payment by the customer is a condition precedent for the seller to deliver or is delivery by the seller a condition precedent for payment.

A **condition subsequent** excuses contractual performance if some future event takes place. A marine insurance policy might terminate coverage for any shipping losses "if war is declared." This is a condition subsequent. Another typical example of this type of condition is the requirement that an insured motorist or homeowner must notify the insurance company

As an employee, you usually have a responsibility to work for a certain amount of time (equivalent to a pay period) before your employer is obligated to pay you. You are entitled to be paid before working the next period. The performance of work is a condition to be paid, and receiving your pay is a condition for you to continue working. Do you see how contractual conditions govern performance?

Figure 9.1 Contractual performance flow chart

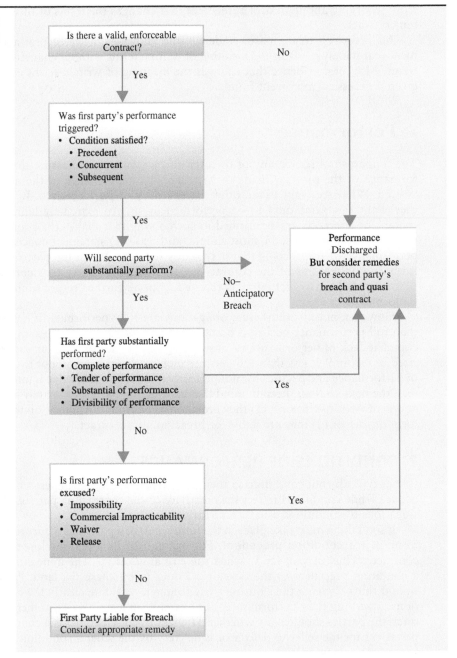

of a claim (from a car accident or homeowner's loss) within a short time period (five days perhaps) of the claim arising from the accident of the loss. Failure to provide this notice relieves the insurance company of its duty to provide coverage.

The distinction between conditions precedent and conditions subsequent can appear quite subtle. The key difference is found in the timing of the duty to perform. A contracting party has no duty to perform prior to a condition precedent being satisfied. Once the condition precedent is met, the duty to perform is owed. The failure to meet a condition subsequent relieves the other contracting party from having to perform the duties previously promised.

What happens if the parties do not have **express conditions** governing performance specified in their contract? Courts may be asked whether **implied conditions** can be read into the parties' obligations to perform. When courts decide the conditions of performance, a common decision can be the parties have a simultaneous duty to perform. In essence, there is a **concurrent condition** of performance. In a contract for the transfer of title to land, the buyer and seller usually expect to meet at a closing event and perform their obligations concurrently. The buyer provides the necessary funds to cover the purchase price while, at the same time, the seller signs and delivers the legal documents transferring ownership.

Most of our everyday purchases involve implied concurrent conditions of performance. While shopping you take items to a cashier and expect to pay and take the items with you. Your contractual duty to pay and the store's contractual duty to deliver are exchanged simultaneously. As business contracts often involve more complicated transactions, issues related to performance require further examination.

> Employers required to notify their insurance companies of claims by employees should provide this notice when an employee files a claim of discrimination with the EEOC.

4. PAYMENT, DELIVERY, SERVICES TENDERED

The preceding sections' content on conditions allows us to examine more fully the order of performance by the parties. Performance often is based on one or more conditions occurring or being satisfied. For example, in a typical contract involving the delivery of goods by a seller and payment of money by a buyer, what is the required order of performance? In essence, who goes first? The best way to answer these questions is to have the contracting parties provide specific guidance in the contract. When the parties fail to provide this level of detail, the law states the buyer's payment is a condition that must be satisfied before the seller has the duty to deliver (§2-511(1)).

Delivery is a legal term referring to the transfer of possession from the seller to the buyer. The buyer and seller may presume to know implicitly how and when the goods will be delivered. Sidebar 9.1 illustrates how the UCC serves as a gap-filler, thereby not leaving the terms of delivery of goods to the parties' uncertain presumptions.

Performance of contractual obligations presents parties and courts with legal issues. The resolution of these issues often requires analysis of principles relating to formation as well as performance of contracts. Case 9.2 involves a typical business transaction. Notice how the court examines the questions of which party made the offer and which one accepted it. The conclusion of this formation issue impacts which party has failed to perform.

The UCC provides valuable guidance to performance issues in contracts for the sales of goods. However, when a contract involves the performance of services, the parties to the contract should take time to provide specific conditions. If their agreement lacks specificity, reasonableness needs to

>> *sidebar* 9.1

Terms of Delivery in the UCC

Suppose your company sells office equipment to a buyer. Further suppose that the contract carefully describes the equipment and the purchase price. However, the contract provides no specific guidance as to when or where the equipment is to be delivered.

The UCC permits and encourages the enforceability of this contract by providing a series of gap-filling provisions. In essence, if the parties fail to write clear instructions on delivery of the equipment, the UCC controls.

The seller's obligation is to tender delivery of the goods, and the buyer's duty is to accept and pay for them (§2-301). The phrase *tender of delivery* means the seller must make the goods available to the buyer. If, as in our example, the contract makes no statement about delivery, the presumption is the buyer must make arrangements to pick up the goods at the location the seller designates (§2-503(1)).

Many buyers may not want to assume the burden of picking up the goods at the seller's location.

Thus, it is common for the buyer and seller to agree the goods will be shipped to the buyer. If the contract does not provide additional details, how does the seller satisfy its obligation to ship the goods? The UCC states the seller satisfies its obligation to ship goods once they are transferred to the shipper for transportation (§2-504). If the goods are damaged in transit, the liability rests on the buyer, not the seller.

To avoid the assumption of risk, experienced buyers may insist on what is called a destination contract. This contract requires the seller to get the goods shipped and delivered to a specific place of business designated by the buyer. The risk of loss for damage to the goods remains with the seller until the goods safely arrive at the buyer's destination (§2-310(1)(b)).

Do you now see why negotiation over the terms of performance, such as shipment and delivery, should be so important to your company?

govern the relationship and performance. For example, let's assume your manufacturing company hires software consultants to oversee the installation and implementation of new programs that hopefully will enhance your overall efficiency. The contract specifies the date for the completion of this work by the consultants; however, the contract does not provide a beginning date.

 case **9.2** >>

VENTURE MEDIA LIMITED PARTNERSHIP v. COLT PLASTICS COMPANY, INCORPORATED
168 F. 3d 484 (4th Cir. 1999)

PER CURIAM: . . . Venture sells cosmetic products through direct-response marketing. Colt manufactures and sells plastic containers for cosmetic products.

In 1994, Venture approached Colt seeking to purchase plastic containers for its line of cosmetic products. Meetings were held between representatives of both Colt and Venture. . . . When all of these issues were settled, Venture began placing orders with Colt.

In its business, Colt uses a number of forms including a Quotation/Proposal Form (Proposal Form) and an Invoice Form (Invoice). . . .

[continued]

Between 1994 and September 1995, Venture ordered from Colt, and Colt manufactured and shipped, plastic containers for Venture's cosmetic products. . . . Venture placed orders with Colt using a purchase order. After manufacturing and shipping the plastic containers requested in the various purchase orders, Colt sent an Invoice to Venture requesting payment. The Invoice stated that payment was "due 30 days from the Invoice date," and "amounts 30 days past due [were] subject" to twelve percent annual interest. This period of time passed with the two companies transacting without incident.

However, in August and early September 1995, Venture felt as if there were problems. The deliveries were arriving late, and Colt refused to increase Venture's line of credit. To resolve these issues, Venture requested a meeting with Colt. At this meeting, Colt assured Venture it would resolve the concerns raised by Venture.

Based on these assurances, on September 21, 1995, Venture sent a purchase order to Colt for plastic containers totaling $339,996.25. The purchase order specified exact quantities, exact prices for each quantity, and the total price. In addition, the purchase order explicitly specified the location where the products should be shipped and stated: "Please notify us immediately if this order cannot be shipped complete on or before 11/03/95." Colt never sent an acknowledgment to Venture but began to manufacture the plastic containers requested in the purchase order.

Between late February and early March 1996, Colt shipped plastic containers aggregating $47,922.18 to Venture in a series of shipments. Colt also sent Invoices for each shipment to Venture. Venture never paid Colt for these deliveries and did not give notice to Colt of any defects in the delivered goods within the thirty-day period required by the Proposal Form. Colt continued to manufacture plastic containers totaling $122,799.59 after the deadline date for delivery specified in Venture's purchase order. Because of the outstanding balance owed by Venture, Colt never shipped these plastic containers to Venture. Colt sold what it could of these products to third parties, but because these plastic containers were specially manufactured for Venture, they were difficult to sell on the open market. Consequently, Colt continues to hold in its inventory $108,793.84 in plastic containers manufactured for Venture.

On December 30, 1996, Venture filed this suit against Colt in the Circuit Court of Maryland for Baltimore County alleging breach of contract. . . . Colt removed the case to the United States District Court for the District of Maryland based on diversity jurisdiction. Colt filed a counterclaim alleging breach of contract and seeking $47,922.18 plus interest for the plastic containers sent to Venture and $108,793.84 for the plastic containers specially manufactured for, but not sent to Venture.

Both parties moved for summary judgment with respect to all claims. The district court granted Colt's motion for summary judgment, and therefore, entered judgment in favor of Colt on Venture's claims and on Colt's counterclaim. . . . On appeal, Venture contends the district court erred when it granted summary judgment in favor of Colt. . . .

The parties agree that a contract existed for the sale of plastic containers amounting to $339,996.25, but vigorously dispute which terms control the sale. According to Venture, a $339,996.25 contract for plastic containers was formed when it sent its purchase order to Colt and Colt began to manufacture the plastic containers. Venture further maintains that Colt breached the contract by: (1) delivering defective plastic containers; (2) delivering damaged plastic containers; (3) failing to deliver the plastic containers by the agreed upon dates; (4) failing to extend Venture a volume purchase discount; and (5) failing to extend Venture's line of credit. In response, Colt contends that a $339,996.25 contract for plastic containers was formed when Colt sent its Proposal Form to Venture and Venture sent its purchase order to Colt. According to Colt, Venture breached the contract when it failed to make payment for the plastic containers that were manufactured and delivered to Venture. Colt further maintains that it never breached its contract with Venture because the plain language of the Proposal Form disposes of Venture's breach of contract allegations.

The district court granted summary judgment in favor of Colt on Venture's breach of contract claim, concluding that a contract was formed when Colt sent the Proposal Form to Venture and Venture sent the purchase order for $339,996.25 of plastic containers to Colt. Further, the district court concluded that Venture breached the contract when it failed to make payment for the plastic containers that Colt manufactured and delivered to Venture. Finally, the district court concluded that Colt did not breach its contract with Venture because the plain language of the Proposal Form was dispositive of Venture's breach of contract allegations. . . .

Under Maryland common law, an offer is "a expression by the offeror . . . that something over which he at least assumes to have control shall be done or happen or shall not be done or happen if the conditions stated in the offer are complied with." An offer must be definite and certain. Further, the intention of the parties is one of the primary factors when deciding whether an offer was made. Therefore, the facts and circumstances of each particular case are crucial.

[continued]

In this case, Colt's Proposal Form was an offer. From 1994 through September 1995, Venture placed purchase orders with Colt for various plastic containers. Throughout this period, Colt sent numerous Proposal Forms to Venture. The Proposal Form explicitly sought acceptance by means of a purchase order. In conformity with this condition, Venture placed all of its orders by means of purchase order. Venture always abided by Colt's terms and never objected to them. Accordingly, we agree with the district court that Colt's Proposal Form was an offer made to Venture.

The Code states that once a certain and definite offer is made, acceptance may be made in any manner that is reasonable. However, an offeror may be particular about the appropriate means of acceptance. Here, Colt's Proposal Form was explicit: the proposal "may be accepted only by written purchase order." Venture abided by this requirement when it submitted its purchase order on September 21, 1995, accepting Colt's offer, thus creating a binding contract between the two companies under the terms of Colt's Proposal Form.

Having determined that Colt's Proposal Form constituted a valid offer and Venture's purchase order constituted a valid acceptance, thereby creating an enforceable contract, we agree with the district court that the contract's terms are dispositive of Venture's breach of contract claim. Accordingly, for the reasons stated above, the district court appropriately granted summary judgment in favor of Colt on Venture's breach of contract claim.

Turning to Colt's counterclaim for breach of contract, the district court awarded Colt $47,922.18 plus $7,524.50 in interest for the plastic containers Colt manufactured and shipped to Venture. Because Venture accepted the shipment, did not object to the quality, and did not make payment, Colt was entitled to summary judgment on its counterclaim for these damages. Further, because the explicit terms of the Invoices sent to Venture by Colt allow interest at a twelve percent annual rate beginning sixty days after the date the Invoice was due, the district court correctly awarded the sales price and interest to Colt in the total amount of $55,446.68.

Colt is also entitled to damages for the plastic containers that it manufactured specifically for Venture. The aggregate contract price for these plastic containers is $122,799.59. Colt has sold some of these containers on the open market but still has $108,793.84 of the plastic containers manufactured for Venture in its inventory. The district court correctly awarded this amount to Colt.

We conclude that the district court properly granted summary judgment in favor of Colt on Colt's counterclaim for breach of contract. The district court properly awarded Colt: (1) $55,446.68 (sales price and interest) for the plastic containers delivered to Venture; and (2) $108,793.84 for the plastic containers that Colt specially manufactured for Venture and has been unable to sell on the open market. . . .

For the reasons stated herein, the judgment of the district court is

Affirmed.

>> CASE QUESTIONS

1. In what businesses are Venture and Colt involved?
2. According to the court, who is the offeror and the offeree in this case?
3. What are the actual offer and acceptance in this factual situation?
4. How does the answer to the preceding question impact the conclusion of which party is entitled to a finding in its favor?
5. Which party is liable to the other?

One party's tender of performance may satisfy a required condition leading to the other party's duty to perform.

Reasonable standards should govern your company and these consultants. Hopefully, effective negotiation will overcome the lack of direction in the contract. The concept of tendering performance may help. To **tender performance** means to offer to perform. When the consultants offer to send a team to your plant next week, they are tendering performance. A reasonable response is to permit this work to begin by allowing the consultants access to your facility. Once work begins, the contract's provisions on when payment is owed will govern your performance.

5. SUBSTANTIAL PERFORMANCE

LO 9-3

Beyond the order of performance as determined through conditions, the degree or amount of performance can become an issue. A party to a contract may not always perfectly perform the duties owed. The more complex a contract is, the more difficult it is for a party to complete every aspect of performance. Courts generally recognize three levels of performance. These levels are summarized in Sidebar 9.2.

>> *sidebar* 9.2

Levels of Performance

1. *Complete Performance* recognizes that a contracting party has fulfilled every duty required by the contract. Payment of money, for example, is a contractual duty of performance that a party can perform completely. A party that performs completely is entitled to a complete performance by the other party and may sue to enforce this right.

2. *Material Breach* is a level of performance below what is reasonably acceptable. A party that has materially breached a contract cannot sue the other party for performance and is liable for damages arising from the breach.

3. *Substantial Performance* represents a less-than-complete performance. However, the work done is sufficient to avoid the claim of a breach. A party who substantially performs may be entitled to a partial recovery under the contract.

Substantial performance is a middle ground between full performance and a breach due to nonperformance. Substantial performance is much more than some performance. It is even greater than significant performance. A very typical example when substantial performance is applicable occurs in service-oriented contracts. The consultants in the software installation/implementation contract should recover for work performed even if the entire contract is not completed on time.

Likewise, a construction contractor who gets a home built but has not finished all the landscaping and finishing details by the due date is not denied a financial recovery. This builder can recover under the contract but remains liable for any damages to the homeowner for delays. It would be unfair, from the legal perspective, to allow the homeowner to refuse to pay the builder because a deadline is missed.

> Substantial performance is close to, but less than, full performance. Some or even significant performance may not satisfy the requirement of substantial performance.

6. DIVISIBILITY OF PERFORMANCE

Up to this point, we have assumed a contract specified aspects of performance by one party followed by the next party's performance. Alternatively, a contract may call for both parties to perform concurrently. It is possible, and indeed quite common, for a contract to be divided into segments or installments. An employment contract is a good example. One party (the employee) performs services for a period of time followed by the other party (the employer) paying the wages that are due. This pattern of recurring conditions precedent allows the employment contract to be divided into parts. This contract is considered to be divisible, typically into segments timed as pay periods.

Many contracts that at first glance appear divisible actually are not. While our consulting contract example may look to be divided into monthly or quarterly periods, the manufacturer would have a good argument that it wants the installation and implementation of the software complete. A portion of the work is not what is desired. The contract calls for all the work to be done. Thus, this contract is not divisible. Similarly most construction contracts are viewed as a whole and not as divisible into installments. The fact that the contract may call for payment to be forthcoming following certain benchmarks are met does not make the contract divisible.

With respect to performance, the benefit of divisibility is to view the duty to perform as a series of smaller contracts. This may reduce the amount of disputes (numbers of them and the dollar figures involved) that arise due to nonperformance of the contract.

> The divisibility or entirety of a contract helps determine when performance of duties should occur.

>> Excuses for Nonperformance

Generally speaking, in contracts the party who refuses to perform a promise can expect to be sued for breaching the agreement. Even beyond the special situations related to performance presented in the previous sections, the law may provide for nonperforming with a valid excuse. If such an excuse for nonperformance exists, there can be no legitimate claim of a breach. The next sections of this chapter present material relevant to most business contracts.

Prior to studying these topics, it is important to revisit the fact there are many ways to discharge a party's obligation under a contract. The most common ways to achieve a discharge follow:

> Remember, a discharge relieves a party from the obligation to perform contractual promises.

1. Complete performance of the contract.
2. Tendering performance if that tender is rejected.
3. Substantial performance.
4. Performance of part of a divisible contract.

In addition, a legitimate excuse for nonperformance can result in a party being discharged from contractual performance.

7. IMPOSSIBILITY OF PERFORMANCE

A party's nonperformance is excused because of **impossibility of performance**. This may occur because of the death of an essential party, the destruction of essential materials, or the subject matter of the contract becomes illegal.

If the subject matter of the contract is destroyed, the contract becomes impossible to perform. When a contract exists for the sale of a building, and the building burns, the seller is discharged from performance. Likewise, when there is a contract for personal services, and the party promising the services becomes ill or dies, the party receives discharge from performances.

> Impossibility of performance is less likely to occur compared to impracticability.

The party that promises performance that becomes illegal is also discharged because of impossibility of performance. Mere increased difficulty or reduced profitability, however, does not constitute impossibility of performance.

8. COMMERCIAL IMPRACTICABILITY

Under the UCC a party to a sale-of-goods contract receives discharge from performance because of **commercial impracticability** (§2–615). The *impracticability* standard is not as difficult to meet as the *impossibility* standard. What constitutes impracticability of performance depends upon the circumstances of the situation. For instance, a manufacturer may be discharged from an obligation to make goods for a buyer when the manufacturer's major source of raw materials is unexpectedly interrupted. But if the raw materials are reasonably available from another supplier, the manufacturer may not receive discharge because of impracticability.

9. WAIVER OR RELEASE

A party may be excused from not performing contractual obligations by the other party to the agreement. When a party intentionally relinquishes a right to enforce the contract, a **waiver** occurs. When a party announces the other party does not have to perform as promised, a **release** exists. The distinction between a waiver and a release is not important when examining the resulting discharge of the contract. Nonperformance of the contract is forgiven and there is no liability for a breach of contract.

To gain some clarity regarding these closely related terms, focus on the timing of the nonperformance. Waivers generally occur after a contracting party fails to perform. In this situation, nonperformance by one party may cause the other party to waiver its right to enforce the contract. The waiver typically is unilateral. The nonbreaching party grants the waiver. A landlord may waive the right to collect a late payment fee when the rent is only two days overdue.

Releases usually occur before a contracting party fails to perform. A release often takes the form of a negotiated contract. The release is bargained for and is supported by consideration. A borrower may seek the lender's release to avoid having to make an interim payment. This borrower may have to agree to pay the entire debt before its original due date to get the lender's release from the interim payment.

>> Breach of Contract

A party that does not live up to the obligation of contractual performance is said to breach the contract. There are several remedies or solutions available for a breach of contract. These include the following:

- Negotiated settlement
- Arbitration
- Various awards, including compensatory, consequential, liquidated, and nominal damages
- Specific performance
- Rescission

You contract with *P* to paint your house for $2,000. *P* does not complete the job, and you hire *R* and pay $3,000. You are entitled to $1,000 from *P* as compensatory damages.

Figure 9.2 *Remedies for breach of contract*

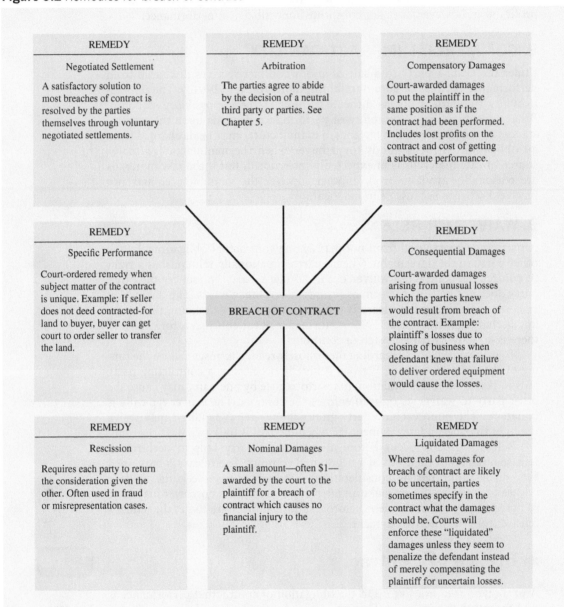

Figure 9.2 provides a summary of these remedies for breach of contract. Note that the choice of one remedy may exclude others. For example, if one choses rescission, one cannot also make a claim for damages.

Awarding money damages is the more common way courts provide remedies to nonbreaching parties. The theory behind such awards rests in putting the damaged person in the same financial position as if the contract was fully performed. Usually compensatory damages suffice to achieve this objective of making a party whole. Occasionally courts will add consequential damages to create a fair remedy. Liquidated, or agreed-upon, damages can simplify disputes when a breach occurs. However, it is important that liquidated damages cannot constitute a penalty for breach; they must be a reasonable attempt to assess actual damages in the face of uncertainty when the contract is formed.

>> *sidebar* 9.3

Opening the Door to Related Liability

In some cases, a breach of contract may coincide with liability for related actions. For example, when software is loaded onto your computer, you have almost certainly agreed to an electronic license for the program's copyright. If you violate the terms of that license in a way that impacts a copyright owner's exclusive rights—e.g., by making more copies of the software than permitted—you not only breach the contract, but also infringe upon the copyright (discussed in more detail in Chapter 11). The license was your relief from copyright claims by the software owner, and by breaching it you remove that protection. On the other hand, if you breach your license agreement in a way that has no impact on a copyright owner's rights, infringement may not be an issue.

The liability for actions associated with a breach of contract can be quite severe. The U.S. Department of Justice (DOJ) has brought cases under the Computer Fraud and Abuse Act based in part on a violation of a website's terms of use. In general, terms of use grant access to a website in exchange for the user agreeing to follow certain rules. When those rules are not followed, the user is engaged in unauthorized access. Criminal prosecution may result depending on what the user does with that access.

Sources: *MDY Indus., LLC v. Blizzard Entertainment, Inc.*, 629 F.3d 928 (9th Cir. 2010); Nick Akerman, "When a Breach of Contract is Evidence of Computer Fraud," *The National Law Journal*, November 29, 2010.

The victim of a contract breach must mitigate damages when possible. Mitigating damages requires the victim to take reasonable steps to reduce them. For example, when a tenant breaches a house lease by moving away before the lease expires, the landlord must mitigate damages by attempting to rent the house to another willing and suitable tenant if such a person is available.

> **Mitigation** is the purposeful reduction of damages; it usually is the responsibility of the nonbreaching party.

At times, money damages are not satisfactory as a remedy. Instead, the nonbreaching party might desire either a return of the value given, which involves the equitable remedy of rescission or restitution. Or a party might request an order that the breaching party specifically perform the contractual promise made, which is known as specific performance.

Efficient Breach   Should you always perform your contractual obligations if at all possible? Scholars have long debated whether performance of contractual duties should be predicated on more than economic benefit. One school of thought suggests that if one monetarily compensates the non-breaching

280   **PART 3**   Legal Foundations for Business

party according to the contract terms, nothing more is required. You may be able to breach, fully compensate the nonbreaching party, and still end up better off. That scenario is termed an efficient breach, because all parties end up either indifferent or in a better position than if the contract was performed. But another view argues that one is morally obligated to carry through on one's promises.

Mortgage contracts provide a current context for considering the issue of efficient breach. This is discussed in sidebar 9.4 below.

>> sidebar 9.4

Walking Away from a Mortgage

In essence, a mortgage is a contract. In such an arrangement, a bank or other lender (mortgagee) has provided the funds for purchasing property (a home) in exchange for the homeowner's (mortgagor) agreement to make payments with interest. Property is pledged as security for the loan. In a "title" state, the lender actually holds the deed until the mortgage is paid, but in a "lien" state, the lender merely has a right to obtain title if payments are not made. In either case, the failure to make payments on a mortgage—a breach of contract—can result in a "foreclosure" wherein the lender takes ownership of the property. In some states, the mortgagor has no further obligation after the mortgagee forecloses.

In a strong economy, when home prices rise, making payments on a mortgage seems like a good economic arrangement for all involved. However, in a bad economy, home prices may fall so quickly that a mortgagee's payments will cover only the inflated portion of the loan for many years. Such a mortgage is said to be "underwater," with the property being worth far less than the amount owed to the lender. When this happens, a homeowner may be inclined to simply walk away from the mortgage, permitting the lender to take over the property and recoup only a part of the amount loaned. To many, this makes economic sense, at least from the perspective on the homeowner. But is it morally wrong?

Consider whether it is acceptable to walk away from a mortgage that is substantially underwater. What would be the impact on the housing market if many people did this? Try to imagine arguments for both sides.

LO 9-6   ## >> Agency Law in Contracts and Other Contexts

Business organizations cannot accomplish anything without the assistance of individuals. An accounting firm does nothing as an organization. The work of the firm is done through the accountants and other employees. Likewise, a local restaurant provides food through the work of servers, cooks, managers, and other employees. In both cases, those employees undertake acts that implicate contract, tort, or criminal law.

The people who get the work done are called *agents,* and the principles presented below are referred to as *agency law.* The actions of agents can have significant consequences to business organizations. The concepts presented in the next four sections form the fundamentals of agency relationships in the transaction of everyday business.

10. TERMINOLOGY

The application of agency law involves the interaction among three parties. Although individuals usually are these parties, agency relationships can involve business organizations. Figure 9.3 illustrates a three-step approach to understanding how the law views the purpose of agency relationship.

First, a **principal** interacts with someone (or some organization) for the purpose of obtaining that second party's assistance. This second party is the **agent.** Principals hire agents to do tasks and represent them in transactions. All employees are agents of the employer/principal, but not all agents are employees. For example, a principal may hire an **independent contractor** to perform a task. Principals do not directly control independent contractors and independent contractors generally work for more than one principal. Examples of independent contractors include attorneys (other than in-house counsel), outside accountants and subcontractors hired to perform construction projects. The nature of their relationship with the principal determines whether employees or independent contractors have authority to contractually bind the principal.

Next, the agent (on behalf of the principal) interacts with a **third party.** Third, the usual legal purpose of the agent is to create a binding relationship between the principal and third party. Typically, the agent wants Step 3 to involve the understanding that any liability created by Steps 1 and 2 is replaced by the new principal–third party relationship. To accomplish this substitution, the agent must remember to comply with the following duties owed to the principal:

Organizations deal with third parties through the actions of agents.

- A duty of loyalty to act for the principal's advantage and not to act to benefit the agent at the principal's expense.
- A duty to keep the principal fully informed.
- A duty to obey instructions.
- A duty to account to the principal for monies handled.

In studying the law of agency, keep in mind that the employer/business organization is the principal and the employee is the agent. Whether employee conduct creates liability for the employer is the usual agency issue facing businesses. Such issues may involve either contracts or torts.

11. CONTRACTUAL LIABILITY FROM AN AGENT'S ACTS

How is a company bound in a contract? For an employee to bind the employer to a contract negotiated with a third party, the employer must

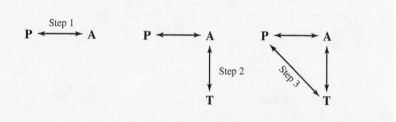

Figure 9.3
Illustration of the agency relationship

have authorized the employee's actions. Contractual authority can take the following forms:

- Actual authority.
- Expressed, written authority.
- Implied authority.
- Apparent authority.

Only when one of these types of authority is present will the principal and the third party become contractually bound.

Actual Authority A simple example helps illustrate the concept of actual authority. Suppose, as an owner of a restaurant, you hire Alex to be an evening manager. You discover that the restaurant is running low on coffee. You write a note to your friend, Terry, the manager of the local grocery store. In this note, you ask Terry to allow Alex to charge $100 worth of coffee to your restaurant's account at the grocery store. You give this note to Alex with instructions to purchase the coffee and deliver the note to Terry. If Terry allows Alex to charge $100 worth of coffee, is your restaurant liable to pay $100 to the grocery store? The answer is yes, because Alex had **actual authority**, which was expressed in writing.

Now suppose a week later, you send Alex to the same grocery store to buy pound cake and yogurt. This time you call Terry on the phone and ask that Alex be allowed to charge the cost of the cake and yogurt. Once again, your restaurant is contractually liable to pay for this purchase since Alex was actually authorized to contract through your expressed oral statement to Terry.

> Specific instructions, whether spoken or written, given by an employer to an employee create actual authority.

>> *sidebar* 9.5

Can Electronic Agents Make Contracts?

In the current business environment, it is common for contracts to be formed electronically. Agency law is not necessarily involved in such agreements. For example, agency may not arise as an issue if a live party accepts a browse-wrap or click-wrap agreement. This is because, although the contract is offered electronically, a person generated it originally. However, what happens if the computer providing the contract can change the terms in accordance with customer input. Or consider the case of an electronic contract that is accepted by a computer program (often referred to as a "bot") on behalf of its creator. Can a contract be formed by these electronic agents?

In general, the answer to the above questions is yes. As a result of recent federal and state legislation, the law supports the ability of electronic agents to bind their live principals. The federal Electronic Signatures in Global and National Commerce Act (ESIGN) provides that a contract may not be denied legal effect "solely because its formation, creation, or delivery involved the action of one or more electronic agents so long as the action of any such electronic agent is legally attributable to the person to be bound." The Uniform Electronic Transactions Act (UETA), adopted by 48 states, provides that "A contract may be formed by the interaction of electronic agents of the parties, even if no individual was aware of or reviewed the electronic agents' actions or the resulting terms and agreements."

Implied Authority   What if, sometime later, you and your co-owner are out of town and Alex is in charge of the restaurant for the evening. Alex, realizing that the tuna salad is in short supply, goes to Terry's grocery store and charges to the restaurant $60 worth of tuna fish. Upon your return, you find a bill from Terry for this purchase. Legally, do you have to pay it? Yes. This time Alex's actions contractually bind the restaurant to Terry since Alex had **implied authority** to do what was necessary for the restaurant's benefit. This implied authority arises from the position Alex holds as evening manager and by the history of the express authority situations.

> Implied authority can be inferred from the acts of an agent who holds a position of authority or who had actual authority in previous situations.

Apparent Authority   Finally, suppose that you terminate Alex's employment. In retaliation, Alex goes to Terry's grocery store and charges a variety of groceries that are consistent with the food your restaurant serves. When you get the bill from Terry, is the restaurant liable? Answer—yes. Even though Alex lacks any actual (expressed or implied) authority, your failure to notify Terry of Alex's termination left Alex with **apparent authority.** Due to the history of Alex's representing your restaurant, it is reasonable for Terry to assume that this incident is one more in the series of Alex's properly charging items to the restaurant's account. To prevent this unwanted liability from occurring, you should have let Terry know that Alex is no longer employed. This notice destroys the existence of apparent authority.

> Remember to notify third parties if an agent no longer works for you; this notice is essential to cut off apparent authority.

It should be noted that in this last scenario, involving the existence of apparent authority, you would have a claim against Alex for the monies you had to pay Terry. Alex's liability to you arises because Alex breached the duty of loyalty owed to the restaurant.

The basic concepts of agency law apply to the operation of business organizations. Sometimes the law provides technical rules, such as those applicable to how partners can bind their partnership. One such special rule is worthy of mention. A partner in a **trading partnership**, that is, one engaged in the business of buying and selling commodities, has the implied authority to borrow money in the usual course of business and to pledge the credit of the firm. A partner in a **nontrading partnership,** such as an accounting or other service firm, has no implied power to borrow money. In the latter case, such authority must be actual before the firm will be bound.

Ratification   What happens when an agent enters into a contract without proper authority? Although the agent does not have the power to bind the principal, the contract may become binding if ratified. **Ratification** occurs when a principal voluntarily decides to honor an agreement, which otherwise would not be binding due to an agent's lack of authority. Returning to the example of the restaurant's evening manager Alex, suppose Alex enters into a contract on behalf of the restaurant to purchase $100,000 worth of kitchen equipment. If Alex had no authority to bind the restaurant, yet you realize that this is a great deal, you could ratify the contract, and follow through with the transaction.

12. TORT LIABILITY FROM AN AGENT'S ACTS

The legal elements of a tort are discussed later, in Chapter 10. For the purpose of this discussion, you should know that a tort is a breach of a duty that causes injury to a person or their property. If you drive your car onto the sidewalk and hit a pedestrian, you are personally liable for the tort of negligence due to your poor driving. Now, suppose the driver was your employee delivering items from your business. Can the injured victim collect damage from you and your business? The answer is found in agency law.

Do know when agents are and are not acting within the scope of employment.

An agent who causes harm to a third party may create legal liability owed by the principal to the third party. The legal test for imposing this "vicarious liability" depends on whether the agent was acting within the scope of employment when the tort occurred. Any time an employee is liable for tortious acts in the *scope of employment,* the employer is also liable. This is because of the tort doctrine of **respondeat superior** ("let the master reply").

The reason for *respondeat superior* is that the employee is advancing the interests of the employer when the tortious act occurs. If the employee is not doing the work, the employer would have to do it. Therefore, the employer is just as liable as the employee when the employee acts tortiously in carrying out the work. In a sense, the employer has set the employee in motion and is responsible for the employee's acts.

Most *respondeat superior* cases involve employee negligence. Note, however, that the employer is strictly liable once the employee's fault is established. And it does not matter that the employer warned the employee against the tortious behavior.

Some *respondeat superior* cases involve an employee's intentional tort. If a store's service representative strikes a customer during an argument over the return of merchandise, the store will be liable under *respondeat superior.* But if the argument concerns football instead of the return of merchandise, the store will not be liable. The difference is that the argument over football is not within the scope of employment.

An agent on a frolic and detour leaves the scope of employment, and the principal is not liable for the agent's actions.

Usually, the only defense the employer has to the strict liability of *respondeat superior* is that the employee was outside the scope of employment. Sometimes this defense is made using the language **frolic and detour.** An employee who is on a frolic or detour is no longer acting for the employer. If, for example, an employee is driving to see a friend when an accident occurs, the employer is not liable.

An employer who must pay for an employee's tort under *respondeat superior* may legally sue the employee for reimbursement. In practice, this seldom happens because the employer carries insurance. Occasionally, an insurer who has paid a *respondeat superior* claim will sue the employee who caused the claim.

The type of business organization in existence determines the extent of responsibility for agents' torts. In essence, partners are liable for all transactions entered into by any partner in the scope of the partnership business and are similarly liable for any partner's torts committed while she or he is acting in the course of the firm's business. Each partner is in effect both an agent of the partnership and a principal, being capable of creating both contract and tort liability for the firm and for copartners and likewise being responsible for acts of copartners. Generally, shareholders of corporations and members of LLCs are protected from tort liability that exceeds the amount of their investment.

13. CRIMINAL LIABILITY

As with torts and contracts, agents can impose criminal liability on business organizations. There are a variety of ways businesspeople and their organizations can be found criminally responsible. The issue of holding businesses criminally liable has been emphasized by the scandals in the beginning of this century. The repercussions of Enron, WorldCom, Tyco, and others are still being felt. And recent cases like the one involving the Galleon Group demonstrate that the emphasis continues.

>> Additional Thought On Contracts

Before concluding your study of contracts, the point made at the beginning of Chapter 8 should be reemphasized. Understanding contracts is critical because they are the key to transacting business. Having an appreciation for contract law may make you a more effective negotiator in some instances. However, as your career advances and you get involved in more complicated business transactions, you will work closely with lawyers to create contractual documentation. Sidebar 9.6 offers some concluding guidance on how to maintain a balanced relationship with your lawyer. Remember, your goal should always be to create contracts that enhance your business activities.

>> *sidebar* 9.6

Suggestions for Businessperson/Lawyer Relationship on the Drafting of Contracts

- Contracts are business documents; they should be in writing whenever possible.
- Use plain English.
- Tell story of relationship; provide timeline of obligations.
- Avoid legalese (whereas; party of the first part, etc.); be careful with "and," "or," "before," "on," "after," "each," "every," etc.

- There should be a flow from section to section.
- Create clear definitions, if necessary.
- Proofread carefully.
- Ask questions about language or issues you do not understand.
- Consistently redraft to update.

>> Key Terms

Actual authority 282	Condition precedent 269	Frolic and detour 284
Agent 281	Condition subsequent 269	Implied authority 283
Apparent authority 283	Delivery 271	Implied conditions 271
Commercial	Discharge 269	Impossibility of
impracticability 277	Duty of performance 269	performance 276
Concurrent condition 271	Express conditions 271	Independent contractor 281

>> Review Questions and Problems

Interpretation of Contracts

1. *Rules of Interpretation*

   Gus contracts to buy a used car from Cars Galore, Inc. The printed contract specifies "no warranties." But Gus and the sales manager of Cars handwrite into the contract a 90-day guarantee on the transmission. If the transmission fails after 60 days, is there a warranty protecting Gus? Explain.

2. *The Parol Evidence Rule*

   Caryn negotiates to buy 50 washers and 50 dryers from the "We-Clean-It Company." These machines are going into laundermats that Caryn operates with her family. Because these machines will be heavily used, Caryn got the company to agree to a one-year warranty instead of the standard 90-day warranty. Following the negotiation, Caryn signs a written contract. Only later, Caryn realizes there is no warranty provision in the written contract. What should Caryn do to be able to enforce the original extended warranty agreement?

Performance

3. *Conditions of Performance*

   (a) Why are conditions important in understanding how and when contracts are performed?

   (b) List the three types of conditions that are most common in contractual performance.

4. *Payment, Delivery, Services Tendered*   └complete material breach substantial perf.

   (a) Explain the role of tender of performance.

   (b) What is the impact of one party tendering its performance?

5. *Substantial Performance*

   Ace Contracting constructs an office building for Realty Enterprises. Realty's tenants quickly find a number of minor problems with the plumbing and insulation of the new building. When Realty contacts Ace about bringing its work up to standard, Ace promises to correct the problems, but never does.   work sufficient to avoid claim of a breach.

   (a) Can Realty rescind the contract?

   (b) What are Realty's legal remedies?   partial recovery

6. *Divisibility of Performance*

   Why is an employment contract usually viewed as being divisible while a construction contract is not considered divisible?

Excuses for Nonperformance

7. *Impossibility of Performance*   death, illegal, subject matter destroyed

   To be a legitimate excuse for nonperformance, impossibility must be real and absolute. What are three examples of factual situations involving real impossibility of performance?

8. *Commercial Impracticability*

   A tripling of prices by an illegal cartel of uranium producers caused Westinghouse Electric Corp. to default on uranium delivery contracts to a number of utility companies. The companies sued and Westinghouse settled. If the case had gone to trial, what defense might Westinghouse have raised to excuse its nonperformance under the contracts?

9. *Waiver or Release*

What do waivers and releases have in common?

Agency Law in Contracts and Other Contexts

agent principal independant contractor.

10. *Terminology*

(a) What are the names given to the three parties typically involved in an agency relationship?

(b) Describe the general purpose of the agency relationship.

11. *Contractual Liability*

For several years, Albert acted as a collection agent for Paulette. Recently, Paulette revoked Albert's authority to collect payments from customers. However, neither Paulette nor Albert told any customers of Albert's termination. Yesterday, Theresa, one of Paulette's customers, paid Albert the money owed to Paulette. Albert never gave this money to Paulette. Is Theresa liable to pay Paulette? Why or why not?

12. *Tort Liability from an Agent's Acts*

Tammy was shopping in Save-a-Lot Grocery Store when Stewart, an employee, brushed Tammy's ankle with a grocery cart. A short time later, while still shopping, Tammy told Stewart that he should say "Excuse me," and then people would get out of his way. Stewart then punched Tammy in the face, knocking her to the floor. If Tammy sues Save-a-Lot, what legal issue must be addressed to determine whether Save-a-Lot is liable?

13. *Criminal Liability*

Describe how business organizations can be found criminally responsible for their actions. What is the way such organizations are punished?

business >> *discussions*

As a new sales representative for Misco Equipment Corporation, you take a customer out to dinner. Before dinner is over, you have shaken hands on a deal to sell the customer nearly a half-million dollars' worth of industrial equipment. In writing up the formal contract the next morning, you discover that you misfigured the equipment's price. Your error could cost Misco $60,000. You telephone your customer and explain the situation.

Is the "deal" you made an enforceable contract?
Does the mistake you made permit you to get out of an enforceable contract?
What do you think will happen in this situation?

Chapter 10. Torts Affecting Business

10

Torts Affecting Business

☐ Learning Objectives

In this chapter you will learn:

10-1. To compare how tort law is related to property.

10-2. To differentiate the three divisions of torts and to generate a theory of why torts are so divided.

10-3. To explain the elements of negligence and to relate these elements to the development of negligence law.

10-4. To analyze why tort litigation is so controversial in society today.

Just as contract law is the way owners exchange what they own in a property-based legal system, so also tort law is an important part of the same system. The property fence protects our use of things. It is part of what we own. But our protected use is not *infinite*. It may be *absolute* but because we live with other people and what is proper to them, we may not use things just anyway we please. We do not have a protected use of a thing if our use harms what others own, including their persons. Tort law helps define where the property fence is when it comes to our use of things. It makes our use legally wrongful and helps anyone injured by our wrongful use to get compensation, called "damages."

The word **tort** means "wrong." Legally, a tort is a civil wrong other than a breach of contract. Tort law sets limits on how people can act and use their resources so they do not violate the right

LO 10-1

*Torts are divided into intentional torts, negligence, and strict liability.

others have to their resources. If you think of property as a type of legal fence surrounding resources, then tort law defines when someone has crossed that fence wrongfully so that compensation is due to the owner.

Legal wrongs inflicted on the resources of others may be crimes as well as torts (see Chapter 12), but the law of tort itself is civil rather than criminal. The usual remedy for a tort is dollar damages. Behavior that constitutes a tort is called *tortious* behavior. One who commits a tort is a *tortfeasor*.

This chapter divides torts into three main categories: intentional torts, negligence torts, and strict liability torts. Intentional torts involve deliberate actions that cause injury. Negligence torts involve injury following a failure to use reasonable care. Strict liability torts impose legal responsibility for injury even though a liable party neither intentionally nor negligently causes the injury.

Important to torts are the concepts of duty and causation. One is not liable for another's injury unless he or she has a *duty* toward the person injured. And, of course, there is usually no liability for injury unless one has *caused* the injury. We explain these concepts under the discussion of negligence, where they are most relevant.

This chapter also covers the topic of damages. The topic concerns the business community because huge damage awards, frequently against businesses, have become common in recent years.

LO 10-2

Intent is the desire to bring about certain results.

>> Intentional Torts

An important element in the following torts is *intent*, as we are dealing with intentional torts. **Intent** is usually defined as the desire to bring about certain results. But in some circumstances the meaning is even broader, including not only desired results but also results that are "substantially likely" to result from an action. Recently, employers who knowingly exposed employees to toxic substances without warning them of the dangers have been sued for committing the intentional tort of battery. The employers did not desire their employees' injuries, but these injuries were "substantially likely" to result from the failure to warn.

The following sections explain the basic types of intentional torts. Sidebar 10.1 lists these torts.

>> *sidebar* 10.1

Types of Intentional Torts

- Assault and battery
- Intentional infliction of mental distress
- Invasion of privacy
- False imprisonment and malicious prosecution
- Trespass
- Conversion
- Defamation
- Fraud
- Common law business torts

1. ASSAULT AND BATTERY

An **assault** is the placing of another in immediate apprehension for his or her physical safety. "Apprehension" has a broader meaning than "fear." It includes the expectation that one is about to be physically injured. The person who intentionally creates such apprehension in another is guilty of the tort of assault. Many times a battery follows an assault. A **battery** is an illegal touching of another. As used here, "illegal" means that the touching is done without justification and without the consent of the person touched.

Hitting someone with a wrench causes physical injury, but as the following case illustrates, the "touching" that constitutes part of a battery need not cause physical injury.

 case **10.1** >>

HARPER v. WINSTON COUNTY
892 So.2d 346 (Ala. Sup. Ct. 2004)

Sandra Wright, the revenue commissioner of Winston County, Alabama, fired her employee, Sherry Harper. Harper sued, claiming among other things that Wright had committed an assault and battery in grabbing her and jerking her arm in trying to force her to go to Wright's office. Before trial, the court granted summary judgment in favor of Wright. The plaintiff, Harper, appealed, and the case reached the Alabama Supreme Court.

SEE, J: . . . Harper argues that the trial court erred in entering a summary judgment in favor of Wright, on Harper's assault and battery claim, because, she claims, she presented substantial evidence in support of her claim. Harper argues that Wright admits that she intentionally grabbed Harper's arm and, she asserts, Wright's grabbing of her arm was offensive. Harper states: "[Wright] jerked my arm and tried to pull me back." She argues that Alabama law does not require that Wright strike or hit her in order for a battery to occur. In response, Wright argues that she merely "took a hold of [Harper's] hand." Wright states that she did not touch Harper in an offensive manner and that she was only trying to coax Harper into stepping into her office so that they could continue their conversation away from the view of the customers and the employees of the Department. The trial court stated in its summary-judgment order that "the undisputed evidence from Sandra Wright clearly points out that the touching was not in any way harmful or offensive, but was instead done in an attempt to bring [Harper] under control."

The plaintiff in an action alleging assault and battery must prove "(1) that the defendant touched the plaintiff; (2) that the defendant intended to touch the plaintiff; and (3) that the touching was conducted in a harmful or offensive manner." In *Atmore Community Hospital*, the plaintiff presented evidence indicating that the defendant "touched her waist, rubbed against her when passing her in the hall, poked her in the armpits near the breast area, and touched her leg." The plaintiff also presented evidence indicating that "each of these touchings was intentional, was conducted with sexual overtones, and was unwelcome." We held that these factual assertions constituted substantial evidence that the defendant had committed a battery.

In *Surrency*, we stated that an actual injury to the body is not a necessary element for an assault-and-battery claim. We also stated that when the evidence as to whether a battery in fact occurred is conflicting, the question whether a battery did occur is for the jury. Quoting *Singer Sewing Machine Co.*, this Court stated:

> "To what acts will constitute a battery in a case like this, the rule is well stated by Mr. Cooley in his work on Torts. He says: 'A successful assault becomes a battery. A battery consists in an injury actually done to the person of another in an angry or revengeful or rude or insolent manner, as by spitting in the face, or in any way touching him in anger, or violently jostling him out of the way, or in doing any intentional violence to the person of another.' *The wrong here consists, not in the touching, so much as in the manner or spirit in which it is done, and the question of bodily pain is important only as affecting damages. Thus, to lay hands on another in a hostile manner is a battery, although no damage follows; but to touch another, merely to attract his attention, is no battery*

[continued]

and not unlawful. And to push gently against one, in the endeavor to make way through a crowd, is no battery; but to do so rudely and insolently is and may justify damages proportioned to the rudeness. . . ."

Alabama courts have recognized that privilege can be a defense to a plaintiff's claim that the defendant battered her. This Court has held that when a merchant suspects a customer of shoplifting, it is reasonable for the merchant's employee to use reasonable force to ensure that the suspected shoplifter is detained.

In this case, there is no question that Wright intended to touch Harper's arm; it is the "manner or spirit" in which Wright touched Harper's arm that is in dispute. Harper testified at the June 13, 2000, hearing that Wright forcefully grabbed her arm. Wright testified that she reached for Harper's arm in an attempt to lead her into her office so they could continue their discussion away from the public area. In *Surrency,* we noted that "to touch another, merely to attract his attention, is no battery and not unlawful. While it is certainly

conceivable that this type of touching is all that occurred in this case, Harper presents substantial evidence to the contrary. Harper testified at her hearing that Wright "jerked" her arm. In her response to Wright's motion for a summary judgment, Harper states that Wright's touch greatly offended her and that this fact is evidenced by the fact that she filed her complaint with the Winston County Commission on May 9, 2000. In her complaint, Harper states that "[Wright] grabbed my arm and tried to force me to go with her." Reviewing the facts in the light most favorable to Harper, as this Court is required to do on an appeal from a summary judgment, we conclude that the question whether a battery occurred in this case—specifically, whether Wright touched Harper in a harmful or offensive manner—is a question of fact for the jury to decide.

We reverse the summary judgment in favor of Wright on Harper's assault-and-battery claim; and we remand this case to the trial court for proceedings consistent with this opinion.

>> CASE QUESTIONS

1. The defendant in this case did not hurt the plaintiff, Harper. Explain why the defendant might still be liable for the tort of battery.

2. Do all touchings constitute a battery? Discuss and give examples to support your conclusion.

3. In litigation what is the difference between a question of law and a question of fact? What does the Alabama Supreme Court decide in this case about whether this alleged battery is a question of law or a question of fact? Discuss.

A store manager who threatens an unpleasant customer with a wrench, for example, is guilty of assault. Actually hitting the customer with the wrench would constitute battery.

2. INTENTIONAL INFLICTION OF MENTAL DISTRESS

This tort usually requires the plaintiff to prove not only mental distress but also physical symptoms.

Intentional **infliction of mental distress** is a battery to the emotions. It arises from outrageous, intentional conduct that carries a strong probability of causing mental distress to the person at whom it is directed. Usually, one who sues on the basis of an intentional infliction of mental distress must prove that the defendant's outrageous behavior caused not only mental distress but also physical symptoms, such as headaches or sleeplessness.

The most common cases of intentional infliction of mental distress (also called *emotional distress*) have concerned employees who have been discriminated against or fired. Many such cases, however, do not involve the type of outrageous conduct necessary for the mental distress tort.

In the business world, other examples of infliction of mental distress come about from the efforts of creditors to extract payment from their debtors. Frequent, abusive, threatening phone calls by creditors might provide the basis for a claim of intentional infliction of mental distress. As torts go, this one is of fairly recent origin. It is a judge-made tort, which furnishes a good example of how the courts are becoming increasingly sensitive to the range of injuries for which compensation is appropriate. In some states, courts have gone so far as to establish liability for carelessly inflicted mental distress, such as the distress of a mother who sees her child negligently run down by a delivery truck.

3. INVASION OF PRIVACY

The tort of **invasion of privacy** is one that is still in the early stages of legal development. As the statutes and court cases recognize it, the tort at present comprises three principal invasions of personal interest. An invasion of any one of these areas of interest is sufficient to trigger liability.

Most commonly, liability will be imposed on a defendant who appropriates the plaintiff's name or likeness for his or her own use. Many advertisers and marketers have been required to pay damages to individuals when pictures of them have been used without authorization to promote products, or when their names and identities have been used without permission for promotional purposes. Before using anyone's picture or name, an advertiser must obtain a proper release from that person to avoid possible liability. See Sidebar 10.2.

> That you can recover damages for misappropriation of likeness illustrates that you own your name and likeness in certain respects.

>> sidebar 10.2

Privacy, Michael Jordan, and Society

Michael Jordan's name is one of the most recognizable in all of sports. Jordan has filed several lawsuits against advertisers who have used his name without permission in connection with the promotion of their products. For instance, he sued Avon for $100 million in connection with a Father's Day promotion that used his identity. Avon and Jordan settled that case. More recently, Jordan sued two Chicago-area grocery stores for using his name in order to attract customers to their stores. Sports and entertainment stars especially often sue businesses that use their identities without permission.

In general, the law considers a right to privacy as "a right to be left alone." But notice how similar a right to privacy is to the property right. Privacy, like property, is a right to exclude others from interfering with something that is privately proper to someone. Would it have been simpler if the law had developed by saying that people have *property* in their identities? Why do you think the law didn't develop this way?

Privacy concerns arose as new technologies like cameras and recorders made it easy to peer into the lives of others. The same concerns continue today with the Internet and computers. Legislatures have passed a variety of laws concerning privacy. As with the common law causes of action mentioned in this section of the text, some of the new privacy acts and statutes don't even mention the word "privacy." Chapter 18 on consumer protection covers some of the new privacy laws. In general, concern about various privacy issues illustrate how law develops to meet changing needs in society.

A second invasion of privacy is the defendant's intrusion upon the plaintiff's physical solitude. Illegal searches or invasions of home or possessions, illegal wiretapping, and persistent and unwanted telephoning can provide the basis for this invasion-of-privacy tort. In one case, a woman even recovered damages against a photographer who entered her sickroom and snapped a picture of her. Employers who enter their employees' homes without permission have also been sued successfully for invasions of privacy. If the invasion of privacy continues, it may be enjoined by the court. Jacqueline Kennedy Onassis sought and obtained an injunction that forbade a certain photographer from getting too close to her and her children. Under this tort, the invasion of physical solitude must be highly objectionable to a reasonable person.

> **Don't** forget that the First Amendment protects you when you publish even highly personal truthful information about public officials and public figures.

The third invasion of personal interest that gives rise to the invasion-of-privacy tort is the defendant's public disclosure of highly objectionable, private information about the plaintiff. A showing of such facts can be the basis for a cause of action, even if the information is true. Thus, publishing in a newspaper that the plaintiff does not pay his or her debts has been ruled to create liability for the defendant creditor. Communicating the same facts to a credit-reporting agency or the plaintiff's employer usually does not impose liability, however. In these cases, there has been no disclosure to the public in general. Also, the news media are protected under the First Amendment when they publish information about public officials and other public figures.

4. FALSE IMPRISONMENT AND MALICIOUS PROSECUTION

> One false imprisonment lawsuit arose when a tow-truck operator towed a car with the driver still in it.

Shoplifting accounts for some $18 billion a year in business losses, almost 1% of retail sales. Claims of **false imprisonment** stem most frequently in business from instances of shoplifting. This tort is the intentional unjustified confinement of a nonconsenting person. Although most states have statutes that permit merchants or their employees to detain customers suspected of shoplifting, this detention must be a reasonable one. The unnecessary use of force, lack of reasonable suspicion of shoplifting, or an unreasonable length of confinement can cause the merchant to lose the statutory privilege. The improperly detained customer is then able to sue for false imprisonment. Allegations of battery are also usually made if the customer has been touched. Not all false imprisonment lawsuits arise because of shoplifting. In one instance a KPMG employee sued for false imprisonment alleging that his manager blocked a door with a chair during a performance review and caused the employee to have to remain in the room against his will.

The tort of **malicious prosecution** is often called *false arrest*. Malicious prosecution arises from causing someone to be arrested criminally without proper grounds. It occurs, for instance, when the arrest is accomplished simply to harass someone. In Albany, New York, a jury awarded a man $200,000 for malicious prosecution. His zipper had broken, leaving his fly open, and a store security guard had him arrested for indecent exposure even after he explained that he had not noticed the problem.

5. TRESPASS

To enter another's land without consent or to remain there after being asked to leave constitutes the tort of **trespass.** A variation on the trespass tort arises when something (such as particles of pollution) is placed on another's land without consent. Although the usual civil action for trespass asks for an injunction to restrain the trespasser, the action may also ask for damages.

Union pickets walking on company property (in most instances), customers refusing to leave a store after being asked to do so, and unauthorized persons entering restricted areas are all examples of trespass. Note that trespass is often a crime as well as a tort. Intentional wrongdoing is frequently criminal.

Trespass concerns the crossing of an owner's boundaries. Today, trespass usually refers to violating the physical boundaries of an owner's land, but in legal history trespass was the legal remedy for direct injuries caused by another to one's person as well. The famous British constitutional historian Frederick Maitland wrote, "Trespass is the fertile mother of actions." By this he meant that many of our modern day causes of action in tort—like battery—come from trespass. Now do you appreciate better the connection of tort law to property in our legal system? In an important sense, we own ourselves and various things we have acquired, and those who violate our boundaries become liable to compensate us.

The reason for emphasizing how tort relates to property is to show you how our legal system has historically centered on the concept of exclusive right, which applies to your person as well as to land and other physical resources.

6. CONVERSION

Conversion is the wrongful exercise of dominion (power) and control over the personal (nonland) resources that belong to another. Conversion deprives owners of their lawful right to exclude others from such resources. The deprivation may be either temporary or permanent, but it must constitute a serious invasion of the owner's legal right. Abraham Lincoln once convinced an Illinois court that a defendant's action in riding the plaintiff's horse for 15 miles was not sufficiently serious to be a conversion since the defendant had returned the horse in good condition. The plaintiff had left the horse with the defendant to be stabled and fed.

Conversion often arises in business situations. Stealing something from an employer is conversion, as is purchasing—even innocently—something that has been stolen. Failing to return something properly acquired at the designated time, delivering something to the wrong party, and destruction or alteration of what belongs to another are all conversions when a deprivation of ownership is serious or long-lived. Even if you intend to return something, if you have converted it you are absolutely liable for any damage done to it. A warehouse operator who improperly transfers stored goods from a designated to a nondesignated warehouse is absolutely liable when a tornado destroys the goods or when a thief steals them.

In one case a student drove a rental car into Mexico although the lease specifically prohibited cross-border driving. When an earthquake destroyed the car while it was parked in Mexico City, the rental company successfully sued the student for conversion.

7. DEFAMATION

Defamation is the publication of untrue statements about another that hold up that individual's character or reputation to contempt and ridicule. "Publication" means that the untruth must be made known to third parties. If defamation is oral, it is called **slander.** Written defamation, or defamation published over radio or television, is termed **libel.**

False accusations of dishonesty or inability to pay debts frequently bring on defamation suits in business relationships. Sometimes, such accusations arise during the course of a takeover attempt by one company of another through an offering to buy stock. In a recent instance, the chairman of one company called the chairman of a rival business "lying, deceitful, and treacherous" and charged that he "violated the standards by which decent men do business." If untrue, these remarks provide a good example of defamation of character. At one major university, a former business professor received a multimillion-dollar settlement following allegations made by university administrators that he had vandalized the new business school. The allegations cost

Is it defamation of character to say that someone is gay or lesbian? How about that someone is of a different race than is correct? Is calling someone a "communist" defamatory?

In 2008, publisher Judith Reagan and her employer News Corporation settled her $100 million lawsuit against News Corporation for defaming her by saying it had fired her because she had made anti-Semitic remarks.

him a deanship at another university. Punitive or punishment damages, as well as actual damages, may be assessed in defamation cases.

Individuals are not the only ones who can sue for defamation. A corporation can also sue for defamation if untrue remarks discredit the way the corporation conducts its business. Untruthfully implying that a company's entire management is dishonest or incompetent defames the corporation.

Nearly one-third of all defamation suits are currently brought by employees against present and former employers. Often these suits arise when employers give job references on former employees who have been discharged for dishonesty. As a result, many employers will now not give job references or will do no more than verify that former employees did work for them.

There are two basic defenses to a claim of defamation. One defense is that the statements made were true. *Truth* is an absolute defense. The second defense is that the statement arose from *privileged communications*. For example, statements made by legislators, judges, attorneys, and those involved in lawsuits are privileged under many circumstances.

Defamation and the First Amendment   Because of the First Amendment, special rules regarding defamation apply to the news media. These media are not liable for the defamatory untruths they print about public officials and public figures unless plaintiffs can prove that the untruths were published with "malice" (evil intent, that is, the deliberate intent to injure) or with "reckless disregard for the truth." Public figures are those who have consciously brought themselves to public attention. See Sidebar 10.3.

>> *sidebar* 10.3

Football Coaches as Public Figures

The U.S. Supreme Court issued the "public official" standard requiring defamation plaintiffs to prove "malice" or "reckless disregard for the truth" in *New York Times v. Sullivan,* 376 U.S. 254 (1964), a case involving criticism of an Alabama police commissioner. The Court extended essentially the same standard to defamation cases against "public figures" in *Curtis Publishing Co. v. Butts,* 388 U.S. 130 (1967). The facts of this case are interesting.

The *Saturday Evening Post,* one of the nation's leading feature story magazines for many years, published a story about the University of Georgia's athletic director and former football coach Wallace ("Wally") Butts and the University of Alabama's football coach Paul ("Bear") Bryant. The *Post* alleged that in a telephone conversation overheard accidentally by an Atlanta insurance salesman, Butts told Bryant how to beat Georgia in an upcoming game. "Before the University of Georgia played the University of Alabama. . . , Wally Butts . . . gave to Bear Bryant

Georgia's plays, defensive patterns, all the significant secrets Georgia's football team possessed." The article continued, "The Georgia players, their moves analyzed and forecast like those of rats in a maze, took a frightful physical beating." Georgia lost the game, and Alabama went on to win the national championship.

Although the conversation between the two coaches may really have involved only a routine request to exchange game films, Butts ended up being forced to resign as athletic director. Both he and Bryant sued the *Post* for defamation. The coaches won their lawsuit, which was appealed to the Supreme Court.

The Court determined that the two coaches were "public figures" and that the First Amendment protected comment about them in much the same way it protected comment about public officials. However, the Court also concluded that the coaches had met their heavy burden of proof. It affirmed the judgment against the *Post.* Within a short time, the *Saturday Evening Post* went out of business.

Plaintiffs' verdicts in media defamation cases are often overturned by trial or appellate judges. In one instance a Houston investment firm, now defunct, sued *The Wall Street Journal,* claiming that a story published by the newspaper caused the firm to go out of business. Following a huge jury verdict, the trial judge threw out $200 million in damages, ruling that the firm had not proved the newspaper published certain statements with knowledge of their falsity or with reckless disregard for the truth.

Plaintiffs' verdicts in defamation cases are often overturned by appellate courts. Because of the constitutional protection given to speech and the media, appellate judges reexamine trial evidence very closely to determine whether the necessary elements of defamation had been proven.

8. FRAUD

Business managers must be alert to the intentional tort of **fraud.** A fraud is an intentional misrepresentation of a material fact that is justifiably relied upon by someone to his or her injury. An intentional misrepresentation means a lie. The lie must be of a material fact—an important one. The victim of the fraud must justifiably rely on the misrepresentation and must suffer some injury, usually a loss of money or other resource one owns.

According to a survey by the Association of Certified Fraud Examiners, U.S. companies lose an average of 6% of their profit to fraud.

Fraud applies in many different situations. Business frauds often involve the intentional misrepresentation of property or financial status. Lying about assets or liabilities in order to get credit or a loan is a fraud. Likewise, intentionally misrepresenting that land is free from hazardous waste when the seller knows that toxic chemicals are buried on the land constitutes fraud.

You can also prove fraud by giving evidence that another has harmed you by failing to disclose a material (important) hidden fact. The fraud of failure to disclose arises when the defendant is under a legal duty to disclose a fact, such as when a defendant seller knows that the foundations of a house are weakened by termites and must disclose this to the buyer.

Likewise, a defendant who has intentionally concealed an important fact and has induced reliance on it to the plaintiff's injury is liable for fraud. Following the financial collapse that began in 2007, hundreds of plaintiffs filed fraud lawsuits against banks, other financial institutions, and various of their executives based on concealment. In one such case, the former chief executive of Countrywide Financial agreed to pay $67.5 million to settle a fraud case brought by the Securities and Exchange Commission. The alleged fraud was the intentional concealment of the risks of subprime mortgages from investors in the then-largest national mortgage lender. Note that not only the common law but also many statutes regulating the financial industry provide for causes of action based on fraud.

In another concealment case, New York State filed a lawsuit based on fraud against Guidant Corporation. The complaint alleged that heart defibrillators manufactured by the company were defective and that the implanted devices had already failed in 28 patients. Further, the complaint asserted that Guidant had known of the defect for several years and concealed this information while continuing to sell the defibrillators. Said New York's former attorney general, "Concealment of negative facts that might influence a consumer to purchase another manufacturer's product is the essence of fraud."

Fraud is not only a tort but a crime as well. Do you understand the difference between torts and crimes? (See Sidebar 10.4.)

>> *sidebar* 10.4

Tort or Crime? Or Both?

Some torts are crimes and some are not. How do we make sense out of this? Crimes, which you will study in Chapter 13, generally require *intent* (also called *willfulness*). The prosecutor has to prove that the defendant intended to cross the proper boundaries (property) established by law. If the primary purpose of the state (government) is to protect people and their resources with the legal fence of property, as was thought by many framers of the Constitution, it becomes clear that most crimes, which are offenses against the proper order (property order) enforced by the government, involve the most serious and intentional crossings of the legal fences that protect people. These crossings injure or harm what belongs to people and the state punishes such harm. But people also deserve compensation because of the injury. That is where tort law comes in.

The most serious torts like assault, battery, conversion, and fraud, which are also frequently crimes, are all intentional. Accidental boundary crossings are usually not criminal unless they are extremely reckless, but when they injure what belongs to an owner, the owner can still get compensation through tort law, for example, through proof of unreasonable and careless boundary crossing called *negligence* (see Sections 11–13). Likewise, certain other accidental boundary crossings that cause injury, like the sale of a defective product, result in the person crossing the legal fence being held *strictly liable,* that is, liable even in the absence of unreasonable behavior in the crossing (see Sections 15–17). However, because these torts are unintentional, they are usually not crimes as well.

Since torts are civil and crimes are, well, criminal in nature, they have different burdens of proof, as explained in Chapter 4. The judge instructs the jury that the plaintiff must prove the tort by a preponderance of the evidence but instructs the jury in a criminal case that the prosecutor must prove the victim's intentional injury by the defendant beyond a reasonable doubt. The burdens of proof are different because to deprive criminal defendants of their freedom is considered much more serious than merely to deprive them civilly of their money. And burdens of proof exist in both civil and criminal cases because to punish a criminal defendant to protect the proper order of the state or to compensate a civil plaintiff for a wrongful boundary crossing involves the taking of something that was previously proper to defendants, whether it is their freedom, their money, or some other resource belonging to them.

Do you understand better now why the same trespass across a legal fence can be both a tort and a crime?

Additional Fraud Examples Fraud also can be committed in the hiring process. For instance, courts have found employers liable for misrepresenting to employees about conditions at a business that later affect employment adversely. In one case, former professional football player Phil McConkey received a $10 million award because his employer misrepresented the status of merger talks with another company. McConkey lost his job the year after he was hired when the two companies merged.

Other instances of business fraud can include:

- Misrepresentation in employment. Screenwriter Benedict Fitzgerald sued actor–director Mel Gibson and his production company for defrauding him into taking a much smaller salary based on their representation that the movie budget was only $4 million–$7 million instead of the estimated $25 million–$50 million that had been actually budgeted.

- Misrepresentation about products. The tobacco industry is beginning to lose lawsuits when plaintiffs allege fraud based on the industry's claiming for years that no tobacco consumption harm had been scientifically proved when it knew that such harm had been established. In 2008, for instance, the Oregon Supreme Court affirmed a $79.5 million punitive damage award in the fraud case of deceased smoker Jesse Williams.

- Concealment about products. Farmers and growers have received over $1 billion from DuPont in settlements based on the damage the fungicide Benlate caused various plants. DuPont allegedly committed fraud by concealing that Benlate could cause crop damage even when the company was asked about the possibility.

- Nondisclosure to third parties about home sale prices. Fannie Mae, the nation's largest investor in home loans, told lenders in 2008 that it considered certain "practices that may distort or artificially inflate" house prices to be potentially fraudulent. Fannie Mae referenced situations where home developers or builders represented that they sold homes in an area for reported high prices but in reality gave back part of the purchase price to buyers. The concern is that such practices can defraud future home buyers in that development into paying higher prices than they actually should and also mislead banks that loan money for home mortgages in the area.

The previous chapter on contracts discussed fraud as voiding a contract. But fraud is also an intentional tort, and one who is a victim of fraud can sue for damages, including punitive or punishment damages. Today many frauds, as well as other intentional torts, occur on the Internet. See Sidebar 10.5.

>> *sidebar* 10.5

Internet Torts

A variety of intentional torts take place on the Internet. Defamation occurs when e-mailers place messages on Listservs or public chatrooms that hold others up to "public contempt or ridicule." Intentional infliction of mental distress arises, for example, when threats are made via e-mail or websites. A jury in Oregon awarded plaintiffs over $100 million when it found that a website threatened abortion providers. When computer hackers break into company databases, trade secrets are easily misappropriated.

Perhaps the most common intentional cyber-related tort is fraud. The Federal Trade Commission has released a list of such frauds or scams that include a variety of pyramid schemes, fraudulent auctions, deceptive travel offers, sale of unmiraculous "miracle" products, health care rip-offs, phony credit card charges, and work-at-home frauds. There was even a "rebate" check sent to consumers that if cashed gave them new Internet service that could not be canceled. The FTC reports that its enforcement actions against Internet scams have risen steadily in recent years.

Fraud and Corporate Governance   Antifraud laws are a major weapon in the enforcement of good corporate governance. Much corporate misgovernance, especially by managers, arises because of misrepresentations of fact about corporate assets or liabilities. These misrepresentations usually induce investors to buy corporate stock shares at higher prices and benefit corporate managers or others inside the corporation who sell their stock. Sometimes a misrepresentation that raises the stock price obtains a bonus or other perk for managers or a loan for the corporation. Usually, a misrepresentation amounts to fraud because investors (who become owners) or lenders rely on it to their injury, that is, they lose some or all of their investment.

Many specific laws create civil and criminal liability for the fraud of corporate managers and other corporate agents. As you think about fraud, remember that it violates the principle of property. One does not acquire proper ownership by defrauding others of their resources. Fraud does not respect the equal property right of others.

9. COMMON LAW BUSINESS TORTS

The label *business torts* embraces different kinds of torts that involve intentional interference with business relations.

> **Do** remember that you can be sued for making statements about a competitor's product that the competitor considers false.

Injurious Falsehood   **Injurious falsehood,** sometimes called *trade disparagement,* is a common business tort. It consists of the publication of untrue statements that disparage the business owner's product or its quality. General disparagement of the plaintiff's business may also provide basis for liability. As a cause of action, injurious falsehood is similar to defamation of character. It differs, however, in that it usually applies to a product or business rather than character or reputation. The requirements of proof are also somewhat different. Defamatory remarks are presumed false unless the defendant can prove their truth. But in disparagement cases the plaintiff must establish the falsity of the defendant's statements. The plaintiff must also show actual damages arising from the untrue statements.

As an example of injurious falsehood, consider the potential harm to Procter & Gamble of the assertions that associated its former logo of moon and stars with satanism. The company threatened to sue a number of individuals. In another instance Warnaco sued Calvin Klein, alleging that Klein had made publicly disparaging remarks about how Warnaco made Calvin Klein clothing under license. The lawsuit alleged that Klein "falsely accused [Warnaco] of effectively 'counterfeiting' Calvin Klein apparel."

Intentional Interference with Contractual Relations   A second type of business tort is **intentional interference with contractual relations.** Probably the most common example of this tort involves one company raiding another for employees. If employees are under contract to an employer for a period of time, another employer cannot induce them to break their contracts. In a variation on this tort, the brokerage firm PaineWebber Group sued Morgan Stanley Dean Witter & Company over PaineWebber's merger agreement with J. C. Bradford & Company. PaineWebber claimed that Morgan Stanley pursued "a carefully planned, broadbased campaign to raid Bradford personnel and interfere with the merger agreement between PaineWebber and Bradford."

> **Don't** induce the employees of another company to come to work for you when they are under contract to work for a period of time.

One of the most famous tort cases in history involved interference with a contract of merger. In that case a jury awarded Pennzoil over $10 billion against Texaco for persuading Getty Oil to breach an agreement of merger with Pennzoil. After Texaco filed for bankruptcy, Pennzoil accepted a settlement of around $3 billion.

>> Negligence

The second major area of tort liability involves unreasonable behavior that causes injury. This area of tort is called **negligence.** In the United States more lawsuits allege negligence than any other single cause of action.

Negligence takes place when one who has a duty to act reasonably acts carelessly and causes injury to another. Actually, five separate elements make up negligence, and the following sections discuss these elements. Sidebar 10.6 also summarizes them. In business, negligence can occur when employees cause injury to customers or others; when those invited to a business are injured because the business fails to protect them; when products are not carefully manufactured; when services, such as accounting services, are not carefully provided; and in many other situations.

>> *sidebar* 10.6

Elements of Negligence

Existence of a duty of care owed by the defendant to the plaintiff.

Unreasonable behavior by the defendant that breaches the duty.

Causation in fact.

Proximate causation.

An actual injury.

---

10. DUTY OF CARE

A critical element of the negligence tort is **duty.** Without a duty to another person, one does not owe that person reasonable care. Accidental injuries occur daily for which people other than the victim have no responsibility, legally or otherwise.

Duty usually arises out of a person's conduct or activity. A person doing something has a duty to use reasonable care and skill around others to avoid injuring them. Whether one is driving a car or manufacturing a product, she or he has a duty not to injure others by unreasonable conduct.

Usually, a person has no duty to avoid injuring others through *nonconduct.* There is no general duty requiring a sunbather at the beach to warn a would-be surfer that a great white shark is lurking offshore, even if the sunbather has seen the fin. There is moral responsibility but no legal duty present.

When there is a special relationship between persons, the situation changes. A person in a special relationship to another may have a duty to avoid unreasonable nonconduct. A business renting surfboards at the beach would probably be liable for renting a board to a customer who was attacked by a shark if it knew the shark was nearby and failed to warn the customer. The special business relationship between the two parties creates a duty to take action and makes the business liable for its unreasonable nonconduct.

*A person doing something has a legal duty to act reasonably to avoid injuring others.

In recent years, negligence cases against businesses for nonconduct have grown dramatically. Most of these cases have involved failure to protect customers from crimes. The National Crime Prevention Institute estimates that such cases have increased tenfold since the mid-1970s.

One famous case involved the Tailhook scandal. A group of male naval aviators was sexually groping female guests as they walked down the hallway at a Hilton hotel. (Remember that an unconsented-to touching is an intentional tort.) One of the females who was sexually touched sued the Hilton hotel for negligence in knowing of the aviators' behavior and failing to protect her. A jury awarded her a total of $6.7 million against Hilton.

The extent of a business's duty to protect customers is still evolving. Note that in Case 10.2 the New Hampshire Supreme Court says that the defendant restaurant has no special relationship to the plaintiff, but still rules that it may have a duty to protect restaurant customers.

 case **10.2** >>

IANNELLI v. BURGER KING CORP.
200 N. H. Lexis 42 (N. H. Sup. Ct. 2000)

MCHUGH, J.: The plaintiffs, Nicholas and Jodiann Iannelli, individually and on behalf of their three children, brought a negligence action against the defendant, Burger King Corporation, for injuries sustained as a result of an assault at the defendant's restaurant. During the late afternoon or early evening hours of December 26, 1995, the Iannelli family went to the defendant's restaurant for the first time. Upon entering the restaurant, the Iannellis became aware of a group of teenagers consisting of five males and two females, whom they alleged were rowdy, obnoxious, loud, abusive, and using foul language. Some in the group claimed they were "hammered." Initially this group was near the ordering counter talking to an employee whom they appeared to know. The Iannellis alleged that one of the group almost bumped into Nicholas. When that fact was pointed out, the teenager exclaimed, "I don't give an F. That's his F'ing problem."

Nicholas asked his wife and children to sit down in the dining area as he ordered the food. While waiting for the food to be prepared, Nicholas joined his family at their table. The teenagers also moved into the dining area to another table. The obnoxious behavior and foul language allegedly continued. One of the Iannelli children became nervous. Nicholas then walked over to the group intending to ask them to stop swearing. As Nicholas stood two or three feet from the closest of the group, he said, "Guys, hey listen, I have three kids." Whereupon, allegedly unprovoked, one or more of the group assaulted Nicholas by hitting him, knocking him to the ground and striking him in the head with a chair.

The plaintiffs argue that a commercial enterprise such as a restaurant has a general duty to exercise reasonable care toward its patrons, which may include a duty to safeguard against assault when circumstances provide warning signs that the safety of its patrons may be at risk. The most instructive case, given the issues presented, is *Walls v. Oxford Management Co.* In *Walls*, a tenant of an apartment complex alleged that the owner's negligent maintenance of its property allowed her to be subjected to a sexual assault in the parking lot. We held that as a general principle landlords have no duty to protect tenants from criminal attacks. In as much as landlords and tenants have a special relationship that does not exist between a commercial establishment and its guests, it follows that the same general principle of law extends to restaurants and their patrons. We recognized in *Walls*, however, that particular circumstances can give rise to such a duty. These circumstances include when the opportunity for criminal misconduct is brought about by the actions or inactions of the owner or where overriding foreseeability of such criminal activity exists.

Viewing the evidence in the light most favorable to the plaintiffs, we must decide whether the behavior of the rowdy youths could have created an unreasonable risk of injury to restaurant patrons that was foreseeable to the defendant. If the risk of injury was reasonably

[continued]

foreseeable, then a duty existed. We hold that the teenagers' unruly behavior could reasonably have been anticipated to escalate into acts that would expose patrons to an unreasonable risk of injury. The exact occurrence or precise injuries need not have been foreseen.

Viewed in a light most favorable to the plaintiffs, the evidence could support a finding that the teenagers' obnoxious behavior in the restaurant was open and notorious. Because the group was engaging in a conversation at times with a restaurant employee, it could be found that the defendant was aware of the teenagers' conduct. The near physical contact between one teenager and Nicholas Iannelli at the counter and the indifference expressed by the group member thereafter could be deemed sufficient warning to the restaurant

manager of misconduct such that it was incumbent upon him to take affirmative action to reduce the risk of injury. The plaintiffs allege that at least one other restaurant patron expressed disgust with the group's actions prior to the assault. The manager could have warned the group about their behavior or summoned the police if his warnings were not heeded.

In summary, the trial court's ruling that as a matter of law the defendant owed no duty to the plaintiffs to protect them from the assault was error. While as a general principle no such duty exists, here it could be found that the teenagers' behavior in the restaurant created a foreseeable risk of harm that the defendant unreasonably failed to alleviate. Accordingly, we **reverse and remand.**

>> CASE QUESTIONS

1. Under the decision in this case, when does a duty arise for the defendant restaurant to protect its customers?
2. What does the court suggest that the restaurant manager should have done in this case that would have satisfied the duty?
3. What do you think is the difference in this case between a "special relationship" duty and the duty of the restaurant?

Note that the duty to act reasonably also applies to professional providers, like doctors, lawyers, CPAs, architects, engineers, and others. In most negligence cases, however, the standard of reasonableness is that of a *reasonable person*. In negligence cases involving professionals, the negligence standard applied is that of the *reasonable professional*. The negligence of professionals is called *malpractice*.

As Sidebar 10.7 suggests, professional negligence is a controversial area of tort law.

11. UNREASONABLE BEHAVIOR—BREACH OF DUTY

At the core of negligence is the unreasonable behavior that breaches the duty of care that the defendant owes to the plaintiff. The problem is how do we separate reasonable behavior that causes accidental injury from unreasonable behavior that causes injury? Usually a jury determines this issue, but negligence is a mixed question of law and fact. Despite the trend for judges to let juries decide what the standard of reasonable care is, judges also continue to be involved in the definition of negligence. A well-known definition by Judge Learned Hand states that negligence is determined by "the likelihood that the defendant's conduct will injure others, taken with

A train rounds a bend but cannot stop in time to avoid running over an intoxicated person who has fallen asleep on the track. A jury is not likely to find the railroad's behavior "unreasonable."

>> sidebar 10.7

Medical Malpractice Crisis

Few people would disagree that physicians are extremely unhappy about the rapidly growing insurance premiums they have to pay. Some physicians have gone on strike; others have left the practice of medicine. The exact causes of the situation, however, are difficult to determine. Consider the following and make your own evaluation.

- Studies suggest between 44,000 and 98,000 people die annually from medical errors.
- A study in the *New England Journal of Medicine* found that 9 out of 10 patients who suffer disability from medical errors go uncompensated.
- In 2004 total payments for medical malpractice claims fell 8.9% nationally.
- As of 2005, 27 states have capped malpractice awards.
- In 2004 malpractice insurance costs for various medical specialties rose between 6.9% and 24.9%.

Question: what would be the impact on the cost of malpractice insurance if physicians had patients sign arbitration clauses before providing service in all but emergency cases? These clauses might provide that disputes with a physician be resolved before an arbitration board appointed by the state medical association. These clauses are currently not widely used and are specifically prohibited by several states. But under the Federal Arbitration Act, the state prohibitions are likely preempted by the federal law because medical practice has a substantial impact on interstate commerce. The Supreme Court has already ruled that law practice has such an impact, so it is likely that medical practice does as well.

Sources: *BusinessWeek*, *The New York Times*, Department of Health and Human Services.

the seriousness of the injury if it happens, and balanced against the interest which he must sacrifice to avoid the risk."

Examples of Negligence Failure to exercise reasonable care can cost a company substantial sums. In one instance the licensed owner of a National Car Rental agency in Indianapolis was ordered to pay $5.5 million to a man who slipped on the floor and broke his hip. To save overtime pay the rental agency had had its floors mopped during, instead of after, normal working hours. Unaware that someone was mopping the floors behind him, the plaintiff had stepped backwards, slipped, and fallen on the wet floor.

In another case arising from unreasonable behavior, Wal-Mart Stores agreed to pay two young girls a settlement of up to $16 million. A store employee had sold the girls' father a shotgun used to kill their mother in spite of the fact that a federal form filled out by the buyer indicated that he was under a restraining order. Federal law bars those under restraining orders from purchasing guns.

Even before the terrorist attacks of 9/11, New York's World Trade Center (WTC) had been bombed. In 2005 a Manhattan jury determined that the Port Authority of New York was negligent in the earlier attack, which involved a blast from a truck filled with explosives that terrorists had driven into the public parking lot under the WTC. Six people died and over a thousand were injured. Is it an example of litigation gone wild to hold the Port Authority liable for a terrorist act? Consider that before the bombing a report commissioned by the Port Authority, which controlled the WTC parking, had specifically warned against such a bombing and recommended: "Eliminate all public parking at the World Trade Center." Citing potential loss of revenue, the Port Authority had declined to follow the report's recommendation.

Willful and Wanton Negligence A special type of aggravated negligence is **willful and wanton negligence.** Although this does not reveal intent, it does show an extreme lack of due care. Negligent injuries inflicted by drunk drivers show willful and wanton negligence. The significance of this type of negligence is that the injured plaintiff can recover punitive damages as well as actual damages. For example, following the *Exxon Valdez* oil spill in Alaska, commercial fishers sued Exxon for damage to their livelihoods. A jury awarded substantial actual and punitive damages when it found that Exxon was willful and wanton in allowing the ship captain to be in charge of the ship when they knew he was an alcoholic.

In 2005 a New Jersey state court awarded a 2-year-old boy $105 million for an accident that left him permanently paralyzed from the neck down. A drunken Giants football fan had caused the accident. Before driving, the fan consumed at least 12 beers sold to him by a Giants Stadium concessionaire. The award for willful and wanton negligence against the concessionaire is the largest ever for the careless sale of alcohol. The award included $30 million in compensatory and $75 million in punitive damages.

Because employers are also liable for the intentional torts of employees in advancing the interests of their employers (see Chapter 14), employers face punitive damage awards in those instances even when they are also liable for simple negligence, or have not acted negligently at all. (See Sidebar 10.8.)

*Willful and wanton negligence allows an injured plaintiff to recover punitive as well as actual damages.

>> *sidebar* 10.8

Strip Search Hoax Costs McDonald's $6.1 Million

The caller identified himself as a police officer and told the McDonald's assistant manager that Louise Ogburn had stolen the purse of a customer who had recently left the restaurant and should be searched. For more than an hour the assistant manager and other McDonald employees detained, searched, and even committed sexual battery against Ogburn at the instruction of the caller. However, the caller was not a police officer and the call was a hoax.

Ogburn sued McDonald's and the jury awarded her a million dollars in actual damages for pain and suffering and $5 million in punitive damages against the company. To understand why McDonald's is liable, you have to understand that numerous instances of such hoaxes were known to the company involving various fast-food restaurants, yet the jury found that the company had not reasonably trained its employees such calls might be hoaxes.

If McDonald's negligence were extreme, that is, willful and wanton, that would justify the $5 million punitive damage award, but McDonald's is also liable for the intentional torts of its employees that justify awarding punitive damages. In this case the employees committed such intentional torts as false imprisonment and battery in the course of Ogburn's detention. Such detention advanced the interests of McDonald's in dealing with dishonest employees and made the intentional acts accompanying Ogburn's treatment the company's responsibility when they turned out to be wrongful.

12. CAUSATION IN FACT

Before a person is liable to another for negligent injury, the person's failure to use reasonable care must actually have "caused" the injury. This observation is not so obvious as it first appears. A motorist stops by the roadside to change a tire. Another motorist drives past carelessly and sideswipes the first as he changes the tire. What caused the accident? Was it the inattention of the second motorist or the fact that the first motorist had a flat tire? Did the argument the second motorist had with her boss before getting in the car cause the accident, or was it the decision of the first motorist to visit one more client that afternoon? In a real sense, all these things caused the accident. Chains of causation stretch out infinitely.

Still, in a negligence suit the plaintiff must prove that the defendant actually caused the injury. The courts term this **cause in fact.** In light of the many possible ways to attribute accident causation, how do courts determine if a plaintiff's lack of care, in fact, caused a certain injury? They do so very practically. Courts leave questions of cause in fact almost entirely to juries as long as the evidence reveals that a defendant's alleged carelessness could have been a substantial, material factor in bringing about an injury. Juries then make judgments about whether a defendant's behavior in fact caused the harm.

A particular problem of causation arises where the carelessness of two or more tortfeasors contributes to cause the plaintiff's injury, as when two persons are wrestling over control of the car which strikes the plaintiff. Tort law handles such cases by making each tortfeasor *jointly and severally* liable for the entire judgment. The plaintiff can recover only the amount of the judgment, but she or he may recover it wholly from either of the tortfeasors or get a portion of the judgment from each.

Approximately 40 states have limited joint and several liability in certain cases, for example, medical injury cases. In these states and types of cases, multiple defendants are each liable usually only for that portion of the damages juries believe they actually caused.

> Many states are currently modifying the common law of torts regarding rules like that of joint and several liability.

13. PROXIMATE CAUSATION

It is not enough that a plaintiff suing for negligence prove that the defendant caused an injury in fact. The plaintiff also must establish proximate causation. **Proximate cause** is, perhaps, more accurately termed *legal cause*. It represents the proposition that those engaged in activity are legally liable only for the *foreseeable* risk that they cause.

Defining proximate causation in terms of foreseeable risk creates further problems about the meaning of the word *foreseeable*. In its application, foreseeability has come to mean that the plaintiff must have been one whom the defendant could reasonably expect to be injured by a negligent act. For example, it is reasonable to expect, thus foreseeable, that a collapsing hotel walkway should injure those on or under it. But many courts would rule as unforeseeable that someone a block away, startled upon hearing the loud crash of the walkway, should trip and stumble into the path of an oncoming car. The court would likely dismiss that person's complaint against the hotel as failing to show proximate causation.

Another application of proximate cause doctrine requires the injury to be caused *directly* by the defendant's negligence. Causes of injury that intervene

> British Petroleum promised $20 billion to pay for claims arising from its oil spill in the Gulf. To date, only about a fifth of that amount has been paid out by claims adjusters. Part of the problem relates to proximate causation. How do claimants prove, for instance, that a falloff in business miles inland is directly caused by the oil spill instead of poor business practice, or for some other reason?

between the defendant's negligence and the plaintiff's injury can destroy the necessary proximate causation. Some courts, for instance, would hold that it is not foreseeable that an owner's negligence in leaving keys in a parked car should result in an intoxicated thief who steals the car, crashing and injuring another motorist. These courts would dismiss for lack of proximate cause a case brought by the motorist against the car's owner. For one of the most famous tort cases in history, see Sidebar 10.9.

>> *sidebar* 10.9

Explosion on the Long Island Railroad

Helen Palsgraf stood on the loading platform on the Long Island Railroad. Thirty feet away, two station guards were pushing a man onto a departing train when one guard dislodged an unmarked package held by the man. The package, which contained fireworks, fell to the ground with a loud explosion.

The explosion caused a heavy scale to fall on Helen Palsgraf, injuring her. She sued the railroad for the negligence of its guard and won at trial and in the appellate court. Three justices of the Court of Appeals (New York's supreme court) agreed with the lower courts: "The act [of the guard] was negligent. For its proximate consequences the defendant is liable."

However, four justices of the Court of Appeals decided that proximate causation was "foreign to the case before us." The majority ruled that what the guard did could not be considered negligence at all in relation to the plaintiff Palsgraf. The guard owed no duty to someone 30 feet away not to push a passenger—even carelessly—onto a train. The Court of Appeals reversed the damage award to the plaintiff.

The famous *Palsgraf* case illustrates the complexity of legal analysis. Question: Was it negligent for the passenger to carry fireworks in a crowded railroad station? Why didn't the plaintiff just recover damages from the passenger?

Source: *Palsgraf v. Long Island R.R.*, 162 N.E. 99 (1928).

---

14. DEFENSES TO NEGLIGENCE

There are two principal defenses to an allegation of negligence: contributory negligence and assumption of risk. Both these defenses are *affirmative defenses*, which means that the defendant must specifically raise these defenses to take advantage of them. When properly raised and proved, these defenses limit or bar the plaintiff's recovery against the defendant. The defenses are valid even though the defendant has actually been negligent.

Contributory Negligence As originally applied, the **contributory negligence** defense absolutely barred the plaintiff from recovery if the plaintiff's own fault contributed to the injury "in any degree, however slight." The trend today, however, in the great majority of states is to offset the harsh rule of contributory negligence with the doctrine of **comparative responsibility** (also called *comparative negligence* and *comparative fault*). Under comparative principles, the plaintiff's contributory negligence does not bar recovery. It merely compares the plaintiff's fault with the defendant's and reduces the damage award proportionally. For example, a jury determined damages at $3.1 million for an Atlanta plaintiff who was run over and dragged by a bus. But the jury then reduced the damage award by 20% ($620,000) on the basis that the plaintiff contributed to his own injury by failing reasonably to look out for his own safety in an area where buses come and go.

Adoption of the comparative negligence principle seems to lead to more frequent and larger awards for plaintiffs. This was the conclusion of a study by the Illinois Insurance Information Service for the year following that state's adoption of comparative negligence.

Contractual notices regarding assumption of the risk are more likely to be enforced if they prominently bring to attention the risk involved.

People injured by a baseball at a baseball game or a golf ball on the golf links also usually assume the risk. Does someone assume the risk of a racing car veering off a race track and going over a barrier and into the crowd?

Assumption of Risk If contributory negligence involves failure to use proper care for one's own safety, the **assumption-of-the-risk** defense arises from the plaintiff's knowing and willing undertaking of an activity made dangerous by the negligence of another. When professional hockey first came to this country, many spectators injured by flying hockey pucks sued and recovered for negligence. But as time went on and spectators came to realize that attending a hockey game meant that one might occasionally be exposed to flying hockey pucks, courts began to allow the defendant owners of hockey teams to assert that injured spectators had assumed the risk of injury from a speeding puck. It is important to a successful assumption-of-the-risk defense that the assumption was voluntary. Entering a hockey arena while knowing the risk of flying pucks is a voluntary assumption of the risk. However, that the injured person has really understood the risk is also significant to the assumption-of-the-risk defense. In one 2007 case, a University softball coach smacked his player in the face with a bat while demonstrating a batting grip to her. She required surgery for multiple fractures of her face and sued the coach and his employer, the university. The court denied the assumption-of-the-risk defense, asserting that it was up to the jury to determine whether the coach had acted negligently in hitting his player. The court observed that the player did not appreciate the risk of being hit by her coach with the bat.

Courts have often ruled that people who imperil themselves while attempting to rescue their own or others' property from a risk created by the defendant have not assumed the risk voluntarily. A plaintiff who is injured while attempting to save his possessions from a fire negligently caused by the defendant is not subject to the assumption-of-the-risk defense.

Assumption of the risk may be implied from the circumstances, or it can arise from an express agreement. Many businesses attempt to relieve themselves of potential liability by having employees or customers agree contractually not to sue for negligence, that is, to assume the risk. Some of these contractual agreements are legally enforceable, but many will be struck down by the courts as being against public policy, especially where a business possesses a vastly more powerful bargaining position than does its employee or customer.

>> Strict Liability in Tort

Strict liability is a catchall phrase for the legal responsibility for injury-causing behavior that is neither intentional nor negligent. There are various types of strict liability torts, some of which are more "strict" than others. What ties them together is that they all impose legal liability, regardless of the intent or fault of the defendant. The next sections discuss these torts and tort doctrines.

15. STRICT PRODUCTS LIABILITY

A major type of strict tort liability is **strict products liability,** for the commercial sale of defective products. In most states any retail, wholesale, or manufacturing seller who sells an unreasonably dangerous defective product that causes injury to a user of the product is strictly liable. For example, if a forklift you are using at work malfunctions because of defective brakes and you run off the edge of the loading dock and are injured, you can sue the retailer, wholesaler, and manufacturer of the product for strict liability. The fact that the retailer and wholesaler may have been perfectly careful in selling the product does not matter. They are strictly liable.

Don't forget that strict products liability applies only against *commercial* sellers.

Strict products liability applies only to "commercial" sellers, those who normally sell products like the one causing injury, or who place them in the stream of commerce. Included as commercial sellers are the retailer, wholesaler, and manufacturer of a product, but also included are suppliers of defective parts and companies that assemble a defective product. Not included as a commercial seller is your next door neighbor who sells you her defective lawnmower. The neighbor may be negligent, for instance, if she knew of the defect that caused you injury and forgot to warn you about it, but she cannot be held strictly liable.

An important concept in strict products liability is that of "defect." Strict liability only applies to the sale of unreasonably dangerous *defective* products. There are two kinds of defects. **Production defects** arise when products are not manufactured to a manufacturer's own standards. Defective brakes on a new car are a good example of a production defect. Another example involves the clam chowder in which a diner found a condom, which led in 2005 to a rapid settlement between the diner and a seafood restaurant chain. **Design defects** occur when a product is manufactured according to the manufacturer's standards, but the product injures a user due to its unsafe design. Lawsuits based on design defects are common but often very controversial. Recent such lawsuits have included one against Ford that claimed Ford should have designed its vans to have a heat-venting system so children accidentally locked in the vans would be safe. Lack of adequate warnings concerning inherently dangerous products can also be considered a design defect. American Home Products settled a wrongful death lawsuit for an estimated $10 million. The lawsuit alleged that the company had not adequately warned users of its diet drug about the risks of hypertension, which had been linked to diet-drug use.

In one case, a jury found the defendant liable when its cleaning product warned users to "vent" rooms being cleaned but failed to say "vent to outside." Vapors from the product injured several people when it was used in a room with a closed circulation venting system.

In practice, strict products liability is useful in protecting those who suffer personal injury or property damage. It does not protect businesses that have economic losses due to defective products. For instance, a warehouse that loses profits because its defective forklift will not run cannot recover those lost profits under strict products liability. The warehouse would have to sue for breach of contract. However, if the forklift defect causes injury to a worker, the worker can successfully sue the forklift manufacturer for strict products liability.

Under strict products liability, contributory negligence is not a defense but assumption of the risk is. The assumption-of-the-risk defense helped protect tobacco manufacturers from health injury liability for many years. Misuse is another defense that defendants commonly raise in product liability cases. Removing safety guards from equipment is a common basis for the misuse defense. Defendants have also argued that if a product meets some federally required standard, it cannot be considered defective. Most courts, however, have ruled that federal standards only set a minimum requirement for safe design and that meeting federal standards does not automatically keep a manufacturer from being sued for strict products liability.

In recent years many states have changed or modified the rules of product liability. See Sidebar 10.10. These changes to the rules of products liability (and modifications to the rules of medical malpractice) are often known generally as "tort reform." The federal government has also enacted tort reform that applies to product liability. As of 2005, federal courts can decide any *class-action* lawsuit involving over $5 million and involving persons from different states. Federal plaintiffs in such class-action lawsuits need no longer claim the usual $75,000 jurisdictional amount.

>> *sidebar* 10.10

Tort Reform

The rapid growth of products litigation during the past two decades has brought forth many calls for "tort reform." Numerous states have changed their laws to modify the tort doctrines discussed in this section and chapter. At the federal level, comprehensive tort reform has been strongly advocated although it has not passed as of this writing. Some of the tort reforms proposed or passed by the states include:

- Permitting only negligence actions against retailers and wholesalers unless the product manufacturer is insolvent.
- Eliminating strict liability recovery for defective product design.
- Barring products liability claims against sellers if products have been altered or modified by a user.

- Providing for the presumption of reasonableness defense in product design cases in which the product meets the **state-of-the-art;** that is, the prevailing industry standards at the time of product manufacture.
- Creating a **statute of repose** that would specify a period (such as 25 years) following product sale after which plaintiffs would lose their rights to bring suits for product-related injuries.
- Reducing or eliminating punitive damage awards in most product liability cases.

Importantly, note that not all, or even most, of these reforms have been adopted by every state.

Another important development in products liability is that in nearly every state product liability case based on design defects, failures to warn adequately and testing inadequacies are now decided according to "reasonableness" standards, making these product liability cases based on the negligence. Consider the following case involving Ford Motor Company's failure to test a seatbelt sleeve.

BRANHAM v. FORD MOTOR CO.
701 S.E.2d 5 (S.C. Sup. Ct. 2010)

Hale was driving several children to her house in her Ford Bronco. No one was wearing a seatbelt. Hale admittedly took her eyes off the road and turned to the backseat to ask the children to quiet down. When she took her eyes off the road, the Bronco veered towards the shoulder of the road, and the rear right wheel left the roadway. She responded by overcorrecting to the left. Her overcorrection caused the Bronco to roll over. One of the children, Jesse Branham, was thrown from the vehicle, was severely injured, and sued Ford Motor Company and Hale. At trial, Branham did not seriously pursue the claim against Hale. The case against Ford was based on two product liability claims, one for failing to test the seatbelt sleeve, and the other a design defect claim related to the vehicle's tendency to rollover. Both of these claims were pursued in negligence and strict liability. The jury found both Ford and Hale responsible and awarded Branham $16 million in actual damages. Only Ford appeals.

KITTREDGE, J.: . . . Branham alleged Ford was negligent "in selling the Bronco II with a defective rear occupant restraint system." At trial, Branham claimed Ford was negligent and also strictly liable in failing to adequately *test* the seatbelt sleeve. The trial court dismissed the strict liability claim on the ground that the seatbelt sleeve was not as a matter of law in a defective condition unreasonably dangerous to the user at the time of manufacture. Based on this premise, Ford contends the companion negligence claim must fail, for all products liability actions, regardless of the stated theory, have common elements. "In a products liability action the plaintiff must establish three things, regardless of the theory on which he seeks recovery: (1) that he was injured by the product; (2) that the product, at the time of the accident, was in essentially the same condition as when it left the hands of the defendant; and (3) that the injury occurred because the product was in a defective condition unreasonably dangerous to the user." Ford, therefore, concludes that the negligence claim (which required Branham to prove that the seatbelt sleeve was in a defective condition unreasonably dangerous to the user) should have been dismissed. We agree.

The trial court determined as a matter of law that the seatbelt sleeve was not in a defective condition unreasonably dangerous to the user. Consequently, the absence of this common, shared element required

the dismissal of the strict liability claim *and* the companion negligence claim. The trial court erred in failing to direct a verdict as to the negligent seatbelt sleeve claim.

We next consider the "handling and stability" design defect claim in strict liability and negligence. We address Ford's two-fold argument that: (1) Branham failed to prove a reasonable alternative design pursuant to the risk-utility test; and (2) South Carolina law requires a risk-utility test in design defect cases to the exclusion of the consumer expectations test. For a plaintiff to successfully advance a design defect claim, he must show that the design of the product caused it to be "unreasonably dangerous." In South Carolina, we have traditionally employed two tests to determine whether a product was unreasonably dangerous as a result of a design defect: (1) the consumer expectations test and (2) the risk-utility test.

In *Claytor v. General Motors Corp.*, this Court phrased the consumer expectations test as follows: "The test of whether a product is or is not defective is whether the product is unreasonably dangerous to the consumer or user given the conditions and circumstances that foreseeably attend use of the product." The *Claytor* Court articulated the risk-utility test in the following manner: "[N]umerous factors must be considered when determining whether a product is unreasonably dangerous, including the usefulness and desirability of the product, the cost involved for added safety, the likelihood and potential seriousness of injury, and the obviousness of danger." In *Bragg v. Hi-Ranger, Inc.*, our court of appeals phrased the risk-utility test as follows: "[A] product is unreasonably dangerous and defective if the danger associated with the use of the product outweighs the utility of the product."

Ford contends Branham failed to present evidence of a feasible alternative design. Implicit in Ford's argument is the contention that a product may only be shown to be defective and unreasonably dangerous by way of a risk-utility test, for by its very nature, the risk-utility test requires a showing of a reasonable alternative design. Branham counters, arguing that under *Claytor* he may prove a design defect by resort to the consumer expectations test or the risk-utility test. Branham also argues that regardless of which test is required, he has met both, including evidence of a feasible alternative design. We agree with Branham's

[continued]

contention that he produced evidence of a feasible alternative design. Branham additionally points out that the jury was charged on the consumer expectations test *and* the risk-utility test.

As discussed above, Branham challenged the design of the Ford Bronco II by pointing to the MacPherson suspension as a reasonable alternative design. A former Ford vice president, Thomas Feaheny, testified that the MacPherson suspension system would have significantly increased the handling and stability of the Bronco II, making it less prone to rollovers. Branham's expert, Dr. Richardson, also noted that the MacPherson suspension system would have enhanced vehicle stability by lowering the vehicle center of gravity. There was further evidence that the desired sport utility features of the Bronco II would not have been compromised by using the MacPherson suspension. Moreover, there is evidence that use of the MacPherson suspension would not have increased costs. Whether this evidence satisfies the risk-utility test is ultimately a jury question. But it is evidence of a feasible alternative design, sufficient to survive a directed verdict motion.

While the consumer expectations test fits well in manufacturing defect cases, we do agree with Ford that the test is ill-suited in design defect cases. We hold today that the exclusive test in a products liability design case is the risk-utility test with its requirement of showing a feasible alternative design. Some form of a risk-utility test is employed by an overwhelming majority of the jurisdictions in this country. States that exclusively employ the consumer expectations test are a decided minority. By our count 35 of the 46 states that recognize strict products liability use some form of risk-utility analysis in their approach to determine whether a product is to effectively design. Four states do not recognize strict liability at all. Those four states are Delaware, Massachusetts, North Carolina, and Virginia.

We believe that in design defect cases the risk-utility test provides the best means for analyzing whether a product is designed defectively. Unlike the consumer expectations test, the focus of a risk-utility test centers upon the alleged defectively designed product. The risk-utility test provides objective factors for a trier of fact to analyze when presented with a challenge to a manufacturer's design. Conversely, we find the consumer expectations test and its focus on the consumer ill-suited to determine whether a product's design is unreasonably dangerous.

Most any product can be made more safe. Automobiles would be safer with disc brakes and steel-belted radial tires than with ordinary brakes and ordinary tires, but this does not mean that an automobile dealer would be held to have sold a defective product merely because the most safe equipment is not installed. By a like token, a bicycle is safer if equipped with lights and a bell, but the fact that one is not so equipped does not create the inference that the bicycle is defective and unreasonably dangerous. There is, of course, some danger incident to the use of any product.

In a product liability design defect action, the plaintiff must present evidence of a reasonable alternative design. The plaintiff will be required to point to a design flaw in the product and show how his alternative design would have prevented the product from being unreasonably dangerous. This presentation of an alternative design must include consideration of the costs, safety and functionality associated with the alternative design. On retrial, Branham's design defect claim will proceed under to the risk-utility test and not the consumer expectations test.

[*Reversed and remanded*]

>> CASE QUESTIONS

1. Since the injured plaintiff was not wearing a seatbelt, why is Ford being sued for failing to test the seatbelt sleeve?
2. It is often said that product liability causes of action, especially negligence and strict liability, are coming together or merging. Discuss this idea in light of the South Carolina Supreme Court's decision.
3. Is the consumer expectations test or the risk utility test more favorable to manufacturers? Explain.
4. Can Branham still win this case? Explain.

16. ULTRAHAZARDOUS ACTIVITY

In most states, the courts impose strict liability in tort for types of activities they call *ultrahazardous*. Transporting and using explosives and poisons fall under this category, as does keeping dangerous wild animals. Injuries caused from artificial storage of large quantities of liquid can also bring strict liability on the one who stores. For an example of the unusual dangers of ultrahazardous activity, see Sidebar 10.11.

Some states have analyzed fireworks-related explosions that cause accidental injury by the standard of ultrahazardous activity.

>> *sidebar* 10.11

The Great Molasses Flood

The Purity Distilling Co. had filled the enormous steel tank on the Boston hillside with two million gallons of molasses to be turned into rum. Unusually warm weather caused the molasses to expand. On January 15, 1919, with sounds like gunfire as the restraining bolts sheared, the tank exploded. A wave of hot molasses 30-feet high raced down the street toward Boston Harbor, faster than people could run, engulfing entire buildings. Before it subsided, 150 people were injured and 21 drowned. "The dead," reported the *Boston Herald*, "were like candy statues."

It took months to clean up the harbor. It took six years to resolve the 125 lawsuits that followed. The artificial storage of large quantities of liquid can be a sticky matter indeed.

Source: Anthony V. Riccio, *Portrait of an Italian-American Neighborhood* (1998).

17. OTHER STRICT LIABILITY TORTS

The majority of states impose strict liability upon tavern owners for injuries to third parties caused by their intoxicated patrons. The acts imposing this liability are called **dram shop acts.** Because of the public attention given in recent years to intoxicated drivers, there has been a tremendous increase in dram shop act cases.

Common carriers, transportation companies licensed to serve the public, are also strictly liable for damage to goods being transported by them. Common carriers, however, can limit their liability in certain instances through contractual agreement, and they are not liable for (1) acts of God, such as natural catastrophes; (2) action of an alien enemy; (3) order of public authority, such as authorities of one state barring potentially diseased fruit shipments from another state from entering their state; (4) the inherent nature of the goods, such as perishable vegetables; and (5) misconduct of the shipper, such as improper packaging.

>> Damages

LO 10-4

One legal scholar concludes that "the crucial controversy in personal injury torts today" is in the area of damages. For dramatic examples of the size of recent awards, refer to Sidebar 10.12. Juries determine the size of damage

>> *sidebar* 10.12

Highest Jury Tort Awards of 2010

EVENT CAUSING INJURY	JURY AWARD IN MILLIONS OF DOLLARS
1. Pharmaceutical products liability causing hepatitis C outbreak.	$505.1
2. Products liability for secondhand asbestos exposure to worker's laundry.	$208.8
3. Verdict against a cigarette company for providing deceased woman free cigarettes when she was a child.	$152
4. Products liability for design defect in a Ford Bronco rollover accident.	$132.5
5. Negligence verdict against a bus company to seven passengers injured or killed while riding in an unlicensed commercial van.	$124.5
6. Verdict against the world's largest law firm involving malpractice and intentional interference with business (contractual) relationships.	$103
7. Products liability against a cigarette company involving lung cancer death.	$ 90.8
8. Products liability for production defect of a carburetor in an airplane crash.	$ 89
9. Negligence in a natural gas explosion causing death at a plant.	$ 82.5
10. Cigarette products liability for lung cancer death.	$ 80

Note: Although virtually ignored in news media headlines, the damages in almost all of these large jury verdicts were reduced significantly. In some instances the judge reduced the damages as a matter of law. In other cases, appeals courts reduced damages or reversed the trial court. In many cases, however, the parties simply negotiated a reduced settlement to avoid the risk of an appeal that upheld or reversed the damages entirely. In reading about large jury verdicts, this final outcome is an important point for you to remember.

awards in most cases, but judges also play a role in damages, especially in damage instructions to the jury and in deciding whether to approve substantial damage awards.

18. COMPENSATORY DAMAGES

Most damages awarded in tort cases compensate the plaintiff for injuries suffered. The purpose of damages is to make the plaintiff whole again, at least financially. There are three major types of loss that potentially follow tort injury and are called **compensatory damages.** They are:

- Past and future medical expenses.
- Past and future economic loss (including property damage and loss of earning power).
- Past and future pain and suffering.

Compensatory damages may also be awarded for loss of limb, loss of consortium (the marriage relationship), and mental distress.

Calculation of damage awards creates significant problems. Juries frequently use state-adopted life expectancy tables and present-value discount tables to help them determine the amount of damages to award. But uncertainty about the life expectancy of injured plaintiffs and the impact of inflation often makes these tables misleading. Also, awarding damages for pain and suffering is an art rather than a science. These awards measure jury sympathy as much as they calculate compensation for any financial loss. The recent dramatic increases in the size of damage awards helps underline the problems in their calculation. One result is that many individuals and businesses are underinsured for major tort liability.

Currently, compensatory damage awards for pain and suffering are very controversial. How do you compensate injured plaintiffs for something like pain which has no market value? Many plaintiffs suffer lifelong pain or the permanent loss of vision, hearing, or mobility. No amount of damages seems large enough to compensate them, yet no amount of damages, however high, will cause their pain and suffering to stop. In 2003, President Bush called for the limitation of tort damages for pain and suffering in a case to $250,000 per person. Do you agree or disagree?

19. PUNITIVE DAMAGES

Compensatory damages are not the only kind of damages. There are also **punitive damages.** By awarding punitive damages, courts or juries punish defendants for committing intentional torts and for negligent behavior considered "gross" or "willful and wanton." The key to the award of punitive damages is the defendant's motive. Usually the motive must be "malicious," "fraudulent," or "evil." Increasingly, punitive damages are also awarded for dangerously negligent conduct that shows a conscious disregard for the interests of others. These damages punish those who commit aggravated torts and act to deter future wrongdoing. Because they make an example out of the defendant, punitive damages are sometimes called *exemplary damages*.

> **Punitive** or exemplary damages arise from intentional torts or extreme "willful and wanton" negligence.

Presently, there is much controversy about how appropriate it is to award punitive damages against corporations for their economic activities. Especially when companies fail to warn of known danger created by their activities, or when cost-benefit decisions are made at the risk of substantial human injury, courts are upholding substantial punitive damage awards against companies. Yet consider that these damages are a windfall to the injured plaintiff who has already received compensatory damages. And instead of punishing guilty management for wrongdoing, punitive damages may end up punishing innocent shareholders by reducing their dividends.

Many court decisions also overlook a very important consideration about punitive damages. Most companies carry liability insurance policies that reimburse them for "all sums which the insured might become legally obligated to pay." This includes reimbursement for punitive damages. Instead of punishing guilty companies, punitive damages may punish other companies, which have to pay increased insurance premiums, and may punish consumers, who ultimately pay higher prices. As a matter of public policy, several states prohibit insurance from covering punitive damages, but the

> "If you were to talk to foreign businesses about what scares them the most about the U.S. judicial process, they would say class actions and punitive damages."
>
> **–Carter G. Phillips, Sidney Austin Brown & Wood (law firm)**

great majority of states permit such coverage. This fact severely undermines arguments for awarding punitive damages against companies for their economic activities.

Consider also that an award of punitive damages greatly resembles a criminal fine. Yet the defendant who is subject to these criminal-type damages lacks the right to be indicted by a grand jury and cannot assert the right against self-incrimination. In addition, the defendant is subject to a lower standard of proof than in a criminal case. However, defendants in tort suits have challenged awards of punitive damages on a constitutional basis. See Sidebar 10.13.

>> *sidebar* 10.13

Punitive Damage Guidelines

In 2003 the Supreme Court determined that $145 million in punitive damages in a case was unconstitutional. In *State Farm v. Campbell,* the Court decided that the large difference between punitive and compensatory damages violated due process. The Court suggested that a single-digit ratio of punitive to compensatory damages (9/1 or less) would be more constitutionally appropriate than a 145/1 ratio.

State Farm v. Campbell also reaffirmed general punitive damage guidelines from an earlier case. The Court stated, in evaluating the appropriateness of punitive damages, that courts should consider:

- "the responsibility of the defendant's conduct (how bad it was),
- the ratio of punitive to actual damages
- how the punitive damages compare with criminal or civil penalties for the same conduct."

Note that juries award punitive damages in only about 2% of litigated cases.

Finally, note that almost no other country in the world except the United States permits civil juries to award punitive damages. For instance, in 2007 an Italian court refused to enforce a $1 million award against an Italian helmet maker whose defective helmet had caused the death of a 15-year-old motorcyclist in Alabama because the award contained punitive damages. However, a few courts in other countries have enforced U.S. punitive damage awards even though courts in their own countries cannot award them.

>> Key Terms

Assault 291	Contributory negligence 307	Fraud 297
Assumption-of-the-risk 308	Conversion 295	Infliction of mental distress 292
Battery 291	Defamation 295	
Cause in fact 306	Design defect 309	Injurious falsehood 300
Comparative responsibility 307	Dram shop act 313	Intent 290
	Duty 301	Intentional interference with contractual relations 300
Compensatory damages 314	False imprisonment 294	

Invasion of privacy 293
Libel 295
Malicious prosecution 294
Negligence 301
Production defect 309
Proximate cause 306

Punitive damages 315
Slander 295
State-of-the-art 310
Statute of repose 310
Strict liability 308
Strict products liability 309

Tort 289
Trespass 294
Willful and wanton
 negligence 305

>> Review Questions and Problems

Intentional Torts

1. *Assault and Battery*

   Under what theory can an employee sue her employer for merely touching her? Explain.

2. *Intentional Infliction of Mental Distress*

   In business the intentional infliction of mental distress tort has most often involved what type of situation?

3. *Invasion of Privacy*

   Explain the three principal invasions of personal interest that make up invasion of privacy.

4. *False Imprisonment and Malicious Prosecution*

   Explain the difference between false imprisonment and malicious prosecution. In what business situation does false imprisonment most frequently arise?

5. *Trespass*

   In recent months, homeowners downwind from International Cement Company have had clouds of cement dust settle on their property. Trees, shrubbery, and flowers have all been killed. The paint on houses has also been affected. Explain what tort cause of action these homeowners might pursue against International.

6. *Conversion*

   Bartley signs a storage contract with Universal Warehouses. The contract specifies that Bartley's household goods will be stored at Universal's midtown storage facility while he is out of the country on business. Later, without contacting Bartley, Universal transfers his goods to a suburban warehouse. Two days after the move, a freak flood wipes out the suburban warehouse and Bartley's goods. Is Universal liable to Bartley? Explain.

7. *Defamation*

   Acme Airlines attempts to get control of Free Fall Airways by making a public offer to buy its stock from shareholders. Free Fall's president, Joan, advises the shareholders in a letter that Acme's president, Richard, is "little better than a crook" and "can't even control his own company." Analyze the potential liability of Free Fall's president for these remarks.

8. *Fraud*

   Fraud can be used to void a contract and as a basis for intentional tort. What is the advantage to a plaintiff of suing for the tort of fraud as opposed to using fraud merely as a contractual defense?

9. *Common Law Business Torts*

   You are concerned because several of your employees have recently broken their employment contracts and left town. Investigation reveals that Sly and Company, your competitor in a nearby city, has paid bonuses to your former employees to persuade them to break their contracts. Discuss what legal steps you can take against Sly.

Negligence

10. *Duty of Care*

    (a) Do you have a duty of care to warn a stranger on the street of the potential danger of broken glass ahead?

(b) Do you have a duty to warn an employee of similar danger at a place of employment? Explain.

11. *Unreasonable Behavior—Breach of Duty*

In litigation who usually determines if the defendant's behavior is unreasonable?

12. *Causation in Fact*

(a) What does it mean to say that "chains of causation stretch out endlessly"?

(b) What is the standard used by the judge in instructing the jury about causation?

13. *Proximate Causation*

Explain the difference between proximate causation and causation in fact.

14. *Defenses to Negligence*

A jury finds Lee, the defendant, liable in a tort case. It determines that José, the plaintiff, has suffered $200,000 in damages. The jury also finds that José's own fault contributed 25% to his injuries. Under a comparative negligence instruction, what amount of damages will the jury award the plaintiff?

Strict Liability in Tort

15. *Strict Products Liability*

While driving under the influence of alcohol, Joe runs off the road and wrecks his car. As the car turns over, the protruding door latch hits the ground and the door flies open. Joe, who is not wearing his seat belt, is thrown from the car and badly hurt. Joe sues the car manufacturer, asserting that the door latch was defectively designed. Discuss the legal issues raised by these facts.

16. *Ultrahazardous Activity*

Through no one's fault, a sludge dam of the Phillips Phosphate Company breaks. Millions of gallons of sludge run off into a nearby river that empties into Pico Bay. The fishing industry in the bay area is ruined. Is Phillips Phosphate liable to the fishing industry? Explain.

17. *Other Strict Liability Torts*

Explain when common carriers are not strictly liable for damage to transported goods.

Damages

18. *Compensatory Damages*

Explain the three types of loss that give rise to compensatory damages.

19. *Punitive Damages*

During a business lunch, Bob eats salad dressing that contains almond extract. He is very allergic to nuts and suffers a severe allergic reaction. There are complications and Bob becomes almost totally paralyzed. Because Bob had instructed the restaurant waiter and the chef that he might die if he ate any nuts, he sues the restaurant for negligence. Discuss the types of damages Bob may recover.

business >> *discussions*

1. You own University Heights Apartments, a business that rents primarily to students. One evening, your tenant Sharon is attacked by an intruder who forces the lock on the sliding glass door of her ground-floor apartment. Sharon's screams attract the attention of Darryl, your resident manager, who comes to Sharon's aid. Together, he and Sharon drive the intruder off, but not before they both are badly cut by the intruder.

> Is the intruder liable for what he has done?
> Do you have legal responsibilities to Sharon and Darryl?
> What should you consider doing at your apartments?

2. You manufacture trunk locks and your major account is a large car company. When an important piece of your equipment unexpectedly breaks, you contact Mayfair, Inc., the only manufacturer of such equipment, and contract to replace it. The Mayfair sales representative assures you orally and in writing that the prepaid equipment will arrive by October 1, in time for you to complete your production for the car company. Instead, there is a union strike in the Mayfair trucking division, and the equipment does not arrive until December 1.

By December 1 the car company has made an agreement with another lock manufacturer. You threaten to sue Mayfair for their failure to deliver on time, but Mayfair reminds you of a contract term that relieves them of contractual liability because of "labor difficulties." Then you learn from a former secretary to the Mayfair sales representative that Mayfair knew that its trucking division was likely to strike. In fact the sales representative and the sales vice president had discussed whether or not to tell you of this fact and decided not to out of concern that you would not place your order.

> Has Mayfair done anything legally wrong?
> Is your legal remedy against Mayfair limited to breach of contract?
> Will you be able to get damages from Mayfair other than a refund of your prepayment? Explain.

Chapter 11. Intellectual Property

Intellectual Property

☐ Learning Objectives

In this chapter you learn:

11-1. To recognize why intellectual property is so important to our economic system and explain how it creates incentives for investment.

11-2. To identify the type of information that is protected by trade secret law and characterize circumstances that constitute misappropriation.

11-3. To list the requirements for a valid patent and recognize important issues in the enforcement of patents.

11-4. To categorize source indicators as trademark types and to differentiate between trademark dilution and infringement.

11-5. To define copyright protection and fair use limitations.

11-6. To describe the basic elements of the international system for protecting intellectual property rights.

In reading the previous chapters, you should have come to understand that the essence of "property" is a certain system of law. **Property** establishes a relationship of legal exclusion between an owner and other people regarding limited resources. It makes a particular resource like a new discovery legally "proper" to the owner rather than someone else.

The concept of ownership is easiest to understand in the context of something physical. You can readily intuit what it means to own a plot of land surrounded by a fence or an automobile, and laws that protect such ownership seem natural. Of course, it is a mistake to think that you can always know the exact boundaries of what is legally proper to you. Your property includes the legal uses of what you own, and the full extent of these uses is frequently unclear. By using what you own, you will at some point collide with the equal right of others to what they own. It is the job of both common law and statutory tort law to determine when you cross the boundary separating your proper use from wrongful injury to what belongs legally to others.

If defining boundaries is a daunting task in the tangible world, consider how much more difficult it is for the intangible. Should individuals or firms be permitted to own information as if it were property? If so, how do we determine the limits? These are important questions, because when property boundaries are unknown or difficult to determine and to enforce, much concern arises about the property system.

The decision to permit the ownership of information is not theoretical. Modern businesses count on the advantage of controlling inventions, expressions, marks, designs and business secrets like marketing plans or a list of customers. The different kinds of intangible, mostly knowledge-based assets that businesses may possess include the following:

- Employee skills and talents
- Production designs, inventions, and technologies
- Processes and methods of business operation
- Reports, manuals, and databases
- Relationships with customers and suppliers and brand identity
- Software
- New product or service research
- Marketing plans

To provide the necessary control, we apply property law to such information through rights like trade secrets, patents, trademarks, and copyrights. Today, intellectual property represents protection of some of the most valuable resources that businesses have. However, against this backdrop of economic significance, we continue to explore the proper boundaries of information ownership.

>> *sidebar* 11.1

The Increasing Importance of Intellectual Property

Knowledge assets are perhaps the most valuable resources of modern businesses. How to make things, how to do things, where to get things, how to sell things, how to buy things, and how to manage people are all vitally important to businesses. To some extent, knowledge assets can be protected by property, and property enables businesses to capture or realize the value of these assets.

Although it is impossible to know the exact value of intellectual property owned by a firm at any given time, there is a general consensus that it constitutes an ever-greater percentage of firm assets.

The information economy, in which some successful businesses never produce a single physical product, has increased the importance of intangible information. In addition, the business community has become more aware of the advantages of intellectual property ownership. Firms are seeking portfolios that are striking in their breadth and diversity. Sports teams and universities vigorously protect trademarks. Social networking services like Facebook even own patents. In the modern business world, it is critical to understand the basics of intellectual property just to compete.

This chapter begins by considering the justification for intellectual property. It then explores the importance of knowledge assets to businesses, followed by the major forms of intellectual property: trade secrets, patents, trademarks, and copyrights. It concludes by reviewing the international legal environment and examining how intellectual property serves the common good.

1. THE JUSTIFICATION FOR INTELLECTUAL PROPERTY `LO 11-1`

The justification for **intellectual property** is the same as for the private property system generally. Property relationships are believed to be more productive in allocating scarce resources and producing new ones than legal relationships that merely divide resources equally.

Abraham Lincoln said that intellectual property couples "the fuel of interest with the fire of genius." He was referring to how an exclusive right to what you acquire and produce gives incentive to create new things, new ways of doing things, and new invention generally. The framers of the U.S. Constitution made sure that Congress could protect intellectual property. Article 1, Section 8, of the Constitution grants Congress the power "[t]o promote the Progress of Science and useful Arts, by securing for limited Times to Authors and Inventors the exclusive Right to their respective Writings and Discoveries." Note that the justification for "securing" an "exclusive Right" is "[t]o promote the Progress of Science [knowledge and creativity] and the useful Arts [inventions]." The Constitution recognizes that exclusive property boundaries promote, or give incentive to, the business production of what people need and want. However, the Constitution also ensures that after "limited Times" defined by Congress, the resources of new expression and invention, which were formerly exclusive to "Authors and Inventors," will be freely available to everyone.

2. INTELLECTUAL PROPERTY AND COMPETITION

The basic economic system of intellectual property is grounded in the idea of incentives. We give firms and individuals the ability to secure property rights if they produce certain types of information. Those property rights provide exclusivity that can lead to market advantages such as the ability to charge premium prices or utilize customer recognition. The possibility of economic return on investment encourages firms and individuals to create more information than they otherwise would.

Conversely, without intellectual property, the pace of creative research and development (R&D) in business would slow dramatically. R&D is expensive. If businesses have to finance R&D and then compete against others who quickly copy the resulting new invention, the businesses paying for R&D will be at a competitive disadvantage.

Countering the benefits of intellectual property protection are certain costs. Property rights in information reduce competition (at least temporarily) that could otherwise increase availability and keep prices low for consumers. Intellectual property systems presume that the long-term benefits of increased information and investment are greater than the short-term costs.

Is intellectual property protection necessary for the production of *all* information? Intuitively, you know this is not true. An artist may paint simply to express herself without any notion of making a profit or excluding others from the work. A university scientist may investigate the mechanism of disease for the notoriety of discovery and the desire to benefit humanity. A blogger may write a post solely for the satisfaction of knowing that it will be shared widely and many people will read it. It is fair to say that intellectual property is believed to *incrementally increase* the production of information and investment over that which would normally occur. Society obtains this benefit in exchange for allowing some information to be controlled through property. The great debate regarding our intellectual property laws is whether they are truly calibrated to provide a net benefit to society.

>> *sidebar* 11.2

The Open Source Alternative

You may have heard of information products like software being distributed under an open source model. This means that the information is shared freely, and individuals and firms are able to build upon it outside of the strict control of the creator. Open source models of information development have been particularly successful in networked communities as exist across the Internet. Some believe that it is a better alternative than intellectual property or contract for producing certain types of information.

Note that open source products are not necessarily divorced from intellectual property rights.

For example, open source software is often offered accompanied by a license that sets certain use limitations. The purpose of the license may be to ensure continued open access and to prevent unauthorized commercialization, which is usually not a property-centric goal. Yet, these open access provisions may be enforced through intellectual property. Failure to adhere to the terms constitutes infringement.

Source: Yochai Benkler, *Coase's Penguin, or, Linux and* The Nature of the Firm, 112 Yale L.J. 369 (2002).

---

3. CAPTURING INTELLECTUAL PROPERTY

The protections of property often do not apply automatically to ownership of intangible knowledge resources. Depending on the type of information, you may be required to undertake certain steps to protect the time, effort, and money spent in developing knowledge in order to transform it into valuable intangible assets. Some intellectual property forms have very strict deadlines for asserting rights or other formal requirements. The failure to follow the rules may mean that information that could have been captured is instead dedicated to the public domain, meaning that anyone can use it. In general, once information is in the public domain, an intellectual property right cannot be applied to recapture it. Firms that do not have an intellectual property strategy in place risk losing valuable assets.

The sections that follow describe the forms of property that protect knowledge-based intangible business resources. Some general principles are conveyed, that can guide you in finding more detailed information. This chapter concludes by examining the right of property and the common good.

  >> Trade Secrets

One of the most common ways of asserting property in knowledge-based intangible business resources is through the trade secret. Trade secret law developed in the common law industrial revolutions of the 1800s. Before this time, the relationship of confidence and trust between skilled artisans (craftspersons) and their apprentices protected what the artisans knew from harmful competition by their former apprentices. But the 1800s brought large factories to the economy. The employees of these factories were not apprentices and at first were free to take their employers' knowledge, leave employment, and compete against their former employers. Trade secret law arose to protect the employers' valuable knowledge. It also facilitated economic development by making employers willing to hire employees who might come into contact with the employers' knowledge.

A **trade secret** is any form of knowledge or information that (1) has economic value from not being generally known to, or readily ascertainable by proper means by, others and (2) has been the subject of reasonable efforts by the owner to maintain secrecy. To violate another's trade secret rights, one must misappropriate the information. This is an important distinction from intellectual property rights that make one liable simply for unauthorized use. The majority of states have adopted the Uniform Trade Secrets Act (UTSA), but some states continue to rely on common law protection. The UTSA does not differ substantially from common law. Let us now examine the two elements of a trade secret.

4. ESTABLISHING THE EXISTENCE OF A TRADE SECRET

As described above, businesses may possess many different forms of valuable knowledge. It may be financial, technical, scientific, economic, or engineering knowledge. When a business has spent time, effort, or money in training skills, preparing materials, making plans, or developing relationships with customers and suppliers, the business may wish that its competitors not have access to this knowledge. However, not all of this knowledge is covered by the law of trade secrets. To protect information as a trade secret, the information must actually be secret, and the business must take *reasonable measures* to keep it so.

A first step in protecting trade secrets is to identify confidential knowledge-based resources. It is useful for all businesses to conduct a *trade secret audit*, which simply lists all the valuable forms of information possessed by the business, including formulas, plans, reports, manuals, research, and knowledge of customers and suppliers. Interestingly, multiple businesses may have trade secret property in substantially the same knowledge. For example, they may each have customer lists that overlap with many of the same names. As long as there are actual or potential competitors who are not aware of all the customer names, the knowledge still has economic value. It has not become general public knowledge just because multiple competitors have overlapping lists.

Having identified potential trade secrets, a business must next assert its property by preserving secrecy. Reasonable measures to preserve secrecy over valuable knowledge resources include physically locking away formulas, research results, blueprints, and various written plans. In the era of e-mail and the Internet, companies routinely protect computer-stored knowledge with protective "firewalls" and encryption to keep hackers from obtaining access. Some companies maintain two different computer systems in order to protect proprietary (owned) knowledge, one connected to the Internet and

> "More than ever before, information is what gives businesses their competitive edge, and they want to make sure that inside dope on products and services doesn't walk out the door."
>
> *–BusinessWeek,*
> **November 12, 2007,**
> **p. 76.**

Trade secret audits help you identify the valuable information that a business produces.

one networked only internally. Employees use the internal network to send messages about matters that are not for public consumption. To protect trade secrets from outsiders, companies often also carefully regulate who can visit the business and what areas of the business visitors can see. Visitors are sometimes required to sign agreements not to disclose to the public what they see and learn in a company they visit.

Business customers, suppliers, and repair technicians—in addition to visitors—may also have access to knowledge that a company values and protects. Like visitors, these parties may also be asked to sign nondisclosure agreements (contracts). As long as a company takes such reasonable measures to prevent the public dissemination of trade secrets, it does not lose its property in knowledge-based resources merely because customers, suppliers, repair technicians, or even visitors come into contact with the secrets.

Establishing the existence of a trade secret is a critical step in controlling valuable knowledge resources. The failure to maintain secrecy, or to prove that the knowledge was secret in the first place, can mean that competitors may be able to access it. Case 11.1 is an illustration of this fundamental requirement.

 case 11.1 >>

NATIONWIDE MUTUAL INSURANCE CO v. MORTENSEN
606 F.3d 22 (2d Cir. 2010)

The file that an insurance company keeps for a customer includes valuable information about the customer's history that informs pricing and policy options. If a competitor obtains that information, it can offer an alternate policy and take away business. Although customer files have economic value, it is essentially the customer's information. That customer can repeat it to anyone else without breaching a duty of confidentiality. Therefore, courts have been reluctant to characterize customer files as a trade secret. However, is a secret created when a company incorporates this information into a secure computer system?

PARKER, J: When each defendant began to work as a Nationwide insurance agent, he or she signed an identical, standard-form contract with Nationwide called an Agent's Agreement. By the terms of the contract, each defendant's relationship with the company was that of an exclusive agent and "independent contractor." Initially, the agents were given a large number of policyholder files of preexisting Nationwide customers. From then on, they serviced these customers and solicited new ones. In the course of this work, they maintained physical policyholder files containing

information relevant to the customers' insurance needs, including documentation that they received from both the customers and Nationwide . . .

The agents also used Nationwide's Agency Office Automation ("AOA") computer system, which they were required to lease from Nationwide. This database linked them with Nationwide's central computers, permitting them to access insurance quotes in real-time, and it gathered and sorted the information collected in the policyholder files. The AOA system was password-protected. . . .

In late 1999 and early 2000, the defendants terminated their agency relationships with Nationwide. In the months leading up to the terminations, they met with representatives of other insurance companies to discuss possible employment. During these meetings, they allegedly shared with the companies information contained in Nationwide's policyholder files concerning prices, computer print-outs of policyholder information from the AOA computer system ("screen prints"), and copies of documents they received from Nationwide relating to their sales and commissions. After terminating the Agent's Agreement, they began to compete with Nationwide by selling policies issued by its competitors. . . .

[continued]

On learning of the defendants' activities, Nationwide filed this suit in diversity, contending that the agents had violated numerous provisions of Connecticut law . . .

Nationwide's primary claim is that the policyholder files retained by the departing agents constitute trade secrets protected by [the Connecticut Uniform Trade Secrets Act (CUTSA)]. . . . While customer lists are within the scope of CUTSA, a number of courts have noted that such materials often lie "on the periphery of the law of trade secrets and unfair competition." . . .

Importantly, although Nationwide contested the agents' right to all of the policyholder files and information in the litigation below, on appeal it focuses exclusively on print-outs that the agents took from the AOA computer system. This strategy was designed, presumably, to strengthen Nationwide's argument that the screen-prints represent proprietary or confidential information [because a significant number of courts have rejected the argument that the agents' policyholder files themselves qualify as trade secrets]. The shift in focus, however, seriously undercuts Nationwide's argument. We must conclude, as a result, that Nationwide's claims with respect to the physical policyholder files have been waived on appeal. . . . Yet at the same time, the company nowhere shows that the AOA screen-prints contain substantially different information from the physical policyholder files. . . .

It is difficult to understand, then, how the screen-prints could be protected as trade secrets when this information could be easily obtained from the physical policyholder files themselves.

In order to qualify as a trade secret, materials cannot be "readily ascertainable by proper means" from another source. . . . The record offers little basis for concluding that the information in the AOA screen-prints was materially different from that contained in the files themselves. . . . On appeal, Nationwide points to no evidence suggesting otherwise. In fact, it is undisputed that the agents generally entered information into the AOA database directly from the physical files maintained at their offices. At most, the AOA database condensed this information into an organized format and permitted an agent to generate Nationwide quotes based on a policyholder's data in real-time. But, at bottom, a screen-print was an electronic compilation of information readily available in the very same office. Simply because the AOA information existed in a different, better-protected format than the physical folders does not elevate it to trade secret status. It is not the medium that matters here, but whether the information itself was adequately protected—and it was not. Because this same information was readily available from another source, it does not qualify as a trade secret as a matter of law. The district court's dismissal is affirmed. . . .

>> CASE QUESTIONS

1. Why was this case tried in federal court rather than in state court?
2. What did the court determine about the trade secret status of the screen-print files?
3. Could Nationwide possess any confidential information regarding its customers, outside of the policyholder files?
4. Can you imagine any other ways that Nationwide could have limited competition from its agents?

5. DEMONSTRATING MISAPPROPRIATION

To be liable in a trade secret case, a defendant must have misappropriated the information in question. Misappropriation obviously occurs when one improperly acquires secret information through burglary, espionage or computer hacking. However, misappropriation also occurs when one discloses information that one was under a duty to keep secret, even if the original acquisition was proper. Such a duty may arise from an employment relationship or a contractual agreement. Additionally, if one acquires a secret from another who has a duty to maintain secrecy, and one knows of that duty, misappropriation has occurred.

Importantly, independent creation does *not* constitute misappropriation. If, through your own effort, you are able to recreate the same information that another considers to be a trade secret, no misappropriation has occurred. In addition, reverse engineering a secret by looking at a product and figuring out how it works or how it is formulated is not misappropriation. An exception to this principle would be if one contractually agreed to keep the information secret.

The fact that secrets can get out through normal product marketing is an important limitation on trade secret rights. For that reason, as discussed below, a patent may provide better protection for a valuable invention embodied in a product, assuming the stringent requirements can be met. On the other hand, if the valuable information relates to processes or techniques that will not be disclosed when a product or service is sold, trade secret rights may be a viable, relatively inexpensive, and long-lived option.

> **Do** remember the role of contractual confidentiality agreements and do not compete agreements in preserving trade secrets.

Employee Mobility and Trade Secrets   Businesses have to take reasonable measures to protect trade secrets even from employees. Employees may leave an employer and use the knowledge they have gained to compete against their former employer, or they may go to work for their former employer's competitors.

Increasingly, employers require employees to sign confidentiality contracts promising not to disclose what they learn in confidence in the workplace. This promise, however, applies only to knowledge that is unknown publicly and amounts to trade secrets. Additionally, not all states presume that former employees are likely to disclose confidential information in a new position. This creates difficulty in establishing misappropriation. Because it may be difficult to establish all of the elements of a trade secret case employers frequently take the additional step of having employees agree not to compete against them if the employees leave their employment.

The law states that employers can enforce agreements (or contractual "covenants") not to compete only when there is a "valid business purpose" for the contract. Generally, this means that employers are protecting trade secrets, or, at least protecting their investment in the training of their employees, which itself can be a trade secret. The laws of unfair competition limit the extent to which employers can prevent employees from competing against them. The contracts and antitrust chapters discuss these limitations in greater detail. You should appreciate, however, how businesses use contracts to ensure recognition of property over intangible resources.

6. CIVIL ENFORCEMENT OF TRADE SECRETS

> The wrongful taking of any kind of intellectual property is called *misappropriation* or *infringement.*

The owner of a trade secret may go into court and get an injunction to prevent others—often former employees—from divulging or using a trade secret. An **injunction** is an order by a judge either to do something or to refrain from doing something. In the case of trade secrets, the injunction orders those who have *misappropriated* the trade secret to refrain from using it or telling others about it. In rare instances the injunction may also order that one delay in taking a new job.

Trade secret owners can also obtain damages against those who misappropriate trade secrets. In 2011, a California jury awarded St. Jude Medical, Inc., $2.3 billion in a dispute against a former employee and rival medical device company, Nervicon. The employee allegedly left St. Jude with documents related to a crystal oscillator, and used the document to help Nervicon create the same device.

7. CRIMINAL ENFORCEMENT OF TRADE SECRETS

In addition to civil enforcement of trade secret boundaries, criminal prosecution can also result from misappropriation of trade secrets. Although various state laws make intentional trade secret misappropriation a crime, the primary criminal prosecutions today result under the federal Economic Espionage Act (EEA). The act makes it a crime to steal (intentionally misappropriate) trade secrets and provides for fines and up to 10 years' imprisonment for individuals and up to a $5 million fine for organizations.

Although one provision of the EEA makes one liable for misappropriation to benefit a foreign government—the act that usually comes to mind when we think of espionage—the law also has a provision that relates to common trade secret theft. The Coca-Cola case in Sidebar 11.3 is an example of an Economic Espionage Act criminal prosecution.

>> *sidebar* 11.3

Soda Secrets

The Coca-Cola Company considers the formula for its namesake drink, also known as Coke, to be a valuable secret. Even though it was created over 100 years ago, the company refuses to disclose the original formula and continues to undertake measures to maintain its secrecy. Through various reformulations, the basic recipe remains confidential according to the company.

However, is it possible to discern the formula for Coca-Cola from a purchased bottle? Science provides the means for characterizing the various elements of chemical compounds, and one would assume that such techniques could be applied to a soft drink to learn its composition. Absent a contract, patent, or employee relationship, this type of reverse engineering does not violate the law. In fact, over the years, several people have claimed to be in possession of the secret formula for Coca-Cola through disclosure or reverse engineering, including the host of

the radio program *This American Life* in 2011. Without a confirmation from the Coca-Cola Company, it is difficult to know for certain how accurate such claims are.

Regardless of whether the actual formula for Coca-Cola is known outside the company, it is certainly true that Coca-Cola can possess protectable trade secrets on newer products. In 2007, a jury convicted a former Coca-Cola secretary for conspiring with others to steal secrets for products in development and sell them to rival Pepsi for $1.5 million. She was sentenced to eight years in prison. The scheme came to light when Pepsi informed the FBI that it received an offer to obtain Coca-Cola's product secrets.

Sources: Robbie Brow & Kim Severson, "Recipe for Coke? One More to Add to the File," *The New York Times*, Feb. 19, 2011; "Ex-Secretary Gets 8-Year Term in Coca-Cola Secrets Case," The Associated Press, May 24, 2007.

330   **PART 3**   Legal Foundations for Business

The following sections discuss other types of intellectual property and the boundaries they establish.

>> *sidebar* 11.4

Federal Government Intellectual Property Enforcement

Although private parties carry out much enforcement of state and federal intellectual property laws, governments also play an important role. In particular, the federal government prosecutes criminal cases involving copyright infringement (referred to as piracy in some cases), trademark infringement (also known as counterfeiting in some cases), and trade secret misappropriation. In 2008, the Prioritizing Resources and Organization for Intellectual Property Act (PRO IP Act) became law, creating a new position for coordinating federal agency intellectual property enforcement known as the Intellectual Property Enforcement Coordinator (IPEC). Agencies that enforce the nations intellectual property laws include the Department of Justice, through its Computer Crime and Intellectual Property Section (CCIPS), the Federal Bureau of Investigation (FBI), and Customs and Border Protection, as well as many others. CCIPS conducts the actual prosecution of intellectual property cases, and a significant amount of information on its work and the relevant laws can be found at www.cybercrime.gov.

Source: PRO IP Act, Pub. L. No. 110-403 (2008).

LO 11-3   **>> Patent Law**

Patents have existed for hundreds of years as property rights, but the term has not always been associated with a new idea. Historically, a patent was any legal monopoly openly issued by the government. In some cases, European monarchs sold "letters of patent" for large sums of money in order to give private persons sole control over such things as the operation of toll roads, river ferries, and profits. However, patents were associated with invention at least as early as the 1400s. The Venetian Patent Act of 1474 is generally considered to be the world's first patent statute for the purpose of rewarding new ideas. Many of its basic principles for protecting inventions are present in modern patent law.

Today, a **patent** is firmly associated with an inventive act, and conveys a right to exclude others from making, using selling or importing the covered invention. The Constitution authorizes Congress to create patents, and Congress has passed numerous laws affecting exclusive patent right, which, of course, is property. Since colonial times, the United States has been a world leader in establishing patent law. Many of the constitutional framers were interested in technology and new invention, and during the Constitutional Convention in Philadelphia, the framers apparently took time off one afternoon to watch a newly invented steamboat cruising on the Delaware River.

In 1790, Thomas Jefferson helped draft the first federal patent law, and he personally invented numerous new devices and ways of doing things. Abraham Lincoln, however, was the first American president to patent an invention. In 1849 he applied for a patent on a system of air chambers to help boats float in shallow water. The disclosure begins:

To all whom it may concern:

Be it known that I, Abraham Lincoln, of Springfield, in the County of Sangamon, in the State of Illinois, have invented a new and improved manner of combining adjustable buoyant air chambers with a steamboat or other vessel for the purpose of enabling their draught of water [how deep the boat sinks in the water] to be readily lessened to enable them to pass over bars, or through shallow water, without discharging their cargoes. . . .

Many other famous Americans have held patents. For an example, see Sidebar 11.5.

>> *sidebar* 11.5

A Famous Writer's Love Affair with Patents

Mark Twain is best known as one of America's most famous writers. His single most profitable property right, however, came not from any of his books but from a 1873 patent issued on a self-pasting scrapbook. In part, his books were not so profitable because of inadequate enforcement of property law (copyright) to protect their copying and sale.

So fond was Mark Twain of patent law that he wrote about it in *A Connecticut Yankee in King Author's Court* (1889). In the book the main character, Hank

Morgan, gets in a barroom brawl and is knocked out. When he wakes up, he is in the time of King Arthur. By predicting a solar eclipse, he gains the king's favor and is appointed the king's "perpetual minister and executive." He later explains:

> [T]he very first official thing I did in my administration—and it was on the very first day of it too—was to start a patent office; for I knew that a country without a patent office and good patent laws was just a crab, and couldn't travel any way but sideways or backways.

---

8. OBTAINING A PATENT

A patent is an exclusive right created by statute and conveyed by the U.S. Patent and Trademark Office (PTO) for a limited period of time. This property applies to inventions, which are new applications of information.

Don't forget that patents apply for only a limited period of time.

Patent Type It is important to understand that there are actually three types of patents granted by the PTO, each with their own distinct subject matter (See Figure 11.1).

An easy way to remember the distinction between a utility patent and a design patent is that the former applies to useful, functional inventions. Such inventions are what most of us think of when we see the word "patent."

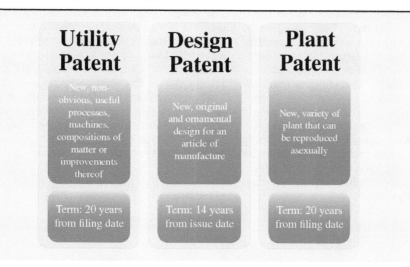

Figure 11.1 *Types of Patents*

On the other hand, design patents apply to the appearance of an article of manufacture, unrelated to its function. They cover subject matter more similar to copyrights (discussed later in this chapter). Plant patents apply to new varieties of asexually reproduced plants. However, it is important to understand that many inventions related to plants may also be protected as utility patents. For example, one or more utility patent rights often cover genetically modified plants. Therefore, just because the subject matter is a plant, the relevant property right is not necessarily a plant patent.

In 2010, the U.S. Patent and Trademark Office received 520,277 patent applications, which is approximately double that received in 1998.

To obtain a patent, an inventor must pay a filing fee and file an application with the PTO. In the case of a utility patent the application must in words and drawings (1) explain how to make and use the basic invention; (2) show why the invention is different from *prior art*, that is, from all previous and related inventions or state of knowledge; and (3) precisely detail the subject matter that the inventor regards as the invention (called *claims*). The PTO assigns a *patent examiner* to consider the application, and there is usually a great deal of communication between the examiner and the applicant over the adequacy of the application's explanations, the scope of the proposed patent (exactly what the patent applies to), and whether the invention even qualifies at all for a patent. The applicant can amend the application, and the process can take several years from start to finish.

In 2011, the President signed into law the *America Invents Act*, the first substantial revision to U.S. patent law since 1999. Among the law's many changes is the eventual switch from a first-to-invent system to a first-inventor-to-file system. This means that, in a contest between two inventors claiming the same patentable idea, the first to get to the patent office will win. On the other hand, the law increases the ability of companies to keep some internal

>> *sidebar* 11.6

Should Utility Patents Always be Presumed Valid?

As noted above, utility patents issue only after a substantial analysis by a professional PTO Examiner. Following such scrutiny, it seems reasonable to give some degree of credit to the process. Patent law accomplishes this by establishing a higher burden of proof for a defendant who wishes to challenge a patent. According to this principle, courts have determined that proof of invalidity must be made by "clear and convincing evidence" instead of the "preponderance of the evidence" standard that exists in most civil cases. This makes it more likely that a patent will be upheld in court.

An increased burden makes sense if the PTO fully considered every issue that the defendant attempts to raise in court. However, what if the defendant finds new evidence of invalidity? Should the clear and convincing standard still apply?

The Supreme Court recently considered this issue in *Microsoft Corp. v. i4i LTD. Partnership*. The case involved software code patented by i4i that Microsoft allegedly incorporated into its word processing software without permission. Microsoft argued that i4i's patent was invalid based on facts not considered by the PTO, even though these facts did not rise to the level of "clear and convincing." The Supreme Court rejected Microsoft's position and decided that clear and convincing evidence of invalidity is necessary in all cases to eliminate an issued patent. The case ensures that utility patents remain strong property rights.

Source: Microsoft Corp. v. i4i LTD. Partnership, 131 S.Ct. 2238 (June 9, 2011)

processes secret and avoid infringing another's patent through "prior user rights." Other provisions in the law are expected to make the patent examination process more efficient, particularly by giving the PTO more control over its funding.

9. PATENTABLE SUBJECT MATTER

After the PTO issues a patent, the patent owner may choose to maintain its exclusivity in the invention. Alternatively, the patentee may license others. However, if another infringes the patent by making, using, selling, or importing the invention without permission, the patent owner may have to defend its property. When the patent owner threatens a lawsuit, it is common for the alleged infringer to respond by attacking the validity of the patent. Validity can be challenged in court or the PTO. If the patent is found invalid, the alleged infringer will win. A finding that a patent is completely invalid in one case is very significant, as it renders the patent invalid against all future defendants, essentially eliminating it.

A *process* is a way of doing something through a series of operations.

Attacking the "subject matter" of a patent is one common way of testing the validity of a patent. Although not unlimited, the subject matter for a potential patent is quite broad. This is particularly true for utility patents. In *Diamond v. Chakrabarty*, 447 U.S. 303 (1980), the Supreme Court ruled that a scientist could cover with a utility patent a genetically modified bacterium that ate hydrocarbons found in oil spills. The Court said, "Congress is free to amend §101 [the subject matter section of the general patent law] so as to exclude from patent protection organisms produced by genetic engineering. . . . Or it may choose to craft a statute specifically designed for such living things. But until Congress takes such action, the language of §101 fairly embraces the respondent's invention." In an example of such congressional action, the 2011 revisions to the patent act explicitly preclude patents covering humans.

One of the most controversial areas of potentially patentable subject matter concerns "processes." What is a process? Is a computer program a process? Are ways of doing business a process? Mere ideas are not a patentable process. Nor are mathematical algorithms or formulas like $E = mc^2$ that express truths about the universe. Historically, business methods like double-entry bookkeeping were considered unpatentable, but they are after all processes, methods for doing things.

In *State Street Bank and Trust Co. v. Signature Financial Group, Inc.*, 149 F.3d 1360 (1998), a federal circuit court that considers all patent appeals from district courts upheld the patent on a data processing system that allowed an administrator to monitor and record the financial information flow and make all calculations necessary for maintaining a mutual fund investment partnership. Following this case, thousands of patents were filed on business-related processes. Subsequently, that court narrowed its ruling asserting that a claim involving mental processes or algorithms is patentable subject matter only if it is tied to a machine or involves the transformation of a physical object. This rule called into question the validity of issued business method patents, and some believed that it could have impacted software as well. In the following case, the Supreme Court considered the viability of "machine or transformation" rule.

case 11.2 >>

BILSKI v. KAPPOS
130 S. Ct. 3218 (2010)

KENNEDY, J: . . . Petitioners' application seeks patent protection for a claimed invention that explains how buyers and sellers of commodities in the energy market can protect, or hedge, against the risk of price changes. The key claims are claims 1 and 4. . . . Claim 1 consists of the following steps:

"(a) initiating a series of transactions between said commodity provider and consumers of said commodity wherein said consumers purchase said commodity at a fixed rate based upon historical averages, said fixed rate corresponding to a risk position of said consumers;

"(b) identifying market participants for said commodity having a counter-risk position to said consumers; and

"(c) initiating a series of transactions between said commodity provider and said market participants at a second fixed rate such that said series of market participant transactions balances the risk position of said series of consumer transactions." . . .

The patent examiner rejected petitioners' application, explaining that it "'is not implemented on a specific apparatus and merely manipulates [an] abstract idea and solves a purely mathematical problem without any limitation to a practical application, therefore, the invention is not directed to the technological arts.'" . . . The Board of Patent Appeals and Interferences affirmed, concluding that the application involved only mental steps that do not transform physical matter and was directed to an abstract idea. . . .

Section 101 . . . specifies four independent categories of inventions or discoveries that are eligible for protection: processes, machines, manufactures, and compositions of matter. "In choosing such expansive terms . . . modified by the comprehensive 'any,' Congress plainly contemplated that the patent laws would be given wide scope." . . . Congress took this permissive approach to patent eligibility to ensure that "'ingenuity should receive a liberal encouragement.'" *Id.,* at 308-309, 100 S. Ct. 2204, 65 L. Ed. 2d 144 (quoting 5 Writings of Thomas Jefferson 75-76 (H. Washington ed. 1871)).

The Court's precedents provide three specific exceptions to §101's broad patent-eligibility principles: "laws of nature, physical phenomena, and abstract ideas." . . . While these exceptions are not required by the statutory text, they are consistent with the notion that a patentable process must be "new and useful." . . .

The §101 patent-eligibility inquiry is only a threshold test. Even if an invention qualifies as a process, machine, manufacture, or composition of matter, in order to receive the Patent Act's protection the claimed invention must also satisfy "the conditions and requirements of this title." §101. Those requirements include that the invention be novel, see §102, nonobvious, see §103, and fully and particularly described, see §112.

The present case involves an invention that is claimed to be a "process" under §101. . . .

Under the Court of Appeals' formulation, an invention is a "process" only if: "(1) it is tied to a particular machine or apparatus, or (2) it transforms a particular article into a different state or thing." 545 F.3d at 954. This Court has "more than once cautioned that courts 'should not read into the patent laws limitations and conditions which the legislature has not expressed.'" . . .

Any suggestion in this Court's case law that the Patent Act's terms deviate from their ordinary meaning has only been an explanation for the exceptions for laws of nature, physical phenomena, and abstract ideas. . . . This Court has not indicated that the existence of these well-established exceptions gives the Judiciary *carte blanche* to impose other limitations that are inconsistent with the text and the statute's purpose and design. Concerns about attempts to call any form of human activity a "process" can be met by making sure the claim meets the requirements of §101.

Adopting the machine-or-transformation test as the sole test for what constitutes a "process" (as opposed to just an important and useful clue) violates these statutory interpretation principles. . . .

Section 101 similarly precludes the broad contention that the term "process" categorically excludes business methods. . . .

The term "method," which is within §100(b)'s definition of "process," at least as a textual matter and before consulting other limitations in the Patent Act and this Court's precedents, may include at least some methods of doing business. . . . The Court is unaware of any argument that the "'ordinary, contemporary, common meaning,'" . . . , of "method" excludes business methods. Nor is it clear how far a prohibition on business method patents would reach, and whether it would exclude technologies for conducting a business more efficiently. . . .

Even though petitioners' application is not categorically outside of §101 under the two broad and atextual approaches the Court rejects today, that does not mean

[continued]

it is a "process" under §101. Petitioners seek to patent both the concept of hedging risk and the application of that concept to energy markets. App. 19-20. Rather than adopting categorical rules that might have wide-ranging and unforeseen impacts, the Court resolves this case narrowly on the basis of this Court's decisions in *Benson, Flook,* and *Diehr,* which show that petitioners' claims are not patentable processes because they are attempts to patent abstract ideas. Indeed, all members of the Court agree that the patent application at issue here falls outside of §101 because it claims an abstract idea. . . .

Today, the Court once again declines to impose limitations on the Patent Act that are inconsistent with the Act's text. The patent application here can be rejected under our precedents on the unpatentability of abstract ideas. The Court, therefore, need not define further what constitutes a patentable "process," beyond pointing to the definition of that term provided in §100(b) and looking to the guideposts in *Benson, Flook,* and *Diehr.*

And nothing in today's opinion should be read as endorsing interpretations of §101 that the Court of Appeals for the Federal Circuit has used in the past. See, *e.g., State Street,* 149 F.3d at 1373; *AT&T Corp.,* 172 F.3d at 1357. It may be that the Court of Appeals thought it needed to make the machine-or-transformation test exclusive precisely because its case law had not adequately identified less extreme means of restricting business method patents, including (but not limited to) application of our opinions in *Benson, Flook,* and *Diehr.* In disapproving an exclusive machine-or-transformation test, we by no means foreclose the Federal Circuit's development of other limiting criteria that further the purposes of the Patent Act and are not inconsistent with its text.

The judgment of the Court of Appeals is affirmed.

10. NOVELTY, NONOBVIOUSNESS, AND UTILITY

To be patentable, it is not enough for something to be appropriate subject matter. An invention must also have certain characteristics. Namely, it must be novel, nonobvious, and useful. An alleged infringer can always defend against an infringement lawsuit by proving that the patent is invalid because the invention is previously known, obvious, or lacks utility.

The characteristic of novelty indicates that something is new and different from the prior art (the previous state of knowledge in the field). The test is met when no single piece of prior art meets all of the elements of an invention's claims. However, under patent law even if an invention is otherwise new, it fails the novelty test if it has been described in a publication, sold, or put to public use more than one year before a patent application on it is filed (the one-year grace period). This limitation exists even if it is the inventor who undertakes such actions. The 2011 revisions to the law apply the one-year grace period only to an inventor's publication, use or sale; activity by others before a patent is filed preclude patentability, even within a year. Note that many countries have no grace period at all.

Nonobviousness refers to the ability of an invention to produce surprising or unexpected results; that is, results not anticipated by prior art. The nonobviousness standard is measured in relation to someone who has ordinary skill in the prior art. For instance, to be patentable a computer hardware invention would need to be nonobvious to an ordinary computer engineer. Importantly, obviousness is assessed as of the date of the application as opposed to later in the litigation. Courts are careful to avoid "highlight" bias, which is the tendency to see any invention as obvious after it is revealed and its significance is known.

Patent litigation over the obviousness of an invention is typically very subjective with each side to the lawsuit producing experts who disagree. Ultimately it is up to the court to determine the state of knowledge existing when the inventor filed the application and whether the invention is nonobvious. See Sidebar 11.7.

Perhaps the most common way of challenging a patent's validity is to claim that the "invention" is obvious to someone with knowledge in the field.

>> *sidebar* 11.7

The Determination of Obviousness

A problem of the patent system is that a single manufactured item like an automobile may have hundreds of patents applying to various parts. Any time an improvement is made on a part by manufacturer X, there is always the possibility that a current patent holder Y will sue claiming infringement. X often responds that Y's patent claim is invalid because it was obvious. If Y's patent claim is obvious, then the fact that X based its new improvement on technology covered by Y's claim is not patent infringement because the patent is invalid.

The Supreme Court faced this situation in *KSR International Co. v. Teleflex, Inc.,* 127 S. Ct. 1727 (2007), a case involving Teleflex's accusation that KSR infringed its patent by adding a new electronic sensor to an adjustable automobile accelerator pedal. Teleflex believed it had a patent that covered the use of electronic sensors along with adjustable automobile accelerator pedals, a combination that did not exist in the prior art. KSR responded by asserting that the patent claim was invalid because the technology of attaching the electronic sensor to the pedal was obvious. In its decision favoring KSR, the Supreme Court rejected a prior decision by the United States Court of Appeals for the Federal Circuit, which deals with patents. That prior case decided that a patent claim is only proved

obvious when some specific reference like a journal article prior to the patent in question teaches, suggests or motivates one of ordinary skill to create the claimed invention (in this case suggesting the attaching of the electronic sensor to an adjustable automobile accelerator pedal prior to the Teleflex patent).

Instead, the Supreme Court observed that a variety of factors could lead a court to conclude legally that a patent was invalid for obviousness. Importantly, the Court said, "We build and create by bringing to the tangible and palpable reality around us new works based on instinct, simple logic, ordinary inferences, extraordinary ideas, and sometimes even genius. These advances, once part of our shared knowledge, define a new threshold for which innovation starts once more. And as progress beginning from higher levels of achievement is expected in the normal course, the results of ordinary innovation are not the subject of exclusive rights under the patent laws. Were it otherwise patents might stifle, rather than promote, the progress of useful arts."

What the Supreme Court has done is to make it somewhat easier to challenge the validity of patents by arguing that patent claims are obvious and that new improvements in technology or designs do not violate patents in the old technology or designs.

Except for patents issued on designs or plants, an invention to be valid must have utility, that is, it must do something useful. Suppose that Acme Laboratory scientists invent a new chemical compound. Until the compound has a use, say, ridding pets of fleas, Acme will be unable to get a utility patent on it. Usefulness was the issue in *Diamond v. Diehr,* 450 U.S. 175 (1981), the first Supreme Court decision to recognize a patent on computer software. The Court stated that the software involved controlled the timing for curing rubber and thus was useful. Since this case, the mathematical algorithms contained in computer software have been patentable if they do something in the real world.

Computer software code has long been copyrightable. The importance of patenting software as opposed to just copyrighting is that the copyright protects only the actual programming code and the look and feel of the program; it does not cover the functionality, which can be copied using different code. But if you patent the actions of the software, you may have a legal monopoly over the way the computer does something, such as controlling rubber curing. Merely changing the code will not keep someone from infringing a patent.

11. PATENT ENFORCEMENT

As the U.S. Constitution specifies, the property represented by patents runs for limited duration. Statutes limit utility patents and plant patents to 20 years from the filing date, and design patents to 14 years from the issue date. When a patent expires, the invention is in the public domain, and others may use it without limitation. Remember that when the patent expires, it is easy to use the invention since the patent application explains exactly how the invention works, including drawings of its construction. The explicit purpose of patent law is to make inventions public following the limited period of legal property right. For the duration of a patent, the owner can sue those who infringe on it. If successful, the owner can get an injunction prohibiting future infringement, damages, including triple damages for willful infringement.

*When a patent expires, the patent is in the *public domain,* and others may use it without limitation.

Complicating the business environment for patents is the fact that they can overlap. Simply owning one is not a license to produce a product or service. A fundamental concept in patent law is that patents only convey the right to exclude others from making, using, selling, and importing the invention. They do not include the right to use the invention. At first glance, the latter point may seem counterintuitive. Can you really own a patent and have no right to make a product that is covered by it? The answer, surprisingly, is yes, and the key to understanding it is to realize that multiple intellectual property rights can cover the same article. There is often more than one patent to a product.

Consider an average cell phone. Imagine that you own a patent that covers touch screen technology, enabling you to open programs and type by placing your fingers on the screen. Now, imagine that your friend owns a patent on technology that allows a phone to switch between hardware buttons and a touch screen. Add another friend who has a patent and perhaps a copyright that cover the phone's operating system (See Figure 11.2). Even though you

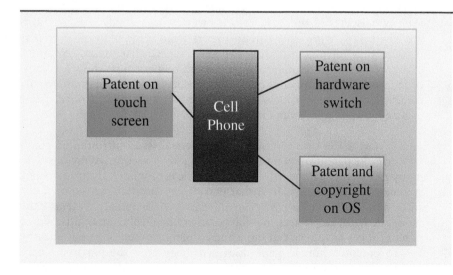

Figure 11.2
Overlapping Intellectual Property Rights

338   **PART 3**   Legal Foundations for Business

The consequences of patent infringement can be high, with two recent cases involving jury awards of over $1 billion. Such awards are often reduced on appeal, but still amount to millions in damages.

own a patent that covers part of a cell phone, you cannot produce the cell phone with the characteristics above without using the rights of others. In reality, of course, cell phones are covered by hundreds of patents as well as other rights. Many licenses are required to produce a single phone. This situation exists to varying degrees with other products.

12. CURRENT ISSUES IN PATENT LAW

What property protects is not always clear. As a patent is an application of property, what patents protect are not always clear. Even when what patents protect is quite certain, the question arises as to whether a property monopoly is appropriate. Consider the following issues.

Some non-practicing patent entities have quite large portfolios, raising concerns on their impact on the marketplace. For example, a company called Intellectual Ventures is reported to own more than 30,000 patents.

Patent Trolls   As described above, patents may overlap to cover a single product, and in some fields the number overlapping rights can be quite large. This makes it difficult to identify and license all of the patents one might infringe. The ambiguity provides an opportunity for one who purchases a patent right simply to sue existing companies, because the damages (from trial or settlement) can be great and the risk to the patent owners relatively small. Out of the belief that such non-practicing patent owners are nothing more than a toll-taker on a bridge, they have been widely referred to as "patent trolls." The pejorative term suggests that non-producing patent owners do not contribute as much to the innovation environment compared to the costs imposed by their enforcement.

As a counter to the patent troll rhetoric, one might consider the fact that non-practicing entities are exercising a legitimate right under their property grant. Patents do not require their owners to actually make and sell an invention. This concept is similar to land property, wherein one may own a plot land but decide not to build anything. However, the overlapping nature of intellectual property sets the stage for greater conflict than with non-producing landowners.

Companies that believe they are disproportionately impacted by troll-like behavior, such as consumer electronics firms, have pushed for reforms. At least two aspects of the 2011 reforms to patent law may reduce troll behavior. The new law prevents patent owners from suing multiple parties merely because they infringe the same patent, a change that makes litigation more expensive for trolls. Going forward, patent owners must show a common set of facts or a case arising out of the same occurrence to join multiple parties in a suit. Additionally, business method patents, as described above, are subject to a new review proceeding if litigated.

"It's a measure of the deeply dysfunctional U.S. patent system that the most sophisticated technology companies have been reduced to investing in patents to defend themselves from one another."

L. Gordon Crovitz in the *Wall Street Journal*, August 22, 2011.

Patenting Genes   Another controversial issue surrounding patent law concerns the patenting of human genes. In part, the controversy arises because many people do not understand what a gene is or what it means to patent one. A gene is a sequence of DNA that occupies a specific location on a chromosome and determines a particular inherited characteristic. Patents can cover the sequence of DNA itself, similar to other chemical compounds. Worldwide, patent offices have received thousands of gene-related patent applications.

To patent a human gene does not mean that the patent holder owns some part of you. Only when the gene has been isolated and purified in a way that can be put to use can someone patent it. Still, many believe that one should not be able to patent basic knowledge about specific genes. They argue that there should be a common use of this knowledge and that its production does not depend on the same incentives that justify other types of patents.

A recent challenge to gene patents has arisen in the context of genes useful for detecting breast cancer. A company called Myriad owns patents covering natural mutations of genes, BRCA1 and BRCA2, that are strongly correlated with breast cancer. Concerned scientists in concert with advocacy groups like the American Civil Liberties Union (ACLU) sued to have the patents declared invalid. To the surprise of many, a federal district court in New York ruled that such gene patents are in fact not patentable subject matter, as they are not materially different from DNA that exists in nature. *Assoc. for Molecular Pathology v. U.S. Patent & Trademark Off.*, 702 F. Supp. 2d 181 (S.D.N.Y. 2010). The decision was largely overturned on appeal by a federal circuit court in July of 2011, but it may be further appealed and eventually reach the U.S. Supreme Court. The outcome of the dispute is extremely important to industries that rely on gene patents, like biotechnology, pharmaceuticals, and even universities.

>> Trademark Law

For thousands of years, people have used marks on what they produce to represent the origin of goods and services. Pottery from ancient Greece, Rome and China often bears the mark of its maker. The same is true for ancient building materials like brick and tile. Today, we generally call such marks **trademarks** and when they indicate a specific producer, the law protects them against use by others.

Trademarks are a form of intellectual property. Like patents you can register them with the PTO, and also like patents, trademarks are some of the most valuable properties that businesses own. McDonald's golden arches, the Nike "swoosh," Coca-Cola, Sony, Facebook, Amazon.com, the Colonel, Exxon, Kodak, Kleenex, the Olympic rings, Rolex, Levi's—the list of famous trademarks is almost endless, but always recognizable.

Although registration systems exist at the federal and state level, it is important to understand that trademark rights come from *use* of the mark in association with goods or services. One can have rights in an unregistered trademark, and even sue for infringement. You cannot presume that, simply because a mark is unregistered, it is open for use in your field. However, this is not to say that registration is irrelevant. Particularly at the federal level under the Lanham Act, registration conveys important advantages. Therefore, it is advisable for a business to pursue a federal trademark registration for its source indicating marks whenever possible.

Recognizability or *distinctiveness* is the function of trademarks. In a world cluttered with stimulation, information, and advertising, trademarks pierce through the clutter and let people know that the goods or services represented are "the real thing"—that they come from one source. They are an information property, exclusively distinguishing the reputation and goodwill of a particular business from that of all other businesses. Trademarks protect

According to a 2010 study by *Interbrand*, the four most valuable brands belong to Coca-Cola, IBM, Microsoft, and Google both businesses and consumers from confusion regarding who makes or provides what. As one recent Federal Court of Appeals case observed:

> Trademarks are designed to inform potential buyers who makes the goods on sale. Knowledge of origin may convey information about a product's attributes and quality, and consistent attribution of origin is vital when vendors reputations matter. Without a way to know who makes what reputations cannot be created and evaluated, and the process of competition will be less effective. *Top Tobacco, L.P. v. North Atlantic Operating Co.*, 509 F. 3d 380, 381 (7th Cir. 2007)

Trademark infringement, which may involve intentional use of the owner's mark or an accidental design of one's own mark too similarly to another's, is a major business problem, especially in the Digital Age when often the only point of contact people have with a goods or service provider is a computer screen.

13. TYPES OF TRADEMARKS

Although state law protects trademarks, this chapter focuses on the federal protection given trademarks by the Lanham Act of 1946. The Lanham Act protects the following marks used to represent a product, service, or organization:

- Trademark—any mark, word, picture, or design that attaches to goods to indicate their source.
- Service mark—a mark associated with a service, for example, LinkedIn.
- Certification mark—a mark used by someone other than the owner to certify the quality, point of origin, or other characteristics of goods or services, for example, the Good Housekeeping Seal of Approval.
- Collective mark—a mark representing membership in a certain organization or association, for example, the National Football League logo.

For convenience, all of these marks will be referred to as trademarks.

>> *sidebar* 11.8

Brands vs. Trademarks

In a marketing class you may have heard the term "brand" used quite frequently. However, in law, the term "trademark" is used. Do these terms have the same meaning, and are they completely interchangeable?

The terms have a long history of association. Branding as a means of marking animals to designate ownership could be considered the original form of trademark. And its modern use related to marking products is derived by analogy to this ancient practice. The term "brand" actually comes from the Anglo-Saxon verb that means "to burn."

In the modern business context, a mark, symbol, or picture that someone refers to as a brand would also qualify in almost all cases as a trademark. A brand is a marketing concept that invokes a corporate strategy to capture a family of products or services in a readily identifiable manner. A trademark is the legal designation given to a mark that serves as a source identifier. It may not be as broad as a brand. Consider, for example, the different models of cars sold under the Ford brand. Each model name likely qualifies as a trademark itself, but may not be considered a separate brand. It is probably fair to say that most brands are trademarks, but not all trademarks are brands.

Source: Sidney A. Diamond, "The Historical Development of Trademarks," 65 *Trademark Reporter* 265 (1975).

Trade Dress Similar to trademarks, and also protected by the Lanham Act, is trade dress. **Trade dress** refers to a color or shape associated with a product or service. The red color scheme of Coca-Cola when associated with the general design of Coca-Cola labeling constitutes trade dress. Trade dress protection prevents Coca-Cola competitors from designing a shape that resembles "Coca-Cola" and attaching the characteristic Coke red to the design in such a way as to confuse potential Coke customers about what they are getting. Trade dress also includes distinctive store decorating motifs (e.g., McDonald's) or package shapes and colors.

> The distinctive "wasp-shaped" Coca-Cola bottle is part of its trade dress.

An important trade dress case is *Two Pesos, Inc. v. Taco Cabana, Inc.,* 505 U.S. 763 (1992). In that case the Supreme Court defined trade dress as "the total image and overall appearance" of a business. The Court upheld a decision that Two Pesos had violated Taco Cabana's trade dress. The Court stated that "trade dress [in this case] may include the shape and general appearance of the exterior of the restaurant, the identifying sign, the interior kitchen floor plan, the décor, the menu, the equipment used to serve food, the servers' uniforms and other features reflecting on the total image of the restaurant." The law protects trade dress from being copied as long as it is distinctive. If it is distinctive and registered, the law protects it even without proof that the public has come to identify the trade dress with a specific source.

14. TRADEMARK REGISTRATION

If one wishes to register a trademark with the PTO, one must use the mark in interstate commerce. Posting the trademark on an Internet website in association with a product or service meets this qualification. Alternatively, an intent-to-use application may be filed, followed by an amended application when actual use begins.

To be registerable, a trademark must be distinctive. The PTO will deny registration in the following circumstances:

- If the mark is the same or similar to a mark currently used on similar related goods, for example, a computer company's cherry mark that resembles the apple mark of Apple Inc.

- If the mark contains certain prohibited or reserved names or designs, including the U.S. flag, other governmental symbols, immoral names or symbols, the names or likenesses of living persons without their consent, and the names or likenesses of deceased American presidents without the permission of their spouses.

- If the mark merely describes a product or service, for example, "Fast Food" for a restaurant franchise.

- If the mark is generic and represents a product or service, for example, "cell phone" for a wireless communication company.

Note that a mark that is descriptive or generic in one context may be unique and distinctive in another. "Apple" appears to be an arbitrary term in the context of consumer electronics because it easily distinguishes the source of one company's products and services from another's. However, it would not be registerable for a fruit stand that sells apples.

As part of the trademark application process, the PTO places a proposed mark in the *Official Gazette,* which gives existing mark owners notice and allows them to object that the proposed mark is similar to their own. If existing mark owners object to the proposed mark's registration, the PTO holds a hearing to resolve the objection and, possibly, to deny registration. Finally, if the PTO determines the mark acceptable, it registers the mark on the *Principal Register.* This registration provides notice of official trademark registration status.

Unlike a patent, which specifies a limited property duration, the trademark enjoys a potentially unlimited protection period. But after six years the trademark owner must notify the PTO that the trademark is still in use. Currently, every 10 years the owner must renew the trademark registration.

The attempt to register certain descriptive terms, or a person's name, presents a special problem. Generally, the PTO will not accept a person's name or a descriptive term for protection on the *Principal Register.* However, there is a process by which a name or descriptive term can achieve full trademark status and protection. If it is listed on the PTO's *Supplemental Register* for five years *and* acquires a secondary meaning, it can then be transferred to the *Principal Register* for full protection.

Secondary meaning refers to a public meaning that is different from its meaning as a person's name or as a descriptive term, a public meaning that makes the name or term distinctive. In the public mind, "Ford" now refers to an automobile rather than a person, "Levi" means jeans rather than a family, and "Disney" refers to a specific entertainment company rather than its founder.

15. TRADEMARK ENFORCEMENT

Trademark law protects the trademark's owner from having the mark used in an unauthorized way. Using a mark that is confusingly similar to the trademark owner's mark violates the law. The standard for liability is proof that a defendant's use has created a "likelihood of confusion" with the plaintiff's trademark. To make this determination, courts use a multi-factored test that considers elements such as the defendant's intent and proof of actual consumer confusion. The law establishes both civil and criminal trademark violation.

Civil violation of a trademark (or a patent) is termed **infringement.** The violator infringes on the trademark's property right through an unintentional or a willful unauthorized use, misappropriating the goodwill and reputation that the trademark represents and confusing the public about the identity of the user. Remedies for civil infringement include a variety of damages, injunctions, prohibiting future infringement, and orders to destroy infringing products in anyone's possession.

The following case illustrates the application of the likelihood of confusion test as well as the extent to which unregistered trade dress can serve as a protectable mark.

case **11.3** >>

LOUISIANA STATE UNIVERSITY v. SMACK APPAREL CO.
550 F.3d 465 (5th Cir. 2008)

REAVLEY, J: . . . The plaintiffs are Louisiana State University (LSU), the University of Oklahoma (OU), Ohio State University (OSU), the University of Southern California (USC), and Collegiate Licensing Company (CLC), which is the official licensing agent for the schools. . . . Each university has adopted a particular two-color scheme as its school colors (purple and gold for LSU, crimson and creme for OU, scarlet and gray for OSU, and cardinal and gold for USC). The Universities have used their respective color combinations for over one hundred years, and the color schemes are immediately recognizable to those who are familiar with the Universities. The schools use these color schemes in many areas associated with university life, including on campus signs and buildings, on printed brochures, journals, and magazines, and on materials sent to potential donors. The Universities also use the color schemes extensively in connection with their athletic programs, particularly on team uniforms, resulting in wide-spread recognition of the colors among college sports fans. Each university operates a successful collegiate football program, and the respective football teams have appeared on numerous occasions in nationally televised football games that have been viewed by millions of people.

The schools also grant licenses for retail sales of products, including t-shirts, that bear the university colors and trademarks. In recent years, the total annual sales volume of products bearing the school colors along with other identifying marks has exceeded $ 93 million for all the Universities combined. The Universities hold registered trademarks in their respective names and commonly used initials. They do not, however, possess registered trademarks in their color schemes.

Smack Apparel Company is located in Tampa, Florida. Since 1998 Smack has manufactured t-shirts targeted toward fans of college sports teams, and it uses school colors and printed messages associated with the Universities on its shirts. Smack sells some of the shirts over the Internet, but most are sold wholesale to retailers and t-shirt vendors. The shirts frequently appear alongside those that have been officially licensed by the Universities. The instant case involves six of Smack's t-shirt designs that concern the appearance of the OU and LSU football teams in the

2004 Sugar Bowl in New Orleans, Louisiana, and the number of national championships previously won by OSU and USC. . . .

The Universities claimed that Smack's products are similar to and competed with goods sold or licensed by the Universities and are sold directly alongside merchandise authorized by the plaintiffs at or near events referenced in the shirts. In this way, according to the Universities, the sale of Smack's products is likely to deceive, confuse, and mislead consumers into believing that Smack's products are produced, authorized, or associated with the plaintiff Universities. The Universities sought injunctive relief, lost profits, damages, costs, and attorneys' fees. . . .

To prevail on their trademark infringement claim, the plaintiffs must show two things. First, they must establish ownership in a legally protectible mark, and second, they must show infringement by demonstrating a likelihood of confusion.

The Lanham Act provides that a trademark may be "any word, name, symbol, or device, or any combination thereof" that is used or intended to be used "to identify and distinguish" a person's goods "from those manufactured or sold by others and to indicate the source of the goods, even if that source is unknown."[15] A mark need not be registered in order to obtain protection because "[o]wnership of trademarks is established by use, not by registration.". . .

The parties correctly agree that a color scheme can be protected as a trademark when it has acquired secondary meaning and is non-functional. . . . Although the parties discuss color at length in their briefs, the Universities do not claim that every instance in which their team colors appear violates their respective trademarks. Instead, the claimed trademark is in the colors on merchandise that combines other identifying indicia referring to the Universities. . . .

Secondary meaning "occurs when, 'in the minds of the public, the primary significance of a [mark] is to identify the source of the product rather than the product itself.'". . .

The record shows that the Universities have been using their color combinations since the late 1800s. The color schemes appear on all manner of materials, including brochures, media guides, and alumni materials associated with the Universities. Significantly, each university features the color schemes on

[continued]

merchandise, especially apparel connected with school sports teams, and such prominent display supports a finding of secondary meaning. . . . The record also shows that sales of licensed products combining the color schemes with other references to the Universities annually exceed the tens of millions of dollars. As for advertising, the district court held that the Universities "advertise items with their school colors in almost every conceivable manner . . ." . . . Furthermore, the district court correctly observed that the school color schemes have been referenced multiple times in newspapers and magazines and that the schools also frequently refer to themselves using the colors. . . . Given the longstanding use of the color scheme marks and their prominent display on merchandise, in addition to the well-known nature of the colors as shorthand for the schools themselves and Smack's intentional use of the colors and other references, there is no genuine issue of fact that when viewed in the context of t-shirts or other apparel, the marks at issue here have acquired the secondary meaning of identifying the Universities in the minds of consumers as the source or sponsor of the products rather than identifying the products themselves.

We think this conclusion is consistent with the importance generally placed on sports team logos and colors by the public. We have previously noted, although not in the context of secondary meaning, that team emblems and symbols are sold because they serve to identify particular teams, organizations, or entities with which people wish to identify. . . . We think this desire by consumers to associate with a particular university supports the conclusion that team colors and logos are, in the minds of the fans and other consumers, source indicators of team-related apparel. By associating the color and other indicia with the university, the fans perceive the university as the source or sponsor of the goods because they want to associate with that source. . . .

Once a plaintiff shows ownership in a protectible trademark, he must next show that the defendant's use of the mark "creates a likelihood of confusion in the minds of potential customers as to the 'source, affiliation, or sponsorship'" of the product at issue. . . . "Likelihood of confusion is synonymous with a probability of confusion, which is more than a mere possibility of confusion." When assessing the likelihood of confusion, we consider a nonexhaustive list of so-called "digits of confusion," including: "(1) the type of mark allegedly infringed, (2) the similarity between the two marks, (3) the similarity of the products or services, (4) the identity of the retail outlets and purchasers, (5) the identity of the advertising media used, (6) the defendant's intent, and (7) any evidence of actual confusion." . . . Courts also consider (8) the degree of care exercised by potential purchasers. . . . No single factor is dispositive, and a finding of a likelihood of confusion need not be supported by a majority of the factors. . . .

After reviewing the record, we conclude that there is no genuine issue of fact that Smack's use of the Universities' color schemes and other identifying indicia creates a likelihood of confusion as to the source, affiliation, or sponsorship of the t-shirts. . . . [T]he digits of confusion—particularly the overwhelming similarity of the marks and the defendant's intent to profit from the Universities' reputation—compel this conclusion. This is so, we have noted, because Smack's use of the Universities' colors and indicia is designed to create the illusion of affiliation with the Universities and essentially obtain a "free ride" by profiting from confusion among the fans of the Universities' football teams who desire to show support for and affiliation with those teams. . . . This creation of a link in the consumer's mind between the t-shirts and the Universities and the intent to directly profit therefrom results in "an unmistakable aura of deception" and likelihood of confusion. . . .

We hold that given the record in this case and the digits of confusion analysis discussed above—including the overwhelming similarity between the defendant's t-shirts and the Universities' licensed products, and the defendant's admitted intent to create an association with the plaintiffs and to influence consumers in calling the plaintiffs to mind—that the inescapable conclusion is that many consumers would likely be confused and believe that Smack's t-shirts were sponsored or endorsed by the Universities. The Universities exercise stringent control over the use of their marks on apparel through their licensing program. It is also undisputed that the Universities annually sell millions of dollars worth of licensed apparel. We further recognize the public's indisputable desire to associate with college sports teams by wearing team-related apparel. We are not persuaded that simply because some consumers might not care whether Smack's shirts are officially licensed the likelihood of confusion is negated. Whether or not a consumer *cares* about official sponsorship is a different question from whether that consumer would likely *believe* the product is officially sponsored. For the foregoing reasons, we conclude that a likelihood of confusion connecting the presence of the Universities' marks and the Universities' themselves was demonstrated in this case.

[continued]

>> CASE QUESTIONS

1. Describe what the universities were seeking to protect as a trademark or trade dress.
2. What evidence supported that the trademarks in question had "secondary meaning"?
3. What factors (or digits) did the court consider most important in its analysis?
4. What could Smack do if it wished to continue selling clothing with the universities' marks?

Trademark owners must be vigilant in protecting their marks because if a trademark becomes **generic,** if it loses its distinctiveness, it also loses its status as a protected trademark. A trademark is most likely to become generic (1) when an owner does not defend against unauthorized use and (2) when the public becomes confused as to whether a term refers to a particular product/service or refers to a general class of products/services. Due to concern that its famous trademark not become generic, Coca-Cola seeks to prevent trademark infringement by employees at soda fountains who without comment give customers other colas when asked for a "Coke." Employers are warned to advise employees to specify that another cola will be substituted if Coke is not available.

As Table 11.1 illustrates, a number of trademarks have been lost because the public came to think of them as generic terms.

To win a trademark infringement lawsuit, a defendant will usually present one of three basic defenses: (1) the mark is not distinctive, (2) there is

Don't forget what it means for a trademark to become **generic.**

table 11.1 >> Trademarks Lost Due to Generic Use

The following generic terms were once trademarks:

Aspirin	Lite Beer
Cellophane	Refrigerator
Cola	Thermos
Escalator	Zipper

To ensure that its well-known trademark not be lost to generic use, the Xerox Corporation spent millions of dollars advertising to the public that *xerox* is a registered trademark and that the term should not be used as a verb (to "xerox" a copy) or as a noun (a "xerox").

Note that a term that is generic in one country may be protectable in another. For example, the term "aspirin" is a protected trademark of Bayer AG in many countries, including Canada.

Business Law 1 Intro. to Contracts, Liability Issues & Intellectual Property

346   **PART 3**   Legal Foundations for Business

The use of trademarked names in this textbook is a "fair use."

little chance of the public's being confused by use of a term trademarked by someone else, or (3) the use is a "fair use." In arguing the first defense, the defendant maintains that the mark is descriptive or generic and that the PTO should not have protected it in the first instance. Alternatively, the defendant argues that the mark has become generic since its trademarking and that it now stands for a class of items. Note that a court can declare a mark invalid even if the PTO accepted registration.

The second defense argues that there is little chance of public confusion over two uses of the same mark. For example, the public is not likely confused between the Ford automobile and the Ford Modeling Agency. But the confusion defense does not always work. In 2010, a federal district court awarded the owners of the Rolls-Royce trademark $2 million against a defendant calling itself "Rolls-Royce USA" for willful infringement in the context of clothing such as t-shirts. Despite the fact that the trademark owners primarily manufacture airplane engines and automobiles, not clothing, confusion was established.

The third defense raised in trademark infringement lawsuits is that of fair use. *Fair use* of a registered trademark is allowed by the Lanham Act and relates to a discussion, criticism, or parody of the trademark, the product, or its owner, for example, in the news media, on the Internet, or in a textbook. The courts have been explicit that the use of a rival's trademark in comparative advertising is also a fair use. You can legally advertise the results of a study that show your product to be superior to a competitor's, even if you mention the competitor's trademarked product by name.

Criminal trademark penalties apply to those who manufacture or traffic in *counterfeit* trademarked products, products such as imitation "Rolex" watches or "Levi" jeans. What makes counterfeiting criminal is the deliberate intent to pass off, or *palm off,* fake products as real by attaching an unauthorized trademark.

Trademarks and the Internet   Cyber technology and the Internet produce a combination of old and new trademark issues. One new issue concerns the relationship between a website domain name registered with the Internet Corporation for Assigned Names and Numbers (ICANN) and a trademark registered with the Patent and Trademark Office. There have been numerous instances in which people attempt to register domain names containing well-known trademarks that did not belong to them. Generally, it is a violation of trademark law to use another's registered mark in your domain name. Further, the Anticyber-squatting Consumer Protection Act of 1999 provides a remedy of statutory damages and transfer of a *famous* trademark domain name to its owner if it was registered in "bad faith." As an alternative to litigation, a trademark owner can pursue an arbitration against an improper domain name registrant. ICANN, an international organization that administers the Internet's addressing system, has a formal dispute resolution policy. ICANN has the authority to cancel or transfer the registration of the losing party.

"The International Chamber of Commerce estimates that the value of counterfeit and pirated products worldwide is about $600 billion, and projects that figure to double by 2015."

–Elizabeth Holmes in
***the Wall Street Journal,* June 30, 2011**

16. TRADEMARK DILUTION

In 1995, Congress passed the Federal Trademark Dilution Act. This law prohibits you from using a mark the same as or similar to another's "famous" trademark so as to dilute its significance, reputation, and goodwill. Even if an owner of a famous trademark cannot prove that the public is confused by another's use of a similar mark (called a "junior" mark), the owner of the "senior" famous trademark can still get an injunction prohibiting further use of the junior mark on the basis of **trademark dilution.** The court also has discretion to award the owner the infringer's profits, actual damages, and attorney's fees if the infringer "willfully intended to trade on the owner's reputation or to cause dilution of the famous mark."

In 2006, Congress passed the Trademark Dilution Revision Act, which established that dilution exists when a defendant creates a "likelihood of dilution." The law was designed, in part, to overrule an earlier Supreme Court decision, *Mosely v. V. Secret Catalogue, Inc.,* which set a higher standard of actual dilution. Thus, it is now slightly easier to win a dilution case.

Remember: only the owners of famous marks can prevail under the Federal Trademark Dilution Act.

>> Copyright Law

LO 11-5

Like patent, **copyright** gives those who have this property a monopoly over the right to exclude others from copying and marketing for a limited period of time. Unlike patent, copyright deals with original *expression* rather than invention. The importance of copyright began with the development of the printing press in the early 1400s, but the first copyright law was the Statute of Anne, enacted in England in 1710. In the United States copyright is authorized in the Constitution, and Congress has revised copyright several times. Until the late 1800s, however, the United States did not recognize foreign copyright laws as they protected the works of foreign authors. As a result, U.S. publishers felt free to publish the works of foreign authors without permission or the payment of fees called *royalties.*

Today the United States has joined most other countries in international agreements, such as the Berne Convention, in protecting the copyright of other nations, but once again copyright has come to a turning point in the road. Digital technology makes it ever easier to copy not only printed material, but music, movies, and software as well. No longer is a large business necessary to copy and distribute copyrighted materials illegally. Individuals can copy materials quickly and almost without cost and send them around the world in a blink of an eye. As you read the following sections on copyright law, keep in mind the new digital age you have entered.

17. COPYRIGHT OWNERSHIP

Copyright law grants property in certain creative expressions that keeps others from reproducing it without the owner's permission. The copyright attaches not to an idea or to facts but to the original *expression* of an idea or facts. Three criteria are necessary for copyright protection to occur:

- A work must be original. It must be created, not copied. Facts are not original, though collections of facts may be, depending on the selection and arrangement.

- The work must be fixed in a tangible medium of expression like a book, canvas, compact disk, hard drive, or flash memory.

- The work must show some creative expression. For example, the Supreme Court ruled in *Feist Publications, Inc. v. Rural Telephone Service Co.,* 499 U.S. 340 (1991), that the mere effort and alphabetic arrangement of names that went into a telephone directory's white pages was insufficiently creative to warrant a copyright.

Copyright laws protect authors rather than inventors. An author creates works of a literary, dramatic, musical, graphic, choreographic, audio, or visual nature. Ranging from printed material to photographs to records and motion pictures, these works receive automatic federal protection under the Copyright Act of 1976 from the moment the author creates them. Importantly, no registration is required to obtain a copyright under federal law. Additionally, notice—for example, a copyright symbol or the word "copyrighted"—is also *not* required. For that reason, businesses are often advised to assume that a work created by another is copyrighted, no matter if it appears freely available without notice.

Companies can be considered authors under copyright law. In fact, when an employee creates a work within the scope of their employment, the employer is automatically the owner and author. This type of work is called a "work-for-hire." It eliminates the need for companies to negotiate the rights to letters, documents, web pages, etc., that employees produce in the course of every day work.

The copyright allows the holder to control the reproduction, display, distribution, and performance of a protected work. The copyright runs for the author's lifetime, plus 70 additional years for an individual, and 95 years from publication or 120 years from creation for a work by a company. Congress has occasionally extended the term for copyrights in existence. The last time was in 1998 under the Copyright Term Extension Act, which added 20 years to the term.

18. COPYRIGHT PROTECTION

An important part of what copyright holders own is a limited resource in the market for their music or other expressions. That means the object of their property right is the market itself.

Although copyright protection attaches at the moment a work is created, an action for copyright infringement cannot be begun unless the author has properly registered the work with the Copyright Office. Unless the work was registered within three months of publication, a copyright owner can obtain statutory damages only if the work is registered before a defendant's infringement. The author may also be able to obtain actual damages, attorney's fees and the infringer's profits. Illegally reproduced copies may also be seized, and willful copyright violations can be a criminal offense.

The Copyright Act specifies that a fair use of copyrighted materials is not an infringement of the owner's property. **Fair use** includes copying for "criticism, comment, news reporting, teaching (including multiple copies for classroom use), scholarship, or research." In determining whether a particular use is a fair one, a court will consider

- The purpose and character of the use, including whether such use is for commercial or nonprofit educational purposes.
- The nature of the copyrighted work.
- The amount and substantiality of the portion used in relation to the copyrighted work as a whole.
- The effect of the use upon the potential market for the copyrighted work.

The determination of a fair use in light of these factors is made on a case-by-case basis. In Case 11.4, the Supreme Court considers whether one song makes a fair use of a previous song's copyrighted lyrics. The fair use being considered concerns *parody,* a form of expression that criticizes by poking fun at something through exaggeration.

case 11.4 >>

CAMPBELL v. ACUFF-ROSE MUSIC, INC.
510 U.S. 569 (1994)

The rap group 2 Live Crew recorded and sold a commercial parody of Roy Orbison's copyrighted song "Oh Pretty Woman." Acuff-Rose Music, Inc., the copyright holder, sued the 2 Live Crew members after nearly a quarter million copies of the recording had been sold. The case came before the Supreme Court after the court of appeals decided that 2 Live Crew's parody had taken too much of "Oh Pretty Woman" to be protected as a fair use.

SOUTER, J: It is uncontested here that 2 Live Crew's song would be an infringement of AcuffRose's rights in "Oh Pretty Woman," under the Copyright Act of 1976, but for a finding of fair use through parody. From the infancy of copyright protection, some opportunity for fair use of copyrighted materials has been thought necessary to fulfill copyright's very purpose, "to promote the Progress of Science and useful Arts. . . ." For as Justice Story explained, "in truth, in literature, in science and in art, there are, and can be, few, if any, things, which in an abstract sense, are strictly new and original throughout. Every book in literature, science and art, borrows, and must necessarily borrow, and use much which was well known and used before."

The first factor in a fair use enquiry is "the purpose and character of the use, including whether such use is of a commercial nature or is for nonprofit educational purposes." The enquiry here may be guided by looking to whether the use is for criticism, or comment, or news reporting, and the like. The central purpose of this investigation is to see, in Justice Story's words, whether the new work merely "supersede[s] the objects" of the original creation, or instead adds something new, with a further purpose or different character, altering the first with new expression, meaning, or message; it asks, in other words, whether and to what extent the new work is "transformative." Although such transformative use is not absolutely necessary for a finding of fair use, the goal of copyright, to promote science and the arts, is generally furthered by the creation of transformative works. Such works thus lie at the heart of the fair use doctrine's guarantee of breathing space within the confines of copyright, and the more transformative the new work, the less will be the significance of other factors, like commercialism, that may weigh against a finding of fair use.

The second statutory factor, "the nature of the copyrighted work," calls for recognition that some works are closer to the core of intended copyright protection than others, with one consequence that fair use is more difficult to establish when the former works are copied. We agree with both the District Court and the Court of Appeals that the Orbison original's creative expression for public dissemination falls within the core of the copyright's protective purposes. This fact, however, is not much help in this case, or ever likely to help much in separating the fair use sheep from the infringing goats in a parody case, since parodies almost invariably copy publicly known, expressive works.

The third factor asks whether "the amount and substantiality of the portion used in relation to the copyrighted work as a whole" are reasonable in relation to the purpose of the copying. The District Court considered the song's parodic purpose in finding that 2 Live Crew had not helped themselves overmuch. The Court of Appeals disagreed, stating that "while it may not be inappropriate to find that no more was taken than necessary, the copying was qualitatively substantial. . . . We conclude that taking the heart of the original and making it the heart of a new work was to purloin a substantial portion of the essence of the original."

Suffice it to say here that, as to the lyrics, we fail to see how the copying can be excessive in relation to its parodic purpose, even if the portion taken is the original's "heart." As to the music, we express no opinion whether repetition of the bass riff is excessive copying, and we remand to permit evaluation of the amount taken, in light of the song's parodic purpose and character, its transformative elements, and considerations of the potential for market substitution sketched more fully below.

The fourth fair use factor is "the effect of the use upon the potential market for or value of the copyrighted work." It requires courts to consider not only the extent of market harm caused by the particular actions of the alleged infringer, but also "whether unrestricted and widespread conduct of the sort engaged in by the defendant . . . would result in a substantially adverse impact on the potential market" for the original. The enquiry "must take account not only of harm to the original but also of harm to the market for derivative works."

[continued]

Although 2 Live Crew submitted uncontroverted affidavits on the question of market harm to the original, neither they, nor Acuff-Rose, introduced evidence or affidavits addressing the likely effect of 2 Live Crew's parodic rap song on the market for a nonparody, rap version of "Oh Pretty Woman." And while Acuff-Rose would have us find evidence of a rap market in the very facts that 2 Live Crew recorded a rap parody of "Oh Pretty Woman" and another rap group sought a license to record a rap derivative, there was no evidence that a potential rap market was harmed in any way by 2 Live Crew's parody, rap version.

It was error for the Court of Appeals to conclude that the commercial nature of 2 Live Crew's parody of "Pretty Woman" rendered it presumptively unfair. No such evidentiary presumption is available to address either the first factor, the character and purpose of the use, or the fourth, market harm, in determining whether a transformative use, such as parody, is a fair one. The court also erred in holding that 2 Live Crew had necessarily copied excessively from the Orbison original, considering the parodic purpose of the use. We therefore reverse the judgment of the Court of Appeals and remand the case for further proceedings consistent with this opinion.

Reversed and remanded.

19. COPYRIGHT IN THE DIGITAL AGE

Under copyright law it is illegal not only to make copies that violate the law but also to assist others in doing so. When copyright holders challenged certain programs that assisted file sharing of materials—mostly, copyrighted music—one case went to the Supreme Court. In *Metro-Goldwyn-Mayer Studios v. Grokster*, 125 S. Ct. 2764 (2005), the Court asserted: "We hold that one who distributes a device with the object of promoting its use to infringe copyright, as shown by clear expression or other affirmative steps taken to foster infringement, is liable for the resulting acts of infringement by third parties." In addition to inducing others to infringe, one can be liable for materially contributing to another's infringement with knowledge of the infringement. Obtaining financial benefit with the ability to supervise the infringement also makes one vicariously liable.

International piracy of copyrighted material is a major problem, but international enforcement efforts are improving slowly.

Criminal prosecutions and civil lawsuits for "file sharing" copyrighted material over the Internet continue. The motion picture and recording industries have been particularly active over the years in pursuing individuals for file sharing. Some excuse file sharing by saying that intellectual property does not diminish the way that tangible property does when someone misappropriates it. But consider this: property is a legal right to exclude, not a physical thing, and the object of a property copyright includes the reproduction of music for commercial profit. The holder of a copyright owns the right to market what is copyrighted, and the market resource is diminished for the copyright owner when file sharers misappropriate music. In the early years of this century, the volume of sales for copyrighted music has declined significantly, largely due to misappropriation.

20. DIGITAL MILLENNIUM COPYRIGHT ACT

Because copyrighted property is easily misappropriated over the Internet, Congress passed a law in 1998 that prohibits certain activities leading to copyright violation. The Digital Millennium Copyright Act (DMCA) makes illegal the effort to get around (circumvent) devices used by copyright owners to keep their works from being infringed. In particular, the act prevents the production, marketing, or sales of a product or service designed to circumvent technological protections of computer software, videos, and compact disks. The act also prevents circumvention of access protections for such products. It further provides a safe-harbor for Internet service providers, protecting them from liability (1) for illegal copies that pass temporarily through their systems and (2) for permanent illegal copies stored in their systems, for example, at a website, if the service provider removes the offending material upon request of a copyright owner. Finally, the act relieves service providers from liability for unintentionally linking to a website that contains infringing materials.

>> *sidebar* 11.9

Knowledge of Users' Infringing Activity

Internet service provides (ISPs), which include companies that provide Internet access as well as those that host content like videos, have protection against claims of contributory infringement so long as they act to address copyright owner claims. For hosting services, the DMCA requires content removal when a copyright owner provides notice. However, ISPs may be obligated to act even before a copyright owner notifies them. Under the act, actual knowledge of infringing works posted by users requires action. Additionally, knowledge of facts or circumstances from which infringement is apparent requires that an ISP remove the infringing content.

When do facts and circumstances make infringement apparent? Is a general knowledge that some users post infringing content enough? This question was addressed in the recent case *Viacom Intern. Inc. v. YouTube, Inc.*, 718 F. Supp. 2d 514 (S.D.N.Y. 2010). Viacom contended that YouTube was aware of infringing activity on its service and did not work sufficiently to eliminate it. The court rejected that argument, stating "Mere knowledge of prevalence of such activity in general is not enough." The court found that YouTube was protected by the DMCA's safe harbor provisions.

Violations of the DMCA permit civil remedies, including injunction, actual damages, and statutory damages. A court can assess triple damages against a repeat offender. Willful circumvention for financial gain can also result in up to 10 years' imprisonment.

>> International Intellectual Property Rights   LO 11-6

To this point, this chapter has presented the basic rules of U.S. intellectual property rights. You may be aware that you can obtain similar rights in other countries. Is such protection automatic once you have protection in the U.S.? Is there an international system for protecting intellectual property? These are essential questions for any modern business. As commerce becomes global, the protection of intellectual property internationally is increasingly important.

There are in fact no fully international intellectual property rights, *per se*. Local or regional law controls the creation and ownership of patents, copyrights, trademarks and trade secrets. However, there are international standards that most industrialized nations have agreed to uphold. The most important source for standards is an international treaty known as the Trade-Related Aspects of Intellectual Property Agreement (TRIPS). This agreement was formed in 1994 as part of the treaty that created the World Trade Organization (WTO). The United States has been a member since the agreement's inception, and was a major force is drafting its provisions. TRIPS requires that member countries provide protection for all of the forms of intellectual property discussed in this chapter. In addition, it sets forth baseline rules for that protection in terms of subject matter, procedure, and enforcement. By virtue of the TRIPS agreement, businesses can count on being able to obtain similar protection for intellectual property in other countries. However, differences in the manner in which counties comply with TRIPS require that companies exercise due care in pursuing international rights.

In addition to substantive protection, international treaties exist that can facilitate filing for rights in several countries at the same time. In the context of patents, there is the Patent Cooperation Treaty (PCT), which allows an applicant to obtain a preliminary international examination and then pursue final rights in multiple countries at the same time. Similarly, trademark owners can pursue rights in several countries at the same time through the Madrid System for International Registration of Marks. Because members of the Berne Convention, described above, are not required to undertake any formalities to obtain copyright protection, no international filing system is necessary. Members agree to provide rights if similar rights are obtained in an author's home country.

In order to monitor and administer certain aspects of international intellectual property agreements, countries have provided authority to certain independent international organizations. The most important two organizations are the WTO and the World Intellectual Property Organization (WIPO). The WTO administers the TRIPS agreement, including the settlement of disputes concerning its interpretation. The WIPO administers the PCT and Madrid System in addition to many other international intellectual property treaties. Both organizations provide much useful information to businesses, and it is worth consulting their respective web resources before pursuing international protection.

>> A Conclusion about Intellectual Property

Intellectual property, like property itself, serves the common good. The U.S. Constitution points this out in Article 1, Section 8, by asserting that the purpose for Congress granting "to authors and inventors the exclusive right to their respective writings and discoveries" is to promote the progress of science and business, which society believes promotes the common good. The framers of the Constitution believed, as do modern economists, that property, including intellectual property, gives incentive for private production of goods and services, which benefits not only the owners providing goods and services, but also to the overall wealth of society.

A property system is only as effective as the mechanism for enforcing it. Without adequate enforcement, a property system cannot function for the common good, and enforcement relies upon more than laws and courts. It depends also on the attitudes of people toward legitimacy of the property. Without social recognition of the exclusive legal fences that are at the heart of the property system and without adequate enforcement of property, the system cannot provide the incentive necessary for private productive effort.

Increasingly, we live in a global society, and the information that is the resource of intellectual property moves easily across national borders. This means that the enforcement of intellectual property is something important to all nations that are part of the global trading system.

>> Key Terms

Copyright 347	Injunction 328	Trade dress 341
Fair use 348	Intellectual property 323	Trademark 339
Generic 345	Patent 330	Trademark dilution 347
Infringement 342	Property 321	Trade secret 325

>> Review Questions and Problems

1. *The Justification for Intellectual Property*
   (a) What is the purpose of patents and copyrights as identified in the Constitution?
   (b) Explain the claim that the pace of research and development of new products would slow if intellectual property right did not protect it.

2. Intellectual Property and Competition
   (a) Explain the balance between intellectual property's rights of exclusion and competition.
   (b) Articulate alternatives to intellectual property for encouraging information creation.

3. Capturing Intellectual Property
   Explain the assertion that businesses can lose rights if they do not diligently assess and pursue intellectual property protection.

Trade Secrets

4. *Trade Secret: Taking Reasonable Measures to Keep the Secret*
   (a) How do trade secrets differ from other applications of property?
   (b) Discuss several ways of preserving trade secrets.

5. Demonstrating Misappropriation
   What types of actions constitute misappropriation under trade secret law?

6. *Trade Secret: Civil Enforcement*
   What are the remedies available for the civil enforcement of trade secrets?

7. *Trade Secret: Criminal Enforcement*
   Why has criminal misappropriation of trade secrets become an issue of greater concern in recent years?

Patent Law

8. *Obtaining a Patent*
   Describe the process for obtaining a patent.

9. *Patentable Subject Matter*
   Through long, expensive research you determine that both a bowling ball and a feather fall at the rate of 32 feet per second in a vacuum. Can you patent this knowledge? Explain.

10. *Nonobviousness, Novelty, and Usefulness*

   (a) Imagine that you discover a long-ignored cure for headaches in an old U.S. medical journal from the 1800s, and you apply for a patent. Explain why a patent examiner would likely reject your application.

   (b) Discuss the patent requirement of nonobviousness.

11. *Patent Enforcement*

   Is it possible for two utility patents owned by different people to cover the same product? Explain.

12. *Current Issues in Patent Law*

   (a) Discuss the propriety of entities that acquire and assert patents but make no product.

   (b) You discover a specific human gene that determines male pattern baldness. Explain what it means to say that you can patent this gene.

Trademark Law

13. *Types of Trademarks*

   Name four types of marks that are often called "trademarks."

14. *Trademark Registration*

   (a) Can you register the name "Fast Food" as a trademark? Explain.

   (b) Under what conditions can you *not* register a mark?

15. *Trademark Enforcement*

   Do you ever "google" something on the Internet? Is the company Google in danger of losing its name as a trademark? Explain.

16. *Trademark Dilution*

   Articulate an example that would constitute trademark dilution, but not infringement. Can you come up with one that constitutes infringement but not dilution?

Copyright Law

17. *Copyright Ownership*

   (a) If you spend the time and effort necessary to alphabetize the names of the students at your school and list their e-mail addresses, can you copyright a printed version? Explain.

   (b) Explain the rights a company has to the works created by its employees.

18. *Copyright Protection*

   Imagine that you are making a presentation to a class on the occurrence of product advertising in film. You display a short clip of a recent film to illustrate your point. Explain how one would argue that this use constitutes a "fair use" of the copyrighted material.

19. *Copyright in the Digital Age*

   Explain why digital copies of works create greater difficulties in controlling infringement.

20. *Digital Millennium Copyright Act*

   Are file-hosting sites like YouTube liable for infringing videos posted by their users?

business >> *discussions*

1. Colonel Cars, Inc., plans to introduce a new speaker complex in the steering wheels of its automobiles. It believes the change will revolutionize the drivers' music-listening enjoyment. The company is also preparing an advertising campaign around the improved listening experience. Both the new steering-wheel speakers and the ad campaign are carefully kept secrets. But Colonel Cars's vice president for marketing is hired by European Motor Works (EMW) to be the president of its international division. Before Colonel Cars can begin its advertising, EMW comes out with an ad campaign centered on—you guessed it—speakers in the steering wheels of its new model cars.

> What is "property"?
> Can a company have property in its marketing plans the way you can have property in your car?
> Can EMW use Colonel Car's marketing plans without permission?

Chapter 12. International Law

12 International Law

▢ Learning Objectives

In this chapter you will learn:

12-1. To understand the legal risk inherent in international transactions, including the requirements of the Foreign Corrupt Practices Act.

12-2. To identify the basic sources of international law and major institutions.

12-3. To consider the importance of free trade agreements on the global economy.

12-4. To grasp the basic methods of transacting international business.

12-5. To realize the complexity of resolving international disputes.

The risks of engaging in global transactions are apparent in the news on a daily basis. From increased prosecutions for bribery to lawsuits involving global operations, the international marketplace is fraught with potential legal issues.

The collapse of Lehman Brothers during the fall of 2008, illustrates the interconnectedness of international business. Lehman's bankruptcy triggered a "cash crunch" around the world, precipitating losses and accelerating the demise of other businesses. The U.S. laws and regulations governing financial institutions immediately were subjected to international scrutiny.

Law is fundamental to business in the United States and throughout the globe. As American businesses become increasingly global in a very competitive international marketplace, some understanding of legal issues in this context is essential. Throughout this text, the importance of *the rule of law* is emphasized. This concept is particularly important for companies doing business abroad. Property rights and contracts must be enforced to minimize risk in international transactions.

The United States enters into treaties and trade agreements to govern competition and the way goods and technology are sold from one country to the next. Every country is interested in developing rules that make its products and services more competitive in the global market. Nation-states and corporations alike are protected by a mutual respect for property and contractual rights.

The goal of American trade policy is to open markets throughout the world. The idea is to create new opportunities for business and also higher living standards. The United States is a party to many trade agreements and is continually negotiating new ones to further open markets to free trade. National economies rely on their ability to export products and services abroad to create jobs and economic growth at home. Companies likewise are continually looking for productive ways to expand their international business. Overall, however, the United States has a huge trade deficit because it buys more than it sells abroad. At the end of 2010, the trade deficit was $497.8 billion. For a chart of the top trading partners with the United States, see Figure 12.1.

This chapter discusses the risks of global trade, with increased emphasis on the pressure for bribes. It then provides a basic understanding about international law and organizations that affect trade, including major trade agreements. Next, it provides an overview of methods of transacting international business and concludes with ways of resolving international disputes. Overall, this chapter should help you understand the issues affecting business in the international landscape.

> "Travel is fatal to prejudice, bigotry, and narrow-mindedness . . . Broad, wholesome, charitable views of men and things cannot be acquired by vegetating in one little corner of the earth all one's lifetime."
>
> **– Mark Twain, American humorist (1857)**

Figure 12.1 *Top Ten Trading Partners with the United States*

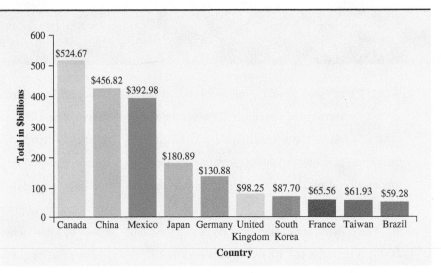

Source: U.S. Census Bureau Statistics for 2010

>> Risks Involved in International Trade

LO 12-1

Because international trade means dealing with different legal systems, cultures, and ways of doing business, there are a number of risks involved. For example, when a firm expends globally, a host of potential risks and concerns are raised, such as:

- What U.S. laws have an "extraterritorial" reach?
- Are property rights enforced?
- Will foreign courts uphold the validity of contracts?
- Is intellectual property protected or is it vulnerable to infringement?
- Are there export or import restrictions on the firm's products?
- Are there risks associated with political instability and/or war?
- What international trade agreements will affect the firm's expansion?
- What national laws (e.g., labor and environmental) affect the firm?
- How should language and cultural differences be bridged?

See Sidebar 12.1 as an example of problems that can arise with outsourcing manufacturing. This section addresses specific concerns about pressures for bribes, expropriation and nationalization, and export controls.

>> *sidebar* 12.1

Problems with Outsourcing in China: Mattel's Massive Toy Recall

 In 2007, Mattel, Inc., recalled over 10 million toys manufactured in China. What was at issue? Lead paint and tiny magnets presented safety hazards for children. At least one U.S. child died and 19 others required surgery after swallowing magnets in the toys. The recall included some of Mattel's most popular toys, including Barbie, Dora, Thomas the Train, Polly Pocket, and *Cars* movie items. The over $33 billion U.S. toy industry heavily relies on manufacturing in China for approximately 80 percent of its toys.

 >> PRACTICAL CONSIDERATIONS FOR BUSINESS

Who is responsible?

What is the best way to address the problem?

Should there be tighter consumer standards?

How can companies better control outsourced manufacturing?

1. PRESSURES FOR BRIBES

Following widespread disclosure of scandalous payments by domestic firms to officials of foreign government, Congress enacted the **Foreign Corrupt Practices Act (FCPA)** in 1977. The law is designed to stop bribery of foreign officials and to prohibit U.S. citizens and companies from making payments to foreign officials whose duties are not "essentially ministerial or clerical" for the purpose of obtaining business. Since 2009, FCPA enforcement increased

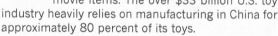

substantially. Any company trading on a U.S. stock exchange can be prosecuted for FCPA violations.

This statute has two principal requirements:

1. Financial records and accounts must be kept "which, in reasonable detail, accurately and fairly reflect the transactions and dispositions of assets" of the business.

2. The business must "devise and maintain a system of internal accounting controls sufficient to provide reasonable assurances" that transactions are being carried out in accordance with management's authorization.

These provisions are intended to correct the previously widespread practice of accounting for bribes as commission payments, payments for services, or other normal business expenses and then illegally deducting the payments on income tax returns.

Many legal observers criticized the FCPA for creating a significantly chilling effect on U.S. companies seeking business in many developing countries where under-the-table payments to government officials are an accepted practice. Indeed, many civil servants in other nations are expected to supplement their salaries in this manner. The U.S. prohibition of such payments is perceived as an attempt to impose U.S. standards of morality in other parts of the world, and it has caused resentment and discrimination against U.S. businesses. Moreover, the FCPA arguably puts U.S. firms at a competitive disadvantage with businesses in other countries that are not operating under similar constraints.

>> *sidebar* 12.2

Turning Back the Tide of Corruption

An international group known as Transparency International generates the Corruption Perceptions Index annually. It ranks 178 countries according to perception of corruption in the public sector. This global coalition against corruption measures perceptions as a reliable measure of the degree of corruption of a country. Here is a sampling of countries from the 2010 report:

Denmark, New Zealand and Singapore tied for #1

Canada #6

Germany #15

United States #22

China #78

Mexico #96

Iraq #175

Afghanistan #176

Myanmar #177

Somalia #178

#1 = least corrupt #178 = most corrupt

Source: Transparency International Corruption Perceptions Index, www.transparency.org

As a result of intensive lobbying by the U.S. business community, Congress amended the FCPA in 1988 in an effort to eliminate ambiguity and uncertainty over what constitutes improper conduct. Although the law still *table 12.1* >> FCPA: Legal or Permissible Payments

The following payments are permissible under the FCPA:

"Facilitating," "expediting," or "grease" payments for "routine government action." Examples include obtaining permits, licenses, or other official documents; processing governmental papers (e.g., visas and work orders); providing police protection; loading and unloading cargo; and scheduling inspections associated with contract performance or transit of goods across country.

Any payments permitted under the written laws of the foreign country.

Travel expenses of a foreign official for the purpose of demonstrating a product or for performing a contractual obligation.

prohibits bribery and corruption, the amendments establish clearer standards for firms to follow in overseas operations. The amendments limit criminal liability for violations of accounting standards to those who "knowingly" circumvent accounting controls or falsify records of corporate payments and transactions. The amendments also clarify the level of detail required in such record keeping and should improve compliance by businesses and enforcement by the government. Moreover, under the new law otherwise prohibited payments to foreign officials may be defended if they were legal under the written laws of the host country or if they cover "reasonable and bona fide" expenses associated with the promotion of the product and the completion of the contract (see Table 12.1).

The FCPA also prohibits corrupt payments through intermediaries. It is unlawful to make a payment to a third party, while knowing that all or a portion of the payment will go directly or indirectly to a foreign official. The term *knowing* includes conscious disregard and deliberate indifference. Additionally, the antibribery provisions of the FCPA apply to foreign firms and persons who take action in furtherance of a corrupt payment while in the United States.

Criminal penalties may be imposed for violations of the FCPA: corporations and other business entities are subject to a fine of up to $2,000,000; officers, directors, stockholders, employees, and agents are subject to a fine of up to $100,000 and imprisonment for up to five years. Fines imposed on individuals may *not* be paid by their employer or principal. The attorney general or the SEC, as appropriate, may also bring a civil action for fines against any firm, as well as any officer, director, employee, or agent of a firm or stockholder acting on behalf of the firm who violates the antibribery provisions. The conduct that violates the antibribery provisions of the FCPA may also give rise to a private cause of action for treble damages under the Racketeer Influenced and Corrupt Organizations Act (RICO). For example, a RICO action could be brought by a competitor who alleges that the bribery caused the defendant to obtain a foreign contract. See Sidebar 12.3 for examples of successful FCPA prosecutions.

Payment of a bribe in violation of the FCPA can buy you jail time.

>> *sidebar* 12.3

FCPA Prosecutions: U.S. Government Success Stories

 Siemens AG paid a record-breaking $800 million for FCPA violations. The total consisted of a $450 million fine to the Department of Justice and $350 million in disgorgement of profits to the Securities and Exchange Commission. Siemens allegedly violated the FCPA by paying $1.36 billion in bribes around the world in connection with obtaining contracts. According to the prosecution, the corruption implicated all levels of management, including senior management, and involved elaborate payment schemes and off-book accounts to conceal payments. The Department of Justice described the level of corruption at Siemens as a "pattern of bribery" that was "unprecedented in scale and geographic reach."

>> OTHER RECENT PROSECUTIONS

Daimler paid a $93.6 million fine and $91.4 million fine for disgorgement of profits. The company and its subsidiaries allegedly made hundreds of improper payments in at least 22 countries, including China and Russia.

Johnson & Johnson agreed to pay $70 million to settle civil and criminal bribery charges involving bribes paid to public doctors and public hospital administrators in Greece, Poland, and Romania.

Baker Hughes paid $44 million following accusations that the company used bribes to win an oil fields contract in Kazakhstan.

IBM agreed to pay $10 million to settle civil bribery charges involving payments by more than 100 employees of a subsidiaries and joint ventures in Asia.

Tyson Foods, Inc., paid $5.2 million in criminal and civil penalties to resolve FCPA allegations involving meat inspectors employed by the Mexican government.

Antonio Perez, a former controller of a Florida-based telecommunications company, pleaded guilty to conspiring to commit FCPA violations and money laundering in connection with payments made to Telecommunications D'Haiti. He was sentenced to two years in prison, to serve an additional two years of supervised release following his prison term, and to forfeit $36,375.

concept >> *summary*

Risks Involved in International Trade

1. The Foreign Corrupt Practices Act seeks to stop the bribery of foreign government officials.
2. Expropriation and nationalization are risks involved in international business.
3. Expert controls seek to balance national security interests against global trade.

2. EXPROPRIATION AND NATIONALIZATION

Creeping expropriation is a series of acts, such as taxes, regulation, or other changes in law that have an expropriatory effect, reducing or eliminating foreign investments.

If a domestic firm is involved in a foreign country to the extent of locating assets there (whether through branches, subsidiaries, joint ventures, or otherwise), it may be subject to the ultimate legal and political risk of international business activity—expropriation. **Expropriation,** as used in the context of international law, is the seizure of foreign-owned property by a government. When the owners are not fairly compensated, the expropriation is also considered to be a *confiscation* of property. Usually, the expropriating government also assumes ownership of the property, so the process includes

nationalization as well. In the United States, the counterpart of expropriation is called the *power of eminent domain.*

This power of a government to take private property is regarded as inherent; yet it is subject to restraints upon its exercise. The U.S. Constitution (as well as the constitutions and laws of most nations) prohibits the government from seizing private property except for "public purposes" and upon the payment of "just compensation."

However, the extent of such protection varies widely. Treaties (or other agreements) between the United States and other countries provide additional protection against uncompensated takings of property. It is customary for international law to recognize the right of governments to expropriate the property of foreigners only when accompanied by "prompt, adequate, and effective compensation." This so-called modern traditional theory is accepted by most nations as the international standard and requires full compensation to the investor including fair market value as a going concern. See Sidebar 12.4 for an example of nationalization.

>> *sidebar* 12.4

ExxonMobil Corp. v. Petróleos de Venezuela: Chavez and Nationalization of the Oil Industry

Venezuelan President Hugo Chavez nationalized the last privately run oil fields in the country in 2007. The government took over four oil projects run by some of the world's biggest petroleum companies, including Exxon Mobil Corp. In his announcement of the takeover, Chavez told cheering workers that foreign oil companies damaged Venezuela's national interests and that reclaiming them represented an historic victory.

Exxon is not taking the loss without a fight. Exxon brought an action against state-owned Petróleos de Venezuela (PDVSA) in the United States. In early 2008, Exxon won a $315 million freeze of PDVSA's assets, as well as a ruling blocking PDVSA's transactions with Britain and the Netherlands, affecting as much as $12 billion in assets. Ultimately, what compensation will Exxon receive for the loss of its assets in Venezuela? Will other foreign oil companies whose assets were nationalized in Venezuela be compensated? The matter is far from resolved and has far-reaching political implications.

Chavez is also taking steps to nationalize utilities, the telecommunications industry, and the Venezuelan subsidiary of Mexican cement company Cemex SEB.

3. EXPORT CONTROLS

Another risk involved in doing business abroad is **export controls** placed on the sale of U.S. strategic products and technology abroad. Controlling the export of such items has been the cornerstone of Western policy since the conclusion of World War II. Most of the attention was focused on preventing the acquisition of technology by the former Soviet Union and its allies. However, since the end of the Cold War the policy rationale behind export controls has been drawn into question, with many Western countries contending they should be eliminated to increase trading opportunities with Russia, China, Eastern Europe, and the Middle East. Indeed, the Coordinating Committee for Multilateral Export Controls (COCOM), an organization created by the major Western nations (including the United States, Europe, and Japan) to control exports, came to an end in 1994.

Exports from the United States to countries such as Cuba, Iran, Libya, North Korea, Sudan, and Syria are restricted.

Query: Should the U.S. lift its trade embargo with Cuba? The EU agreed to lift its sanctions against Cuba in June 2008.

Since that time, a new organization supported by 33 countries, known as the Wassanaar Arrangement, has come into existence to help control the spread of both military and dual-use technology to unstable areas of the world. Participating nations seek, through their national policies, to ensure that transfer of conventional arms and strategic goods and technologies do not destabilize regional and international security. The 2002 plenary meeting of the Wassanaar Arrangement, held in Vienna, resulted in several significant initiatives to combat terrorism. The member countries agreed on several measures aimed at intensifying cooperation to prevent terrorist groups and individuals from acquiring arms and strategic goods and technologies.

The U.S. export control system currently is regulated by the Department of State and the Department of Commerce under authority provided by the Export Administration Act and the Arms Export Control Act. The Department of Defense also plays a key role in determining the technology to be controlled as does the U.S. Customs Service in the enforcement of the controls. Significant criminal and administrative sanctions may be imposed upon corporations and individuals convicted of violating the law.

>> *sidebar* 12.5

Export Control Reform

The Comprehensive Iran Sanctions, Accountability, and Divestment Act of 2010 makes significant improvements for the nation's export enforcement authorities. This law harmonizes the different maximum export control criminal penalties under four different statutes. It also permanently restores the Department of Commerce's export enforcement authorities.

On November 9, 2010, the President signed Executive Order 13558, establishing an Export Enforcement Coordination Center (EECC) among the Departments of State, the Treasury, Defense, Justice, Commerce, Energy, and Homeland Security, as well as elements of the Intelligence Community. The Department of Homeland Security will administer the EECC. The EECC is designed to:

- Prevent conflicts in criminal and administrative enforcement operations and coordination of industry enforcement outreach activity.

- Provide a conduit between federal law enforcement agencies and the U.S. intelligence community.
- Serve as the primary point of contact between enforcement agencies and export licensing agencies for enforcement and licensing matters.
- Resolve interagency conflicts not settled in the field.
- Establish governmentwide statistical tracking capabilities for U.S. export enforcement activities.

The goal of this reform is to harmonize business practices and processes across the export enforcement agencies.

Source: www.export.gov/ecr/eg_main_027618.asp

According to the U.S. Export Control and Related Border Security Assistance (EXBS) Program, exporters should be aware of the following "red flags":

- A *customer* is reluctant to provide end-use/user information; is willing to pay cash for high-value shipments; has little background in the relevant business; declines normal warranty/service/installation; or orders products incompatible with the business.

- *A shipment* involves a private intermediary in a major weapons sale; shipments are directed to entities with no connection to the buyer; requests for packing are inconsistent with the normal mode of shipping; or circuitous or illogical routing.

- *The end-user* requests equipment inconsistent with inventory; spare parts in excess of projected needs; the end-use is at variance with standard practices; a middleman from a third country places the order; or the end-user refuses to state whether the goods are for domestic use, export, or re-export.

In 2000, the U.S. government extended the Export Administration Act and raised the penalties for violators. The export control agenda for the twenty-first century remains focused on maintaining national security and reducing the proliferation of weapons, while also facilitating U.S. competitiveness in the global economy.

The successful prosecution of two leading American aerospace companies, Hughes Electronics and Boeing Satellite Systems, illustrates the government's commitment to vigorous export control to prevent harmful proliferation of weapons. The companies paid a record $32 million in penalties to settle charges in connection with 123 alleged violations of export control laws regarding the transfer of rocket and satellite data to China.

However, the future of the U.S. system remains in doubt with many proposals pending in Congress to reform and limit the current export control system. Over the past several years, these controls have become an extremely controversial topic in the international business community. Export controls make successful business deals more difficult because foreign buyers may be reluctant to trade with a U.S. firm due to the red tape involved in obtaining governmental approval as compared with Europe or Japan.

>> *sidebar* 12.6

Twenty-First Century Pirates

 According to the International Maritime Bureau, in 2010, pirates hijacked 53 ships worldwide and took 1,181 hostages in 445 attacks—a 10 percent rise from 2009. Most of the hijackings occurred in the Gulf of Aden. A study by One Earth Future estimates that maritime piracy costs between $7 and $12 billion a year. In early 2011, Somali pirates were still holding 31 ships and over 700 crewmembers. Other violent attacks were reported in the South China Sea off of Indonesia, Bangladesh, and Nigeria.

Sources: "Pirates Seized Record 1,181 Hostages in 2010," *Report BBC News* (Jan. 1, 2011) and One Earth Future at www.oneearthfuture.org/.

>> International Law and Organizations

What is "international law"? Inasmuch as there is no "world government" or "world legislature," international law is not created the same way as domestic law. International law is found in a variety of sources, including U.S. domestic law, national laws of other countries, international agreements, treaties, and even in what is called "customary international law." Customary international law involves principles that are widely practiced and acknowledged by many civilized nations to be law.

In the landmark case of *The Paquette Habana* (1900), the United States Supreme Court held that "[i]nternational law is part of our law, and must be ascertained and administered by the courts of justice of appropriate jurisdiction as often as questions of right depending upon it are duly presented for their determination."

International organizations, such as the United Nations, the World Trade Organization, and the European Union, directly impact international business transactions. Agreements entered into by the United States, including the Convention on the International Sale of Goods, the North American Free Trade Agreement, and the Dominican Republic-Central American Free Trade Agreement also affect the global sale of goods. These agreements facilitate trade and minimize risk for business.

>> *sidebar* 12.7

What Are Corporate Codes of Conduct?

Corporate codes of conduct are policy statements adopted by companies to define ethical standards for their conduct. These are completely voluntary, often addressing topics such as:

- Forced labor.
- Child labor.
- Discrimination.
- Health and safety of workers.
- Freedom of association and collective bargaining.
- Hours of work, wages, benefits, and overtime compensation.
- Working conditions.
- Environmental issues.
- Monitoring and enforcement of the code of conduct.

Recognizing that there are different legal and cultural environments around the world, companies often develop a code of conduct to establish a foundation for their standards in international business. Seeking to promote global corporate citizenship, the United Nations developed the Global Compact, a voluntary code of conduct supported by companies and organizations around the world. For a list of participants, see www.globalcompact.org. Many major corporations engaging in global operations, including Microsoft, GAP, Inc., and Cisco Systems, Inc., also have supplier or vendor codes of conduct. These codes allow companies to set standards for their suppliers and vendors consistent with the companies' mission and values.

LO 12-2

4. SOURCES OF INTERNATIONAL LAW

What are the principles or rules of international law that apply to a particular contract or dispute? Generally, international law is classified as either **public international law** or **private international law.** Public international law examines relationships between nations and uses rules that are binding on all countries in the international community. Private international law examines relationships created by commercial transactions and utilizes international agreements, as well as the laws of nations to resolve business disputes. Business managers are primarily concerned with private international law issues.

Public International Law   Article 38 of the Statute of the **International Court of Justice (ICJ)** is the traditional place for ascertaining what is public international law. However, in contrast to what you learned in Chapter 1 regarding U.S. cases, the decisions made by the ICJ, the World Court, do not create binding rules of law or precedent in future cases.

The ICJ is the judicial branch of the United Nations and sits at The Hague in the Netherlands. It consists of 15 judges representing all of the world's major legal systems. The judges are elected by the U.N. General Assembly and the Security Council after having been nominated by national groups, not governments. No more than one judge may be a national of any country.

The ICJ has not been a major force in settling disputes since it began functioning in 1946. The ICJ renders, on average, only one contested decision per year and one advisory opinion every two years. There has been widespread reluctance to resort to the ICJ as a forum for resolving international disputes for several reasons. First, only countries have access to the Court. Private parties or corporations may not directly present claims before the Court. No device exists under U.S. law by which a firm or individual can compel the U.S. government to press a claim on its behalf before the ICJ. Furthermore, only countries that have submitted to the Court's jurisdiction may be parties, since there is no compulsory process for forcing a country to come before the Court. A country may choose to accept the Court's jurisdiction only when the use of the Court may suit its own interests. Moreover, the ICJ has no enforcement authority and must rely on diplomacy or economic sanctions against countries that breach international law. For these reasons, infractions of international law often are settled through diplomacy or arbitration, rather than by the presentation of formal charges to the ICJ.

Of course, deciding whether international law has been violated is often a very difficult question. Article 38 sets forth the following order of importance for determining what is international law in a given case:

> The Court, whose function is to decide in accordance with international law such disputes as are submitted to it, shall apply:
>
> a. *International Conventions*, whether general or particular, establishing rules expressly recognized by the contesting states;
>
> b. *International Custom*, as evidence of a general practice accepted as law;
>
> c. *The General Principles of Law* recognized by civilized nations;
>
> d. *Judicial Decisions and the Teachings of the Most Highly Qualified Publicists* of various nations, as subsidiary means for the determination of rules of law.

International Conventions are similar to legislation or statutes and represent formal agreements between nations. International Custom describes common legal practices followed by nations in working with each other over a long period of time. General Principles of Law may be found in national rules common to the countries in a dispute. Finally, Judicial Decisions and Teachings, although not binding, may be used for guidance in resolving a dispute. See Sidebar 12.8 for an example of an ICJ decision and the interplay with U.S. courts.

The ICJ's hearings are open to the public, unless one of the parties asks for the proceedings to be *in camera* or the Court so decides. The hearings take place in the Great Hall of Justice in the Peace Palace, in The Hague.

Business Law 1 Intro. to Contracts, Liability Issues & Intellectual Property

>> *sidebar* 12.8

Medellin v. Texas (2008): The U.S. Supreme Court and the International Court of Justice (ICJ)

What is the effect of an ICJ judgment in the United States? In a 6–3 ruling, the U.S. Supreme Court held that President Bush went too far when he decreed that the states must abide by a 2004 decision by the ICJ. The ICJ found that several dozen Mexican citizens sentenced to death in the United States had not been given the assistance of Mexican diplomats that they were entitled to under the Vienna Convention.

The case in question involved Jose Medellin, a onetime Houston gang member who took part in the rape and murder of two teenaged girls. After he was arrested, and read his Miranda Rights, Medellin

confessed to the crimes, including revealing particularly egregious details. The conviction was challenged because law enforcement authorities failed to inform him of his right under the Vienna Convention.

In the majority opinion, Chief Justice Roberts states that neither the defendant nor his supporters "have identified a single nation that treats ICJ judgments as binding in domestic courts." In response, Mexico has asked the ICJ to declare that the United States "must provide review and reconsideration of the convictions and sentences" consistent with its 2004 decision.

Do include choice of law and forum selection clauses in all international contracts.

Eight UN Millennium Development Goals:

1. Eradicate extreme poverty and hunger.
2. Achieve universal primary education.
3. Promote gender equality and empower women.
4. Reduce child mortality.
5. Improve maternal health.
6. Combat HIV/AIDS, malaria, and other diseases.
7. Ensure environmental sustainability.
8. Develop a global partnership for development.

Private International Law Private international law is represented by the laws of individual nations and the multilateral agreements developed between nations to provide mutual understanding and some degree of continuity to international business transactions. Even in purely domestic business deals, the law is rarely predictable or certain. When different national laws, languages, practices, and cultures are added to the transaction, the situation can become very unstable for international business.

International law can be complicated and a single business transaction can involve several companies in different nations. For example, a contract dispute between a Chinese manufacturer, an American wholesaler, and a Canadian retailer could potentially involve the law of all three countries. Which law controls? The answer could affect the outcome of the case. Determining which nation's court may hear the case can be difficult. For this reason, most international contracts contain choice of law and forum provisions to eliminate this uncertainty.

5. INTERNATIONAL ORGANIZATIONS

Several international organizations play important roles in the development of political, economic, and legal rules for the conduct of international business. The two primary organizations are the United Nations and the World Trade Organization. Additionally, the European Union plays an important role in international trade.

United Nations Established after World War II, the **United Nations** has grown considerably from the 51 founding nations. Almost every country in the world is a member today. The Charter of the United Nations sets forth as its primary goal "to save succeeding generations from the scourge of war" and, to that end, authorizes "collective measures for the prevention and removal of threats to the peace, and for the suppression of acts of aggression or other breaches of the peace."

The General Assembly is composed of every nation represented in the United Nations and permits each country to cast one vote. The real power in the United Nations rests in the Security Council, which is composed of 15 member states. The Security Council has the power to authorize military action and to sever diplomatic relations with other nations. The five permanent members of the Council (United States, Russia, China, France, and United Kingdom) have veto power over any action proposed in the Council. France and Russia used the threat of a veto in 2003 to force the United States to go forward with the war in Iraq without clear United Nations' authority. Although the United States contended that its authority for war came from previously passed UN resolutions regarding Iraq, the U.S. government was disturbed by the veto threat. The failure of the United Nations to dictate the resolution of the U.S.-Iraq conflict created serious questions about the future authority and role of the United Nations in international conflicts.

A number of organizations affiliated with the United Nations have authority over activities that directly affect international business. The United Nations Commission on International Trade Law (UNCITRAL) was created in 1966 to develop standardized commercial practices and agreements. One of the documents drafted by UNCITRAL is the Convention on the International Sale of Goods, which is discussed in more detail later in this chapter. UNCITRAL has no authority to force any country to adopt any of the conventions or agreements that it proposes. The United Nations Conference on Trade and Development (UNCTAD) deals with international trade reform and the redistribution of income through trading with developing countries. UNCTAD drafted both the Transfer of Technology Code and the Restrictive Business Practices Code, which are largely ignored by most nations.

At the Bretton Woods Conference of 1944, two important institutions were also created under the auspices of the United Nations. The **International Monetary Fund (IMF)** encourages international trade by maintaining stable foreign exchange rates and works closely with commercial banks to promote orderly exchange policies with members. The **World Bank** promotes economic development in poor countries by making loans to finance necessary development projects and programs.

For more information about current projects at the World Bank and IMF, see www.worldbank.org/ and www.imf.org/.

> "The human spirit is indomitable. Each individual matters. The seeds of policies and innovations planted today can influence tomorrow. And free men and women can move the world."
>
> **–Robert B. Zoellick, president of the World Bank Group (2008)**

World Trade Organization

Every nation has the right to establish its own trading policies and has its own national interests at stake when dealing with other nations. Ultimately, after years of economic conflict, many countries concluded that their own interests could be served best by liberalizing trade through reduced tariffs and free markets. The **General Agreement on Tariffs and Trade (GATT)** was originally signed by 23 countries after World War II and represented the determination of a war-weary world to open trade and end the protection of domestic industries. Since GATT was created in 1948, it has undergone eight major revisions, including the 1994 Uruguay Round, which culminated in the creation of the **World Trade Organization (WTO)** as an umbrella organization to regulate world trade. The 1994 agreement was signed by 125 countries.

The WTO is an international organization which, as its primary purpose, seeks to resolve trade disputes between member nations. The WTO administers the GATT but does not have the authority to regulate world trade in any manner it desires. The WTO expects nations to avoid unilateral trade wars and rely on GATT dispute settlement procedures to avert conflict. At the heart of the 1994 Uruguay Round are several enduring GATT principles:

1. Nondiscrimination (treating all member countries equally with respect to trade).
2. National treatment (countries not favoring their domestic products over imported products.
3. Elimination of trade barriers (reducing tariffs and other restrictions in foreign products).

Under the WTO, existing tariffs are reduced and the agreement extends GATT rules to new areas such as agricultural products and service industries. The WTO further restricts tariffs on textiles, apparel, and forest products. It also requires countries to upgrade their intellectual property laws to protect patents and copyrights and to guard against the piracy of items such as computer software and videotapes.

Another important aspect of the WTO is the **Agreement on Trade-Related Aspects of Intellectual Property Rights (TRIPS)**, including trade in counterfeit goods. Recognizing that there are widely different standards for the protection of intellectual property, as well as a lack of a multilateral framework of rules for dealing with counterfeit goods, the WTO directly addressed this issue with TRIPS. This agreement discusses the applicability of GATT principles and those of relevant international property agreements in an effort to strengthen the protection of intellectual property in the international sphere.

The WTO has the power to hear disputes involving member states. The United States has been involved in a number of disputes. For example, the United States brought an action against the European Union claiming that the Europeanwide restrictions on genetically modified food violate WTO rules. Additionally, the United States brought a successful challenge against Mexico; the WTO held that Mexico's beverage tax on soft drinks made with imported sweeteners is discriminatory. Under the beverage tax, soft drinks made with cane sugar are tax exempt. Because the beverage tax discriminates against U.S. products, it is contrary to WTO rules.

If a nation does not comply with a WTO ruling, the organization has the power to impose sanctions. Like any international institution, compliance by the most powerful trading nations is necessary to give the WTO credibility.

The WTO faces opposition from antiglobalization protesters. There are many reasons to support the WTO and the important role it plays in trade. Concerns, however, are raised by opponents who are concerned about human rights, environmental, and labor issues. Tensions between developed and developing nations are hindering negotiations to cut tariffs. Overall, the future of the WTO is uncertain. The cooperation of member states is critical to its success in liberalizing trade.

The European Union   The European Union is an economic and political partnership between 27 democratic European countries. In 1957, six

The WTO is the only global international trade organization dealing with the rules of trade between nations.

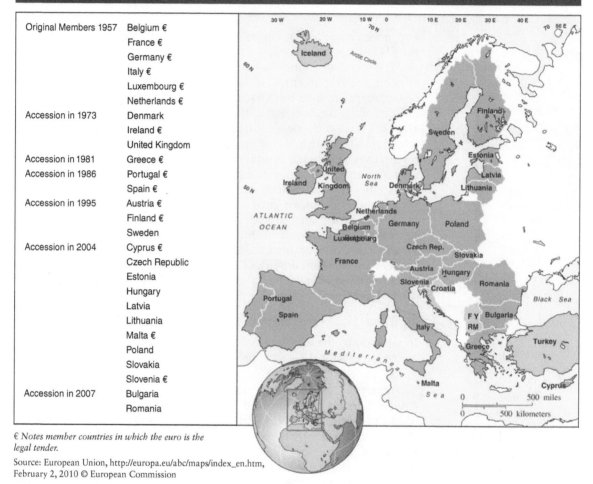

table 12.2 >> Twenty-Seven European Union Member States

Original Members 1957	Belgium €
	France €
	Germany €
	Italy €
	Luxembourg €
	Netherlands €
Accession in 1973	Denmark
	Ireland €
	United Kingdom
Accession in 1981	Greece €
Accession in 1986	Portugal €
	Spain €
Accession in 1995	Austria €
	Finland €
	Sweden
Accession in 2004	Cyprus €
	Czech Republic
	Estonia
	Hungary
	Latvia
	Lithuania
	Malta €
	Poland
	Slovakia
	Slovenia €
Accession in 2007	Bulgaria
	Romania

€ *Notes member countries in which the euro is the
legal tender.*

Source: European Union, http://europa.eu/abc/maps/index_en.htm,
February 2, 2010 © European Commission

European countries, Belgium, France, Germany, Luxembourg, and the Netherlands signed the Treaty of Rome, creating the European Community. Six
successive enlargements created the **European Union (EU)**, as it is known
today. See Table 12.2 for a complete list of states, accession dates, and those
countries using the euro as legal tender. Negotiations are ongoing with Croa-
tia, the Republic of Macedonia, and Turkey about possible membership in
the EU.

Europe's mission in the twenty-first century is to:

- Provide peace, prosperity, and stability for its peoples.
- Overcome the divisions on the continent.
- Ensure that its people live in safety.
- Promote balanced economic and social development.
- Meet the challenges of globalization and preserve the diversity of the peo-
  ples of Europe.

• Uphold the values that Europeans share, such as sustainable development and a sound environment, respect for human rights, and the social market economy.

For more detailed information about these goals, see the official website of the EU at http://europa.eu.

The major institutions of the EU are the Council of Ministers, the Commission, the Parliament, and the Court of Justice. The Council is composed of one representative from each member state. The Council coordinates the policies of the member states in a variety of areas from economics to foreign affairs. The Commission consists of individuals who represent the will and interests of the entire EU, rather than specific national concerns. Elected representatives from each member state compose the Parliament, which plays an active role in drafting legislation that has an impact on the daily lives of its citizens. The Parliament, for example, has addressed environmental protection, consumer rights, equal opportunities, transport, and the free movement of workers, capital, services, and goods. Parliament also has joint power with the Council over the annual budget of the European Union. Finally, the Court of Justice decides the nature and parameters of EU law. Justices are appointed by the Council, and each member state has a justice seated on the Court.

> The aims of the European Union are: "Peace, prosperity and freedom for its 495 million citizens—in a fairer, safer world."

LO 12-3

6. MAJOR AGREEMENTS AFFECTING TRADE

In addition to the international institutions discussed in this chapter, a number of international agreements also facilitate trade.

> The U.S. Trade Representative is a Cabinet member who serves as the president's principal trade adviser, negotiator, and spokesperson on trade issues. See www.ustr.gov for current trade news.

Convention on the International Sale of Goods   The **Convention on the International Sale of Goods (CISG)** outlines standard international practices for the sale of goods. It took several years to develop, and represents many compromises among nations that follow a variety of practices in the area of contracts. Effective in 1988, it has been adopted by the United States and most of the other countries that engage in large quantities of international trade. The CISG represents the cumulative work of over 60 nations and international groups and is widely accepted around the globe.

The CISG applies to contracts for the commercial sale of goods (consumer sales for personal, family, or household use are excluded) between parties whose businesses are located in different nations, provided that those nations have adopted the convention. If a commercial seller or buyer in the United States, for example, contracts for the sale of goods with a company located in another country that also has adopted the CISG, the convention and not the U.S. Uniform Commercial Code (UCC) applies to the transaction.

Under the CISG, a significant degree of freedom is provided for the individual parties in an international contract. The parties may negotiate contract terms as they deem fit for their business practices and may, if desired, even opt out of the CISG entirely. One of the most interesting provisions in the CISG includes a rule that contracts for the sale of goods need not be in writing. The

> "We must continue to open markets if we want our exports to grow. . . . Open markets create higher paying jobs and help support the prosperity of American workers, farmers, and entrepreneurs."
>
> **–Susan C. Schwab, U.S. Trade Representative (2008)**

CISG also provides that in contract negotiations an acceptance that contains new provisions that do not materially alter the terms of the offer becomes part of the contract, unless the offeror promptly objects to the change. The CISG sets forth the fundamental elements that will materially alter a contract such as price, payment, quality, and quantity of the goods, place and time of delivery of goods, provisions related to one party's liability to the other, and methods for settling disputes. Since international transactions typically involve sophisticated parties, the CISG also makes it easier to disclaim warranties on goods than under traditional U.S. law. The CISG does not resolve all areas of contract law; parties are still subject to local laws and customs, which makes international agreements complex and tricky to negotiate.

North American Free Trade Agreement The passage of the **North American Free Trade Agreement (NAFTA)** in 1993 set in motion increased trade and foreign investment and opportunities for economic growth in the United States, Mexico, and Canada. Free trade is at the core of NAFTA, through the reduction and eventual elimination of tariffs and other barriers to business between these three countries. NAFTA also provides for a dispute settlement mechanism that makes it easier to resolve trade disputes between the three countries. Based upon concerns that cheap labor and poor environmental controls might cause U.S. firms to relocate to Mexico, side agreements also were reached to improve labor rights and environmental protection in Mexico. Since its enactment, NAFTA has expanded shipments of U.S. goods to Mexico and Canada, as well as Mexican and Canadian exports to the United States.

Central America-Dominican Republic Free Trade Agreement Similar to NAFTA, the passage of the **Central America-Dominican Republic Free Trade Agreement (CAFTA-DR)** in 2005 opened up many opportunities for business in Central America. CAFTA-DR is a comprehensive trade agreement between Costa Rica, El Salvador, Guatemala, Honduras, Nicaragua, the Dominican Republic, and the United States. This agreement is designed to eliminate the barriers on products trades between the member countries. Prior to CAFTA-DR, many exports of American goods to Central America faced high tariffs. This trade agreement is a step to create a fairer playing field for American exports.

Jimmy Carter supported the passage of CAFTA-DR as a "chance to reinforce democracies in the region."

Recent Free Trade Agreements The United States is continually seeking opportunities to open global trade. In October 2011, Congress passed free trade agreements for three key markets: Colombia, Panama, and South Korea. The agreement with Colombia was the most controversial. According to the U.S. Trade Representative's office, this agreement is important (1) To open a significant new export market; (2) to level the playing field for American business, farmers, ranchers, and workers; (3) to strengthen peace, democracy, freedom, and reform; (4) to promote economic growth and poverty reduction; and (5) to anchor longstanding ties with a vital regional ally. Opponents to the Colombia agreement argued that the agreement does not contain adequate provisions to address labor concerns and human rights violations, including violence against union members.

concept >> *summary*

International Law and Organizations

1. International law is classified as either public or private.
2. The International Court of Justice is the traditional place for determining public international law.
3. The World Trade Organization regulates world trade for member nations.
4. The Convention on the International Sale of Goods governs international practices for the sale of goods.
5. The European Union has evolved into the most important economic force in Europe.
6. The North American Free Trade Agreement has substantially expanded trade with Mexico and Canada.

>> *sidebar* 12.9

Philip Morris: Restrictions Affecting Their Global Business

With more and more anti-smoking laws in the United States and general public opposition to smoking, global markets are increasingly important to tobacco giant Philip Morris. What kinds of issues does it face abroad?

- Limits on cigarette advertising in Britain
- More detailed health warnings in South America
- Higher cigarette taxes in the Philippines and Mexico
- Prohibitions on store displays in Ireland and Norway
- The World Health Organization Framework Convention on Tobacco Control, a public health treaty ratified by 171 nations
- Mandatory health warnings that cover 80 percent of cigarette packages in Uruguay

Alleging that its tobacco regulations are excessive, Philip Morris sued the government of Uruguay. Philip Morris also brought an action against Brazil, arguing that the images the government wants to put on cigarette packages "vilify" tobacco companies.

Sources: Duff Wilson, "Cigarette Giants in Global Fight on Tighter Rules," *The New York Times* (Nov. 13, 2010); World Health Organization Framework Convention on Tobacco Control, www.who.int/fctc/en/.

LO 12-4 >> **Methods of Transacting International Business**

A U.S. business that wants to engage in international trade is presented with an almost limitless array of possibilities. Choosing a method of doing business in foreign countries not only requires understanding the factors normally involved in selecting an organization and operating a business domestically but also demands an appreciation of the international trade perspective. Depending upon the country, type of export, and amount of export involved in a particular transaction, international trade may involve direct foreign sales, licensing agreements, franchise agreements, or direct foreign investment.

7. FOREIGN SALES

The most common approach for a manufacturer to use when trying to enter foreign markets is to sell goods directly to buyers located in other countries. However, with foreign sales, increased uncertainty over the ability to enforce the buyer's promise to pay for goods often requires that more complex arrangements for payment be made than with the usual domestic sale. International sales involve many risky legal issues. Commonly, an **irrevocable letter of credit** is used to ensure payment. Transactions using such a letter involve, in addition to a seller and buyer, an *issuing bank* in the buyer's country. The buyer obtains a commitment from the bank to advance (pay) a specified amount (i.e., the price of the goods) upon receipt, from the carrier, of a **bill of lading,** stating that the goods have been shipped. The issuing bank's commitment to pay is given, not to the seller directly, but to a *confirming bank* located in the United States from which the seller obtains payment. The confirming bank forwards the bill of lading to the issuing bank in order to obtain reimbursement of the funds that have been paid to the seller. The issuing bank releases the bill of lading to the buyer after it has been paid, and with the bill of lading the buyer is able to obtain the goods from the carrier. Use of a letter of credit in the transaction thus reduces the uncertainties involved. The buyer need not pay the seller for goods prior to shipment, and the seller can obtain payment for the goods immediately upon shipment.

There is no room in documentary transactions for substantial performance. All of the duties and responsibilities of parties must be evaluated based upon the documents tendered, and these documents must comply *strictly* with the letter of credit. The tradition and purpose of the letter of credit in international transactions is demonstrated in Case 12.1, where the issue of notice became the central issue for the court.

Do learn more about the traditions, culture, and etiquette of a host nation before you travel, including business card protocol.

 case 12.1 >>

VOEST-ALPINE TRADING USA v. BANK OF CHINA
288 F. 3d 262 (5th Cir. 2002)

Jiangyin Foreign Trade Corporation ("JFTC"), a Chinese company, agreed to purchase 1,000 metric tons of styrene monomer from Voest-Alpine Trading USA Corporation ("Voest-Alpine"), an American company. At Voest-Alpine's insistence, JFTC obtained a letter of credit from the Bank of China for the purchase price of $1.2 million. The letter of credit provided for payment to Voest-Alpine after it delivered the monomer and presented several designated documents to the Bank of China. By the time Voest-Alpine was ready to ship its product, the market price of styrene monomer had dropped significantly from the original contract price. JFTC asked for a price concession, but Voest-Alpine

refused. After shipping the monomer to JFTC, Voest-Alpine presented the documents specified in the letter of credit to Texas Commerce Bank ("TCB"), which would forward the documents to the Bank of China. TCB noted several discrepancies between what Voest-Alpine presented and what the letter of credit required. Because it did not believe any of the discrepancies would warrant refusal to pay, Voest-Alpine instructed TCB to present the documents to the Bank of China "on approval," meaning that JFTC would be asked to waive the problems.

The Bank of China received the documents. The bank notified TCB that the documents contained

[continued]

several discrepancies and that it would contact JFTC about acceptance. On August 15, 1995, TCB, acting on behalf of Voest-Alpine, responded that the alleged discrepancies were not adequate grounds for dishonoring the letter of credit and demanded payment. On August 19, the Bank of China reiterated its position that the documents were insufficient and stated: "Now the discrepant documents may have us refuse to take up the documents according to article 14(B) of UCP 500." JFTC refused to waive the discrepancies, and the Bank of China returned the documents to TCB on September 18, 1995.

CLEMENT, J.: Voest-Alpine filed the instant action for payment on the letter of credit.

The Bank of China's primary contention on appeal is that the district court erroneously concluded that the bank failed to provide proper notice of refusal to Voest-Alpine. In order to reject payment on a letter of credit, an issuing bank must give notice of refusal to the beneficiary no later than the close of the seventh banking day following the day of receipt of the [presentation] documents. If the Bank of China did not provide timely notice, it must honor the letter of credit despite any questions as to Voest-Alpine's compliance.

The Bank of China received Voest-Alpine's documents on August 9. Since August 12 and 13 were Chinese banking holidays, the deadline for giving notice of dishonor was August 18. The Bank of China's only communication before the deadline was its telex of August 11. Accordingly, the issue is whether that telex provided notice of refusal. The bank's August 11 telex stated:

> Upon checking documents, we note the following discrepancy:
>
> 1. Late presentation.
> 2. Beneficiary's name is differ (*sic*) from L/C.
> 3. B/L should be presented in three originals (*sic*) i/o duplicate, triplicate.
> 4. Inv. P/L. and cert. Of origin not showing "original."
> 5. The date of surver (*sic*) report later than B/L date.
> 6. Wrong L/C no. in fax copy.
> 7. Wrong destination in cert. Of origin and beneficiary's cert.
>
> We are contacting the applicant for acceptance of the relative discrepancy. Holding documents at your risk and disposal.

The district court found that the telex failed to provide notice of refusal because (1) the bank did not explicitly state that it was rejecting the documents; (2) the bank's statement that it would contact JFTC about accepting the documents despite the discrepancies holds open the possibility of acceptance upon waiver and indicates that the Bank of China has not refused the documents; and (3) the Bank of China did not even mention refusal until its August 19 telex in which it wrote: "Now the discrepant documents may have us refuse to take up the documents according to article 14(B) of UCP 500." In light of these circumstances, the district court concluded that the August 11 telex was merely a status report, the bank would not reject the documents until after it consulted JFTC, and the bank did not raise the possibility of refusing payment on the letter of credit until August 19. Accordingly, the district court held that the Bank of China forfeited its right to refuse the documents and was obligated to pay Voest-Alpine.

We find ample evidence supporting the district court's decision. The court's determination that the August 11 telex did not reject the letter of credit is based primarily on the Bank of China's offer to obtain waiver from JFTC. The offer to solicit a waiver, the district court reasoned, suggests that the documents had not in fact been refused but might be accepted after consultation with JFTC. In reaching this conclusion, the district court relied heavily on the testimony of Voest-Alpine's expert witness on international standard banking practices. [The expert] testified that the bank's telex would have given adequate notice had it not contained the waiver clause. The waiver clause, he explained, deviated from the norm and introduced an ambiguity that converted what might otherwise have been a notice of refusal into nothing more than a status report. Faced with this evidence, the district court correctly decided that the Bank of China noted discrepancies in the documents, and, instead of rejecting the letter of credit outright, contacted JFTC for waiver.

Viewed in the context of standard international banking practices, the Bank of China's notice of refusal was clearly deficient. The bank failed to use the standard language for refusal, failed to comply with generally accepted trade usages, and created ambiguity by offering to contact JFTC about waiver, thus leaving open the possibility that the allegedly discrepant documents might have been accepted at a future date. Accordingly, the district court properly found that the August 11 telex was not an adequate notice of refusal. Since we agree with the district court that the bank failed to provide timely notice, we need not reach the question of whether the alleged discrepancies warranted refusal.

The Bank of China failed to provide Voest-Alpine with adequate notice that it was refusing payment on the letter of credit. Without a valid excuse for nonpayment, the bank is liable for the full amount of the letter of credit and for VoestAlpine's legal fees. Accordingly, we affirm the judgment of the district court.

Affirmed.

[continued]

>> CASE QUESTIONS

1. Why is the issue of "timely notice" so important in the case?
2. What is the primary importance of a letter of credit?
3. Why did the court rule against Bank of China?

8. LICENSES OR FRANCHISES

In appropriate circumstances, a domestic firm may choose to grant a foreign firm the means to produce and sell its product. The typical method for controlling these transfers of information is the **license** or **franchise** contract. In this manner, intangible property rights, such as patents, copyrights, trademarks, or manufacturing processes, are transferred in exchange for royalties in the foreign country. A licensing arrangement allows the international business to enter a foreign market without any direct foreign investment. Licensing often is used as a transitional technique for firms expanding international operations since the risks are greater than with foreign sales but considerably less than with direct foreign investment. Licensing and franchise agreements also must follow the local laws where they operate.

Licensing technology or the sale of a product to a foreign firm is a way to expand the company's market without the need for substantial capital. The foreign firm may agree to this arrangement because it lacks sufficient research and development capability or the management skills or marketing strategies to promote the product alone. Of course, as with all international trade agreements, there is some level of risk. The licensor must take care to restrict the use of the product or technology to agreed-upon geographic areas and must take adequate steps to protect the confidential information that is licensed to the foreign firm so that third parties cannot exploit it.

Each day, McDonald's serves an average of 64 million customers worldwide.

Subway is one of the fastest growing franchises with over 34,000 restaurants in 97 countries.

9. DIRECT FOREIGN INVESTMENT

As a business increases its level of international trade, it may find that creation of a **foreign subsidiary** is necessary. Most countries will permit a foreign firm to conduct business only if a national (individual or firm) of the host country is designated as its legal representative. Since this designation may create difficulties in control and result in unnecessary expense, the usual practice for multinational corporations is to create a foreign subsidiary in the host country. The form of subsidiary most closely resembling a U.S. corporation is known as a *société anonyme (S.A.)* or, in German-speaking countries, an *Aktiengesellschaft (AG)*. Other forms of subsidiaries may also exist that have characteristics of limited liability of the owners and fewer formalities in their creation and operation.

Creation of a foreign subsidiary may pose considerable risk to the domestic parent firm by subjecting it to foreign laws and the jurisdiction of foreign courts. An industrial accident in Bhopal, India, where hundreds of people were killed and thousands injured as a result of toxic gas leaks from a chemical plant, resulted in lawsuits against both the Indian subsidiary corporation and Union Carbide, the parent firm in the United States. Union Carbide agreed to pay more than $450 million to settle outstanding claims and compensate the victims of the disaster.

In many instances, however, the only legal or political means a firm has to invest directly in a foreign country is to engage in a **joint venture** with an entity from that host country. A host country's participant may be a private enterprise or, especially in developing countries, a government agency or government-owned corporation. Many foreign countries favor joint ventures because they allow local individuals and firms to participate in the benefits of economic growth and decrease the risk of foreign domination of local industry. Many of the developing countries require that the local partner have majority equity control of the venture and also insist on joint ventures with government participation.

>> *sidebar* 12.10

Chiquita Brands International: Payments to Death Squads for "Protection"

Chiquita Brands International pled guilty to doing business with the United Self-Defense Forces of Colombia (UAC), a right-wing paramilitary group in Colombia. Prosecutors said the banana company made $1.7 million in "protection payments" to this death squad, which is reportedly responsible for some of Colombia's worst massacres. In 2001, the U.S. State Department declared that UAC was an "international terrorist group," making it a violation of U.S. law to conduct business with the group. To settle the charges, Chiquita paid $25 million, arguing that it had no choice but to pay protection money to prevent the UAC from turning death squads loose on its banana workers.

Families of over 350 people thought to have been killed by UAC are suing Chiquita in U.S. federal court seeking $7.86 billion in civil damages. The families claim that Chiquita aided and abetted terrorism, war crimes, and crimes against humanity because of its financial support of UAC. In May 2011, the seven pending lawsuits were consolidated into one action involving allegations of over 4,000 killings of Colombian nationals. In June 2011, the federal judge in Florida overseeing the litigation denied Chiquita's motion to dismiss some of the claims brought under the ATCA and Torture Victim Protection Act. The judge rejected Chiquita's argument that the case should be dismissed because it could have foreign policy implications.

Colombia's attorney general has also threatened to seek extradition of eight Chiquita executives to face criminal prosecution.

LO 12-5   ## >> Resolving International Disputes

International law can be complicated, and a single business transaction may involve several companies in different nations. For example, a contract dispute between a Chinese manufacturer, an American wholesaler, and a Canadian retailer could potentially involve the law of all three countries. Which law controls? What jurisdiction has the power to resolve the dispute? The answers to these questions could affect the outcome of the case. As such, most international contracts contain choice of law and forum provisions to eliminate this uncertainty. This section addresses the limitations on suing foreign governments in the United States, issues raised when suing foreign firms in the United States, and international arbitration options.

10. ALIEN TORT CLAIMS ACT

The **Alien Tort Claims Act (ATCA)**, enacted in 1789, grants jurisdiction to U.S. federal district courts over "any civil action by an alien for a tort only, committed in violation of the law of nations or a treaty of the United States." For nearly 200 years, the law lapsed into obscurity. In the last 20 years, however, it has been revived in a number of human rights contexts, including claims brought against U.S. global companies. An essential aspect of a successful claim under the ATCA is to demonstrate that the acts committed violate the law of nations. This prompts many unanswered legal questions in the international labor context. What constitutes the "law of nations"? In general, the law of nations is embodied in international agreements, treaties, and conventions. ATCA actions have been alleged against many U.S. companies, including Bridgestone, Chevron, Del Monte, Drummond Company, Dyncorp, ExxonMobil, Gap, Inc., Texaco, Inc., Unocal Corp., Wal-Mart, and, most recently, Yahoo. Claims typically involve allegations of forced labor, but may also include other human rights abuses such as murder, rape, torture, unlawful detention, and kidnapping. It is not unusual for these cases to also allege that acts were committed by paramilitaries hired by the company.

> The ATCA is viewed by some as a way to hold U.S. companies responsible for their participation in human rights abuses abroad.

 case 12.2 >>

KIOBEL v. ROYAL DUTCH PETROLEUM, CO.
621 F.3d 111 (2nd Cir. 2010)

Nigerian residents filed a class action under the Alien Tort Claims Act (ATCA) or Alien Tort Statute (ATS) alleging that Dutch, British and Nigerian corporations engaged in oil exploration and production aided and abetted the Nigerian government in committing human rights abuses in violation of the law of nations. In 2004, the U.S. Supreme Court endeavored to clarify the scope of the ATCA. In his opinion, Justice Souter stated "judicial power should be exercised on the understanding that the door is still ajar subject to vigilant door-keeping, and thus open to a narrow class of international norms today." (542 U.S. 692, 729). Relying on the Sosa decision, defendants moved to dismiss this action. In September 2006, the District Court dismissed plaintiffs' claims for aiding and abetting property destruction; forced exile; extrajudicial killing; and violations of the rights to life, liberty, security and association. The District Court reasoned that customary international law did not define those violations with the particularity required by Sosa. The District Court denied defendants' motion to dismiss with respect to the remaining claims of aiding and

abetting arbitrary arrest and detention' crime against humanity; and torture or cruel, inhuman, and degrading treatment. The District Court certified its entire order for interlocutory appeal.

JOSÉ A. CABRANES, CIRCUIT JUDGE: Once again we consider a case brought under the Alien Tort Statute ("ATS"), 28 U.S.C. §1350,FN1 a jurisdictional provision unlike any other in American law and of a kind apparently unknown to any other legal system in the world. Passed by the first Congress in 1789, the ATS lay largely dormant for over 170 years. Judge Friendly called it a "legal Lohengrin"—"no one seems to know whence it came." Then, in 1980, the statute was given new life, when our Court first recognized in *Filartiga v. Pena-Irala* that the ATS provides jurisdiction over (1) tort actions, (2) brought by aliens (only), (3) for violations of the law of nations (also called "customary international law" including, as a general matter, war crimes and crimes against humanity-crimes in which the perpetrator can be called "*hostis humani generis,* an enemy of all mankind." . . .

[continued]

Because appellate review of ATS suits has been so uncommon, there remain a number of unresolved issues lurking in our ATS jurisprudence—issues that we have simply had no occasion to address in the handful of cases we have decided in the thirty years since the revival of the ATS. This case involves one such unresolved issue: Does the jurisdiction granted by the ATS extend to civil actions brought against corporations under the law of nations? . . .

Plaintiffs are residents of Nigeria who claim that Dutch, British, and Nigerian corporations engaged in oil exploration and production aided and abetted the Nigerian government in committing violations of the law of nations. They seek damages under the ATS, and thus their suit may proceed only if the ATS provides jurisdiction over tort actions brought against corporations under customary international law. A legal culture long accustomed to imposing liability on corporations may, at first blush, assume that corporations must be subject to tort liability under the ATS, just as corporations are generally liable in tort under our domestic law (what international law calls "municipal law"). But the substantive law that determines our jurisdiction under the ATS is neither the domestic law of the United States nor the domestic law of any other country. By conferring subject matter jurisdiction over a limited number of offenses defined by *customary international law,* the ATS requires federal courts to look beyond rules of domestic law—however well-established they may be—to examine the specific and universally accepted rules that the nations of the world treat as binding *in their dealings with one another. . . .*

Accordingly, absent a relevant treaty of the United States-and none is relied on here-we must ask whether a plaintiff bringing an ATS suit against a corporation has alleged a violation of customary international law. The singular achievement of international law since the Second World War has come in the area of human rights, where the subjects of customary international law—*i.e.,* those with international rights, duties, and liabilities-now include not merely *states,* but also *individuals.* This principle was most famously applied by the International Military Tribunal at Nuremberg. . . .

From the beginning, however, the principle of individual liability for violations of international law has been limited to natural persons—not "juridical" persons such as corporations-because the moral responsibility for a crime so heinous and unbounded as to rise to the level of an "international crime" has rested solely with the individual men and women who have perpetrated it. . . .

In short, because customary international law imposes individual liability for a limited number of international crimes—including war crimes, crimes against humanity (such as genocide), and torture—we have held that the ATS provides jurisdiction over claims in tort against individuals who are alleged to have committed such crimes. As we explain in detail below, however, customary international law has steadfastly rejected the notion of corporate liability for international crimes, and no international tribunal has ever held a corporation liable for a violation of the law of nations. We must conclude, therefore, that insofar as plaintiffs bring claims under the ATS against corporations, plaintiffs fail to allege violations of the law of nations, and plaintiffs' claims fall outside the limited jurisdiction provided by the ATS. We emphasize that the question before us is not whether corporations are "immune" from suit under the ATS: That formulation improperly assumes that there is a norm imposing liability in the first place. Rather, the question before us, as the Supreme Court has explained, "is whether international law extends the scope of liability for a violation of a given norm to the perpetrator being sued, if the defendant is a private actor such as a corporation or individual." Looking to international law, we find a jurisprudence, first set forth in Nuremberg and repeated by every international tribunal of which we are aware, that offenses against the law of nations (*i.e.,* customary international law) for violations of human rights can be charged against States and against individual men and women but not against juridical persons such as corporations. As a result, although customary international law has sometimes extended the scope of liability for a violation of a given norm to individuals, it has *never* extended the scope of liability to a corporation. . . .

Accordingly, insofar as plaintiffs in this action seek to hold only corporations liable for their conduct in Nigeria (as opposed to individuals within those corporations), and only under the ATS, their claims must be dismissed for lack of subject matter jurisdiction. . . .

Conclusion

The ATS provides federal district courts jurisdiction over a tort, brought by an alien only, alleging a "violation of the law of nations or a treaty of the United States." 28 U.S.C. §1350. When an ATS suit is brought under the "law of nations," also known as "customary international law," jurisdiction is limited to those cases alleging a violation of an international norm that is "specific, universal, and obligatory." *Sosa v. Alvarez-Machain,* 542 U.S. 692, 732, 124 S.Ct. 2739, 159 L.Ed.2d 718 (2004). . . .

To summarize, we hold as follows:

(1) Since *Filartiga,* which in 1980 marked the advent of the modern era of litigation for violations of human rights under the Alien Tort

[continued]

Statute, all of our precedents—and the Supreme Court's decision in *Sosa,* 542 U.S. at 732 n. 20 require us to look to international law to determine whether a particular class of defendant, such as corporations, can be liable under the Alien Tort Statute for alleged violations of the law of nations.

(2) The concept of corporate liability for violations of customary international law has not achieved universal recognition or acceptance as a norm in the relations of States with each other. . . . Inasmuch as plaintiffs assert claims against corporations only, their complaint must be dismissed for lack of subject matter jurisdiction.

>> CASE QUESTIONS

1. What kinds of claims can be brought under the Alien Tort Statute?
2. Why does the Second Circuit reject imposing liability on corporations?
3. What are the ramifications of the decision?

11. SUING FOREIGN GOVERNMENTS IN THE UNITED STATES

The doctrine of **sovereign immunity** provides that a foreign sovereign is immune from suit in the United States. Under the doctrine of sovereign immunity, the foreign sovereign claims to be immune from suit entirely based on its status as a state.

Until approximately 1952, this notion was absolute. From 1952 until 1976, U.S. courts adhered to a *restrictive theory* under which immunity existed with regard to sovereign or public acts but not with regard to private or commercial acts. In 1976, Congress enacted the **Foreign Sovereign Immunities Act (FSIA),** which codifies this restrictive theory and rejects immunity for *commercial acts* carried on in the United States or having direct effects in this country.

Sovereignty is defined as the supreme, absolute, and uncontrollable power by which any state is governed.

The Supreme Court held that the doctrine should not be extended to foreign governments acting in a commercial capacity and "should not be extended to include the repudiation of a purely commercial obligation owed by a foreign sovereign or by one of its commercial instrumentalities." This interpretation recognizes that governments also may act in a private or commercial capacity and, when doing so, will be subjected to the same rules of law as are applicable to private individuals. A nationalization of assets, however, probably will be considered an act in the "public interest" and immune from suit under the FSIA.

12. SUING FOREIGN FIRMS IN THE UNITED STATES

As foreign products and technology are imported into the United States, disputes may arise over either the terms of contract or the performance of the goods. To sue a foreign firm in the United States, the Supreme Court held that the plaintiff must establish "minimum contacts" between the foreign defendant and the forum court. The plaintiff must demonstrate that exercise of

382   **PART 3**   Legal Foundations for Business

Although punitive damages may be awarded in U.S. courts against a foreign company doing business in the United States, it may be difficult or impossible to enforce the award in the company's home country. Outside of the United States, very few countries allow punitive damage awards, which are viewed as a "peculiarity of American law."

personal jurisdiction over the defendant "does not offend traditional notions of fair play and substantial justice."

Once the plaintiff decides to sue in the United States, he or she also must comply with the terms of the Hague Service Convention when serving the foreign defendant notice of the lawsuit. The Hague Service Convention is a treaty that was formulated "to provide a simpler way to serve process abroad, to assure that defendants sued in foreign jurisdictions would receive actual and timely notice of suit, and to facilitate proof of service abroad." Many countries, including the United States, follow this convention. The primary requirement of the agreement is to require each nation to establish a central authority to process requests for service of documents from other countries. After the central authority receives the request in proper form, it must serve the documents by a method prescribed by the internal law of the receiving state or by a method designated by the requester and compatible with the law.

>> *sidebar* 12.11

The Reach of U.S. Law: *Spector v. Norwegian Cruise Line, Ltd.* 545 U.S. 119 (2005)

Issue: Whether foreign-flagged cruise ships serving U.S. ports must comply with the public accommodations provisions in Title III of the Americans with Disabilities Act.

Key Facts: Disabled plaintiffs and their companions alleged that physical barriers on the Norwegian Cruise Line Ltd. (NCL) ships denied them access to various equipment, programs, and facilities on the ships. They sought injunctive relief

requiring NCL to remove certain barriers that obstructed their access to the ships' facilities.

Procedural History: The district court found that foreign-flagged cruise ships *are* subject to the ADA. The Fifth Circuit Court of Appeals *reversed*.

Outcome: The U.S. Supreme Court reversed, holding that Title III of the ADA is applicable to foreign-flag cruise ships in U.S. waters.

In Case 12.3, the court considers a lawsuit against a foreign firm over whether U.S. employment laws can be imposed on its domestic employees. Also, see Sidebar 12.11 for another example of the reach of U.S. law.

---

 case 12.3 >>

MORELLI v. CEDEL
141 F. 3d 39 (2d Cir. 1998)

CUDAHY, J.: This appeal requires us to decide whether the domestic employees of certain foreign corporations are protected under the Age Discrimination and Employment Act of 1967 (the ADEA), and, if so, whether a foreign corporation's foreign employees are counted for the purpose of determining whether the corporation has enough employees to be subject to the ADEA. We answer both questions in the affirmative.

[continued]

After the defendant fired the plaintiff, the plaintiff sued the defendant. The plaintiff's amended complaint asserted that the defendant violated the ADEA, the Employment Retirement Security Act (ERISA), and New York State's Human Rights Law. The district court dismissed the complaint on the grounds that the defendant was not subject to the ADEA.

As alleged in the complaint, the facts relevant to this appeal are as follows. The plaintiff, Ida Morelli, was born on April 11, 1939. The defendant is a Luxembourg bank. On or about June 29, 1984, the defendant hired the plaintiff to work in its New York office. On or about February 26, 1993, the plaintiff became an assistant to Dennis Sabourin, a manager in the defendant's New York office. Mr. Sabourin summoned the then 54-year-old plaintiff to his office on January 18, 1994, handed her a separation agreement, and insisted that she sign it.

Under the terms of the separation agreement, the plaintiff would resign, effective April 30, 1994. She would continue to receive her salary and benefits until the effective date of her resignation, but she would be relieved of her duties as an employee, effective immediately. Both the defendant and the employee would renounce all claims arising out of "their past working relationship." Mr. Sabourin told the plaintiff that she would receive the three months' severance pay, medical coverage for three months, and her pension only on the condition that she sign the agreement on the spot. The plaintiff had never seen the separation agreement before and had no warning that she was going to be asked to resign. But in the face of Mr. Sabourin's ultimatum, she did sign the agreement immediately and returned it to him. The defendant, however, never provided her with a pension distribution.

The ADEA was enacted to prevent arbitrary discrimination by employers on the basis of age. In order to determine whether the defendant is subject to the ADEA, we must first determine whether the ADEA generally protects the employees of a branch of a foreign employer located in the United States.

[T]he ADEA provides that the prohibitions of [the ADEA] shall not apply where the employer is a foreign person not controlled by an American employer. At a minimum, this provision means that the ADEA does not apply to the foreign operations of foreign employers—unless there is an American employer behind the scenes. An absolutely literal reading of [the statute] might suggest that the ADEA also does not apply to the domestic operations of foreign employers. But the plain language is not necessarily decisive if it is inconsistent with Congress' clearly expressed legislative purpose. Congress' purpose was not to exempt the domestic workplaces of foreign employers from the ADEA's prohibition of age discrimination. . . .

We have previously concluded that even when a foreign employer operating in the United States can invoke a Friendship, Commerce and Navigation treaty to justify employing its own nationals, this does not give the employer license to violate American laws prohibiting discrimination in employment. Although the Supreme Court vacated our judgment in that case on the grounds that the defendant could not invoke the treaty, the Court observed that "the highest level of protection afforded by commercial treaties" to foreign corporations operating in the United States is generally no more than "equal treatment with domestic corporations." Here equal treatment would require that antidiscrimination rules apply to foreign enterprises' U.S. branches, since defending personnel decisions is a fact of business life in contemporary America and is a burden that the domestic competitors of foreign enterprise have been required to shoulder. Also, U.S. subsidiaries of foreign corporations are generally subject to U.S. antidiscrimination laws, and, absent treaty protection—not an issue in this case—a U.S. branch of a foreign corporation is not entitled to an immunity not enjoyed by such subsidiaries.

Cedel will still not be subject to the ADEA by virtue of its U.S. operations unless Cedel is an "employer" under the ADEA. A business must have at least twenty "employees" to be an "employer." Cedel maintains that, in the case of foreign employers, only domestic employees should be counted. The district court agreed, and, since Cedel had fewer than 20 employees in its U.S. branch, the court granted Cedel's motion to dismiss for lack of subject matter jurisdiction without considering the number of Cedel's overseas employees.

The district court reasoned that the overseas employees of foreign employers should not be counted because they are not protected by the ADEA. But there is no requirement that an employee be protected by the ADEA to be counted; an enumeration, for the purpose of ADEA coverage of an employer, includes employees under age 40, who are also unprotected. The nose count of employees relates to the scale of the employer rather than to the extent of protection.

Cedel contends that because it has fewer than 20 employees in the United States, it is the equivalent of a small U.S. employer. This is implausible with respect to compliance and litigation costs; their impact on Cedel is better gauged by its worldwide employment. Cedel would not appear to be any more a boutique operation in the United States than would a business with ten employees each in offices in, say, Alaska and Florida, which would be subject to the ADEA. Further, a U.S. corporation with many foreign employees but

[continued]

fewer than 20 domestic ones would certainly be subject to the ADEA.

Accordingly, in determining whether Cedel satisfies the ADEA's 20-employee threshold, employees cannot be ignored merely because they work overseas.

We therefore vacate the judgment on the plaintiff's ADEA count.

So ordered.

>> CASE QUESTIONS

1. What is the purpose behind the ADEA?
2. How did the court find that the ADEA covered a U.S. branch of a foreign employer?
3. Why did the court count foreign employees of the firm in determining whether the employer was subject to the ADEA?

>> *sidebar* 12.12

Chevron and Texaco in Ecuador: $18 Billion Judgment

In February 2011, an Ecuadorian court in Lago Agrio rendered an $18 billion judgment against Chevron for alleged environmental damage. Chevron's subsidiary, Texaco Petroleum Co. (TexPet), conducted oil operations in Chevron. Chevron claims that TexPet fully remediated its share of environmental impacts arising from oil production and that any remaining environmental issues are the responsibility of Ecuador's state-owned oil company, Petroecuador.

Chevron is appealing the Ecuadorian verdict on the grounds that it "lacks scientific merit and that it ignores overwhelming evidence of fraud and corruption." Chevron also claims that it was not afforded due process in Ecuador.

>> SUBSEQUENT EVENTS

- Southern District of New York Judge Lewis Kaplan issued a preliminary injunction "enjoining and restraining" the plaintiffs from enforcing the ruling anywhere in the world.
- An International Tribunal from the Permanent Court of Arbitration in The Hague ordered Ecuador to suspend the enforcement or recognition of the judgment.
- Chevron filed a Racketeer Influenced and Corrupt Organizations Act against Steven Donziger (the plaintiffs' lead U.S. lawyer), Ecuadorian lawyer Pablo Fajardo, environmental activist Luis Yanza, and three organizations, including Amazon Watch.

The documentary *Crude* presents the controversial story of the environmental damage and the ensuing complicated litigation.

13. INTERNATIONAL ARBITRATION

International businesses now are focusing on the need for new methods of resolving international commercial disputes and, as a result, are frequently resorting to the use of arbitration. The advantages of arbitration in domestic transactions, previously discussed in Chapter 5, are more pronounced in international transactions where differences in languages and legal systems make litigation costs still more costly.

The United Nations Convention on the Recognition and Enforcement of Foreign Arbitral Awards of 1958 (New York Convention), adopted in more than 50 countries, encourages the use of arbitration in commercial agreements made by companies in the signatory countries. Under the New York Convention it is easier to compel arbitration, where previously agreed upon by the parties, and to enforce the arbitrator's award once a decision is reached.

Once the parties to an international transaction agree to arbitrate disputes between them, the U.S. courts are reluctant to disturb that agreement. In the case of *Mitsubishi Motors v. Soler Chrysler-Plymouth* (1985) the Supreme Court upheld an international agreement even where it required the parties to arbitrate all disputes, including federal antitrust claims. The Court decided that the international character of the undertaking required enforcement of the arbitration clause even as to the antitrust claims normally heard in a U.S. court.

There are many advantages to arbitrating international disputes. The arbitration process likely will be more streamlined and easier for the parties to understand than litigating the dispute in a foreign court. Moreover, the parties can avoid the unwanted publicity that often results in open court proceedings. Finally, the parties can agree, before the dispute even arises, on a neutral and objective third party to act as the arbitrator. Several organizations, such as the International Chamber of Commerce in Paris and the Court of International Arbitration in London, provide arbitration services for international disputes.

China International Economic and Trade Arbitration Commission

The China International Economic and Trade Arbitration Commission (CIETAC) is a permanent arbitration institution established to resolve economic and trade disputes arising in China. The parties must agree in writing to submit their dispute for arbitration. Here is a sample arbitration clause recommended by CIETAC:

> Any dispute arising from or in connection with this Contract shall be submitted to CIETAC for arbitration, which shall be conducted in accordance with the Commission's arbitration rules in effect at the time of applying for arbitration. The arbitral always is final and binding upon both parties.

Frequently, the parties will also stipulate the location of the arbitration; the language of the proceeding; the number of arbitrators; the nationality of the arbitrators; the method of selecting the arbitrators; and the law governing the contract. For more information, including a current list of arbitrators and their areas of expertise, see www.cietac.org.

The World Intellectual Property Organization: Arbitration and Mediation Center

The World Intellectual Property Organization (WIPO) Arbitration and Mediation Center hears cases involving domain name disputes and cybersquatting. The Uniform Domain Name Dispute Resolution Policy (UDRP) went into effect in 1999. Since that time, over 8,350 disputes involving 127 countries and some 16,000 domain names have been handled by the WIPO.

Many UDRP cases involve high-value, well-known brands. In fact, cases involving most of the 100 largest international brands by value have been heard by the WIPO. Well-known individuals, including Madonna, Julia Roberts, Eminem, Pamela Anderson, J K Rowling, Morgan Freeman, and Lance Armstrong have used the WIPO's services. For more information about WIPO cases, see www.wipo.int.

>> Key Terms

Agreement on Trade-Related Aspects of Intellectual Property Rights (TRIPS) 370

Alien Tort Claims Act (ATCA) 379

Bill of lading 375

Central America-Dominican Republic Free Trade Agreement (CAFTA-DR) 373

Convention on the International Sale of Goods (CISG) 372

European Union (EU) 371

Export controls 363

Expropriation 362

Foreign Corrupt Practices Act (FCPA) 359

Foreign Sovereign Immunities Act (FSIA) 381

Foreign subsidiary 377

Franchise 377

General Agreement on Tariffs and Trade (GATT) 369

International Court of Justice (ICJ) 367

International Monetary Fund (IMF) 369

Irrevocable letter of credit 375

Joint venture 378

License 377

Nationalization 363

North American Free Trade Agreement (NAFTA) 373

Private international law 366

Public international law 366

Sovereign immunity 381

United Nations 368

World Bank 369

World Trade Organization (WTO) 369

>> Review Questions and Problems

Risks Involved in International Trade

1. *Pressures for Bribes*

    XYZ Company, a U.S. firm, is seeking to obtain business in Indonesia. XYZ learns that one of its major competitors, a German firm, is offering a key Indonesian governmental official a trip around the world for choosing their firm in the transaction. Can XYZ report this bribe to the Department of Justice and have the German firm prosecuted under the Foreign Corrupt Practices Act?

2. *Expropriation and Nationalization*

    Explain the "modern traditional theory" of compensation related to the taking of private property by a foreign government.

3. *Export Controls*

    (a) Why is the future of export controls in doubt?

    (b) What are some of the dangers associated with having an inadequate export control regime as nations combat terrorism?

International Law and Organizations

4. *Sources of International Law*

    (a) What are the essential differences between the International Court of Justice and the U.S. Supreme Court?

    (b) How does the ICJ determine international law?

5. *International Organizations*

    (a) What are the three major principles of the World Trade Organization?

    (b) Has adherence to those principles improved international trade?

    (c) Describe the organization of the European Union.

    (d) How is it similar to the structure of the government of the United States?

6. *Major Agreements Affecting Trade*

    (a) How does the CISG facilitate international sales of goods?

    (b) How do free trade agreements, such as NAFTA and CAFTA-DR, benefit U.S. businesses?

Methods of Transacting International Business

7. *Foreign Sales*

    BMW, a German buyer, opens an irrevocable letter of credit in favor of Goodyear, an American seller, for the purchase of tires on BMW automobiles. BMW confirms the letter of credit with Goodyear's bank in New York, JPMorgan Chase. How will the seller obtain payment?

8. *Licenses or Franchises*
   (a) How should a licensor protect its investment in a foreign country?
   (b) Is licensing a less risky approach for the seller than direct foreign investment?
9. *Direct Foreign Investment*
   What are the advantages and disadvantages of a joint venture with a foreign firm?

Resolving International Disputes

10. *Alien Tort Claims Act*
    Several citizens of Colombia filed an action in the U.S. against Super Bananas, a U.S. company that owns the banana plantation where the individuals worked. In their complaint, the plaintiffs allege that they were threatened, beaten and tortured by Super Banana's security guards when they tried to unionize. Do they have an actionable claim under the ATCA?
11. *Suing Foreign Governments in the United States*
    Belgium arrests an American citizen, while he is visiting Brussels, on suspicion that he is an international drug smuggler. After a thorough investigation, Belgium realizes that it has arrested the wrong person. Can the American citizen successfully sue Belgium in the United States for false arrest?
12. *Suing Foreign Firms in the United States*
    What is the primary requirement of the Hague Service Convention and how does it help a plaintiff when filing a lawsuit?
13. *International Arbitration*
    Why are arbitration clauses in international agreements favored by the courts and likely to be enforced when conflicts arise between the contracting parties?

business >> *discussions*

1. XYZ Company is a U.S. firm that makes communication software used in a variety of consumer goods manufactured and sold in the United States. XYZ recently learned that one of the manufacturing firms it supplies, ABC Company, is exporting finished goods to a country where U.S. goods and component parts are prohibited because of numerous conflicts with the U.S. government.

Does XYZ have any moral or legal responsibility in this case?
How should XYZ protect itself under these circumstances?
Should American business practices be impacted by conflicts between governments?

2. Hello-Hello is a U.S. telecommunications company with global operations. Sophia is an assistant vice president of Hello-Hello. She is dispatched to China to handle two situations. First, a shipment of 500 cases of cell phones is stalled in customs. She is assigned the task of getting the goods out of customs and into retail stores. Sophia learns through the grapevine that customs officials expect $5 (U.S. per case) to help "speed things along." Second, she is instructed by her boss to do "whatever is necessary" to secure cell tower permits from local officials in two outlying areas. A local agent suggests that she give him $500,000 in cash so they can get to know the officials better. When Sophia asks him what the money will be used for, he tells her that he wants to take them out to dinner, maybe on a weekend outing in the city, and that he generally needs "flexibility."

Should Sophia call the home office to ask for advice?
If her boss says to pay the money, should she do it?
What potential legal problems are presented by the payments?

Chapter 20. Discrimination Employment

20

Discrimination in Employment

Learning Objectives

In this chapter you will learn:

20-1. To discuss the general provisions of Title VII, enforcement procedures, and the differences between disparate treatment and disparate impact.

20-2. To understand the specific kinds of discrimination prohibited by Title VII.

20-3. To discuss employment practices that may be challenged.

20-4. To apply other federal statutes protecting against employment discrimination.

20-5. To realize that state laws may offer additional protection against workplace discrimination.

Laws prohibiting discrimination exist at both the federal and state levels. The opening sections of the chapter focus on antidiscrimination laws at the federal level. Title VII of the Civil Rights Act of 1964 (including its amendments) is the principal such law. It prohibits certain discrimination based on race, sex, color, religion, and national origin. Next, employment practices that may be challenged as discriminatory are considered. Other antidiscrimination laws covered are the Civil Rights Act of 1866 (referred to as Section 1981), the Age Discrimination in Employment Act, Americans with Disabilities Act, the Genetic Information Nondiscrimination Act and the Uniformed Services Employment and Reemployment Act. The chapter concludes with a discussion of trends in employment discrimination litigation and a section on employment discrimination, corporate governance, and the broad sense of property.

>> The Civil Rights Act of 1964

"That all men are created equal" was one of the "self-evident" truths recognized by the Founding Fathers in the Declaration of Independence. However, equality among all our citizens clearly has been an ideal rather than a fact. The Constitution itself recognizes slavery by saying that slaves should count as "three fifths of all other Persons" for determining population in House of Representatives elections. And of course, that all *men* are created equal says nothing about women, who did not even get a constitutionally guaranteed right to vote until 1920.

Nowhere have effects of inequality and discrimination been felt more acutely than in the area of job opportunity. Historically, common law permitted employers to hire and fire virtually at will, unless restrained by contract or statute. Under this system, white males came to dominate the job market in their ability to gain employment and their salaries and wages.

Although the Civil Rights Act of 1866 contains a provision that plaintiffs now widely use in employment discrimination cases, such use is relatively recent. Passage of labor law in the 1920s and 1930s marks the first significant federal limitation on the relatively unrestricted right of employers to hire and fire. Then, in connection with the war effort, President Franklin D. Roosevelt issued executive orders in 1941 and 1943 requiring a clause prohibiting racial discrimination in all federal contracts with private contractors. Subsequent executive orders in the 1950s established committees to investigate complaints of racial discrimination against such contractors. Affirmative action requirements on federal contracts followed from executive orders of the 1960s.

The most important statute eliminating discriminatory employment practices, however, is the federal Civil Rights Act of 1964, as amended by the Equal Employment Opportunity Act of 1972, the Pregnancy Discrimination Act of 1978, and the Civil Rights Act of 1991.

> Historically, common law permitted employers to hire and fire at will. At-will employment still applies today unless modified by legislation.

1. GENERAL PROVISIONS

The provisions of Title VII of the Civil Rights Act of 1964 apply to employers with 15 or more employees, labor unions, and certain other employers. The major purpose of these laws is to eliminate job discrimination based on race, color, religion, sex, or national origin. Discrimination for any of these reasons is a violation of the law, except that employers, employment agencies, and labor unions can discriminate on the basis of religion, sex, or national origin where these are **bona fide occupational qualifications (BFOQs)** reasonably necessary to normal business operations. Title VII also permits discrimination if it results unintentionally from a seniority or merit system.

The types of employer action in which discrimination is prohibited include:

> **Don't** forget that a defense to intentional discrimination is that such discrimination is a BFOQ.

- Discharge.
- Refusal to hire.
- Compensation.
- Terms, conditions, or privileges of employment.

> According to the Seventh Circuit Court of Appeals, denial of overtime can constitute an adverse employment action sufficient to trigger Title VII.

Employment *agencies* are prohibited from either *failing to refer* or from *actually referring* an individual for employment on the basis of race, color, religion, sex, or national origin. This prohibition differs from the law binding *employers,* where it is unlawful only to fail or refuse to hire on discriminatory grounds—the affirmative act of hiring for a discriminatory reason is apparently not illegal. For example, assume that a contractor with a government contract seeks a qualified African American engineer and requests an employment agency to refer one. The agency complies with the request. Unless a white applicant was discriminated against, the employer likely did not break the law; but the employment agency, by referring on the basis of color, unquestionably *did* violate Title VII.

Employers, unions, and employment agencies are prohibited from discriminating against an employee, applicant, or union member because he or she has made a charge, testified, or participated in an investigation or hearing under the act or otherwise opposed any unlawful practice.

Note that regarding general hiring, referrals, advertising, and admissions to training or apprenticeship programs, Title VII allows discrimination only on the basis of religion, sex, or national origin and only where these considerations are bona fide occupational qualifications. For example, it is legal for a Baptist church to refuse to engage a Lutheran minister. EEOC guidelines on sex discrimination consider sex to be a bona fide occupational qualification, for example, where it is necessary for authenticity or genuineness in hiring an actor or actress. The omission of *race* and *color* from this exception must mean that Congress does not feel these two factors are ever bona fide occupational qualifications.

Additional exemptions exist with respect to laws creating preferential treatment for veterans and hiring based on professionally developed ability tests that are not designed or intended to be used to discriminate. Such tests must bear a relationship to the job for which they are administered, however.

> Discriminating in employment on the basis of race or color can almost never be a BFOQ.

2. ENFORCEMENT PROCEDURES

The Civil Rights Act of 1964 created the Equal Employment Opportunity Commission (EEOC). This agency has the primary responsibility of enforcing the provisions of the act. The EEOC is composed of five members, not more than three of whom may be members of the same political party. They are appointed by the president, with the advice and consent of the Senate, and serve a five-year term. In the course of its investigations, the EEOC has broad authority to hold hearings, obtain evidence, and subpoena and examine witnesses under oath.

Under the Equal Employment Opportunity Act of 1972, the EEOC can file a civil suit in federal district court and represent a person charging a violation of the act. However, it must first exhaust efforts to settle the claim. Remedies that may be obtained in such an action include reinstatement with back pay for the victim of an illegal discrimination and injunctions against future violations of the act by the defendant. See Figure 20.1 for a breakdown of charges received by the EEOC.

The 1991 Amendments In 1991 Congress amended the Civil Rights Act to allow the recovery of compensatory and punitive damages of up to $300,000 per person. These damages are in addition to other remedies such as job reinstatement (depending on the size of the employer) and back pay or front pay. Compensatory damages include damages for the pain and suffering of discrimination. Punitive damages are appropriate whenever discrimination

> "[M]ajor American businesses have made clear that the skills needed in today's increasingly global marketplace can only be developed through exposure to widely diverse people, cultures, ideas, and viewpoints."
>
> **–Justice Sandra Day O'Connor,** *Grutter v. Bollinger,* **539 U.S. 306, 330 (2003)**

> Under Title VII, a plaintiff can recover up to $300,000 in punitive and compensatory damages for *intentional* discrimination. Back pay damages can further add to that amount.

Figure 20.1 *What Kinds of Claims Are Being Filed with the EEOC?*

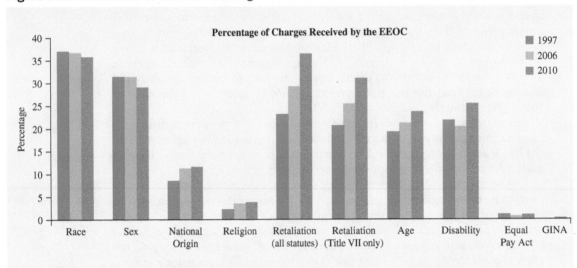

In 1997, the EEOC received 80,680 total charges, in 2006, it received 75,768 charges, and in 2010, it received 99,922 charges.

Source: EEOC Charge Statistics FY1997–2010, www.eeoc.gov/eeoc/statistics/enforcement/charges.cfm.

occurs with "malice or with reckless or callous indifference to the federally protected rights of others." The 1991 amendments allow compensatory and punitive damages *only* when employers are guilty of *intentional* discrimination.

In enacting Title VII of the Civil Rights Act of 1964, Congress made it clear that it did not intend to preempt states' fair employment laws. Where state agencies begin discrimination proceedings, the EEOC must wait 60 days before it starts action. Furthermore, if a state law provides relief to a discrimination charge, the EEOC must notify the appropriate state officials and wait 60 days before continuing action.

An employee must file charges of illegal discrimination with the EEOC within 180 days after notice of the unlawful practice. If the employee first filed in a timely fashion with a state fair employment practices commission, the law extends the time for filing with the EEOC to 300 days.

Do remember that the three types of cases permitted under Title VII are for (1) disparate treatment, (2) disparate impact, and (3) retaliation.

Winning a Title VII Civil Action   To win a Title VII civil action, a plaintiff must initially show that steps taken by the employer likely had an illegally discriminatory basis, such as race. Generally, the plaintiff must prove either disparate (unequal) treatment or disparate impact. In proving **disparate treatment,** the plaintiff must convince the court that the employer *intentionally* discriminated against the plaintiff. If discrimination is a substantial or motivating factor, an employer's practice is illegal even though other factors (such as customer preference) also contributed. Even if the plaintiff proves disparate treatment, the defendant can win by showing that all or substantially all members of the plaintiff's class *cannot* perform the duties of the job. This defense is the BFOQ defense mentioned in Section 1 of this chapter.

In a **disparate impact** case the plaintiff must prove that the employer's practices or policies had a discriminatory effect on a group protected by Title VII. The employer can defeat the plaintiff's claim by proving the

business necessity defense. This defense requires that the employer prove that the practices or policies used are job related and based on business necessity. However, the plaintiff can still establish a violation by showing that other policies would serve the legitimate interests of business necessity without having undesirable discriminatory effects.

A third type of discrimination case concerns **retaliation.** It is illegal for employers to retaliate against employees for making discrimination charges, giving testimony in a discrimination case, or in any way participating in a discrimination investigation. Such retaliation discrimination involves employers taking "adverse employment actions" against employees, such as firing employees or transferring them to less desirable jobs.

What are ways a company can avoid retaliation claims? As illustrated in Figure 20.1, retaliation claims are on the rise. There are a number of steps an employer can take to address allegations of discrimination without triggering a retaliation claim:

- Treat complaints seriously as soon as they are made.
- Investigate the complaint.
- Be sure managers and other employees know and follow the company's policies on discrimination, including harassment.
- Follow-up with the complainant, including explaining how the company will address the problem.
- Create an atmosphere in which the complainant and others with information feel comfortable coming forward with information or other complaints.
- Never take adverse action against a complainant or witnesses, based on information obtained in the investigation.

These straightforward steps go a long way to create an atmosphere of fairness and head off additional claims based on retaliation.

Before the 1991 Civil Rights Act amendments, employees or the EEOC sometimes claimed that proving racial or gender statistical imbalances in a workforce established illegal discrimination. They claimed that such imbalances showed illegal discrimination, much like disparate impact discrimination, even in the absence of proof of an employer's discriminatory intent. However, the 1991 amendments state that the showing of a statistically imbalanced workforce is not enough *in itself* to establish a violation of Title VII.

If an employee who complains about discrimination is transferred to the night shift, even without a loss of pay, he may have a claim for retaliation under Title VII. *Burlington Northern and Santa Fe Railroad Co. v. White,* 548 U.S. 53 (2007).

 case **20.1** >>

THOMPSON v. NORTH AMERICAN STAINLESS, LP
562 U.S. __ (2011)

After petitioner Thompson's fiancée, Miriam Regalado, filed a sex discrimination charge with the Equal Employment Opportunity Commission (EEOC) against their employer, respondent North American Stainless (NAS), NAS fired Thompson. He filed his own charge and a subsequent suit under Title VII of the Civil Rights Act, claiming that NAS fired him to retaliate against Regalado for filing her charge. The District Court granted NAS summary judgment on the ground that third-party retaliation claims were not

[continued]

permitted by Title VII, which prohibits discrimination against an employee "because he has made a [Title VII] charge." The en banc Sixth Circuit affirmed, reasoning that Thompson was not entitled to sue NAS for retaliation because he had not engaged in any activity protected by the statute. By a vote of 8-0, the Supreme Court overturned the Court of Appeals. (Justice Kagan took no part in the consideration of the case.)

SCALIA, J.: Until 2003, both petitioner Eric Thompson and his fiancée, Miriam Regalado, were employees of respondent North American Stainless (NAS). In February 2003, the Equal Employment Opportunity Commission (EEOC) notified NAS that Regalado had filed a charge alleging sex discrimination. Three weeks later, NAS fired Thompson.

Thompson then filed a charge with the EEOC. After conciliation efforts proved unsuccessful, he sued NAS in the United States District Court for the Eastern District of Kentucky under Title VII of the Civil Rights Act of 1964, 78 Stat. 253, 42 U. S. C. §2000e *et seq.,* claiming that NAS had fired him in order to retaliate against Regalado for filing her charge with the EEOC. The District Court granted summary judgment to NAS, concluding that Title VII "does not permit third party retaliation claims." 435 F. Supp. 2d 633, 639 (ED Ky. 2006). After a panel of the Sixth Circuit reversed the District Court, the Sixth Circuit granted rehearing en banc and affirmed by a 10-to-6 vote. 567 F. 3d 804 (2009). The court reasoned that because Thompson did not "engag[e] in any statutorily protected activity, either on his own behalf or on behalf of Miriam Regalado," he "is not included in the class of persons for whom Congress created a retaliation cause of action." . . .

Title VII provides that "[i]t shall be an unlawful employment practice for an employer to discriminate against any of his employees . . . because he has made a charge" under Title VII. 42 U. S. C. §2000e–3(a). The statute permits "a person claiming to be aggrieved" to file a charge with the EEOC alleging that the employer committed an unlawful employment practice, and, if the EEOC declines to sue the employer, it permits a civil action to "be brought . . . by the person claiming to be aggrieved . . . by the alleged unlawful employment practice." §2000e–5(b), (f)(1). It is undisputed that Regalado's filing of a charge with the EEOC was protected conduct under Title VII. In the procedural posture of this case, we are also required to assume that NAS fired Thompson in order to retaliate against Regalado for filing a charge of discrimination. This case therefore presents two questions: First, did NAS's firing of Thompson constitute unlawful retaliation? And second, if it did, does Title VII grant Thompson a cause of action?

With regard to the first question, we have little difficulty concluding that if the facts alleged by Thompson are true, then NAS's firing of Thompson violated Title VII. In *Burlington N. & S. F. R. Co.* v. *White,* 548 U. S. 53 (2006), we held that Title VII's antiretaliation provision must be construed to cover a broad range of employer conduct. We reached that conclusion by contrasting the text of Title VII's antiretaliation provision with its substantive antidiscrimination provision. . . . Title VII's antiretaliation provision prohibits any employer action that "well might have dissuaded a reasonable worker from making or supporting a charge of discrimination." *Id.,* at 68 (internal quotation marks omitted). We think it obvious that a reasonable worker might be dissuaded from engaging in protected activity if she knew that her fiancé would be fired. Indeed, NAS does not dispute that Thompson's firing meets the standard set forth in *Burlington.* Tr. of Oral Arg. 30. NAS raises the concern, however, that prohibiting reprisals against third parties will lead to difficult line-drawing problems concerning the types of relationships entitled to protection. Perhaps retaliating against an employee by firing his fiancée would dissuade the employee from engaging in protected activity, but what about firing an employee's girlfriend, close friend, or trusted co-worker? . . .

Although we acknowledge the force of this point, we do not think it justifies a categorical rule that third-party reprisals do not violate Title VII. As explained above, we adopted a broad standard in *Burlington* because Title VII's antiretaliation provision is worded broadly. We think there is no textual basis for making an exception to it for third-party reprisals, and a preference for clear rules cannot justify departing from statutory text. We must also decline to identify a fixed class of relationships for which third-party reprisals are unlawful. We expect that firing a close family member will almost always meet the *Burlington* standard, and inflicting a milder reprisal on a mere acquaintance will almost never do so, but beyond that we are reluctant to generalize. . . .

The more difficult question in this case is whether Thompson may sue NAS for its alleged violation of Title VII. The statute provides that "a civil action may be brought . . . by the person claiming to be aggrieved." ". . . to be aggrieved" to bring "a civil action." It is arguable that the aggrievement referred to is nothing more than the minimal Article III standing, which consists of injury in fact caused by the defendant and remediable by the court. See *Lujan* v. *Defenders of Wildlife,* 504 U. S. 555, 560–561 (1992). But Thompson's claim undoubtedly meets those requirements, so if that is indeed all that aggrievement consists of, he may sue. . . .

We hold that the term "aggrieved" in Title VII incorporates this test, enabling suit by any plaintiff with

[continued]

an interest "arguably [sought] to be protected by the statutes," *National Credit Union Admin. v. First Nat. Bank & Trust Co.,* 522 U. S. 479, 495 (1998) (internal quotation marks omitted), while excluding plaintiffs who might technically be injured in an Article III sense but whose interests are unrelated to the statutory prohibitions in Title VII. Applying that test here, we conclude that Thompson falls within the zone of interests protected by Title VII. Thompson was an employee of NAS, and the purpose of Title VII is to protect employees from their employers' unlawful actions. Moreover,

accepting the facts as alleged, Thompson is not an accidental victim of the retaliation—collateral damage, so to speak, of the employer's unlawful act. To the contrary, injuring him was the employer's intended means of harming Regalado. Hurting him was the unlawful act by which the employer punished her. In those circumstances, we think Thompson well within the zone of interests sought to be protected by Title VII. He is a person aggrieved with standing to sue.

Reversed and remanded.

>> CASE QUESTIONS

1. What are the key facts of this case?
2. What were the two issues before the Supreme Court?
3. What did the Court decide? What is the rationale for the decisions?

3. DISCRIMINATION ON THE BASIS OF RACE OR COLOR

`LO 20-2`

The integration of African Americans into the mainstream of American society is the primary objective of the Civil Rights Act of 1964. Title VII, which deals with employment practices, is the key legal regulation for achieving this goal. Without equal employment opportunities, African Americans can hardly enjoy other guaranteed rights, such as access to public accommodations.

Title VII prohibits discriminatory employment practices based on race or color that involve *recruiting, hiring,* and *promotion* of employees. Of course, intentional discrimination in these matters is illegal, but, as previously stated, policies with disparate impact are also forbidden. Such discrimination arises from an employer's policies or practices that apply equally to everyone but that discriminate in greater proportion against minorities and have no relation to job qualification.

Examples of disparate impact on race include:

- Using personnel tests that have no substantial relation to job qualification, which have the effect of screening out minorities.
- Denying employment to unwed mothers, when minorities have a higher rate of illegitimate births than whites.
- Refusing to hire people because of a poor credit rating, when minorities are disproportionately affected.
- Giving hiring priority to relatives of present employees, when minorities are underrepresented in the workforce.

Often at issue in disparate impact cases is whether a discriminatory policy or practice relates to job qualification. Courts require proof, not mere assertion, of job relatedness before upholding an employer's discriminatory personnel test or other practice.

Lockheed Martin settled a race discrimination and retaliation lawsuit for $2.5 million in 2008. The case alleged a racially hostile work environment at several job sites, including threats of lynching and the use of the "N-word."

The law also prohibits discrimination in *employment conditions* and *benefits*. EEOC decisions have found such practices as the following to be violations:

- Permitting racial insults in the work situation.
- Maintaining all-white or all-black crews for no demonstrable reasons.
- Providing better housing for whites than blacks.
- Granting higher average Christmas bonuses to whites than blacks for reasons that were not persuasive to the commission.

>> *sidebar* 20.1

Hithon v. Tyson Foods, Inc.: The Use of the Word "Boy"

John Hithon and Anthony Ash, African American men, worked at a Tyson Foods plant in Alabama. When two supervisor positions opened up, they were passed over for promotion and two white men from other plants were hired. Believing that the failure to be promoted resulted from racial prejudice, Hithon and Ash filed an employment discrimination claim against their employer.

As part of their case, the plaintiffs produced evidence that their white boss used the term "boy" when referring to them. Is the use of the term *boy* racially discriminatory?

In 2002, an Alabama jury awarded Hithon and Ash $250,000 each in compensatory damages and $1.5 million in punitive damages. After a magistrate overruled the jury's verdict, Hilton and Ash appealed. On appeal, the 11th Circuit determined that an adult African American man being called "boy" alone was

not discriminatory unless it was preceded by "black" or "white."

The U.S. Supreme Court unanimously reversed the 11th Circuit's decision, stating:

> Although it is true that the disputed word will not always be evidence of racial animus, it does not follow that the term, standing alone, is always benign . . . The speaker's meaning may depend on various factors including context, inflection, tone of voice, local custom and historical usage.

Thereafter, another Alabama jury found in favor of Hithon, awarding him $35,000 in back pay, $300,000 in compensatory damages for his mental anguish and $1 million in punitives. The District Court vacated the punitive damage award. Both sides appealed. On appeal, the 11th Circuit voted 2-1 entering a judgment in favor of Tyson Foods. The majority said that the evidence did not support Hithon's argument.

Researchers revealed racial bias in hiring based on an applicant's name. The study tracked response rates to resumes sent to 1,300 help-wanted ads. The authors found that white-sounding names (such as Anne, Emily, Allison, Neil, Todd, and Matthew) are 50 percent more likely to get called for an initial interview than applicants with African American-sounding names (such as Tamika, Latoya, Latonya, Tyrone, Tremayne, and Rasheed). Additionally, race affects the degree to which applicants benefit from having more experience and credentials. The study showed that white applicants with higher-quality resumes received 30 percent more callbacks than whites with lower-quality resumes. By contract, African American applicants experienced only 9 percent more callbacks for the same improvement in credentials.

It is important to appreciate that Title VII prohibits employment discrimination against members of all races. In one recent case, a federal court jury awarded a white senior air traffic official $500,000 in damages against the Federal Aviation Administration. The official charged the FAA had demoted

> The State of New York has outlawed the display of a noose as a threat, punishable by up to four years in prison.

him and replaced him with an African American following complaints that blacks were underrepresented in senior management levels. Note that this case did not involve affirmative action.

case **20.2** >>

RICCI v. DESTEFANO
557 U.S.__ (2009)

New Haven, Conn. (City), uses objective examinations to identify those firefighters best qualified for promotion. When the results of such an exam to fill vacant lieutenant and captain positions showed that white candidates had outperformed minority candidates, a rancorous public debate ensued. Confronted with arguments both for and against certifying the test results—and threats of a lawsuit either way—the City threw out the results based on the statistical racial disparity. Petitioners, white and Hispanic firefighters who passed the exams but were denied a chance at promotions by the City's refusal to certify the test results, sued the City and respondent officials, alleging that discarding the test results discriminated against them based on their race in violation of, inter alia, Title VII of the Civil Rights Act of 1964. The defendants responded that had they certified the test results, they could have faced Title VII liability for adopting a practice having a disparate impact on minority firefighters. The District Court granted summary judgment for the defendants, and the Second Circuit affirmed. Justice Sotomayor was on the Second Circuit at the time of that decision. Justice Kennedy wrote the majority opinion in which Chief Justice Roberts, and Justices Scalia, Thomas and Alito joined.

Justice Ginsburg filed a dissenting opinion in which Justices Stevens, Souter and Breyer joined. In her dissent, Justice Ginsburg notes that firefighting is "a profession in which the legacy of racial discrimination casts an especially long shadow" and that the facts of this case should be assessed "against this backdrop of entrenched inequality."

KENNEDY, J.: In the fire department of New Haven, Connecticut—as in emergency-service agencies throughout the Nation—firefighters prize their promotion to and within the officer ranks. An agency's officers command respect within the department and in the whole community; and, of course, added responsibilities command increased salary and benefits. Aware of the intense competition for promotions, New Haven, like many cities, relies on objective examinations to identify the best-qualified candidates. In 2003, 118 New Haven firefighters took examinations to qualify for promotion to the rank of lieutenant or captain. Promotion examinations in New Haven (or City) were infrequent, so the stakes were high. The results would determine which firefighters would be considered for promotions during the next two years, and the order in which they would be considered. Many firefighters studied for months, at considerable personal and financial cost.

When the examination results showed that white candidates had outperformed minority candidates, the mayor and other local politicians opened a public debate that turned rancorous. Some firefighters argued the tests should be discarded because the results showed the tests to be discriminatory. They threatened a discrimination lawsuit if the City made promotions based on the tests. Other firefighters said the exams were neutral and fair. And they, in turn, threatened a discrimination lawsuit if the City, relying on the statistical racial disparity, ignored the test results and denied promotions to the candidates who had performed well. In the end the City took the side of those who protested the test results. It threw out the examinations.

Certain white and Hispanic firefighters who likely would have been promoted based on their good test performance sued the City and some of its officials. Theirs is the suit now before us. The suit alleges that, by discarding the test results, the City and the named officials discriminated against the plaintiffs based on their race, in violation of both Title VII of the Civil Rights Act of 1964, 78 Stat. 253, as amended, 42 U. S. C. §2000e *et seq.*, and the Equal Protection Clause of the Fourteenth Amendment. The City and the officials defended their actions, arguing that if they had certified the results, they could have faced liability under Title VII for adopting a practice that had a disparate

[continued]

impact on the minority firefighters. The District Court granted summary judgment for the defendants, and the Court of Appeals affirmed.

We conclude that race-based action like the City's in this case is impermissible under Title VII unless the employer can demonstrate a strong basis in evidence that, had it not taken the action, it would have been liable under the disparate-impact statute. The respondents, we further determine, cannot meet that threshold standard. As a result, the City's action in discarding the tests was a violation of Title VII. In light of our ruling under the statutes, we need not reach the question whether respondents' actions may have violated the Equal Protection Clause. . . .

Title VII of the Civil Rights Act of 1964, 42 U. S. C.§2000e *et seq.,* as amended, prohibits employment discrimination on the basis of race, color, religion, sex, or national origin. Title VII prohibits both intentional discrimination (known as "disparate treatment") as well as, in some cases, practices that are not intended to discriminate but in fact have a disproportionately adverse effect on minorities (known as "disparate impact"). . . . The Civil Rights Act of 1964 did not include an express prohibition on policies or practices that produce a disparate impact. But in *Griggs* v. *Duke Power Co.,* 401 U. S. 424 (1971), the Court interpreted the Act to prohibit, in some cases, employers' facially neutral practices that, in fact, are "discriminatory in operation." *Id.,* at 431. The *Griggs* Court stated that the "touchstone" for disparate impact liability is the lack of "business necessity": "If an employment practice which operates to exclude [minorities] cannot be shown to be related to job performance, the practice is prohibited." . . . Twenty years after *Griggs,* the Civil Rights Act of 1991, 105 Stat. 1071, was enacted. The Act included a provision codifying the prohibition on disparate-impact discrimination. That provision is now in force along with the disparate-treatment section already noted. Under the disparate-impact statute, a plaintiff establishes a prima facie violation by showing that an employer uses "a particular employment practice that causes a disparate impact on the basis of race, color, religion, sex, or national origin." 42 U. S. C. §2000e–2(k)(1)(A)(i). An employer may defend against liability by demonstrating that the practice is "job related for the position in question and consistent with business necessity." *Ibid.* Even if the employer meets that burden, however, a plaintiff may still succeed by showing that the employer refuses to adopt an available alternative employment practice that has less disparate impact and serves the employer's legitimate needs. . . . Petitioners allege that when the CSB refused to certify the captain and lieutenant exam results based on the race of the successful

candidates, it discriminated against them in violation of Title VII's disparate-treatment provision. The City counters that its decision was permissible because the tests "appear[ed] to violate Title VII's disparate impact provisions." . . . The same interests are at work in the interplay between the disparate-treatment and disparate-impact provisions of Title VII. Congress has imposed liability on employers for unintentional discrimination in order to rid the workplace of "practices that are fair in form, but discriminatory in operation." *Griggs, supra,* at 431. But it has also prohibited employers from taking adverse employment actions "because of" race. §2000e–2(a)(1). Applying the strong-basis-in-evidence standard to Title VII gives effect to both the disparate-treatment and disparate-impact provisions, allowing violations of one in the name of compliance with the other only in certain, narrow circumstances. The standard leaves ample room for employers' voluntary compliance efforts, which are essential to the statutory scheme and to Congress's efforts to eradicate workplace discrimination. See *Firefighters, supra,* at 515. And the standard appropriately constrains employers' discretion in making race-based decisions: It limits that discretion to cases in which there is a strong basis in evidence of disparate-impact liability, but it is not so restrictive that it allows employers to act only when there is a provable, actual violation.

Resolving the statutory conflict in this way allows the disparate-impact prohibition to work in a manner that is consistent with other provisions of Title VII, including the prohibition on adjusting employment-related test scores on the basis of race. . . . The racial adverse impact here was significant, and petitioners do not dispute that the City was faced with a prima facie case of disparate-impact liability. On the captain exam, the pass rate for white candidates was 64 percent but was 37.5 percent for both black and Hispanic candidates. On the lieutenant exam, the pass rate for white candidates was 58.1 percent; for black candidates, 31.6 percent; and for Hispanic candidates, 20 percent. The pass rates of minorities, which were approximately one half the pass rates for white candidates, fall well below the 80-percent standard set by the EEOC to implement the disparate-impact provision of Title VII. . . .

There is no genuine dispute that the examinations were job-related and consistent with business necessity. . . . On the record before us, there is no genuine dispute that the City lacked a strong basis in evidence to believe it would face disparate-impact liability if it certified the examination results. In other words, there is no evidence—let alone the required strong basis in evidence—that the tests were flawed because they were not job-related or because other, equally valid

[continued]

and less discriminatory tests were available to the City. Fear of litigation alone cannot justify an employer's reliance on race to the detriment of individuals who passed the examinations and qualified for promotions. The City's discarding the test results was impermissible under Title VII, and summary judgment is appropriate for petitioners on their disparate-treatment claim. . . . Many of the candidates had studied for months, at considerable personal and financial expense, and thus the injury caused by the City's reliance on raw racial statistics at the end of the process was all the more severe. Confronted with arguments both for and against certifying the test results—and threats of a lawsuit either way—the City was required to make a difficult inquiry. But its hearings produced no strong evidence of a disparate-impact violation, and the City was not entitled to disregard the tests based solely on the racial disparity in the results.

Reversed.

>> CASE QUESTIONS

1. Explain how the case involved both issues of disparate treatment and disparate impact?
2. If you were representing the City of New Haven, would you have certified the test results? Why or why not?
3. What is the basis for the Supreme Court's holding?

>> *sidebar* 20.2

Abercrombie & Fitch's $40 Million Diversity Lesson

In 2005, Abercrombie & Fitch (A&F) settled a discrimination lawsuit with over 10,000 class members. The suit alleged hiring discrimination against Latino, African American, and Asian American applicants. The checks ranged from several hundred to several thousand dollars each, totaling $40 million. The settlement agreement also requires A&F to:

- Set "benchmarks" (*not* quotas) for hiring and promotion of women, Latinos, African Americans, and Asian Americans.
- Stop targeting fraternities, sororities, or specific colleges for recruitment.

- Hire 25 recruiters who will focus on seeking women and minority employees.
- Implement a new internal complaint procedure.
- Create marketing materials reflecting diversity.

What is A&F saying about diversity now? According to Mike Jeffries, A&F's Chairman and CEO, "Diversity and inclusion are key to our organization's success."

In 2011, Abercrombie was sued again for discrimination. This time, a Muslim woman claims that she was fired for refusing to remove her hijab at work.

4. DISCRIMINATION ON THE BASIS OF NATIONAL ORIGIN

Title VII's prohibition against national origin discrimination protects various ethnic groups in the workplace. In a recent case, the court ruled that Title VII had been violated when a bakery employee of Iranian descent was called "Ayatollah" in the workplace by the assistant manager and other employees. After he complained, he was fired. In 2005, the EEOC reported that employees of Middle Eastern descent had filed almost a thousand

Approximately 1.2 million Americans are of Middle Eastern or Arab descent, according to the U.S. Census.

656   **PART 5**   The Employer-Employee Relationship

discrimination complaints against employers since the terrorist bombings of in September 11, 2001.

Don't forget that a policy requiring employees to speak English will violate Title VII as disparate impact unless it is justified by *business necessity*.

Discrimination concerning the speaking of a native language frequently causes national-origin lawsuits under Title VII. For instance, courts have ruled illegal an employer's rule against speaking Spanish during work hours when the employer could not show a business need to understand all conversations between Hispanic employees. On the other hand, some courts have held that if jobs require contact with the public, a requirement that employees speak some English may be a business necessity.

Direct foreign investment in the United States has doubled and redoubled in recent years. This increasing investment has presented some unusual issues of employment discrimination law. For instance, many commercial treaties with foreign countries give foreign companies operating in the United States the right to hire executive-level employees "of their choice." Does this mean that foreign companies in the United States can discriminate as to their managerial employees on a basis forbidden under Title VII? The Supreme Court has partially resolved this issue by ruling that the civil rights law applied to a Japanese company that did business through a subsidiary incorporated in this country.

>> *sidebar* 20.3

National Origin Discrimination: Problematic Ethnic Slurs

The EEOC brought a lawsuit on behalf of Mexican immigrant workers at Sam's Club who claimed they were harassed about their national origin *by a co-worker who is Mexican American.* Among the allegations:

- At least nine female workers of Mexican descent and one woman married to a Mexican were subjected to ethnic slurs and derogatory remarks.
- The insults were made on a "near daily" basis, including being called "f----n' wetbacks" and references to Mexicans only being good to clean the harasser's home.

- The harasser also threatened to report three of the victims to immigration authorities, despite their legal status.
- The victims complained about the hostile work environment but this "only intensified the harassment and led to intimidation."

Wal-Mart Stores agreed to pay $440,000 to settle this case.

Source: EEOC Press Release, Wal-Mart to Pay $440,000 to Settle EEOC Suit for Harassment of Latinos, April 14, 2011, www.eeoc.gov/eeoc/newsroom/release/4-14-11.cfm

---

5. DISCRIMINATION ON THE BASIS OF RELIGION

Note that religious corporations, associations, or societies can discriminate in all their employment practices on the basis of religion, but not on the basis of race, color, sex, or national origin. Other employers cannot discriminate on the basis of religion in employment practices, and they must make reasonable accommodation to the religious needs of their employees if it does not result in undue hardship to them.

In one case the Supreme Court let stand a lower court ruling that employees cannot be required to pay union dues if they have religious objections to unions. The case determined that a union violated Title VII by forcing a company to fire a Seventh Day Adventist who did not comply with a collective bargaining agreement term that all employees must pay union dues. The union argued unsuccessfully that it had made reasonable accommodation to the worker's religious beliefs by offering to give any dues paid by him to charity. However, in another case the Supreme Court ruled that a company rightfully fired an employee who refused to work on Saturdays due to religious belief. The Court said that the company did not have to burden other employees by making them work Saturdays.

A growing source of religious discrimination lawsuits concerns employees who for religious reasons refuse to perform some task required by the employer. For example, in one case a vegetarian bus driver refused to distribute hamburger coupons on his bus, asserting religious beliefs. When his employer fired him, he sued. The parties settled the case for $50,000. Note that even if an employer wins such a lawsuit, it can be extremely expensive to defend.

As mentioned earlier, since the 9/11 bombings religious discrimination against Muslim employees has risen steeply. In 2003 the EEOC settled a complaint by four Muslim machine operators against Stockton Steel of California for $1.1 million. The four operators claimed they were given the worst jobs, ridiculed during their prayers, and called names like "camel jockey" and "raghead."

UPS paid $46,000 to settle a religious discrimination case for failing to accommodate the Rastafarian religious beliefs of an employee whose religious beliefs prohibited him from cutting his hair or shaving his beard to comply with UPS policy.

In the case of employees of Arab descent, note the close connection between national origin discrimination and religious discrimination.

>> *sidebar* 20.4

Workplace Discrimination Against Muslims

About 25 percent of the religious discrimination claims filed with the EEOC are brought by Muslims, even though Muslims make up only 2 percent of the U.S. population. Complaints include:

- Somali immigrants working at a meatpacking company who were cursed for being Muslim; had blood, meat, and bones thrown at them; and were interrupted during prayer breaks.
- Dress policies forbidding headwear, prohibiting Muslim women from wearing headscarves, also called hijabs.
- Name-calling, including: "terrorist," "Osama," "camel jockey," and "towel head."

What steps should employers take to accommodate Muslims in the workplace? If it will not cause undue hardship, employers should consider allowing the following kinds of accommodations:

- Prayer breaks with the understanding that Muslims pray five times a day for approximately five to 15 minutes.
- Headscarves for women if they do not create a safety issue.
- Facial Hair for men.
- Vacation days for religious holidays such as *Eid al-Fitr* and *Eid al-Adha*.

Overall, as is the case with any form of illegal discrimination, employers should be vigilant and take action to ensure that the workplace is free from discriminatory animus.

6. DISCRIMINATION ON THE BASIS OF SEX

Historically, states have enacted many laws designed supposedly to protect women. For example, many states by statute have prohibited the employment of women in certain occupations such as those that require lifting heavy objects. Others have barred women from working during the night or more than a given number of hours per week or day. A federal district court held that a California state law that required rest periods for women only was in violation of Title VII. Some statutes prohibit employing women for a specified time after childbirth. Under EEOC guidelines, such statutes are not a defense to a charge of illegal sex discrimination and do not provide an employer with a bona fide occupational qualification in hiring standards. Other EEOC guidelines forbid employers:

- To classify jobs as male or female.
- To advertise in help-wanted columns that are designated male or female, unless sex is a bona fide job qualification.

Query: Could Victoria's Secret stores legally hire only women for certain positions?

Similarly, employers may not have separate male and female seniority lists.

Whether sex is a bona fide occupational qualification (and discrimination is thus legal) has been raised in several cases. The courts have tended to consider this exception narrowly. In the following instances involving hiring policy, *no* bona fide occupational qualification was found to exist:

- A rule requiring airline stewardesses, but not stewards, to be single.
- A policy of hiring only females as flight cabin attendants.
- A rule against hiring females with preschool-age children, but not against hiring males with such children.
- A telephone company policy against hiring females as switchers because of the alleged heavy lifting involved on the job.

In the telephone company case, the court held that for a bona fide occupational qualification to exist, there must be "reasonable cause to believe, that is, a factual basis for believing, that all or substantially all women would be unable to perform safely and efficiently the duties of the job involved." The Supreme Court has indicated that for such a qualification to exist, sex must be provably relevant to job performance.

Other examples of illegal sex discrimination include:

- Refusing to hire a female newscaster because "news coming from a woman sounds like gossip."
- Allowing women to retire at age 50, but requiring men to wait until age 55.
- Failing to promote women to overseas positions because foreign clients were reluctant to do business with women.

The much-talked about Hooters restaurant case involved a lawsuit filed by men in Illinois and Maryland who were denied jobs. Hooters paid $3.75 million to settle the lawsuit. The settlement allows Hooters to continue employing voluptuous and scantily clad female "Hooters Girls," but they must create and fill a few other support jobs, like bartenders and hosts, without regard to gender.

The largest gender discrimination case was brought as a class action against Wal-Mart and Sam's Club. In 2011, the U.S. Supreme Court refused to certify the class. For more information about this case, see Case 4.2 in Chapter 4.

>> *sidebar* 20.5

Gender Bias in Corporate America

Here are some examples of gender bias cases brought by women against major U.S. firms:

- **Novartis Pharmaceuticals Corp.**—After finding discrimination against women employees in pay, promotion and pregnancy policies, a New York jury awarded the plaintiffs $3,367,250 in compensatory damages and $250 million in punitive damages. In his closing argument, the plaintiffs' lawyer told the jury that the evidence proved that Novartis "tolerated a culture of sexism, a boys' club atmosphere." Novartis subsequently settled the remaining gender bias claims, agreeing to a settlement of approximately $152.5 million to current and former female sales representatives.

- **Morgan Stanley**—In 2004, the firm agreed to pay $54 million to settle a gender discrimination suit brought by a former bond saleswoman.

- **Goldman Sachs Group, Inc.**—Three former female employees have sued Goldman Sachs in 2010, alleging "systemic" violations of female employees' rights, including allegations of excluding women from golf outings and other work-related social events, push-up contests, and retaliation after complaining about being groped by a male colleague after an outing at a topless bar. The suit alleges that the decentralized structure gives managers "unchecked discretion" in assigning pay and responsibilities.

- **Citigroup**—Six current and former female employees sued Citigroup alleging that it engages in "pervasive discrimination and retaliation" against female employees during the 2008 layoffs. Calling the firm an "outdated 'boys' club,'" it allegedly systematically discriminates against women at all levels.

Sexual Harassment A common type of illegal sex discrimination in the workplace is **sexual harassment.** The typical sexual harassment case involves a plaintiff who has been promised benefits or threatened with loss if she or he does not give sexual favors to an employment supervisor. Such a case is also called a *quid pro quo* (this for that) case. Under Title VII and agency law, an employer is liable for this sex discrimination.

Another type of sexual harassment is the **hostile work environment,** one in which co-workers make offensive sexual comments or propositions, engage in suggestive touching, show nude pictures, or draw sexual graffiti. The Supreme Court in *Meritor Savings Bank v. Vinson* ruled that Title VII prohibits "an offensive or hostile working environment," even when no economic loss occurs. By so ruling, the Court acknowledged that the work environment itself is a condition of employment covered by Title VII.

The Supreme Court also addressed the hostile work environment issue in *Harris v. Forklift Systems, Inc.* Specifically, the Court was asked to determine whether, before a person could sue under Title VII, a hostile work environment had "to seriously affect [his or her] psychological well-being" or "cause injury." The Court ruled that illegal sexual harassment goes beyond that which causes "injury." It includes any harassment reasonably perceived as "hostile and abusive."

Is all sexually offensive conduct between employees illegal? The answer is no, although an employee's company may choose to forbid and punish all

> Think of sexual harassment discrimination in terms of (1) quid pro quo cases and (2) hostile work environment cases.

> Well-known talk show hosts Maury Povich and Bill O'Reilly both have been accused of sexual harassment in multimillion-dollar lawsuits. O'Reilly settled the case for an undisclosed amount.

such conduct. In 2005 the Supreme Court in *Clarke County School District v. Breeden* summarized when offensive sexual conduct becomes illegal:

> [S]exual harassment is actionable under Title VII only if it is so severe or pervasive as to alter the conditions of the victim's employment and create an abusive working environment.

The Court continued:

> Workplace conduct is not measured in isolation; instead, whether an environment is sufficiently hostile or abusive must be judged by looking at all the circumstances, including the frequency of the discriminatory conduct; its severity; whether it is physically threatening or humiliating, or a mere offensive utterance; and whether it unreasonably interferes with an employee's work performance.

16.4% of all sexual harassment claims—or 2,094 claims—were filed by men in 2009.

It is not uncommon for a discrimination lawsuit to involve multiple kinds of claims. A good example of this is a recent case against Cracker Barrel, in which the restaurant agreed to pay $2 million to settle a lawsuit alleging sexual harassment, racial harassment, and retaliation by 51 current or former employees. On behalf of the workers, the EEOC alleged that male co-workers and managers subjected female workers to unwelcome and offensive sexual comments and touching. According to the EEOC, "Black employees said that they experienced racially charged language in the workplace, including 'spear chucking porch monkey,' 'you people,' and the 'n-word.'" In addition to the monetary settlement, Cracker Barrel must train all employees in its stores about harassment.

>> *sidebar* 20.6

Vulgar Workplace Language & Sexual Harassment

Can vulgar language, *even if it is not specifically directed at an individual,* be actionable as sexual harassment under Title VII? Yes—according to the 11th Circuit Court of Appeals. The plaintiff, Ingrid Reeves, worked at a sales company, C.H. Robinson. Reeves alleged that she was subjected to hearing her male co-workers call other women names such as "b***h," "wh**e" and "c**t" on a daily basis. She also claimed that there were repeated vulgar discussions about female body parts and a pornographic image of a woman in the office. Reeves complained to her co-workers, her supervisor, and top company executives, but the offensive conduct was "accepted and tolerated."

According to the 11th Circuit, "if Reeves's account is to be believed, C.H. Robinson's workplace was more than a rough environment—indiscriminately vulgar, profane, and sexual. Instead, a just reasonably could find that it was a workplace that exposed Reeves to disadvantageous terms or conditions of employment to which members of the other sex were not exposed." Moreover, the court stated that it was no defense to assert "that the workplace may have been vulgar and sexually degrading before Reeves arrived."

For more information, see, *Reeves v. C.H. Robinson Worldwide, Inc.,* 07-10270 (11th Cir. Jan. 20, 2010), available at www.ca11.uscourts.gov/opinions/ops/200710270op2.pdf.

Employer's Defense to Hostile Environment   Is an employer always liable when fellow employees create a hostile environment based on gender? The answer is that the employer is not always legally responsible for a hostile environment. The employer may have a defense. Courts have ruled that an employer is liable to a plaintiff employee for a hostile working environment created by fellow employees only when the employer knows of the problem and fails to take prompt and reasonable steps to correct it, such as by moving the harassers away from the plaintiff employee. The employer can defend itself by proving the employer exercised reasonable care to prevent and correct promptly any sexually harassing behavior, and the plaintiff employee unreasonably failed to take advantage of any preventive or corrective opportunities provided by the employer.

Remember Title VII says that an employer is liable for discriminatory practices only if an employee files a complaint concerning them with the EEOC within 180 days of their happening (within 300 days if the employee has first filed with a state fair employment practices commission). Employers are liable for acts that occurred before 180 days of EEOC filing if they are part of a single hostile environment that continued within the 180-day period.

> **Don't** forget that employers are liable if plaintiffs prove quid pro quo harassment. But employers may have a defense to hostile environment harassment.

Pregnancy Discrimination Act   The Pregnancy Discrimination Act amended the Civil Rights Act in 1978. Under it, employers can no longer discriminate against women workers who become pregnant or give birth. Thus, employers with health or disability plans must cover pregnancy, childbirth, and related medical conditions in the same manner as other conditions are covered. The law covers unmarried as well as married pregnant women. It also states that an employer cannot force a pregnant woman to stop working until her baby is born, provided she is still capable of performing her duties properly. And the employer cannot specify how long a leave of absence must be taken after childbirth. Coverage for abortion is not required by the statute unless an employee carries to term and her life is endangered or she develops medical complications because of an abortion. If a woman undergoes an abortion, though, all other benefits provided for employees, such as sick leave, must be provided to her.

> Men as well as women may be subject to illegal sex discrimination.

Note that sex discrimination applies to discrimination against men as well as women. For example, under the Pregnancy Discrimination Act the Supreme Court ruled unlawful an employer's health insurance plan that covered the pregnancies of female employees but did not cover the pregnancies of male employees' wives.

>> *sidebar* 20.7

Pregnancy Discrimination: Claims on the Rise

The EEOC reports that pregnancy-related claims are consistently increasing:

YEAR	CLAIMS RECEIVED
1997	3977
2000	4160
2003	4649
2007	5587
2010	6119

What does a woman need to bring a successful claim? She must prove that her pregnancy or her status as a mother motivated the employer's adverse action.

In 2007, the EEOC sued Bloomberg LP, the news and financial services company, alleging discrimination against women who became pregnant and took maternity leave. The complaint alleges that Bloomberg engaged in a pattern of demoting and reducing the pay of women after they were pregnant. Other allegations included that some women were subjected to stereotyping about their abilities to do work while they were tending to family and caregiver responsibilities.

For more information, see www.eeoc.gov/types/pregnancy.html.

662   **PART 5**   The Employer-Employee Relationship

According to the census statistics, women earned 77 cents on the male dollar in 2008. April 20th is now Equal Pay Day in the U.S. to highlight awareness of this ongoing discrepancy.

Equal Pay Act   Historically, employers have paid female employees less than males, even when they held the same jobs. In 1964, women earned only 59 cents for every dollar earned by males. By 2008, female employees earned just 77 cents for every dollar earned by males.

Federal legislation prohibits sex discrimination in employment compensation under both Title VII and the Equal Pay Act of 1963. Administered by the EEOC, the Equal Pay Act prohibits an employer from discriminating on the basis of sex in the payment of wages for equal work performed. For jobs to be equal, they must require "equal skill, effort, and responsibility" and must be performed "under similar working conditions." Discrimination is allowed if it arises from a seniority system, a merit system, a piecework production system, or any factor other than sex.

The focus of Equal Pay Act cases is whether the male and female jobs being compared involve "equal" work. Courts have recognized that *equal* does not mean *identical*; it means *substantially* equal. Thus, courts have ruled "equal" the work of male barbers and female beauticians and of male tailors and female seamstresses. Differences in male and female job descriptions will not totally protect employers against charges of equal-pay infractions. The courts have held that "substantially equal" work done on different machines would require the employer to compensate male and female employees equally.

One court ruled that an employer could pay male physician assistants more than female nurses because the physician assistants had administrative duties that nurses did not have to perform.

The Supreme Court has ruled that discriminatory male and female pay differences can also be illegal under Title VII. In *County of Washington v. Gunther,* the Court decided that plaintiffs can use evidence of such pay differences to help prove intentional sex discrimination, even when the work performed is not substantially equal. Relying on the *Gunther* case, at least one lower court has held that women must be paid equally with men who perform comparable work. A federal district court ruled that the state of Washington discriminated against secretaries (mostly women) by paying them less than maintenance and other personnel (mostly men). However, the **comparable worth** theory is highly controversial, and other courts have not agreed with the theory. Equal Pay Act cases tend to rely heavily on statistical analysis of disparities.

In a landmark Equal Pay Act decision, *Ledbetter v. Goodyear Tire & Rubber Co., Inc.* (2007), a sharply divided Supreme Court rejected the pro-employee paycheck-accrual theory of pay discrimination previously accepted by many courts. Simply stated, employees must file an EEOC charge within 180 or 300 days (depending on their state) after each discriminatory pay decision or forever lose their claim. For more details about the controversial *Ledbetter* case, see Sidebar 20.8.

Examples of successful Equal Pay Act cases include one against Wal-Mart and another against the New York Corrections Department. In the first case, a pharmacist who claimed Wal-Mart fired her after asking to be paid the same as her male colleagues won nearly a $2 million award against Wal-Mart. Wal-Mart argued that it fired the pharmacist for leaving the pharmacy unattended and allowing a technician to use her computer security code to issue prescriptions, including a fraudulent prescription for a painkiller. Countering this argument, the pharmacist argued that the prescription incident

>> *sidebar* 20.8

Did the Supreme Court Get It Wrong? Fallout Over the *Ledbetter* Case

Lilly Ledbetter worked for Goodyear for nearly 20 years. During that time, Ledbetter and other salaried employees received or were denied raises based on their supervisors' evaluation of their performance. Near the end of her tenure at Goodyear, Ledbetter discovered that her pay was significantly less—as much as 40 percent less—than her male counterparts. Ledbetter then filed a charge with the EEOC.

>> PROCEDURAL HISTORY

The district court allowed Ledbetter to present evidence of her entire 19-year career at Goodyear. A jury found in her favor, awarding both compensatory and punitive damages. The Eleventh Circuit reversed and the Supreme Court (5–4) affirmed the decision that a Title VII pay discrimination claim cannot be based on any pay decision that occurred outside of the EEOC charging period.

>> DISSENTING VIEWS

Justice Ruth Bader Ginsberg wrote a spirited dissent (joined by Justices Stevens, Souter, and Breyer) arguing that "[p]ay disparities often occur . . . in small increments" and "cause to suspect that discrimination is at work develops only over time." She continued, asserting that discriminatory disparities in pay, like hostile work environment claims, rest not on "one particular paycheck, but on 'the cumulative effect of individual acts.'" Incensed about the majority opinion, Justice Ginsberg read her dissent aloud from the bench.

>> LEGISLATIVE RESPONSE

The first piece of legislation President Obama signed into law was the Lilly Ledbetter Fair Pay Act of 2009. The Ledbetter Act extends the time for employees to bring gender discrimination claims challenging pay or promotion decision.

took place 18 months before her termination and more severe infractions by her male counterparts were unpunished. In the second case, the EEOC settled an Equal Pay Act suit against the New York Department of Corrections for nearly $1 million. The EEOC alleged that female employees were receiving less benefits than their male counterparts.

Sexual Orientation Discrimination   Title VII does not prohibit discrimination against employees based on their sexual orientation, or whether they are gay, lesbian, bisexual, transgendered, or heterosexual. The word *sex* in Title VII refers only to gender, whether someone is female or male. A quarter of the states, however, and numerous cities do forbid discrimination based on sexual orientation, and Congress could amend Title VII to protect employees from such discrimination. Already, thousands of companies ranging from American Express, Coca-Cola, and J. P. Morgan Chase Bank to Ford, General Motors, and Chrysler, offer domestic partner benefits to all employees without regard to sexual orientation.

Although the House of Representatives voted 235–184 to pass the Employment Non-Discrimination Act of 2007, banning employment discrimination on the basis of sexual orientation, it has not yet become federal law. See Sidebar 20.9 for other developments in sexual orientation laws and protections.

>> *sidebar* 20.9

Sexual Orientation Discrimination: State and Local Laws

Although there is no federal protection prohibiting sexual orientation in the workplace based on sexual orientation, many private employers—especially those who operate in many states—have company policies prohibiting sexual orientation discrimination. Consider these facts and legal developments:

- The majority of Fortune 500 companies provide health insurance for domestic partners of their employees.
- According to Human Rights Campaign, a gay political group, more than 7,000 employers offer domestic partner benefits.
- *State laws.* Twenty states and the District of Columbia have laws that currently prohibit sexual orientation discrimination in private employment:

California, Colorado, Connecticut, Hawaii, Illinois, Iowa, Maine, Maryland, Massachusetts, Minnesota, Nevada, New Hampshire, New Jersey, New Mexico, New York, Oregon, Rhode Island, Vermont, Washington, and Wisconsin. Some of these states also specifically prohibit discrimination based on gender identity.

- *Local laws.* More than 180 cities and counties nationwide prohibit sexual orientation discrimination in at least some workplaces.

For more information and a state-by-state list of antidiscrimination laws, including city and county ordinances, see the Lambda Legal Defense and Education Fund website at www.lambdalegal.org.

>> Employment Practices That May Be Challenged

In studying the Civil Rights Act, we can usefully consider several specific employment practices that employees or job applicants may challenge as discriminatory. These practices include:

- Setting testing and educational requirements.
- Having height and weight requirements for physical labor.
- Maintaining appearance requirements.
- Practicing affirmative action.
- Using seniority systems.

The following sections take a close look at these practices.

7. QUESTIONNAIRES, INTERVIEWS, TESTING, AND EDUCATIONAL REQUIREMENTS

Employers have used a number of tools to help them find the right person for the right job. Among these tools are questionnaires, interviews, references, minimum educational requirements (such as a high school diploma), and personnel tests. However, employers must be extremely careful not to use tools that illegally discriminate. For example, Rent-A-Center, a Dallas-based appliance-rental company, agreed to pay more than $2 million in damages to more than 1,200 job applicants and employees who were asked questions about their sex lives and religious views in a 500-item true-false questionnaire. Plaintiffs claimed the questionnaire discriminated illegally on the basis of gender and religion and that it violated their privacy.

Interviews can also discriminate illegally, and personnel interviewers must be well trained. One study indicated that interviewers can be biased even if they are not aware of it. The study showed that the interviewers tended to select males over females for sales positions because the interviewers *subconsciously* related sales success with height, and males are on the average taller than females. References may not be so reliable, either. A previous employer's letter may reflect personal biases against an applicant that were not related to job performance.

At the other extreme, an employer may give a poor employee a top recommendation because of sympathy or fear of a lawsuit in case the letter is somehow obtained by the employee. Advocates of personnel tests in the selection process feel they are very valuable in weeding out the wrong persons for a job and picking the right ones. They believe reliance on test results eliminates biases that interviewers or former employers who give references may have.

Tests, however, can have a *disparate impact* on job applicants, discriminating on the basis of race, sex, color, religion, or national origin. Setting educational standards such as requiring a high school diploma for employment can also have a disparate impact. To avoid discrimination challenges, employers must make sure that all testing and educational requirements are job related and necessary for the business.

Most employment practices that discriminate illegally do so because of their disparate impact.

In the past, some employers have "race normed" employment tests. *Race norming* is the practice of setting two different cutoff test scores for employment based on race or one of the other Title VII categories. For example, on a race-normed test, the minimum score for employment of white job applicants might be set at 75 out of 100. For minority applicants, the minimum score might be set at 65. *The Civil Rights Act amendments of 1991 specifically prohibit the race norming of employment tests.*

Don't forget that for employers to race-norm employment tests violates Title VII.

8. HEIGHT AND WEIGHT REQUIREMENTS

Minimum or maximum height or weight job requirements apply equally to all job applicants, but if they have the effect of screening out applicants on the basis of race, national origin, or sex, the employer must demonstrate that such requirements are validly related to the ability to perform the work in question. For example, maximum size standards would be permissible, even if they favored women over men, if the available work space were too small to permit large persons to perform the duties of the job properly. Most size requirements have dictated minimum heights or weights, often based on a stereotyped assumption that a certain amount of strength that smaller persons might not have probably was necessary for the work. In one case, a 5-foot, 5-inch, 130-pound Hispanic won a suit against a police department on the basis that the department's 5-foot, 8-inch minimum height requirement discriminated against Hispanics, who often are shorter than that standard. He was later hired when he passed the department's physical agility examination, which included dragging a 150-pound body 75 feet and scaling a 6-foot wall.

9. APPEARANCE REQUIREMENTS

Walt Disney World has detailed instructions for employees on "The Disney Look," including eyewear, body piercing, earlobe expansion, facial hair, fingernails, hear length, and sideburns. The goal is to look "friendly, approachable, and knowledgeable."

Employers often have set grooming standards for their employees. Those regulating hair length of males or prohibiting beards or mustaches have been among the most common. Undoubtedly, motivation for these rules stems from the feeling of the employer that the image it projects to the public through its employees will be adversely affected if their appearance is not "proper." It is unclear whether appearance requirements are legal or illegal, since there have been rulings both ways. However, in 2000 the EEOC filed a lawsuit in Atlanta against FedEx Corporation for firing a bearded delivery driver who refused to shave in violation of a company policy that permitted beards only when medically necessary. The driver's Islamic beliefs required males to wear beards, and the lawsuit alleged that FedEx's policy constituted religious discrimination.

The burden of proof in a disparate impact case requires the employer to prove that appearance is a business necessity.

In another case, a black employee argued that he was wrongfully fired for breaking a company rule prohibiting beards. Dermatologists testified that the plaintiff had a condition called "razor bumps" (which occurs when the tightly curled facial hairs of black men become ingrown from shaving) and that the only known cure was for him not to shave. Although the federal appeals court found that the plaintiff was prejudiced by the employer's regulation, it held in favor of the company, ruling that its *slight racial impact* was justified by the *business necessity* it served. A conflicting opinion in still another case upheld an employee's right to wear a beard because of razor bumps.

10. AFFIRMATIVE ACTION PROGRAMS AND REVERSE DISCRIMINATION

Since the 1940s, a series of presidential executive orders have promoted non-discrimination and **affirmative action** by employers who contract with the federal government. The authority for these orders rests with the president's executive power to control the granting of federal contracts. As a condition to obtaining such contracts, employers must agree contractually to take affirmative action to avoid unlawful discrimination in recruitment, employment, promotion, training, rate of compensation, and layoff of workers.

It is not unusual for an employment ad to state that the company is an "affirmative action/ equal opportunity employer." Some ads also state: "Women and underrepresented minorities are encouraged to apply."

The affirmative action requirement means that federally contracting employers must actively recruit members of minority groups being underused in the workforce. That is, employers must hire members of these groups when there are fewer minority workers in a given job category than one could reasonably expect, considering their availability. In many instances, employers must develop written affirmative action plans and set goals and timetables for bringing minority (or female) workforces up to their percentages in the available labor pool.

The Labor Department administers executive orders through its Office of Federal Contract Compliance Programs (OFCCP). The OFCCP can terminate federal contracts with employers who do not comply with its guidelines and can make them ineligible for any future federal business. For instance, it required Uniroyal, Inc., to give its female employees an estimated $18 million in back pay to compensate for past employment discrimination. The alternative was elimination of $36 million of existing federal contracts and ineligibility for future federal business.

The Labor Department has eased OFCCP regulations on 75 percent of the firms that do business with the federal government. Firms with fewer than 250 employees and federal contracts of under $1 million no longer must prepare written affirmative action plans for hiring women and minorities. The OFCCP has also begun to limit its use of back pay awards to specific individuals who can show an actual loss due to violation of OFCCP guidelines.

Private Employer Affirmative Action   Not all affirmative action programs arise under federal contracting rules. Courts also impose affirmative action on private employers to overcome a history of prior discrimination. Sometimes private employers voluntarily adopt affirmative action or agree to it with unions. These affirmative action programs can give rise to claims of **reverse discrimination** when minorities or women with lower qualifications or less seniority than white males are given preference in employment or training. Even though such programs are intended to remedy the effects of present or past discrimination or other barriers to equal employment opportunity, white males have argued that the law does not permit employers to discriminate against *them* on the basis of race or sex any more than it allows discrimination against minorities or women.

In *United Steelworkers of America v. Weber,* the Supreme Court ruled legal under Title VII a voluntary affirmative action plan between an employer and a union. The plan required that at least 50 percent of certain new work trainees be black. The Court noted that the plan did not require that white employees be fired or excluded altogether from advancement. It was only a temporary measure to eliminate actual racial imbalance in the workforce.

Note the difference between taking affirmative action and setting a "quota." Affirmative action is taken to help correct historic workforce imbalances and usually has target goals that are pursued for a limited time. On the other hand, quotas set rigid standards for various groups, such as that 50 percent of the workforce must be female. The 1991 Civil Rights Act amendments prohibit the setting of quotas in employment.

The EEOC has issued guidelines intended to protect employers who set up affirmative action plans. These guidelines indicate that Title VII is not violated if an employer determines that there is a reasonable basis for concluding that such a plan is appropriate and the employer takes *reasonable* affirmative action. For example, if an employer discovers that it has a job category where one might expect to find more women and minorities employed than are actually in its workforce, the employer has a reasonable basis for affirmative action.

In *Adarand Constructors, Inc. v. Pena,* the Supreme Court emphasized that government-imposed affirmative action plans are subject to *strict judicial scrutiny* under equal protection guaranteed by the Fifth and Fourteenth Amendments. To be constitutional, such plans must now be supported by a *compelling interest.* The *Adarand* decision will make it constitutionally difficult to justify some government-imposed affirmative action plans. Much litigation has followed that tests the constitutionality of various plans.

In California voters approved the controversial Proposition 209. In relevant part it says that "the state shall not discriminate against, or grant preferential treatment to, any individual or group on the basis of race, sex, color, ethnicity, or national origin in the operation of public employment,

Do remember that the justification for affirmative action is the historic discrimination against protected groups.

In 2005, a federal jury found that the New Orleans district attorney discriminated against 43 white employees by firing them and replacing them with African Americans.

Voluntary affirmative action plans by private employers *may* violate Title VII but do *not* violate constitutional equal protection because they are not "state action."

public education, or public contracting." The Supreme Court refused to hear an appeal from a lower court decision that upheld Proposition 209 against constitutional challenge and the assertion it violated federal civil rights law. Although Proposition 209 *does not* affect private employer affirmative action plans required by federal law, it does illustrate the current opposition that many Americans have to affirmative action. Polls show that almost three-fourths of the general population disapproves of affirmative action. Nearly 50 percent of African Americans also oppose it.

11. SENIORITY SYSTEMS

Seniority systems give priority to those employees who have worked longer for a particular employer or in a particular line of employment of the employer. Employers may institute seniority systems on their own, but in a union shop they are usually the result of collective bargaining. Their terms are spelled out in the agreement between the company and the union. Seniority systems often determine the calculation of vacation, pension, and other fringe benefits. They also control many employment decisions such as the order in which employees may choose shifts or qualify for promotions or transfers to different jobs. They also are used to select the persons to be laid off when an employer is reducing its labor force. As a result of seniority, the last hired are usually the first fired. Decisions based on seniority have been challenged in recent years as violating the laws relating to equal employment opportunity. Challenges often arose when recently hired members of minority groups were laid off during periods of economic downturn. Firms with successful affirmative action programs often lost most of their minority employees.

Section 703(h) of the Civil Rights Act of 1964 provides that, in spite of other provisions in the act, it is not an unlawful employment practice for an employer to apply different employment standards under a bona fide (good-faith) seniority system if the differences are not the result of an *intention* to discriminate. In *Memphis Fire Dept. v. Stotts* the Supreme Court ruled that discrimination resulting from application of a seniority system was lawful even when it affected minorities hired or promoted by affirmative action.

> Title VII specifically allows employers to adopt seniority systems even when they may operate to discriminate against protected groups.

>> Other Statutes and Discrimination in Employment

Although the Civil Rights Act of 1964 is the most widely used antidiscrimination statute, there are other important antidiscrimination laws. They include the Civil Rights Act of 1866, the Age Discrimination in Employment Act, the Americans with Disabilities Act, and various state and local laws. The following sections examine these laws.

12. CIVIL RIGHTS ACT OF 1866

An important federal law that complements Title VII of the 1964 Civil Rights Act is the Civil Rights Act of 1866. One provision of that act, known as **Section 1981** (referring to its U.S. Code designation, 42 U.S.C. §1981), provides that "all persons . . . shall have the same right to make and enforce contracts . . . as enjoyed by white citizens." Since union memberships and employment relationships involve contracts, Section 1981 bans racial discrimination in these areas.

The courts have interpreted Section 1981 as giving a private plaintiff most of the same protections against racial discrimination that the 1964 Civil Rights Act provides. In addition, there are at least two advantages to the plaintiff who files a suit based on Section 1981. First, there are no procedural requirements for bringing such a suit, whereas there are a number of fairly complex requirements plaintiffs must follow before bringing a private suit under Title VII. For instance, before a plaintiff can file a lawsuit against an employer, the plaintiff must file charges of discrimination with the EEOC and obtain a notice of right to sue from the agency. By using Section 1981, a plaintiff can immediately sue an employer in federal court without first going through the EEOC.

Unlimited Damages   A second advantage to Section 1981 is that under it the courts can award unlimited compensatory and punitive damages. There are no capped limits as there are under Title VII. As a practical matter, parties alleging racial discrimination usually sue under both Section 1981 and Title VII.

Note that Section 1981 does not cover discrimination based on sex, religion, national origin, age, or handicap. As interpreted by the courts, this section applies only to *racial* discrimination. However, what is race? The Supreme Court has held that being of Arabic or Jewish ancestry constitutes "race" as protected by Section 1981. The Court stated that when the law was passed in the nineteenth century, the concept of race was much broader than it is today. Race then included the descendants of a particular "family, tribe, people, or nation." Has the Court opened the door for a white job applicant to sue a black employer for discrimination under Section 1981?

In *Patterson v. McLean,* the Supreme Court interpreted Section 1981 to apply only to the actual hiring or firing of employees based on race. Under this interpretation, Section 1981 did not offer protection against discrimination such as a hostile working environment. But the Civil Rights Act amendments of 1991 redefined Section 1981 to include protection against discrimination in "enjoyment of all benefits, privileges, terms and conditions of the contractual relationship." Thus Section 1981 now also protects against hostile environment discrimination. In 2008, the Supreme Court also extended Section 1981 to claims of retaliation for complaining about race discrimination.

Denny's restaurants have been repeatedly sued for black customers claiming Denny's violated their civil rights. Denny's has paid more than $54 million to settle the lawsuits.

Don't forget that Section 1981 is why racial discrimination is subject to damages far in excess of the $300,000 limit imposed on individuals under Title VII.

Under Section 1981, "race" includes ethnic or national groups.

13. DISCRIMINATION ON THE BASIS OF AGE

The workforce is "graying." The U.S. Census Bureau projects that by 2010 over 51 percent of the workforce will be 40 years of age or older. As percentages of older workers rise in coming years, so will the increase in complaints about age discrimination.

Neither the Civil Rights Act nor the Equal Employment Opportunity Act forbids discrimination based on age. However, the Age Discrimination in Employment Act (ADEA) does. It prohibits employment discrimination

"Age bias is still a persistent problem in the 21st century workplace."

–Spencer H. Lewis, EEOC district director

against employees ages 40 and older, and it prohibits the mandatory retirement of these employees. Only certain executives and high policymakers of private companies can be forced into early retirement. Specifically, "bona fide" executives and high-level policy makers age 65 and older who are entitled to receive annual retirement benefits of at least $44,000 a year are subject to mandatory retirement policies. The ADEA applies to employers with 20 or more employees. The ADEA also invalidates retirement plans and labor contracts that violate the law.

Types of Age Discrimination

The ADEA recognizes both disparate treatment and disparate impact discrimination. The Supreme Court has upheld a jury's finding of disparate treatment in an age discrimination case. The employer had said the employee "was so old [he] must have come over on the Mayflower" and that he "was too damn old to do his job." When the employer later fired the employee, the jury found for the employee in spite of the employer's assertion that it had fired the employee for reasons other than age.

The Supreme Court has also stated that the ADEA recognizes disparate impact in age discrimination cases. The city of Jackson, Mississippi, had awarded pay raises to junior ranks of police officers that were substantially higher than the pay raises given to more senior ranks. These raises had the impact of discriminating on the basis of age. Older officers received lower pay raises because they were mostly in senior ranks.

However, the Supreme Court stated that disparate impact alone did not prove illegality under the ADEA. The city of Jackson was merely attempting to match the salaries offered to junior officers in nearby cities, which was a "reasonable factor other than age." See Sidebar 20.10 for an example of illegal mandatory retirement policy.

Employer Defenses in ADEA Cases

The employer defenses to age discrimination, disparate treatment, and disparate impact differ slightly from the defense in Title VII cases.

For instance, under the ADEA age is seldom recognized as the basis for a bona fide occupational qualification. It is recognized that as people grow older, their physical strength, agility, reflexes, hearing, and vision tend to diminish in quality. However, this generally provides no legal reason for discriminating against older persons as a class. Although courts will uphold job-related physical requirements if they apply on a case-by-case basis, they frequently find as illegal those policies that prohibit the hiring of persons beyond a maximum age or that establish a maximum age beyond which employees are forced to retire for physical reasons. Thus, one court ruled that a mandatory retirement age of 65 was illegally discriminatory as applied to the job of district fire chief. In an exception to the general rule, one court has ruled that age can be a BFOQ in a case where the airlines imposed a maximum age for hiring new pilots. The court observed that the Federal Aviation Administration mandated a retirement age for pilots.

Willful violations of the ADEA allow courts to impose double damage awards against employers.

The ADEA also does not require the employer to prove a "business necessity" in order to successfully defend an age discrimination case of disparate impact. All the employer need do is establish that a "reasonable factor other than age" accounted for the discriminatory impact. Further, unlike under Title VII, the employer's defense of a reasonable factor other than age cannot be defeated by the employee's showing of a less discriminatory way of achieving the employer's purpose.

Remedies under the ADEA Courts have disagreed on whether remedies for violation of the ADEA include, in addition to reinstatement and wages lost, damages for the psychological trauma of being fired or forced to resign illegally. One federal district court awarded $200,000 to a victim of age discrimination who was an inventor and scientist, for the psychological and physical effects suffered from being forced into early retirement at age 60. Also awarded were out-of-pocket costs of $60,000 and attorneys' fees of $65,000. Note that *willful* violations of the act permit discrimination victims to be awarded *double damages*.

Note an important exception to this general rule about remedies under the ADEA. In accordance with the Supreme Court case *Kimel v. Florida Board of Regents* (2000), a plaintiff cannot recover money damages against a state entity. State law, however, may offer additional remedies for age discrimination perpetrated by a state.

>> *sidebar* 20.10

Did You Read the Law? A Law Firm Runs Afoul of the ADEA

The EEOC filed a lawsuit against Sidley Austin Brown & Wood ("Sidley Austin"), a major Chicago-based international law firm, alleging that it violated the ADEA when it selected 32 "partners" for expulsion from the firm on account of their age or forced them to retire.

After over two years of litigation, Sidley Austin agreed to pay $27.5 million to the former partners. The firm also agreed to refrain from "terminating,

expelling, retiring, reducing the compensation of or otherwise adversely changing the partnership status of any partner because of age" or "maintaining any formal or informal policy or practice requiring retirement as a partner or requiring permission to continue as a partner once the partner has reached a certain age."

Source: EEOC Press Releases.

14. DISCRIMINATION ON THE BASIS OF DISABILITIES

According to a Harris poll, two-thirds of all disabled Americans between the ages of 16 and 64 are not working, even though most of them want to work. To help those with disabilities obtain work, Congress in 1990 passed the Americans with Disabilities Act (ADA). Thereafter, the U.S. Supreme Court rendered a number of employer–friendly decisions restricting the scope of the ADA's protection. Responding to criticism that the U.S. Supreme Court unreasonably restricted the ADA's scope, Congress passed the ADA Amendments Act of 2008, effective January 1, 2009 and, in 2011, the EEOC released its final regulations. The ADA is now expanded to protect a broader group of individuals.

To prevent disability discrimination, the ADA prohibits employers from requiring a preemployment medical examination or asking questions about the job applicant's medical history. Only after a job offer has been extended

It is now easier to establish a "disability" within the definition of the ADA and employers need to be prepared to make reasonable accommodations.

672   **PART 5**   The Employer-Employee Relationship

can the employer condition employment on the employee's responses to *job related* medical questions.

The concept of "disability" includes mental disabilities and diseases as well as physical impairment.

The ADA prohibits employer discrimination against job applicants or employees based on (1) their having a disability, (2) their having a disability in the past, or (3) their being *regarded as* having a disability. The ADA defines **disability** as "any physical or mental impairment that substantially limits one or more of an individual's major life activities." "Substantially limits" now requires a lower degree of limitation than was previously applied by the courts.

"Physical and mental impairment" includes physical disorders and conditions, disease, disfigurement, amputation affecting a vital body system, psychological disorders, mental retardation, mental illness, and learning disabilities. An individual can demonstrate that he or she is "regarded as" having a disability by establishing that he or she has been subjected to an action prohibited by the ADA "because of an actual or perceived physical or mental impairment whether or not the impairment limits or is perceived to limit a major life activity."

Impairments, such as cancer, that are substantially limiting when active remain so despite being in remission.

"Major life activities" include such activities as "caring for oneself, performing manual tasks, seeing, hearing, eating, sleeping, walking, standing, lifting, bending, speaking, breathing, learning, reading, concentrating, thinking, communicating and working." The definition also includes the operation of any major body function, including functions of the immune system, normal cell growth, and digestive, bowel, bladder, neurological, brain, respiratory, circulatory, endocrine, and reproductive functions. The determination of whether an impairment substantially limits a major life activity must be made without regard to the "ameliorative effects of mitigating measures"—that is, individuals who use medications, artificial limbs, or hearing aids qualify for protection under the ADA, even though those measures may overcome the limiting effects of an impairment. (Ordinary eyeglasses and contact lenses are specifically excluded from this list by the amendments to the ADA.) The ADA also states that an individual with an impairment that is "transitory and minor," defined as having an actual or expected duration of six months or less, does not fall under the ADA. However, individuals with impairments that are episodic or in remission, such as epilepsy, diabetes, or cancer are not barred from coverage under the ADA.

According to the American Bar Association's *Mental & Physical Disability Law Reporter,* employers prevailed in 94.5 percent of 327 disability discrimination cases decided in federal courts across the United States in 2002.

Not included by the ADA as protected disabilities are homosexuality, sexual behavior disorders, compulsive gambling, kleptomania, and disorders resulting from *current* drug or alcohol use. The emphasis on current drug or alcohol use means that employees who have successfully recovered or are successfully recovering from drug or alcohol disabilities are protected from employment discrimination.

Individuals with HIV or AIDS are protected by the ADA. Persons who are discriminated against because they are regarded as being HIV-positive are also protected.

The ADA prohibits employers of 15 or more employees (also unions with 15 or more members and employment agencies) from discriminating against the qualified disabled with respect to hiring, advancement, termination, compensation, training, or other terms, conditions, or privileges of employment. **Qualified disabled** are defined as those with a disability who, with or without reasonable accommodation, can perform the essential functions of a particular job position. Employers must make reasonable accommodation only for the *qualified* disabled.

Reasonable Accommodation under the ADA The ADA does not require employers to hire the unqualified disabled, but they must make reasonable accommodation so qualified disabled employees can succeed in the workplace. **Reasonable accommodation** is the process of adjusting a job or work environment to fit the needs of disabled employees. It may include:

- Making the work facilities accessible and usable to disabled employees.
- Restructuring jobs or modifying work schedules.
- Purchasing or modifying necessary equipment for use by the disabled.
- Providing appropriate training materials or assistance modified to fit the needs of disabled employees.

Note that an employer need make only reasonable accommodation for disabled employees. The employer can plead *undue hardship,* defined as "an action requiring significant difficulty or expense," as a reason for not accommodating the needs of disabled employees. The ADA specifies that in evaluating undue hardship, the cost of the accommodation, the resources of the employer, the size of the employer, and the nature of the employer's business be considered.

Businesses must reasonably accommodate not only *employees* for their disabilities under the ADA but also customers and others who use public facilities such as hotels, restaurants, theaters, schools (even private ones), most places of entertainment, offices providing services, and other establishments doing business with the public. The Supreme Court ruled that the Professional Golf Association had to accommodate golfer Casey Martin, who suffered a walking disability because of a circulatory disorder, by allowing him to use a golf cart in PGA tournaments. The Court held (1) that PGA tournaments were open to any member of the public who paid a qualifying fee and participated successfully in a qualifying tournament and (2) that accommodating Casey Martin by allowing him to use a golf cart while other golfers walked a tournament course did not "fundamentally alter the nature" of PGA tournament events.

>> *sidebar* 20.11

Chipotle Mexican Grill: Must Accommodate Disabled Patrons

 The ADA prohibits discrimination in employment and in public accommodations. Maurizio Antoninetti, a patron of the Chipotle Mexican Grill, complained that a 45-inch barrier at Chipotle restaurants blocked his view of the counter, preventing him from inspecting each dish, choosing his order, and watching it be prepared.

Chipotle argued that it accommodated the needs of customers in wheelchairs by bringing them spoonfuls of their preferred dish for inspection before ordering.

This fell short of being adequate. The Ninth Circuit Court of Appeals held that the barrier "subjects disabled customers to a disadvantage that non-disabled customers do not suffer." The U.S. Supreme Court denied certiorari. Chipotle is retrofitting its restaurants with new counters to eliminate concerns regarding wheelchair accessibility.

The remedies under the ADA are basically the same remedies available under Title VII.

Remedies under the ADA Remedies under the ADA are basically the same remedies available under the Civil Rights Act, including hiring, reinstatement, back pay, injunctive relief, and compensatory and punitive damages. As with the Civil Rights Act, a plaintiff must first seek administration remedies with the EEOC. Compensatory and punitive damages are not available for policies that mere have disparate impact. They are available for intentional discrimination and for other employer actions such as failing to make reasonable accommodation for known job applicant or employee disabilities.

The ADA replaces the Rehabilitation Act of 1973 as the primary federal law protecting the disabled. However, the Rehabilitation Act, which applies only to employers doing business with the government under a federal contract for $2,500 or more, still requires that such employers have a qualified affirmative action program for hiring and promoting the disabled.

15. GENETIC DISCRIMINATION

The **Genetic Information Nondiscrimination Act (GINA)**, effective November 2009, prohibits covered employers from firing, refusing to hire, or otherwise discriminating against individuals on the basis of their genetic information, and from discriminating against employees and applicants on the basis of a family member's genetic information. Genetic information includes information about an individual's genetic tests; genetic information about genetic tests of an individual's family members; information about the manifestation of a disease or disorder in an individual's family history; request for or receipt of genetic services; and genetic information of a fetus and the genetic information of any embryo held by the individual or a family member.

"Covered employers" is defined as all employers subject to Title VII. The act further prohibits the limitation, segregation, or classification of employees in such a way "that would deprive or tend to deprive any employee of employment opportunities or otherwise adversely affect the status of the employee as an employee, because of genetic information with respect to the employee."

Under GINA, it is unlawful for an employer to "request, require, or purchase genetic information with respect to an employee or the family member of an employee," with limited exceptions.

GINA also has ramifications for group health plans and health insurance companies. Although many states have already enacted similar legislation, GINA establishes a federal baseline for protection against employment discrimination based on genetic information.

In November 2010, the EEOC published final regulations implementing Title II of GINA, which protects applicants for employment, current employees, former employees, apprentices, trainees and labor organization members against discrimination based on their genetic information. The EEOC regulations, which became effective on January 11, 2011, are intended to:

- Prohibit the use of genetic information in employment decisions
- Restrict employers from requesting, requiring, or purchasing genetic information

- Require that genetic information be maintained as a confidential medical records and place strict limits on the disclosure of genetic information
- Provide remedies for individuals whose genetic information is acquired, used or disclosed in violation of GINA

Tests that are considered to be "genetic tests" under GINA include:

- Tests that might determine if a person is genetically disposed to breast cancer, colon cancer or Huntington's Disease
- Amniocentesis and newborn screening
- Carrier screening for cystic fibrosis, sickle cell anemia, spinal muscular dystrophy, and fragile X syndrome
- DNA testing to detect genetic markers associated with ancestry information

>> *sidebar* 20.12

Protecting Against Inadvertent Acquisition of Medical Information in Violation of GINA

Employers should incorporate the following language into FMLA and other forms to establish a defense to any claim that it wrongfully obtained genetic information in response to an otherwise lawful request for medical information:

The Genetic Information Nondiscrimination Act of 2008 (GINA) prohibits employers and other entities covered by GINA Title II from requesting or requiring genetic information of an individual or family member of the individual, except as specifically allowed by this law. To comply with this law, we are asking that you not provide any genetic information when responding to this request for medical information. 'Genetic information' as defined by GINA, includes an individual's family medical history, the results of an individual's or family member's genetic tests, the fact that an individual or an individual's family member sought or received genetic services, and genetic information of a fetus carried by an individual or an individual's family member or an embryo lawfully held by an individual or family member receiving assistive reproductive services.

16. DISCRIMINATION IN GETTING AND KEEPING HEALTH INSURANCE

A new act prohibits group health plans and health insurance issuers from discriminating against employees based on certain factors. The Health Insurance Portability and Accountability Act (HIPAA) forbids group plans and issuers from excluding an employee from insurance coverage or requiring different premiums based on the employee's health status, medical condition or history, genetic information, or disability.

The act primarily prevents discrimination against individual employees in small businesses. Before the act, individual employees with an illness like cancer or a genetic condition like sickle cell anemia were sometimes denied coverage in a new health plan. The small size of the plan deterred insurers from covering individual employees whose medical condition might produce large claims. The act denies insurers the right to discriminate on this basis. It also guarantees that insured employees who leave their old employer and join a new employer are not denied health insurance. As of this writing, the exact meanings of many HIPAA provisions are still unclear.

Note, however, that the act only applies to prevent discrimination in group health insurance plans. It does not apply to individuals who purchase individual health insurance. Congress is considering legislation to extend HIPAA's antidiscrimination provisions to individual insurance. Behind HIPAA and proposals for new legislation is the concern that new forms of genetic testing will allow insurers and employers to identify and discriminate against individuals who may in the future develop certain medical conditions.

17. OTHER FEDERAL LEGISLATION

Other federal legislation dealing with employment discrimination includes the National Labor Relations Act of 1936. The National Labor Relations Board has ruled that appeals to racial prejudice in a collective bargaining representation election constitute an unfair labor practice. The NLRB has also revoked the certification of unions that practice discriminatory admission or representation policies. Additionally, employers have an obligation to bargain with certified unions over matters of employment discrimination. Such matters are considered "terms and conditions of employment" and are thus mandatory bargaining issues.

Finally, various other federal agencies may prohibit discriminatory employment practices under their authorizing statutes. The Federal Communications Commission, for example, has prohibited employment discrimination by its licensees (radio and TV stations) and has required the submission of affirmative action plans as a condition of license renewal.

LO 20-5   18. STATE ANTIDISCRIMINATION LAWS

State antidiscrimination laws may permit discrimination lawsuits against employers of fewer than 15 employees, the minimum number for a lawsuit under federal Title VII.

According to a study by the Rudd Center at Yale University, discrimination against overweight people, particularly women, is as common as racial discrimination.

Federal laws concerning equal employment opportunity specifically permit state laws imposing additional duties and liabilities. In recent years, fair employment practices legislation has been introduced and passed by many state legislatures. When the federal Equal Employment Opportunity Act became effective, 40 states had such laws, but their provisions varied considerably. A typical state act makes it an unfair employment practice for any employer to refuse to hire or otherwise discriminate against any individual because of his or her race, color, religion, national origin, or ancestry. If employment agencies or labor organizations discriminate against an individual in any way because of one of these reasons, they are also guilty of an unfair employment practice. State acts usually set up an administrative body, generally known as the Fair Employment Practices Commission, which has the power to make rules and regulations and hear and decide charges of violations filed by complainants.

State antidiscrimination laws sometimes protect categories of persons not protected by federal law. For example, some protect persons from employment discrimination based on weight.

As discussed earlier, state and local law may prohibit sexual orientation discrimination in the workplace (see Sidebar 20.9). Other state and local laws prohibit employment discrimination based on weight (e.g., Michigan; Santa Cruz and San Francisco, California; and Washington DC). Michigan's antidiscrimination discrimination law also includes height and weight.

State law may also supplement Title VII, offering remedies to victims of sexual harassment. In New York, for example, former Knicks team executive Anucha Browne Sanders sued the owner of the New York Knicks and Madison Square Garden for discrimination using Title VII, as well as New York State Human Rights Law, New York Executive Law §296, and the Administrative Code of the City of New York §8-107, which prohibit unlawful discriminatory practices. After hearing testimony about crude racial and sexual insults and unwanted advances from coach Isiah Thomas, a jury awarded Sanders $11.6 million.

As indicated in Chapter 10 on torts, discrimination plaintiffs can also sue employers under various state common law causes of action, like negligence, assault, battery, intentional infliction of mental distress, invasion of privacy, and defamation. Under common law, plaintiffs may be able to receive unlimited compensatory and punitive damages, and greater numbers of plaintiffs seem to be suing under common law. In Las Vegas a jury awarded over $5 million against the Hilton Hotel and in favor of a plaintiff who had been sexually groped at an aviators' Tailhook convention. The jury determined that the hotel had been negligent in failing to provide adequate security.

Do remember that discrimination lawsuits can be based on multiple causes of action, including common law ones.

19. TRENDS IN EMPLOYMENT DISCRIMINATION AND LITIGATION

Several current trends in employment discrimination and litigation will require close attention from managers in the coming years. These trends highlight the fact that the workforce is increasingly diverse and that new managers must be alert to the full impact of antidiscrimination laws. They also show the effects of new technology.

Surge in Private Lawsuits Private lawsuits alleging discrimination in employment surged in recent years, more than tripling. Several factors account for the rapid increase. The 1991 revision of the Civil Rights Act to support punitive and compensatory damages has encouraged employees to sue their employers. The passage of the Americans with Disabilities Act has led to a new area of discrimination lawsuits, and some 50 million Americans, according to a conservative estimate, may legally qualify as disabled. Finally, as the large generation of baby boomers ages in the workforce, more lawsuits arise under the Age Discrimination in Employment Act. In the new century, these trends continue, making it ever more important for business managers to understand the law prohibiting discrimination in employment. See Sidebar 20.13 for an interesting study about female CEOs.

>> *sidebar* 20.13

Is It Important to Investors If the CEO Is a Man or a Woman?

The clear answer is, unfortunately, "Yes" according to a study by Lyda Bigelow and Judi McLean Parks at the Olin School of Business, Washington University in St. Louis.

Bigelow and McLean Parks created a prospectus for a fictitious company about to go public, along with a set of qualifications for the company's CEO. To determine if gender played a role in the decision, they gave half of the potential investors information with a female CEO and the other half a male CEO—the qualifications, however, were the same. Only the name and gender were different. They then asked individuals with a background in finance to consider investing in the company.

The researchers found that the CEO's gender clearly affected potential investors. For example, the study showed that the participants were inclined to invest up to three times more with the company with the male CEO. Executive compensation was also an issue. The participants in the study indicated that they would pay the female CEO 14 percent less than her male counterpart.

Perhaps even more disturbing, female CEOs were evaluated more harshly in other very subjective categories. Although the only difference given in the study was gender, participants deemed female CEOs as less competent leaders in a variety of realms, including handling a crisis and dealing with the company's board of directors.

Overall, the study showed that participants viewed male CEOs as more favorable representatives of the company in the public eye.

Source: *U.S. News and World Report,* www.usnews.com/usnews/biztech/articles/060508/8investment_bias.htm.

Arbitration in Employment Discrimination Disputes Arbitration is usually cheaper, quicker, and less public than litigation. Accustomed to using arbitration clauses in contracts with customers and suppliers, many employers also have begun placing arbitration clauses in employment contracts and personnel handbooks. These clauses require arbitration in employment discrimination disputes and with other employment controversies.

The Federal Arbitration Act (see Chapter 5) prefers arbitration over litigation, but that act may not apply to certain employment contracts. The EEOC has issued a policy statement concluding that "agreements that mandate binding arbitration of discrimination claims as a condition of employment are contrary to the fundamental principles" of antidiscrimination laws.

However, without specifically discussing the EEOC's policy statement, the Supreme Court has upheld arbitration clauses in certain employment discrimination cases. In *Circuit City Stores, Inc. v. Adams,* 532 U.S. 105 (2001), the Supreme Court decided that the Federal Arbitration Act did not prohibit enforceability of the following arbitration provision, which an employee had signed in his job application:

> I agree that I will settle any and all previously unasserted claims, disputes or controversies arising out of or relating to my application or candidacy for employment, employment and/or cessation of employment with Circuit City, *exclusively* by final and binding *arbitration* before a neutral arbitrator. By way of example only, such claims include claims under federal, state, and local statutory or common law, such as the Age Discrimination in Employment Act, Title VII of the Civil Rights Act of 1964, as amended, including the amendments of the Civil Rights Act of 1991, the Americans with Disabilities Act, the law of contract and the law of tort.

Congress may ultimately decide whether binding arbitration as a condition of working for an employer is an acceptable part of the employment contract. In the meantime, employers who wish to have employment disputes, including discrimination disputes, arbitrated should consider the following:

- Paying employees separately from the employment contract to sign arbitration agreements.
- Ensuring that arbitration agreements allow for the same range of remedies contained in the antidiscrimination laws.
- Allowing limited discovery in arbitration, which traditionally has no discovery process.
- Permitting employees to participate in selecting neutral, knowledgeable professional arbitrators instead of using an industry arbitration panel.
- Not requiring the employee to pay arbitration fees and costs.

These steps should go far toward eliminating many of the objections to the arbitration of employment discrimination disputes.

Proper arbitration agreements should continue to be considered as a business response to discrimination in employment disputes. Interestingly, at least one study has found that employees alleging discrimination win more often before arbitration panels than before juries and only two-thirds of the time.

Insuring against Employment Discrimination Claims

Employers commonly insure against many potential liabilities. However, the general liability policies carried by many businesses, which cover bodily injury and property damage, often do not insure against intentional torts. Intent is a key element in many employment discrimination claims. In addition, general policies may not cover the back pay or damages for mental anguish that many discrimination plaintiffs seek. As a result, employers are beginning to ask for and get employment practices liability insurance, a type of insurance aimed specifically at discrimination claims.

Even with the availability of the new insurance, not all types of employment discrimination can be insured against in every state. States like New York and California do not permit companies to insure against "intentional acts." Disparate treatment discrimination is an example of such an act. Similarly, some states do not permit companies to insure against punitive damages that can arise in intentional violations of Title VII. Managers should also be aware that what the new policies cover and what they exclude vary widely.

> Insurance policies are more likely to insure against disparate impact claims rather than disparate treatment claims. Do you understand why?

concept >> *summary*

Illegal Employment Practices

Unless bona fide occupational qualifications or business necessity can be proved, federal law prohibits recruiting, hiring, promoting, and other employment practices that involve disparate treatment or produce a disparate impact on the basis of:

Race or color.
National origin.
Religion.

Sex.
Test scores and educational requirements.
Height and weight.
Appearance.
Age.
Disabilities.

>> Key Terms

Affirmative action 666
Bona fide occupational
   qualifications (BFOQs) 646
Business necessity defense 649
Comparable worth 662
Disability 672
Disparate impact 648

Disparate treatment 648
Genetic Information
   Nondiscrimination Act
   (GINA) 674
Hostile work environment 659
Qualified disabled 672

Reasonable
   accommodation 673
Retaliation 649
Reverse discrimination 667
Section 1981 668
Seniority system 668
Sexual harassment 659

>> Review Questions and Problems

The Civil Rights Act of 1964

1. *General Provisions*

   Martel, a competent male secretary to the president of ICU, was fired because the new president of the company believed it is more appropriate to have a female secretary.

   (a) Has a violation of the law occurred?

   (b) Assume that a violation of the law has occurred and Martel decided to take an extended vacation after he was fired. Upon his return seven months later, Martel filed suit in federal district court against ICU, charging illegal discrimination under the Civil Rights Act of 1964. What remedies will be available to him under the act?

2. *Enforcement Procedures*

   Muscles-Are-You, Inc., a bodybuilding spa targeted primarily toward male bodybuilders, refused to hire a woman for the position of executive director. The spa's management stated that the executive director must have a "macho" image to relate well with the spa's customers. Discuss whether it is likely that the spa has violated Title VII.

3. *Discrimination on the Basis of Race or Color*

   Does Title VII prohibit employment discrimination against members of all races? Explain.

4. *Discrimination on the Basis of National Origin*

   Ace Tennis Co. hires only employees who speak English. Does this policy illegally discriminate against Hispanic job applicants who speak only Spanish? Discuss.

5. *Discrimination on the Basis of Religion*

   Ortega, an employee of ABC, Inc., recently joined a church that forbids working on Saturdays, Sundays, and Mondays. Ortega requested that his employer change his work schedule from eight-hour days, Monday through Friday, to ten-hour days, Tuesday through Friday. Ortega's request was refused because the employer is in operation only eight hours per day, five days a week. After a month during which Ortega failed to work on Mondays, he was fired. The employer stated that "only a full-time employee would be acceptable" for Ortega's position. What are Ortega's legal rights, if any?

6. *Discrimination on the Basis of Sex*

   A male supervisor at Star Company made repeated offensive sexual remarks to female employees. The employees complained to higher management, which ignored the complaints. If the company does not discharge or otherwise penalize the employee, has it violated Title VII? Discuss.

Employment Practices That May Be Challenged

7. *Questionnaires, Interviews, Testing, and Educational Requirements*

   Jennings Company, which manufactures sophisticated electronic equipment, hires its assembly employees on the basis of applicants' scores on a standardized mathematics aptitude test. It has been shown that those who score higher on the test almost always perform better on the job. However, it has also been demonstrated that the use of the test in hiring employees has the effect of excluding African Americans and other minority groups. Is this practice of the Jennings Company prohibited by the Civil Rights Act of 1964?

8. *Height and Weight Requirements*

    (a) An employer hires job applicants to wait tables in the Executive Heights Restaurant only if they are over 6 feet tall. Does this policy likely violate Title VII? Explain.

    (b) If a class of job applicants under 6 feet sues the employer, will it likely get compensatory and punitive damages? Explain.

9. *Appearance Requirements*

    Silicon Products requires all male employees to wear their hair "off the collar." Does this policy violate Title VII? Discuss.

10. *Affirmative Action Programs and Reverse Discrimination*

    Kartel, Inc., found that historically African Americans had been significantly underrepresented in its workforce. It decided to remedy the situation and place African Americans in 50 percent of all new job openings. Discuss the legality of Kartel's action.

11. *Seniority Systems*

    Are seniority systems in the workplace legal under Title VII if in fact they discriminate on the basis of gender or race? Explain.

Other Statutes and Discrimination in Employment

12. *Civil Rights Act of 1866*

    When is it an advantage for a plaintiff to use Section 1981 as the basis for discrimination litigation as contrasted with using Title VII?

13. *Discrimination on the Basis of Age*

    Cantrell, the controller of Xylec's, Inc., was forced to retire at age 58 due to a general company policy. Although Cantrell has a company pension of $50,000 per year, she believes that her lifestyle will soon be hampered due to inflation, since the pension provides for no cost-of-living increases. What are Cantrell's rights, if any?

14. *Discrimination on the Basis of Disabilities*

    Ralph is a systems analyst for the Silicon Corporation, a major defense contractor. When Ralph's co-workers learn that he has AIDS, six of them quit work immediately. Fearing that additional resignations will delay production, the company discharges Ralph. Discuss whether or not the company acted legally.

15. *Genetic Discrimination*

    Amy learns that she has the "breast cancer gene." Devastated, she shares the news with her supervisor. A few days later, Amy receives a harsh employment evaluation—the first of her career—criticizing her handling of a client matter. Two weeks later, Amy is fired. Amy cannot understand how she went from being a model employee with strong performance reviews to unemployed in such a short time. Does she have any claim against her employer?

16. *Discrimination in Getting and Keeping Health Insurance*

    Why does Title VII not apply to preventing discrimination in the getting and keeping of health insurance?

17. *Other Federal Legislation*

    Do employers have an obligation to negotiate with groups of employees over issues of discrimination? Explain.

18. *State Antidiscrimination Laws*

    Explain how state antidiscrimination laws protect workers in situations where federal laws do not.

19. *Trends in Employment Discrimination and Litigation*

    Can arbitration agreements be used to keep employees from litigating discrimination issues? Discuss.

business >> *discussions*

1. When Maria Suarez got her new job, she was happy. As an oil rigger, she would make enough money to support herself and her two children. But after a week of working with a primarily male crew, her happiness was gone. Her co-workers were the reason. At first the men made unwelcome comments about her body. Then sexual graffiti mentioning her name appeared. When she came to work one morning a nude female picture was pinned to one of the rigs. Her name had been scrawled across the bottom. Maria complained to the crew foreman, who referred her to the site manager. "Let's ignore it for a while," he told Maria. "It's just good fun. The men are testing you. You've got to fit in."

What are Maria's legal rights in this situation?
What would you do if you were the site manager?
Do you think Maria should just try to "fit in"?

2. Delivery Quik, Inc., delivers packages to small retail stores from a central distribution point in a major metropolitan area. Drivers both load and unload their packages, some of which weigh close to 100 pounds. Although equipment helps the drivers in their tasks, there is still considerable lifting necessary. Delivery Quik has a policy that drivers must stand at least 6 feet tall and weigh no less than 180 pounds. All drivers must retire at age 45 and have at least a high school education.

Does the height, weight, age, and education policy discriminate illegally?
How would you change the policy?
If your customers prefer male drivers, does their preference mean that the company can hire only males as drivers?

Chapter 21. Employment Laws

21

Employment Laws

☐ Learning Objectives

In this chapter you will learn:

21-1. To identify major employment laws and their significance for employers and employees.

21-2. To explain the scope and limits of the employment-at-will doctrine.

21-3. To understand the limits of privacy in the workplace and the role of workers' compensation laws.

21-4. To discuss ways an employer should document employee performance in anticipation of potential employee litigation.

I n addition to the employment discrimination laws detailed in Chapter 20, there are many other employment laws pertaining to the employer–employee relationship. This chapter surveys a number of important employment laws. As you read, consider how these laws contribute to the employment law framework in the United States. Most of the laws discussed are federal laws. However, it is important to understand that states and local governments may also have employment laws. One major example of this is workers' compensation laws. Each state has its own laws addressing accidental workplace injuries. Lastly, in light of the practical reality of defending against employee lawsuits, this chapter suggests ways that employers should document employee performance, so that they are prepared for potential litigation by current and former employees.

>> *sidebar* 21.1

Fair Labor Standards Act: To Pay or Not to Pay Overtime?

The number of FLSA cases is on the rise. Here are points to consider regarding overtime pay to be in compliance with the law:

- **Hourly or Salaried?** It is not uncommon for an employer to pay a salary to an employee who should be paid hourly. "Executive employees" may be paid a salary of at least $455 per week *if* (1) the employee's primary duty is managing the enterprise, or managing a customarily recognized department or subdivision of the enterprise; (2) the employee must customarily and regularly direct the work of at least two or more other full-time employees or their equivalent; (3) the employee must have the authority to hire or fire other employees, or the employee's suggestions and recommendations as to the hiring, firing, advancement, promotion, or any other change of status of other employees must be given particular weight.

- **Employee or Independent Contractor?** Because the FLSA requires employers to pay non-exempt employees overtime compensation for hours worked in excess of 40 hours per week, employers are sometimes tempted to classify these workers as "independent contractors" to avoid overtime pay.

Although each individual's damages may not be substantial, an employer may face a FLSA collective action involving many workers who are misclassified. Workers are increasingly aware of their rights under wage and hour laws, especially when it comes to overtime pay.

For more information see the U.S. Department of Labor, Wage and Hour Division, *FairPay Overtime Initiative,* available at www.dol.gov/whd/regs/compliance/fairpay/.

>> Employment Laws

A complete review of all laws and regulations that impact how employers and employees interact is beyond our scope. The following sections address some of these laws and examine some current issues arising in many companies. Table 21.1 provides a list of some of the major employment laws and the purpose of each. Chapter 20 focused on the first category of laws, those addressing discrimination. This chapter discusses a range of employment laws from the Fair Labor Standards Act to retirement and pension laws. Chapter 22 then details labor laws, the last category in the table.

Employment laws are among the most emotionally and politically charged topics. The reason tempers flare and even violence happens is that these laws go to the heart of how business makes a profit and how people make a living.

1. MINIMUM WAGES AND MAXIMUM HOURS

The federal government regulates wages and hours through the **Fair Labor Standards Act (FLSA).** Originally enacted in 1938, the FLSA establishes a minimum wage, overtime pay, record-keeping requirements, and child labor standards. The FLSA has been repeatedly amended to keep it up to date. For example, effective May 25, 2007, the FLSA was amended to increase the federal minimum wage in three steps:

- To $5.85 per hour effective July 24, 2007.
- To $6.55 per hour effective July 24, 2008.
- To $7.25 per hour effective July 24, 2009.

table 21.1 >> Summary of Major Federal Employment Laws

Law	Purpose
Civil Rights Acts, Equal Employment Opportunity Act, Pregnancy Discrimination Act, Americans with Disabilities Act, Age Discrimination in Employment Act, and Genetic Nondiscrimination Act	• Provide national policy governing employment discrimination.
Fair Labor Standards Act (FLSA)	• Provides hourly minimum wage and maximum number of hours before overtime is owed. • Provides restrictions on child labor.
Worker Adjustment and Retraining Notification Act (WARN Act)	• Provides restrictions on plant closings and mass layoffs.
Family Medical Leave Act (FMLA)	• Provides unpaid leave to care for a newborn child, an adopted child, to care for a family member, or for serious health conditions.
Uniformed Services Employment and Reemployment Rights Act (USERRA)	• Provides reemployment rights after performing uniformed service. • Provides those serving in the military the right to be free from discrimination and retaliation based on uniformed service.
Occupational Safety and Health Act (OSHA)	• Provides standards for a safe and healthy working environment.
Social Security Act	• Provides unemployment compensation. • Provides disability benefits.
Employment Retirement Income Security Act (ERISA)	• Provides requirements for private pension plans.
Electronic Communications Privacy Act	• Provides standards to protect privacy.
Railway Labor Act, Norris-LaGuardia Act, Wagner Act, Taft-Hartley Act, and Landrum-Griffin Act	• Provide national policy for governing the union-management relationship.

Additionally, overtime pay at a rate of not less than one and one-half times the employee's regular rate of pay is required after 40 hours of work in a workweek. For example, if an employee earns $8 an hour, the overtime pay must be at least $12 per hour. Employers of "tipped employees" must pay a cash wage of at least $2.13 per hour if they claim a tip credit against their minimum wage obligation. If the employee's tips combined with the cash wage do not meet the minimum hourly wage, the employer must make up the difference (with certain conditions). Many states provide for minimum wages higher than the federal rate. Employers are legally required to pay whichever minimum wage is higher. The FLSA does not require breaks or meal periods to be given to workers. Some states, however, may require breaks or meal periods.

The highest state minimum wages: Washington at $8.02; California and Massachusetts at $8.00 per hour.

Employers should use care to properly classify workers as either "employees" or "independent contractors."

>> *sidebar* 21.2

Internship Programs under the FLSA

Individuals who participate in "for-profit" private sector internships or training programs may do so without compensation. Under what circumstances should interns be paid? According to the Department of Labor, six criteria must be applied when making the determination:

1. The internship, even though it includes actual operation of the facilities of the employer, is similar to training which would be given in an educational environment.
2. The internship experience is for the benefit of the intern.
3. The intern does not displace regular employees, but works under close supervision of existing staff.
4. The employer that provides the training derives no immediate advantage from the activities of the intern; and on occasion its operations may actually be impeded.
5. The intern is not necessarily entitled to a job at the conclusion of the internship .
6. The employer and the intern understand that the intern is not entitled to wages for the time spent in the internship.

If all of the factors listed above are met, an employment relationship *does not exist* under the FLSA, and the minimum wage and overtime provisions *do not apply* to the intern.

Source: U.S. Department of Labor, Wage and Hour Division, *Fact Sheet #71: Internship Programs Under the Fair Labor Standards Act*, April 2010, available at www.dol.gov/whd/regs/compliance/whdfs71.pdf.

Although a minimum wage and a maximum workweek of 40 hours before overtime is owed seems straightforward, there are many exceptions and factual situations complicating the general rules. In Case 21.1, the Supreme Court addresses the legal issue of how an employer is to count work hours. As you read the case, note that the courts count minutes to determine the overall amount in this "donning and doffing" case. In 2008, a Wisconsin federal court certified a similar donning/doffing class-action against Kraft Foods.

 case **21.1** >>

IBP, INC. v. ALVAREZ
546 U.S. 21 (2005)

This case actually is the consolidation of two cases. At issue in both cases is the calculation of the workday for the purposes of distinguishing between regular and overtime hours under the Fair Labor Standards Act (FLSA). Both cases involve meat processing companies and whether the employer must count the time workers spend putting on (donning) and taking off (doffing) required protective gear as a part of the workday. Also at issue are the minutes the workers walk from the locker room area to the production area. The Court analyzes the Fair Labor Standards Act and its amendment. Specifically, the Court notes that the Portal-to-Portal Act of 1947 emphasizes that the workday begins when workers engage in their principal activities. This law attempted to make it clear that employers are not

[continued]

liable to pay workers for the time they spend walking on the employers' property from a time clock to the actual workplace or for any time spent in preliminary or postliminary activities to the workers' principal working activities.

STEVENS. J.: . . . IBP, Inc. (IBP), is a large producer of fresh beef, pork, and related products. . . . All production workers must wear outer garments, hardhats, hairnets, earplugs, gloves, sleeves, aprons, leggings, and boots. Many of them, particularly those who use knives, must also wear a variety of protective equipment for their hands, arms, torsos, and legs; this gear includes chain-link metal aprons, vests, Plexiglass armguards, and special gloves. IBP requires its employees to store their equipment and tools in company locker rooms, where most of them don their protective gear.

Production workers' pay is based on the time spent cutting and bagging meat. Pay begins with the first piece of meat and ends with the last piece of meat. Since 1998, however, IBP has also paid for four minutes of clothes-changing time. In 1999, respondents, IBP employees, filed this class action to recover compensation for preproduction and postproduction work, including the time spent donning and doffing protective gear and walking between the locker rooms and the production floor before and after their assigned shifts.

After a lengthy bench trial, the District Court for the Eastern District of Washington held that donning and doffing of protective gear that was unique to the jobs at issue were compensable under the FLSA because they were integral and indispensable to the work of the employees who wore such equipment. Moreover, consistent with the continuous workday rule, the District Court concluded that, for those employees required to don and doff unique protective gear, the walking time between the locker room and the production floor was also compensable because it occurs during the workday. . . .

The District Court proceeded to apply these legal conclusions in making detailed factual findings with regard to the different groups of employees. For example, the District Court found that, under its view of what was covered by the FLSA, processing division knife users were entitled to compensation for between 12 and 14 minutes of preproduction and postproduction work, including 3.3 to 4.4 minutes of walking time. The Court of Appeals agreed with the District Court's ultimate conclusions on these issues. . . .

IBP does not challenge the holding below that . . . the donning and doffing of unique protective gear are "principal activities" under the Portal-to-Portal Act. . . . Thus,

the only question for us to decide is whether the Court of Appeals correctly rejected IBP's contention that the walking between the locker rooms and the production areas is excluded from FLSA coverage by the Portal-to-Portal Act. . . .

IBP emphasizes that our decision in *Anderson v. Mt. Clemens Pottery Co.,* 66 S. Ct. 1187, may well have been the proximate cause of the enactment of the Portal-to-Portal Act. In that case we held that the FLSA mandated compensation for the time that employees spent walking from time clocks located near the plant entrance to their respective places of work prior to the start of their productive labor. In IBP's view, Congress's forceful repudiation of that holding reflects a purpose to exclude what IBP regards as the quite similar walking time spent by respondents before and after their work slaughtering cattle and processing meat. Even if there is ambiguity in the statute, we should construe it to effectuate that important purpose.

This argument is also unpersuasive. There is a critical difference between the walking at issue in *Anderson* and the walking at issue in this case. In *Anderson* the walking preceded the employees' principal activity; it occurred before the workday began. The relevant walking in this case occurs after the workday begins and before it ends. Only if we were to endorse IBP's novel submission that an activity can be sufficiently "principal" to be compensable, but not sufficiently so to start the workday, would this case be comparable to *Anderson*. . . .

For the foregoing reasons, we hold that . . . any walking time that occurs after the beginning of the employee's first principal activity and before the end of the employee's last principal activity . . . is covered by the FLSA.

Barber Foods, Inc. (Barber), operates a poultry processing plant in Portland, Maine, that employs about 300 production workers. These employees operate six production lines and perform a variety of tasks that require different combinations of protective clothing. They are paid by the hour from the time they punch in to computerized time clocks located at the entrances to the production floor.

Petitioners are Barber employees and former employees who brought this action to recover compensation for alleged unrecorded work covered by the FLSA. Specifically, they claimed that Barber's failure to compensate them for (a) donning and doffing required protective gear and (b) the attendant walking and waiting violated the statute.

After extensive discovery, the Magistrate Judge issued a comprehensive opinion analyzing the facts

[continued]

in detail, and recommending the entry of partial summary judgment in favor of Barber. That opinion, which was later adopted by the District Court for Maine, included two critical rulings.

First, the Magistrate held that "the donning and doffing of clothing and equipment required by the defendant or by government regulation, as opposed to clothing and equipment which employees choose to wear or use at their option, is an integral part of the plaintiffs' work [and therefore are] not excluded from compensation under the Portal-to-Portal Act as preliminary or postliminary activities."

Second, the Magistrate rejected petitioners' claims for compensation for the time spent before obtaining their clothing and equipment. Such time, in the Magistrate's view, "could [not] reasonably be construed to be an integral part of employees' work activities any more than walking to the cage from which hairnets and earplugs are dispensed. . . ." Accordingly, Barber was "entitled to summary judgment on any claims based on time spent walking from the plant entrances to an employee's workstation, locker, time clock or site where clothing and equipment required to be worn on the job is to be obtained and any claims based on time spent waiting to punch in or out for such clothing or equipment." . . .

[The Court then reviews the findings of the District Court, which held for Barber, and the 1st Court of Appeals, which affirmed, saying that Barber is not responsible to pay for and count toward the FLSA maximum hours the time the workers spent waiting to put on protective gear, the time these workers spent actually putting on the protective gear, and the time these workers spent walking to the actual work site. Based on the holding in *IBP,* the Court quickly decided the 1st Circuit was wrong with respect to the time workers spent donning and doffing protective gear and walking to and from the locker room and workplace. The Court then concentrates on the issue of how to handle the time workers might spend waiting to get their protective gear.]

Petitioners also argued in the Court of Appeals that the waiting time associated with the donning and doffing of clothes was compensable. The Court of Appeals disagreed, holding that the waiting time qualified as a "preliminary or postliminary activity" and thus was excluded from FLSA coverage by the Portal-to-Portal Act. Our analysis . . . demonstrates that the Court of Appeals was incorrect with regard to the predoffing waiting time. Because doffing gear that is "integral and indispensable" to employees' work is a "principal activity" under the statute, the continuous workday rule mandates that time spent waiting to doff is not affected by the Portal-to-Portal Act and is instead covered by the FLSA.

The time spent waiting to don—time that elapses before the principal activity of donning integral and indispensable gear—presents the quite different question whether it should have the effect of advancing the time when the work-day begins. Barber argues that such predonning waiting time is explicitly covered by the Portal-to-Portal Act, which, as noted above, excludes "activities which are preliminary to or postliminary to [a] principal activity or activities" from the scope of the FLSA.

By contrast, petitioners maintain that the predonning waiting time is "integral and indispensable" to the "principal activity" of donning, and is therefore itself a principal activity. However, unlike the donning of certain types of protective gear, which is always essential if the worker is to do his job, the waiting may or may not be necessary in particular situations or for every employee. It is certainly not "integral and indispensable" in the same sense that the donning is. It does, however, always comfortably qualify as a "preliminary" activity.

We thus do not agree with petitioners that the predonning waiting time at issue in this case is a "principal activity". . . . As Barber points out, the fact that certain preshift activities are necessary for employees to engage in their principal activities does not mean that those preshift activities are "integral and indispensable" to a "principal activity." . . . For example, walking from a time clock near the factory gate to a workstation is certainly necessary for employees to begin their work, but it is indisputable that the Portal-to-Portal Act evinces Congress's intent to repudiate *Anderson's* holding that such walking time was compensable under the FLSA. We discern no limiting principle that would allow us to conclude that the waiting time in dispute here is a "principal activity," without also leading to the logical (but untenable) conclusion that the walking time at issue in *Anderson* would be a "principal activity" and would thus be unaffected by the Portal-to-Portal Act. . . .

In short, we are not persuaded that such waiting—which in this case is two steps removed from the productive activity on the assembly line—is "integral and indispensable" to a "principal activity" that identifies the time when the continuous workday begins. . . .

For the reasons stated above, we affirm the judgment of the Court of Appeals for the Ninth Circuit. We affirm in part and reverse in part the judgment of the Court of Appeals for the First Circuit, and we remand the case for further proceedings consistent with this opinion.

So ordered.

[continued]

>> CASE QUESTIONS

1. What is the split between the circuit courts that this case attempts to resolve?
2. Why are companies willing to litigate the issue of what counts and doesn't count as workday activities when so few minutes are likely involved?
3. What three holdings does the Court announce in this case?

The FLSA also sets wage, hours worked, and safety requirements for minors (individuals under age 18). The rules vary depending upon the particular age of the minor and the particular job involved. As a general rule, the FLSA sets 14 years of age as the minimum age for employment, and limits the number of hours worked by minors under the age of 16. In 2008, the FLSA was amended to increase penalties against employers who violate child labor laws. The penalties increased from $11,000 to $50,000 for each FLSA violation leading to the serious injury or death of a child worker. The increased fines are subject to doubling for repeated or willful violations.

>> *sidebar* 21.3

Break Time for Nursing Moms

The FLSA now requires break time for nursing mothers. Employers are required to provide "reasonable break time for an employee to express breast milk for her nursing child for 1 year after the child's birth each time such employee has need to express the milk."

Employers are also required to provide a functional space for expressing breast milk that is "shielded from view and free from intrusion from co-workers and the public." A bathroom, even a private one, is not a permissible location under the FLSA.

Employers with fewer than 50 employees are not subject to the FLSA break time requirement *if* compliance with the provision would impose an undue hardship.

Employers are not required to compensate nursing mothers for breaks taken for the purpose of expressing milk. However, if the employer already provides compensated breaks, an employee who uses that break time to express milk must be compensated in the same way that other employees are compensated for break time.

Source: U.S. Department of Labor, Wage and Hour Division, *Fact Sheet #73 Break Time for Nursing Mothers under the FLSA*, December 2010, available at www.dol.gov/whd/regs/compliance/whdfs73.htm.

 case **21.2** >>

KASTEN v. SAINT-GOBAIN PERFORMANCE PLASTICS CORP.
53 U.S. ___ (2011)

Petitioner Kasten brought an antiretaliation suit against his former employer, respondent (Saint-Gobain), under the Fair Labor Standards Act of 1938 (Act), which provides minimum wage, maximum hour, and overtime pay rules; and which forbids employers "to discharge . . . any employee because such employee

[continued]

has filed any complaint" alleging a violation of the Act, 29 U. S. C. §215(a)(3). In a related suit, the District Court found that Saint-Gobain violated the Act by placing timeclocks in a location that prevented workers from receiving credit for the time they spent donning and doffing work related protective gear.

In this suit Kasten claims that he was discharged because he orally complained to company officials about the timeclocks. The District Court granted Saint-Gobain summary judgment, concluding that the Act's antiretaliation provision did not cover oral complaints. The Seventh Circuit affirmed. Justice Breyer delivered the opinion of the Court in which Chief Justice Roberts, and Justices Kennedy, Ginsburg, Alito and Sotomayor joined. Justice Scalia filed a dissenting opinion in which Justice Thomas joined in part. Justice Kagan took no part in the consideration or decision of the case.

BREYER, J.: The Fair Labor Standards Act of 1938 (Act) sets forth employment rules concerning minimum wages, maximum hours, and overtime pay. 52 Stat. 1060, 29 U. S. C. §201 *et seq.* The Act contains an antiretaliation provision that forbids employers

> "to discharge or in any other manner discriminate against any employee because such employee has *filed any complaint* or instituted or caused to be instituted any proceeding under or related to [the Act], or has testified or is about to testify in such proceeding, or has served or is about to serve on an industry committee." §215(a)(3) (emphasis added).

We must decide whether the statutory term "filed any complaint" includes oral as well as written complaints within its scope. We conclude that it does.

I The petitioner, Kevin Kasten, brought this antiretaliation lawsuit against his former employer, Saint-Gobain Performance Plastics Corporation. Kasten says that where Kasten and other workers put on (and take off) their work-related protective gear and the area where they carry out their assigned tasks. That location prevented workers from receiving credit for the time they spent putting on and taking off their work clothes—contrary to the Act's requirements. In a related suit the District Court agreed with Kasten, finding that Saint-Gobain's "practice of not compensating . . . for time spent donning and doffing certain required protective gear and walking to work areas" violated the Act. *Kasten v. Saint-Gobain Performance Plastics Corp.*, 556 F. Supp. 2d 941, 954 (WD Wis. 2008). In this suit Kasten claims unlawful retaliation. He says that Saint-Gobain discharged him because he orally complained to Saint-Gobain officials about the timeclocks.

In particular, Kasten says that he repeatedly called the unlawful timeclock location to Saint-Gobain's attention— in accordance with Saint-Gobain's internal grievance resolution procedure. See Brief for Petitioner 4 (quoting Saint-Gobain's Code of Ethics and Business Conduct as imposing upon every employee "the responsibility to report . . . suspected violations of . . . any applicable law of which he or she becomes aware"); *id.,* at 4–5 (quoting Saint-Gobain's Employee Policy Handbook as instructing employees with "questions, complaints, and problems" to "[c]ontact" their "supervisor[s] immediately" and if necessary "take the issue to the next level of management," then to the "local Human Resources Manager," then to "Human Resources" personnel at the "Regional" or "Headquarters" level).

Kasten adds that he "raised a concern" with his shift supervisor that "it was illegal for the time clocks to be where they were" because of Saint-Gobain's exclusion of "the time you come in and start doing stuff"; he told a human resources employee that "if they were to get challenged on" the location in court, "they would lose"; he told his lead operator that the location was illegal and that he "was thinking about starting a lawsuit about the placement of the time clocks"; and he told the human resources manager and the operations manager that he thought the location was illegal and that the company would "lose" in court. Record in No. 3:07–cv–00686–bbc (WD Wis.), Doc.87–3, pp. 31–34 (deposition of Kevin Kasten). This activity, Kasten concludes, led the company to discipline him and, in December 2006, to dismiss him.

Saint-Gobain presents a different version of events. It denies that Kasten made any significant complaint about the timeclock location. And it says that it dismissed Kasten simply because Kasten, after being repeatedly warned, failed to record his comings and goings on the timeclock.

For present purposes we accept Kasten's version of these contested events as valid. See *Scott* v. *Harris,* 550 U. S. 372, 380 (2007). That is because the District Court entered summary judgment in Saint-Gobain's favor. . . . Kasten sought certiorari. And in light of conflict among the Circuits as to whether an oral complaint is protected, we granted Kasten's petition. . . . The sole question presented is whether "an oral complaint of a violation of the Fair Labor Standards Act" is "protected conduct under the [Act's] anti-retaliation provision." Pet. for Cert. i. The Act protects employees who have "filed any complaint," 29 U. S. C. §215(a)(3), and interpretation of this phrase "depends upon reading the whole statutory text, considering the purpose and context of the statute, and consulting any precedents or authorities that inform the analysis,"

[continued]

Dolan v. *Postal Service,* 546 U. S. 481, 486 (2006). This analysis leads us to conclude that the language of the provision, considered in isolation, may be open to competing interpretations. But considering the provision in conjunction with the purpose and context leads us to conclude that only one interpretation is permissible. We begin with the text of the statute. The word "filed" has different relevant meanings in different contexts. . . .The bottom line is that the text, taken alone, cannot provide a conclusive answer to our interpretive question. The phrase "filed any complaint" might, or might not, encompass oral complaints. We must look further. . . .

Why would Congress want to limit the enforcement scheme's effectiveness by inhibiting use of the Act's complaint procedure by those who would find it difficult to reduce their complaints to writing, particularly illiterate, less educated, or overworked workers? . . . In the years prior to the passage of the Act, illiteracy rates were particularly high among the poor. . . . To limit the scope of the antiretaliation provision to the filing of written complaints would also take needed flexibility from those charged with the Act's enforcement. It could prevent Government agencies from using hotlines, interviews, and other oral methods of receiving complaints. . . . To fall within the scope of the antiretaliation provision, a complaint must be sufficiently clear and detailed for a reasonable employer to understand it, in light of both content and context, as an assertion of rights protected by the statute and a call for their protection. This standard can be met, however, by oral complaints, as well as by written ones. . . .

Second, given Congress' delegation of enforcement powers to federal administrative agencies, we also give a degree of weight to their views about the meaning of this enforcement language. . . . The Secretary of Labor has consistently held the view that the words "filed any complaint" cover oral, as well as written, complaints. . . . The EEOC has set forth a similar view in its Compliance Manual . . . These agency views are reasonable. They are consistent with the Act. . . . We conclude that the Seventh Circuit erred in determining that oral complaints cannot fall within the scope of the phrase "filed any complaint" in the Act's antiretaliation provision. We leave it to the lower courts to decide whether Kasten will be able to satisfy the Act's notice requirement. We vacate the Circuit's judgment and remand the case for further proceedings consistent with this opinion.

Reversed and remanded.

>> CASE QUESTIONS

1. What was the question before the Court?
2. What is the basis for the Court's holding?
3. Based on the facts in the case, what will Kasten need to prove his claim on remand?

2. THE WARN ACT

The Worker Adjustment and Retraining Notification Act (WARN) became law in 1989. Known as the **WARN Act,** this law requires employers to provide notice of plant closings and mass layoffs. This notice must be given in writing and be delivered at least 60 days prior to closing a work site or conducting mass layoffs. The WARN notice must be given to employees or their bargaining representatives (such as a union), the state's dislocated worker unit, and the elected chief officer of the local government impacted.

The WARN notice is required of employers with 100 or more employees. Workers who work less than half-time are not counted to determine this threshold level of 100. Employees entitled to receive the WARN notice include

The WARN notice allows impacted employees and communities some time to prepare for the negative impact of a plant closing or mass layoff.

694   **PART 5**   The Employer-Employee Relationship

According to the AFL-CIO, "Layoffs continue at a pace of 1.5 million impacted workers every year and almost half a million have been idled by mass layoffs in the first three months" of 2008.

those who are hourly, salaried, supervisory, and managerial. In essence all workers, even part-time, are entitled to receive the notice.

The WARN notice covers plant closings and mass layoffs involving loss of employment. Covered plant closings are defined as the shutting of an employment site resulting in a loss of employment of 50 or more employees during any 30-day period. A mass layoff requires the WARN notice if 500 or more employees lose their jobs in a 30-day period. This notice also must be given if between 50 and 499 employees are laid off if the number terminated make up at least 33 percent of the employer's workforce. Although they are entitled to receive any applicable WARN notice, less than half-time employees are not counted to reach the requirement of 50 for plant closings or the thresholds for mass layoffs. A loss of employment includes (1) termination of employment, (2) layoff exceeding 6 months, or (3) a reduction in an employee's work time of more than 50 percent in each month for six months.

The WARN notice must be provided even if the numbers in the preceding paragraph are not satisfied if there are two or more plant closings or mass layoffs in a 90-day period that when taken together satisfy the threshold numbers. The sale of a business may or may not require the WARN notice. Any required notice prior to the sale being completed is the responsibility of the seller. The buyer of the business assumes this responsibility after the date of the closing.

The penalty for failure to comply with the WARN notice is back pay to employees to cover the required 60-day period. Each day of the 60-day period that an employer fails to provide written notice to the local government can result in a $500 fine.

When an employer is replacing striking employees in large numbers, the WARN notice is not required. Employers may avoid the need to provide 60-day notice if it can show its business is faltering and to give notice of a plant closing would adversely impact its ability to get financing. Also, unforeseen business circumstances may justify a less than 60-day WARN notice for either plant closing or layoffs. Finally, natural disasters, such as storms, floods, and earthquakes, may justify a less than 60-day notice for a plant closing or mass layoff.

3. THE FAMILY AND MEDICAL LEAVE ACT

"With the Family Medical Leave Act, the United States at last joined more than 150 other countries in guaranteeing workers some time off when a baby is born or a family member is sick."

—President Bill Clinton in *My Life*

On February 5, 1993, Bill Clinton signed his first piece of legislation as president. This was the **Family and Medical Leave Act (FMLA).** While the details of this law have been called burdensome to business, it has provided eligible employees who work for covered employers to take up to 12 weeks of unpaid leave during any 12-month period if one or more of the following events occur:

• Birth and care of a newborn child of the employee.

• Placement with employee of a son or daughter for adoption or foster care.

• Care of an immediate family member with a serious health condition.

• Employee is unable to work due to a serious health condition.

The provisions relating to birth, adoption, and foster care apply to both female and male employees. Increasingly, men are opting to take leave to care for children. See Sidebar 21.4 for FMLA facts and statistics. An immediate family member is a spouse, minor child, or parent of the employee. Under the FMLA, the employee's parents in law do not qualify as an immediate family member. And the employee's children who are over 18 years old do not qualify as an immediate family member, unless that child is incapable of self-care due to a mental or physical disability that limits one or more of the major life activities as defined in the Americans with Disabilities Act. For a more thorough discussion of the ADA, see Chapter 20. In 2008, the FMLA was expanded to include leave related to a family member's military service. The law grants employees up to 26 weeks of unpaid leave to care for a family member in the military who has incurred a serious illness or injury, and allows employees to take their current 12-week FMLA leave entitlement "for any qualifying exigency" arising out of the fact that a family member is on or has been notified that he or she is being called to active duty in support of a contingency operation. The Department of Labor has the responsibility of issuing regulations related to these changes, including defining "any qualifying exigency."

The parents of a 23-year-old injured so severely in an accident that he is paralyzed are eligible for family medical leave.

On June 23, 2010, the Department of Labor announced that benefits available to parents of newborns and newly adopted children under the FMLA may apply to same-sex couples.

>> sidebar 21.4

FMLA: Facts and Statistics

>> WHO TAKES FMLA LEAVE?

About 62 percent of workers qualify to take leave under the FMLA.
Over 50 million people have taken FMLA leave.

>> WHY DO PEOPLE TAKE FMLA LEAVE?

To care for their own serious illness: 52 percent.
To care for a seriously ill family member: 31 percent.
To take care of a new child: 26 percent (29 percent women and 23 percent men).

>> HOW HAS FMLA IMPACTED EMPLOYERS?

98 percent of eligible employees return to work for the same employer after returning from FMLA leave.

89 percent of covered businesses report that the FMLA has a neutral or positive effect on employee morale.

90 percent of covered businesses reported that the FMLA had either a neutral or positive effect on business profitability.

Sources: *U.S. Department* of Labor's 2000 Report *Balancing the Needs of Families and Employers: Family and Medical Leave Surveys 2000 Update*; Nicole Casta's "Highlights of the 2000 U.S. Department of Labor Report: Balancing the Needs of Families and Employers: Family and Medical Leave Surveys," and the National Partnership for Women & Families' 2005 Report "Facts about the FMLA: What Does It Do, Who Uses It, and How."

Covered employers are those who employ 50 or more employees for each working day of 20 or more calendar weeks during either the current or preceding year. Eligible employees have worked for their employer for at least 12 months and have worked at least 1,250 hours during the preceding 12 months. The 12-month work period does not have to be consecutive

To satisfy the requirement that the employer have 50 employees, all persons who work for the employer within 75 miles can be counted.

months. An employee satisfies this requirement so long as that employee has worked for the employer at least a total of 12 months. Furthermore, eligible employees must work at a location where at least 50 employees are employed.

The FMLA places a number of responsibilities on the employer. These responsibilities include notifying the employees that they are eligible for family medical leave and designating in writing when the employee has requested such leave. The employer may request a medical certification that a qualifying event has occurred in the employee's life, but the employer is not entitled to review the actual medical records of the employee.

>> *sidebar* 21.5

EEOC: Best Practices Recommendations on Work/Family Balance

As part of an ongoing attempt to avoid discrimination against workers with caregiving responsibilities, sometimes called "family responsibilities discrimination," the EEOC issued a document on best practices. Those recommendations include the following:

- Be aware of and train managers about the legal obligations that may impact decisions about the treatment of workers with caregiving responsibilities.
- Develop, disseminate, and enforce a strong EEO policy that clearly addresses the types of conduct that might constitute unlawful discrimination.
- Ensure that managers at all levels are aware of and comply with the organization's work-life policies.
- Respond to complaints of caregiver discrimination efficiently and effectively.
- Protect against retaliation.

The document also encourages employers to develop "flexible work policies," which studies have demonstrated have a "positive impact on employee engagement organizational productivity and profitability."

Case to Consider: *Chadwick v. Wellpoint, Inc.* (1st Cir. 2009), in which the court held that "unlawful sex discrimination occurs when an employer takes an adverse job action on the assumption that a woman, because she is a woman, will neglect her job responsibilities in favor of her presumed childcare responsibilities." The plaintiff in *Chadwick* was the mother of young triplets. She was passed over for promotion and the position was given to a woman with two older children. The First Circuit held that the district court erred in granting summary judgment in favor of the employer and, accordingly reversed and remanded the case for further proceedings.

Source: EEOC, *Employer Best Practices for Workers with Caregiving Responsibilities*, 2009, available at www.eeoc.gov/policy/docs/caregiver-best-practices.html.

Once family medical leave is granted, the employer must keep the employee's job available for when the leave is up and the employee returns to work. In essence, the employee who qualifies for family medical leave is not supposed to be disadvantaged by the fact that the leave was taken. For example, if the employer gives a bonus for perfect attendance, the employee on family medical leave should be awarded this bonus, assuming perfect attendance other than the leave period. If a bonus is based on the amount of sales, the FMLA does not require the employer to award sales that the employee would have made if not on family medical leave.

Employees who believe they have been denied their rights under the FMLA can sue the employer in federal district court for equitable and monetary damages. Such an employee may sue for reinstatement or may seek damages or both.

>> *sidebar* 21.6

Are States Immune from Certain FMLA Claims?

>> CASE TO WATCH: *COLEMAN V. MARYLAND COURT OF APPEALS*

On June 27, 2011, the U.S. Supreme Court granted certiorari in this case to decide whether a State can be sued under the Family Medical Leave Act where the employee is seeking leave due to his or her own serious health condition.

> *Key Facts:* Daniel Coleman was an employee of the Maryland Court of Appeals for six years. In August 2007, he sent a letter requesting sick leave for a documented medical condition. The request was denied and Mr. Coleman was given an ultimatum: resign or be terminated. In this complaint, Mr. Coleman claimed that his FMLA leave was denied in retaliation for his complaints of wrongdoing in the office.

> *Procedural History:* The District Court granted defendants' motion to dismiss, including plaintiffs'

FMLA claims, holding that "the FMLA's self-care provisions did not validly abrogate Eleventh Amendment immunity." The Fourth Circuit affirmed.

Explanation: The Eleventh Amendment of the U.S. Constitution bars claims in federal court against an unconsenting state and any governmental units that are arms of the state unless Congress has abrogated immunity. To do so, Congress must make clear its intent to abrogate and must act in accordance with a valid exercise of power. The Supreme Court's decision should address whether a State can be sued under the FMLA in cases involving self-care.

For ongoing information about this case and official documents, see www.scotusblog.com/case-files/cases/coleman-v-maryland-court-of-appeals/.

---

4. UNIFORMED SERVICES EMPLOYMENT AND REEMPLOYMENT RIGHTS ACT

The **Uniformed Services Employment and Reemployment Rights Act (USERRA)** protects the rights of individuals who voluntarily or involuntarily leave employment positions to undertake military service or certain types of service in the National Disaster Medical System. Specifically, USERRA provides reemployment rights following a period of service if:

- The individual held a civilian job
- The employee informed the employer that he/she was leaving the job for service in the uniformed services
- The period of service did not exceed five years (with exceptions)
- The release from service was under "honorable conditions"
- The individual reports back to the civilian employer in a timely manner or submits a timely application for reemployment

An international survey of 173 countries revealed that the United States is only one of four countries that does not guarantee any paid leave for new mothers. The other countries are Liberia, Papua New Guinea, and Swaziland. Source: Project on Global Working Families' 2007 Report "Work, Family, and Equity Index."

698   **PART 5**   The Employer-Employee Relationship

Those eligible to be reemployed must be restored to the job and receive benefits that would have been attained had there not been an absence due to military service. USERRA protects those performing uniformed service from discrimination in:

- Initial employment
- Reemployment
- Retention in employment
- Promotion
- Any benefit of employment

Employers may not retaliate against anyone assisting in the enforcement of USERRA rights, even if that person has no service connection.

USERRA also contains health insurance provisions. Covered individuals who leave a job to perform military service have the right to elect to continue existing employer-based health plan coverage for up to 24 months. For those who do not elect to continue coverage, they have the right to be reinstated in the employer's health plan when reemployed, generally without any waiting periods or exclusions (except for service connected illnesses or injuries). Federal law required employers to notify employees of their rights under USERRA, including by displaying government notices.

>> *sidebar* 21.7

Rand Study: Invisible Wounds of War

Rand, a non-profit global think tank, conducted a study of U.S troops to determine the effects of their service. Since October 2001, approximately 1.64 million U.S. troops have been deployed for operations in Iraq and Afghanistan. The study assessed the post-deployment health-related needs. Major findings:

- About 19 percent of returning veterans report symptoms consistent with a diagnosis of post-traumatic stress disorder (PTSD) or depression.
- About 20 percent reported having suffered a probably traumatic brain injury while deployed.
- Only about half of those who need treatment for PTSD and depression actually seek it, and slightly more than half of those who receive treatment get care that meets minimal clinical standards.

- Concerns about confidentiality and career issues were major reasons why many veterans did not seek treatment.
- Removing such barriers to care and delivering treatment supported by scientific evidence can improve recovery rates and reduce societal costs.

Taking into consideration these issues, the U.S. Department of Labor issued *Hiring Veterans: A Step-by-Step Toolkit for Employers* to help employers working with transitioning service members. The guide includes information about available resources and developing effective strategies to hire veterans.

Source: Rand, *Invisible Wounds of War: Psychological and Cognitive Injuries, Their Consequences, and Services to Assist Recovery*, 2008, available at www.rand.org/health/feature/forty/invisible_wounds.html.

case 21.3 >>

STAUB v. PROCTOR HOSPITAL
562 U.S. ___ (2011)

This case contains a reference to the Seventeenth Century fable, "The Monkey and the Cat" by French poet Jean de la Fontine. In that fable, a monkey persuades an unsuspecting cat to extract some chestnuts from a fire. The monkey absconds with the nuts, leaving the cat with only a burnt paw. Under the cat's paw theory of liability, an employer may be held liable when a biased non-decision maker (the monkey) influences an unbiased decision maker (the cat) to take action he or she would not otherwise take.

While employed as an angiography technician by respondent Proctor Hospital, petitioner Staub was a member of the United States Army Reserve. Both his immediate supervisor (Mulally) and Mulally's supervisor (Korenchuk) were hostile to his military obligations. Mulally gave Staub disciplinary warning, which included a directive requiring Staub to report to her or Korenchuk when his cases were completed. After receiving a report from Korenchuk that Staub had violated the Corrective Action, Proctor's vice president of human resources (Buck) reviewed Staub's personnel file and decided to fire him. Staub filed a grievance, claiming that Mulally had fabricated the allegation underlying the warning out of hostility toward his military obligations, but Buck adhered to her decision. Staub sued Proctor under the Uniformed Services Employment and Reemployment Rights Act of 1994 (USERRA). He contended not that Buck was motivated by hostility to his military obligations, but that Mulally and Korenchuk were, and that their actions influenced Buck's decision. A jury found Proctor liable and awarded Staub damages, but the Seventh Circuit reversed, holding that Proctor was entitled to judgment as a matter of law because the decision maker had relied on more than Mulally's and Korenchuk's advice in making her decision. The U.S. Supreme Court unanimously reversed. Justice Kagan did not take part in the decision.

SCALIA, J.: We consider the circumstances under which an employer may be held liable for employment discrimination based on the discriminatory animus of an employee who influenced, but did not make, the ultimate employment decision.

Petitioner Vincent Staub worked as an angiography technician for respondent Proctor Hospital until 2004, when he was fired. Staub and Proctor hotly dispute the facts surrounding the firing, but because a jury found for Staub in his claim of employment discrimination against Proctor, we describe the facts viewed in the light most favorable to him. While employed by Proctor, Staub was a member of the United States Army Reserve, which required him to attend drill one weekend per month and to train full time for two to three weeks a year. Both Janice Mulally, Staub's immediate supervisor, and Michael Korenchuk, Mulally's supervisor, were hostile to Staub's military obligations. . . .

On April 2, 2004, Angie Day, Staub's co-worker, complained to Linda Buck, Proctor's vice president of human resources, and Garrett McGowan, Proctor's chief operating officer, about Staub's frequent unavailability and abruptness. McGowan directed Korenchuk and Buck to create a plan that would solve Staub's "availability' problems." But three weeks later, before they had time to do so, Korenchuk informed Buck that Staub had left his desk without informing a supervisor, in violation of the January Corrective Action. Staub now contends this accusation was false: he had left Korenchuk a voicemail notification that he was leaving his desk. Buck relied on Korenchuk's accusation, however, and after reviewing Staub's personnel file, she decided to fire him. The termination notice stated that Staub had ignored the directive issued in the January 2004 Corrective Action.

Staub challenged his firing through Proctor's grievance process, claiming that Mulally had fabricated the allegation underlying the Corrective Action out of hostility toward his military obligations. Buck did not follow up with Mulally about this claim. After discussing the matter with another personnel officer, Buck adhered to her decision.

Staub sued Proctor under the Uniformed Services Employment and Reemployment Rights Act of 1994, 38 U. S. C. §4301 *et seq.*, claiming that his discharge was motivated by hostility to his obligations as a military reservist. His contention was not that Buck had any such hostility but that Mulally and Korenchuk did, and that their actions influenced Buck's ultimate employment decision. A jury found that Staub's "military status was a motivating factor in [Proctor's] decision to discharge him," App. 68a, and awarded $57,640 in damages.

The Seventh Circuit reversed, holding that Proctor was entitled to judgment as a matter of law. 560 F. 3d 647. The court observed that Staub had brought a "'cat's

[continued]

paw' case," meaning that he sought to hold his employer liable for the animus of a supervisor who was not charged with making the ultimate employment decision. . . . Here, however, Staub is seeking to hold liable not Mulally and Korenchuk, but their employer. Perhaps, therefore, the discriminatory motive of one of the employer's agents (Mulally or Korenchuk) can be aggregated with the act of another agent (Buck) to impose liability on Proctor. . . . Thus, if the employer's investigation results in an adverse action for reasons unrelated to the supervisor's original biased action (by the terms of USERRA it is the employer's burden to establish that), then the employer will not be liable. But the supervisor's biased report may remain a causal factor if the independent investigation takes it into account without determining that the adverse action was, apart from the supervisor's recommendation, entirely justified. We are aware of no principle in tort or agency law under which an employer's mere conduct of an independent investigation has a claim-preclusive effect. Nor do we think the independent investigation somehow relieves the employer of "fault." The employer is at fault because one of its agents committed an action based on discriminatory animus that was intended to cause, and did in fact cause, an adverse employment decision. . . . motivated by antimilitary animus that is *intended* by the supervisor to cause an adverse employment action, and if that act is a proximate cause of the ultimate employment action, then the employer is liable under USERRA . . . Applying our analysis to the facts of this case, it is clear that the Seventh Circuit's judgment must be reversed. Both Mulally and Korenchuk were acting within the scope of their employment when they took the actions that allegedly caused Buck to fire Staub. A "reprimand . . . for workplace failings" constitutes conduct within the scope of an agent's employment. *Faragher* v. *Boca Raton,* 524 U. S. 775, 798–799 (1998). As the Seventh Circuit recognized, there was evidence that Mulally's and Korenchuk's actions were motivated by hostility toward Staub's military obligations. There was also evidence that Mulally's and Korenchuk's actions were causal factors underlying Buck's decision to fire Staub. Buck's termination notice expressly stated that Staub was terminated because he had "ignored" the directive in the Corrective Action. Finally, there was evidence that both Mulally and Korenchuk had the specific intent to cause Staub to be terminated. Mulally stated she was trying to "get rid of" Staub, and Korenchuk was aware that Mulally was "out to get" Staub. Moreover, Korenchuk informed Buck, Proctor's personnel officer responsible for terminating employees, of Staub's alleged noncompliance with Mulally's Corrective Action, and Buck fired Staub immediately thereafter; a reasonable jury could infer that Korenchuk intended that Staub be fired. The Seventh Circuit therefore erred in holding that Proctor was entitled to judgment as a matter of law.

It is less clear whether the jury's verdict should be reinstated or whether Proctor is entitled to a new trial. The jury instruction did not hew precisely to the rule we adopt today; it required only that the jury find that "military status was a motivating factor in [Proctor's] decision to discharge him." App. 68a. Whether the variance between the instruction and our rule was harmless error or should mandate a new trial is a matter the Seventh Circuit may consider in the first instance.

Reversed and Remanded.

>> CASE QUESTIONS

1. How does the "cat's paw" theory of liability apply to this case?
2. What is the Court's rationale for reversing the Seventh Circuit?
3. Could the rationale in this case be applied to Title VII cases?

5. OCCUPATIONAL SAFETY AND HEALTH ADMINISTRATION

Occupational Safety and Health Administration (OSHA) has jurisdiction over complaints about hazardous conditions in the workplace. Employers are required to comply with OSHA standards to furnish a workplace free

>> *sidebar* 21.8

New OSHA Crowd Management Safety Guidelines

In 2008, a temporary maintenance worker was pushed to the ground and suffocated to death after approximately 2,000 holiday shoppers broke through Walmart's glass doors. The shoppers were racing to buy sharply discounted televisions, computers and other gifts. OSHA filed a citation against Walmart, alleging that it did not furnish a workplace "free from recognizable hazard" that were likely to cause death or serious physical harm to an employee due to "crowd crush." Walmart was fined $7,000 and was required to take steps to correct the hazard. Although the fine is *de minimus* for Walmart, concerned about the ramifications for future crowd-attracting events, the retailer appealed. The fine was upheld on appeal.

As a result of this incident, OSHA issued *Crowd Control Guidelines* in November 2010. The detailed guidelines address steps to be taken during planning, pre-event setup, the sales event and in emergency situations. Considerations include staffing plans, emergency contacts, training workers in crowd management, using barricades or ropes with adequate breaks or turns, using wristbands, tickets or an Internet lottery for "hot items," and ensuring adequate communication between employees, customers, and emergency personnel.

Specific measures implemented by Walmart include issuing tickets for hot items, placing employees on platforms to direct customers, using steel barriers in zig-zag patters in front to the store to guide customers into the store in an orderly fashion—avoiding a shoving and crushing mass trying to enter the store.

For more about OSHA's new rules, see *Crowd Control Guidelines* at www.osha.gov/OshDoc/data_General_Facts/Crowd_Control.pdf.

from recognized hazards. Employees have the right to request an OSHA inspection if they believe that there are unsafe and unhealthful conditions in the workplace. Employees making complaints who are subjected to retaliation or discrimination by their employers may also file a complaint with OSHA. There is no private cause of action under OSHA, which means that an employee cannot sue an employer for damages based on an OSHA violation.

OSHA investigates a wide variety of workplace hazards. For example, following the deaths of 20 workers in 2008 in construction accidents in New York City, OSHA is sending inspectors there in an effort to increase safety and improve working conditions. OSHA inspectors will examine cranes and high-rise construction sites. In addition to the inspections, OSHA sent notices to employers' insurance and workers' compensation carriers. Citations involving training violations at unionized sites will also be sent to the unions representing workers and to their training funds. The U.S. House Education and Labor Committee is reviewing the sufficiency of OSHA's construction enforcement. OSHA is also investigating The Atlanta Ballet following the fall of a 17-year-old dancer wearing a panda costume during a performance of "The Nutcracker" at the Fox Theater in Atlanta. The dancer, who fell about 12 feet into the empty orchestra pit, suffered serious injuries, requiring spinal surgery. OSHA conducted over 38,000 inspections in 2006.

>> *sidebar* 21.9

OSHA's Severe Violator Enforcement Program

Under the Obama administration, OSHA is increasing its focus on enforcing safe workplaces. One significant step was releasing the Severe Violator Enforcement Program (SVEP) draft directive to concentrate resources on "inspecting employers who have demonstrated indifference" to their OSHA obligations "by willful, repeated, or failure-to-abate violations." If an employer engages in this behavior in one of the following four areas, it is at risk for being placed in the SVEP:

1. Fatality and/or catastrophic situations, such as three or more hospitalizations or the death of an employee

2. Non-fatality and/or catastrophic situations in which the employer has exposed the employee to one of the most severe workplace hazards, including "high gravity serious violations" such as fall hazards, combustible dust hazards and lead hazards

3. Hazards due to the potential release of a highly hazardous chemical

4. Any violation that is deemed "egregious" under current OSHA regulations

The SVEP casts a wide enforcement net, applying to employers of all sizes.

Source: OSHA, Severe Violator Enforcement Program Directive, available at www.osha.gov/dep/svep-directive.pdf.

6. PENSION PLANS AND HEALTH CARE

In 1974, Congress passed and President Nixon signed the Employee Retirement Income Security Act (ERISA). This law attempts to protect employees whose employers have voluntary pension plans. These protections include disclosure of information about the management of and fiduciary relationships within the plan. Since ERISA, the federal government has enacted a number of other laws directed at protecting employees' health care. Among these laws are Consolidated Omnibus Budget Reconciliation Act (COBRA), which was passed in 1986, and provides that employees can continue to purchase health insurance even after their employment is terminated. The Health Insurance Portability and Accountability Act (HIPAA) became law in 1996 and protects employees who have preexisting health conditions when they change jobs.

For more details about these laws, visit www.dol.gov/dol/topic/health-plans/erisa.htm#content

During the early part of this century, we have seen a new crisis arising. This involves businesses who are changing their defined-benefit retirement plans to private individual accounts, such as 401(k) plans. A number of companies have gone into bankruptcy and have sought permission to cancel retirement plans. It appears a very real competitive advantage is to be a new company that is not burdened by large pension plans obligations. For example, many of the legacy airlines, such as Delta, United, and Northwest, have gone into and come out of bankruptcy in the hope that they will be competitive with newer airlines, which do not have the large obligation of paying the pensions of thousands of retirees. Sidebar 21.10 provides detail of a major company's changes in pension plans.

>> *sidebar* 21.10

Changes in Pension Plans

IBM announced that beginning in 2008, it would freeze its workers' pension plan and begin offering only 401(k) retirement accounts. This announcement by IBM indicates that even financially healthy companies are moving away from defined-benefit plans, which pay retirement benefits based on the employee's income and years of service. IBM operates the third largest retirement plan with $48 billion in assets.

General Electric has the second largest, and General Motors' retirement plan is the largest. This announcement by IBM causes a lot of speculation regarding other companies. Much of the public will watch General Motors with interest since its largest parts supplier, Delphi, already has filed for bankruptcy.

Source: Mary Williams Walsh, "IBM to Freeze Pension Plans to Trim Costs," *The New York Times*, January 6, 2006.

7. LIMITATIONS ON EMPLOYMENT AT WILL

LO 21-2

Historically, unless employees contracted for a definite period of employment (such as for one year), employers were able to discharge them without cause at any time. This is called the **employment-at-will doctrine.**

During the 1930s, employers began to lose this absolute right to discharge employees whenever they desired. The Labor-Management Relations Act prohibited employers from firing employees for union activities. Now, many federal laws limit employers in their right to terminate employees. Table 21.2 provides a listing of some of these laws. Some states also prohibit employers

table 21.2 >> Federal Statutes Limiting Employment-at-Will Doctrine

Statute	Limitation on Employee Discharge
Labor-Management Relations Act	Prohibits discharge for union activity or for filing charges under the act.
Fair Labor Standards Act	Forbids discharge for exercising rights guaranteed by minimum-wage and overtime provisions of the act.
Occupational Safety and Health Act	Prohibits discharge for exercising rights under the act.
Civil Rights Act	Makes illegal discharge based on race, sex, color, religion, or national origin.
Age Discrimination in Employment Act	Forbids age-based discharge of employees over age 40.
Employee Retirement Income Security Act	Prohibits discharge to prevent employees from getting vested pension rights.
Clean Air Act	Prevents discharge of employees who cooperate in proceedings against an employer for violation of the act.
Clean Water Act	Prevents discharge of employees who cooperate in proceedings against an employer for violation of the act.
Consumer Credit Protection Act	Prohibits discharge of employees due to garnishment of wages for any one indebtedness.
Judiciary and Judicial Procedure Act	Forbids discharge of employees for service on federal grand or petit juries.

704   **PART 5**   The Employer-Employee Relationship

by statute from discharging employees for certain reasons, such as for refusing to take lie detector examinations.

Courts, too, have begun limiting the at-will doctrine. Under contract theory, several courts have stated that at-will employment contracts (which are not written and are little more than an agreement to pay for work performed) contain an implied promise of good faith and fair dealing by the employer.

Do understand that any commitments stated in an employee handbook are viewed by courts as a contractual promise by the employer.

Other courts have ruled that the employer's publication of an employee handbook can change the nature of at-will employment. They have held the employer liable for breach of contract for discharging an employee in violation of statements made in the handbook about discharge procedures.

Many contract and tort exceptions to employment at will have involved one of three types of employer behavior:

- Discharge of employee for performance of an important public obligation, such as jury duty.
- Discharge of employee for reporting employer's alleged violations of law (whistleblowing). The recent financial reform legislation, Dodd-Frank, includes financial incentives to blow the whistle for a broad range of wrongdoing from securities and accounting fraud to bribery allegations. (See Sidebar 21.11 for information about IRS whistleblowers.)
- Discharge of employee for exercising statutory rights.

>> *sidebar* 21.11

IRS Whistleblowers Rewards Program

In 2006, the IRS amended its whistleblower statute to encourage the reporting of tax fraud perpetrated by individuals and corporations. Pursuant to 26 U.S.C. §7623, whistleblowers have an enforceable right to a reward when they report significant tax violations. A person who provides information regarding tax law violations under the IRS Whistleblower Law is known as a whistleblower. To be eligible to recover compensation from the IRS, a person must bring information to the Internal Revenue Service's attention. The whistleblower may receive compensation only from monies actually collected based on the information provided.

Under the IRS Whistleblower Reform Law, a person can receive a reward of between 15 percent and 30 percent of the total collected proceeds (including penalties, interest, additions to tax, and additional amounts). If the IRS moves forward with an administrative or judicial action based on information brought by a whistleblower, the whistleblower is eligible to receive at least 15 percent and up to a cap of 30 percent of the recovery, depending on the whistleblower's contribution to the prosecution

of the action. The IRS may give awards of lesser amounts under certain circumstances (i.e., when the fraud has already been publicly disclosed and the whistleblower is not an original source).

>> WHAT ARE THE MOST COMMON TAX FRAUD SCHEMES?

- Failing to report income earned in a foreign stock exchange.
- Participating in bogus income tax shelters.
- Hiding or transferring assets or income out of the United States.
- Overstating deductions.
- Making false entries in books and records.
- Claiming personal expenses as business expenses.
- Claiming false deductions.
- Underreporting tip income.
- Paying employees in cash.
- Keeping two sets of books.

Most of the cases that limit at-will employment state that the employer has violated *public policy*. What does it mean to say that an employer has violated public policy? Is it a court's way of saying that most people no longer support the employer's right to do what it did?

Limitations on discrimination and employment at will evidence a growing concern for the rights of employees in their jobs and may suggest a trend that could lead to some type of broad, legally guaranteed job security. In recent years, unions have also increasingly focused on job-security issues in their bargaining with employers.

>> *sidebar* 21.12

Privacy, Technology and Social Media

Technology and social media are raising ongoing issues about privacy in the workplace. Both employers and employees are dealing with how to navigate these issues. Here are a few examples:

- The U.S. Supreme Court unanimously found that notwithstanding a city policy officer's reasonable expectation of privacy in text messages received on a pager provided by the City, the City did not violate his privacy rights under the Fourth Amendment by reviewing transcripts of those text messages. In this case, many of the messages were not work related and were sexually explicit. (*City of Ontario v. Quon*, 560 U.S. __ (2010).)

- Employers may review an applicant's Facebook, MySpace, or LinkedIn pages to learn more about potential employees during the recruitment and hiring process.

- Many employers now have documented policies pertaining to their employees' use of social media sites while on the job.

- When using social media sites, employers must use care not to base a decision on something learned that cannot legally be used to make an employment decision.

---

8. WORKERS' PRIVACY

LO 21-3

Individual privacy is such an important part of individual freedom that both legal and ethical questions regarding privacy are bound to multiply in the computer age. While debate continues concerning the need for further federal privacy legislation, many states have passed their own privacy-related statutes. Several states guarantee workers access to their job personnel files and restrict disclosure of personal information to third parties.

Concerns for individual privacy also contributed to passage of the Electronic Communications Privacy Act of 1986 and the 1988 Employee Polygraph Protection Act. Under this latter federal law, private employers generally are forbidden from using lie detector tests while screening job applicants. Current employees may not be tested randomly but may be tested as a result of a specific incident or activity that causes economic injury or loss to an employer's business. The act permits private security companies to test job applicants and allows companies that manufacture or sell controlled substances to test both job applicants and current employees. The Labor Department may seek fines of up to $10,000 against employers who violate the act. Employees are also authorized to sue employers for violating the act.

Don't rely on an expectation of privacy in the workplace; employers may monitor e-mail systems they provide.

Another important privacy concern involves drug testing. At present there is no uniform law regarding the drug testing of employees. Many private companies conduct such testing. However, some states have placed some limits on a private company's right to test for drugs.

Unlike the U.S., workers in other jurisdictions, such as the European Union, enjoy a much higher expectation of privacy in the workplace.

Public employees are protected from some drug testing by the Fourth Amendment's prohibition against *unreasonable* searches. However, exactly when drug tests are unreasonable is subject to much debate in the courts. In general, public employees may be tested when there is a proper suspicion that employees are using illegal drugs that impair working ability or violate employment rules. Courts have also upheld drug testing as part of required annual medical exams.

>> *sidebar* 21.13

Is There Any Reasonable Expectation of Privacy in the Workplace?

There is very little expectation of privacy in the American workplace. For example, of the employers surveyed:

- 73 percent monitored e-mail messages.
- 66 percent monitored Web surfing.
- 48 percent monitored with video surveillance.
- 45 percent monitored keystrokes and keyboard time.
- 43 percent monitored computer files.

Of those employers, a number reported firing employees for violating policies regarding use of the Internet (30 percent), e-mail (28 percent), or phones (6 percent).

Source: 2007 Electronic Monitoring & Surveillance Survey (released February 2008) by the American Management Association and The ePolicy Institute.

---

9. WORKER'S COMPENSATION ACTS

In Chapter 10, you learned about torts. What happens, however, if a worker is injured at work? Around the turn of the century, the tort system was largely replaced in the workplace by a series of workers' compensation acts. These statutes were enacted at both the state and federal level, and they imposed a type of strict liability on employers for accidental workplace injuries suffered by their employees. The clear purpose of these statues was to remove financial losses of injury from workers and redistribute them onto employers and ultimately onto society.

Even if an employee's contributory negligence or assumption of risk leads to an accidental injury, the employee still receives workers' compensation.

Remember workers' compensation is a form of insurance required by the states.

If you are injured at work, report the accident immediately.

History **Workers' compensation** laws are state statutes designed to protect employees and their families from the risks of accidental injury, death, or disease resulting from their employment. They were passed because the common law did not give adequate protection to employees from the hazards of their work. At common law, anyone was liable in tort for damages resulting from injuries caused to another as a proximate result of negligence. If an employer acted unreasonably and his or her carelessness was the proximate cause of physical injury suffered by an employee, the latter could sue and recover damages from the employer. However, the common law also provided the employer with the means of escaping this tort liability in most cases through three defenses:

- Assumption of the risk
- Contributory negligence
- The fellow-servant rule

For example, assume that the employer knowingly instructed workers to operate dangerous machinery not equipped with any safety devices, even though it realized injury to them was likely. A worker had his arm mangled when it was caught in the gears of one of these machines. Even though the employer was negligent in permitting this hazardous condition to persist, if the worker was aware of the dangers that existed, he would be unable to recover damages because he knowingly *assumed the risk* of his injury. In addition, if the injury were caused by *contributory negligence* of the employee as well as the negligence of the employer, the action was defeated. And, if the injury occurred because of the negligence of another employee, the negligent employee, rather than the employer, was liable because of the *fellow-servant rule*.

The English Parliament passed a workers' compensation statute in 1897. Today all states have such legislation, modeled to a greater or lesser degree on the English act. These laws vary a great deal from state to state as to the industries subject to them, the employees they cover, the nature of the injuries or diseases that are compensable, the rates of compensation, and the means of administration. In spite of wide variances in the laws of the states in this area, certain general observations can be made about them.

The System   State workers' compensation statutes provide a system to pay workers or their families if the worker is accidentally killed or injured or incurs an occupational disease while employed. To be compensable, the death, illness, or injury must arise out of and in the course of the employment. Under these acts, the negligence or fault of the employer in causing an on-the-job injury is not an issue. Instead, these laws recognize the fact of life that a certain number of injuries, deaths, and diseases are bound to occur in a modern industrial society as a result of the attempts of businesses and their employees to provide the goods and services demanded by the consuming public. This view leads to the conclusion that it is fairer for the consuming public to bear the cost of such mishaps rather than to impose it on injured workers.

Workers' compensation laws create strict liability for employers of accidentally injured workers. Liability exists regardless of lack of negligence or fault, provided the necessary association between the injuries and the business of the employer is present. The three defenses the employer had at common law are eliminated. The employers, treating the costs of these injuries as part of the costs of production, pass them on to the consumers who created the demand for the product or service being furnished.

Workers' compensation acts give covered employees the right to certain cash payments for their loss of income due to accidental, on-the-job injuries. In the event of a married employee's death, benefits are provided for the surviving spouse and minor children. The amount of such awards usually is subject to a stated maximum and is calculated by using a percentage of the wages of the employee. If the employee suffers permanent, partial disability, most states provide compensation both for injuries that are scheduled in the statute and those that are nonscheduled. As an example of the former, a worker who loses a hand might be awarded 100 weeks of compensation at $95 per week. Besides scheduling specific compensation for certain specific injuries, most acts also provide compensation for nonscheduled ones based upon the earning power the employee lost due to his or her injury. In addition to the above payments, all statutes provide for medical benefits.

In some states, employers have a choice of covering their workers' compensation risk with insurance or of being self-insured (that is, paying all claims directly) if they can demonstrate their capability to do so. Approximately 20 percent of compensation benefits are paid by self-insurers. In other states, employers pay into a state fund used to compensate workers entitled to benefits. In these states, the amounts of the payments are based on the size of the payroll and the experience of the employer in having claims filed against the system by its employees. Workers' compensation laws are usually administered exclusively by an administrative agency called the industrial commission or board, which has quasi-judicial powers. Of course, the ruling of such boards is subject to review by the courts of the jurisdiction in the same manner as the actions of other administrative agencies.

Tests for Determining Compensation   The tests for determining whether an employer must pay workers' compensation to an employee are simply:

1. Was the injury accidental?
2. Did the injury arise out of and in the course of employment?

Because workers' compensation laws benefit workers, courts interpret them liberally to favor workers. In recent years, cases have tended to expand employers' liability. For instance, courts have held that heart attacks (as well as other common ailments in which the employee has had either a preexisting disease or a physical condition likely to lead to the disease) are compensable as "accidental injuries." One ruling approved an award to a purchasing agent who became mentally ill because she was exposed to unusual work, stresses, and strains.

Her "nerve-racking" job involved a business whose sales grew over sixfold in 10 years. Factors contributing to her "accidental injury" included harsh criticism by her supervisor and long hours of work. Likewise, the courts have been liberal in upholding awards that have been challenged on the grounds that the injury did not arise "out of and in the course of employment." Courts routinely support compensation awards for almost any accidental injury that employees suffer while traveling for their employers. A Minnesota Supreme Court decision upheld a lower court award of compensation to a bus driver. On a layover during a trip, the driver had been shot accidentally in a tavern parking lot following a night on the town.

Exclusive Remedy Rule   Recently, some courts have been liberal in their interpretations of the **exclusive remedy rule.** This rule, which is written into all compensation statutes, states that an employee's sole remedy against an employer for workplace injury or illness shall be workers' compensation. In the past few years, courts in several important jurisdictions have created exceptions to this rule. Note that these exceptions recognize in part that workers' compensation laws do not adequately compensate badly injured workers.

Since workers' compensation laws apply only to accidentally injured workers, the exclusive remedy rule does not protect employers who intentionally injure workers. But the issue arises as to how "intentional" such an injury has to be. What if an employer knowingly exposes employees to a chemical that may cause illness in some employees over a long term?

The Future of State Workers' Compensation Currently, many problems confront the state workers' compensation system. Fifty separate non-uniform acts make up the system. Many acts exclude from coverage groups such as farmworkers, government employees, and employees of small businesses. Many state legislatures have enacted changes in their compensation laws. However, states that have broadened coverage and increased benefits have greatly boosted the cost of doing business within their borders. This discourages new businesses from locating within these states and encourages those already there to move out.

In the last decade, workers' compensation payments have tripled. Many workers exaggerate their injuries to get compensation. At the same time, compensation payments to seriously injured workers are often inadequate, and this has led to attempts to get around the exclusive remedy rule.

As our national economy moves from a manufacturing to a service emphasis, the nature of injuries suffered under workers' compensation programs begins to change. In particular, the number of mental stress claims rises. The National Council on Compensation Insurance states that these claims have increased fivefold in the past few years. Problems of proving (or disproving) mental stress claims bring new concerns for the workers' compensation system.

A major problem concerns slowly developing occupational diseases. Many toxic chemicals cause cancer and other diseases only after workers have been exposed to them over many years. Often it is difficult or impossible for workers or their survivors to recover workers' compensation for such diseases. One solution to the problems confronting the workers' compensation system would be federal reform. Those advocating such reform have put forth several plans, but Congress has shown little inclination so far to adopt a uniform federal act.

>> *sidebar* 21.14

Workplace Issues Related to Medical Marijuana

The use of medical marijuana is raising a range of workplace issues. Sixteen states and the District of Columbia have statutes decriminalizing the use of marijuana for medical purposes. This is creating a range of questions for employers in those states:

- Are random drug tests problematic under the Americans with Disabilities Act?

- Employers have a "general duty" to provide a safe workplace under OSHA, so can they terminate a worker who tests positive for THC?

- How do these laws affect an employers' obligations under the federal Drug-Free Workplace Act of 1988 if they are receiving federal contracts?

- If a employees are legally using medical marijuana outside of the workplace, yet tests positive at work, can they be fired?

This is an evolving area of the law and one that employers need to be mindful of as they make decisions involving workers who are using medical marijuana.

---

10. EMPLOYMENT ELIGIBILITY VERIFICATION

In accordance with the federal Immigration Reform and Control Act of 1986 ("IRCA"), all U.S. employers must complete and retain Form I-9 **Employment Eligibility Verification** forms for each individual they hire in the United

States. Both citizens and noncitizens must complete the form. The employer is required to examine the employment eligibility and identify document(s) an employee presents to determine whether the document(s) reasonably appear to be "genuine." Acceptable documents that establish both identity and employment authorization include:

- U.S. Passport or U.S. Passport Card
- Permanent Resident Card or Alien Registration Receipt Card
- Foreign passport that contains a temporary I-551 stamp or temporary I-551 printed notation on a machine-readable visa
- An Employment Authorization document that contains a photograph

If none of these documents are available, a worker may use a combination of documents specified by federal law. Employers must use care to determine that the documents appear genuine, but not to go overboard and be liable for "document abuse" or discriminatory practices related to verification. The U.S. Citizen and Immigration Services broadly categorizes document abuse into four categories:

1. Improperly requesting that employees produce more documents than are required by Form I-9 to establish the employee's identity and employment authorization
2. Improperly requesting that employees present a particular document, such as a "green card," to establish identity and/or employment authorization
3. Improperly rejecting documents that reasonably appear to be genuine and to relate to the employee presenting them
4. Improperly treating groups of applicants differently when completing Form I-9, such as requiring certain groups of employees who look or sound "foreign" to present particular documents to the employer

The completed forms must be retained by the employer either for three years after the date of hire or for one year after employment is terminated, whichever is later.

>> *sidebar* 21.15

Arizona Law on Hiring Foreign Workers Is Upheld

By a 5-3 vote, the U.S. Supreme Court ruled in *Chamber of Commerce v. Whiting*, 563 U.S. ___ (2011) that the federal Immigration Reform and Control Act (IRCA) law does *not* pre-empt the Arizona statute that penalizes employers who knowingly hire unauthorized foreign workers. The Legal Arizona Workers Act provides that the licenses of state employers that knowingly or intentionally employ unauthorized aliens may be, and in certain circumstances must be, suspended or revoked. The law also requires all Arizona employers to use E-Verify, an Internet-based system that provides instant verification of work authorization.

The U.S. Chamber of Commerce, along with various business and civil rights organizations, challenged the Arizona law. The Court reasoned that Arizona's licensing law falls well within the confines of the authority Congress chose to leave to the States and therefore is not expressly preempted.

11. EMPLOYEE LAWSUITS

LO 21-4

Despite the presence of many examples of the employer's violating an employment law, most employers strive to obey the law. They still risk lawsuits, however, including many brought by unsatisfactory employees who have been disciplined, denied promotion, or discharged. How can employers protect themselves from unjustified employee lawsuits?

One important protection against unjustified employee lawsuits is an established system of adequate documentation. Sometimes called the **paper fortress,** this documentation consists of job descriptions, personnel manuals, and employee personnel files.

Before handing anyone an employment application, the employer should insist that the potential candidate carefully study a job description. A well-written job description will help potential applicants eliminate themselves from job situations for which they lack interest or qualification, thus preventing employers from having to dismiss them later and risking lawsuits.

Once a new employee is hired, the employer should give the employee a personnel manual. This manual should include information about employee benefits and should also outline work rules and job requirements. The employer should go over the manual with the employee and answer any questions. Clear identification of employer expectations and policies helps provide a defense against employee lawsuits if subsequent discipline or discharge of the employee becomes necessary. The employer should ask that the employee sign a form indicating receipt of the manual and an understanding of the employer's explanation of its contents.

The employer should enter this form, with all other documentation relevant to an employee's work history, into the employee's personnel file. Regular written evaluations of employee performance should also be entered into the personnel file. A chronological record of unsatisfactory work performance is a very useful defense against unjustified lawsuits following discipline, denial of promotion, or discharge.

Another piece of documentation that helps justify employer decisions is the written warning. Anytime an employee breaks a work rule or performs unsatisfactorily, the employer should issue the employee a written warning and place a duplicate in the personnel file. The warning should explain specifically what work rule the employee violated. In addition, employers should either have an employee sign that he or she has received a written warning or else note in the personnel file that the employee has received a copy of it. The employer should also give the employee the opportunity to place a letter of explanation in the personnel file.

Taking any disciplinary action without documentation fails to build the record for increased sanctions in the future.

Laws discussed in this chapter and the next one should not prevent employers from discharging unsatisfactory employees. In an actual termination conversation, however, the employer should provide the employee with specific reasons for discharge, taken from the personnel file. Detailed documentation is vital in successfully responding to unjustified employee lawsuits. Even better is to prevent them in the first place through the development, enforcement, and review of company policies that promote legal compliance.

See Sidebar 21.16 for practical suggestions for employers to prevent employee lawsuits.

>> *sidebar* 21.16

What Can Employers Do to Avoid Employment Litigation?

There are a number of steps that employers can take to avoid employment litigation, including:

- Implementing workplace policies and procedures, and training employees to understand the rules and apply them consistently. The policies should cover how to prevent sexual harassment and other forms of discrimination and how to report the same.
- Conducting regular candid performance evaluations, with clear feedback to employees.
- Investigating all complaints thoroughly, never taking any adverse action against persons making honest complaint.

- Documenting all employee incidents, including disciplinary issues and other problems, in each employee's personnel file.
- Being fair and objective when dealing with employees. Being upfront and honest about action taken in the workplace, including termination, helps employees understand the rationale for the action.

Keep these practical suggestions in mind as you study discrimination in Chapter 20, and realize how many workers could potentially assert one or more discrimination claims against their employer.

>> Key Terms

Employment Eligibility
    Verification 709
Employment-at-will doctrine 703
Exclusive Remedy Rule 708
Fair Labor Standards Act
    (FLSA) 686

Family and Medical Leave Act
    (FMLA) 694
Occupational Safety and
    Health Administration
    (OSHA) 700
Paper fortress 711

Uniformed Services
    Employment and
    Reemployment Rights Act
    (USERRA) 697
WARN Act 693
Workers' Compensation 706

>> Review Questions and Problems

Employment Laws

1. *Minimum Wages and Maximum Hours*
    (a) What federal law establishes the minimum wage and the hours in a work week?
    (b) What is the minimum wage and what is considered the maximum work week?
    (c) What is required regarding overtime compensation or time off?

2. *The WARN Act*
    To show your understanding of the WARN notice, answer these questions:
    (a) Who are the covered employers?
    (b) What format is required for a WARN notice?
    (c) When must the WARN notice be given?
    (d) To whom must the WARN notice be delivered?

3. *The Family and Medical Leave Act*
    In the sixth month of her pregnancy, Suzanne was advised by her doctors to slow down the hectic pace of her consulting career. Upon this advice, Suzanne requested and was granted by

her employer 12 weeks of medical leave. During the tenth week of this leave, Suzanne had a healthy baby. How much family leave is Suzanne entitled to take under the FMLA to care for her newborn?

4. *Uniformed Services Employment and Reemployment Rights Act*

Robert left his position as commercial airline pilot to undertake his duties in the Marine Reserves for a tour of duty in Iraq. When he returns home a year later, his employer apologetically tells him that they filled his position during his absence and they "will call" when something comes available. They also express concern about his ability to fly commercial jets because he has not flown in the last year. What legal recourse does Robert have, if any?

5. *Occupational Safety and Health Administration*

Larry, a machine operator, is concerned that the cardboard baler he is working on should have a safety shield to protect his arms from the moving parts. He is also worried that if he reports his concerns, he will be put on the night shift. What should he do? Does he have any protection if he reports the issue?

6. *Pension Plans and Health Care*

Why has the aging of the "baby boom" generation put so much pressure on the financial stability of historically successful companies?

7. *Limitations on Employment at Will*

Terry was hired as an assistant manager by the Assurance Manufacturing Company. There was no specific time period related to Terry's employment. During Terry's first day at work, the personnel director of Assurance gave Terry a copy of the employee's handbook. In this handbook, Assurance stated that no employee would be terminated without a justifiable explanation. Five months after beginning work at Assurance, Terry was notified that after an additional two weeks there would be no further job for Terry at Assurance. When Terry asked why this termination was occurring, the personnel director told Terry, "Under state law no reason for termination has to be given. In essence, you are an employee only for as long as Assurance desires." What is the best argument Terry can make that the employment-at-will doctrine is not applicable in this situation? Explain.

8. *Workers' Privacy*

John Hancock Life Insurance Company instructed its employees to create passwords to protect their e-mail accounts. Employees also were told to create personal folders for messages they send and receive. After a company investigation, Nancy and Joanne were terminated as John Hancock employees for using their e-mail accounts to send sexually explicit messages. These employees sued John Hancock for wrongful discharge on the basis that the company's investigation had violated their rights of privacy. Was John Hancock entitled to examine these employees' e-mail accounts?

9. *Workers' Compensation Acts*

If Sam fails to wear a hard hat, as required by Super Construction, Inc., his employer, and is injured by a falling hammer, can he recover workers' compensation from Super Construction, Inc.? Your answer should explain the basis for recovering workers' compensation.

10. *Employment Eligibility Verification*

Sophia's Glam Designs needs to hire 100 new workers to manufacture a new line of back-to-school outfits. The company received hundreds of applications for the positions. Simone, Sophia's Glam Designs Human Resources Manager, requires all new hires to complete an I-9 and to produce a valid passport or green card to prove employment eligibility. When one worker attempts to use a combination of a Georgia driver's license and a social security card, Simone refuses to accept the documents. Because of the large amount of workers hired, she wants to use documents she feels comfortable verifying and streamline the documentation process. Is this permissible?

11. *Employee Lawsuits*
   (a) What is meant by the phrase "paper fortress"?
   (b) How does maintaining a paper fortress aid the employer when the employee claims unfair treatment?

business >> *discussions*

1. You just had one of those days—exciting and overwhelming. As your company's director of human relations, you have dealt with an employee asking how much leave he can take when his wife has their first baby next month. A phone call from the company's CFO involved discussions of potential layoffs in order to "make the budget." A group of employees came to meet with you, and they indicated they were talking with union organizers as a way to combat the company's policy of monitoring phone calls and e-mail messages. Another group of employees expressed their feelings that they were not being paid for all the time they worked.

Before heading home, you take a few minutes to reflect and ask yourself the following questions:

How is the workday calculated?
What legal requirements have to be met before layoffs can occur?
What is the company's responsibility to educate employees about their rights under the Family and Medical Leave Act?
Can your company properly monitor its employees' phone calls and e-mail messages?

Chapter 22. Labor-Managment Relationship

22 Labor-Management Relationship

☐ Learning Objectives

In this chapter you will learn:

22-1. To understand the role unions play in the U.S. labor market.

22-2. To describe the development of early labor law, focusing on The Clayton Act, The Railway Labor Act, and The Norris-LaGuardia Act.

22-3. To appreciate the significance of The Wagner Act, including the creation of the National Labor Relations Board and unfair labor practices by management.

22-4. To recognize how The Taft-Hartley Act amended labor law to balance the power between labor and management, including the recognition of unfair labor practices by unions.

Chapters 20 and 21 pertain to "employment law," the area of the law that controls how employers must treat applicants for employment, employees, and former employees. As you know, employment law encompasses a wide variety of employer-employee workplace issues. This chapter focuses on *labor laws*, the area of the law designed to equalize the bargaining power between employers and employees. Specifically, labor law prohibits employers and unions from engaging in specified "unfair labor practices" and establishes an obligation of both parties to engage in good-faith collective bargaining. Labor laws pertain to the relationships between employers and unions, granting employees the right to unionize and allowing employers and employees to engage in certain activities (such as strikes, picketing, seeking injunctions, lockouts). These laws regulating labor-management relations are largely a product of the New Deal era of the 1930s.

Although union membership is not as large as it once was in the United States, unions are alive and well with active agendas on behalf of their members. They are also high-profile advocates during political elections and on labor-related topics such as international trade. A number of free trade agreements discussed in Chapter 12, faced vocal opposition from labor unions. Despite their smaller numbers, labor unions continue to be formidable in the United States.

LO 22-1

>> Labor Laws

The National Education Association is the largest union with 2.7 million members.

"The basic principle that brings us here today is that American workers cannot win a better life unless more workers belong to unions."

–Statement of five union presidents announcing the Change to Win Coalition

"Forming this coalition is a step in the wrong direction because it's the first step toward a truly divided labor movement. Splitting the AFL-CIO will mean less power for workers."

–Gerald W. McEntree, president of the American Federation of State, County and Municipal Employees

What is your reaction to the word *union?* Do your thoughts have a mostly positive or negative connotation? Society's reaction and the government's response to the union movement have varied over time. Thus, your reaction is not right or wrong; it is likely formed by where you were raised and what your parents did to support you. Children of business managers probably have a very different perspective of unions, than children of workers whose wages were increased and job security strengthened through the efforts of union bargaining agents.

A union is basically workers organizing their collective voices to increase their ability to communicate with their employer. As a concept, a union is neither good nor bad. How the concept is utilized makes all the difference in one's view of unions.

Does such a viewpoint really matter today? Haven't unions outlived their usefulness? These questions and other similar ones are very much in today's public debate. Interestingly, this debate is occurring among union leaders as well. The statistics tell a varied story. Often cited is the declining percentage of the workforce that is unionized. However, Table 22.1 illustrates that story is more complex due to the decline in private employees being offset by the growth of public employees who are union members.

The largest unions in the United States represent teachers, government employees, and service workers. The focus on how much time and money are dedicated to recruiting new members through intensive organizing campaigns at the work site versus through political efforts caused a split in the AFL-CIO, labor's longtime unified voice. Five of the larger unions formed a group called Change to Win. See Sidebar 22.1 for union statistics.

The goal of labor laws is successful **collective bargaining**, the process by which labor and management negotiate and reach agreements on matters of importance to both. Such matters include wages to be paid workers, hours to be worked, and other terms and conditions of employment. Collective

table 22.1 >> Statistics on Union Membership

Year	Private		Public		Total Membership	
1953	35.7%*	15,540,000	11.6%	770,000	32.5%*	16,310,000
1975	26.3	16,397,000	39.6	5,810,000	28.9	22,207,000*
2004	7.9	8,205,000	36.6	8,131,000*	12.5	15,472,000
2010	6.9	7,100,000	36.2	7,600,000	11.9	14,700,000

*Record highs
Source: www.lraonline.org/econ_stats.org.

>> *sidebar* 22.1

2010 Statistics on Union Membership

According to the Department of Labor, the number of workers belonging to a union declined by 612,000 in 2010 to 14.7 million. Public support for unions has also dropped. Other statistics:

- Union members accounted for 11.9 percent of all employed wage and salary workers. (In 1983, the first year data was available, union membership was 20.1 percent.)
- Education, training, and library occupations had the highest unionization rate among all occupations (37.1 percent).

- Among demographic groups, the union membership rate was highest for black men and lowest for Hispanic women.
- Union membership varies substantially by state. For example, New York had the highest union membership rate (24.2 percent) and North Carolina had the lowest (3.2 percent).

Source: Bureau of Labor Statistics Jan. 21, 2011, www.bls.gov/news.release/pdf/union2.pdf.

bargaining can be successful only if the bargaining power of the parties is equal. Most laws regulating labor-management relations seek to equalize this bargaining power. As a result, some laws add to the bargaining position of labor and others add to that of management.

These laws have been passed when Congress perceived that one side's bargaining power was excessive. As in any balancing process, it is very difficult to hit the right middle point. Thus, as you read the following sections understand that the labor-management relationship is a delicate one involving many nuances. Table 22.2 lists the major federal labor laws.

1. LAWS BEFORE 1935

LO 22-2

Until 1935, Congress viewed management as having greater bargaining power in the labor-management relationship. This view certainly was justified since the union movement historically was met with strong and swift reprisals by employers. It was not uncommon in the 1800s and early 1900s for workers who tried to unionize to be fired or, worse, beaten, even killed. This treatment of workers engaged in unacceptable behavior, from the employers' viewpoint, certainly kept management in a strong bargaining position and prevented unions from growing. In a series of "prolabor" laws, Congress took action to correct the inequalities. It did so by passing the following:

- The Clayton Act.
- The Railway Labor Act.
- The Norris-LaGuardia Act.

The Clayton Act The first federal statute of any importance to the labor movement is the **Clayton Act** of 1914, which was passed principally to strengthen the antitrust laws. Between 1890 (when the Sherman Antitrust Act was passed) and 1914, labor unions were weak in their ability to represent employees. At least one reason for the relative strength enjoyed by management was the fact that it could and did argue that employees acting together were restraining trade illegally under the Sherman Act.

"With all their faults, trade unions have done more for humanity than any other organization of men that ever existed. They have done more for decency, for honesty, for education, for the betterment of the race, for the developing of character in men, than any other association of men."

–Clarence Darrow,
***The Railroad Trainman* (1909)**

table 22.2 >> Federal Laws Governing Labor-Management Relations

Year	Statute	Major Provisions
1914	Clayton Act	1. Exempted union activity from the antitrust laws.
1926	Railway Labor Act	1. Governs collective bargaining for railroads and airlines.
		2. Created the National Mediation Board to conduct union elections and mediate differences between employers and unions.
1932	Norris-LaGuardia Act	1. Outlawed yellow-dog contracts.
		2. Prohibited federal courts from enjoining lawful union activities, including picketing and strikes.
1935	Wagner Act (National Labor Relations Act)	1. Created the National Labor Relations Board (NLRB).
		2. Authorized the NLRB to conduct union certification elections.
		3. Outlawed certain conduct by management as unfair to labor (five unfair labor practices).
		4. Authorized the NLRB to hold hearings on unfair labor practices and correct wrongs resulting from them.
1947	Taft-Hartley Act (Labor-Management Relations Act)	1. Outlawed certain conduct by unions as six unfair labor practices.
		2. Provided for an 80-day cooling-off period in strikes that imperil national health or safety.
		3. Allowed states to enact right-to-work laws.
		4. Created the Federal Mediation and Conciliation Service to assist in settlement of labor disputes.
1959	Landrum-Griffin Act (Labor-Management Reporting and Disclosure Act, LMRDA)	1. Created a Bill of Rights for union members.
		2. Requires reports to the secretary of labor.
		3. Added to the list of unfair labor practices.

Do recall that the Clayton Act is considered an antitrust law (see Chapter 16). Congress can use one law to impact various legal areas.

The Clayton Act stated that antitrust laws regulating anticompetitive contracts did not apply to labor unions or their members in lawfully carrying out their legitimate activities. This exemption covered only *legitimate* union practices. Although the Clayton Act exempted employees from the claim that they were restraining trade through unionization, this law did not expressly grant employees the protected right to join a union. Therefore, the Clayton Act did not balance the bargaining power between labor and management. The latter group remained the stronger one.

The Railway Labor Act Among the first industries to unionize were the railroads. In 1926, Congress enacted the **Railway Labor Act** to encourage collective bargaining in the railroad industry. The goal was to resolve labor disputes that might otherwise disrupt transportation and result in violence. The act was later extended to airlines; today it applies to both air and rail transportation. It established the three-member **National Mediation Board,** which must designate the bargaining representative for any given bargaining unit of employees in the railway or air transport industries. The board generally does this by holding representation elections. Specifically, when the parties to a dispute over proposed contract terms in the transportation industry cannot reach an agreement concerning rates of pay or working conditions, the National Mediation Board must attempt mediation of their differences. If mediation does not resolve their differences, the board encourages voluntary arbitration. If the parties refuse arbitration and the dispute is likely to disrupt interstate commerce substantially, the board informs the president, who then appoints a special emergency board. This emergency board lacks judicial power, but it encourages the parties to reach an agreement by investigating the dispute and publishing its findings of fact and recommendations for settlement. During the investigation, which lasts 30 days, and for an additional 30 days after the report is issued, business is conducted without interruption. The parties, however, have no duty to comply with the special board's proposals. Thus, if no new collective bargaining agreement is reached after the 60-day period, lockouts by management and strikes by workers become legal.

The Railway Labor Act has played a vitally important role in balancing the labor-management relationship in the transportation industries. However, due to this act's limited application, the management of businesses outside the transportation industry generally continued to have superior bargaining power following 1926.

The Norris-LaGuardia Act   Because of management's superior bargaining power, prior to 1932 management often made it a condition of employment that employees agree not to join a labor union. Such agreements became known as **yellow-dog contracts** because any employee who would forsake the right to join fellow employees in unionization was considered a cowardly scoundrel (yellow dog). Passed in 1932, the **Norris-LaGuardia Act** made yellow-dog contracts illegal. In essence, management no longer could explicitly deny an employee the right to unionize.

Seeking injunctions to stop concerted activities had remained an important tool of management in fighting the growth of labor unions. The Norris-LaGuardia Act listed specific acts of persons and organizations participating in labor disputes that were not subject to federal court injunctions. Federal courts cannot enjoin:

- Striking or quitting work.
- Belonging to a labor organization.
- Paying strike or unemployment benefits to participants in a labor dispute.
- Publicizing the existence of a labor dispute or the facts related to it (including picketing).
- Assembling peaceably to promote interests in a labor dispute.
- Agreeing with others or advising or causing them to do any of the above acts without fraud or violence.

Although the Norris-LaGuardia Act greatly restricts the use of injunctions in labor disputes, it does not prohibit them altogether. An injunction may be issued to enjoin illegal strikes, such as ones by public employees. In addition, a party seeking an injunction in a labor dispute must meet the test of a stringent, clean-hands rule. No restraining order will be granted to any

> "It is one of the characteristics of a free and democratic nation that it has free and independent labor unions."
>
> **–Franklin Delano Roosevelt**

The timing of the law (1932) likely limited its impact on helping unions. During the Depression, people were more concerned about finding a job than they were about joining a union.

person who fails to comply with any obligation imposed by law or who fails to make every reasonable effort to settle the dispute.

The Norris-LaGuardia Act restricts the use of federal court injunctions in labor disputes; it does not limit the jurisdiction of state courts in issuing them. The Supreme Court has upheld the jurisdiction of a state court to enjoin a union's work stoppage and picketing in violation of a no-strike clause in its collective bargaining agreement.

>> *sidebar* 22.2

Three Pro-Union Executive Orders

During his first month in office, President Obama signed three Executive Orders aimed at reversing Bush-era rules viewed as "anti-union." The Executive Orders:

- Prevent federal contractors from being reimbursed for expenses for their activities undertaken to influence workers deciding whether to unionize and engage in collective bargaining
- Require successor federal contractors, and their subcontractors, to offer jobs to current workers when contractors change

- Reverse a Bush order requiring federal contractors to notify workers that they can limit their financial support of unions that are serving as their exclusive bargaining representatives.

Unions are very supportive of these measures. From a management perspective, these Executive Orders take a very different approach to government contracts, with a much greater emphasis on the interest of organized labor.

LO 22-3

>> The Wagner Act

"Long ago we stated the reason for labor organizations. We said that they were organized out of the necessities of the situation . . . that [a] union was essential to give laborers opportunity to deal on an equality with their employer."

–NLRB v. Jones & Laughlin Steel Corp., 301 U.S. 1 (1937)

The labor movement received its greatest stimulus for growth with the enactment in 1935 of the National Labor Relations Act, known as the **Wagner Act.** Perhaps most significantly, Congress explicitly affirmed labor's right to organize and to bargain collectively. Recognizing that a major cause of industrial strife was the inequality of bargaining power between employees and employers, Section 7 of the act states:

> Employees shall have the right to self-organization, to form, join, or assist labor organizations, to bargain collectively through representatives of their own choosing, and to engage in concerted activities for the purpose of collective bargaining or other mutual aid or protection.

In addition to this Section 7 right to unionize, the Wagner Act contains several other key provisions:

- Creating the National Labor Relations Board (NLRB) to administer the act.
- Providing employees the right to select a union to act as their collective bargaining agent.
- Outlawing certain conduct by employers that generally has the effect of either preventing the organization of employees or emasculating their unions where they do exist; these forbidden acts are called *unfair labor practices.*

- Authorizing the NLRB to conduct hearings on unfair labor practice allegations and, if unfair practices are found to exist, to take corrective action including issuing cease and desist orders and awarding dollar damages to unions and employees.

2. THE NATIONAL LABOR RELATIONS BOARD

Established by the Wagner Act, the **National Labor Relations Board (NLRB)** operates as an independent agency of the U.S. government. This section discusses the organizational structure of the NLRB, its jurisdiction, and its quasi-judicial function. Section 10 examines the NLRB's authority to certify unions as the collective bargaining representative of employees. After this introduction to the NLRB, the remainder of the chapter will illustrate the significant role this agency plays in balancing the labor-management relationship.

NLRB Organization The NLRB consists of five members, appointed by the president with the advice and consent of the Senate, who serve staggered terms of five years each. In addition, there is a general counsel of the board who supervises board investigations and serves as prosecutor in cases before the board. The general counsel supervises operations of the NLRB so that the board itself may perform its quasi-judicial function of deciding unfair labor practice cases free of bias. Administrative law judges are responsible for the initial conduct of hearings in unfair labor practice cases.

The general counsel also is responsible for conducting representation elections. In addition, the general counsel is responsible for seeking court orders requiring compliance with the board's orders and represents the board in miscellaneous litigation. The board determines policy questions, such as what types of employers and groups of employees are covered by the labor law.

Jurisdiction Congress gave the NLRB jurisdiction over any business "affecting commerce." However, the following personnel are exempt from the NLRB's authority:

- Governmental employees.
- Persons covered by the Railway Labor Act.
- Independent contractors.
- Agricultural laborers.
- Household, domestic workers.
- Employees who work for their spouse or parents.

In FY2010, the NLRB processed more unfair labor practices, levied more fines and processed more petitions for certification and decertification than it did the previous year.

The NLRB cannot exercise its powers over all business because it has a limited budget and time constraints. Sidebar 22.3 describes the guidelines the NLRB uses to decide which businesses to regulate. As a result of these self-imposed restrictions, federal labor laws do not apply to many small businesses. The management of these businesses may still need to know what state labor laws require of them. See Case 22.1 for an example of a recent NLRB decision.

"If capitalism is fair then unionism must be. If men have a right to capitalize their ideas and the resources of their country, then that implies the right of men to capitalize their labor."

–Frank Lloyd Wright

>> *sidebar* 22.3

NLRB Assumes Jurisdiction over the Following

- Nonretail operations with an annual outflow or inflow across state lines of at least $50,000.
- Retail enterprises with a gross volume of $500,000 or more a year.
- Enterprises operating office buildings if the gross revenues are at least $100,000 per year.
- Transportation enterprises furnishing interstate services.
- Local transit systems with an annual gross volume of $250,000.
- Newspapers that subscribe to interstate news services, publish nationally syndicated features, or advertise nationally sold products and have a minimum annual gross volume of $250,000.

- Communication enterprises that operate radio or television stations or telephone or telegraph services with a gross volume of $100,000 or more per year.
- Local public utilities with an annual gross volume of $250,000 per year or an outflow or inflow of goods or services across state lines of $50,000 or more per year.
- Hotel and motel enterprises that serve transient guests and gross at least $500,000 in revenues per year.
- All enterprises whose operations have a substantial impact on national defense.
- Nonprofit hospitals.
- Private universities and colleges.

case 22.1 >>

THE GUARD PUBLISHING COMPANY D/B/A THE REGISTER-GUARD AND EUGENE NEWSPAPER GUILD, CWA LOCAL 37194.
Cases 36–CA–8743–1, 36–CA–8849–1, 36–CA–8789–1, and 36–CA–8842–1 (2007)

CHAIRMAN BATTISTA AND MEMBERS LIEBMAN, SCHAUMBER, KIRSANOW, AND WALSH: In this case, we consider several issues relating to employees' use of their employer's e-mail system for Section 7 purposes. First, we consider whether the Respondent violated Section 8(a)(1) by maintaining a policy prohibiting the use of e-mail for all "non-job-related solicitations." Second, we consider whether the Respondent violated Section 8(a)(1) by discriminatorily enforcing that policy against union-related e-mails while allowing some personal e-mails, and Section 8(a)(3) and (1) by disciplining an employee for sending union-related e-mails. Finally, we consider whether the Respondent violated Section 8(a)(5) and (1) by insisting on an allegedly illegal bargaining proposal that would prohibit the use of e-mail for "union business."

After careful consideration, we hold that the Respondent's employees have no statutory right to use the Respondent's e-mail system for Section 7 purposes. We therefore find that the Respondent's

policy prohibiting employee use of the system for "non-job-related solicitations" did not violate Section 8(a)(1).

With respect to the Respondent's alleged discriminatory enforcement of the e-mail policy, we have carefully examined Board precedent on this issue. As fully set forth herein, we have decided to modify the Board's approach in discriminatory enforcement cases to clarify that discrimination under the Act means drawing a distinction along Section 7 lines. We then address the specific allegations in this case of discriminatory enforcement in accordance with this approach.

Finally, we find that the Respondent did not insist on its bargaining proposal prohibiting the use of e-mail for "union business." Therefore, we dismiss the allegation that the Respondent insisted on an illegal subject in violation of Section 8(a)(5) and (1).

. . .

[continued]

FACTS

A. The Respondent's Communications Systems Policy

The Respondent publishes a newspaper. The Union represents a unit of about 150 of the Respondent's employees. The parties' last collective-bargaining agreement was in effect from October 16, 1996 though April 30, 1999. When the record closed, the parties were negotiating, but had not yet reached a successor agreement.

In 1996, the Respondent began installing a new computer system, through which all newsroom employees and many (but not all) other unit employees had e-mail access. In October 1996, the Respondent implemented the "Communications Systems Policy" (CSP) at issue here. The policy governed employees' use of the Respondent's communications systems, including e-mail. The policy stated, in relevant part:

> Company communication systems and the equipment used to operate the communication system are owned and provided by the Company to assist in conducting the business of The Register-Guard. Communications systems are not to be used to solicit or proselytize for commercial ventures, religious or political causes, outside organizations, or other non-job-related solicitations.

The Respondent's employees use e-mail regularly for work-related matters. Throughout the relevant time period, the Respondent was aware that employees also used e-mail to send and receive personal messages. The record contains evidence of e-mails such as baby announcements, party invitations, and the occasional offer of sports tickets or request for services such as dog walking. However, there is no evidence that the employees used e-mail to solicit support for or participation in any outside cause or organization other than the United Way, for which the Respondent conducted a periodic charitable campaign.

B. Prozanski's E-Mails and Resulting Discipline

Suzi Prozanski is a unit employee and the union president. In May and August 2000, Prozanski received two written warnings for sending three e-mails to unit employees at their Register-Guard e-mail addresses. The Respondent contends that the e-mails violated the CSP.

. . .

POSITIONS OF THE PARTIES

The General Counsel

The General Counsel argues that under *Republic Aviation Corp. v. NLRB,* 324 U.S. 793 (1945), rules limiting employee communication in the workplace should be evaluated by balancing employees' Section 7 rights and the employer's interest in maintaining discipline. The General Counsel contends that e-mail cannot neatly be characterized as either "solicitation" or "distribution." Nevertheless, e-mail has become the most common "gathering place" for communications on work and nonwork issues. Because the employees are rightfully on the employer's property, the employer does not have an indefeasible interest in banning personal e-mail just because the employer owns the computer system. The General Counsel distinguishes the Board's decisions that find no Section 7 right to use an employer's bulletin boards, telephones, and other equipment[6] on the basis that those cases did not involve interactive, electronic communications regularly used by employees, nor did they involve equipment used on networks where thousands of communications occur simultaneously. However, the General Counsel concedes that the employer has an interest in limiting employee e-mails to prevent liability for inappropriate content, to protect against system overloads and viruses, to preserve confidentiality, and to maintain productivity.

The General Counsel therefore proposes that broad rules prohibiting nonbusiness use of e-mail should be presumptively unlawful, absent a particularized showing of special circumstances. The General Counsel would evaluate other limitations on employee e-mail use (short of a complete ban) on a case-by-case basis.

With respect to whether an employer may prohibit employees from sending union-related e-mails while allowing other personal e-mails, the General Counsel notes that this conduct would violate Section 8(a)(1) under current Board precedent. The General Counsel disagrees with the Respondent's contention that employees communicating about a union are working on behalf of an "outside organization."

. . .

The Respondent

The Respondent argues that there is no Section 7 right to use the Respondent's e-mail system. E-mail, as part of the computer system, is equipment owned by the Respondent for the purpose of conducting its business. The Respondent notes that under Board precedent, an employer may restrict the nonbusiness use of its equipment. The Respondent argues that *Republic Aviation* and other cases dealing with oral solicitation are inapposite because they do not involve use of the employer's equipment. The Respon-

[continued]

dent observes that the Union and employees here have many means of communicating in addition to e-mail.

With respect to whether an employer has discriminatorily enforced its e-mail prohibition, the Respondent argues that the correct comparison is not between personal e-mails and union-related e-mails. Rather, the Respondent argues that in order to determine whether discriminatory enforcement has occurred, the Board should examine whether the employer has banned union-related e-mails but has permitted outside organizations to use the employer's equipment to sell products, to distribute "persuader" literature, to promote organizational meetings, or to induce group action. The Respondent argues that under this standard, the enforcement of the CSP against Prozanski was not discriminatory.

ORDER

The National Labor Relations Board orders that the Respondent, The Guard Publishing Company d/b/a The Register-Guard, Eugene, Oregon, its officers, agents, successors, and assigns, shall

1. Cease and desist from

(a) Discriminatorily prohibiting employees from using the Respondent's electronic communications systems to send union-related messages.

(b) Maintaining an overly broad rule that prohibits employees from wearing or displaying union insignia while working with customers.

(c) Issuing written warnings to, or otherwise discriminating against, any employee for supporting the Eugene Newspaper Guild, CWA Local 37194 or any other labor organization.

(d) In any like or related manner interfering with, restraining, or coercing employees in the exercise of the rights guaranteed them by Section 7 of the Act.

2. Take the following affirmative action necessary to effectuate the policies of the Act.

(a) Rescind the rule prohibiting circulation department employees from wearing or displaying union insignia while working with customers.

(b) Within 14 days from the date of this Order, rescind the unlawful warning issued to Suzi Prozanski on May 5, 2000, remove from its files any reference to the unlawful warning, and within 3 days thereafter notify Prozanski in writing that this has been done and that the warning will not be used against her in any way. . . .

>> CASE QUESTIONS

1. What was the employer's policy at issue?
2. Why was the policy challenged?
3. What was the General Counsel's argument?
4. What was the employer-Respondent's argument?
5. What are the implications of the decision?

Quasi-Judicial Authority In Sections 4, 9, and 10 of this chapter, you will study the various unfair labor practices. Congress granted the NLRB the authority to conduct the quasi-judicial hearings that are required to investigate and to enforce sanctions if these unfair labor practices occur.

This authority is extensive in that NLRB has discretion to order whatever action is necessary to correct the unlawful practice. However, as Sidebar 22.4 illustrates, there are limits to the NLRB's authority to order remedial actions.

>> *sidebar* 22.4

Limitation of NLRB's Remedies

After presenting documents that verified his legal status to work in the United States, Jose Castro was hired by Hoffman Plastic Compounds, Inc. Castro participated in a union-organizing campaign at the Hoffman facility where he worked. Hoffman laid off Castro and others engaged in this organizing effort. When it was presented with this factual situation, the National Labor Relations Board (NLRB) ordered Hoffman to reinstate Castro (and the other employees) with back pay. During a compliance hearing before an NLRB administrative law judge (ALJ), Castro acknowledged that he did not have the proper paperwork to be a legal alien eligible to work. In essence, Castro admitted that he has used another person's birth certificate to get a driver's license and social security number. Because of these admissions, the ALJ concluded that the NLRB could not award Castro reinstatement and back pay. Castro appealed to the full board, which reversed the ALJ and awarded back pay. Hoffman sought review by the Court of Appeals for the D.C. Circuit. This court upheld the NLRB's award of back pay.

Upon further review, the U.S. Supreme Court reversed the NLRB's decision. It concluded that back pay awarded to illegal aliens would "encourage the successful evasion of apprehension by immigration authorities, condone prior violations of the immigration laws, and encourage future violations."

Source: *Hoffman Plastic Compounds, Inc. v. NLRB*, 535 U.S. 137 (2002).

3. CERTIFICATION OF UNIONS

An employer may voluntarily recognize that its workers want to have a certain labor union represent them. The employer is free to agree to bargain with the union as the collective bargaining representative of the employees. In actuality, such voluntary recognition occurs in relatively few situations. More common is the NLRB's certification of a union as the bargaining agent for a group of employees. This certification process is the result of an election or occurs through authorization cards. These certification processes are discussed in the next two subsections.

Certification Elections Elections are by secret ballot and are supervised by the NLRB. The board decides what unit of employees is appropriate for purposes of collective bargaining and therefore which employees are entitled to vote in the election. It may select the total employer unit, craft unit, plant unit, or any subdivision of the plant.

Obviously, how the board exercises its discretion in this regard may be crucial to the outcome of a given election. If all 100 workers at one plant operated by an employer desire to organize but 400 out of 500 at another of the employer's plants do not, designation of the total employees as the one appropriate bargaining unit would ensure that both plants would remain nonunion.

The NLRB conducts elections upon receipt of a petition signed by at least 30 percent of the employees. In addition, an employer may file a petition for selection of an initial representative. An employer may also file a petition for an election to invalidate certification of an incumbent union. It must show that it doubts, in good faith, the continued support of the union by a majority of the employees. Votes to certify a union or to rescind a union's authority also take place by petition.

Despite the declining percentage of the workforce that is unionized, unions are winning a greater percentage of the certification elections being held.

After a NLRB election, another is not permitted for one year, regardless of whether the union wins or loses the certification vote. Within the term of a collective bargaining agreement or three years after it has been signed, whichever period is shorter, no elections may take place.

Certification through Cards A union seeking to represent employees may solicit cards from them indicating their willingness for the union to represent them. An employer may then recognize the union as the bargaining agent for its employees if the cards are signed by a majority of the employees. Employers do not need to recognize the union based on a majority card showing and always have the option to insist on an election. But once an employer recognizes the union—no matter how informally—the employer is bound by the recognition and loses the right to seek an election.

Cards also may substitute for an election if certain conditions are met. The NLRB may issue a bargaining order based on such cards if the cards are unequivocal and clearly indicate that the employee signing the card is authorizing the union to represent him or her. The general counsel of the NLRB does not need to prove that the employees read or understood the cards. If a card states on its face that it authorizes collective bargaining, counts for that purpose, unless there is clear proof that the employee was told that it would not be used for that purpose.

>> *sidebar* 22.5

Unfair Labor Practice? *The NLRB v. Boeing*

In April 2011, the NLRB filed a complaint against Boeing, Co., claiming that Boeing illegally punished the union by building an assembly line for its 787 Dreamliner jet in South Carolina instead of Washington state. The NLRB seeks to compel Boeing to move the work to Boeing's unionized plant in Washington, away from its new $1billion nonunion plant in South Carolina.

The complaint is drawing criticism from business groups who see the NLRB action as overreaching. Since 1995, three strikes shut down Boeing's facilities near Seattle. In 2008, the work stoppage lasted for eight weeks costing Boeing $2 billion. In connection with the decision, Boeing's Jim McNerney commented on "the negative financial impacts" to Boeing of "strikes happening every three or four years in Puget Sound." The NLRB claims that Boeing engaged in an illegal act of retaliation against strikers in Washington, aimed at intimidating them not to strike in the future.

Consider: Did Boeing engage in an unfair labor practice?

4. UNFAIR LABOR PRACTICES BY MANAGEMENT

Remember that Congress desired to strengthen the bargaining power of labor unions when it passed the Wagner Act in 1935. A principal means of accomplishing this goal was through the creation of five unfair labor practices by management. These practices are summarized as follows:

- Interfering with union activities.
- Dominating a labor organization.
- Discriminating based on union affiliation.
- Discriminating as a result of NLRB proceedings.
- Refusing to bargain in good faith.

Conduct may be, and often is, a violation of more than one of the listed unfair labor practices. Indeed, most violations constitute interference with the right to engage in concerted activity (the first category). For example, retaliation against a union leader for filing charges would constitute a violation of both the first and fourth categories.

Interfering with Unionization   The first unfair labor practice has two distinct parts. First, it is unfair for an employer to interfere with the efforts of employees to form, join, or assist labor organizations. The second part covers interfering with "concerted activities for mutual aid or protection." This violation does not have to involve a union; the act protects any group of employees acting for their mutual aid and protection.

The first part of this unfair labor practice by management is a catchall intended to guarantee the right of employees to organize and join unions. It clearly prohibits "scare" tactics such as threats by employers to fire those involved in organizing employees or threats to cut back on employee benefits if employees succeed in unionizing. In addition, less obvious activities are outlawed, such as requiring job applicants to state on a questionnaire whether they would cross a picket line in a strike. An employer cannot engage in any conduct calculated to erode employee support for the union.

Interference with unionization may take the form of a carrot as well as a stick. The conferring of benefits by an employer may be an unfair labor practice. In one case, the employer reminded its employees two weeks before a representation election that the company had just instituted a "floating holiday" that employees could take on their birthdays. The union lost the election, but the NLRB set it aside. It was an unfair labor practice for the employer to engage in conduct immediately favorable to employees. The conduct interfered with the freedom of choice for or against unionization.

Case 22.2 illustrates how an unfair labor practice allegation arises. Note that the issue of a union's status as a certified bargaining agent becomes intertwined with management's duty to refrain from interfering with an employee's right to engage in union activity.

case **22.2** >>

ALLENTOWN MACK SALES AND SERVICE, INC. v. NATIONAL LABOR RELATIONS BOARD
522 U.S. 359 (1998)

SCALIA, J.: Under long-standing precedent of the National Labor Relations Board, an employer who believes that an incumbent union no longer enjoys the support of a majority of its employees has three options: to request a formal, Board-supervised election, to withdraw recognition from the union and refuse to bargain, or to conduct an internal poll of employee support for the union. The Board has held that the latter two are unfair labor practices unless the employer can show that it had a "good faith reasonable doubt" about the union's majority support. We must decide whether the Board's standard for employer polling is rational and consistent with the National Labor Relations Act, and whether the Board's factual determinations in this case are supported by substantial evidence in the record.

Mack Trucks, Inc., had a factory branch in Allentown, Pennsylvania, whose service and parts employees

[continued]

were represented by Local Lodge 724 of the International Association of Machinists and Aerospace Workers, AFL-CIO. Mack notified its Allentown managers in May of 1990 that it intended to sell the branch, and several of those managers formed Allentown Mack Sales, Inc., the petitioner here, which purchased the assets of the business on December 20, 1990, and began to operate it as an independent dealership. From December 21, 1990, to January 1, 1991, Allentown hired 32 of the original 45 Mack employees.

During the period before and immediately after the sale, a number of Mack employees made statements to the prospective owners of Allentown Mack Sales suggesting that the incumbent union had lost support among employees in the bargaining unit. In job interviews, eight employees made statements indicating, or at least arguably indicating, that they personally no longer supported the union. In addition, Ron Mohr, a member of the union's bargaining committee and shop steward for the Mack Trucks service department, told an Allentown manager that it was his feeling that the employees did not want a union, and that "with a new company, if a vote was taken, the Union would lose." And Kermit Bloch, who worked for Mack Trucks as a mechanic on the night shift, told a manager that the entire night shift (then 5 or 6 employees) did not want the union.

On January 2, 1991, Local Lodge 724 asked Allentown Mack Sales to recognize it as the employees' collective-bargaining representative, and to begin negotiations for a contract. The new employer rejected that request by letter dated January 25, claiming a "good faith doubt as to support of the Union among the employees." The letter also announced that Allentown had "arranged for an independent poll by secret ballot of its hourly employees to be conducted under guidelines prescribed by the National Labor Relations Board." The poll, supervised by a Roman Catholic priest, was conducted on February 8, 1991; the union lost 19 to 13. Shortly thereafter, the union filed an unfair-labor-practice charge with the Board.

The Administrative Law Judge (ALJ) concluded that Allentown was a successor employer to Mack Trucks, Inc., and therefore inherited Mack's bargaining obligation and a presumption of continuing majority support for the union. The ALJ held that Allentown's poll . . . violated §§8(a)(1) and 8 (a)(5) of the National Labor Relations Act (Act) because Allentown did not have an "objective reasonable doubt" about the majority status of the union. The Board adopted the ALJ's findings, . . . agreed with his conclusion, . . . [and] ordered Allentown to recognize and bargain with Local 724.

On review in the Court of Appeals for the District of Columbia Circuit, Allentown challenged both the

facial rationality of the Board's test for employer polling and the Board's application of that standard to the facts of this case. The court enforced the Board's bargaining order. . . . We granted certiorari.

Allentown challenges the Board's decision in this case on several grounds. First, it contends that because the Board's "reasonable doubt" standard for employer polls is the same as its standard for unilateral withdrawal of recognition and for employer initiation of a Board-supervised election (a so-called "Representation Management," or "RM" election), the Board irrationally permits employers to poll only when it would be unnecessary and legally pointless to do so. Second, Allentown argues that the record evidence clearly demonstrates that it had a good-faith reasonable doubt about the union's claim to majority support. Finally, it asserts that the Board has abandoned the "reasonable doubt" prong of its polling standard, and recognizes an employer's "reasonable doubt" only if a majority of the unit employees renounce the union. . . . Allentown argues that it is irrational to require the same factual showing to justify a poll as to justify an outright withdrawal of recognition, because that leaves the employer with no legal incentive to poll. Under the Board's framework, the results of a poll can never supply an otherwise lacking "good-faith reasonable doubt" necessary to justify a withdrawal of recognition, since the employer must already have that same reasonable doubt before he is permitted to conduct a poll. . . . While the Board's adoption of a unitary standard for polling, RM elections, and withdrawals of recognition is in some respects a puzzling policy, we do not find it so irrational as to be "arbitrary [or] capricious" within the meaning of the Administrative Procedure Act. The Board believes that employer polling is potentially "disruptive" to established bargaining relationships and "unsettling" to employees, and so has chosen to limit severely the circumstances under which it may be conducted. The unitary standard reflects the Board's apparent conclusion that polling should be tolerated only when the employer might otherwise simply withdraw recognition and refuse to bargain. . . .

If it would be rational for the Board to set the polling standard either higher or lower than the threshold for an RM election, then surely it is not irrational for the Board to split the difference.

The Board held Allentown guilty of an unfair labor practice in its conduct of the polling because it had not demonstrated that it held a reasonable doubt, based on objective considerations, that the Union continued to enjoy the support of a majority of the bargaining unit employees. We must decide whether that conclusion is supported by substantial evidence

[continued]

on the record as a whole. Put differently, we must decide whether on this record it would have been possible for a reasonable jury to reach the Board's conclusion. . . .

[The Court reviewed the facts and determined that the evidence supported the petitioner's doubt that the majority of its employees supported the union.] We conclude that the Board's "reasonable doubt" test for employer polls is facially rational and consistent with the Act. But the Board's factual finding that Allentown Mack Sales lacked such a doubt is not supported by substantial evidence on the record as a whole. The judgment of the Court of Appeals for the D.C. Circuit is therefore reversed, and the case is remanded with instructions to deny enforcement.

Reversed and remanded.

>> CASE QUESTIONS

1. What event occurred that allowed the representation of employees by a union to be called into question?
2. What were the findings and order by the NLRB?
3. What issues were presented to the Supreme Court?
4. Why does the Court agree with the NLRB about a unitary standard of "reasonable doubt" for refusing to bargain, polling employees, and requesting a decertification election?
5. How does the Court differ with the NLRB in this case?
6. Do you agree with the Court analyses and conclusions?

Interfering With Concerted Activities The term **concerted activity** is given a liberal interpretation in order to create a climate that encourages unionization, collective bargaining, and all that may flow from such activity. For example, some employees refused to work after a heated grievance meeting. They followed their supervisors onto the workroom floor and continued to argue loudly until they were ordered a second time to resume work. The employer issued letters of reprimand alleging insubordination. This was an unfair labor practice. The protection of employee conduct at grievance meetings is extended to a brief cooling-off period following an employer's termination of such a meeting. Protection of employees' participation in the meetings themselves would be seriously threatened if the employer could at any point call an immediate halt to the operation of the law simply by declaring the meeting ended.

The concerted-activity concept is quite extensive. In one case, an employer was investigating theft by employees. One employee asked that a union representative be present during her interview. She was refused. The Supreme Court held that the employee had a right to representation when there was a perceived threat to her employment security. The presence of a representative assures other employees in the bargaining unit that they, too, can obtain aid and protection if they wish when there appears to be a threat to their job security. Refusing the assistance at the interview was an unfair labor practice.

In addition, the right to engage in concerted activity has been expanded to cover the actions of a sole employee under certain circumstances. If an employee has a grievance that may affect other workers, that employee has rights protected by the concerted-activity language of this unfair labor practice, even though no other worker participates in the activity.

Dominating a Labor Organization

The second unfair labor practice prohibits the domination of a labor organization by employers or their contribution of financial or other support to any union. Under the Wagner Act, any organization of employees must be completely independent of their employers. In the case of a controversy between competing unions, employers must remain strictly neutral. It is an unfair labor practice for the employer to support a union by giving it a meeting place; providing refreshments for union meetings; permitting the union to use the employer's telephone, secretary, or copying machine; or allowing the union to keep cafeteria or vending-machine profits.

Discriminating Based on Union Affiliation

The Supreme Court has held that an employer who reports the possible existence of illegal aliens to the Immigration and Naturalization Service engages in an unfair labor practice when that report is closely associated with the employees' approval of a labor union as their bargaining agent.

Under the third unfair labor practice, an employer may neither discharge nor refuse to hire an employee to either encourage or discourage membership in any labor organization. Nor may the employer discriminate regarding any term or condition of employment for such purposes. The law does not oblige an employer to favor union members in hiring employees. It also does not restrict him or her in the normal exercise of any employer's right to select or discharge employees. However, the employer may not abuse that right by discriminatory action based on union membership or activities that encourage or discourage membership in a labor organization.

A company may not go partially out of business because some of its employees have organized, nor may it temporarily close that portion of its business that has unionized. If a company closes one plant because a union is voted in, such action discourages union activity at other plants. Partial closings to "chill" unionism are unfair labor practices.

Discriminating as a Result of NLRB Proceedings

The fourth unfair labor practice, prohibits discharge or from other reprisals by their employers because they are enforcing their rights under the Wagner Act by filing charges or giving testimony in NLRB proceedings. This protection prevents the NLRB's channels of information from evaporating by employer intimidation of complainants and witnesses. An employer cannot refuse to hire a prospective employee because charges have been filed by him or her.

The main defense of any employer accused of reprisal is that he or she discharged or discriminated against the employee for some reason other than filing charges or giving testimony. Most often such cases boil down to trying to prove what motivated the company in pursuing its course of action. If the company can convince the NLRB that the employee was discharged because of misconduct, low production, personnel cutbacks necessitated by economic conditions, or other legitimate considerations, the company will be exonerated. Otherwise, it will be found guilty of this unfair labor practice.

Refusing to Bargain in Good Faith

Take-it-or-leave-it demands in a negotiation are considered bad-faith bargaining.

The fifth unfair labor practice occurs when management refuses to bargain with the collective bargaining representative of its employees. The Wagner Act did not define the phrase "to bargain collectively." Judicial decisions have added the concept of *good faith* to bargaining. To comply with the requirement that they bargain collectively in good faith, employers must approach the bargaining table with fair and open minds and a sincere intent to find a basis of agreement.

The employer's duty to bargain collectively includes a duty to provide relevant information needed by a union for the proper performance of its duties as the employees' bargaining representative. For example, data about job related safety and health must be furnished so that the union can safeguard its members' health and safety.

A more fundamental issue inherent in the requirement that parties bargain collectively is: "About what?" Must the employer bargain with the union about all subjects and all management decisions in which the union or the employees are interested? Are there subjects and issues upon which management is allowed to act alone? See Sidebar 22.6 for a discussion about the "Writers Strike."

Refusing to meet at reasonable times with representatives of the other party, refusing to reduce agreements to writing, and designating persons with no authority to negotiate as representatives at meetings are examples of this unfair labor practice.

>> sidebar 22.6

This Was No Joke: The Writers Guild of America Strike

In November 2007, more than 12,000 film, television, and radio writers joined together in the Writers Guild of America strike against the Alliance of Motion Picture and Television Producers, a trade organization representing nearly 400 American film and television producers.

>> WHAT WAS AT ISSUE?

The most contentious issues at stake: DVD residuals, union jurisdiction over animation and reality program writers, and compensation for "new media," content written for or distributed through emerging digital technology, including the Internet.

>> HOW MUCH DID THE STRIKE COST?

According to an NPR report, the strike cost the economy of Los Angeles an estimated $1.5 billion.

The "Big Four" networks (ABC, CBS, FOX, and NBC) suffered ad shortfalls and declines in prime time ratings.

>> WHAT WAS THE OUTCOME OF THE DISPUTE?

On February 12, 2008, the strike concluded after the parties reached an agreement creating formulas for revenue-based residuals in new media, providing access to deals and financial data to help writers evaluate and enforce the formulas, and establishing the principle for the writers "When they get paid, we get paid." Another outcome was the solidarity that developed throughout the group from the most successful writers to those fighting to get into the business.

For more information about the agreement, see http://unitedhollywood.blogspot.com/.

In answering these questions, the law divides issues into two categories—**compulsory bargaining issues** and **voluntary bargaining issues.** Compulsory, or mandatory, bargaining issues are those concerned with wages, hours, and other terms and conditions of employment. Although the parties may voluntarily consider other issues, the refusal by either to bargain in good faith on such other permissive matters is not an unfair labor practice.

Classifying an issue as *compulsory* or *voluntary* is done on a case-by-case basis. For example, questions relating to fringe benefits are compulsory bargaining issues because they are "wages." The NLRB and the courts are called on to decide whether management and labor must bargain with each other on a multitude of issues. A good example of a case in which bargaining was required is *Ford Motor Co. v. NLRB* (441 U.S. 488).

Employees of the Ford Motor Company belong to the United Auto Workers. Ford provides in-plant cafeterias and vending machines as two ways to ensure its employees with food services. An independent caterer managed both the cafeterias and vending machines. This caterer informed Ford that the

The 73,000 United Automobile Workers went on strike at General Motors in 2007, seeking job security during restructuring of the company. GM is seeking to lower its cost structure and to have a more flexible workforce to compete with other automakers such as Toyota and Honda.

increased costs associated with these food services required food prices to go up. When Ford notified the union representative of these food cost increases, the union requested bargaining be held over the food prices and services.

Ford refused to bargain, and the union filed a charge with the NLRB alleging Ford's refusal to bargain in good faith, which is an unfair labor practice. The NLRB concluded that in-plant food and related services are "other terms and conditions of employment." Therefore, Ford must negotiate with the union over this compulsory bargaining issue. The Supreme Court's review of these facts results in the NLRB's ruling being affirmed.

A party to labor negotiations may present a demand to bargain about a voluntary issue as long as this issue does not have to be resolved before the parties can resolve compulsory bargaining issues. Tying a voluntary bargaining issue to a compulsory bargaining issue results in a failure to bargain in good faith and is in effect an unfair labor practice.

Courts tend to defer to the special expertise of the NLRB in classifying collective bargaining subjects, especially in the area of "terms or conditions of employment." Examples of board rulings holding that issues such as union dues checkoff; health and accident insurance; safety rules; merit pay increases; incentive pay plans; Christmas and other bonuses; stock purchase plans; pensions; paid vacations and holidays; the privilege of hunting on a reserved portion of a paper company's forest preserve; proposals for effective arbitration and grievance procedures; and no-strike and no-lockout clauses are compulsory bargaining issues.

Remember that neither the employer nor the union must make concessions to the other concerning a mandatory subject of bargaining. The law only demands that each negotiate such matters in good faith with the other before making a decision and taking unilateral action. If the parties fail to reach an agreement after discussing these problems, each may take steps that are against the wishes and best interests of the other party. For example, the employer may refuse to grant a wage increase requested by the union, and the union is free to strike.

>> sidebar 22.7

Fired! Venting About the Boss on Facebook

Can you imagine calling your supervisor a "scumbag" or comparing him to a psychiatric patient? Dawnmarie Souza, an employee of American Medical Response of Connecticut, Inc. (AMR), criticized her supervisor on her Facebook page. Souza was terminated for violating AMR's policy, which states: "Employees are prohibited from making disparaging, discriminatory or defamatory comments when discussing the Company or the employee's supervisors, co-workers and/or competitors." The policy also prohibits "Rude or discourteous behavior to a client or co-worker."

The NLRB issued a complaint claiming that AMR's firing was an unfair labor practice. The NLRB also alleged that AMR's Internet policies were overly broad and interfere with an employee's right to engage in protected activities under the NLRA.

The NLRB settled the case, requiring AMR to "revise its Internet policy to allow workers to discuss wages, hours and working conditions with co-workers outside of the workplace; and refrain from disciplining or discharging employees for engaging in those discussions." AMR reached a separate, private settlement with Souza.

The NLRB's complaint is available at www.employmentlawalert.com/uploads/file/PDF Complaint.pdf.

>> The Taft-Hartley Act

The Wagner Act opened the door for the rapid growth of the union movement. From 1935 to the end of World War II, the strength and influence of unions grew substantially. Where, prior to the Wagner Act, employers had the greater advantage in bargaining power, by 1946 many persons felt the pendulum had shifted and that unions, with their ability to call nationwide, crippling strikes, had the better bargaining position. To balance the scale, the Labor-Management Relations Act (the **Taft-Hartley Act**) was enacted in 1947 to amend the Wagner Act.

The purposes of the Taft-Hartley Act are to ensure the free flow of commerce by eliminating union practices that burden commerce and to provide procedures for avoiding disputes that jeopardize the public health, safety, or interest. It recognizes that both parties to collective bargaining need protection from wrongful interference by the other and that employees sometimes need protection from the union itself. Finally, it sought to protect the public interest in major labor disputes. Congress authorized the creation of the Federal Mediation and Conciliation Service to help achieve the goals of the Taft-Hartley Act. Members of this service are available to assist the parties in settling labor disputes.

5. EIGHTY-DAY COOLING-OFF PERIOD

Somewhat like the 60-day period provided under the Railway Labor Act, the Taft-Hartley Act provides for an *80-day cooling-off period* following certain procedures. This provision's intent is to limit the adverse impact of the nationwide strikes by steelworkers, mineworkers, autoworkers, and longshoremen that can paralyze the economy. When a threatened or actual strike or lockout affecting an entire industry or substantial part thereof will, if permitted to occur or to continue, imperil the national health or safety, the 80-day period may be enforced. The procedure starts with the president recognizing the emergency and appointing a board of inquiry to obtain facts about the threatened or actual strike or lockout. The board studies the situation and reports back to the president. If the board finds that the national health or safety is indeed affected by the strike, then the president, through the attorney general, goes to the federal court for an injunction ordering the union to suspend the strike (or the company to suspend the lockout) for 80 days.

During the 80-day period, the Federal Mediation and Conciliation Service works with the labor-management parties to try to achieve an agreement. If during this time the reconciliation effort fails, the presidential board holds new hearings and receives the company's final offer. The union members are then allowed to vote on this final proposal by the company. If they vote for the new proposal, the dispute is over and work continues as usual. If they vote against the proposal, the workers may again be called out on strike. At this point, the strike may continue indefinitely until the disagreement causing it is resolved by collective bargaining or unless there is additional legislation by Congress to solve the problem.

Experience has shown that disputes are often settled during the 80-day period. The injunction provided for in the Taft-Hartley Act may not be used for all strikes and lockouts. This injunction is limited to *national emergency* strikes and lockouts, those that involve national defense or key industries or have a substantial effect on the economy.

In its attempt to balance the bargaining power between labor unions and management, the Taft-Hartley Act:

- Provides for an *80-day cooling-off period* in strikes that imperil the nation's health or safety.

- Reinforces the employer's freedom of speech in labor-management relations.

- Outlaws the *closed-shop* concept but permits *union shops* in the absence of a state *right-to-know* law.

- Permits suits by union members for breach of contract against unions.

- Creates six unfair labor practices by unions.

President George W. Bush used this provision to end the longshoremen's strike on the West Coast in 2002.

>> *sidebar* 22.8

Tweeting His Way to Termination

The *Arizona Daily Star* fired one of its public safety reporters for inappropriate and unprofessional tweets, including the following:

- "You stay homicidal, Tucson. See Star Net for the bloody deets."
- "What?!?!? No overnight homicide? WTF? You're slacking Tucson."
- "Suggestion for new Tucson-area theme song: Droening [sic] pool's 'let the bodies hit the floor'."
- "I'd root for daily death if it always happened in close proximity to Gus Balon's."
- "Hope everyone's having a good Homicide Friday, as one Tucson police officer called it."
- "My discovery of the Red Zone channel is like an adolescent boy's discovery of h . . . let's just hope I don't end up going blind."

Even after Human Resources encouraged the reporter to discuss concerns with colleagues instead of Twitter and his managing editor told him that he should not make comments on social media that could damage the paper's reputation, the reporter continued to tweet. The *Arizona Daily Star* did not have a written policy about using Twitter.

The reporter was fired. What was the position of the NLRB? In a memorandum, the NLRB stated "The charging party's conduct was not protected and concerted: It did not relate to the terms and conditions of his employment or seek to involve other employees in issues related to employment."

6. FREE SPEECH

Employers complained that the Wagner Act violated their right of free speech. Statements by management formed the basis of unfair labor practices claims. To meet this objection, Congress, in Taft-Hartley, added the following provision:

> 8(c) The expressing of any views, argument, or opinion, or the dissemination thereof, whether in written, printed, graphic, or visual form, shall not constitute or be evidence of an unfair labor practice under any of the provisions of this Act, if such expression contains no threat of reprisal or force or promise of benefit.

This provision gives employers limited free speech, at best. It is difficult to make statements that cannot be construed as a threat or a promise. For example, if an employer predicts dire economic events as a result of unionization, such may be an illegal threat if the employer has it within his or her power to make the prediction come true. Whether particular language is coercive or not often depends on the analysis of the total background of facts and circumstances in which it was uttered. To be forbidden, the statements of an employer need not be proved to have been coercive in fact but only to have had a reasonable tendency to intimidate employees under the circumstances.

An employer's threats to withdraw existing benefits if employees unionize is not speech protected by Section 8(c). However, mere predictions and prophecies are protected. For example, in one case an employer's speeches and handbills during the union's organizational campaign stated its intention to fight the union in every legal way possible and to "deal hard" with the union at arm's length if it were voted in. The employer also warned that employees could be permanently replaced if the union called an economic strike. This language was held to fall within the protection of Section 8(c).

The right of free speech guaranteed by the Taft-Hartley Act applies to labor unions as well as employers. However, there is a rule prohibiting either side from making election speeches on company time to massed assemblies of employees within 24 hours before an election.

>> *sidebar* 22.9

Restricting Workplace Speech: Setting the Parameters

These NLRB cases shed light on the kinds of speech restrictions that are permissible—or not—in the workplace. Section 7 of the National Labor Relations Act (NLRA) guarantees that *all* employees (regardless of union status) have the right to engage in "concerted activities for the purpose of . . . mutual aid or protection."

The Policy: Employees are prohibited from discussing work conditions, wages, benefits, and discipline.

NLRB Decision: This policy is illegally broad and violates the NLRA by promulgating a confidentiality rule prohibiting employees from discussing disciplinary information, grievances and complaints, performance evaluations, or salary information with any persons outside the company or with fellow employees.

See *Double Eagle Hotel & Casino,* 341 NLRB No. 17 (January 20, 2004), upheld by the 10th Cir (2005); see also *Longs Drug Stores California, Inc.,* 347 NLRB No 45 (2006).

The Policy: Maintenance of work rules prohibit the use of "abusive and profane language," "verbal, mental, and physical abuse," and "harassment . . . in any way."

NLRB Decision: The rule is lawful and could not reasonably be understood as interfering with employees' Section 7 rights. The rule is lawful because it is based on the employer's legitimate right to establish a "civil and decent" workplace to protect itself from liability for workplace harassment. *Lutheran Heritage Village-Livonia,* 343 NLRB No. 75 (2004).

---

7. UNION SHOP—MEMBERSHIPS AND FEES

The Wagner Act's strong support of unionization gave unintended bargaining power to unions with respect to an employer's hiring practices. In many bargaining situations, the union became so strong that it successfully insisted on management's hiring only union members. In essence, to apply for a prospective job, a person would have to join the union. These situations became known as **closed shops.**

One of the major changes brought about by the Taft-Hartley Act was outlawing of the closed shop. This act still permitted the **union shop.** In a union shop contract, also known as a **union security clause,** the employer agrees that after an employee is hired that employee must join the union as a condition of continued employment. The Taft-Hartley Act, prohibits such a requirement until the thirtieth day after employment begins.

Through a series of cases, the Supreme Court clarified the limited mandatory relationship created by the inclusion of the union security clause in a contract. This type of relationship requires that the union members pay reasonable membership fees and dues. In turn, the union can use these fees and dues only for collective bargaining, contract administration, and grievance activities. Unions are not allowed to use members' dues to support political activities.

One of the sections of the Taft-Hartley Act most distasteful to unions is 14(b), which outlaws the union shop in states that have adopted a right-to-work law. **Right-to-work laws** prohibit agreements requiring membership in a labor organization as a condition of continued employment of a person who was not in the union when hired. Approximately 20 states have right-to-work laws

Right-to-work laws are mostly in the South and Southwest, areas that historically have been antiunion.

today. Workers in these states who do not belong to a union may not be required to pay representation fees to the union that represents the employees. However, such workers are subject to the terms of the collective bargaining agreement, and the union must handle their grievances, if any, with management.

8. SUITS AGAINST UNIONS

Many suits against unions are by members alleging a breach of the duty of fair representation.

Section 301 of the Taft-Hartley Act provides that suits for breach of a contract between an employer and a labor organization can be filed in the federal district courts without regard to the amount in question. A labor organization is responsible for the acts of its agents and may sue or be sued. Any money judgment against it is enforceable only against its assets and not against any individual member. Moreover, individuals cannot be sued for actions such as violating no-strike provisions of a collective bargaining contract.

In addition, members may sue their union and recover the money damages they suffer because of an illegal strike. If a union activity is both an unfair labor practice and a breach of a collective bargaining agreement, the NLRB's authority is not exclusive and does not destroy the jurisdiction of courts under Section 301 of the Taft-Hartley Act.

Since workers cannot bargain individually when represented by a union, the union has an implied duty of fair representation to act reasonably, with honesty of purpose, and in good faith. The union must represent all the employees in the bargaining unit, including those who are nonunion, impartially and without hostile discrimination. Failure to do so may give rise to a lawsuit.

The duty of fair representation applies not only to the *negotiation* of a collective bargaining agreement but also to the *administration* of the agreement. Unions must fairly represent employers in disputes with the employer regarding the *interpretation* and *application* of the terms of an existing contract.

An employee may file suit against the union and its representatives for damages resulting from breach of their duty of fair representation in processing his or her grievance against the employer. A union may not process a grievance in an arbitrary, indifferent, or careless manner.

Finally, a union member may sue a local union for failing to enforce the international union's constitution and bylaws. Thus, Section 301 of the Taft-Hartley Act authorizes an employer to sue a union for breach of contract as well as employees to sue to enforce either the union-management collective bargaining agreement or a union contract with a member.

>> *sidebar* 22.10

Making A Point: Union Protests With Giant Inflatable Rats

 Over the last two decades, giant inflatable rats—as tall as 25 feet—have gained popularity as symbols of anti-union activity. The rats make a graphic visual statement in connection with union protests against companies that hire nonunion workers or do not pay union wages.

In one such protest, the Sheet Metal Workers International Association Local 15 staged a mock funeral in front of a Florida hospital along with a giant rat. That case involved using a staffing agency that employed nonunion workers.

The NLRB ruled that the rats are legally permissible, that the tactic does not violate labor law and is protected speech. Ironically, the manufacturer of the balloons is allegedly a nonunion company.

9. UNFAIR LABOR PRACTICES BY UNIONS

Perhaps more than with any other provision of the Taft-Hartley Act, Congress attempted to balance the bargaining power in the labor-management relationship by enacting six unfair labor practices by unions. These balance the unfair labor practices by management in the Wagner Act, as discussed in Section 4. Six unfair labor practices by unions are:

- Restraining or coercing an employee to join a union or an employer in selecting representatives to bargain with the union.
- Causing or attempting to cause the employer to discriminate against an employee who is not a union member unless there is a legal union shop agreement in effect.
- Refusing to bargain with the employer if it is the NLRB-designated representative of the employees.
- Striking, picketing, or engaging in secondary boycotts for illegal purposes.
- Charging new members excessive or discriminatory initiation fees when there is a union shop agreement.
- Causing an employer to pay for work not performed (featherbedding).

Three of these illegal practices can be presented in a summary fashion due to the preceding discussions in this chapter or because they have very little impact today. The third unfair labor practice by unions is complementary to the fifth unfair labor practice by management. In essence, Congress requires unions to bargain in good faith as is required of management. The fifth unfair labor practice by unions simply means that unions cannot take advantage of the union shop agreement by charging unreasonable dues or fees when members and nonmembers are obligated to pay them. Today, the sixth unfair labor practice, involving *featherbedding*, or payment for work not actually performed, is of less importance than when it was enacted in 1947.

The other unfair labor practices by unions are presented in the following subsections.

Restraining or Coercing an Employee into Joining a Union This unfair labor practice includes misconduct by unions directed toward employees. The law makes it illegal for a union to restrain or coerce employees in the exercise of their rights to bargain collectively, just as it is an unfair labor practice by employers to interfere with the same rights. Employees also are guaranteed the right to *refrain* from union activities unless they are required to join the union by a legal union shop agreement.

Causing an Employer to Discriminate against a Non-Union Member If a legal union shop agreement is in effect, a labor organization may insist that the employer observe its terms. But even when a legal union shop contract is in effect, the law prohibits a union from attempting to cause an employer to discriminate against an employee who has been denied membership or had his or her membership terminated for some reason other than failure to pay the dues and initiation fees uniformly required of all members. And even if an employee is a member, the union may not cause the employer to discriminate against him or her for not following union rules. This prohibition prevents the use of the union shop as a means of intimidating employees who were at odds with union officials over their policies.

Striking or Picketing for Illegal Purposes or Engaging in Secondary Boycotts Jurisdictional strikes are unfair labor practices. A **jurisdictional strike** is used to force an employer to assign work to employees in one craft union rather than another. Since the dispute is between the two unions and not with the employer, the law requires that such disputes be submitted to the NLRB by the unions.

It is also an unfair labor practice for a union to threaten or to coerce by picketing, for example, an employer to recognize or bargain with one union if another one has been certified as the representative of its employees.

It is an unfair labor practice for a union to threaten, coerce, or restrain a third person not party to a labor dispute for the purpose of causing that third person to exert pressure on the company involved in the labor dispute. This law requires that strikes and picketing be directed at the employer with which the union actually has a labor dispute.

An example of illegal secondary activity occurs when a union induces the employees of an employer to strike or engage in a concerted refusal to use, handle, or work on any goods or to perform any service to force the employer to stop doing business with some third person. For example, assume that a supplier (like a bakery) has a workforce that is nonunionized. A customer (i.e., a grocery store) has employees who belong to a union. This union would like to be the bargaining representative for the supplier's employees. It would be an illegal secondary boycott for this union to have its members either strike or picket the grocery store on the basis of it selling nonunionized baked goods from the bakery in the hope that the grocery store would discontinue its buying from this bakery. The union must deal directly with the bakery.

>> *sidebar* 22.11

Change to Win: Securing the American Dream

Unions and over 5.5 workers united in *Change to Win* with a mission to "unite the 50 million workers in Change to Win affiliate industries whose jobs cannot be outsourced and who are vital to the global economy."

Their goal: Securing the American Dream for *all* working people.

>> WHICH UNIONS ARE MEMBERS?

International Brotherhood of Teamsters (IBT)

Service Employees International Union (SEIU)

United Farm Workers of America (UFW)

United Food and Commercial Workers International Union (UFCW)

UNITE HERE

>> WHAT ARE THE MAIN ISSUES?

- Jobs and wages.
- Health care.
- Retirement security.
- Freedom to join together in unions.
- Employee Free Choice Act (EFCA).
- Immigrant workers' rights.
- Workplace health and safety.
- Trade and globalization.

2011 Campaigns:

- Fair Treatment for Farmworkers
- Making Change at Walmart
- Clean and Safe Ports

Source: www.changetowin.org/

10. AMENDMENTS

Congressional hearings in the 1950s uncovered widespread corruption, violence, and lack of democratic procedures in some labor unions. As a result, Congress passed the **Landrum-Griffin Act,** or Labor-Management Reporting and Disclosure Act (LMRDA), in 1959. Its provisions constitute a "bill of rights" for union members and provide for union reform. Also in this act, Congress included some amendments to the unfair labor practices by management and unions.

In essence, in its continuing attempt to balance the bargaining power in the labor-management relationship, Congress added one unfair labor practice by management and two by unions.

Agreeing to Engage in a Secondary Boycott You should recall from your reading in the preceding section that unions cannot engage in secondary boycotts. Technically, nothing in that unfair labor practice, as enacted in the Taft-Hartley Act, prohibited a union and an employer from agreeing to engage in a secondary boycott. The original restriction applied only to the unilateral acts of the union. The Landrum-Griffin Act clarified the concern over secondary boycotts by prohibiting a union-management agreement that would adversely impact a neutral third party.

It is also an unfair labor practice for both the employer involved and the union to enter into a **hot-cargo contract.** A hot-cargo contract is one in which an employer voluntarily agrees with a union that the employees should not be required by their employer to handle or work on goods or materials going to or coming from an employer designated by the union as "unfair." Such goods are said to be hot cargo. These clauses were common in trucking and construction labor contracts. The law thus forbids an employer and a labor organization to make an agreement under which the employer agrees to stop doing business with any other employer.

Picketing When Not Certified In certain cases it is illegal for unions to force an employer to recognize or bargain with the union if it is not currently certified as the duly authorized collective bargaining representative. The purpose is to reinforce the effectiveness of the election procedures employed by the NLRB by outlawing certain tactics used by unions backed by only a minority of the employees of a particular employer. Thus, picketing to force an employer to recognize an uncertified union is an unfair labor practice in the following cases:

1. When the employer has lawfully recognized another union as the collective bargaining representative of its employees.
2. When a valid representation election has been conducted by the NLRB within the past 12 months.
3. When picketing has been conducted for an unreasonable time, in excess of 30 days, without a petition for a representation election being filed with the NLRB.

Including these amendments by the Landrum-Griffin Act, the law on unfair labor practices is summarized in the following concept summary. Remember, as you review these materials, Congress used three laws to create

742 **PART 5** The Employer-Employee Relationship

these lists. The first five items on management's side were enacted in 1935. The first six on the union side came in 1947. The sixth item on the left side and the last two items on the right side were added in 1959.

concept >> *summary*

Unfair Labor Practices

>> BY MANAGEMENT

1. Interfering with unionization and concerted activities by employees.
2. Dominating a union or contributing to it, financially or otherwise.
3. Discriminating in hiring or tenure of employees on the basis of union affiliation.
4. Discriminating against employees who seek to enforce their Wagner Act rights.
5. Refusing to bargain collectively in good faith.
6. Agreeing with a labor organization to engage in a secondary boycott.

>> BY UNIONS

1. Restraining or coercing an employee to join a union.
2. Causing an employer to discriminate against a nonunion member.
3. Refusing to bargain collectively in good faith.
4. Striking, picketing, or engaging in secondary boycotts for illegal purposes.
5. Charging excessive or discriminatory fees.
6. Causing an employer to pay for work not performed.
7. Picketing to force an employer to recognize or bargain with an uncertified union.
8. Agreeing with an employer to engage in a secondary boycott.

>> Key Terms

Clayton Act 719	Landrum-Griffin Act 741	Taft-Hartley Act 735
Closed shop 737	National Labor Relations	Union security clause 737
Collective bargaining 718	Board (NLRB) 723	Union shop 737
Compulsory bargaining	National Mediation	Voluntary bargaining
issue 733	Board 720	issue 733
Concerted activity 731	Norris-LaGuardia Act 721	Wagner Act 722
Hot-cargo contract 741	Railway Labor Act 720	Yellow-dog contract 721
Jurisdictional strike 740	Right-to-work law 737	

>> Review Questions and Problems

Labor Laws

1. *Law before 1935*
   (a) What is the specific purpose of (1) the Clayton Act, (2) the Railway Labor Act, and (3) the Norris-LaGuardia Act?
   (b) Why did these laws not increase laborers' bargaining power to the degree that is considered equal to management's bargaining power?

The Wagner Act

2. *National Labor Relations Board*

   Describe the nature and limitations of the NLRB's jurisdiction.

3. *Certification of Unions*

   The NLRB conducted a certification election, and the union won by a vote of 22–20. Management refused to bargain with this union.

   The reason for this refusal to recognize the union as the employees' bargaining agent was that the union had used "recognition slips" as a means of indicating the employees' support for the union. Several employees testified that they signed these slips to avoid the payment of the initiation fee. Further, at least a few employees indicated that they thought they had to vote for the union since they had signed a recognition slip. Should the NLRB set aside this election of the union? Explain.

4. *Unfair Labor Practices by Management*

   (a) List the five unfair labor practices created by the Wagner Act.

   (b) Describe a situation for each of these unfair labor practices.

The Taft-Hartley Act

5. *Eighty-Day Cooling-Off Period*

   (a) Under what circumstances is the president authorized to order parties in a labor dispute back to work for 80 days?

   (b) Describe the procedures that must be followed to invoke this cooling-off period.

6. *Free Speech*

   The personnel director of your company has been asked to talk with the employees about the benefits and detriments of voting for or against the union in an upcoming certification election. What should this director keep in mind about the Free Speech Clause in the Taft-Hartley Act? Explain.

7. *Union Shop—Memberships and Fees*

   Pat lives in a state that has enacted a right-to-work law. The company that employs her has recognized the United Clerical Workers (UCW) as the bargaining representative of its workers. The union has sought to collect union dues or their equivalent from Pat. Is she required to pay them? Why or why not?

8. *Suits against Unions*

   Ed is discharged for allegedly stealing property from his employer. He asks his union to have him reinstated because his discharge violates the collective bargaining agreement in force. However, the union does not investigate the incident until it is too late to file a request for arbitration under the collective bargaining agreement. Assuming that Ed is innocent of the charges, does he have any rights against the union? Explain.

9. *Unfair Labor Practices by Unions*

   (a) List the six unfair labor practices created by the Taft-Hartley Act.

   (b) Describe a situation for each of these unfair labor practices.

10. *Amendments*

    (a) What were two basic purposes for Congress's passing the Landrum-Griffin Act?

    (b) What are the additional unfair labor practices added by this law?

business >> *discussions*

1. For years, your small electronics company has given all its employees one week's pay and a turkey each Christmas. But now a recession is eroding profitability and the company is operating at a significant loss, so you consider canceling the Christmas presents for this year. The employees have just voted for union representation, and the extra pay and turkeys are not mentioned in the collective bargaining agreement.

Is a Christmas gift still purely a management decision?
Are you in trouble if you cancel the turkeys?
What is the union's role in the decision?

2. Sarah works at a small accounting firm. The firm's handbook contains the following policy:

Employees are prohibited from discussing their salary, bonuses, or any other forms of compensation, including benefits and vacation time.

Sarah is very careful not to violate the policy but, after she becomes married to her co-worker Bill, Sarah realizes that her salary is 20 percent less than Bill's salary. Bill and Sarah were hired at the same time and at the same position level. Sarah is even more upset when she learns that Bill started at the higher salary on his first day on the job. When Sarah asks her boss about the difference, she is terminated.

What potential claims could Sarah assert against her employer?
What defenses should the employer raise?

>> appendix III

>> The Constitution of the United States of America

We, the People of the United States, in Order to form a more perfect Union, establish Justice, insure domestic Tranquility, provide for the common defense, promote the general Welfare, and secure the Blessings of Liberty to ourselves and our Posterity, do ordain and establish this Constitution for the United States of America.

Article I

Section 1. All legislative Powers herein granted shall be vested in a Congress of the United States, which shall consist of a Senate and House of Representatives.

Section 2. The House of Representatives shall be composed of Members chosen every second Year by the People of the several States, and the Electors in each State shall have the Qualifications requisite for Electors of the most numerous Branch of the State Legislature.

No Person shall be a Representative who shall not have attained the Age of twenty five Years, and been seven Years a Citizen of the United States, and who shall not, when elected, be an Inhabitant of that State in which he shall be chosen.

Representatives and direct Taxes shall be apportioned among the several States which may be included within this Union, according to their respective Numbers, which shall be determined by adding the whole Number of free Persons, including those bound to Service for a Term of Years, and excluding Indians not taxed, three-fifths of all other Persons. The actual Enumeration shall be made within three Years after the first Meeting of the Congress of the United States, and within every subsequent Term of ten Years, in such Manner as they shall by Law direct. The Number of Representatives shall not exceed one for every thirty Thousand, but each State shall have at Least one Representative; and until such enumeration shall be made, the State of New Hampshire shall be entitled to chuse three, Massachusetts eight, Rhode Island and Providence Plantations one, Connecticut five, New-York six, New Jersey four, Pennsylvania eight, Delaware one, Maryland six, Virginia ten, North Carolina five, South Carolina five, and Georgia three.

When vacancies happen in the Representation from any State, the Executive Authority thereof shall issue Writs of Election to fill such Vacancies.

The House of Representatives shall chuse their Speaker and other Officers; and shall have the sole Power of Impeachment.

Section 3. The Senate of the United States shall be composed of two Senators from each State, chosen by the Legislature thereof, for six Years; and each Senator shall have one Vote.

Immediately after they shall be assembled in Consequence of the Election, they shall be divided as equally as may be into three Classes. The Seats of the Senators of the first Class shall be vacated at the Expiration of the second Year, of the second Class at the Expiration of the fourth Year, and of the third Class at the Expiration of the sixth Year, so that one third may be chosen every second Year; and if Vacancies happen by Resignation, or otherwise, during the Recess of the Legislature of any State, the Executive thereof may make temporary Appointments until the next Meeting of the Legislature, which shall then fill such Vacancies.

No Person shall be a Senator who shall not have attained to the Age of thirty Years, and been nine Years a Citizen of the United States, and who shall not, when elected, be an Inhabitant of that State for which he shall be chosen.

The Vice President of the United States shall be President of the Senate, but shall have no Vote, unless they be equally divided.

The Senate shall chuse their other Officers, and also a President pro tempore, in the Absence of the Vice President, or when he shall exercise the Office of the President of the United States.

The Senate shall have the sole Power to try all Impeachments. When sitting for that Purpose, they shall be on Oath or Affirmation. When the President of the United States is tried, the Chief Justice shall preside: and no Person shall be convicted without the Concurrence of two-thirds of the Members present.

Judgment in Cases of Impeachment shall not extend further than to removal from Office, and disqualification to hold and enjoy any Office of honor, Trust or Profit under the United States: but the Party convicted shall nevertheless be liable and subject to Indictment, Trial, Judgment and Punishment, according to Law.

Section 4. The Times, Places and Manner of holding Elections for Senators and Representatives, shall be prescribed in each State by the Legislature thereof: but the Congress may at any time by Law make or alter such Regulations, except as to the Places of chusing Senators.

The Congress shall assemble at least once in every Year, and such Meeting shall be on the first Monday in December, unless they shall by Law appoint a different Day.

Section 5.   Each House shall be the Judge of the Elections, Returns and Qualifications of its own Members, and a Majority of each shall constitute a Quorum to do Business; but a smaller Number may adjourn from day to day, and may be authorized to compel the Attendance of absent Members, in such Manner, and under such Penalties as each House may provide.

Each House may determine the Rules of its Proceedings, punish its Members for disorderly Behaviour, and, with the concurrence of two thirds, expel a Member.

Each House shall keep a Journal of its Proceedings, and from time to time publish the same, excepting such Parts as may in their Judgment require Secrecy; and the Yeas and Nays of the Members of either House on any question shall, at the Desire of one-fifth of those Present, be entered on the Journal.

Neither House, during the Session of Congress, shall, without the Consent of the other, adjourn for more than three days, nor to any other Place than that in which the two Houses shall be sitting.

Section 6.   The Senators and Representatives shall receive a Compensation for their Services, to be ascertained by Law, and paid out of the Treasury of the United States. They shall in all Cases, except Treason, Felony and Breach of the Peace, be privileged from Arrest during their Attendance at the Session of their respective Houses, and in going to and returning from the same; and for any Speech or Debate in either House, they shall not be questioned in any other Place.

No Senator or Representative shall, during the Time for which he was elected, be appointed to any civil Office under the Authority of the United States, which shall have been created, or the Emoluments whereof shall have been encreased during such time; and no Person holding any Office under the United States, shall be a Member of either House during his Continuance in Office.

Section 7.   All Bills for raising Revenue shall originate in the House of Representatives; but the Senate may propose or concur with Amendments as on other Bills.

Every Bill which shall have passed the House of Representatives and the Senate, shall, before it become a Law, be presented to the President of the United States; If he approve, he shall sign it, but if not he shall return it, with his Objections to that house in which it shall have originated, who shall enter the Objections at large on their Journal, and proceed to reconsider it. If after such Reconsideration two thirds of that House shall agree to pass the Bill, it shall be sent, together with the Objections, to the other House, by which it shall likewise be reconsidered, and if approved by two thirds of that House, it shall become a Law. But in all such Cases the Votes of both Houses shall be determined by Yeas and Nays, and the Names of the Persons voting for and against the Bill shall be entered on the Journal of each House respectively. If any Bill shall not be returned by the President within ten Days (Sundays excepted) after it shall have been presented to him, the Same shall be a Law, in like Manner as if he had signed it, unless the Congress by their Adjournment prevent its Return, in which Case it shall not be a Law.

Every Order, Resolution, or Vote to which the Concurrence of the Senate and House of Representatives may be necessary (except on a question of Adjournment) shall be presented to the President of the United States; and before the Same shall take Effect, shall be approved by him, or being disapproved by him, shall be repassed by two thirds of the Senate and House of Representatives, according to the Rules and Limitations prescribed in the Case of a Bill.

Section 8.   The Congress shall have the Power to lay and collect Taxes, Duties, Imposts and Excises, to pay the Debts and provide for the common Defence and general Welfare of the United States; but all Duties, Imposts and Excises shall be uniform throughout the United States;

To borrow Money on the credit of the United States;

To regulate Commerce with foreign Nations, and among the several States, and with the Indian Tribes;

To establish an uniform Rule of Naturalization, and uniform Laws on the subject of Bankruptcies throughout the United States;

To coin Money, regulate the Value thereof, and of foreign Coin, and fix the Standard of Weights and Measures;

To provide for the Punishment of counterfeiting the Securities and current Coin of the United States;

To establish Post Offices and post Roads;

To promote the Progress of Science and useful Arts, by securing for limited Times to Authors and Inventors the exclusive Right to their respective Writings and Discoveries;

To constitute Tribunals inferior to the supreme Court;

To define and punish Piracies and Felonies committed on the high Seas, and Offenses against the Law of Nations;

To declare War, grant Letters of Marque and Reprisal, and make rules concerning Captures on Land and Water;

To raise and support Armies, but no Appropriation of Money to that use shall be for a longer Term than two Years;

To provide and maintain a Navy;

To make Rules for the Government and Regulation of the land and naval Forces;

To provide for calling forth the Militia to execute the Laws of the Union, suppress Insurrections and repel Invasions;

To provide for organizing, arming and disciplining, the Militia, and for governing such Part of them as may be employed in the Service of the United States, reserving to the States respectively, the Appointment of the Officers, and the Authority of training the Militia according to the discipline prescribed by Congress;

To exercise exclusive Legislation in all Cases whatsoever, over such District (not exceeding ten Miles square) as may, by Cession of particular States, and the acceptance of Congress, become the Seat of the Government of the United States, and to exercise like Authority over all Places purchased by the Consent of the Legislature of the State in which the Same shall be, for the Erection of Forts, Magazines, Arsenals, dock Yards, and other needful buildings;—And

To make all Laws which shall be necessary and proper for carrying into Execution the foregoing Powers, and all other Powers vested by the Constitution in the Government of the United States, or in any Department or Officer thereof.

Section 9.   The Migration or Importation of such Persons as any of the States now existing shall think proper to admit, shall not be prohibited by the Congress prior to the Year one thousand eight hundred and eight, but a Tax or Duty may be imposed on such Importation, not exceeding ten dollars for each Person.

The Privilege of the Writ of Habeas Corpus shall not be suspended, unless when in Cases of Rebellion or Invasion the public Safety may require it.

No Bill of Attainder or ex post facto Law shall be passed.

No Capitation, or other direct, Tax shall be laid, unless in Proportion to the Census or Enumeration herein before directed to be taken.

No Tax or Duty shall be laid on Articles exported from any State.

No Preference shall be given by any Regulation of Commerce or Revenue to the Ports of one State over those of another: nor shall Vessels bound to, or from, one State, be obliged to enter, clear, or pay Duties in another.

No Money shall be drawn from the Treasury, but in Consequence of Appropriations made by Law; and a regular Statement and Account of the Receipts and Expenditures of all public Money shall be published from time to time.

No Title of Nobility shall be granted by the United States: And no Person holding any Office or Profit or Trust under them, shall, without the Consent of the Congress, accept of any present, Emolument, Office, or Title, of any kind whatever, from any King, Prince, or foreign State.

Section 10.   No State shall enter into any Treaty, Alliance, or Confederation; grant Letters of Marque and Reprisal; coin Money; emit Bills of Credit; make any Thing but gold and silver Coin a Tender in Payment of Debts; pass any Bill of Attainder, ex post facto Law, or Law impairing the Obligation of Contracts, or grant any Title of Nobility.

No State shall, without the Consent of the Congress, lay any Imposts or Duties on Imports or Exports, except what may be absolutely necessary for executing its inspection Laws: and the net Produce of all Duties and Imposts, laid by any State on Imports or Exports, shall be for the Use of the Treasury of the United States; and all such Laws shall be subject to the Revision and Control of the Congress.

No State shall, without the Consent of Congress, lay any Duty of Tonnage, keep Troops, or Ships of War in time of Peace, enter into any Agreement or Compact with another State, or with a foreign Power, or engage in War, unless actually invaded, or in such imminent Danger as will not admit of delay.

Article II

Section 1.   The executive Power shall be vested in a President of the United States of America. He shall hold Office during the Term of four Years, and, together with the Vice President, chosen for the same Term, be elected as follows:

Each State shall appoint, in such Manner as the Legislature thereof may direct, a Number of Electors, equal to the whole Number of Senators and Representatives to which the State may be entitled in the Congress: but no Senator or Representative, or Person holding an Office or Trust or Profit under the United States, shall be appointed an Elector.

The Electors shall meet in their respective States, and vote by Ballot for two Persons, of whom one at least shall not be an Inhabitant of the same State with Themselves. And they shall make a List of all the Persons voted for, and of the Number of Votes for each; which List they shall sign and certify, and transmit sealed to the Seat of the Government of the

United States, directed to the President of the Senate. The President of the Senate shall, in the Presence of the Senate and House of Representatives, open all the Certificates, and the Votes shall then be counted. The Person having the greatest Number of Votes shall be the President, if such Number be a Majority of the whole Number of Electors appointed; and if there be more than one who have such Majority, and have an equal Number of Votes, then the House of Representatives shall immediately chuse by Ballot one of them for President; and if no Person have a Majority, then from the five highest on the List the said House shall in like Manner chuse the President. But in chusing the President, the Votes shall be taken by States, the Representation from each State having one Vote; a quorum for this Purpose shall consist of a Member or Members from two thirds of the States, and a Majority of all the States shall be necessary to a Choice. In every Case, after the Choice of the President, the Person having the greatest Number of Votes of the Electors shall be the Vice President. But if there should remain two or more who have equal Votes, the Senate shall chuse from them by Ballot the Vice President.

The Congress may determine the Time of chusing the Electors, and the Day on which they shall give their Votes; which Day shall be the same throughout the United States.

No Person except a natural born Citizen, or a Citizen of the United States, at the time of the Adoption of this Constitution, shall be eligible to the Office of President; neither shall any Person be eligible to that Office who shall not have attained to the Age of thirty five Years, and been fourteen Years a Resident within the United States.

In Case of the Removal of the President from Office, or of his Death, Resignation, or Inability to discharge the Powers and Duties of the said Office, the Same shall devolve on the Vice President, and the Congress may by Law provide for the Case of Removal, Death, Resignation, or Inability, both of the President and Vice President, declaring what Officer shall then act as President, and such Officer shall act accordingly, until the Disability be removed, or a President shall be elected.

The President shall, at stated Times, receive for his Services, a Compensation, which shall neither be increased nor diminished during the Period for which he shall have been elected, and he shall not receive within that Period any other Emolument from the United States, or any of them.

Before he enter on the Execution of his Office, he shall take the following Oath or Affirmation:—"I do solemnly swear (or affirm) that I will faithfully execute the Office of President of the United States, and will to the best of my Ability, preserve, protect and defend the Constitution of the United States."

Section 2. The President shall be Commander in Chief of the Army and Navy of the United States, and of the Militia of the several States, when called into the actual Service of the United States; he may require the Opinion, in writing, of the principal Officer in each of the executive Departments, upon any Subject relating to the Duties of their respective Offices, and he shall have Power to grant Reprieves and Pardons for Offenses against the United States, except in Cases of Impeachment.

He shall have Power, by and with the Advice and Consent of the Senate, to make Treaties, providing two thirds of the Senators present concur; and he shall nominate, and by and with the advice and consent of the Senate, shall appoint Ambassadors, other public Ministers and Consuls, Judges of the supreme Court, and all other Officers of the United States, whose Appointments are not herein otherwise provided for, and which shall be established by Law: but the Congress may by Law vest the Appointment of such inferior Officers, as they think proper, in the President alone, in the Courts of Law, or in the Heads of Departments.

The President shall have the Power to fill up all Vacancies that may happen during the Recess of the Senate, by granting Commissions which shall expire at the End of their next Session.

Section 3. He shall from time to time give to the Congress Information of the State of the Union, and recommend to their Consideration such Measures as he shall judge necessary and expedient; he may, on extraordinary Occasions, convene both Houses, or either of them, and in Case of Disagreement between them, with Respect to the Time of Adjournment, he may adjourn them to such Time as he shall think proper; he shall receive Ambassadors and other public Ministers; he shall take Care that the Laws be faithfully executed, and shall Commission all the Officers of the United States.

Section 4. The President, Vice President, and all civil Officers of the United States, shall be removed from Office on Impeachment for, and Conviction of, Treason, Bribery, or other high Crimes and Misdemeanors.

Article III

Section 1. The judicial Power of the United States, shall be vested in one supreme Court, and in such inferior Courts as the Congress may from time to time ordain and establish. The Judges, both of the supreme and inferior Courts, shall hold their Offices during good Behaviour, and shall, at stated Times, receive for their Services, a Compensation, which shall not be diminished during their Continuance in Office.

Section 2. The judicial Power shall extend to all Cases, in Law and Equity, arising under this Constitution, the Laws of the United States, and Treaties made, or which shall be made, under their Authority;—to all Cases affecting Ambassadors, other public Ministers and Consuls;—to all Cases of admiralty and maritime Jurisdiction;—to Controversies to which the United States shall be a Party;—to Controversies between two or more States;—between a State and Citizens of another State;—between Citizens of different States;—between Citizens of the same State claiming Lands under Grants of different States, and between a State, or the Citizens thereof, and foreign States, Citizens or Subjects.

In all Cases affecting Ambassadors, other public Ministers and Consuls, and those in which a State shall be Party, the supreme Court shall have original Jurisdiction. In all the other Cases before mentioned, the supreme Court shall have appellate Jurisdiction, both as to Law and Fact, with such Exceptions, and under such Regulations as the Congress shall make.

The Trial of all Crimes, except in Cases of Impeachment, shall be by Jury; and such Trial shall be held in the State where the said Crimes shall have been committed; but when not committed within any State, the Trial shall be at such Place or Places as the Congress may by Law have directed.

Section 3. Treason against the United States, shall consist only in levying War against them, or in adhering to their Enemies, giving them Aid and Comfort. No Person shall be convicted of Treason unless on the Testimony of two Witnesses to the same overt Act, or on Confession in open Court.

The Congress shall have Power to declare the Punishment of Treason, but no Attainder of Treason shall work Corruption of Blood, or Forfeiture except during the Life of the Person attainted.

Article IV

Section 1. Full Faith and Credit shall be given in each State to the public Acts, Records, and judicial Proceedings of every other State. And the Congress may by general Laws prescribe the Manner in which such Acts, Records and Proceedings shall be proved, and the Effect thereof.

Section 2. The Citizens of each State shall be entitled to all Privileges and Immunities of Citizens in the several states.

A person charged in any State with Treason, Felony, or other Crime, who shall flee Justice, and be found in another State, shall on Demand of the executive Authority of the State from which he fled, be delivered up, to be removed to the state having Jurisdiction of the Crime.

No Person held to Service or Labour in one State, under the Laws thereof, escaping into another, shall, in Consequence of any Law or Regulation therein, be discharged from such Service or Labour, but shall be delivered up on Claim of the Party to whom such Service or Labour may be due.

Section 3. New States may be admitted by the Congress into this Union; but no new State shall be formed or erected within the Jurisdiction of any other State, nor any State be formed by the Junction of two or more States, or Parts of States, without the Consent of the Legislatures of the States concerned, as well as of the Congress.

The Congress shall have Power to dispose of and make all needful Rules and Regulations respecting the Territory or other Property belonging to the United States; and nothing in this Constitution shall be so construed as to Prejudice any Claims of the United States, or of any particular State.

Section 4. The United States shall guarantee to every State in this Union a Republican form of Government, and shall protect each of them against Invasion; and on Application of the Legislature, or of the Executive (when the Legislature cannot be convened) against domestic Violence.

Article V.

The Congress, whenever two thirds of both Houses shall deem it necessary, shall propose Amendments to this Constitution, or, on the Application of the Legislatures of two thirds of the several States, shall call a Convention for proposing Amendments, which, in either Case, shall be valid to all Intents and Purposes, as Part of this Constitution, when ratified by the Legislatures of three fourths of the several States, or by Conventions in three fourths thereof, as the one or the other Mode of Ratification may be proposed by the Congress; Provided that no Amendment which may be made prior to the Year One thousand eight hundred and eight shall in any Manner affect the first and fourth Clauses in the Ninth Section of the first Article; and that no State, without its Consent, shall be deprived of its equal Suffrage in the Senate.

Article VI.

All Debts contracted and Engagements entered into, before the Adoption of this Constitution, shall be as valid against the United States under this Constitution, as under the Confederation.

This Constitution, and the Laws of the United States which shall be made in Pursuance thereof; and all Treaties made, or which shall be made, under the Authority of the United States, shall be the supreme

Law of the Land; and the Judges in every State shall be bound thereby, any Thing in the Constitution or Laws of any State to the Contrary notwithstanding.

The Senators and Representatives before mentioned, and the Members of the several State Legislatures, and all executive and judicial Officers, both of the United States and of the several States, shall be bound by Oath or Affirmation, to support this Constitution; but no religious Test shall ever be required as a Qualification to any Office or public Trust under the United States.

Article VII. The Ratification of the Conventions of nine States, shall be sufficient for the Establishment of this Constitution between the States so ratifying the Same.

Amendment I [1791]. Congress shall make no law respecting an establishment of religion, or prohibiting the free exercise thereof; or abridging the freedom of speech, or of the press; or the right of the people peaceably to assemble, and to petition the Government for a redress of grievances.

Amendment II [1791]. A well regulated Militia, being necessary to the security for a free State, the right of the people to keep and bear Arms, shall not be infringed.

Amendment III [1791]. No Soldier shall, in time of peace be quartered in any house, without the consent of the Owner, nor in time of war, but in a manner to be prescribed by law.

Amendment IV [1791]. The right of the people to be secure in their persons, houses, papers, and effects, against unreasonable searches and seizures, shall not be violated, and no Warrants shall issue, but upon probable cause, supported by Oath or affirmation, and particularly describing the place to be searched, and the persons or things to be seized.

Amendment V [1791]. No person shall be held to answer for a capital, or otherwise infamous crime, unless on a presentment or indictment of a Grand Jury, except in cases arising in the land or naval forces, or in the Militia, when in actual service in time of War or public danger; nor shall any person be subject for the same offense to be twice put in jeopardy of life or limb; nor shall be compelled in any criminal case to be a witness against himself, nor be deprived of life, liberty, or property, without due process of law; nor shall private property be taken for public use without just compensation.

Amendment VI [1791]. In all criminal prosecutions, the accused shall enjoy the right to a speedy and public trial, by an impartial jury of the State and district wherein the crime shall have been committed, which district shall have been previously ascertained by law, and to be informed of the nature and cause of the accusation; to be confronted with the Witnesses against him; to have compulsory process for obtaining witnesses in his favor, and to have the Assistance of counsel for his defense.

Amendment VII [1791]. In suits at common law, where the value in controversy shall exceed twenty dollars, the right of trial by jury shall be preserved, and no fact tried by a jury, shall be otherwise re-examined in any Court of the United States, than according to the rules of the common law.

Amendment VIII [1791]. Excessive bail shall not be required, nor excessive fines imposed, nor cruel and unusual punishments inflicted.

Amendment IX [1791]. The enumeration in the Constitution, of certain rights, shall not be construed to deny or disparage others retained by the people.

Amendment X [1791]. The powers not delegated to the United States by the Constitution, nor prohibited by it to the States, are reserved to the States respectively, or to the people.

Amendment XI [1798]. The Judicial power of the United States shall not be construed to extend to any suit in law or equity, commenced or prosecuted against one of the United States by Citizens of another State, or by Citizens or Subjects of any Foreign State.

Amendment XII [1804]. The Electors shall meet in their respective states and vote by ballot for President and Vice-President, one of whom, at least, shall not be an inhabitant of the same state with themselves; they shall name in their ballots the person voted for as President, and in distinct ballots the person voted for as Vice-President, and they shall make distinct lists of all persons voted for as President, and of all persons voted for as Vice-President, and of the number of votes for each, which lists they shall sign and certify, and transmit sealed to the seat of the government of the United States, directed to the President of the Senate;—The President of the Senate shall, in the presence of the Senate and House of Representatives, open all the certificates and the votes shall then be counted;—The person having the greatest number of votes for President, shall be the President, if such number be a majority of the whole number of Electors appointed; and if no person have such majority, then from the persons having the highest numbers not exceeding three on the list of those voted for as President, the House of Representatives shall choose immediately, by ballot, the President. But in choosing the President, the votes shall be taken by states, the representation from each state having one vote; a quorum for this purpose shall consist of a member or members from two-thirds of the states, and a majority of all the states shall be necessary to a choice. And if the House of Representatives shall not choose a President whenever the right of choice shall devolve upon them, before the fourth day of March next following, then the Vice-President shall act as President. The person having the greatest number of votes as Vice-President, shall be the Vice-President, if such number be a majority of the whole number of electors appointed, and if no person have a majority, then from the two highest numbers on the list, the Senate shall choose the Vice-President; a quorum for the purpose shall consist of two-thirds of the whole number of Senators, and a majority of the whole number shall be necessary to a choice. But no person constitutionally ineligible to the office of President shall be eligible to that of the Vice-President of the United States.

Amendment XIII [1865]

Section 1. Neither slavery nor involuntary servitude, except as a punishment for crime whereof the party shall have been duly convicted, shall exist within the United States, or any place subject to their jurisdiction.

Section 2. Congress shall have power to enforce this article by appropriate legislation.

Amendment XIV [1868]

Section 1. All persons born or naturalized in the United States, and subject to the jurisdiction thereof, are citizens of the United States and of the State wherein they reside. No State shall make or enforce any law which shall abridge the privileges or immunities of citizens of the United States; nor shall any State deprive any person of life, liberty, or property, without due process of law; nor deny to any person within its jurisdiction the equal protection of the laws.

Section 2. Representatives shall be appointed among the several States according to their respective numbers, counting the whole number of persons in each State, excluding Indians not taxed. But when the right to vote at any election for the choice of electors for President and Vice President of the United States, Representatives in Congress, the executive and judicial officers of a State,

or the members of the Legislature thereof, is denied to any of the male inhabitants of such State, being twenty-one years of age, and citizens of the United States, or in any way abridged, except for participation in rebellion, or other crime, the basis of representation therein shall be reduced in the proportion which the number of such male citizens shall bear to the whole number of male citizens twenty-one years of age in such State.

Section 3. No person shall be a Senator or Representative in Congress, or elector of President and Vice President, or hold any office, civil or military, under the United States, or under any State, who, having previously taken an oath, as a member of Congress, or as an officer of the United States, or as a member of any State legislature, or as an executive or judicial officer of any State, to support the Constitution of the United States, shall have engaged in insurrection or rebellion against the same, or given aid or comfort to the enemies thereof. But Congress may by a vote of two-thirds of each House, remove such disability.

Section 4. The validity of the public debt of the United States, authorized by law, including debts incurred for payment of pensions and bounties for services in suppressing insurrection or rebellion, shall not be questioned. But neither the United States nor any State shall assume or pay any debt or obligation incurred in aid of insurrection or rebellion against the United States, or any claim for the loss or emancipation of any slave; but all such debts, obligations and claims shall be held illegal and void.

Section 5. The Congress shall have the power to enforce, by appropriate legislation, the provisions of this article.

Amendment XV [1870]

Section 1. The right of citizens of the United States to vote shall not be denied or abridged by the United States or by any State on account of race, color, or previous condition of servitude.

Section 2. The Congress shall have power to enforce this article by appropriate legislation.

Amendment XVI [1913].

The Congress shall have power to lay and collect taxes on incomes, from whatever sources derived, without apportionment among the several States, and without regard to any census or enumeration.

Amendment XVII [1913].

The Senate of the United States shall be composed of two Senators from each State, elected by the people thereof, for six years; and each Senator shall have one vote.

The electors in each State shall have the qualifications requisite for electors of the most numerous branch of the State legislatures.

When vacancies happen in the representation of any State in the Senate, the executive authority of such State shall issue writs of election to fill such vacancies: *Provided,* That the legislature of any State may empower the executive thereof to make temporary appointments until the people fill the vacancies by election as the legislature may direct.

This amendment shall not be so construed as to affect the election or term of any Senator chosen before it becomes valid as part of the Constitution.

Amendment XVIII [1919]

Section 1.   After one year from the ratification of this article the manufacture, sale, or transportation of intoxicating liquors within, the importation thereof into, or the exportation thereof from the United States and all territory subject to the jurisdiction thereof for beverage purposes is hereby prohibited.

Section 2.   The Congress and the several States shall have concurrent power to enforce this article by appropriate legislation.

Section 3.   This article shall be inoperative unless it shall have been ratified as an amendment to the Constitution by the legislatures of the several States, as provided in the Constitution, within seven years from the date of the submission hereof to the States by the Congress.

Amendment XIX [1920].   The right of

citizens of the United States to vote shall not be denied or abridged by the United States or by any State on account of sex.

Congress shall have power to enforce this article by appropriate legislation.

Amendment XX [1933]

Section 1.   The terms of the President and the Vice President shall end at noon on the 20th day of January, and the terms of Senators and Representatives at noon on the 3d day of January, of the years in which such terms would have ended if this article had not been ratified; and the terms of their successors shall then begin.

Section 2.   The Congress shall assemble at least once in every year, and such meeting shall begin at noon on the 3d day of January, unless they shall by law appoint a different day.

Section 3.   If, at the time fixed for the beginning of the term of the President, the President elect shall have died, the Vice President elect shall become President. If

a President shall not have been chosen before the time fixed for the beginning of his term, or if the President elect shall have failed to qualify, then the Vice President elect shall act as President until a President shall have qualified; and the Congress may by law provide for the case wherein neither a President elect nor a Vice President shall have qualified, declaring who shall then act as President, or the manner in which one who is to act shall be selected, and such person shall act accordingly until a President or Vice President shall have qualified.

Section 4.   The Congress may by law provide for the case of the death of any of the persons from whom the House of Representatives may choose a President whenever the right of choice shall have devolved upon them, and for the case of the death of any of the persons from whom the Senate may choose a Vice President whenever the right of choice shall have devolved upon them.

Section 5.   Sections 1 and 2 shall take effect on the 15th day of October following the ratification of this article.

Section 6.   This article shall be inoperative unless it shall have been ratified as an amendment to the Constitution by the legislatures of three-fourths of the several States within seven years from the date of its submission.

Amendment XXI [1933]

Section 1.   The eighteenth article of amendment to the Constitution of the United States is hereby repealed.

Section 2.   The transportation or importation into any State, Territory, or possession of the United States for delivery or use therein of intoxicating liquors, in violation of the laws thereof, is hereby prohibited.

Section 3.   This article shall be inoperative unless it shall have been ratified as an amendment to the Constitution by conventions in the several States, as provided in the Constitution, within seven years from the date of the submission hereof to the States by the Congress.

Amendment XXII [1951]

Section 1.   No person shall be elected to the office of the President more than twice, and no person who has held the office of President, or acted as President, for more than two years of a term to which some other person was elected President shall be elected to the office of President more than once. But this Article shall not apply to any person holding the office of President when this Article was proposed by the Congress, and shall not prevent any person who may be holding the office of President, or acting as President, during the term within which this Article becomes operative from holding the office of President or acting as President during the remainder of such term.

Section 2.   This article shall be inoperative unless it shall have been ratified as an amendment to the Constitution by the legislatures of three-fourths of the several States within seven years from the date of its submission to the States by the Congress.

Amendment XXIII [1961]

Section 1.   The District constituting the seat of Government of the United States shall appoint in such manner as the Congress may direct:

A number of electors of President and Vice President equal to the whole number of Senators and Representatives in Congress to which the District would be entitled if it were a State, but in no event more than the least populous State; they shall be in addition to those appointed by the States, but they shall be considered, for the purposes of the election of President and Vice President, to be electors appointed by a State; and they shall meet in the District and perform such duties as provided by the twelfth article of amendment.

Section 2.   The Congress shall have power to enforce this article by appropriate legislation.

Amendment XXIV [1964]

Section 1.   The right of citizens of the United States to vote in any primary or other election for President or Vice President, for electors for President or Vice President, or for Senator or Representative in Congress, shall not be denied or abridged by the United States or any State by reason of failure to pay poll tax or any other tax.

Section 2.   The Congress shall have power to enforce this article by appropriate legislation.

Amendment XXV [1967]

Section 1.   In case of the removal of the President from office or of his death or resignation, the Vice President shall become President.

Section 2.   Whenever there is a vacancy in the office of the Vice President, the President shall nominate a Vice President who shall take the office upon confirmation by a majority vote of both Houses of Congress.

Section 3.   Whenever the President transmits to the President pro tempore of the Senate and the Speaker of the House of Representatives his written declaration that he is unable to discharge the powers and duties of his office, and until he transmits to them a written declaration to the contrary, such powers and duties shall be discharged by the Vice President as Acting President.

Section 4.   Whenever the Vice President and a majority of either the principal officers of the executive departments or of such other body as Congress may by law provide, transmit to the President pro tempore of the Senate and the Speaker of the House of Representatives their written declaration that the President is unable to discharge the powers and duties of his office, the Vice President shall immediately assume the powers and duties of the office as Acting President.

Thereafter, when the President transmits to the President pro tempore of the Senate and the Speaker of the House of Representatives his written declaration that no inability exists, he shall resume the powers and duties of his office unless the Vice President and a majority of either the principal officers of the executive departments or of such other body as Congress may by law provide, transmit within four days to the President pro tempore of the Senate and the Speaker of the House of Representatives their written declaration that the President is unable to discharge the powers and duties of his office. Thereupon Congress shall decide the issue, assembling within forty-eight hours for that purpose if not in session. If the Congress, within twenty-one days after receipt of the latter written declaration, or, if Congress is not in session, within twenty-one days after Congress is required to assemble, determines by two-thirds vote of both houses that the President is unable to discharge the powers and duties of his office, the Vice President shall continue to discharge the same as Acting President; otherwise, the President shall resume the powers and duties of his office.

Amendment XXVI [1971]

Section 1.   The right of citizens of the United States, who are eighteen years of age or older, to vote shall not be denied or abridged by the United States or any State on account of age.

Section 2.   The Congress shall have power to enforce this article by appropriate legislation.

Amendment XXVII [1992]. No law, varying the compensation for the services of the Senators and Representatives shall take effect, until an election of Representatives shall have intervened.

>> glossary

Abatement Decrease, reduction, or diminution.

Acceptance The contractual communication of agreeing to another's offer. The acceptance of an offer creates a *contract.*

Accession Property acquired by adding something to an owned object.

Accessory A term used at the state level that is similar to "aiding and abetting." Accessory to a crime generally is either before the criminal act or after it.

Accord and satisfaction Payment of money, or other thing of value, usually less than the amount demanded, in exchange for cancellation of a debt that is uncertain in amount.

Actual authority The authority a principal expressly or implicitly gives to an agent in an agency relationship. This authority may be written, spoken, or derived from the circumstances of the relationship.

Ad infinitum Without limit; endlessly.

Adjudication The judicial determination of a legal proceeding.

Adjustment Under the Bankruptcy Act the procedure followed when a debtor's debts are partly reduced and partly rearranged for repayment.

Administrative agency An organization, usually a part of the executive branch of government, that is created to serve a specific purpose as authorized by the legislative branch. An agency's function usually is characterized as quasi-legislative or quasi-judicial.

Administrative law The legal principles involved in the workings of administrative agencies within the regulatory process.

Administrative law judge The individual employed by an administrative agency who is in charge of hearing the initial presentations in a quasi-judicial case.

ADRs An abbreviation for alternative dispute resolution systems that may be used in lieu of litigation.

Ad substantiation program A program of the Federal Trade Commission under which the FTC demands that an advertiser substantiate any claims made in advertising. Even if the claims are not provably untrue, they are considered deceptive if they cannot be substantiated.

Ad valorem According to value.

Adverse possession Property ownership acquired through open, notorious, actual, exclusive, continuous, and wrongful possession of land for a statutorily prescribed period of time.

Advisory opinion A formal opinion by a judge, court, regulatory agency, or law officer upon a question of law.

Affidavit A sworn written statement made before an officer authorized by law to administer oaths.

Affirmative action Positive steps taken in order to alleviate conditions resulting from past discrimination or from violations of a law.

Affirmative action program A program designed to promote actively the position of minority workers with regard to hiring and advancement.

Affirmative defenses Defenses that must be raised and proved by the defendant.

A fortiori Even more clearly; said of a conclusion that follows with even greater logical necessity from another that is already included in the argument.

Agent The person who on behalf of a principal deals with a third party.

Agreement on Trade-Related Aspects of Intellectual Property Rights (TRIPS) The WTO agreement that discusses the applicability of GATT principles and intellectual property agreements in the international sphere.

Aiding and abetting A criminal action that arises from association with and from assistance rendered to a person guilty of another criminal act.

Alien corporation A corporation created under the authority of a foreign country.

Alien Tort Claims Act (ATCA) The federal law that grants jurisdiction to U.S. federal district courts over any civil action by an alien for a tort only, committed in violation of the law of nations or a treaty of the United States.

Alter-ego theory One method used by courts to pierce the corporate veil when a shareholder fails to treat the corporate organization as a separate legal entity.

Amicus curiae A friend of the court who participates in litigation though not a party to the lawsuit.

Annual percentage rate A rate of interest that commercial lenders charge persons who borrow money. This rate is calculated in a standardized fashion required by the Truth-in-Lending Act.

Annuity A contract by which the insured pays a lump sum to the insurer and later receives fixed annual payments.

Answer The responsive pleading filed by a defendant.

Apparent authority The authority that a third party in an agency relationship perceives to exist between the principal and the agent. In fact, no actual authority does exist. Sometimes also called *ostensible authority*.

Appeal The right of the litigation parties to have the legal decisions of the trial judge reviewed by an appellate court.

Appellant The party seeking review of a lower court decision.

Appellate court A court that decides whether a trial judge has made a mistake of law.

Appellee The party responding to an appeal; the winner in the trial court.

Apportionment The concept used by states to divide a company's taxable income so that no one state burdens a company with an unfair tax bill.

Arbitration Submission of a dispute to an extrajudicial authority for decision.

Arbitrator The individual or panel members authorized by disputing parties to resolve a dispute through the arbitration process.

Arguendo For the sake of argument.

Articles of incorporation The legal document that forms the application for a state charter of incorporation.

Articles of organization The document used to create a limited liability company. Its purpose corresponds to the purpose of the articles of partnership and the articles of incorporation.

Articles of partnership Another name for a formally drafted partnership agreement.

Artisan's lien The lien that arises in favor of one who has expended labor upon, or added value to, another person's personal property. The lien allows the person to possess the property as security until reimbursed for the value of labor or materials. If the person is not reimbursed, the property may be sold to satisfy the claim.

Assault The intentional creation of immediate apprehension of injury or lack of physical safety.

Assignee A third party, who is not an original contracting party, to whom contractual rights or duties or both are transferred. This party may enforce the original contract.

Assignment A transfer of contractual rights.

Assignor An original contracting party who assigns or transfers contractual rights or duties or both to a third party.

Assumed-name statute A state law that requires partners to make a public filing of their identities if their partnership operates under a name that does not reveal the partners' identities.

Assumption of risk Negligence doctrine that bars the recovery of damages by an injured party on the ground that such a party acted with actual or constructive knowledge of the hazard causing the injury.

Attachment The term *attachment* has three meanings. First, attachment is a method of acquiring in rem jurisdiction of a nonresident defendant who is not subject to the service of process to commence a lawsuit. By "attaching" property of the nonresident defendant, the court acquires jurisdiction over the defendant to the extent of the value of the property attached. Second, attachment is a procedure used to collect a judgment. A plaintiff may have the property of a defendant seized, pending the outcome of a lawsuit, if the plaintiff has reason to fear that the defendant will dispose of the property before the court renders its decision. Third, attachment is the event that creates an enforceable security interest under the Uniform Commercial Code (UCC). In order that a security interest attach, there must be a signed, written security agreement, or possession of the collateral by the secured party; the secured party must give value to the debtor; and the debtor must maintain rights in the collateral.

Award The decision announced by an arbitrator.

Bailee In a bailment, the person who takes possession of an object owned by another and must return it or otherwise dispose of it.

Bailment An owner's placement of an object into the intentional possession of another person with the understanding that the other person must return the object at some point or otherwise dispose of it.

Bailor In a bailment, the person who transfers possession of tangible, personal property to another person with the understanding that the other person must return the object at some point or otherwise dispose of it.

Bait-and-switch promotion An illegal promotional practice in which a seller attracts consumer interest by promoting one product, the "bait," then once interest has been attracted switches it to a second, higher-priced product by making the "bait" unavailable or unattractive.

Balance of trade   The difference between the amount of exports and imports of goods by a nation. A favorable balance would indicate more exports than imports. The United States has run an unfavorable balance of trade for several years.

Bank Merger Acts   Federal laws passed in 1960 and 1966 that require approval of the appropriate administrative agency prior to the merger of banks.

Bankruptcy   Traditionally, the financial condition where debts exceed assets and one is unable to pay debts as they mature.

Bankruptcy crime   An action involving the falsification of documents filed in a bankruptcy case.

Bargained for   A term used in conjunction with the requirement of contractual consideration to represent the exchange of benefits and burdens between the contracting parties.

Battery   The cause of action for physical contact that is not consented to and is offensive.

Beneficiary   A person entitled to the possession, use, income, or enjoyment of an interest or right to which legal title is held by another; a person to whom an insurance policy is payable.

Best evidence rule   A principle requiring that the original of a document be submitted to the court as proof of the document's contents.

Beyond a reasonable doubt   The burden of proof required in a criminal case. The prosecution in a criminal case has the burden of proving the defendant is guilty, and the jury must have no reasonable doubt about the defendant's guilt. See also *Burden of proof.*

Bilateral contract   An agreement that contains mutual promises, with each party being both a promisor and a promisee.

Bill of lading   A document issued by a carrier indicating that goods to be shipped have been received by the carrier.

Bill of particulars   In legal practice, a written statement furnished by one party to a lawsuit to another, describing in detail the elements upon which the claim of the first party is based.

Biodegradable   Capable of being decomposed by organic action.

Blue sky laws   Securities law enacted by States.

Bona fide   In good faith; innocently; without fraud or deceit.

Bona fide occupational qualification (BFOQ)   A qualification that permits discriminatory practices in employment if a person's religion, sex, or national origin is reasonably related to the normal operation of a particular business.

Brand   A marketing device that distinguishes one firm's products and services from another's. In general, brands are synonymous with trademarks under the law. See *Trademark.*

Breach of contract   A party's failure to perform some contracted-for or agreed-upon act, or failure to comply with a duty imposed by law.

Bribery   The offering, receiving, or soliciting of something of value for the purpose of influencing the action of an official in the discharge of his or her public or legal duties.

Brief   A written document produced by a party for a reviewing court that contains the facts, propositions of law, and argument of a party. It is in this document that the party argues the desired application of the law and any contentions as to the rulings of the lower court.

Browse-wrap agreement   An agreement proposed on a website that may be accepted by an explicit act, such as clicking an agreement button or simply using the service. Related forms are known as "click-wrap" and "shrink-wrap" agreements.

Bubble concept   A procedure by which the Environmental Protection Agency (EPA) allows a business to treat its entire plant complex as though encased in a bubble. The business suggests its own methods of cleanup, provided the total pollution does not exceed certain limits.

Bulk transfer   A transfer made outside the ordinary course of the transferor's business involving a major part of the business's inventory. Bulk transfers are subject to Article 6 of the Uniform Commercial Code (UCC).

Burden of proof   The term *burden of proof* has two meanings. It may describe the party at a trial with the burden of coming forward with evidence to establish a fact. The term also describes the party with the burden of persuasion. This party must convince the judge or jury of the disputed facts in issue or else lose that issue. There are various degrees of proof. See also *Beyond a reasonable doubt, Preponderance of evidence,* and *Clear and convincing proof.*

Burglary   Theft by breaking and entering.

Business judgment rule   A legal principle used by the courts to uphold the decisions of corporate directors and officers who have exercised good faith and due care in their business practices.

Business necessity defense   An affirmative defense under Title VII of the Civil Rights Act. It is raised to disparate impact claims and asserts that a facially neutral but discriminatory policy is job related.

Buy and sell agreement   A contract, usually among partners, but perhaps among shareholders, wherein one party agrees to buy the ownership interest held by another party or the first party agrees to sell such an interest to the other party. These contractual provisions help provide for a transition of owners without harming the business of the organization.

Buyer in the ordinary course of business   A buyer who buys from someone who ordinarily sells such goods in his or her business.

Capacity   Mental ability to make a rational decision that includes the ability to perceive and appreciate all relevant facts. A required element of a contract.

Cap and trade   A pollution policy that caps allowable pollution at a certain amount, distributes the rights to engage in that pollution, then allows the owners of the rights to trade them.

Case law   The legal principles that are developed by appellate judges through their written opinions. See *Common law.*

Categorical imperative   A concept by the philosopher Kant that a person should never act in a certain way unless he or she is willing to have everyone else act in the same way.

Caucus   The name used for a private meeting between a mediator and one of the parties involved in a mediation.

Cause in fact   The actual cause of an event; the instrument that is the responsible force for the occurrence of a certain event. A required element of a tort.

Cause of action   This phrase has several meanings, but it is commonly used to describe the existence of facts giving rise to a judicially enforceable claim.

Caveat emptor   Let the buyer beware; rule imposing on a purchaser the duty to inform him- or herself as to defects in the property being sold.

Caveat venditor   Let the seller beware; it is the seller's duty to do what the ordinary person would do in a similar situation.

Cease and desist order   The sanction that may be issued by an administrative agency to prevent a party from violating the law.

Celler-Kefauver amendment   Passed in 1950 to amend the Clayton Act by broadening the scope of Section 7 on mergers and acquisitions.

Central America-Dominican Republic Free Trade Agreement (CAFTA-DR)   An agreement between the United States, Costa Rica, El Salvador, Guatemala, Honduras, Nicaragua, and the Dominican Republic designed to eliminate trade barriers.

Certification mark   A mark used by someone other than its owner to certify the quality, point of origin, or other characteristic of goods or services. The Good Housekeeping "Seal of Approval" is an example.

Certiorari   A Latin word that means "to be informed of." This is the name of a writ that a higher court grants permitting the review of a lower court's ruling.

Changing conditions defense   A defense to a price discrimination (Section 2 of the Clayton Act) case wherein the defendant seeks to justify charging different customers different prices due to a change in the conditions of the product or marketplace.

Charter   The legal document issued by a state when creating a new corporation.

Circuit court   This term frequently is used to describe two distinct courts. First, the appellate courts in the federal court system often are called circuit courts of appeals. Second, the trial courts of general subject matter jurisdiction in some state court systems also are referred to as circuit courts.

Citation   The reference identifying how to find a case.

Civil law   The area of law governing the rights and duties between private parties as compared with the criminal law. This term also describes the system of codifying law in many countries as compared with the judicial orientation of the common law system.

Civil rights   The area of law designed to protect an individual's right to freedom from discrimination. In employment, this area of law prohibits unequal treatment based on race, color, national origin, religion, and sex.

Class-action suit   A method of litigation that allows one or more plaintiffs to file a lawsuit on behalf of a much larger group of persons, all of whom have a common interest in the claims being litigated.

Clayton Act   Legislation passed in 1914 that exempts labor unions from the Sherman Act. This law expanded the national antitrust policy to cover price discrimination, exclusive dealings, tying contracts, mergers, and interlocking directors.

Clean-hands doctrine   An equitable principle that requires a party seeking an equitable remedy to be free from wrongdoing.

Clear and convincing proof   A burden of proof that requires the party with the burden to establish clearly the existence of the alleged facts. This burden requires more proof than merely having a preponderance of evidence on one's side.

Closed shop   A contractual agreement between an employer and a union that all applicants for a job with the employer will have to join the union. This type of agreement was outlawed by the Taft-Hartley Act.

Closely held   An organization that is owned by only a few people.

Code   A compilation of legislation enacted by a federal, state, or local government.

Colgate doctrine   The legal principle that allows a form of vertical price fixing in that manufacturers may maintain the resale price of their products by announcing their pricing policy and refusing to deal with customers who fail to comply with the policy.

Collateral   The valuable thing put up by someone to secure a loan or credit.

Collective bargaining   The process used by an employer and a union representing employees to discuss and resolve differences so that the parties can agree to a binding contract.

Collective mark   A mark representing membership in a certain organization or association. The "union label" is an example.

Commerce clause   A provision in Article I, Section 8, of the U.S. Constitution that grants the federal government the power to regulate business transactions.

Commercial impracticability   A Uniform Commercial Code (UCC) defense to contractual nonperformance based on happenings that greatly increase the difficulty of performance and that violate the parties' reasonable commercial expectations.

Commercial speech   Speech that has a business-oriented purpose. This speech is protected under the First Amendment, but this protection is not as great as that afforded to noncommercial speech.

Common law   That body of law deriving from judicial decisions as opposed to legislatively enacted statutes and administrative regulations.

Comparable worth   Jobs that, although different, produce substantially equal value for the employer.

Comparative negligence   A doctrine that compares the plaintiff's contributory fault with the defendant's fault and allows the jury to reduce the plaintiff's verdict by the percentage of the plaintiff's fault.

Comparative responsibility   A doctrine that compares the plaintiff's contributory fault with the defendant's fault and allows the jury to reduce the plaintiff's verdict by the percentage of the plaintiff's fault. Also called *comparative negligence.*

Compensatory damages   Usually awarded in breach-of-contract cases to pay for a party's losses that are a direct and foreseeable result of the other party's breach. The award of these damages is designed to place the nonbreaching party in the same position as if the contract had been performed.

Complaint   In legal practice, the first written statement of the plaintiff's position and allegations, which initiates the lawsuit.

Complete performance   Degree of performance recognizing that each contracting party has performed every duty required by the contract.

Compulsory bargaining issue   Mandatory bargaining issue regarding wages, hours, or other terms or conditions of employment. Refusal to engage in good-faith bargaining with regard to these issues is an unfair labor practice.

Concealment   An intentional misrepresentation of a material fact occurring through the silence of a party.

Concerted activities   Those activities involving an agreement, contract, or conspiracy to restrain trade that may be illegal under the Sherman Antitrust Act.

Concurrent conditions   Mutual conditions under which each party's contractual performance is triggered by the other party's tendering (offering) performance.

Condition precedent   An event in the law of contracts that must occur before a duty of immediate performance of the promise arises. Contracts often provide that one party must perform before there is a right to performance by the other party. For example, completion of a job is often a condition precedent to payment for that job. One contracting party's failure to perform a condition precedent permits the other party to refuse to perform, cancel the contract, and sue for damages.

Condition subsequent   A fact that will extinguish a duty to make compensation for breach of contract after the breach has occurred.

Conduct   Under the Uniform Commercial Code (UCC) the conduct of contracting parties (i.e., their actions) is important in determining the meaning of a sales contract.

Confiscation The seizure of property without adequate compensation.

Conflict The common occurrence in life when two or more points of view exist.

Conflict of law Rules of law the courts use to determine that substantive law applies when there is an inconsistency between laws of different states or countries.

Confusion Property ownership that arises when identical masses of objects, such as grain, are mixed together.

Conglomerate merger The merger resulting when merging companies have neither the relationship of competitors nor that of supplier and customer.

Consent order Any court or regulatory order to which the opposing party agrees; a contract of the parties entered upon the record with the approval and sanction of a court.

Consequential damages The amount of money awarded in a breach-of-contract case to the non-breaching party to pay for the special damages that exceed the normal compensatory damages. Lost opportunities may create consequential damages if the breaching party was aware of the special nature of the contract.

Consequentialism An ethical system that concerns itself with the moral consequences of actions. Also called *teleology*.

Consideration An essential element in the creation of a contract obligation that creates a detriment to the promisee or a benefit to the promisor.

Consolidation The process by which two or more corporations are joined to create a new corporation.

Conspiracy A combination or agreement between two or more persons for the commission of a criminal act.

Constitution When capitalized, the term refers to the U.S. federal Constitution, which sets out the basic framework for federal government and, as amended, for individual rights.

Constitutional law The legal issues that arise from interpreting the U.S. Constitution or a state constitution.

Constitutional relativity The idea that constitutional interpretation is relative to the time in which the Constitution is being interpreted.

Constructive discharge The event of an employee resigning because the employer has made working conditions too uncomfortable for continued employment.

Consumer An individual who buys goods and services for personal use rather than for business use.

Consumer Financial Protection Bureau (CFPB) A federal regulatory agency established by the Consumer Financial Protection Act of 2010. The CFPB has authority over federal financial consumer law.

Consumer investigative report A report on a consumer's character, general reputation, mode of living, etc., obtained by personal interviews in the community where the consumer works or lives.

Contempt of court An order by a judge to punish wrongdoing with respect to the court's authority.

Contingency fee An arrangement whereby an attorney is compensated for services in a lawsuit according to an agreed percentage of the amount of money recovered.

Contract A legally enforceable promise.

Contract clause The constitutional provision that prohibits states from enacting laws that interfere with existing contracts. The Supreme Court has refused to interpret this clause in an absolute manner.

Contract law The law of legally enforceable promises.

Contribution The right of one who has discharged a common liability to recover from another also liable the proportionate share of the common liability.

Contributory negligence A failure to use reasonable care by the plaintiff in a negligence suit.

Controlling person The person who has the control of, or is controlled by, the issuer of securities in securities laws.

Convention on the International Sale of Goods (CISG) The agreement that sets forth standard international practices for the sale of goods.

Conversion An unlawful exercise of dominion and control over another's property that substantially interferes with property rights.

Cooling-off period A time provided by the Taft-Hartley Act during which labor and management must suspend the work stoppage (strike or lockout) and continue their working relationship while negotiating a resolution of the dispute. This period is for 80 days.

Copyright A statutorily created property in creative expression that protects authors.

Corporate codes of conduct Policy statements adopted by companies to define ethical standards for their conduct.

Corporate governance A term that has at least two meanings. One relates to how business

782   Glossary

organizations are created and managed. A second concerns how the various levels of government regulate business organizations as they transact business.

Corporation   An artificial, but legal, person created by state law. As a business organization, the corporation's separation of owners and managers gives it a high level of flexibility.

Corrective advertising   A Federal Trade Commission (FTC) remedy that requires companies that have advertised deceptively to run ads that admit the prior errors and correct the erroneous information.

Cost justification defense   A defense to a price discrimination (Section 2 of the Clayton Act) case wherein the defendant seeks to justify charging different customers different prices due to that defendant's costs varying because of the differing quantities purchased by the customers.

Counterclaim   Any claim filed by the defendant in a lawsuit against the plaintiff in the same suit.

Counterdefendant   The party involved in litigation against whom a counterclaim is filed. This party is the original plaintiff.

Counteroffer   An offer made in response to another's offer. Usually made in place of an acceptance. A counteroffer usually terminates an offer.

Counterplaintiff   The party involved in litigation who files a counterclaim. This party is the original defendant who is making a claim against the original plaintiff.

Course of dealing   The way parties to a contract have done business in the past. Important in helping to determine the meaning of a contract for the sale of goods.

Courts of appeal   A court that reviews decisions by lower courts.

Covenant   An agreement or promise in writing by which a party pledges that something has been done or is being done. The term is often used in connection with real estate to describe the promises of the grantor of the property.

Covenant not to compete   An agreement in which one party agrees not to compete directly with the business of the other party; may be limited by geography or length of time.

Criminal law   That area of law dealing with wrongs against the state as representative of the community at large, to be distinguished from civil law, which hears cases of wrongs against persons.

Cross-examination   The process of questioning a witness by the lawyer who did not call the witness to testify on behalf of that lawyer's client.

Cruel and unusual punishment   Protection against such punishment is provided by the Eighth Amendment of the U.S. Constitution. To be cruel and unusual, the punishment must be disproportionately harsh when compared to the offense committed.

Damages   Monetary compensation recoverable in a court of law.

D.B.A.   Doing business as.

Decree   The decision of a court of equity.

Deed   A document representing the title or ownership of land.

Deeds of trust   A type of document to secure an extension of credit through an interest in the land.

Defamation   The publication of anything injurious to the good name or reputation of another.

Default   The failure of a defendant to answer a plaintiff's complaint within the time period allowed by the court. Upon the defendant's default, a judgment is entered in the plaintiff's favor.

Defect   Something that makes a product not reasonably safe for a use that can be reasonably anticipated.

Defendant   The party involved in a lawsuit that is sued; the party required to respond to the plaintiff's complaint.

Deficiency   In a land based security interest, the amount of the loan which remains unpaid after the land has been sold.

Defined benefit plan   A money-purchase plan that guarantees a certain retirement income based on the employee's service and salary under the Employee Retirement Income Security Act. The benefits are fixed, and the contributions vary.

Defined contribution plan   A money-purchase plan that allows employers to budget pension costs in advance under the Employee Retirement Income Security Act. The contribution is fixed, and the benefits vary.

Delivery   The physical transfer of something. In sale-of-goods transactions, delivery is the transfer of goods from the seller to the buyer.

Demurrer   A formal statement by the defendant that the facts alleged by the plaintiff are insufficient to support a claim for legal relief in common law pleading.

De novo judicial review   A proceeding wherein the judge or hearing officer hears the case as if it had not been heard before.

Deontology   An ethical system that affirms an absolute morality. Also called *formalism*.

Deposited acceptance rule   The contractual doctrine that a binding acceptance of an offer occurs when a mailed acceptance is irrevocably placed with the postal service.

Deposition   A discovery process outside the court's supervision that involves the sworn questioning of a potential witness. This oral questioning is reduced to a written form so that a record is established.

Derivative action   A lawsuit filed by a shareholder of a corporation on behalf of the corporation. This action is filed to protect the corporation from the mismanagement of its officers and directors.

Derivative suit   A lawsuit filed by one or more shareholders of a corporation against that organization's management. This suit is brought to benefit the corporation directly and its shareholders indirectly.

Design defect   A defect arising when a product does not meet society's expectation for a safely designed product.

Design patent   A property right awarded for a new, original and ornamental design for an article of manufacture.

Dicta   Statements made in a judicial opinion that are not essential to the decision of the case.

Digital Millennium Copyright Act   A 1998 federal law that provides a safe harbor from contributory copyright infringement for Internet service providers and creates liability for breaking the locks that protect copyrighted works.

Directed verdict   A motion for a directed verdict requests that the judge direct the jury to bring in a particular verdict if reasonable minds could not differ on the correct outcome of the lawsuit. In deciding the motion, the judge will view in the light most favorable to the nonmoving party, and if different inferences may be drawn by reasonable people, then the court cannot direct a verdict. In essence, a directed verdict removes the jury's discretion.

Direct examination   The process of questioning a witness conducted by the lawyer who called the witness to testify on behalf of that lawyer's client.

Directors   Those individuals who are elected by the shareholders to decide the goals and objectives for the corporate organization.

Disability   Any physical or mental impairment that substantially limits a major life activity.

Disaffirm   To void. Used to describe a minor's power to get out of a contract because of age.

Discharge   In bankruptcy the forgiving of an honest debtor's debts. In contract law an act that forgives further performance of a contractual obligation.

Discovery   Procedures by which one party to a lawsuit may obtain information relevant to the case from the other party or from third persons.

Discretionary function exception   An exception to the waiver of the doctrine of sovereign immunity. Officials of administrative agencies are exempt from personal liability if their performance or lack thereof is based on a discretionary function.

Discrimination in effect   The discriminatory result of policies that appear to be neutral.

Disparate impact   A term of employment litigation that refers to the disproportionate impact of a policy neutral on its face on some protected class (e.g., race or sex).

Disparate treatment   A term of employment litigation that refers to the illegal discriminatory treatment of an individual in some protected class (e.g., race or sex).

Dispute   The circumstance when a party in conflict claims the right to do or have something and the other party denies, rejects, or ignores the claim.

Dissolution   The cancellation of an agreement, thereby rescinding its binding force. A partnership is dissolved anytime there is a change in partners. A corporation's dissolution occurs when that business entity ceases to exist.

Diversity of citizenship   The plaintiffs filing a lawsuit must be from states different from those of the defendants. This requirement, along with over $75,000 at stake, is one method a federal court gains jurisdiction over the subject matter of a lawsuit.

Divestiture   The antitrust remedy that forces a company to get rid of assets acquired through illegal mergers or monopolistic practices.

Docket   A book containing a brief summary of all acts done in court in the conduct of each case.

Doctrine of abstention   A principle used by federal courts to refuse to hear a case. When used by the federal courts, the lawsuit involved is sent to the state court system.

Domestic corporation   A business organization created by the issuance of a state charter that operates in the state that issued the charter.

Domicile   That place that a person intends as his or her fixed and permanent legal residence; place of permanent abode, as contrasted with a residence, which may be temporary; a person can have a number of residences but only one domicile; the state of incorporation of a corporation.

Donee beneficiary   A noncontracting third party who receives as a gift the benefits of a contract made between two other parties. This third party is empowered to enforce the contract to ensure the receipt of the contract's benefits.

Dormant commerce clause concept The impact of the commerce clause as a means of limiting state and local governments' powers to regulate business activities.

Double jeopardy A constitutional doctrine that prohibits an individual from being prosecuted twice by the same governing body based on the same factual situation.

Double tax A disadvantage of a corporate form of organization in that the corporation must pay a tax on the money earned and the shareholder pays a second tax on the dividends distributed.

Dram shop acts Statutes adopted in many states that impose strict liability upon tavern owners for injuries to third parties caused by their intoxicated patrons.

Due diligence defense A defense that experts may assert in a 1933 Securities Act case involving the failure to register securities or the failure to provide accurate documents. The expert utilizing this defense attempts to prove his or her reasonable investigation into all available information.

Due process Fundamental fairness. As applied to judicial proceedings, adequate notice of a hearing and an opportunity to appear and defend in an orderly tribunal.

Due process clause A provision found in the Fifth and Fourteenth Amendments of the U.S. Constitution. This clause assures all citizens of fundamental fairness in their relationship with the government.

Dumping The practice of selling foreign goods in one country at less than the comparable price in the country where the goods originated.

Duress Action by a person that compels another to do what he or she would not otherwise do. It is a recognized defense to any act that must be voluntary in order to create liability in the actor.

Duty A legal obligation imposed by the law.

Duty of performance In contract law the legal obligation of a party to a contract.

Duty of reasonable care The legal duty owed under negligence doctrine.

Easement The right of one other than the owner of land to some use of that land.

Economic boycott Used in three basic forms (primary, secondary, and tertiary), a practice aimed at cutting off trade opportunities for enemy countries.

Eighty-day cooling-off period A provision in the Taft-Hartley Act that allows the president to require that laborers continue working and that the laborers' representatives and management continue bargaining for at least 80 days during which it is intended that federal mediation will resolve the dispute. This provision can be utilized by the president only when there is a determination that the work stoppage is adversely affecting the national health and safety.

Ejusdem generis Of the same kind or class; a doctrine of legislative interpretation.

Embezzlement The fraudulent appropriation by one person, acting in a fiduciary capacity, of the money or property of another.

Eminent domain The government's constitutional power to take private property for public use upon the payment of just compensation.

Emissions reduction banking The policy stating that businesses that lower pollution beyond the requirements of the law may use the additional reductions in the future.

Employment at will A hiring for an indefinite period of time.

En banc Proceedings by or before the court as a whole rather than any single judge.

Endangerment of workers A criminal act that involves placing employees at risk with respect to their health and safety in the work environment.

Enforceable contract A contract that can be enforced in court.

Enjoin To require performance of, or abstention from, some act through issuance of an injunction.

Environmental impact statement A filing of documents required by the National Environmental Policy Act that forces governmental agencies to consider the environmental consequences of their actions.

Equal protection clause A provision in the Fourteenth Amendment of the U.S. Constitution that requires all citizens to be treated in a similar manner by the government unless there is a sufficient justification for the unequal treatment.

Escrow A deed, bond, or deposit that one party delivers for safekeeping by a second party who is obligated to deliver it to a third party upon the fulfillment of some condition.

Establishment clause A provision in the First Amendment of the U.S. Constitution that prohibits the federal government from establishing any government-supported religion or church.

Estate The bundle of rights and powers of real property ownership.

Estoppel   The legal principle that one may not assert facts inconsistent with one's own prior actions.

Ethics   A systematic statement of right and wrong together with a philosophical system that both justifies and necessitates rules of conduct.

European Union (EU)   Created by the Treaty of Rome, an organization that seeks to facilitate the free movement of goods, services, labor, professions, transportation, and capital among European countries.

Exclusive dealing   A buyer agrees to purchase a certain product exclusively from the seller or the seller agrees to sell all of his or her production to the buyer.

Exclusive remedy rule   The rule that limits an injured employee's claim against the employer to workers' compensation.

Exculpatory clause   A provision in a contract whereby one of the parties attempts to relieve itself of liability for breach of a legal duty.

Exculpatory contract   A contract that excuses one from accepting responsibility or blame. For example, a contract that excuses one from having to accept liability for one's negligence or another's injury or loss.

Exculpatory no   The doctrine that merely denying guilt is not a criminal lie in response to a question from an agency of the federal government. This doctrine is no longer valid.

Executed contract   A contract that is fully accomplished or performed, leaving nothing unfulfilled.

Execution   To carry out some action to completion. With respect to enforcing a court's judgment, an execution involves the seizure of the debtor's property, a sale of the property, and the payment of proceeds to the creditor.

Executory contract   An agreement that is not completed. Until the performance required in a contract is completed, it is executory.

Exemplary damages   Punitive damages. Monetary compensation in excess of direct losses suffered by the plaintiff that may be awarded in intentional tort cases where the defendant's conduct deserves punishment.

Exhaustion of remedies   A concept used in administrative law that requires any party to an administrative proceeding to give the administrative agency every opportunity to resolve the dispute before appealing to the court system.

Expectation of privacy   The expectation that one will not be observed by the state.

Experience rating system   A system of sliding taxation under which employers are charged less unemployment compensation tax as they lay off fewer workers due to economic conditions.

Export controls   Action taken on a national and multilateral basis to prevent the exportation of controlled goods and technology to certain destinations.

Express authority   Actual authority that arises from specific statements made by the principal to the agent.

Express conditions   Conditions that are explicitly set out in a contract.

Express contract   A contract in which parties show their agreement in words.

Express warranty   Any statement of fact or promise about the performance of a product made by a seller.

Expropriation   A foreign government's seizure of privately owned property.

Extortionate picketing   Picketing by employees in an attempt to force an employer to pay money to union officials or other individuals when these payments provide personal benefit to the officials or individuals instead of benefiting the union membership generally.

Extradition   The process that one state uses to have another state transfer to the jurisdiction of the first state a person accused of criminal activities.

Failing-company doctrine   A merger between a failing company and a competitor may be allowed, although such a merger would be illegal if both companies were viable competitors.

Fair Labor Standards Act (FLSA)   Originally passed in 1938, this law provides basic protections for employees, including the minimum wage and maximum number of hours before overtime must be paid.

Fair use   A statutorily permitted use of another's copyright for criticism, comment, news reporting, teaching, scholarship, or research.

False advertising   Untrue and fraudulent statements and representations made by way of advertising a product or a service.

False imprisonment   The tort of an intentional, unjustified confinement of a nonconsenting person who knows of the confinement.

Family and Medical Leave Act (FMLA)   This law, which became effective in 1993, allows eligible workers up to 12 weeks of unpaid leave in any

12-month period to care for a newborn baby, to care for a child placed for adoption or foster care, to care for an immediate family member with a serious health condition, or when the employee is unable to work because of a serious health condition.

Family resemblance test A legal principle used to determine whether or not promissory notes or other similar investment opportunities are securities.

Featherbedding A term used in the labor laws to describe workers who are paid although they do not perform any work. Under the Taft-Hartley Act, featherbedding is an unfair labor practice by unions.

Federal Employer's Liability Act The federal act covering transportation workers that establishes an employer's liability to employees for negligence.

Federalism A term used to describe the vertical aspect of the separation of powers. The coexistence of a federal government and the various state governments, with each having responsibilities and authorities that are distinct but overlap, is called federalism.

Federal question cases Litigation involving the application or interpretation of the federal Constitution, federal statutes, federal treaties, or federal administrative agencies. The federal court system has subject matter jurisdiction over these issues.

Federal Rules of Civil Procedure A law passed by Congress that provides the procedural steps to be followed by the federal courts when handling civil litigation.

Federal Trade Commission (FTC) The federal regulatory agency that enforces the Federal Trade Commission Act of 1914 and various antitrust and consumer protection laws.

Federal Trade Commission Act Passed in 1914, this legislation created the Federal Trade Commission (FTC) and authorized it to protect society against unfair methods of competition. The law was amended in 1938 (by the Wheeler-Lea amendment) to provide the FTC with authority to regulate unfair or deceptive trade practices.

Fee schedule A plan, usually adopted by an association, that establishes minimum or maximum charges for a service or product.

Fee simple The maximum bundle of rights, or estate, permitted by law.

Fellow-servant doctrine The doctrine that precludes an injured employee from recovering damages from his employer when the injury resulted from the negligent act of another employee.

Felony A criminal offense of a serious nature, generally punishable by death or imprisonment in a penitentiary; to be distinguished from a misdemeanor.

Fiduciary One having a duty to act for another's benefit in the highest good faith.

Finance charge Any charge for an extension of credit, which specifically includes interest, service charges, and other charges.

Financing statement An established form that a secured party files with a public officer, such as a state official or local court clerk, to perfect a security interest under the Uniform Commercial Code (UCC). It is a simple form that contains basic information such as a description of the collateral, names, and addresses. It is designed to give notice that the debtor and the secured party have entered into a security agreement.

Firm offer An offer in signed writing by a merchant to buy or sell goods; it gives assurances that the offer will be held open for acceptance under the Uniform Commercial Code (UCC).

Fixture Personal property that has become real property, generally through physical attachment (annexation).

Focus group A group acting as a mock jury; attorneys present cases to such a group to get the members' feedback on the merits of the various arguments presented.

Foreclosure If a mortgagor fails to perform his or her obligations as agreed, the mortgagee may declare the whole debt due and payable, and she or he may foreclose on the mortgaged property to pay the debt secured by the mortgage. The usual method of foreclosure authorizes the sale of the mortgaged property at a public auction. The proceeds of the sale are applied to the debt.

Foreign corporation A business organization, created by the issuance of a state charter, that operates in states other than the one issuing the charter.

Foreign Corrupt Practices Act (FCPA) A U.S. law that seeks to ban the payment of bribes to foreign officials in order to obtain business.

Foreign Sovereign Immunities Act (FISA) A federal law passed in 1976 that codifies the restrictive theory of *sovereign immunity* and rejects immunity for commercial acts carried on in the United States or having direct effects in this country.

Foreign subsidiary A practice common in a multinational corporation that conducts part of its business operations in a foreign country.

Formalism   An ethical system that affirms an absolute morality. Also called *deontology.*

Forum non conveniens   The doctrine under which a court may dismiss a lawsuit in which it appears that for the convenience of the parties and in the interest of justice the action should have been brought in another court.

Franchise   A marketing technique whereby one party (the franchisor) grants a second party (the franchisee) the right to manufacture, distribute, or sell a product using the name or trademark of the franchisor.

Fraud   A false representation of fact made with the intent to deceive another that is justifiably relied upon to the injury of that person.

Free exercise clause   A provision in the First Amendment of the U.S. Constitution that allows all citizens the freedom to follow or believe any religious teaching.

Frolic and detour   The activity of an agent or an employee who has departed from the scope of the agency and is not, therefore, a representative of his or her employer.

Full faith and credit clause   A provision in the U.S. Constitution that requires a state to recognize the laws and judicial decisions of all other states.

Full-line forcing   An arrangement in which a manufacturer refuses to supply any portion of the product line unless the retailer agrees to accept the entire line.

Functional discount   A reduction in price as the result of the buyer's performing some service that usually is provided by the seller.

Garnishment   A legal proceeding whereby a creditor may collect directly from a third party who is obligated to the debtor.

General Agreement on Tariffs and Trade (GATT)   An international treaty that requires member countries to abide by the principles of open and free trade.

General counsel   An individual who is responsible for coordinating all law-related issues, such as the quasi-judicial hearings in administrative agencies. This term is also used to describe the principal lawyer of a company.

General partner   The owner of a limited partnership that enjoys the control of the partnership's operation. This type of partner is personally liable for the debts of the limited partnership.

General partnership   A business organization wherein all owners (partners) share profits and losses and all are jointly and severally liable for the organization's debts.

Generic   To lose distinctiveness in reference to the source of goods and thus to lose trademark protection.

Genetic Information Nondiscrimination Act (GINA)   Prohibits covered employers from firing, refusing to hire, or otherwise discriminating against individuals on the basis of their genetic information or a family member's genetic information.

Geographic extension merger   A combining of companies involved with the same product or service that do not compete in the same geographical regions or markets.

Geographic market   The relevant section of the country affected by a merger.

Gift   Transfer of ownership by intent and the delivery of the object gifted.

Going bare   A professional practicing (in her or his field of expertise) without liability insurance.

Good, the   In philosophy the moral goals and objectives that people choose to pursue.

Good faith   Honesty in dealing; innocence; without fraud or deceit.

Good-faith meeting-of-competition defense   A bona fide business practice that is a defense to a charge of violation of the Robinson-Patman Act. The Robinson-Patman Act is an amendment to the Clayton Act, which outlaws price discrimination that might substantially lessen competition or tends to create a monopoly. This exception allows a seller in good faith to meet the equally low price, service, or facility of a competitor. The good-faith exception cannot be established if the purpose of the price discrimination has been to eliminate competition.

Goods   Tangible (touchable), movable personal property.

Greenmail   Forcing a corporation to buy back some of its own stock at an inflated price to avoid a takeover.

Guardian   One charged with the duty of care and maintenance of another person such as a minor or incompetent under the law.

Guardian *ad litem*   A guardian appointed to prosecute or defend a lawsuit on behalf of an incompetent or a minor.

Guidelines   A result of an administrative agency's quasi-legislative function that assists parties being regulated to understand the agency's functions and intentions. Guidelines do not have the force of the law, but they can be helpful in anticipating the application of an agency's regulations.

Habeas corpus   The name of a writ that orders one holding custody of another to produce that individual before the court for the purpose of determining whether such custody is proper.

Hearsay evidence   Evidence of statements made or actions performed out of court that is offered to prove the truth thereof.

Hearsay rule   The exclusion, with certain exceptions, of hearsay evidence because of the lack of opportunity to cross-examine the original source of the evidence.

Holding   The precise legal response in an opinion by an appellate court on an issue of law raised on appeal.

Holder in due course   One who has acquired possession of a negotiable instrument through proper negotiation for value, in good faith, and without notice of any defenses to it. Such a holder is not subject to personal defenses that would otherwise defeat the obligation embodied in the instrument.

Horizontal merger   Merger of corporations that were competitors prior to the merger.

Horizontal price fixing   A per se illegal agreement among competitors as to the price all of them will charge for their similar products.

Horizontal territorial agreement   An arrangement between competitors with respect to geographical areas in which each will conduct its business to the exclusion of the others. This type of agreement is illegal per se under the Sherman Act.

Hostile working environment   Under Title VII an environment where co-workers make offensive sexual comments or propositions, engage in suggestive touching, show nude pictures, or draw sexual graffiti.

Hot-cargo contract   An agreement whereby an employer agrees to refrain from handling, using, selling, transporting, or otherwise dealing in the products of another employer or to cease doing business with any other person.

Illegal search and seizure   The area covered by the Fourth Amendment that protects individuals and organizations from unreasonable intrusion without a court-issued warrant.

Immunity   Status of exemption from lawsuits or other legal obligations.

Implied authority   Actual authority that is incidental to express authority.

Implied conditions   Conditions to a contract that are implied by law rather than by contractual agreement.

Implied contract   A legally enforceable agreement inferred from the circumstances and conduct of the parties. Also called an *implied-in-fact contract.*

Implied-in-fact contract   A legally enforceable agreement inferred from the circumstances and conduct of the parties.

Implied-in-law contract   A quasi-contract.

Implied warranty   A warranty implied by law rather than by express agreement of the parties to a contract.

Implied warranty of fitness for a particular purpose   An implied Uniform Commercial Code (UCC) warranty that arises when a buyer specifies a purpose for a product, then relies on the seller's skill and judgment to select the product.

Implied warranty of habitability   A warranty implied by law in a number of states that guarantees the quality of new home construction.

Implied warranty of merchantability   A warranty (implied) that the goods are reasonably fit for the general purpose for which they are sold.

Impossibility of performance   A defense to contractual nonperformance based on special circumstances that render the performance illegal, physically impossible, or so difficult as to violate every reasonable expectation the parties have regarding performance.

Incidental beneficiary   A person who may incidentally benefit from the creation of a contract. Such a person cannot enforce any right to incidental benefit.

Incorporators   Those individuals who are responsible for bringing a corporation into being.

Indefiniteness   When the terms of an agreement are not sufficiently specific, the agreement does not rise to the level of a contract because of the doctrine of indefiniteness.

Indictment   A document issued by a grand jury formally charging a person with a felony.

Individual retirement account   A retirement account for persons who can make either tax deductible contributions, which are taxed on withdrawal, or contributions that are taxed, which produce tax-free withdrawals. This latter type of account is known as a Roth IRA.

Industry guide   An issue of the Federal Trade Commission (FTC) defining the agency's view of the legality of an industry's trade practice.

Infliction of mental distress   An intentional tort of the emotions that causes both mental distress and physical symptoms as a result of the defendant's outrageous behavior.

Information   A written accusation by the prosecutor presented in court charging an accused person with a crime.

Infringement   The tort establishing violation of intellectual property rights.

Injunction   A court order directing a party to do or to refrain from doing some act.

Injurious falsehood   A statement of untruth that causes injury or damage to the party against whom it is made.

In pari materia   Concerning the same subject matter. A rule of statutory construction that two such statutes will be construed together.

In personam   The jurisdiction of a court to affect the rights and duties of a specific individual.

In rem   The jurisdiction of a court to affect property rights with respect to a specific thing.

Insider   A person who owns 10 percent or more of a company or who is a director or officer of the company; a term used in securities law. This term is also used to describe a person possessing nonpublic information.

Intangible property   Something that represents value but has no physical attributes, such as a copyright, patent, or franchise right.

Intellectual property   A type of property in information and its application or expression. Patents and copyrights are examples.

Intent   A legal doctrine indicating that parties meant to do what they did.

Intentional interference with contractual relations   The tort of causing another to break a contract.

Intentional tort   Noncontractual legal wrong caused by one who desires to cause the wrong or where the wrong is substantially likely to occur from the behavior.

Intent to defraud   Applies to an individual who knowingly and willfully makes a misrepresentation of a material fact that is relied on and thereby causes injury or harm.

Interference with contractual relations   A business tort in which persons are induced to breach binding agreements.

International Court of Justice   The judicial branch of the United Nations, which sits at The Hague in the Netherlands and consists of 15 judges representing the world's major legal systems.

International Monetary Fund   An international economic organization.

Interpleader   A legal procedure by which one holding a single fund subject to conflicting claims of two or more persons may require the conflicting claimants to come into court and litigate the matter between themselves.

Interrogatory   A written question submitted by one party to another in a lawsuit; a type of discovery procedure.

Inter se   Between themselves.

Intestate   A person who dies without a will.

Invasion of privacy   A tort based on misappropriation of name or likeness, intrusion upon physical solitude, or public disclosure of objectionable, private information.

Investigative consumer report   A consumer report under the Fair Credit Reporting Act that arises when a credit reporting agency goes beyond reporting financial transactions and also reports the habits and practices of someone seeking credit or a job.

Involuntary petition   The document filed by a creditor to initiate bankruptcy proceedings against a debtor.

Irreconcilable conflicts   When a state or local law requires something different than a federal law or regulation and both laws cannot be satisfied. Under Commerce Clause analysis, the state or local law is declared invalid and void.

Irrevocable letter of credit   Reduces the risk to parties in cases where business is extended across national borders between strangers by providing guarantees of payment and delivery of goods.

Issuer   The term in securities law for an individual or business organization offering a security for sale to the public.

Jointly and severally liable   The legal principle that makes two or more people, usually partners, liable for an entire debt as individuals or in any proportional combination.

Joint tenancy   A property ownership that is undivided (common) and equal between two or more owners. Permits survivorship.

Joint venture   Two or more persons or business organizations agreeing to do business for a specific and limited purpose.

Judgment   Official adjudication of a court of law.

Judgment notwithstanding the verdict   The decision of a court that sets aside the verdict of a jury and reaches the opposite result.

Judgment on the pleadings   A principle of litigation, in the form of a motion, whereby one party tests the validity of the allegations contained in the complaint and answer. Upon this motion a judge might determine that the pleadings contain no issues of fact or law and thus grant a judgment prior to a trial.

Judicial activism   An activist judge tends to abide by the following judicial philosophies: (1) The political process cannot adequately handle society's difficult issues; (2) the courts can correct society's ills through the decision-making process; (3) following precedent is not crucial; and (4) "judge-made law" is often necessary to carry out the legislative intent of the law. See also *Judicial restraint.*

Judicial admission   An exception under the statute of frauds allowing courts to enforce oral contracts when a party acknowledges the oral promise in a formal judicial/court environment.

Judicial restraint   A judge who abides by the judicial restraint philosophy (1) believes that the political process, and not the courts, should correct society's ills; (2) decides an issue on a narrow basis, if possible; (3) follows precedent whenever possible; and (4) does not engage in "judge-made law" but interprets the letter of the law. See also *Judicial activism.*

Judicial review   The power of courts to declare laws enacted by legislative bodies and actions by the executive branch to be unconstitutional.

Jurisdiction   The power and authority of a court or other governmental agency to adjudicate controversies and otherwise deal with matters brought before it.

Jurisdictional strike   A stoppage of work that arises from a dispute between two or more unions as to what work should be assigned to the employees belonging to the disputing unions. This work stoppage is an unfair labor practice. This dispute between the unions should be resolved by the NLRB.

Jurisprudence   The science of the law; the practical science of giving a wise interpretation of the law.

Jury instruction   A statement made by the judge to the jury informing them of the law applicable to the case the jury is bound to accept and apply.

Kickbacks   Payments made to a person who has facilitated a transaction.

Knowingly   Intentionally.

Laches   Defense to an equitable action based on the plaintiff's unreasonable delay in bringing the action.

Landrum-Griffin Act   The federal law passed in 1959 that provides union members with a "Bill of Rights" and requires union officers to file reports with the Department of Labor. This law, which is known as the Labor-Management Reporting and Disclosure Act, also added unfair labor practices by unions.

Land sales contract   A type of document to secure an extension of credit through an interest in the land purchased.

Lanham Act   A federal law regulating unfair methods of competition regarding trademarks.

Larceny   The unlawful taking of personal property with the intent to deprive the right owner of this property.

Law   The rules of the state backed up by enforcement.

Law of agency   That body of law concerning one's dealing with another on behalf of a principal.

Law of nations   The law embodied in international agreements, treaties, and conventions.

Leading question   A question that indicates the appropriate answer because of the way or manner in which it is asked. Typically, such questions are allowed during the cross-examination of a witness but not during the direct examination.

Leashold estate   The property granted to tenants (lessees) by a landlord (lessor).

Legacy   A gift of money under a will. It is a type of bequest, which is a gift of personal property. The word *devise* is used in connection with real property distributed by will.

Legal capacity   The ability of a business organization to sue and be sued in its own name rather than having to sue or be sued in the name of its owners.

Legal clinic   A term referring to a law firm that specializes in low-cost, generally routine legal procedures.

Legislation   Laws passed by an elected body such as Congress, a state legislation, or local council/commission. Those laws enacted at the federal and state levels are called statutes. At the local level, such laws are often referred to as ordinances.

Legislative history   A technique used by courts in interpreting statutes. Courts often examine the record of the legislators' debate in an attempt to determine what was intended by the legislation.

Letter of credit   A document commonly used in international transactions to ensure payment and delivery of goods.

Libel   A defamatory written statement communicated to a third party.

License   A common method of controlling product or technology transfers across national borders.

Lien   A claim to an interest in property in satisfaction of a debt or claim.

Life estate   A property that grants land ownership for the lifetime of a specified person.

Limited liability   This term is used to describe the exposure of business owners to pay the debts of their businesses when such exposure does not exceed the owner's investment in the business.

Limited liability company (LLC)   A type of business organization that has characteristics of both a partnership and a corporation. The owners of an LLC are called members, and their personal liability is limited to their capital contributions. The LLC, as an organization, is not a taxable entity.

Limited liability partnership   A hybrid business partnership.

Limited partners   Those owners of a limited partnership who forgo control of the organization's operation in return for their liability being limited to the amount of their investment.

Limited partnership   A partnership in which one or more individuals are general partners and one or more individuals are limited partners. The limited partners contribute assets to the partnership without taking part in the conduct of the business. Such individuals are liable for the debts of the partnership only to the extent of their contributions.

Limited personal liability   See *Limited liability*.

Liquidated damages clause   A contractual provision that specifies a predetermined amount of damages or a formula for such a determination to be utilized if a breach of contract occurs.

Liquidation   The process of winding up the affairs of a business for the purpose of paying debts and disposing of assets. May be voluntary or under court order.

Litigation   The process of utilizing the court system to resolve a legal dispute.

Long-arm statute   A state statute that gives extra-territorial effect to process (summon) in specified cases. It allows state courts to obtain jurisdiction in civil actions over defendants who are beyond the border of the state provided the defendants have minimum contact with the state sufficient to satisfy due process.

Mailbox rule   The rule that an acceptance is effective once it is sent. See *Deposited acceptance rule*.

Mail fraud   The use of the United States Postal Service or any interstate carrier to conduct fraudulent activities with the intent to deprive an owner of property.

Malfeasance   Doing of some wrongful act.

Malice   The state of mind that accompanies the intentional doing of a wrongful act without justification or excuse.

Malicious prosecution   An action for recovery of damages that have resulted to person, property, or reputation from previous unsuccessful civil or criminal proceedings that were prosecuted without probable cause and with malice.

Manager   A person designated and charged with day-to-day operations of a Limited Liability Company.

Mandamus   A court order directing the holder of an office to perform his or her legal duty.

Mandatory arbitration   A form of resolving a dispute, as an alternative to litigation, that is required by a statute.

Manifest system   A documentary system required by the Resource Conservation and Recovery Act. Used in the disposal of toxic chemicals.

Market extension merger   An acquisition in which the acquiring company increases its market through product extension or geographical extension.

Master   The term used in an agency relationship to describe the principal (employer) of a servant (employee) who is involved in a tort.

Material breach   A level of performance below what is reasonably acceptable. A substantial failure, without excuse, to perform a promise that constitutes the whole or part of a contract. A party who has materially breached cannot sue the other party for performance and is liable for damages.

Mayhem   Unlawfully depriving a human being of a member of his or her body.

Mechanic's lien   A lien on real estate that is created by statute to assist suppliers and laborers in collecting their accounts and wages. Its purpose is to subject the owner's land to a lien for material and labor expended in the construction of buildings and other improvements.

Med-Arb   An abbreviation for an alternative dispute resolution system that involves parties going through mediation and agreeing to resolve as many issues as possible. These parties agree that any matters not resolved in the mediation process will then be arbitrated.

Mediation   An alternative to litigation whereby a third party attempts to assist the disputing parties in reaching a settlement. The third-party mediator lacks authority to impose on the parties a binding solution to the dispute.

Mediator   An individual who assists disputing parties in their efforts to resolve their differences. Mediators must rely on their persuasive abilities since they have no authority to settle the dispute.

Members   The individuals or business entities that belong to a limited liability company.

Merchant   A term used in the Uniform Commercial Code to describe parties to a contract that regularly do business in the goods being sold and purchased.

Merger   The extinguishment of a corporate entity by the transfer of its assets and liabilities to another corporation that continues in existence.

Minimum rationality   A legal test used by courts to test the validity of governmental action, such as legislation, under the equal protection clause of the U.S. Constitution. To satisfy this test, the government needs to demonstrate that there is a good reason for the government's action.

Minimum wage   Minimum hourly wages, established by Congress under the Fair Labor Standards Act, to maintain the health, efficiency, and general well-being of workers.

Ministerial duty   An example of a definite duty regarding that nothing be left to discretion or judgment.

Minitrial   An alternative dispute resolution system that involves lawyers presenting both sides of a business dispute to the executives of the organizations involved.

Mirror image rule   The common law rule that the terms of an acceptance offer must mirror exactly the terms of the offer. Any variation of terms would make the attempted acceptance a counteroffer.

Misappropriation   A term referring to the wrongful taking of what belongs to an owner. Often used in intellectual property law.

Misappropriation theory   The legal doctrine supported by the Securities and Exchange Commission (SEC) and the courts that any person who shares nonpublic information with another party or who trades on the information violates the securities laws if that information was intended to be kept confidential.

Misdemeanor   A criminal offense of less serious nature than a felony, generally punishable by fine or jail sentence other than in a penitentiary.

Misfeasance   A misdeed or trespass.

Misrepresentation   An untrue manifestation of fact by word or conduct; it may be unintentional.

Mitigate   To lessen the consequences of. Usually used to refer to the contractual duty to lessen damages following breach of contract.

Mock trial   An alternative dispute resolution system that involves lawyers presenting their clients' cases to a group of citizens who render their opinion about the relative merits of the parties' positions.

Monopoly   Exclusive control of a market by a business entity.

Morality   The values of right and wrong.

Mortgage   1. A transfer of an interest in property for the purpose of creating a security for a debt. 2. A type of security interest in land, usually securing an extension of credit.

Mortgagor   The owner of land who places a mortgage on it.

Motion   The process by which the parties make written or oral requests that the judge issue an order or ruling.

Mutual assent   A contractual doctrine requiring that the minds of the contracting parties must meet before there exists a binding contract.

Mutual mistake   A situation in which parties to a contract reach a bargain on the basis of an incorrect assumption common to both parties.

Nationalization   A claim made by a foreign government that it owns expropriated property.

National Labor Relations Board (NLRB)   The federal administrative agency created in 1935 to conduct certification/decertification elections of unions and to conduct quasi-judicial hearings arising from the labor-management relationship.

National Mediation Board   Created by the Railway Labor Act, this federal agency is to help the parties resolve labor-management disputes arising in transportation industries.

Natural law   A philosophy of law that says certain legal rules can be reasoned out from nature itself and always hold true.

Necessaries of life   Food, clothing, shelter, medical care, and, in some states, education. A minor is legally responsible to pay a reasonable value for purchased necessaries of life.

Negligence   A person's failure to exercise reasonable care that foreseeably causes another injury.

Negotiable instrument or document   A special type of written promise to pay money (instrument) or deliver goods (document). Personal defenses do not apply against the holder in due course of a negotiable instrument or document.

Negotiated settlement A voluntary but binding agreement that settles a legal dispute, such as one involving a contractual breach or a tort lawsuit.

Negotiation The process used to persuade or coerce someone to do or to stop doing something.

Nexus A logical connection.

NLRB National Labor Relations Board.

Noerr-Pennington doctrine This doctrine exempts from the antitrust laws concerted efforts to lobby government officials regardless of the anticompetitive purposes. It is based on the First Amendment freedom of speech.

No-fault laws Laws barring tort actions by injured persons against third-party tortfeasors and requiring such persons to obtain recovery from their own insurers.

Nolo contendere A plea entered by the defendant in a criminal case that neither admits nor denies the crime allegedly committed but, if accepted by the court, permits the judge to treat the defendant as guilty.

Nonprofit corporation A corporation that must return all profits to the organization for use in future operations. Such corporations are often exempt from federal income tax.

Nontrading partnership A business organization made up of two or more partners engaged in buying and selling goods.

Norris-LaGuardia Act The federal legislation adopted in 1932 that attempted to increase union membership by prohibiting the use of injunctions issued by federal courts against certain union activities and by outlawing yellow-dog contracts.

North American Free Trade Agreement (NAFTA) An agreement reached in 1993 among the United States, Mexico, and Canada to increase economic growth through mutual trade.

Noscitur a sociis The principle that the scope of general words is defined by specific accompanying words; a doctrine of legislative interpretation.

Notary public A public officer authorized to administer oaths and certify certain documents.

Notice Communication sufficient to charge a reasonable person with knowledge of some fact.

Novation The substitution of a new contract in place of an old one.

Nuisance A physical condition constituting an unreasonable and substantial interference with the rights of individuals or the public at large.

Obligee One who is entitled to receive a payment or performance under a contract.

Obligor One who is obligated to pay or perform under a contract.

Obstruction of justice A criminal act involving the interference of the administration of the laws during the investigations and conduct of trials.

Occupational Safety and Health Administration (OSHA) The organization that has jurisdiction over complaints about hazardous conditions in the workplace.

Offer A contractual communication that contains a specific promise and a specific demand. The offer initiates the process of making a contract.

Officers Those individuals appointed by directors of a corporation to conduct the daily operations of the corporate organization.

Oligopoly Control of the supply and price of a commodity or service in a given market by a small number of companies or suppliers.

Opinion The decision of a judge, usually issued in a written form.

Option A contractual arrangement under which one party has for a specified time the right to buy certain property from or sell certain property to the other party. It is essentially a contract to not revoke an offer.

Oral argument Attorneys appear in person before the appellate court to explain orally to the court their position in the case and answer the court's questions about the case.

Ordinance The legislative enactment of a city, county, or other municipal corporation.

Organizers The parties responsible for bringing a limited liability company into existence. These parties correspond to the functions of incorporators with respect to corporations.

Overbreadth doctrine A principle used by courts to invalidate legislation that is broader in scope than is necessary to regulate an activity. This doctrine may be utilized to protect constitutional rights, such as freedom of speech, against a wide sweep of some governmental action.

Overt act An essential element of a crime. Without this action by a party, the intent to engage in criminal activity is not wrongful.

Ownership The term refers to the exclusive legal right to possess, transfer, and use resources. It is a synonym for "property."

Paper fortress   A term referring to the documentation an employer should keep about an employee's performance.

Parker v. Brown doctrine   The name given to the state action exemption to the Sherman Act. See also *State action exemption*.

Parol evidence   Legal proof based on oral statements; with regard to a document, any evidence extrinsic to the document itself.

Parol evidence rule   Parol evidence is extrinsic evidence. In contracts, the parol evidence rule excludes the introduction of evidence of prior written or oral agreements that may vary, contradict, alter, or supplement the present written agreement. There are several exceptions to this rule. For example, when the parties to an agreement do not intend for that agreement to be final and complete, then parol evidence is admissible.

Partnership   A business organization involving two or more persons agreeing to conduct a commercial venture while sharing its profits and losses.

Part performance   The contractual doctrine that says when a buyer of land has made valuable improvements in it or has paid part or all of the purchase price, the statute of frauds does not apply to prevent an oral land sales contract from being enforceable.

Patent   A statutorily created property in inventions and discoveries. See *Utility patent, Design patent,* and *Plant patent.*

Pattern of racketeering   Under RICO, two or more similar acts of organized crime in a ten year period.

Pay-for-play   A term referencing the need for one to have to pay to get performed a duty that an official, frequently a government official, is already obligated to perform, for example, an appointment by the official. Pay for play usually indicates official corruption.

Per capita   By or for each individual.

Per curiam   By the court; said of an opinion expressing the view of the court as a whole as opposed to an opinion authored by any single member of the court.

Peremptory challenge   The power granted each party to reject a limited number of potential jurors during voir dire examination. No reason for the rejection need be given.

Perfection   The status ascribed to security interests after certain events have occurred or certain prescribed steps have been taken, e.g., the filing of a financing statement.

Perjury   The giving of false testimony under oath.

Per se   In itself.

Per se illegality   Under the Sherman Act, agreements and practices are illegal only if they are unreasonable. The practices that are conclusively presumed to be unreasonable are per se illegal. If an activity is per se illegal, only proof of the activity is required, and it is not necessary to prove an anticompetitive effect. For example, price fixing is per se illegal. See also *Rule of reason.*

Personal jurisdiction   The power of a court over the parties involved in the litigation process.

Personal property   All property that does not involve land and interests in land.

Petitioner   The party filing either a case in equity or a petition for a writ of *certiorari* before a supreme court.

Petit jury   The fact-finding body during a trial. Also called a trial or traverse jury.

Petty offenses   Criminal acts that are viewed as minor and thus are typically punished by a fine only.

Piercing the corporate veil   The legal doctrine used by courts to disregard the existence of a corporation, thereby holding the shareholders personally liable for the organization's debts.

Plaintiff   The person who initiates a lawsuit.

Plan termination insurance   The insurance required by federal law on regulated pension plans. It protects against plan termination that leaves pension benefits underfunded.

Plant patent   A property right awarded for a new variety of plant that can be produced asexually. Note that inventions involving plants may be protected as utility patents. See *Utility patent.*

Pleadings   The system for defining and narrowing the issues by parties who file formal documents stating their respective positions in a lawsuit.

Plenary   Entire; complete in all respects.

Point source   Any source of air pollution that must be licensed under the Clean Air Act.

Police power   The authority a state or local government has to protect the public's health, safety, morals, and general welfare.

Positional bargaining   A method of negotiation that focuses on the parties exchanging offers, with concessions being made so that parties find a middle ground. The seller refers to the last offer made as its bottom line, and the buyer refers to the last offer made as its top dollar.

Possession   Dominion and control over property; the holding or detention of property in one's own power or command.

Postdispute arbitration clause Can be applicable to arbitration, mediation, or other methods of ADR; such a clause is signed by parties that are already in dispute.

Posteffective period As it relates to an initial public offering of securities, this is the period during which the securities may by sold. This period usually follows a twenty-day waiting period.

Precedent A prior judicial decision relied upon as an example of a rule of law.

Predatory conduct An anticompetitive action that is intended to drive competitors out of business. A common example occurs when a business lowers its prices in the hope of gaining such a large market share that it can then raise prices without the fear of competition.

Predatory pricing A policy of lowering the price charged to customers for the purpose of driving competitors out of business. Typically, this policy involves prices that are below the seller's costs of the products sold with resulting losses to the seller.

Predispute arbitration clause Applicable to ADR systems agreed to by contracting parties prior to a dispute arising; usually this clause is a part of the original contract between the parties.

Preemption A condition when a federal statute or administrative rule governs an issue to the extent that a state or local government is prohibited from regulating that area of law.

Preemptive right A corporation's shareholder's right to maintain the same percentage ownership of the organization whenever newly authorized stock is sold.

Preferred stock A type of stock issued by a corporation that entitles the owner to receive a dividend before owners of common stock.

Prefiling period As it relates to an initial public offering of securities, this is that period of time prior to the filing of a registration statement with the SEC.

Prejudicial error An error in judicial proceedings that may have affected the result in the case.

Preponderance of evidence In the judgment of the jurors, evidence that has greater weight and overcomes the opposing evidence and presumptions.

Presumption of innocence The basis of requiring the government to prove a criminal defendant's guilt beyond a reasonable doubt.

Prevention of significant deterioration A rule implemented under the Clean Air Act that prohibits the degradation of air quality in regions where air quality is better than required by primary air quality standards.

Price discrimination A seller charging different purchasers different prices for the same goods at the same time.

Price fixing An agreement or combination by which the conspirators set the market price, whether high or low, of a product or service whether being sold or purchased.

Prima facie On the face of it; thus, presumed to be true unless proved otherwise.

Primary air quality standards The standards necessary to protect human health. Secondary air quality standards are stricter standards necessary to protect various environmental amenities.

Primary jurisdiction A doctrine used by reviewing courts to determine whether a case is properly before the courts or whether it should be heard by an administrative agency first since such an agency might have expertise superior to the courts'.

Principal The person who gives an agent authority.

Principled, interest-based, negotiations A method of negotiation that focuses on the parties' interests as opposed to positions. The language used to describe this bargaining includes options, alternatives, objective criteria, and relationships.

Prior consideration Service or gift from the past that presently induces one to make a promise. Prior consideration does not enable that promise to bind one. It is not legal consideration.

Prior restraint A principle applicable under the freedom of press and speech clauses of the First Amendment of the U.S. Constitution. The courts have announced decisions that encourage governments to allow the publication or expression of thoughts rather than to restrain such thoughts in advance of their publication or expression.

Private international law A body of rules that deal with controversies between private persons, such as those created by commercial transactions.

Private law A classification of legal subject matters that deals most directly with relationships between legal entities. The law of contracts and the law of property are two examples of this classification.

Private nuisance An unreasonable use of one's land so as to cause substantial interference with the enjoyment or use of another's land.

Private Securities Litigation Reform Act (PSLRA) A 1995 federal statute that limits the recovery for securities violations against third parties who are not directly responsible for the violation. For example, only the Securities and Exchange Commission can pursue these claims. This law also requires lead plaintiffs in class-action securities suits and restricts recovery of damages and attorneys fees.

Privilege   A special advantage accorded by law to some individual or group; an exemption from a duty or obligation generally imposed by law.

Privileged communication   A rule of evidence that protects conversations that society deems to be confidential. For example, a witness cannot be required to disclose communications between an attorney and a client.

Privileges and immunities clause   A provision found in Article IV and the Fourteenth Amendment of the U.S. Constitution that prevents a state government from discriminating in favor of its citizens and against citizens from another state. This clause, while not interpreted to be absolute, has emphasized national rather than state citizenship.

Privity   Interest derived from successive relationship with another party; a contractual connection.

Probable cause   The reasonable basis on which law enforcement officials convince a judge that criminal activity has occurred. This is the basis that must be satisfied before a judge will issue a criminal search warrant.

Procedural due process   The process or procedure ensuring fundamental fairness that all citizens are entitled to under the U.S. Constitution.

Procedural law   The body of rules governing the manner in which legal claims are enforced.

Product extension merger   A merger that extends the products of the acquiring company into a similar or related product but one that is not directly in competition with existing products.

Production defect   A defect arising when a product does not meet its manufacturer's own standards.

Product liability   The liability that sellers have for the goods they sell.

Prohibiting discrimination   A standard of review under the Commerce Clause that can invalidate state and local laws. When state and local laws discriminate against or negatively impact interstate commerce, such laws are invalid and void.

Promise   A commitment or willingness to be bound to a contract obligation.

Promissory estoppel   Court enforcement of an otherwise unbinding promise if injustice can be avoided only by enforcement of the promise. A substitute for consideration.

Property   A bundle of private, exclusive rights in people to acquire, possess, use, and transfer scarce resources.

Property law   The law of the legal fence that establishes exclusive right in someone called an owner.

Proportionality review   The process that appellate courts use to determine the appropriateness of a criminal sentence.

Prospectus   The legal document required by the 1933 Securities Act to be made available to potential purchasers of securities.

Pro tanto   So far as it goes.

Proximate causation   The doctrine that limits an actor's liability to consequences that could reasonably be foreseen to have resulted from the act.

Protestant ethic   A set of beliefs urging that human desire and indulgence be bent to God's will through hard work, self-denial, and rational planning.

Proximate cause   In tort law and legal requirement that an act foreseeably causes an injury.

Proxy   The legal document whereby a shareholder appoints an agent to vote the stock at a corporation's shareholders' meeting.

Public international law   A body of rules that examines relationships among nations and seeks to bind them to common principles in the international community.

Public law   A classification of legal subject matters that regulates the relationship of individuals and organizations to society.

Publicly held   A business organization that has hundreds, if not thousands, of owners who can exchange their ownership interests on public exchanges.

Public nuisance   An owner's use of land that causes damage or inconvenience to the general public.

Public policy   Accepted standards of behavior. For instance, a contract is illegal if it violates public policy.

Punitive damages   Monetary damages in excess of a compensatory award, usually granted only in intentional tort cases where defendant's conduct involved some element deserving punishment. Also called *exemplary damages.*

Purchase money security interest (PMSI)   A security interest given to the party that loans the debtor the money that enables the debtor to buy the collateral.

Qualified disabled   A disabled person who can perform the duties of a job.

Qualified pension plan   A private retirement plan that gains favorable income tax treatment from the Internal Revenue Service (IRS). A qualified pension plan allows for the deduction of contributions made to fund the plan. Also, earnings from fund investments are not taxable, and employees defer personal income tax liability until payments are received after retirement. To qualify, the plan must cover a high percentage of workers (usually 70 percent) or cover classifications of employees that do not discriminate in favor of management or shareholders.

Quantity discount   The practice of giving a lower per unit price to businesses that buy a product in volume than to their competitors that do not.

Quasi-contract   A quasi-contract, often referred to as an implied-in-law contract, is not a true contract. It is a legal fiction that the courts use to prevent unjust enrichment and wrongdoing. Courts permit the person who conferred a benefit to recover the reasonable value of that benefit. Nonetheless, the elements of a true contract are not present.

Quasi-judicial   Administrative actions involving factual determinations and the discretionary application of rules and regulations.

Quasi-legislative   This term describes the rule-making functions of administrative agencies.

Quasi-strict scrutiny   A legal test used by courts to test the validity of governmental action, such as legislation, under the equal protection clause of the U.S. Constitution. To satisfy this test, the government needs to demonstrate that the purpose of the action is substantially related to an important governmental objective.

Quick-look analysis   A process of review used by courts in antitrust cases to determine the legality of an anticompetitive act. This analysis is something greater than the per se determination of illegality and less than the full consideration of the rule of reason analysis.

Quid pro quo   The exchange of one thing of value for another.

Quitclaim deed   The transfer by deed of all the grantor's rights, title, and interest in property.

Quo warranto   An action brought about by the government to test the validity of some franchise, such as the privilege of doing business as a corporation.

Racketeering   A crime under RICO involving a pattern of actions that are indictable under state or federal laws.

Railway Labor Act   The federal law passed in 1926 to encourage collective bargaining in the railroad industry. The law also created the National Mediation Board.

Ratification   What occurs when a principal voluntarily decides to honor an agreement.

Ratio decidendi   Logical basis of judicial decision.

Real property   Property in land and interests in land.

Reasonable accommodation   The actions that an employer must take under Title VII of the Civil Rights Act and under the Americans with Disabilities Act to adapt employment conditions to an employee's religious belief or disability.

Reciprocal dealing   A contract in which two parties agree to mutual actions so that each party can act as both a buyer and a seller. The agreement violates the Clayton Act if it results in a substantial lessening of competition.

Redlining   An act or refusal to act that results in a discriminatory practice. For example, refusing to make loans in low-income areas can discriminate against minorities in granting credit.

Reformation   A contractual remedy exercised by a court to correct a mistake of drafting or some other nonessential mistake. After reformation the parties remain bound to the contract.

Registration statement   The legal document required to be filed with the Securities and Exchange Commission (SEC) prior to securities being offered for sale to the public.

Reimbursement   Restoration; to pay back or repay that expended; the act of making one whole.

Rejection   The refusal of an offer. A rejection terminates an offer.

Release   The relinquishment of a right or claim against another party.

Remand   The return of a case by an appellate court for further action by the lower court.

Remedial statute   Legislation designed to provide a benefit or relief to a victim of a violation of law.

Remedy   The action or procedure that is followed in order to enforce a right or to obtain damages for injury to a right; the means by which a right is enforced or the violation of a right is prevented, redressed, or compensated.

Reorganization   The legal process of forming a new corporation after bankruptcy or foreclosure.

Replevin   An action for the recovery of goods wrongfully taken or kept.

Representational standing   The requirements that must be satisfied for an organization to have the right to file a lawsuit on behalf of its members.

Request for an admission   A method of discovery used to narrow the issues to be litigated by having a party request that the other party admit the facts that are not in dispute.

Request for production of documents   A method of discovery whereby one party asks the other to provide documents for the requesting party's review.

Requirements contract A contract under which the buyer agrees to buy a certain item only from the seller.

Res A thing, object, or status.

Resale price maintenance Manufacturer control of a brand- or trade-name product's minimum resale price.

Rescind To cancel or annul a contract and return the parties to their original positions.

Rescission A contractual remedy that cancels the agreement and returns the consideration exchanged to each party.

Res ipsa loquitur The thing speaks for itself. A rule of evidence whereby negligence of the alleged wrongdoer may be inferred from the mere fact that the injury occurred.

Res judicata The doctrine that deems a former adjudication conclusive and prevents a retrial of matters decided in the earlier lawsuit.

Respondeat superior The doctrine imposing liability on one for torts committed by another person who is in his or her employ and subject to his or her control.

Respondent The party answering a petition for a writ of *certiorari* in the Supreme Court.

Restitution A contractual remedy involving one party returning to another the value previously received.

Restraint of trade Monopolies, combinations, and contracts that impede free competition.

Restrictive covenants Private agreements that restrict land use.

Retaliation Striking back against someone for what they did to you. Used in labor law, employment discrimination cases, and whistle-blowing as part of a doctrine prohibiting an employer from firing or taking other adverse actions against employees for reporting the employer to federal agencies for violating various laws.

Retaliatory trade practices Actions by aggrieved nations responding to tariffs and other unfair trade restrictions imposed by foreign governments.

Reverse Overturn or vacate the judgment of a court.

Reverse discrimination The advancement and recruitment of minority workers ahead of similarly qualified nonminority workers.

Revocation The contractual communication of withdrawing an offer.

RICO The Racketeer Influenced and Corrupt Organizations Act.

Right of redemption The right to buy back. A debtor may buy back or redeem his or her mortgaged property when he or she pays the debt.

Right-to-work law A state statute that outlaws a union shop contract—one by which an employer agrees to require membership in the union sometime after an employee has been hired as a condition of continued employment.

Robbery Illegally taking something by force.

Robinson-Patman Act The amendment to Section 2 of the Clayton Act covering price discrimination. As originally adopted, the Robinson-Patman Act outlawed price discrimination in interstate commerce that might substantially lessen competition or tends to create a monopoly.

Rule against perpetuities The rule that prohibits an owner from controlling what he or she owns beyond a life in being at the owner's death, plus 21 years.

Rule of law The general and equal application of laws, even to lawmakers.

Rule of first possession The rule that says one becomes an owner by reducing to possession previously unowned objects or abandoned objects.

Rule of reason Under the Sherman Act, contracts or conspiracies are illegal only if they constitute an unreasonable restraint of trade or attempt to monopolize. An activity is unreasonable if it adversely affects competition. An act is reasonable if it promotes competition. The rule of reason requires that an anticompetitive effect be shown. See also *Per se illegality*.

Rules of evidence The laws governing the admission of evidence, such as testimony and documents, during the trial of a case.

Sale of business doctrine The legal principle in securities law that might be used to remove the sale of corporate stock from the securities laws' protection if the purchaser of such stock is to operate the business instead of relying on others to do so.

Sanctions Penalties imposed for violation of a law.

Sarbanes-Oxley Act of 2002 The law enacted to correct inadequacies in the law that existed and allowed numerous examples of corporate fraud. In essence, through increased criminal sanctions and specific requirements, this law attempts to make corporate CEOs more responsible.

Say-on-pay A policy of companies that allow the compensation of executives to be reviewed by shareholders.

Scheme to defraud   A plan to misrepresent a material fact in order to obtain something, usually money, from another.

Scienter   With knowledge; particularly, guilty knowledge.

Scoping   A regulatory step required of a federal agency by the Council on Environmental Quality. Before preparing an environmental impact statement, an agency must designate which environmental issues of a proposed action are most significant.

S corporation   A business organization that is formed as a corporation but, by a shareholders' election, is treated as a partnership for taxation purposes.

Search warrant   A court order required by the Fourth Amendment of the U.S. Constitution to be obtained from government officials prior to private property being searched or seized.

Secondary air quality standards   Clean Air Act standards designed to protect environmental quality other than human health.

Secondary boycott   Conspiracy or combination to cause the customers or suppliers of an employer to cease doing business with that employer.

Section 1981   That provision of the Civil Rights Act of 1866 that forbids racial discrimination in the making of contracts.

Section 402A   That section of the Second Restatement of Torts that imposes strict liability on product sellers who sell a product in a "defective condition unreasonably dangerous to the user or consumer or his property."

Section 5   Section of the Federal Trade Commission act which authorizes the commission to regulate unfair or deceptive acts or practices in trade.

Secured transactions   Any credit transaction creating a security interest; an interest in personal property that secures the payment of an obligation.

Securities Act of 1933   The federal law that regulates (through disclosure requirements) the initial sale of securities to the public.

Securities and Exchange Commission (SEC)   The federal administrative agency that regulates the securities industry.

Securities Exchange Act of 1934   The federal law that regulates sales (other than the initial sale) of securities. This law governs the resale of securities whether by individuals or through brokers and exchanges.

Security   Under the securities law, an investment in which the investor does not participate in management.

Security interests   An application of property that gives someone an interest in what belongs to another, usually to secure an extension of credit.

Self-regulation   An entire industry's regulation of itself, as opposed to government regulation of the businesses in the industry.

Seller   In commercial law, a person who sells or contracts to sell goods.

Seniority system   A plan giving priority to employees based on the length of time an employee has worked for an employer. An employer may apply different standards pursuant to a good-faith seniority system if the differences are not the result of an intention to discriminate.

Sentencing guidelines   Adopted by the U.S. Sentencing Commission as a means of standardizing the sentences given to similar criminals committing similar crimes.

Separation of powers   The doctrine that holds that the legislative, executive, and judicial branches of government function independently of one another and that each branch serves as a check on the others.

Servant   The person hired to act on behalf of a principal in an agency relationship.

Service mark   Any mark, word, picture, or design that attaches to a service and indicates its source.

Set-off   A counterclaim by a defendant against a plaintiff that grows from an independent cause of action and diminishes the plaintiff's potential recovery.

Sexual harassment   Under Title VII, for an employer or workplace supervisor to promise benefits or threaten loss if an employee does not give sexual favors.

Shareholders   The owners of corporations. Typically these owners vote on major decisions impacting their corporations, most commonly the election of a board of directors.

Shark repellent   Corporate action to make a threatened acquisition unattractive to the acquiring company.

Shelf registration   The process in securities law under Securities and Exchange Commission (SEC) Rule 415 that allows an issuer to satisfy the registration statement requirements, thereby allowing the issuer immediately to offer securities for sale.

Sherman Act   An 1890 congressional enactment designed to regulate anticompetitive behavior in interstate commerce.

Short-swing profits   The proceeds gained by an insider buying and selling, or vice versa, securities within a six-month time period. Such profits are considered to be illegal.

Simplified employee pension   A type of pension permitted by the Revenue Act of 1978. Under this pension type, employers contribute up to a specified amount to employee individual retirement accounts.

Slander   An oral defamatory statement communicated to a third person.

Small-claims court   A court of limited jurisdiction, usually able to adjudicate claims up to a certain amount, such as $3,000, depending on the state.

Social contract theory   A theory by John Rawls that proposes a way for constructing a just society.

Sole proprietorship   The simplest form of business organization, created and controlled by one owner.

Sovereign immunity   A doctrine of state and international law that permits a foreign government to claim immunity from suit in the courts of other nations.

Sovereignty   The supreme, absolute, and uncontrollable power by which any state is governed.

Specific performance   Equitable remedy that requires defendants in certain circumstances to do what they have contracted to do.

Stakeholder theory   Ethical theory which asserts that in order to be ethical a business must take into consideration not only the making of a profit but the impacts of the business on all interests that are affected by the business.

Standing   The doctrine that requires the plaintiff in a lawsuit to have a sufficient legal interest in the subject matter of the case.

Standing to sue   The requirement that a plaintiff must satisfy by demonstrating a personal interest in the outcome of litigation or an administrative hearing.

Stare decisis   The doctrine that traditionally indicates that a court should follow prior decisions in all cases based on substantially similar facts.

State action exemption   The Sherman Act exemption of the sovereign action of a state that replaces competition with regulation if the state actively supervises the anticompetitive conduct.

State-of-the-art defense   A defense that the defendant's product or practice was compatible with the current state of technology available at the time of the event in question.

States' relations article   Article IV of the U.S. Constitution. Among its purposes, this article prevents a state from favoring its citizens over the citizens of another state, thereby making the United States one nation as opposed to 50 subgroups.

Status quo   The conditions or state of affairs at a given time.

Statute   A legislative enactment.

Statute of frauds   Legislation that states that certain contracts will not be enforced unless there is a signed writing evidencing the agreement.

Statute of limitations   A statute that sets a date after which a lawsuit may not be brought. The statute begins running after the happening of a certain event, such as the occurrence of an injury or the breach of a contract.

Statute of repose   A statute that applies to product liability cases. It prohibits initiation of litigation involving products more than a certain number of years (e.g., 25) following their manufacture.

Statutory construction   The rules courts use in interpreting the meaning of legislation.

Strict liability   The doctrine under which a party may be required to respond in tort damages without regard to such party's use of due care.

Strict products liability   The cause of action under which commercial sellers of defective products are held liable without negligence.

Strict scrutiny   A legal test used by courts to test the validity of governmental action, such as legislation, under the equal protection clause of the U.S. Constitution. To satisfy this test, the government needs to demonstrate that there is a compelling state interest justifying the government's action.

Structured settlement   A periodic payment of damages, usually taking the form of a guaranteed annuity.

Subject matter jurisdiction   The authority of a court to hear cases involving specific issues of law.

Submission   The act or process of referring an issue to arbitration.

Subpoena   A court order directing a witness to appear or to produce documents in his or her possession.

Substantial performance   Degree of performance recognizing that a contracting party has honestly attempted to perform but has fallen short. One who has substantially performed is entitled to the price promised by the other less that party's damages.

Substantive due process   The use of the due process provision of the U.S. Constitution to make certain that the application of a law does not unfairly deprive persons of property rights.

Substantive law A body of rules defining the nature and extent of legal rights.

Summary judgment A judicial determination that no genuine factual dispute exists and that one party to the lawsuit is entitled to judgment as a matter of law.

Summons An official notice to a person that a lawsuit has been commenced against him or her and that he or she must appear in court to answer the charges.

Superfund The Comprehensive Environmental Response, Compensation, and Liability Act of 1980.

Supremacy clause Article VI of the U.S. Constitution, which states that the Constitution, laws, and treaties of the United States shall be the "supreme law of the land" and shall take precedence over conflicting state laws.

Supreme Court The highest appellate court.

Surety One who incurs a liability for the benefit of another. One who undertakes to pay money in the event that his or her principal is unable to pay.

Symbolic speech Nonverbal expression.

Taft-Hartley Act The federal law enacted in 1947 to increase the bargaining power of management by creating unfair labor practices by unions, by outlawing the closed shop, by creating an 80-day cooling-off period, by permitting states to adopt right-to-work laws, and by creating the Federal Mediation and Conciliation Service.

Tangible property Physical property.

Teleology An ethical system that concerns itself with the moral consequences of actions. Also called *consequentialism*.

Tenancy in common A property ownership that is undivided (common) but not necessarily equal between two or more owners.

Tender offer An invited public offer by a company or organization to buy shares from existing shareholders of another public corporation under specified terms.

Tender performance The offer by one contracting party to perform a promise; usually associated with the offer to pay for or to ship items under the contract.

Testator One who has made a will.

Third party One who enters into a relationship with a principal by way of interacting with the principal's agent.

Third-party beneficiaries Persons who are recognized as having enforceable rights created for them by a contract to which they are not parties and for which they have given no consideration.

Third-party defendant A party who is not a party (plaintiff or defendant) to the original litigation. Typically, a defendant might file a claim against a third party stating that if the defendant is liable to the plaintiff, then this third party will be liable to the defendant.

Tippee A person who learns of nonpublic information about a security from an insider.

Title A synonym for ownership. Sometimes represented as a document.

Tombstone ad An advertisement announcing the public offering of securities; these usually run during the waiting period.

Tort A civil wrong other than a breach of contract.

Trade disparagement The publication of untrue statements that disparage the plaintiff's ownership of property or its quality.

Trade dress A legal doctrine giving someone ownership of a distinctive overall appearance or look and feel of a product or service.

Trademark A statutorily created property in a mark, word, picture, or design that attaches to goods and indicates their source.

Trademark dilution Using someone's trademark in such a way so as to reduce the value of the trademark's significance, reputation, and goodwill, even if the public is not confused by the use.

Trade practice regulation A term generally referring to laws that regulate competitive practices.

Trade secret Any formula, pattern, machine, or process of manufacturing used in one's business that may give the user an opportunity to obtain an advantage over its competitors. Trade secrets are legally protectable.

Trade usage Refers to the particular use of a word in business that may differ from its common use.

Trading partnership A business organization made up of two or more partners engaged in providing services.

Treason Breach of allegiance to one's government, specifically by levying war against such government or by giving aid and comfort to the enemy.

Treaty of Rome A historic agreement reached by six European countries in 1957 to achieve economic unity in the European Community. The latter is now known as the European Union, and its membership has grown to 15 nations.

Glossary

Treble damages   See *Triple damages.*

Trespass   An act done in an unlawful manner so as to cause injury to another; an unauthorized entry upon another's land.

Trial court   The level of any court system that initially resolves the dispute of litigants. Frequently, but not always, a jury serves as a fact-finding body while the judge issues rulings on the applicable law.

Triple damages (or treble damages)   An award of damages allowable under some statutes equal to three times the amount found by the jury to be a single recovery.

Trust   A fiduciary relationship whereby one party (trustee) holds legal title for the benefit of another (beneficiary).

Trustee   One who holds legal title to property for the benefit of another.

Truth in lending   A federal law that requires the disclosure of total finance charges and the annual percentage rate for credit in order that borrowers may be able to shop for credit.

Tying contract   A contract that ties the sale of one piece of property (real or personal) to the sale or lease of another item of property.

Ultra vires   Beyond the scope of corporate powers granted in the charter.

Unconscionable   In the law of contracts, provisions that are oppressive, overreaching, or shocking to the conscience.

Underwriter   The party that, in securities law, guarantees the issuer that the securities offered for sale will be sold.

Undue burden   Under the Civil Rights Act of 1964 and the Americans with Disabilities Act an employer need not take action that is excessively costly or creates excessive inefficiency in order to accommodate an employee's religious beliefs or disability. This is the concept of undue burden.

Undue influence   Influence of another destroying the requisite free will of a testator or donor, which creates a ground for nullifying a will or invalidating a gift. A contract will not be binding if one party unduly influences the other since the parties have not dealt on equal terms.

Unenforceable contract   A contract that cannot be enforced in court.

Unfair competition   A group of statutory torts that include misappropriation of trademarks, patent violations, and copyright breaches. One aspect of the Federal Trade Commission's authority. Section 5 of the FTC Act makes unfair methods of competition illegal.

Unfair labor practices   Activities by management or labor unions that have been declared to be inappropriate by the Wagner Act and Taft-Hartley Act, respectively.

Uniform Commercial Code (UCC)   The most successful attempt to have states adopt a uniform law. This code's purpose is to simplify, clarify, and modernize the laws governing commercial transactions.

Uniformed Services Employment and Reemployment Rights Act (USERRA)   The act which protects the rights of individuals who voluntarily or involuntarily leave employment positions to undertake military service.

Unilateral contract   A contract in which the promisor does not receive a promise as consideration; an agreement whereby one makes a promise to do, or refrain from doing, something in return for a performance, not a promise.

Unilateral mistake   Arises when only one of the parties to a contract is wrong about a material fact. It is not usually a basis for rescinding a contract.

Union security clause   The contractual provision that creates a union shop agreement. This clause requires any person hired as an employee to join the union representing the employees.

Union shop   This term applies, in labor law, to an agreement by management and labor that all employees of a business will be or become union members. Union shops are not allowed in states with right-to-work laws.

United Nations   The principal political organization of the world.

Unreasonable search and seizure   A violation of the Fourth Amendment of the U.S. Constitution that occurs when a valid search warrant is not obtained or when the scope of a valid warrant is exceeded.

Usury   A loan of money at interest above the legal rate.

Utilitarianism   A form of consequentialist ethics.

Utility patent   A property right awarded for a new and non-obvious process, machine, or composition of matter that has a useful function.

Valid contract   A contract that contains all of the proper elements of a contract.

Venue   The geographical area over which a court presides. Venue designates the court in which the case should be tried. Change of venue means moving to another court.

Verdict Findings of fact by the jury.

Vertical merger A merger of corporations where one corporation is the supplier of the other.

Vertical price fixing An agreement between a seller and a buyer (for example, between a manufacturer and a retailer) to fix the resale price at which the buyer will sell goods.

Vertical territorial agreement Arrangement between a supplier and its customers with respect to the geographical area in which each customer will be allowed to sell that supplier's products. This type of agreement is analyzed under the rule of reason to determine whether it violates the Sherman Act. Limitations on intrabrand competition may be permitted if there is a corresponding increase in interbrand competition.

Vested rights Rights that have become so fixed that they are not subject to being taken away without the consent of the owner.

Voidable contract Capable of being declared a nullity, though otherwise valid.

Void contract A contract that is empty, having no legal force; ineffectual, unenforceable.

Voir dire The preliminary examination of prospective jurors for the purpose of ascertaining bias or interest in the lawsuit.

Voluntary arbitration A method of resolving a dispute, as an alternative to litigation, that the parties agree to utilize. This agreement may be made before or after a dispute arises.

Voluntary bargaining issue Either party may refuse to bargain in good faith regarding matters other than wages, hours, and other terms and conditions of employment. This refusal does not constitute an unfair labor practice. An issue over which parties may bargain if they choose to do so.

Voluntary petition The document filed by a debtor to initiate bankruptcy proceedings.

Wagner Act The federal law passed in 1935 that recognizes employees' rights to organize. This law also created the National Labor Relations Board and defined unfair labor practices by management. It is formally known as the National Labor Relations Act.

Waiting period As it relates to an initial public offering of securities, this is the period of time that follows the filing of documents with the SEC and that precedes when the securities can be sold. Unless the SEC objects and extends this period of time, the waiting period lasts only 20 days.

Waiver An express or implied relinquishment of a right.

WARN Act The Worker Adjustment and Retraining Notification Act of 1989; this law requires employers to give notice of plant closings and mass layoffs.

Warrant A judicial authorization for the performance of some act.

Warranty of authority An agent's implied guarantee that he or she has the authority to enter into a contract. The agent is liable for breaching the warranty if he or she lacks proper authority.

Warranty of merchantability A promise implied in a sale of goods by merchants that the goods are reasonably fit for the general purpose for which they are sold.

Wheeler-Lea amendment Legislation passed in 1938 that expanded the Federal Trade Commission's authority to protect society against unfair or deceptive practices.

White-collar crime Violations of the law by business organizations or by individuals in a business-related capacity.

White knight A slang term that describes the inducement of a voluntary acquisition when an involuntary acquisition is threatened. The voluntary acquisition group is a white knight since it saves the corporation from an unfriendly takeover.

Willful and wanton negligence Extremely unreasonable behavior that causes injury.

Willfully With intent to defraud or deceive.

Wire fraud The use of radio, television, telephone, Internet, or other wired forms of communication to conduct fraudulent activities with the intent to deprive an owner of property.

Workers' compensation A plan for the compensation for occupational diseases, accidental injuries, and deaths of employees that arise out of employment. Compensation includes medical expenses and burial costs and lost earnings based on the size of the family and the wage rate of the employee.

Work rules A company's regulations governing the workplace, the application of which often becomes an issue in the ability of employees to organize for their mutual benefit and protection.

World Bank The world's principal financial institution.

World Intellectual Property Organization A specialized agency of the United Nations that administers certain intellectual property treaties and provides related educational resources.

804   Glossary

World Trade Organization (WTO)   Mechanism for enforcing the General Agreement on Tariffs and Trade that allows GATT member countries to bring complaints and seek redress.

Wright-Line doctrine   Establishes procedures for determining the burden of proof in cases involving mixed motivation for discharge.

Writ of certiorari   A discretionary proceeding by which an appellate court may review the ruling of an inferior tribunal.

Writ of habeas corpus   A court order to one holding custody of another to produce that individual before the court for the purpose of determining whether such custody is proper.

Yellow-dog contract   An agreement in which a worker agrees not to join a union and that discharge will result from a breach of the contract.

Zoning ordinance   Laws that limit land use based usually on residential, commercial, or industrial designations.

Online Supplements

ConnectPlus Legal Environment of Business One-Semester online Access for The Legal and Regulatory Environment of Business, 16th Edition

McGraw-Hill Connect® is a web-based assignment and assessment platform that gives students the means to better connect with their coursework, with their instructors, and with the important concepts that they will need to know for success now and in the future. With Connect, instructors can deliver assignments, quizzes and tests easily online. Students can practice important skills at their own pace and on their own schedule.

GETTING STARTED:

To get started in Connect, you will need the following:

1. Your instructor's unique Connect URL

    Sample of Connect URL
    http://www.mcgrawhillconnect.com/class/instructorname_section_name

2. Connect Access Code

    Using a Print Book? Your access code will appear at the back of the book. Reference your Table of Contents for an exact page number.

    Using an eBook? Once you have purchased your Create eBook, you will automatically have access to Connect. Simply go to your instructor's unique URL and sign in using the username and password you established when accessing your Create eBook.

REGISTRATION AND SIGN IN:

- Go to the Connect Website address provided by your instructor.
- Click **Register Now**.
- Enter your email address.
    - **TIP:** If you already have a McGraw-Hill account, you will be asked for your password and will not be required to create a new account.
- Enter your access code (This access code appears on the back cover of the Create book and is only redeemable once.)
- Follow the on-screen instructions.
    - **TIP:** Please choose your Security Question carefully. We will ask you for this information if you forget your password.
- When registration is complete, click on **Go to Connect Now**.
- You are now ready to use **Connect.**

Need Help?
Contact us online: www.mcgrawhillconnect.com/support
Give us a call: 1-800-331-5094